THE SOCIAL MEDIA BIBLE

THE SOCIAL MEDIA BIBLE

SECOND EDITION

LON SAFKO

TACTICS, TOOLS, AND STRATEGIES FOR BUSINESS SUCCESS

WILEY

John Wiley & Sons, Inc.

ISBN 978-0-470-62397-8 (paper)
ISBN 978-0-470-91268-3 (ebk)
ISBN 978-0-470-91269-0 (ebk)
ISBN 978-0-470-91270-6 (ebk)

Printed in the United States of America

10 9 8 7 6 5 4 3 2 1

CONTENTS

 theSocialMediaBible.com

CONTENTS

PART II
Tools

PART III
Strategy

This project was the largest and most passionate undertaking of my career, and using social media to create a book on social media was by far the most enlightening.

When I first created the plan to write a book on social media, I thought it was going to be another typical business book: 250 pages, 20-plus chapters, 50,000 words, the typical business book formula.

Then I realized that it was not only in my best interest to use social media, but also in a way, that I should use social media to create this book. I knew that if I asked the business community what they wanted in a book and wrote it that way, the book would be successful and it was. What I didn't know at the time was the magnitude of the journey I was about to undertake.

We brought the initial concept of the book on social media to more than 1,000 people. They were mostly professionals with annual incomes over $100,000; most had college degrees, from associates up to PhDs.

Of more than 1,000 surveyed, 66.4 percent said that they could not define what social media was, while 99.1 percent said that they knew social media would have a significant effect on them and their businesses. Let me restate this: Two-thirds of these professionals didn't know what it was, but nearly 100 percent knew it was going to affect them. This is whom this book is dedicated to.

By using user-generated content and feedback, I also learned that the business community didn't want just another vertical business book; they wanted something much more comprehensive. They asked for a book that first explains: What are all of these things we keep hearing about? What's a blog, a vlog, a podcast? What is a "trusted network" and "wisdom of the crowds"? What is LinkedIn, MySpace, Flickr, and YouTube? So this became the blueprint for Part I, which in itself is a business book on the tactics of social media.

They then asked for a guide. They asked: Who are the players? Where do I post a video or a podcast? What's the most used photo sharing site? So this became the second business book, or guide to the social media players. This section is Part II, the Tools.

theSocialMediaBible.com

Finally, they wanted a book that could pull all of this together answering the questions: How do I use social media in my business? How can I incorporate this in my business plan? How do I make money using social media? Where's the ROI? How will this change the way I do business? This became Part III of the book, Strategy.

In the first edition, we took an academic approach to this strategy section; providing tried and true methods of determining your specific strategy using SWOT Analysis (Strengths, Weaknesses, Opportunities, and Threats), USP (Unique Selling Position), and other proven marketing techniques.

During the past year, I have had the opportunity to speak with such companies as NCO, Levi Strauss, Nike, United Airlines, PepsiCo, Coca-Cola, Dial, Intel, Scott's, Frito-Lay, General Mills, L'Oréal, Kraft, Dannon, Omaha Steaks, Unisys (Burroughs), La Quinta, Lilly, dozens of entrepreneurs, governmental agencies, and nonprofits. The one run-on question they had in common was: "How do I put together a strategy that includes my conventional media, integrates social media, determines what social media tools I should use, find the resources, and measure my success?"

So in this edition, the Part III, Strategy, section has been completely rewritten. In this new section, I give you "The Five Steps to Social Media Success," which addresses all of the questions asked earlier in five easy steps. This new section is down and dirty and in the weeds, and what you will get out of it is what you are willing to put into it. I ask you to look at things most marketing, PR, and upper management never want to discuss: The cost of customer acquisition and the actual ROI of each of your existing marketing campaigns and efforts.

Once you determine your ROI, and cost-of-customer-acquisition on your existing marketing, you can now better reallocate existing resources; both human and financial to marketing that is significantly more effective, social media.

I approached John Wiley & Sons, Inc., with a concept of three full-sized business books (two business books sandwiching a guide). They trusted the "wisdom of the crowds" and the result is *The Social Media Bible*.

The Social Media Bible is an aggregation of blogs, vlogs, podcasts, wikis, e-mails, and conversations. *The Social Media Bible* is a collection of other books and resources. It's a collection because I could never profess to be an expert in the social media category as identified, including all of their nuances. I can't even profess that I am an expert in any one category. What I have done is pulled together information that many people have contributed. A word of caution: Be very wary of anyone who does call herself an expert or guru in social media, because she is not.

Thank you to Jimmy Wales for creating Wikipedia and the Wikimedia Foundation and to all of the people from around the world who have contributed to Wikipedia, providing such a valuable resource of cumulative human knowledge.

I want to personally thank all of the nearly 40 corporate partners who shared their expert insights in both the book and their executive conversations at www.theSocialMediaBible.com, the 23 technical editors, and the 28 ROI of Social Media vignettes authors.

A heartfelt thank you goes out to my company partners and closest friends, Geoff Clough and Linh Tang, who picked up the slack at the companies, allowing me to write and often to vent. Thank you also goes to Evo Terra for his *Podcasting For Dummies* book, bloggers like David Risley for his top 50 blog tips, and to my friends and colleagues, including Cindy and Steve Bauer for their cabin hideaway in the mountains of Pinetop, Arizona, which prevented my writer's block from setting in, again; Joanne Zimakas for her incredible transcription skills and attention to detail of the more than 24 continuous hours of executive interviews; and thank you to Jay Allen Video for his incredible talent for making me look and sound good in your amazing videos.

I also want to sincerely thank Lindsay Lipman, who was the project manager on this edition. Lindsay's attention to detail and people skills made it possible to pull together up-to-the-minute, highly technical, and sensitive information from more than 80 different contributors in an amazingly short time. Lindsay, thank you for all of your hard work and dedication.

My personal gratitude also goes out to the staff of John Wiley & Sons, Inc., for all of the "wisdom" of that crowd, and especially to Peter Booth Wiley for his support and contributions, without which this book would have never been published. Also, thank you to: Matt Holt for believing in and fighting for this unusual book; Kim Dayman for her marketing and design insights, which really put the polish on the design; Shannon Vargo for her incredible author-wrangling skills, which allowed the book to be published; Christine Moore for her insightful and meticulous editing talent, which made this book intelligible; Beth Zipko for pulling it all together to make the book complete; and Lauren Freestone for making this book look good!

And I want to mostly thank my amazing wife, Sherrie, for working so hard both at work and around the house, for without her painting the deck, trimming the bushes, skimming the pool, and just taking care of business, I never would have been free from distraction and able to write. So Sherrie, "Forever and for always. . . ."

I hear the orchestra beginning to play, signaling that my time is up. So . . . THANK YOU EVERYONE WHO CONTRIBUTED TO MAKE THIS A COLLECTIVE SUCCESS!

—Lon Safko

Welcome to the second edition of *The Social Media Bible*. As you can see from the size of this book, I have done everything possible to include the latest up-to-date information and all of the tools used throughout the entire world of social media. This has been a daunting task, to say the least.

If you think the content of this book might not be as fresh or relevant as possible because social media is constantly reinventing itself, you will find that not to be true. This book presents all of the tools and techniques that social media has to offer while also discussing the reason these social tools are so effective.

Why a vlog (video) is the most effective form of marketing will never change. The psychological impact of your customers and prospects watching and listening to you on video is at the core of human nature. The techniques you use to create a podcast will be the same five years from now. The importance of building trusted relationships that result in sales will be the same long after you retire. Maybe some of the tools might change, but the rest of the content will still be relevant decades from now.

This book is truly a product of social media, user-generated content, and wisdom of the crowds. Literally, more than a hundred people directly participated in the creation of this text. Some by editing the grammar, some by creating original content, some by contributing original content, some by adding their content to wikis, blogs, web pages, news articles, some by editing my content with new technologies and a different perspective. This truly was a collaborative effort by experts from around the world.

Even the actual design of the book was user generated. Before embarking on this project, I simply asked my audience, you, what you wanted in a business book on social media. After surveying nearly a thousand people, you told me you didn't want just another business book on social media, you wanted three different books. Three different business books in one: Tactics, Tools, and Strategies for Business Success.

theSocialMediaBible.com

Part I—Tactics

The first book you asked for was a book on the Tactics of social media that explain what a *vlog*, a *podcast*, a *blog, lifecasting, followers, flaming, tags, SEO* and *SEM*, and *pass along*, are. You asked that the book describe where it came from, where it is, and where is the technology going. You asked for the features and benefits of every type of social media marketing, what tools you should use, and the psychological benefits of each.

Part II—Tools

The second book you wanted was a guide, or a list, of all of the major Tools of the trade. You wanted a list of the Top 100-plus companies that provide the software, the apps, the web sites, the text messaging, the virtual worlds, the game platforms, the mobile marketing insights, e-mail marketing providers, and content sharing sites.

Then you asked for a third book, a book on Strategy. You told me that once you read the first book and understood all of the different ways you could perform social media marketing and now that you've read the second book showing 100-plus of the top technology and service providers, you wanted to know how can you apply all of this newly gained knowledge to develop a successful social media marketing strategy.

You asked that this third book be comprehensive, but in a simple-to-implement, step-by-step process of developing a successful social media marketing plan. While this process needed to be easy to follow and easy to implement, it also had to be applicable to the one-person entrepreneurial company as well as the Fortune 500. It had to be effective when applied to B2C (Business-to-Consumer) and also to the B2B (Business-to-Business) companies. It had to be pertinent if being used to develop a strategic marketing plan for an individual and a corporation. And, it had to apply equally to both for-profit and nonprofit entities, including governmental agencies. And, finally, the plan needed to work for marketing and public relations, but also for customer service and for the internal customers, your employees.

That's what this delivers . . . all three books in one.

Part III—Strategy

In the Part III, Strategy, section of the first edition of *The Social Media Bible*, we took a more academic approach to developing a strategic marketing plan for you and your company. We discussed the age-old SWOT analysis, the four pillars of social media application, and gave the reader exercises to perform. While all of that information and that type of approach is completely valid and useful, you asked that I get down and dirty and give you exactly what you need to develop a successful strategy plan, no more, no less. In this edition, the entire third book has been replaced with The Five Steps to Social Media Success. While it looks like there are only five steps to developing a successful strategy, there still is quite a bit of homework you will need to do to ensure the success of your strategic plan. The amount of work you wish to put into developing your plan will determine the level of your plan's ultimate success. Like most everything else, you will get out of it what you put in to it.

The Five Steps to Social Media Success

The Five Steps to Social Media Success are synergistic, in which the total is greater than the sum of its parts, or the success you will realize is greater than the work necessary to complete your plan. This is true because the plan is comprehensive and because social media is incredibly effective.

The Five Steps to Social Media Success include:

Step 1: Analyze Your Existing Media. In this step, I ask you to list every marketing plan, strategy, and campaign you are currently executing. I want you to look at expenses and the number of new customers that that strategy generates. Then divide to determine your "Cost of Customer Acquisition."

Step 2: The Social Media Trinity. This step asks you to push aside all of the social media noise and hype and focus on the three most important categories of social media: blogging, microblogging, and social networks. Get into the weeds with these three. I'll show you the payoff.

Step 3: Integrate Strategies. Step 3 discusses how you need to completely integrate The Social Media Trinity into your existing marketing strategy, in detail.

Step 4: Resources. "Where do I find the resources to implement this totally new strategy?" is the most-asked question I get at my keynotes from the one-person shop all the way up to the Fortune 500. I'll show you the answer.

Step 5: Implement and Measure. This final step is how you can implement your successful social media strategy plan and includes a very important part of the step that is most often skipped, measurement. They say, "You can't manage what you don't measure." This is true.

If you don't measure your marketing campaign's success, how will you know what the ROI (Return on Investment) or what the CCA (Cost of Customer Acquisition) is? How will you know what you should keep doing and what you should stop doing? How will you know where the most effective use of your limited resources is? I will show you that also.

Social Media Experts

Since the first edition of *The Social Media Bible* came out, I have been amazed and equally appalled by the vast number of people calling themselves "Social Media Experts" or "Social Media Gurus." Please beware of anyone calling themselves an "expert." It took me years and more than 800 pages to bring an overview of what social media is.

It was the exercise of having to create a book as comprehensive as this for me to understand social media as well as I do. If not for the book, I might have focused on two or three of the hundreds of tools social media has to offer and called myself an expert.

When I first began creating this book, I quickly realized that I was not an expert and that no one could be, not in every category of social media marketing. That's when I realized I needed to reach out to the social media community, identify all of the vertical experts, experts in their respective fields, and ask them to teach me what they knew and to share their personal expertise and knowledge.

I identified nearly 50 different experts, who covered the entire list of social media genres. These names ranged from Biz Stone, the inventor of Twitter; to Matt Mullenweg, inventor of WordPress; to Gary "V," social media marketer extraordinaire; to senior vice presidents of YouTube, MySpace, Flickr, Google, Microsoft, and Yahoo!. This list even included such dignitaries as Peter Wiley, the chairman of the board at John Wiley & Sons, Inc., and Vint Cerf, the real inventor of the Internet.

I called each of these extraordinary experts and spent 30 to 45 minutes with each of them, having them explain why they invented their technology, why they are passionate about what they do, and how businesses are profiting from the use of their social media tools. These are what I call "Expert Insights."

I have taken excerpts of those conversations with the industry's greats and placed them throughout every chapter in both Part I and Part II of this book. There is a lot more to the conversations than I had room for in this book. For the entire conversation transcripts, go to www.theSocialMedia Bible.com.

If you prefer audio, there are the actual recorded conversations for you to listen to and download to your iPod or burn to a CD to listen to on a CD player in your home or in your car. If these interviews were played back to back, they would run for more than 24 continuous hours. As the owner of this book, I'm making all of them available to you for free.

The ROI of Social Media

The next most-asked questions at my keynotes are "Where's the ROI in social media marketing?" and "How much should I be spending on social media marketing?" My answer is always, remove the term *social media* from those questions and ask them again: "Where's the ROI in marketing?" and "How much should I be spending on marketing?"

Social media isn't a tool box of silver bullets given to us by aliens, it's just a new set of technologies and concepts that we need to add and integrate into our existing marketing strategy. And, there is always an ROI to marketing.

In this second edition of *The Social Media Bible*, I went back to you, my audience, and asked for user generated content. I asked for your stories of how you have used social media and have realized a positive, measurable ROI.

In each of the chapters in both Part I and Part II, I have included what I call "The ROI of Social Media," 500-word vignettes, or brain candy. These stories are of actual people just like you and me, who have used social media effectively, sharing stories in small bite-sized examples of the power of social media marketing. They range from small nonprofit organizations trying to raise money all the way up to the PR Team at OfficeMax. Here's actual proof of social media effectiveness.

Chapter Commandments

In each of the chapters throughout Part I of this book, I conclude with The Commandments for that category where appropriate. These commandments include tips, how-tos, and dos and don'ts when using that category of marketing tools. These are helpful quick lists that can make you more proficient using social media and help you to avoid the pitfalls of this often unintuitive form of marketing.

Readings and Resources

Lastly, I have taken the time in each chapter to identify as many good books I can find in each of the social media categories. There are a surprising number of good books written on every aspect of social media. As this book had to cover every topic in social media and I couldn't add a single page,[*] these Readings and Resources will provide a comprehensive list of vertical and more specific books on that particular subject matter.

www.theSocialMediaBible.com

As I discussed earlier, the techniques, strategies, and concepts in this book will never become obsolete or outdated; some of the tools and companies providing those tools, however, might. As I also mentioned, we could not physically deliver any more information in a single book; three books and more than 800 pages are our limit. I still want to give you more than I can deliver in this format. TheSocialMediaBible.com is designed to be a resource that will allow you to access as much additional information as your brain will allow.

As an owner of this book, you will have access to the transcripts and podcasts mentioned earlier, clickable links where you can read about an example in this book, see the web link to the example, and either type the link in yourself, or just go to the web site, select the chapter, and all of the links printed in the book are there for you to click on.

I have also provided you with direct links and discounts to many of the companies mentioned in the book along with access to all of the major booksellers where you can find the many books mentioned in the Readings and Resources.

This web site will be an ever-changing, ever-evolving source for you to access the very latest news, products, services, and resources for the worlds of social media.

The entire content of this tome is focused on using these social tools to market you, your company, your products, and your services, by identifying where the conversations are happening, listening to those conversations, and participating in those conversations, which leads to building connections, relationships, and trust, which ultimately leads to sales.

---

[*]I was told by John Wiley & Sons, Inc.'s production and design department that I could not add a single page to this book because if I did, the binding would split. This is the biggest book with the most content that the binding would allow.

This second edition of *The Social Media Bible* was designed and developed by your direction. My philosophy is, ask your customers what they want, deliver it with excellence, and your product will sell. I asked, I listened, you spoke, I delivered. Enjoy, grow, and profit!

—Lon Safko
www.theSocialMediaBible.com
www.ExtremeDigitalMarketing.com
www.LonSafko.com

TACTICS

Part I of this book is all about the tactics of social media. In these chapters I discuss what are all of the many components of social media, What is a blog, a podcast, virtual worlds, lifecasting, mobile marketing, photo sharing, and more.

It is important to understand the terminology, the technology, the application, and the companies providing those services. While this section is not a how-to, it does explain a great deal of the details and techniques to becoming proficient at each application.

Let's start with the basics, "What Is Social Media?"

CHAPTER 1

What Is Social Media?

Social media is the media we use to be social. That's it.

That really is the short answer. The story is in the tactics of each of the hundreds of technologies, all of the tools that are available for you to connect with your customers and prospects, and the strategies necessary to use these tactics and tools effectively.

Ask Your Audience

When I began writing this book I wanted to hear what my audience wanted in a book. I have written six previous books and I knew there was a standard formula for writing a typical business book: 250 pages, 23 chapters, 3,000 words per chapter. But I wasn't sure if this book should follow that formula. Did the audience for a bible on social media want a typical business book? So, I asked them.

I knew that if I asked my audience and delivered what they wanted, it would be a success. Go figure, ask your customers what they want in a product. Then, you told me some interesting facts. First, you didn't want another typical business book on social media. You asked for three books in one: Tactics, in which everything is explained; Tools, with which they can find a comprehensive list of all the companies providing social media services; and Strategy, with which you can apply all that you have learned from Part I and Part II.

This approach of listening to my customers obviously worked. *The Social Media Bible*, First Edition, sold out in the first four days across the country, has been among the top 20 best-selling books in America, and has hit the number two best-selling book spot in its category on Amazon.

The second fact I learned was from the first two questions on the survey, "Can you define social media?" and "Do you believe that social media would have a significant impact on you and your business?"

What I learned by asking my audience these two questions was that 66.4 percent said that they couldn't define social media and the remaining third lied. If it takes me nearly 50 chapters and more than 800 pages to define social media, they didn't know, not even the social media "experts" and "gurus."

The second really interesting fact I learned was that 99.1 percent, nearly everyone, said they knew social media was going to have a significant impact on them personally and their businesses.

These two statistics told me and the publisher that two-thirds of everyone interviewed didn't know what social media was, but that it was coming for them.

So What Is It?

The first part of the terminology, *social*, refers to the instinctual needs we humans have to connect with other humans. We have been doing that in one form or another since our species began. We have a need to be around and included in groups of similar like-minded people with whom we can feel at home and comfortable sharing our thoughts, ideas, and experiences.

The second part of that term refers to the *media* we use with which we make those connections with other humans. Whether they are drums, bells, the written word, the telegraph, the telephone, radio, television, e-mail, web sites, photographs, audio, video, mobile phones, or text messaging, media are the technologies we use to make those connections.

The application of the terminology *social media* in this book is about how we can use all of these technologies effectively to reach out and connect with other humans, create a relationship, build trust, and be there when the people in those relationships are ready to purchase our product offering.

What social media is not is a box of silver bullets given to us by aliens that will instantly solve all of our marketing woes and create instant wealth for all involved. Too many people are viewing social media as a foreign and strange set of technologies that they may or may not want to use to market themselves, their companies, their products, and their services.

In my keynotes, two questions always asked are, "Should I be doing social media marketing?" My answer is "Remove the term *social media* and ask it again. Should I be doing marketing?" See how ridiculous that sounds. The second question is, "How much should I spend on social media marketing?" I reply with "Remove the term *social media* again. How much should I spend on marketing?" And, of course, the answer to both is "Yes, and as much as you can!"

Social media is only a new set of tools, new technology that allows us to more efficiently connect and build relationships with our customers and prospects. It's doing what the telephone, direct mail, print advertising, radio, television, and billboards did for us up until now. But social media is exponentially more effective.

Why Social Media?

The reason social media is so much more effective than the conventional marketing that we've done for the last 6,000 years is that it's two-way communication, not pontification. Since we've been selling goats in the desert, we would stand on a rock and shout out the features and benefits of owning a goat. And, if we chose our words correctly and hit enough of the audience's psychological hot buttons, our prospect would become a customer. Nothing has changed in 6,000 years. Until now.

There is what I call "A Fundamental Shift in Power." It's a shift from pontification to two-way communication and it's a shift about which we no longer control our corporate message. No longer does the consumer trust corporate messages. They don't trust and don't want to hear our commercials any longer. They want their information from people they know, have a relationship with, and share a bond with through trust. They want to be educated by, hear their news from, and get their product reviews by people they know and trust. They want to share their experiences, both good and bad, with people who trust them.

With this Fundamental Shift comes a new way to communicate. The new way to sell is not to sell at all. In fact, if you use social media to sell, you will get "flamed." Social media marketing is all about listening first, understanding the conversation, and then speak last.

Social media marketing is like going to a networking event, a party, a trade show, sporting event, church, or anywhere that large groups of people gather. When you enter you will see small groups of three to five people huddled together. Let's now suppose we use our conventional marketing approach.

You walk up to the group, interrupt everyone, announce your name, and start telling everyone what you do for a living, what you sell, and that they should buy from you! It's the radio car commercials that yell at you from their echo chamber "Sunday! Sunday! Sunday!"; you've heard them. What will happen?

You probably will make everyone angry at you, everyone would walk away, and you might get slapped in the lips. Because that type of behavior in a social situation is completely inappropriate. Let's rewind and try the new marketing approach.

You enter the room, choose a group, walk up to that group and say nothing. You listen first. You understand what is already being said and when you have something of value to contribute to that conversation, you wait for a break, and politely share your ideas. The reaction to this approach is significantly better. At that moment you now become part of that group, that network, and you instantly have credibility and trust.

Then as the conversation continues, eventually someone will ask you, "So, what do you do?" Bingo! Now you can share what you do, a little about your product or service, and pause. Someone in that group will more than likely ask another question about your company or its offering, and if someone in that group is in the buying part of the *sales funnel*, he will ask for your card and you have made your sale. If he isn't in the *buy* part of the funnel, he will remember you when he is. Isn't this why you go to networking events? Marketing using social media is exactly the same. More on the sales funnel later.

Whether it's a social network like Facebook or LinkedIn, Twitter or blogging, it's about participating in that conversation and being there with a relationship when your prospect is ready to buy.

As you can see, social media is completely different from standing on a rock and shouting your message, but it really is a more natural and more comfortable way to sell. By building relationships through social media, you build a more lasting trusted relationship that will result in more sales, fewer returns, and greater word of mouth.

Remember the statistics from my Customer Concentric 101 presentation? Studies have shown that: An angry customer will tell up to 20 other people about a bad experience. A satisfied customer shares good experiences with 9 to 12 people. It costs five times as much to get a new customer as it does to keep an existing one. And customers will spend up to 10 percent more for the same product if they have an existing relationship.

Word of Mouth at the Speed of Light

The statistic that "An angry customer will tell up to 20 other people about a bad experience . . . ," that's face to face. With the use of social media like blogs, Twitter, and Facebook, those 20 people can quickly become 20,000 or even 200,000!

Here's an example about Dave Carroll, a country and western singer and songwriter who had an unpleasant experience with United Airlines and used a video on YouTube to "tell a few people." At the time this chapter was written, Carroll's telling of his story to "a few people" through social media had grown to 8,380,000!

On March 31, 2008, Dave Carroll and his band, Sons of Maxwell, were flying on United Airlines from Nova Scotia to Nebraska when just after landing in Chicago O'Hare, a passenger sitting behind Carroll noticed the baggage handlers throwing his guitar around the tarmac. Carroll immediately notified three flight attendants, but "was met with indifference." When Carroll arrived in Omaha, he found his $3,500 710 Taylor acoustic guitar smashed.

Over the next several months, Carroll called United representatives in Chicago and India (go figure), who told Carroll that United wasn't responsible and would do nothing to help Carroll. Carroll spent $1,200 to repair his guitar, bringing it only "to a state that it plays well but has lost much of what made it special."

The last straw for Carroll was when a United representative, Ms. Irlweg, sent Carroll an e-mail denying Carroll his claim because he didn't file it in the right place or at the right time. United even refused to compensate Carroll by giving him $1,200 in travel vouchers.

Carroll told Ms. Irlweg that he would create a music video with his band and take it to the people using social media. Carroll then created a 4-minute–37-second complaint video called "United Breaks Guitars." Irlweg was unimpressed. The video was posted on YouTube on July 6, 2009, and within 24 hours received more than 500 comments and 24,000 views. To date, Carroll's first of three videos has been viewed by more than 8,380,000 people, while his three videos have had more than 9,500,000 viewers!

Here's Dave Carroll's web site where you can view all three videos and hear the story in his own words, www.davecarrollmusic.com.

That's what I call "Word of Mouth at the Speed of Light!"

Not all social media is used for complaints. Here's a personal story I have about airline customer service I experienced myself.

I was traveling with my public relations assistant while traveling back to New York last year on a press tour before this book was released. We had different flight times for the same day.

My flight was on time and uneventful, while hers was late leaving the gate. The gate attendant for Continental Airlines announced that her flight was running 15 minutes late, but they would board the aircraft as soon as it was serviced. She immediately took out her cell phone and Twittered a tweet "Continental Airlines, 15 minutes late. What else is new?"

They serviced the aircraft and began boarding. As she entered the aircraft, a flight attendant stepped up to her and asked, "Are you Ms. Vega?" When she replied yes, the attendant handed her a glass of Champagne and apologized for any inconvenience. OMG! That's customer service.

This never became a music video, but I have told more than 10,000 people, and I am sure that they have told their networks, who told their networks, and on and on. Just by mounting Twitter and listening to their customers, Continental received positive press that was exponentially the cost of the one glass of Champagne.

These are examples of two-way communications, listening to your customers, the power of peer-to-peer, Word of Mouth at the Speed of Light, and the Fundamental Shift in Power.

Other Customers

The most obvious use for social media is for marketing, sales, public relations, and communications. Remember, social media is about communicating with your customers. Social media is a set of highly effective tools for customer service, business-to-business (B2B), and internal communications.

Marketing and sales is in part responsible for prospects converting to customers, but in many cases it's what happens after the sales that encourages existing customers to purchase again and, as you read earlier, encourage prospects to become customers. An angry customer will tell up to 20 other people about a bad experience. A satisfied customer shares good experiences with 9 to 12 people. If you are in customer service, social media is a must. It's the perfect tool for staying connected with your customers after the sale.

B2B

If you are a company that sells B2B (business-to-business), then social media has to be an integral part of your strategy. I have been in marketing for nearly three decades and while many insist that B2B is significantly different from B2C (business-to-consumer), I disagree. There are some subtle differences, but in B2B, the second B is still a C. The reseller is still a consumer or customer.

I agree that there is some information that should be between you and your reseller such as pricing, training, and customer support, but the majority of your conversation would benefit your end user. Set up a password-protected web site and direct SMS text messaging for that content and freely distribute the rest.

Internal Customers

Don't forget about your internal customers, your employees. They want to feel like they are connected and part of the organization. Social media is an amazing set of tools that allow you to communicate directly to and with your employee base. Use Yammer as an internal, behind-the-firewall Twitter for text messages only your employees can read. Use Jott for team collaboration. Use video sharing for messages from the corner office, the "C" suite. Use photo sharing for all of your employees to exchange photos, ideas, memories, and a sense of team. Use audio podcasts in human resources to give employees updates on benefits, retirement, and their 401(k).

15 Social Media Categories

Another innate human characteristic is to put items in categories; the more items there are, the more there is a need to organize them. You can see my attempt to categorize the entire world of social media in Table 1.1. This was not an easy feat, but I think you will agree it works.

Table 1.1   The 15 Social Media Categories

Category Title	Tactics Chapters	Tools Chapters
Social Networking	Chapter 2	Chapter 23
Publish	Chapters 3–8	Chapter 24
Photo Sharing	Chapter 9	Chapter 25
Audio	Chapters 10–11	Chapter 26
Video	Chapters 12–13	Chapter 27
Microblogging	Chapter 14	Chapter 28
Livecasting	Chapter 15	Chapter 29
Virtual Worlds	Chapter 16	Chapter 30
Gaming	Chapter 17	Chapter 31
Productivity Applications	All Chapters	Chapter 32
Aggregators	Chapter 18	Chapter 33
RSS	Chapter 18	Chapter 34
Search	Chapter 19	Chapter 35
Mobile	Chapter 21	Chapter 36
Interpersonal	Chapter 22	Chapter 37

Category Descriptions and Their Tools

As you can see from the preceding table, these categories translate nicely across both Parts I and II. For example, in Part I, Tactics, Chapter 2, I discuss social networking in great detail, while in Part II, Tools, in Chapter 23, I present all of the major players in social networking.

Category 1: Social Networking

Social networking is as old as humans have been around. Just as in nearly every other species, humans have an instinctual need to be with, communicate with, and share thoughts, ideas, and feelings about their daily lives. Only the tools with which we communicate have changed over the millennia.

This category discusses the many platforms we use today in social media to connect, share, educate, interact, and build trust.

Category 2: Publish

The ability to accurately publish or record our conversations to pass on to future generations is a relatively new concept. For thousands of years, stories containing myths, legends, laws, and mores of a group or society has been passed down through oral reiteration, or storytelling. There have been clay tablets, papyrus, hieroglyphs, handwriting, the printing press, movable type, lithography, computers, desktop publishing, print-on-demand, forums, e-mail, web pages, blogs and comments, text messaging, photo and video sharing, voicemail, and Twitter; what's next?

Category 3: Photo Sharing

Napoleon Bonaparte is sometimes credited with having expressed the idea that "A picture is worth a thousand words," and if that's true, then Flickr's photographs are worth, well $4,000,000,000 \times 1,000$ . . . way too many zeros for me! Flickr now houses more than four billion photographs, and that doesn't count Picasa, SmugMug, PhotoSwarm, or the many other photo sharing sites.

Ever since there were photographs, people were sharing them with each other. Sharing photos are a way of capturing moments in time, which captures the emotions that we can share with others. Simply by looking at a photograph we get a rush of emotions, memories, and a recollection of that very moment that we can share.

Category 4: Audio

Audio is a very powerful medium. It's easier to digest than text and evoke mental images that video doesn't allow. Do you listen to the radio? Have you ever heard a book on CD? Have you ever heard Edgar Allan Poe's work read aloud?

Audio allows us to sit back and allow the author or orator to slowly spoon-feed us content with inflection, dramatic pauses, and human nuances of him being right there in the room speaking to us. While we listen to the cadence of the words being formed into sentences and thoughts, we can imagine the associated images and watch them play out in our minds to form the story the author is trying to portray.

Category 5: Video

If a picture is worth 1,000 words, then at 25 frames (pictures) per second, video adds up to 1.5 million words per minute! That's why everyone loves video!

Video is the preferred choice of medium for relaying information overall. After a hard day at work, do you pick up a book, turn on the radio, or settle down in front of the television for a good movie or uplifting sitcom? Most likely we turn to the television to coast through some nightly brain candy.

People love video because it's the next best thing to being in the same room with someone who is sharing his or her knowledge and experiences. You can hear the words, imagine the images she is conveying, and also watch and become involved in the video that is taking place at that moment. We can see what the author is explaining, and become emotionally involved in the scene. We can hear the actors' inflections while experiencing their facial expressions and body language. It is estimated that 55 percent of all communication comes from body language, while 38 percent from voice, and only 7 percent from the words themselves.

Category 6: Microblogging

Microblogging is no more than text messaging on steroids. With the demise of Pownce, for the most part we're talking about Twitter for open text communication and Yammer for internal or behind-the-firewall communication. The reason for Twitter's success was best put by Samuel Clemens (Mark Twain), when he said in the late nineteenth century, "I apologize for the length of my correspondence. Given more time, it would have been shorter."

We love the 140-character bite-sized messages because we can read and comprehend them in about five seconds. In that short amount of time, we can fully understand what the writer is trying to convey. With text messaging, you don't have the opportunity to drone on and on as we do in our e-mail correspondence. With Twitter, we read it, comprehend it, and move on.

Category 7: Livecasting

Livecasting isn't for everyone, but those who livecast are passionate about it. My friend Jody Gnant livecasted her life for nine full months, 24/7. Chris Pirello has been uStream'n his livecast of himself for years. Both have built a tremendous following and skyrocketed their music and careers.

Livecasting is broadcasting video live. It could be 24 hours a day or just for a simple one-hour television show. Livecasting is the ultimate in reality television and it's available for free to everyone. So if you've always dreamed of creating and starring in your own television show, the companies in this chapter can help you realize your dream.

Category 8: Virtual Worlds

When organizations such as the American Cancer Society, CNN, Dell, Disney, Harvard, IBM, MTV, Reuters, Starwood Hotels, Sun Microsystems, Toyota, and Wells Fargo are all participating in virtual worlds, there must be something to it.

The American Cancer Society has actually raised $650,000 in real dollar donations during their time there. IBM holds their monthly engineers' meetings at their headquarters in Second Life where engineers from all over the world meet, talk, exchange ideas, and watch presentations.

I have some oceanfront land and a two-story Mediterranean mansion in Second Life in which the first floor is a virtual store where you can purchase three-dimensional Internet advertising (paper models). My three developers meet me there from time to time to discuss projects and design ideas. They are in the Ukraine and I have never met them face-to-face other than our time in Second Life.

Category 9: Gaming

Online gaming may seem like an odd category for *The Social Media Bible,* but it really isn't. Did you know that 17 million people are playing Halo 3 or an additional 17 million playing World of Warcraft? Any time you can measure a target audience in the millions, you need to be there.

Many Fortune 1000 companies have participated in gaming as a way to build brand recognition. Hewlett-Packard puts up billboards in auto racing games. An author friend of mine had a game developed for his web site for the release of his new book that cost only a couple of thousand dollars, but now has an 18 percent conversion rate on buying his book. And mobile phone game apps is one of the fastest-growing app categories for smart phones.

Category 10: Productivity Applications

The companies highlighted here offer the widest range of features of any category in *The Social Media Bible*. These are all part of the wide range of productivity tools. These tools include event management, VoIP telecommunications, peer to peer downloads, alerts, word processing and spreadsheets in the cloud, and even online surveys.

Category 11: Aggregators

In this chapter of the book, I highlight Aggregators, web sites that allow you to choose what type of content you want to see, where you want it to come from, present it to you all in an organized page, and do it automatically all of the time. Aggregators allow you to see all of the new blogs, web pages, news, audio, photo, and video updates all in one convenient web page location. This is like having an automated worldwide web clipping service and news agency at your fingertips And, it's free.

Category 12: RSS

RSS, or Really Simple Syndication, is the name of the technology and also the name of just one of the technology providers. An RSS feature on a blog or web site allows you to sign up and automatically get notified whenever there is an update to the site including a new blog or news. Rather than having to go from site to site every day checking to see if new content has been posted, RSS notifies you when it has. RSS automatically feeds you new content from only the sites you want it from, and only when that content is new.

Try RSS by clicking the RSS button on your favorite blog site or try the Google landing page that aggregates RSS feeds from blogs, web pages, airlines, weather, or any changing information of interest to you.

Category 13: Search

Internet search is one of the most important functions of the Internet. How else would you be able to find the one page you are looking for out of the one trillion Google-indexed web pages? SEO, or Search Engine Optimization, is as important as ever. And, as the number of web and blog pages grows, search will become even more integral to your Internet experience and to your customers and prospects.

If you want your customers and prospects to be able to find you and your company, you have to make it easy for them. SEO, tags, fresh content, external reputable links (Link Love), and keyword density, all add to your company's web and blog pages' Google Juice.

Category 14: Mobile

Mobile marketing is the fastest-growing segment of technology-driven marketing. Kakul Srivastava, the general manager for Flickr, told me that there are three cell phones for every man, woman, and child on the planet. With that kind of technology penetration, you and your company needs to be participating.

Mobile phones are less expensive than laptops, desktops, and broadband, and are completely portable. Not many people in Third World countries can afford to have an Internet-connected PC, but they can all afford a mobile phone. It's through this technology that people from around the world are staying in touch with one another, accessing their e-mail, sending photos, audio, video, blogging, and surfing the Web.

Category 15: Interpersonal

This is another category of seemingly unrelated technology. The common thread, however, is that they are all tools that allow you to connect and communicate with your customers and prospects. Some companies provide the means to host a meeting for your employees or perform a webbing for 1,000 people. Some allow you to use the Internet like a free telephone service. Others allow you to convert your voice into text messages to be sent to your e-mail and other team members.

The ROI of Social Media

Pioneer's Holiday Promotion Achieves 60 Percent Click-Through Rate (CTR) Using Forums to Target Influential Automotive Enthusiasts

Background

Advertisers face the same dilemma every holiday season: How to be visible when consumers are inundated.

Strategy

Pioneer Electronics (USA) Inc. overcame that hurdle with room to spare. A holiday-themed rebate offer for Pioneer In-Dash Navigation models achieved a 60 percent click-through rate by using PostRelease to target automotive enthusiasts in online forums.

Implementation

PostRelease provides an automated way to insert sponsored posts into relevant forum discussion threads.

Pioneer Electronics turned to PostRelease to help promote its holiday rebate offers for its new flagship AVIC-Z110BT and AVIC-X910BT navigation systems. The two companies crafted a sponsored forum post that included product images, direct links to the product web pages, and the rebate page on Pioneer's web site.

The campaign ran as a sticky post—meaning the post remained in the lead position—in relevant audio-related discussion categories in 55 automotive-themed forums, from November 2 to November 9, 2009. The post was clearly marked as from PostRelease and Pioneer and, once unstuck, moved down the page as a regular forum post would. It remains part of the forum content for the life of the forum.

Opportunity

People on product-related online forums are ripe audiences for product-specific messages and offers. Consumers visit these types of forums expressly to discuss products, so they're open to relevant sponsored messages and they're more likely to respond.

Conclusion

The one-week campaign continues to drive traffic even after completion, because PostRelease posts remain archived and accessible for the life of the forum.

In fact, sponsored forum posts, clearly marked as advertisements, increase in ability to drive response over time—by an average of more than 100 percent one year after a paid campaign has ended, according to an analysis conducted by PostRelease. After 60 days, the total number of click-throughs increased by an average of 40 percent, and after 180 days, they increased by an average of 77 percent.

(continued)

(*continued*)

The reason for this residual traffic: forum posts contain content that can be discovered in search engine results, driving traffic to the ad not only from the audience of the forum in which it appears, but also directly from organic search listings.

Consumers don't have to be browsing a particular forum to discover an advertiser's message there. If a post offers useful content, it's likely to show up when it is relevant to a consumer's search for information—boosting traffic to the ad and to the forum. The click-through rates increase over time because posts are discovered by people who are actively searching for that content, and therefore are highly motivated to click through.

See one of Pioneer's posts here: http://g35driver.com/forums/g35-37-sedan-v36-2007/313580-200-rebate-pioneer-navigation-holiday-rebate.html#post4671215.

The top five forums to generate the most clicks and reads for Pioneer's holiday campaign were ClubFrontier.com, Camaroz28.com, DuraMaxForum.com, Z06Vette.com, and 300CForums.com.

No other online medium gives advertisers as precise a target as forums do.

Justin Choi
www.PostRelease.com

Justin Choi is president of PostRelease (www.PostRelease.com) and author of the white paper "Online Forums: Social Marketing with Proven Results." He can be reached at justin@postrelease.com.

Expert Insight

Peter Booth Wiley, chairman of the board, John Wiley & Sons, Inc.
www.wiley.com

Peter Booth Wiley

Not only is this book about social media, but the creation of the book is a form of social media. . . . This is a pioneering piece of work. It's been a little more than a year since we last spoke, and in that short period of time, things have changed radically. You could say we spoke pre-Kindle and now we are post-Kindle and post-iPad, and Wiley is doing things today that we were only talking about just a few years and months back. . . .

. . . I am a member of the sixth generation of Wileys involved in the publishing business; our company is 203 years old. There is a seventh generation, including two of my sons, both of whom are working in social media at Wiley. I've been the chairman of the board since 2002. Prior to joining our board of directors in 1984, I was a magazine publisher and a newspaper reporter and columnist, a writer of articles for magazines, and the author of five books. I am currently working on the revision of my last title, a guide to the architecture and history of San Francisco. Once the print version is completed, my daughter and I—we're coauthors—will work on a web site through which people taking the walking tours in the book will be able to access additional information and visuals about the buildings they are looking at. In the spirit of social media, we are giving our readers the ability to comment on what they are reading and seeing, which we can later add to our content. . . .

. . . Back in the 1800s when our company was founded, social media was writing a letter, which was handed to somebody on a horse or stagecoach. It would take roughly four days for a letter to go from, say, Virginia to New York; and in the wet, muddy seasons, it probably went by ship. . . . Sending a letter and getting a response was a very tenuous interaction. Now we've got information and creative ideas flying through the air at the speed of electrons with the ability to interact immediately. . . .

. . . In the 1950s, we began experimenting with introducing computers into the business. Twenty-five years ago, we tried to understand and experiment with computers and networks really aggressively, and our ideas about what we should be doing as a business came from our authors, our customers, and our technical advisors. We listened very carefully to them about new ways of accessing and shaping information and what they thought was going to happen. . . .

. . . We also continue to create a culture internally at Wiley that permits our colleagues to build products and related capabilities, including what we now call social experiences, or social media. We're working on capabilities that help authors share the necessary content with our customers and capabilities that help our customers find exactly the information they need in the format they want. We are helping our intermediaries (brick-and-mortar stores, online print and e-book resellers, wholesalers, et cetera) deliver the content to our customers quickly in the appropriate format. We are also building capabilities that help us internally to work collectively and that help our authors and partners interact with us and with members of their communities. . . .

. . . We use social networks (electronically, before we used them in an interpersonal way) to understand who you are and what you are capable of. So in our initial conversation when you told me of your history in the world of technology, I was very impressed. And so Step One is: "Okay, I recognize that this guy is somebody who has been right on the cutting edge himself." Step Two

(continued)

(continued)

is to use our social network to evaluate your capabilities and your proficiency in whether you are going to be able to deliver a manuscript that we'll be able to sell. . . .

. . . We built responsible risk-taking into the organization quite a while ago. The progression to where we are today in terms of digital media has not been in a straight line, and we've made mistakes at times by being ahead of the curve. I think what we've learned is it's best to be on the leading edge, rather than the bleeding edge, because we've spent time on the bleeding edge. . . .

. . . With the rapid rise of new forms of social media, we're thinking more about how we market our products. Traditionally, we talked about our author's "platform." . . . What's Lon's platform? By which we mean: "Does he speak regularly at conferences? How big are they? Is he going to get on *Oprah*? Is he going to get on *Good Morning America*? Will his books be reviewed in the *New York Times Book Review*? Sadly, the print newspaper book review is fading fast. Television, yes, it works to a degree. I think it's very effective at times. . . .

. . . We've also had experiences with other authors going on high-profile television programs and not selling a lot of books. Now we're looking more at networks, at an author's social media network, trying to understand the way in which an author creates his or her own community digitally and how we can communicate with that community to share with people what the book's all about. . . .

Another interesting thing is the understanding that the way in which an author writes his book, the connections he builds aggregating content and editing it, is creating his platform. No longer is it "Here's a book, write a marketing plan." The authoring and marketing experiences are interacting.

Of course, as a commercial publisher we are interested in metrics. So we are interested in seeing the evolution of the effectiveness of marketing and the effectiveness of networks. And I think we are at an early stage with that, but I really look to the libraries and their interaction with publishers. They are able to measure usage. Say they license a hundred journals from us; they can look at which of those journals are being used. So the librarians are saying, "Okay, I've got these hundred journals and ninety-eight of them are used heavily. Let's review the two that are used less and decide whether to replace them with other journals or whether they should remain in the collection even though there is a low usage rate."

So, there are metrics being developed, and over time. . . .

. . . But let's go back to what we were talking about earlier, about the way you are creating this book, because this tells us a lot about where publishing is now and what its future could be like.

I wrote my last book in 2000. An editor asked me to write it. I sent the manuscript to the publisher. The publisher reviewed it and edited it and sent it to production. Production designed it and laid it out. It went to the printer, then to marketing and sales, to the wholesale and retail intermediaries. And then it ended up in the customer's lap.

That's a very traditional print-on-paper model. Right now we are moving to a continuous process of content development and delivery. We have a favorite graphic that we use at a lot of meetings. It's about Frommer's. We're one of the leading travel publishers, and we've created this circle called the Travel Cycle, which illustrates how we interact with our customers at different points in their travel experience. So the first part of the cycle is when, you, the traveler, *dream* about where you are going to go. You look at travel newsletters, magazines, online forums, blogs; so right now we're publishing travel newsletters, online forums, and blogs about travel.

And then you *plan* your trip; and we are publishing guidebooks and travel web sites with text, photos, video, podcasts, recommendations, interactive maps, and custom PDF guides.

And then you *go* on your trip; and when you're traveling, we continue to interact with you with audio walking tours, iPhone guides, and map and airport guide applications.

And then after you come *back* from your trip, you share with other travelers your experience via online trip journals and photo albums, and you post your reviews and ratings, all on Wiley travel sites. So there is a continuous process of interaction here, rather than the linear process I described earlier. And when you add to that what you are doing with *The Social Media Bible,* which is working with the community (your community) to develop content and review and refine the content, you have a completely different publishing model. . . .

WileyPLUS is our online teaching and learning environment that integrates the entire digital textbook with resources to fit every learning style. Instructors are able to choose and assign the material that fits their syllabus, and students who want more information have access to the full eBook and accompanying learning materials. . . . WileyPLUS provides students with immediate feedback and redirects them to specific areas for review if they don't understand what they are being taught.

. . . Equally important, particularly right now during a recession when institutions of higher education are packed with new students, WileyPLUS gives instructors an option to select only the materials they need, while keeping costs down.

To listen to or read the entire Executive Conversation with Peter Booth Wiley, go to www
.theSocialMediaBible.com.

Credits

The ROI of Social Media was provided by:

Justin Choi, www.PostRelease.com

Expert Insight was provided by:

Peter Booth Wiley, chairman of the board, John Wiley & Sons, Inc., www.wiley.com

CHAPTER 2

Say Hello to Social Networking

What's in It for You?

A *trusted network* is a group of like-minded people who have come together in a common place to share thoughts, ideas, and information about themselves. These groups sometimes include more than 100 million registered users that host more than 10 billion photographs—as with social networking site Facebook (www.facebook.com). A trusted network can also be as small as a single, influential person.

These social networks develop the trust that ultimately creates influence among your consumers. By developing and cultivating networks, your organization can create an opportunity to develop the trust that may result in more sales.

The desire to participate in conversation and influence prospects prompted the writing of a "Sales Manifesto" for a Fortune 500 client by James Burnes, vice president of development and strategy, Internet strategy, of creative services firm MediaSauce. The following excerpt showcases the need for embracing networks to drive business:

> Why do we sell the same way we always have? Because it's safe and reliable. Because it's what we know. Because we've become entrenched in thinking that what we have to say is what our customers want to hear. Because it has worked for the past (insert number) years!

> But the world is rapidly evolving. Advertising, messaging, and communication behaviors are changing more quickly than how we tell our story. Worse, our messaging is competing more and more with the noise that overwhelms our target customers every day/hour/minute/second of their lives. Customers are tuning out

our old messages while social media and the Internet connect them with information that bypasses our expensive marketing communications strategies.

The old tried-and-true tactics of the past (insert number again!) years, like our flashy direct mail pieces, our witty trade media advertisements or those well written, but terribly expensive brochures, aren't setting us apart.

Worse, they aren't even being looked at. They're being ignored. And we're becoming irrelevant. We're becoming part of the noise.

Can we stop being noise and become relevant again? Yes! Absolutely we can. But we have to have a new way of speaking to our customers. We have to differentiate ourselves from the rest of the world and be fresh and exciting.

We need to transform the way we touch our clients, and integrate ourselves into the very fabric of what they do every day. We have to embrace social networks, digital connections, and the online experience and build an organization that embraces conversation and transparency.

We need to take advantage of a new approach to selling, where we are problem solvers and the "go to" team for our prospects whenever a project arises that we contribute to. Everyone sells [product]. We have to be bigger than our [product]. We have to solve our client's pain points.

We need to get digital. We need to take advantage of the tools digital and social media can provide us to open up new channels and speak to prospects on the business issues and problems they are trying to solve.

We need to tell our story in a way that doesn't just interrupt our clients, but engages them and gives them a reason to pass it along. We need to be viral, innovative, non-traditional, and aggressive in how we seek out new business.

How will we do it? By embracing the opportunities that social media offer us to become connected to our customers. We're going to build a culture where communicating, engaging and embracing the feedback, positive and negative, make us a better organization.

Burnes's manifesto showcases the need for transformation, and how social networks and those connections play a critical role in your business.

You will see a common theme throughout the chapters in *The Social Media Bible* that discusses people's tendency to congregate around Internet technology to exchange information and grow into larger, trusted like-minded networks. By definition, the Internet *itself* was the first electronic trusted network. When ARPAnet (see Chapter 19, Spotlight on Search (Search Engine Optimization) for more information about ARPAnet) connected its first group of computers together to share files, everyone assumed that their fellow users would follow a certain protocol, respect each other's files, and share the same interests.

(To hear Executive Conversation Interviews from Angela Courtin, senior vice president of marketing entertainment and content for MySpace; Krista Canfield, public relations manager for LinkedIn; Kyle Ford, the director of product marketing for Ning; and Bill Jula, founder of Fast Pitch!, go to www.theSocialMediaBible.com.)

The social networking site phenomenon has completely and rapidly changed the way that people interact—in regard to personal and professional relationships. And anytime there is a tool that millions of people in one place at one time, all with common interests, are clamoring to use, you, as a businessperson, need to understand it and be a part of it.

Back to the Beginning

Social networks have been around for as long as there have been humans to create them. When people were still living in caves and traveling in clans and tribes, those were the trusted social networks in which people banded together to cooperatively work, live, and protect one another. The group was counted on for protection. The words *society, tribe, clan, team, group, pod, school, flock, colony, troop, drove, clash, caravan, mob, pounce, band, quiver, pack, congregation, litter, bevy, gaggle, herd, Americans, Europeans, Latinas, family, caucus, pro ball teams, New Yorkers, Catholics, Presbyterians,* and even a *business of ferrets* all refer to social networks with similar interests and a common bond—and most important, trust.

These are the groups that help people make life's most important—and not-so-important—decisions. Before you see a movie or go to a restaurant, don't you consult your trusted network of friends and, now, web sites? If you are looking for a job, whom do you go to first? Most likely your trusted network of friends and colleagues. If you are buying a new car, you go to trusted networks of fellow drivers and informational web sites.

Any time a group of people with similar interests and collaborative trust gather in one place, businesspeople need to be participating. In fact, businesspeople also need to provide and *be* that very trusted network for the product or service. Understanding social networks is actually a twofold process that requires participating in other networks as well as becoming one for customers and prospects. In fact, the best way to understand social networks is to first participate in one. There are literally thousands of different kinds available today that you can join for free both on- and offline. But since the focus of social media is online, these are the groups upon which this chapter concentrates. The big two are the aforementioned sites MySpace and Facebook, with LinkedIn coming in as the largest professional network. These sites have amassed a great number of members, all with one common interest and goal: to socialize. Since Facebook has declined to participate in *The Social Media Bible*, MySpace and LinkedIn serve as the main examples for this chapter. Another emerging site called Fast Pitch! is a great derivation on the professional social network theme, as a site designed for companies as opposed to individual businesspeople.

What You Need to Know

A social network, trusted network, virtual community, e-community, or online community is a group of people who interact through newsletters, blogs, comments, telephone, e-mail, and instant messages, and who use text, audio, photographs, and video for social, professional, and educational purposes. The social network's goal is to build trust in a given community.

Virtual communities that utilize Web 2.0 technologies to create and develop contacts have been described as *Community 2.0*. Social networking and strong bonds have been forged online since the early days of USENET (see Chapter 19, Spotlight on Search (Search Engine Optimization) for more information on USENET), and usually depend upon collective interaction and exchange between users. The ability to intermingle with like-minded individuals instantly—from anywhere on the globe—has considerable benefits.

Every social network has different levels of interaction and participation among members. This can range from adding comments or tags to a blog (see Chapter 7, The Ubiquitous Blog) or message board posts (see Chapter 6, The Internet Forum), to competing against other people in online video games such as MMORPGs (see Chapter 17, Gaming the System: Virtual Gaming).

Life Cycle

A membership life cycle for online social networks begins when members initiate their life in a community as visitors, lurkers, or trolls (see Chapter 6, The Internet Forum, for more information). After becoming comfortable, people become novices and participate in the community dialogue. Once they've contributed for a period of time, they become regulars; and oftentimes, these regulars will break through a barrier and become leaders. Members who have been participating in the network for a while and eventually depart are known as elders. The amount of time it takes to become an elder depends on the culture of the site. It can take only a few months or more than a year. This life cycle can be applied to many social networks such as bulletin boards, blogs, and wiki-based communities like Wikipedia.

The following examples of each of the phases in the membership life cycle uses the photo sharing site Flickr:

- *Lurkers* observe the community and view photo content. They do not add to the community content or comments, and they occasionally visit the site to look at photos that someone has suggested.

- *Novices* are just beginning to engage in the community. They start to provide content and tentatively participate in a few threads. Such users make a few comments, become somewhat involved, and will even post some photos of their own.

- *Insiders* consistently add to the community discussion, comments, and content. They interact with other members and regularly post photos. They make a concerted effort to comment, rate, and participate with other members' material.

- *Leaders* are recognized as veteran participants. They connect with the regulars and are recognized as "contributors to watch." A leader would not consider viewing another member's photos without commenting on them, and he or she will often correct another member's behavior when the community considers it inappropriate. Leaders will reference other members' photos in their comments as a way to cross-link content.

- *Elders* leave the network for a variety of reasons. Maybe their interests have changed, or perhaps the community has moved in a direction that doesn't sit well with them. Their departure may be due to lack of time, lack of interest, or any number of other factors.

Contributing

There are many reasons that people want to contribute to social and knowledge-sharing networks like blogs and wikis (see Chapter 8, The Wisdom of the Wiki). In fact, the number of individuals who spend a great deal of time contributing to such web sites is pretty amazing. People usually become motivated to contribute valuable information to the group with the expectation that one will receive useful help or information and recognition in return. This kind of reciprocation is particularly important to many online contributors. Some individuals may also freely contribute valuable information because they get a sense of contribution and a feeling of having some influence over their environment. Social psychology dictates that people are social beings who are gratified by the fact that they receive direct responses to their input. Blogs are a good example of this kind of immediate acknowledgment, whereby readers can instantly comment on and participate in live content.

Dunbar's Number

In 1993, evolutionary psychologist Dr. Robin I. M. Dunbar of the Human Evolutionary Biology Research Group of the University College London anthropology department made an important discovery about the workings of social networks and human interaction. Dunbar proposed that the cognitive limit to the number of people with whom one person can maintain stable social relationships was 150. These are relationships in which individuals know who each person is, and how each person relates to every other person. The size of a typical social network is constrained to about 150 members because of possible limits in the capacity of the human communication channel.

Through the use of social media tools and social networking; however, this number has grown to maybe many hundreds. And by linking your network to each of your contacts' networks, your effective number of usable contacts can be in the millions.

Remember, social networking isn't about allowing everyone who requests to link to you be allowed to do so. It's not about the number of your contacts, but rather about the value that each one brings. Do you think it might be important to mention influencers in this instance?

Social Network Examples

The best way to explain how a social network works is to describe a few specific social networks. The big three social networks are Facebook with

425 million members, MySpace with 76 million users, and LinkedIn with 60 million users. Facebook is by far the most popular and widely used social network. Here are just a few statistics on Facebook:

- Has 425 million users
- More than 35 million users update their status each day
- More than 3 billion photos are uploaded each month
- More than 5 billion pieces of content including blog posts, news, web links, notes, photos, and so on, are shared each week
- More than 3.5 million events are created each month
- More than 1.5 million businesses have Fan Pages
- More than 20 million people become "fans" of fan pages every day

MySpace

MySpace is currently the biggest and most popular social network on the Internet, and has more than 185 million members. Owned by Fox Interactive Media (which is part of Rupert Murdoch's News Corporation), it is an international interactive web site that allows its members to create a user-submitted network of friends, personal profiles, blogs, groups, photos, music, and videos (see Figure 2.1).

In August 2003, several employees of eUniverse—and members of the then-popular social networking site Friendster—saw the potential for this kind of site's popularity and launched MySpace. Not to be distracted by the usual start-up issues, this team's success was due in part to their complete infrastructure—including finance, human resources, technical expertise, bandwidth, and server capacity. Founder, chairman, and CEO of eUniverse Brad Greenspan oversaw the MySpace project, with help from MySpace team members Chris DeWolfe (its first CEO), Tom Anderson (MySpace president), and Josh Berman—as well as a team of programmers and other resources provided by eUniverse (including the key technical expert Toan Nguyen, who helped stabilize the MySpace platform).

Since the very first MySpace users were obviously eUniverse staff members, the company held contests to see who could recruit the most new members. Employees then used the company's resources to market MySpace to the masses. eUniverse utilized its own 20-million-member base of e-mail subscribers to quickly make MySpace the most successful social network of its time.

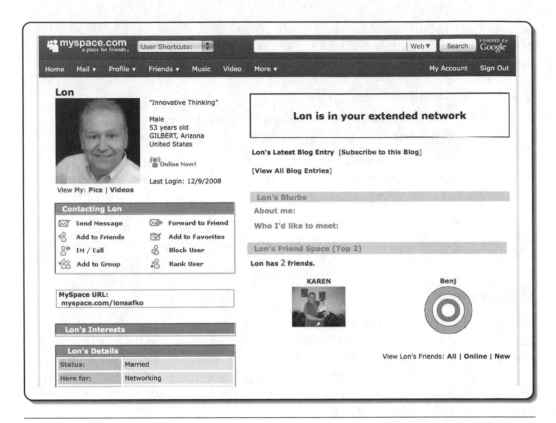

FIGURE 2.1 MySpace

In 2002, YourZ.com—designed to be a leading online data storage and sharing site and casualty of the dot-bomb era—owned the original MySpace .com domain. At that time, MySpace CEO Chris DeWolfe and a friend, while at YourZ.com, owned the MySpace URL and had intentions of creating a hosting site. DeWolfe believed that they should charge for MySpace membership, whereas eUniverse CEO Brad Greenspan felt that it was necessary to keep MySpace free and open in order to make it a large and successful community. It turned out that Brad was right.

DeWolfe and several other employees were later able to purchase equity in the new MySpace entity and its parent company eUniverse, which was renamed Intermix Media shortly before it was acquired in July 2005 by News Corporation—the parent company of Fox Broadcasting and other media enterprises. Fox acquired MySpace for $580 million, of which $327 million was directly attributed to the value of MySpace.

Driven by tapping into the U.K. music scene, MySpace launched its U.K. version in January 2006, followed by a Chinese version shortly thereafter.

REVENUE MODEL

As can be seen with many of the other social networking sites and social media tools, the revenue models are fairly simple: paid subscription, free with advertising, and free with paid upgrades (aka "Freemium"). MySpace chose the free with advertising revenue model with no paid services. The site's overwhelming success through advertising revenue is due to its technique of mining the largest user database, second only to Yahoo!. This practice allows for highly targeted advertising that taps into its huge database of behavioral data, which serves up very specific and selected ads to each individual user.

On August 8, 2006, Google signed a $900 million deal with MySpace whereby Google would provide its Google Search and advertising tools to the site. MySpace has also provided opportunity and hundreds of thousands of dollars in revenue to other, smaller companies that created added functionality through accessories, plug-ins, and widgets—including Slide, RockYou!, and YouTube.

MYSPACE FEATURES

Profile. MySpace profiles contain two standard text sections: "About Me" and "Who I'd Like to Meet." The member's profile also contains "Interests" and "Details" sections. Within the "Details" section, "Status" and "Zodiac Sign" are always on display if the profile holder fills them out. Each profile also contains a blog with standard fields for content, comments, emoticons, and multimedia.

MySpace members may also upload images, one of which can be chosen as their default image—the one that is seen on the profile's main page, search page, and the image that will appear alongside the user's name on their comments, messages, and other personal input. The user can also embed Flash, music, and video. MySpace also provides a blogging capability that has been one of the site's most popular features since its inception.

Comments. Another popular feature of MySpace is the User's Friends Space comments section. This is where the "friends," or contacts of a given member, can leave comments for all of the other viewers to see. As with most every blog, MySpace users can read and approve any comment and have the option to delete any comment before it is posted.

Customization. One of the most popular and powerful MySpace features is the user's ability to customize one's own profile page. This high-level interface allows a member with no programming experience whatsoever to simply drag, drop, and click one's way through creating a very unique web page with its own look and feel, fonts, colors, and rich media content. By utilizing MySpace Music and MySpace Videos, the user is just one click away from programming this multimedia content into her or his own web page.

Music. One of MySpace's unique hooks is that it provides profiles designed specifically for musicians and bands. These profiles differ from the average users', since they allow artists to upload as many as six MP3 songs of their own creation. MySpace has provided the very popular SNOCAP to unsigned musicians to upload, share, and even sell their music. And by using the trusted social networking environment that MySpace provides, many artists have created huge followings of fans and supporters. MySpace has even launched its own record label—MySpace Records—which is intended to assist and discover previously unknown talented artists. In fact, more than eight million artists have already been discovered.

Bulletins. These types of posts are published on bulletin boards on which everyone can read the content. They are useful for contacting your entire list of friends without sending individual messages to each. A bulletin can be about you posting new photos, an event like a party, a book or movie review, or just something new about you that you want all of your friends to know about (see Chapter 6, The Internet Forum).

Groups. The MySpace Groups feature allows a collection of users to share a common page and message board. Anyone can create a group, and a group's moderator can approve or deny anyone from joining. Some examples of MySpace groups are a special hobby such as surfing or scrapbooking, an illness support group, or the fans of a particular band.

MySpace IM. In spring 2006, MySpace introduced the stand-alone software MySpaceIM—the company's own brand of instant messenger. MySpaceIM uses the member's account information to log in to its service. MySpaceIM users get instant notification of new MySpace messages, friend requests, and comments, which can be received on their computer, their PDA, or even their mobile telephone. This way, they can stay in constant contact with all of their MySpace friends.

MySpace TV. In the first quarter of 2007, MySpace introduced its version of YouTube, MySpaceTV. MySpace is also talking about providing this content on conventional television. MySpace inked a deal in 2008 to distribute original video content internationally on www.reuters.com/article/idUSN0929275920080410 and http://news.cnet.com/8301-10784_3-9915692-7.html.

MySpace Mobile. MySpace fully understands the importance of the mobile telephone, and has created a variety of ways in which users can experience MySpace content on their cell phones. American cell phone provider Helio released a series of mobile telephones in 2006 whereby MySpace members can access and edit their own profiles as well as viewing others' in MySpace Mobile. UIEvolution, a company that provides cross-platform access to data, and MySpace have also developed a mobile version of MySpace that works on a wider range of carriers, including AT&T, Vodafone, and Rogers Wireless. Of course, these apps are also available for the iPhone, Android, BlackBerry, and other popular smart phones. (For more information on mobile telephone marketing, see Chapter 21, The Formidable Fourth Screen (Mobile).)

MySpace News. In April 2007, MySpace launched a service called MySpace News that allows users to link to and display reports from their favorite RSS news feeds. MySpace News also lets members rank each news story by vote. As it is with Digg, a community-based news article popularity web site that combines social bookmarking, blogging, and syndication, the more votes a story gets, the higher up the page it moves. (For more information on RSS, see Chapter 18, RSS—Really Simple Syndication Made Simple.)

MySpace Classifieds. In August 2006, MySpace added full-service classified advertising that lets you buy and sell, find a job, and more—like you would see in any newspaper or online classified ads. MySpace Classifieds grew 33 percent in the first year alone.

MySpace Karaoke. On April 29, 2008, MySpace launched its MySpace Karaoke (ksolo.myspace.com), a feature that allows users to upload to their profile page their favorite audio recordings of themselves singing Karaoke. Friends of the user can then view and rate the performances. MySpace president Tom Anderson has stated that the video version is now available.

MySpace Polls. MySpace Polls is a feature that allows users to post polls on their profile and share them with other users. You can create your own unique polls such as for baby names, video of the week, favorite holiday, favorite Christmas movie, long hair or short hair, hottest guys, who is the best athlete, and so on.

MySpace Forum. MySpace also provides its users with the ability to create and participate in forums such as automotive; business and entrepreneurs; campus life; career center; comedy; computers and technology; culture, arts, and literature; fashion; filmmakers; food and drink; games; and so on. (For more information on forums, see Chapter 6, The Internet Forum.)

Politics. Every 2008 presidential hopeful—from the most popular candidate to the lesser-known, minor-party participants—created a MySpace profile in the hopes of soliciting younger voters. Their profiles featured blogs, photos, and videos, and several involved and engaged their constituents in their campaigns through MySpace forums and features. Many people believe that Barack Obama's zeal for MySpace and social media had a significant impact on his voter turnout, which may have swayed the election in his favor.

Candidates aren't the only group that has used the power of MySpace connections. Political organizations such as Greenpeace, the ACLU, and Food Not Bombs have created MySpace profiles to keep in touch with and engage their membership base to keep in contact, to post events and information about proposed new legislation, and to inform, educate, and just build community.

Child Safety Issues. MySpace senior vice president Angela Courtin has made it very apparent that child safety is a matter of the utmost importance—and that MySpace takes every step possible to protect kids. For one thing, a user must be at least 14 years old to create an account on MySpace, and age groups for 14- and 15-year olds are automatically set to private. Members who are 16 years old and older have the option of setting their profiles to public or private, which means that no one can view or message a member under the age of 16. MySpace will also delete any profile and block the IP address of anyone suspected of inappropriate behavior.

LinkedIn

LinkedIn is an online professional contact database that was founded in December 2002 and launched in May 2003. The site allows its members to create a profile and network with the other 25 million LinkedIn members from over 150 industries. LinkedIn was established by former PayPal vice president Reid Hoffman, who is currently the company's president of product and chairman of the board. Dan Nye, previously executive vice president and general manager, investment management, of Advent Software, serves as its CEO (see Figure 2.2).

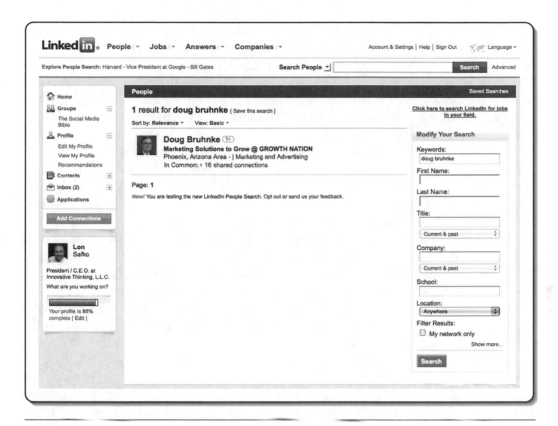

FIGURE 2.2 LinkedIn

The typical LinkedIn member is 41 years old with an average household income of $109,704. Sixty-four percent of members are male, and 80.1 percent are college graduates. Job title breakdowns are as follows: chairperson, 7.8 percent; executive or senior vice president, 6.5 percent; senior management, 16 percent; middle management, 18 percent; and 50 percent are decision makers.

FEATURES

The purpose of LinkedIn is to provide an online professional contact database of its members, and to allow them to link their profiles with those of people whom they know and trust—their connections. The LinkedIn user can invite anyone who is a LinkedIn member to connect with them. This list of connections then increases exponentially in value, due to the connections of your connections and their connections.

The LinkedIn value proposition is often referred to as the Kevin Bacon effect. This makes reference to a popular trivia game called *Six Degrees of Kevin Bacon,* in which a player names an actor in a movie, then an actor who has starred with that actor, then an actor who has starred with the second actor. This continues until you have named an actor who has also starred with Kevin Bacon within six contacts, or degrees, of separation. The concept for the game stemmed from a 1994 comment by Bacon that he had "worked with everybody in Hollywood or someone who's worked with them." The surprising part is that this always seems to work—not just with Kevin Bacon, but with anyone. This is based on the unproven, but amazingly effective idea that everyone on the planet can be connected through a chain of acquaintances by only four other people in between.

Primary or first connections on LinkedIn—people whom the user knows directly and to whom they are immediately linked—can be viewed and contacted at any time. Second-degree connections are contacts that the people you know, know; and third-degree connections are the contacts that *they* know, and so on. This continuous linking allows the LinkedIn member to see connections and be part of a trusted network that would otherwise be impossible to establish.

Members use LinkedIn to find jobs and business opportunities in response to recommendations from a contact in their network. Employers can list job opportunities and search for potential candidates, and job seekers can review the profiles of the person who is hiring to discover who in their first-, second-, or even third-connection contact list can introduce them. This design permits the member to see the relationships, but only contact someone they don't know through the chain of people they do know—a process that protects the privacy and integrity of the members from spamming and unwanted solicitation, and an approach that builds trust within the network.

If this is the first time you have heard of the LinkedIn six-degrees approach, it may seem confusing to you. A real-life example may help, from the content-creation stage for *The Social Media Bible*. When creating the list of Executive Conversations for *The Social Media Bible* web site, one of the authors of the first edition of this book researched and listed *New York Times* best-selling authors, CEOs, founders, and senior vice presidents of the largest companies in the world within the social media ecosphere. But how was a telephone call arranged with the CEO of a Fortune 500 company? How does one possibly walk in off the street, get past the gatekeepers, and begin a chat with a company founder or president? It doesn't typically happen, but if you *know* people—or know people who know people—it could take place. (See James Burnes, MediaSauce, for an example: blog www.blog.mediasauce.com/2009/01/09/linked-in-is-a-sales-secret-weapon. Go to www.theSocialMediaBible.com for "clickable links.")

When writing Chapter 16, Virtual Worlds—Real Impact, Second Life was identified as the largest virtual world player in this space. The CEO of Second Life is Mark Kingdon—a natural subject for an interview. A LinkedIn search turned up Kingdon, and the site showed that he was three degrees separated from one of the authors of the previous edition. The chain of acquaintances revealed a direct contact named Doug Bruhnke, who was directly connected to someone named Steve, whom Bruhnke had worked with in the past. And Steve had gone to college with Mark Kingdon. Bingo!

Now, what do you think the odds were of getting in touch with Kingdon through a close friend and colleague? Very good, of course. And—given that there is good reason—what are the odds that his friend would pass an e-mail on to an old college roommate? Very good again. Sure enough, within 30 minutes of the initial contact with Doug, the author received a call from Mark Kingdon. That's the power of LinkedIn, and that's the power of belonging to one or more trusted networks.

Answers. LinkedIn has a feature called Answers (similar to Yahoo! and Google's Answers features), where users get to toss out a question to the entire community. This free feature is a very effective way of solving your most complex problems, and finding answers to questions like: Who has a shopping cart solution for a medium-sized online company, or where can one find an attorney who understands international copyright law, or does anyone know how to import products from China?

Groups. Like many other social and professional networks, LinkedIn has searchable Groups wherein a member can create a group about a particular topic—and other members can join the group to discuss a common interest or industry, hobby, college, religion, or political viewpoint. LinkedIn Groups are similar to forums (see Chapter 6, The Internet Forum for more on this topic).

What about events and jobs?

Other. In addition to groups, forums, and personal connections, LinkedIn also offers its members the ability to conduct their own polls. Similar to the MySpace Polls, LinkedIn allows you to create and execute your own polls. Send them to your network, and it's free; send them outside your network, and you pay $50 minimum per response. In February 2008, the site launched a mobile version that gives access to LinkedIn over a mobile telephone and is available in six different languages: Chinese, English, French, German, Japanese, and Spanish.

BusinessWeek blogger Jon Fine wrote in his blog Coolfer: "What Do You Get for Two Million MySpace Friends and 26 Million Streams?"

Atlantic rapper T.I. has passed 2 million MySpace friends, his MySpace page has over 82.6 million views, and his hit single "Whatever You Like" has over 27 million streams at MySpace. Right now all of the songs at his MySpace page are collectively getting well over 1 million streams per day and to date have streamed over 138 million times.

How does all that translate into cash?

Contextual advertising on a MySpace page can bring in $15,000 per day if visitors listen to 1.5 million streams (which T.I. will easily exceed today). Those streams would generate even more revenue if the songs had an Amazon.com buy button (which they do not yet have). That's $105,000 in ad revenue for one week. Album sales, assuming a 15/85 digital/physical split, brought in (roughly) $5.42 million. First-week sales of "Whatever You Like" brought in $235,000 (ignoring here a la carte sales from other tracks on the album, as well as ringtones). The total of the three is $5.76 million. That's $3.75 per MySpace friend (again, not including ringtones). . . .

For the complete article, go to www.coolfer.com/blog/archives/2008/10/what_do_you_get.php, or go to www.theSocialMediaBible.com to click the link.

Providers

There are a lot of different social network platforms, and a host of various social network providers. You can even create your own network with web sites like Ning, which allows you to create your own branded MySpace-type pages, or host your own social network with WordPress's BuddyPress (see Chapter 5, The World of Web Pages, and Chapter 7, The Ubiquitous Blog). The sheer volume and variation of providers are too numerous to list here, but some examples are Fast Pitch!, which is a professional network focused on your company instead of the individual (go to www.theSocialMediaBible.com to hear Bill Jula's (founder of Fast Pitch!) Executive Conversation). Then there are ACTORSandCREW, AdultFriendFinder, Advogato, ANobii, aSmallWorld, ASUIsTalking, Avatars United, Badoo, Bahu, Bebo, Biip, BlackPlanet, Boomj.com, Broadcaster.com, Buzznet, CafeMom, Cake Financial, Capazoo, Care2, Classmates.com, Cloob, College Tonight, DeviantART, DontStayIn, Elftown, Eons.com, Erotas Online, Espinthebottle,

Experience Project, Facebook, Faceparty, Fetlife, Flixster, Flickr, Fotolog, Friends Reunited, Friendster, Frühstückstreff, Fubar, Gaia Online, Gather, Geni.com, Goodreads, Gossipreport.com, Grono.net, GuildCafe, Habbo, hi5, Hospitality Club, Hyves, imeem, IRC-Galleria, itsmy, iWiW, Jaiku, Jammer Direct, kaioo, Last.fm, Library Thing, lifeknot, LinkedIn, LiveJournal, Livemocha, LunarStorm, MEETin, Meetup .com, MiGente.com, Mixi, mobikade, MocoSpace, MOG, Multiply, Muxlim, MyChurch, MyHeritage, MySpace, myYearbook, Nasza-klasa.pl, Netlog, Nettby, Nexopia, Ning, Odnoklassniki.ru, OkCupid, Orkut, OneWorldTV, OUTeverywhere, Parlus, Passado, Passportstamp, Pingsta, Plaxo, Playahead, Playboy U, Plurk, ProfileHeaven, quarterlife, RateItAll, Ravelry, Reunion.com, Ryze, scispace.net, Shelfari, Skyrock, Sonico.com, Soundpedia, Stickam, Student.com, StudiVZ, Tagged .com, Taltopia, TravBuddy.com, Travellerspoint, tribe.net, Trombi .com, Tuenti.com, Twitter, V Kontakte, Vampirefreaks, Vox, WAYN, WebBiographies, Windows Live Spaces, Wis.dm, Xanga, XING, Xiaonei, Yelp, Inc., and Youmeo.

To view Top Social Media Sites (ranked by unique worldwide visitors eBizMBA, June 2010), please visit www.ebizmba.com/articles/social-networking-websites.

The ROI of Social Media

Southwest Airlines Generates Top Sales and Web Site Traffic Days Using Social Media

Background

In July 2007, Southwest Airlines joined Twitter. Shortly thereafter, the airline began source coding all of the links it distributed in its tweets. Then, sometime in 2008, something amazing happened. Southwest Airlines Emerging Media managers Paula Berg and Christi Day discovered that seven customers had clicked from Twitter through to southwest.com and made a purchase that week. A whopping *seven*! Their excitement was quickly deflated when a colleague suggested that they *not* report their findings because the number "was so small." Technically, the colleague was right. Relative to the millions of people that book travel on southwest.com each year, seven didn't sound very impressive. But while the number was small, the potential was huge!

(continued)

(*continued*)

Strategy

Continue to engage with customers on Twitter, build a following, cultivate relationships, and monitor activity. In the meantime, bang down internal doors to make colleagues understand the revenue potential of Twitter and other social media channels, commit more resources and staffing power to the airline's social media efforts, and develop appropriate sale opportunities to test in said channels.

Implementation

In 2009, less than a year later, Southwest launched a 48-hour fare sale using nothing more than social media and public relations to promote it—no paid advertising—and achieved its top two sales and web site traffic days in the airline's 38-year history. If anyone thought it was an anomaly, three months later, they did it again.

Opportunity

Inspire organizational change and drive revenue with increased investment in social media.

Conclusion

Anyone who works in social media sees its power and possibility every day. The ultimate challenge is finding ways to persuade peers and leaders to take risks, pursue new opportunities, and make the long-term investment required to succeed. Measurement and reporting can be powerful tools in gaining resources and support, but charts and graphs are just numbers on a page, and they don't predict the future. When measuring and reporting social media, it's essential to not just report past activity but to read between the numbers to spot trends, patterns, and possibilities. Reporting social media should, at times, be like reporting the weather—ignoring what the numbers were yesterday and focusing instead on what the numbers could be tomorrow—and then using that information to educate, inspire, and drive the organizational change needed to meet the needs and possibilities of the changing media landscape.

Paula Berg, Southwest.com

Expert Insight

**Gretchen Howard, director of online sales
and operations, Google AdWords,
www.google.com/corporate/execs.html**

Gretchen Howard

. . . I'm a director at Google and I work on online sales and operations and I've been at Google for about two and a half years. I had a varied path before I landed at Google. I worked in financial services and also in consulting before that. . . .

. . . Sure, let's start with an acronym that you mentioned from the start, Search Engine Marketing, or SEM. Search Engine Marketing is really not intermixed with online advertising. It refers to programs that enable advertisers to run relevant ads alongside search results. So when users perform queries on a search engine, such as Google, online advertisement will also come up. . . .

. . . These onlines are featured advertisements that you're talking about; this is what we call AdWords. So AdWords is just Google's online advertising program. And we really like to describe AdWords as, it may sound a little corny, but I like to explain it as a matchmaking service that can match businesses and customers. They're really the tools that connect businesses to a product and services that sell and customers who are looking for those specific products and services, and online. And it's really done by matching relevant products and services to customers' search queries, and the thing that excites me most about AdWords is that it's highly targeted and cost effective. So it's a measurable system that helps advertisers, both large and small, find their customers online. . . .

. . . It's all about relevance, and so it's really easy to set up. One thing, just to take you quickly through how it works: When you go to www.google.com/adwords, you selected "daily budget," you create an ad. And you target your ad by choosing keywords and a geographic location, and then you let it run. So it's a cost-per-click model, which means advertisers only pay when users click on their ads. And then they are delivered to the advertiser's web site.

So a click can be as low as one cent and you can modify your daily budget at any time. So you're not trapped into a large fee at any time. . . .

. . . It's a pay-per-click model, and that's why our philosophy is that all advertising should be relevant, targetable, and cost effective. And that's why the pay-per-click model comes in because it holds us accountable and not the advertisers with customers. . . .

(continued)

(*continued*)

. . . The other thing that it does is it really levels the playing field. And so it offers this powerful, measurable solution to the needs of both small and niche businesses, as well as large brand advertisers. So in some ways it really democratizes the Web, which is just ground-breaking. . . .

. . . And it doesn't matter how specific. I mean the more specifically someone's looking for something, the easier they're going to find exactly what they're looking for. And so the user experience and the customer experience are both important to their business, and it helps both Google and the online advertisers, as well. So it's really a win-win situation. . . .

. . . So we have an ad traffic quality team and they're constantly at EQ. We have a three-stage system for detecting invalid clicks. The three features are (1) proactive real-time filters, (2) proactive offline analysis, and (3) reactive investigation. And this combined approach is really the essence of click-fraud management. The goal is to cap the net of invalid clicks efficiently, live, in order to have a high degree of competence so that actual malicious behavior is effectively filtered out.

So by proactively filtering these clicks, potentially worth hundreds of millions of dollars every year, we're able to provide a very effective protection against attempted click-fraud, and we take it very seriously. . . .

. . . Google has devoted significant resources and expertise to developing proactive and technically sophisticated measures to filter invalid clicks before advertisers are ever charged for them. We recognize that advertiser satisfaction, from an advertiser's point of view is extremely important. So we investigate every click-fraud claim that comes in to us and we really try to respond to those advertisers' requests as appropriately and timely as possible. . . .

. . . And if we don't catch it proactively (and we do catch most of them proactively) we will absolutely credit advertisers retroactively because the last thing we want is for advertisers to be negatively affected by click-fraud in any way. . . .

. . . But I think this integrity is so key to the essence of our business that it's extremely important for our customer experience and our advertiser experience to be top notch. . . .

. . . AdWords actually is very easy to get started. I like to break it down into three main steps. First: As in any time you're creating an advertising campaign, especially an online marketing campaign, I think the first step and advice that I always give people is, "Know your audience; identify your goals." Precision is the key to search advertising. You want to reach the right advertisers at the right time.

Take a good look at the products or services you are selling and the customers who are buying them. You'd be amazed at how many people don't know who their target audience is and this is an essential first step. Then, once you have a clear sense of your business, you need to focus on how to reach those customers and you'll need to understand and define what your ultimate goal is, so you can actually measure success.

Then you can look to target specific languages or geographic locations that your business serves, and that could be your region or that could be global. . . .

. . . That's one of the beauties of online advertising. You can change your geographic targeting at any time. So you can expand or contract or actually make seasonal changes based on geographic trends as well. . . .

. . . I think, you know, if you are someone in northern California and you're selling a snowboard, you can have a huge presence in the winter in northern California, but in the summer it's a slow time. So why not market those snowboards to folks in New Zealand where it's winter in your summer? So it's a great way to discount the seasonality of your business. . . .

. . . And that leads me to point Number Two and how to get started. It's the second tip that I tell people: "You really have to create effective campaigns." So the first step in that is choosing powerful keywords. Really start brainstorming and expand your list as broadly as possible, and then narrow your focus. Try to think like your customers do and use two- to four-word combinations instead of general words so you really target the audience that you're going after.

The other piece is that advertisers need to write what I call, "Got-to-Click" ads. So those are ads that users feel *compelled* to click on and learn more. Get to the point quickly, convey key product benefits, like free shipping or promotion; and then use "strong calls to action" such as "buy now" or "sign up today" and really direct users to the landing piece on your site that most relates to your ad. And not just to the general landing page, but make it as specific as possible so people get to the information that they are looking after and so they don't have to navigate further once they reach your web site. . . .

. . . Keep the complexity out of the interaction and you will have many more sales than you ever dreamed possible. And I think that's a great point.

The third step is, "Track, test, adopt, and thrive." You really need to adopt an attitude where you're continually looking at the data that the online advertising provides you, and you continue to experiment. The online advertising environment is really dynamic and you can look at your marketing results and keep a close eye on statistics. And again, this is different from any other form of advertising.

You can leverage conversion-tracking software. Lots of people provide free software and at Google it's the Google Analytic product, but there's lots of

(*continued*)

(*continued*)

tools like Google Analytic that provide data that will allow you to glean insight into your web site and how to improve it and make changes so you can achieve your goals. . . .

. . . I think using two- to four-word combinations instead of general words is . . . helps you become more targeted to reach that very specific audience, and it is usually much cheaper than a general keyword. . . .

. . . There are lots of other kinds of advertising we do. You can do print campaigns and you can do TV campaigns. . . .

. . . You can do audio campaigns, but I think that will take another whole session when there's time. But we're always looking at ways we can be innovative and, again, bring that targeted, measurable approach to general advertising. . . .

. . . AdSense is (and this is not my area of expertise) the team that manages our relationships with publishers. So they manage something called the "Content Network." The best example of this is to think about the *New York Times*. They have an online presence and they run AdSense advertisements on that page from various publishers that are relevant to the content in their stories.

So if you're online on the NewYorkTimes.com and you're reading a story about dogs, there might be [an] advertisement shown from different pet food providers. And that's why we call these publishers, such as the *New York Times,* our AdSense publishers. . . .

. . . Anyone can put AdWords or AdSense ads on their blog and basically anytime someone clicks through an ad from your published site, such as a blog, part of that revenue that's derived from clicking through that ad is shared with the publisher. . . .

. . . It's great for blogs and any type of publishers to actually have that relationship with Google, and it also provides valuable advertisements to their users based on the subject that they're writing about. . . .

. . . You can start at Google.com/Adword; you select a daily budget. That's how much you want to spend per day. You actually create an ad, you write a text ad, and then you choose your keywords and geographic location, and that's it! You let it run. So it's really quite easy to set up. You don't have to be tech-savvy to do it. There is a wizard that will take you through step by step. But there are some common mistakes that people do when setting up an account that I'd be happy to walk through if that's an interest. . . .

To listen to or read the entire Executive Conversation with Gretchen Howard, go to www.theSocialMediaBible.com.

For additional Expert Insight excerpts on this subject, go to www
.theSocialMediaBible.com:

- Chris Pirillo, geek and technology enthusiast
- Robert Scoble, famous blogger and author
- Kyle Ford, director, product marketing, Ning
- Stephanie Ichinose, director of communications for Yelp

Commandments

1. **Thou shalt create profiles and groups.**

    Go the most popular social networking sites—MySpace, LinkedIn, Facebook, Fast Pitch!—and create profiles and groups before someone else takes your names. Then create more profiles on lesser-known sites as well.

2. **Thou shalt use Open Social.**

    Google's Open Social–Open ID program will allow you to create a social networking profile and propagate it with just a click of the mouse. Just go to a new social networking web site, create a profile, and click Open Social ID and the profile is completely filled in. This will save you a lot of time typing in the same information over and over for each profile. (It seems strange not to mention Facebook Connect, since it's pretty ubiquitous at this point.)

3. **Thou shalt participate.**

    Start out by reading the comments on a few selected sites and listen to where the conversation is headed. Once you have an idea about how to appropriately respond, then participate.

4. **Thou shalt build your own network.**

    Start building a following with your blog. Comment on other blogs and join in the conversation. Then consider building your own group or social network by using Ning or WordPress Group Platform.

Conclusion

The key to networking—as with all of the social media tools—is to participate. Go to the sites mentioned in this chapter—LinkedIn, MySpace, Facebook, Flickr, YouTube—and any other social network platform you can think of and create your profile and groups. If you don't, someone else will take your name or industry group—and it will be lost forever. Use Google Open Social or Open ID, which will allow you to fill in new profiles with the click of a button and will save you a great deal of time.

Robert Scoble, famous Microsoft blogger, continuously says that to be successful in networking, first listen, then participate. It's like being at a social gathering.

So—join the party! You wouldn't walk into a party, step over to a group of people talking, interrupt, and immediately start telling them about yourself. (Well, maybe once.) But this is how people are currently marketing; and it's not really working that well. First, you have to actually be at the party. Then, you walk over, listen for a while, and then join in on the conversation with something valuable and appropriate to add. Social media marketing for businesses is exactly the same thing. To repeat, because it's important: You first have to be at the party, and then select a group, listen to them—and *then* join in with something valuable. That's how you build community, and that's how you build trust both offline and online.

To hear all of the Expert Interviews, go to www.theSocialMediaBible .com.

Readings and Resources

Baker, Wayne E. *Achieving Success through Social Capital: Tapping the Hidden Resources in Your Personal and Business Networks*. (Hoboken, NJ: John Wiley & Sons, Inc.)

Barney, Darin. *The Network Society*. (Hoboken, NJ: John Wiley & Sons, Inc.)

Basagni, Stefano, Marco Conti, Silvia Giordano, and Ivan Stojmenoviç, eds. *Mobile Ad Hoc Networking*. (Hoboken, NJ: John Wiley & Sons, Inc.)

Belle, Deborah (ed.). *Children's Social Networks and Social Supports*. (Hoboken, NJ: John Wiley & Sons, Inc.)

Brogan, Chris, and Julien Smith. *Trust Agents: Using the Web to Build Influence, Improve Reputation, and Earn Trust*. (Hoboken, NJ: John Wiley & Sons, Inc.)

Castells, Manuel. *The Rise of the Network Society: The Information Age: Economy, Society, and Culture*, Volume I, 2nd ed. with a New Preface. (Hoboken, NJ: John Wiley & Sons, Inc.)

Cross, Robert L., and Robert J. Thomas. *Driving Results through Social Networks: How Top Organizations Leverage Networks for Performance and Growth*. (Hoboken, NJ: John Wiley & Sons, Inc.)

Dixit, Sudhir, and Ramjee Prasad (eds.). *Technologies for Home Networking*. (Hoboken, NJ: John Wiley & Sons, Inc.)

Durland, Maryann M., and Kimberly A. Fredericks. *Social Network Analysis in Program Evaluation: New Directions for Evaluation*, No. 107. (Hoboken, NJ: John Wiley & Sons, Inc.)

Engelbrecht, Andries P. *Fundamentals of Computational Swarm Intelligence*. (Hoboken, NJ: John Wiley & Sons, Inc.)

Evans, Dave. *Social Media Marketing: The Next Generation of Business Engagement*. (Hoboken, NJ: John Wiley & Sons, Inc.)

Fraser, Matthew, and Soumitra Dutta. *Throwing Sheep in the Boardroom: How Online Social Networking Will Transform Your Life, Work and World*. (Hoboken, NJ: John Wiley & Sons, Inc.)

Goldsmith, Stephen, Gigi Georges, and Tim Glynn Burke. *The Power of Social Innovation: How Civic Entrepreneurs Ignite Community Networks for Good*. (Hoboken, NJ: John Wiley & Sons, Inc.)

Grewe, Lynne. *Open Social Network Programming*. (Hoboken, NJ: John Wiley & Sons, Inc.)

Halpern, David. *Social Capital*. (Hoboken, NJ: John Wiley & Sons, Inc.)

Hart, Ted, James M. Greenfield, and Sheeraz D. Haji. *People-to-People Fund-Raising: Social Networking and Web 2.0 for Charities*. (Hoboken, NJ: John Wiley & Sons, Inc.)

Jue, Arthur L., Jackie Alcalde Marr, and Mary Ellen Kassotakis. *Social Media at Work: How Networking Tools Propel Organizational Performance*. (Hoboken, NJ: John Wiley & Sons, Inc.)

Kanter, Beth, and Allison Fine. *The Networked Nonprofit: Connecting with Social Media to Drive Change*. (Hoboken, NJ: John Wiley & Sons, Inc.)

Lacy, Kyle. *Twitter Marketing For Dummies*. (Hoboken, NJ: John Wiley & Sons, Inc.)

Lewis, Ted G. *Network Science: Theory and Applications*. (Hoboken, NJ: John Wiley & Sons, Inc.)

Nanton, Carmela R., and Mary V. Alfred (eds). *Social Capital and Women's Support Systems: Networking, Learning, and Surviving: New Directions for Adult and Continuing Education*, No. 122. (Hoboken, NJ: John Wiley & Sons, Inc.)

Oakes, J. Michael, and Jay S. Kaufman (eds). *Methods in Social Epidemiology*. (Hoboken, NJ: John Wiley & Sons, Inc.)

Poynter, Ray. *The Handbook of Online and Social Media Research: Tools and Techniques for Market Researchers*. (Hoboken, NJ: John Wiley & Sons, Inc.)

Reagan, Dusty. *Twitter Application Development For Dummies*. (Hoboken, NJ: John Wiley & Sons, Inc.)

Sarason, Seymour B., and Elizabeth M. Lorentz. *Crossing Boundaries: Collaboration, Coordination, and the Redefinition of Resources*. (Hoboken, NJ: John Wiley & Sons, Inc.)

Silver, David. *The Social Network Business Plan: 18 Strategies That Will Create Great Wealth*. (Hoboken, NJ: John Wiley & Sons, Inc.)

Simon, Phil. *The Next Wave of Technologies: Opportunities from Chaos*. (Hoboken, NJ: John Wiley & Sons, Inc.)

Singh, Shiv. *Social Media Marketing For Dummies*. (Hoboken, NJ: John Wiley & Sons, Inc.)

Turner, Bryan. *The New Blackwell Companion to Social Theory*. (Hoboken, NJ: John Wiley & Sons, Inc.)

Downloads

For your free downloads associated with *The Social Media Bible*, go to www.theSocialMediaBible.com, and enter your ISBN number located on the back of the book above the bar code. Be sure to enter the dashes.

Credits

The ROI of Social Media was provided by:

Paula Berg, Southwest.com

Expert Insight was provided by:

Gretchen Howard, director of online sales and operations, Google AdWords, www.google.com/corporate/execs.html

Technical edits were provided by:

Lynne Johnson, www.lynnedjohnson.com

CHAPTER 3

Everyone's a Publisher

What's in It for You?

This chapter is intended to introduce the concept of "Everyone's a Publisher." The fact that anyone can publish anything from text, to audio, to photos, to video and make it instantly available to millions of people from around the world is an amazing feat. Then to be able to do this instantly and for free is even more amazing. With the advent of the World Wide Web and the Internet, anyone can type into their web log, or blog, all of their thoughts and simply by hitting the "publish" button distribute that content around the world. It's "Word of Mouth at the Speed of Light."

Included in this overview are web pages, forums, blogs, and wikis. Here are some reasons you need to be aware of each of these:

Chapter 5—The World of Web Pages

In July of 2008, Google hit a milestone, when they recorded one trillion (that's 1,000,000,000,000) unique URLs (web pages)!

Chapter 6—The Internet Forum

The Internet Forum or electronic bulletin boards was one of the very first ways we had electronic textual conversations. The Gaia Online (www.big-boards.com/rd/60/) Animation (game) role-playing community contained 1,739,069,705 posts and 21,379,149 members. That's 1.7 billion posts by more than 21 million members.

Chapter 7—The Ubiquitous Blog

Technorati is currently tracking more than 112.8 million blogs, with an additional 72,820,000 (72.8 million) Chinese blogs as counted by The China Internet Network Information Center (www.cnnic.cn/html/Dir/2007/12/27/4954.htm).

Chapter 8—The Wisdom of the Wiki

Wikipedia, the online, user-generated, user-edited encyclopedia contained more than 9.25 million articles in approximately 250 languages. In March of 2010, there were 220,603 individual English articles. If the

FIGURE 3.2   Middle Babylonian Legal Tablet from Allah in Its Envelope

Source: http://en.wikipedia.org/wiki/File:CunEnv.jpg

soft clay at different angles was gradually augmented with pictographic writing, which used a sharp stylus. These two systems were eventually replaced about 2700–2500 BC by using a wedge-shaped stylus (cuneiform) to write.

Papyrus Scrolls and Hieroglyphs

Writing was very important for maintaining the Egyptian empire. Many scholars believe that Egyptian hieroglyphs came into existence shortly after

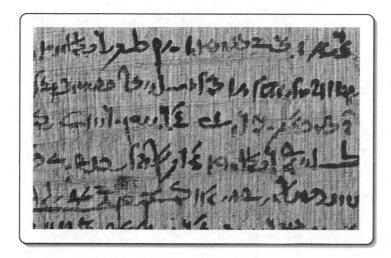

FIGURE 3.3 Papyrus Scroll

Source: http://en.wikipedia.org/wiki/File:Papyrus.jpg

Sumerian script. Going into the service of pharisaic, temple, and military authorities, only people from certain backgrounds were trained in literacy and were educated to become elite scribes.

Papyrus

Papyrus is the earliest form of paper, which is the word's origin. Papyrus is a thick, paper-like material produced from the spongy center of the stem or pith of the papyrus plant, which was a wetland rush, grass, or sedge that was abundant in the Nile Delta of Egypt.

The Dead Sea Scrolls, the most famous papyrus scrolls ever found, are a collection of about 900 documents, including texts from the Hebrew Bible. These amazing scrolls were discovered on the northwest shore of the Dead Sea in Israel in eleven caves in and around the ruins of the ancient settlement of Khirbet Qumran between 1947 and 1956. They include the oldest known surviving copies of biblical and extra-biblical documents from the late Second Temple Judaism. Theses scrolls are written in Hebrew, Aramaic, and Greek and are written on both parchment and papyrus that date between 150 and 70 BC.

Woodblock Printing

Woodblock printing is a technique that originated in China as a method of printing text, images, or patterns on textiles and later on paper and used throughout East Asia The examples date to before 220 BC, and from Egypt as far back as 400 BC.

Movable Type

Movable type is the system of printing called typography that uses movable individual letters or punctuation to reproduce a document.

Bi Sheng invented the first known movable type system in China in 1040, from wood. Later in 1230, metal movable type was invented in Korea during the Goryeo Dynasty, which produced the Jikji in 1377. This is the world's oldest printed book created using movable metal type.

The Gutenberg Printing Press

Around 1440, a German goldsmith, Johannes Gutenberg, invented a complete printing system using a screw press and a form of metal movable type, from which he cast his type pieces from an alloy of lead, tin, and antimony. These are the same ingredients still used today.

For the first time ever, his newly invented hand mold made the precise and rapid creation of metal movable type in large quantities possible. This was a key element in the profitability of printing. His mechanization of bookmaking led to the first mass production of books in history. A single Gutenberg printing press could produce 3,600 pages per day. This compared to 40 pages by hand printing and only a few by hand copying.

Lithography

Lithography is a method for printing using limestone, or a metal plate with a completely smooth surface. As a low-cost method of publishing theatrical works, lithography was created by Bavarian author Alois Senefelder in 1796.

LaserWriter Printer

It took another 200 years before Hewlett-Packard invented the laser printer in 1969. The laser printer, now a common type of computer printer rapidly produces high quality text and graphics on plain paper by the direct scanning of a laser beam across the printer's photoreceptors. This was not only the most important invention in self-publishing in our lifetimes, but ever.

For the first time in history, nearly anyone could afford this relatively inexpensive system that when connected to a computer, could produce newspapers, flyers, and books indistinguishable from professional print houses. In January 1985, Apple Computer announced their first laser printer for the Macintosh and Macintosh Office. The LaserWriter was one of the first laser printers available to the mass market. This printer had a 300 dots-per-inch resolution and a printing speed of four pages per minute, and along with the GUI-based (Graphic User Interface) Macintosh, publishing software Aldus PageMaker, and Adobe PostScript, this combination would ultimately transform the printing industry and create the whole new industry of computer desktop publishing (DTP) revolution.

Note: I was the general manager for an Apple retail store in 1985 when the Apple LaserWriter was first introduced. For $2,495, anyone could connect a Mac to it and begin publishing. I worked with a woman who was a customer who became able to create her own town newspaper, the Benton City Press in Washington State. She would use her Mac Plus to lay out the newspaper at her home office and come to our store to print each page from our LaserWriter at $1 per page. Once she was happy with the layout she would take these pages to the printer and in 24 hours, she had her town's newspaper. I knew at that moment that publishing was going to change forever.

Self-Publishing

With the advent of the Internet, sharing information and documents is as easy as clicking a button. With digital printing and no longer the need for movable type or metal plates, printing can also be done with the click of a mouse. This ease of printing lead to two major breakthroughs in publishing: print-on-demand and self-publishing.

Print-On-Demand

Now that computers and digital data have infiltrated the publishing industry, it's now easy to print one book. Previously, with the extreme labor intensity of movable type, setting up an entire book could take months of man-hours. Today, it's a click away. Large printers no longer have to do "print runs" of books, they can print one or print many and they do this on demand. This has allowed for anyone to produce a professionally printed and bound book in very small quantities.

Note: Printing this way has become so easy, publishers like John Wiley & Sons, Inc., now will create custom textbooks for teachers and professors. The teacher can specify that he would like, say, Chapters 4, 5, and 10 from one textbook and Chapters 6, 9, and 12 from another and actually create his own custom textbook.

Self-publishing, to a writer, is an incredibly powerful concept. Self-publishing solves an author's biggest dilemma: How do you get my words to a wide audience, and maybe earn some money while doing so. Self-publishing allows you, the author, to publish your book while controlling every aspect of authoring and creates the physical book. Many self-publishing services offer a range of professional editorial, marketing, and self-publishing services authors expect from a traditional publisher. Self-publishing helps you get your manuscript off your desk and into the marketplace.

Note: This, *The Social Media Bible,* Second Edition, is my seventh published book. My first two books I published were self-published: *Gratuitous Serendipity,* and *Life Is But a Dream* (both available at Amazon). At the time, they cost $199 and were really easy to produce. I used an online service called iUniverse (www.iuniverse.com). I already had the content written and they provided the template. I simply inserted my Table of Contents where it said Table of Contents, and my frontmatter where it said Front Matter. Within a few days, I had two professionally printed, softcover books available at most booksellers.

What You Need to Know

Rather than trying to duplicate all of the different "What You Need to Knows" from the next four chapters, I am going to let you jump ahead and find out in greater detail.

The ROI of Social Media

PI Social Media Network's Hive/Cross Pollination

Introduction

The PI Social Media Network includes the Procurement Insights and PI Window on Business Blogs, the PI Window on Business Show on Blog Talk Radio, and the PI Inquisitive Eye and TV2 Young Entrepreneurs Internet TV Channels. The PI Window on Business is a featured show on Blog Talk Radio.

The combined syndicated reach through affiliations with social media sites such as Blog Talk Radio (which has more than seven million listeners each month), Evan Carmichael (500,000 visitors monthly) as well as various social networking groups and forums has enabled the PI Social Media to connect with an ever-expanding audience of readers, listeners, and now viewers.

Background

The PI Social Media Network's origins began with the launch of the Procurement Insights Blog in May 2007. The Blog was created as a means of providing various magazines and publications with a single site access to our articles and reports.

Procurement Insights is today the top-sponsored blog in its industry sector in terms of the number of total sponsors.

As a means of building upon and expanding the reach of the Procurement Insights Blog, the PI Window on Business Show was launched in March 2009. Within three months, it was a featured show across the entire Blog Talk Radio Network.

In June 2009, the PI Window on Business Blog was launched as an adjunct support for the show. Within the first six months, the total number of site visitors cracked the 10,000 mark on a monthly basis.

Based on the cross-pollination between venues both within and external to the PI Social Media Network, the Procurement Insights Blog realized an 1,100 percent increase in blog visitors in the past 30 days, while both the PI Window on Business Show and Blog have seen equally impressive growth.

The PI Social Media Network recently launched two Internet TV Channels as well as corresponding blogs.

Strategy

The hive/cross-pollination concept or theory is based on the observation that individuals will likely choose at most one or two primary social networks as their preferred platforms. That is, they will spend the majority of their social networking time interacting within these main "hives."

While they may venture out into the vast social media–social networking world visiting countless other networks, similar to the honey bee, these forays are ultimately geared toward gathering information and insights to bring back to the hive to share with their established community of contacts.

Simply put, while static, single sites (regarding blogs, Web sites, and so forth) that limit their cross-pollination activities to providing somewhat passive links to other similarly myopic single site blogs or Web sites, have failed to recognize that market dynamics change, and that you have to connect with the audience through their preferred venue points.

Implementation

The PI Social Media and its service offerings provide our clients with an ability to transition from the traditional and largely ineffective broadcasting model of yesterday, to the relationship-centric conversational marketing world of social media.

(continued)

(*continued*)

Opportunity

The opportunity afforded the PI Social Media Network, through its services both in the present as well as in the foreseeable future, has been proven by the steady and sustained growth in readership, listener, and viewer base.

Through this expanded and diverse reach that leverages venues such as blogs, Internet Radio, Internet TV, and social networks, the company's increasing revenue base reflects the model's effectiveness—even during a slow economic period.

Conclusion

The following are the links to the various franchises within the PI Social Media Network:

Procurement Insights (Blog)
http://procureinsights.wordpress.com/
PI Window on Business (Blog)
http://piwindowonbusiness.wordpress.com/pi-window-on-business-show-100th-episode-special/

Jon W. Hansen

http://piwindowonbusiness.wordpress.com/book-resource-center/
jon-hansen-host-pi-window-on-business-show

Expert Insight

Tony Mamone, CEO and founder, *Zimbio*, www.zimbio.com

Tony Mamone

. . . We keep growing; it's just a fun thing to be a part of and definitely infectious here in the office just to watch our stats every month going up and up.

I think we did about 13 million unique visitors last month, so . . . I guess we need to change the tag line to "more than 10 million readers a month." . . .

. . . *Zimbio* is an interactive magazine. We focus on topics in popular culture, so we cover things like style and entertainment and sports and current events.

My background . . . I guess there's a long story and a short story; I'll go somewhere in the middle. I'm an engineer by training, but have now moved more into a business role. I have an interest and passion for Internet content and have been involved with it for quite a while now, starting off with a project that launched the site FindArticles.com, which was a poor man's version of Lexis Nexis, so it was a way to search magazine archives and look up full-text articles of popular journals and magazines.

I loved that project, really enjoyed working on it, and the site was ultimately sold to CNet. And a few years ago, I decided I wanted to get my hands back into an entrepreneurial effort and create something from scratch, and as I thought about opportunities with my partner we saw real opportunities to do something interesting and innovative in the magazine publishing space.

So, hence, *Zimbio*. And a big part of what we do here at *Zimbio* is we are trying to create the most popular and influential magazine published in the world. We start with our flagship property in Zimbio.com. It's quite different from traditional print magazines. In a lot of ways from a reader's perspective, it's not too dissimilar from what you would find in a *People* or *Vogue*, or *Elle* or *Newsweek*, but the way we create it is fundamentally different.

We try to leverage technology to automate a lot of the publishing, and we tap into our members and our readers to actually write and create much of the content. . . .

. . . [I]t's hard to get specific stats, but our best guess is that we're one of the 10 most popular magazines on the Internet right now. There are definitely a few that are above us. . . . *People* and *Time* and *Newsweek* still trump *Zimbio*, but we've passed a lot of great brands.

We are more popular than *Entertainment Weekly*, or *Sports Illustrated*, or *US Weekly Online;* and so we focus heavily on digital distribution. We don't have a print version right now. It's not necessarily something that we're going to want because as we look forward and look at what magazine publishing needs to be in 10 years, we believe that the core focus will be digital; and will . . . strip away the need for paper and ink and will sort of move toward the digital distribution model. And so we've just really focused our efforts there and we're doing quite well. . . .

. . . I think the Internet is the core focus and it will be the growth engine for the industry. At the same time, I think that print has a place, especially with magazines. There's just something fun about flipping through the glossy pages of *Rolling Stone* or checking out photos on the beach. I think there will be a place for print; I just believe the core focus of the industry and the growth engine for the industry will be digital. . . .

. . . When we started the demographic, it was a very, sort of Internet-savvy user. People that were surfing and finding these social media sites and, as we've grown, as you approach 10 million-plus readers a month, you start to look a lot more like a mass media play; so at this point our readership is really a

(continued)

(*continued*)

broad spectrum of folks who tend to be in the 18- to 34-year-old range. That's where our core concentration is, but they are really evenly spread between males and females and they're also a worldwide audience.

About 50 percent of our audience is here in the United States, but we also have an awful lot of readers in Canada and the U.K. and India and Australia, and other English-speaking markets.

Our aspirations are that hopefully in the not-too-distant future we will start to offer other languages as well and we'll truly become a global brand. So it's a pretty big spectrum of folks that check out *Zimbio* and for different purposes. It's really a consumer magazine and consumer destination site. An awful lot of people are checking it out. . . .

. . . We've got lots of folks in Ireland and all over Europe. And it's kind of fun for me as an employee of the company. I get to come in every day and check out what the most popular stories were. And a lot of times it's a rugby player in Australia, or it's an actress who's quite famous in a different market that I haven't heard of. So it's sort of a neat way to stay up to date, not only on popular culture here in the United States but popular culture worldwide. . . .

. . . I think the magazine publishing industry, and really publishing in general, is such a robust industry; there are so many publications out there and most readers tend to have many different magazines that they like to read. It's not a one-stop shop. It's not quite as cutthroat as other industries can be. There are plenty of people who read *Zimbio* and they also read a handful of other online magazines, and they subscribe to print; and so there's a little less of the, sort of, cutthroat nature that you might find if it were a conventional publication.

That said, you know I think many of the print magazines and the magazine publishers are starting to look at new media companies as a wave of growth that they're not seeing in their traditional business.

So as folks like the *New York Times* and *Time* start to evaluate their businesses and see that certain profit margins are going away and certain lines of their business aren't growing, you know they're a big company and they're looking for strategic areas of growth. Hopefully *Zimbio* boils up on their radar screen as an example of something that's working. . . .

. . . For my day-to-day job when I come into the office I don't think about what the exit strategy for *Zimbio* is. I think about what we're trying to build. And that is a longer-term view; it's not this year, it's five to ten years from now. What do we want the company to be and what do we want the brand to represent and how are we going to build an audience and how are we going to attract a readership and a contributor base that's going to volunteer and continue to work on and improve the site and the content.

And that's just such a fun project that I'm not at all anxious and not in a rush to find an exit for the company. I'm really just having a great time building it. . . .

. . . If you walk up and down the magazine aisle at your supermarket and check out the headlines on the covers, it's a pretty good representation of what you'd find on *Zimbio*. We . . . actually cover a very broad spectrum of topics. You can find things on home dècor, pets, and health topics and business topics. But our core focus is on four main categories: style, entertainment, current events, and sports.

And if you look into each of those categories on *Zimbio*, one thing that's unique about the way we cover this is that we tend to cover very specific and niche topics within those categories. So instead of covering celebrities, we cover very specific celebrities. Instead of covering sports, or even certain teams or leagues, we cover the actual athletes.

And what we try to do when you come to an athlete's section on *Zimbio*, is we try to show you a very diverse perspective, so you get a collection of photos and articles about a specific person or specific athlete, or a specific actress, a specific politician . . . and it allows you to deep drill and deep dive into one person who is making the news and making headlines, or that you're interested in. . . .

. . . There's a real craft to this and there's a history. If you look at the history of media, there are many different publications that have discovered that people like to read about other people. That's where it really gets interesting, and especially for a magazine where it's mostly reading and you're sort of just browsing because you've got some time and you're interested in a topic. It's just great to get into the details of how people make decisions, and which people are involved in which stories. That's an angle that we like to take and it's really worked for us here at *Zimbio*. . . .

. . . Let me tell you a little story about the history of *Zimbio* and how we started, and sort of lead up to how we generate our content today.

When we first started, we really fully embraced user-submitted content. That was the core and 100 percent focus of the site as we launched. And we were encouraging people to submit articles and photos and write polls, and so forth. And for the first six to twelve months of the company's history, we continued to just focus on user-generated content.

It allowed us to grow and allowed us to get started and the nice thing about starting a company that's focused on user-generated content is you don't need a lot of front cash, or capital, in order to get started; and so you can begin to build a community and nurture that community . . . and it starts to take shape.

And as we started to grow, we really started to reach out to some of our readers and try and get a better sense for what value they were finding in the site. And as we talked to folks and as we watched them use *Zimbio*, we discovered that . . . they were indifferent to the source of the content. What they were interested in was high quality content and they wanted to see diverse

(*continued*)

(*continued*)

perspectives on each story. So one thing that we offered that other folks didn't was that if they came to read the story about Obama street art and the graffiti artists that were drawing these amazing pieces of art about Barack Obama's candidacy, they saw three or four or five, or even more, different authors writing about it. And that was intriguing to them and was something that they liked. As we dug under the covers and peeled back what was going on there, we discovered that sometimes user-generated or user-submitted content was the best source. But other times there were traditional media sources out there, which we could license or find that would add to the mix.

And so where we have evolved to is we now offer a hybrid between citizen journalism and traditional media. So on *Zimbio* you'll find articles written by everyday people just like you, who want to share their opinion and have taken the time to write an article, or submit pieces of content that they feel are important and noteworthy. And you'll also find licensed articles from traditional sources, like *The Guardian,* or Associated Press, or Reuters, or *BusinessWeek.* And we try to mix the two, so that for each reader who comes to the site we can offer them the best of content that we have at our disposal. And that includes professional photography, it includes articles, news, and it includes opinion pieces by our membership. . . .

To listen to or read the entire Executive Conversation with Tony Mamone, go to www .theSocialMediaBible.com.

Conclusion

The most important concept you come away from this chapter with is that during the past 35,000 years of printed communication, we are living in a time when we have the most incredible tools at our fingertips, nearly all of these tools are free to produce your content, distribution is instantaneous, around the world, and at the speed of light, your readers can access your content at no cost, and . . . Everyone can be a publisher!

To hear all of the Expert Interviews, go to www.theSocialMediaBible.com.

Readings and Resources

Rich, Jason R. *Self-Publishing For Dummies.* (Hoboken NJ: John Wiley & Sons, Inc.)

See also Readings and Resources for Chapter 5—The World of Web Pages, Chapter 6—The Internet Forum, Chapter 7—The Ubiquitous Blog, and Chapter 8—The Wisdom of the Wiki.

Downloads

For your free downloads associated with *The Social Media Bible,* go to www.theSocialMediaBible.com, select Downloads, and enter your ISBN number located on the back of the book above the bar code. Be sure to enter the dashes.

Credits

The ROI of Social Media was provided by:

Jon W. Hansen, http://piwindowonbusiness.wordpress.com/book-resource-center/jon-hansen-host-pi-window-on-business-show

Expert Insight was provided by:

Tony Mamone, CEO and founder, *Zimbio,* www.zimbio.com

CHAPTER 4

It's Not Your Father's E-Mail

What's in It for You?

Do you think you know e-mail? Probably—since most people have been e-mailing for about a decade and a half now. Even before there was e-mail, companies were sending messages asking others in their trusted networks to look at their web site or buy their products. And although spam (called by other names, such as "junk mail" or "rubbish") had existed in bulletin boards (see Chapter 6, The Internet Forum, and Chapter 5, The World of Web Pages), it—and other commercial marketing messages—came to fruition in an especially strong manner through the birth of e-mail. After all, there isn't any other form of advertising that has a more reliable return on investment (ROI) than e-mail. What other marketing medium allows you to reach 5,000 to 50,000 of your potential customers for (nearly) free or a very inexpensive price with the help of an e-mail service provider?

When e-mail is used correctly, its conversion rate—the rate at which it turns potential customers into actual customers—can be phenomenal. It has the power to exponentially exceed the results generated by conventional direct mail, newspaper, magazine, and cost-prohibitive radio and television advertising. The Internet is one of the very few media formats that actually allows advertisers to count how many impressions, responses, conversations, and pass-alongs their ads produce, and thereby determine *exactly* how many sales can be attributed to each e-mail campaign.

E-mail is one of the oldest forms of digital social media, and it is by far one of the most effective ways to stay in touch with your customers, transact with them, resolve their issues, recruit new customers, and develop your trusted network—oh, and by the way, it's practically free.

theSocialMediaBible.com

That's the incredible value of the Internet. Everything can be measured. Companies can test and perfect which image works best, which headline is more effective, and which offer drives the most sales. This is why major corporations are moving the majority of their advertising budgets to online ventures. According to the *Silicon Valley Insider*, newspaper ad revenue has been declining at an alarming rate. The prediction is that newspaper ad revenue will continue to drop from $42 billion in 2007 to only $10 billion by 2017. That's a $32 billion loss in offline advertising—and for good reason.

Back to the Beginning

The earliest form of e-mail goes back to the beginning of the 1960s. Single computer electronic mail—such as SNDMSG[1]—simply appended a file on an existing one on the same computer. Then, by opening that file, you could read what others had appended to it.

The first actual e-mail resembling present-day e-mails was sent around 7:00 PM in the autumn of 1971 as a test created by a programming engineer employed by Bolt, Beranek and Newman named Ray Tomlinson, who had been chosen by the U.S. Defense Department to build the ARPAnet: The first major computer network, and the predecessor to today's Internet. Ray was working in Cambridge, Massachusetts, on Network Control Protocol (NCP) for a time-sharing system called TENEX and CPYNET when he sent his first e-mail between two side-by-side PDP-10 computers. He addressed it to himself, and he recalls the message most likely contained the text "QWERTYUIOP," from the row of keys on his computer.

By the end of 1972, Tomlinson's two e-mail software packages—called SNDMSG and READMAIL—had become an industry standard, right down to Tomlinson's first use of the @ in e-mail addresses. When Ray was asked why he chose the @ sign, he explained, "The 'at' sign just makes sense. The purpose of the 'at' sign indicated a unit price (for example, 10 items @ $1.95). I used the 'at' sign to indicate that the user was 'at' some other host rather than being local." And when he was asked about spam—well, he said that he had never anticipated that.

---

1. The Send Message (SNDMSG) command was one instruction and function of Ray Tomlinson's mail program that was first used in 1971 for TENEX. Another component was READMAIL. SNDMSG was used to send Electronic Mail from one user to another.

Table 4.1   Direct Mail versus E-Mail Marketing[a]

Measurement	Direct Mail	E-Mail
Development Time	3–6 weeks	2 days
Cost Per Unit	$1.25	$0.10
Response Rate	0.1–2%[b]	5–15%[c]

[a] This doesn't mean that abandoning direct mail completely is the right choice for everyone. If you are selling RVs, for example, you had better keep sending direct mail pieces, since your typical buying demographic is older and not necessarily e-mail savvy. (However, an interesting note: The U.S. Census Bureau reports important changes for the coming years in the aging of the population. By 2050, one in five residents will be aged 65 or over, up from one in nine today. Refer to Part II of this book to determine which social media tool works best for your company, products, and demographics.)

[b] That's the same thing as taking 1,000 of your direct mail pieces, selecting one from the stack, and throwing the remaining 999 pieces into the trash.

[c] Some e-mail campaigns with which the author is familiar have reached as high as a 34 percent open rate.

What You Need to Know

As mentioned previously, the overwhelming reason for the popularity and widespread use of e-mail is its ROI and effectiveness, and of course, the fact that it's nearly free. According to the Forrester DMA Gartner Group, e-mail marketing is significantly more effective than direct mail marketing. Some specific findings are in Table 4.1.

Table 4.2 shows some additional statistics from an industry survey of 2,700 marketers that states their primary goals for using e-mail in their marketing programs.

Table 4.2   Primary Goals for E-Mail Marketing Programs

Build relationships with existing customers	60%
Acquire new customers	41%
Sell products and services	32%
Provide information	31%
Build the brand	25%
Drive traffic to a web site	21%
Up-sell and cross-sell to existing customers	18%

Source: www.MarketingProfs.com e-mail Marketing Benchmark Survey.

Inbox	E-mail
The Wall Street Journal Online	WSJ@listserv.punchline.net [on behalf of Wall Street Journal]
Sony Electronics	sonyelectronics@sony.m0.net
E-nnouncements from T. ...	noReply@rps-updates.troweprice.com
Hewlett-Packard	[Hewlett-Packard] us-specials@your.HP.com

FIGURE 4.1 From Line

These numbers are a surprise in that the highest usage of e-mail marketing isn't necessarily sales, but rather to build relationships with existing customers. The second-highest-rated use was to acquire new customers, and the primary use of e-mail for these marketers was to build and maintain their trusted network.

E-Mail Terminology

Here are some important and often-used terms with which you should become familiar so you can maximize your e-mail marketing campaigns.

- *From line:* The sender of the e-mail is the first thing recipients look at. There are two components: What is displayed in the inbox and what is displayed when the e-mail is opened (see Figure 4.1).
- *Subject line:* The headline seen before opening the message gives a brief description of the subject of the e-mail. Recipients often decide whether to open an e-mail based on the contents of the subject line (see Figure 4.2).

From	Subject Line
JCPenney	Home Sale: Redecorate with Savings
Quill.com	Look inside for sale offers selected just for you
Staples Newsletter	Regina, here's your July newsletter
Lands' End	DESIGN YOUR OWN JEANS

FIGURE 4.2 Subject Line

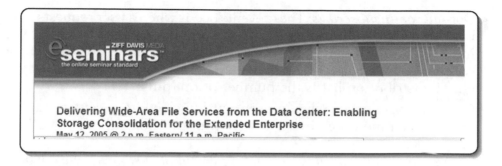

Delivering Wide-Area File Services from the Data Center: Enabling
Storage Consolidation for the Extended Enterprise
May 12, 2005 @ 2 p.m. Eastern/ 11 a.m. Pacific

FIGURE 4.3 Preview Pane

- *Preview pane:* This element in many e-mail programs allows the recipient to view the first few lines of a message. This is also a big factor in getting the recipient to open the message (see Figure 4.3).

- *Open rate:* This statistic measures how many recipients opened the e-mail message, and either enabled the images or clicked on a link.

  This only works for HTML e-mails, because text-only messages have no images (unless, of course, you send a text-based message and ask your clients to click "receipt," which they are not likely to do). This is only the first of several necessary steps that you must take in order to convert readers of an e-mail message to visitors to your web site, and ultimately purchasers of your product.

- *Click-throughs:* These measure the recipients who clicked on a link or an image in an e-mail, thereby opening the hyperlinked web page for additional content. Each link in an e-mail can usually be tracked separately.

- *Pass-alongs:* These are the number of recipients who forward your message along to a friend or colleague.

- *Bounces:* E-mails classified as *bounces* did not reach their destination and were bounced back to the sender.

- *Hard bounces:* These e-mails have been sent to a domain or e-mail address that no longer exists (or never did). You must have a system for deleting hard bounces immediately.

- *Soft bounces:* As opposed to hard bounces, soft bounces present a temporary condition that renders the e-mail undeliverable, the two main reasons for which are usually a full mailbox or a down server. You should resend soft bounces four times, and then delete the address from your e-mail list.

- *Opt-outs or unsubscribes:* These events occur when a user requests not to be included on your e-mail list. This can be done after receiving your initial e-mail, or by having a permission box prechecked. The number of recipients who ask to have their e-mail address removed from your e-mail distribution list is the number of opt-outs.

- *Opt-ins:* These occur when a user actively elects to receive e-mails or promotional messages by checking an opt-in box, which can also be prechecked.

    Be aware that typically, less than 5 percent of customers will opt out of receiving e-mail messages, and less than 10 percent will opt in. An exception is the case of guest books, which typically have a 57 percent opt-in rate—and which can have a dramatic effect on responses to your e-mail.

- *Double opt-in or explicit permission:* Think of this as a double-dog-dare-ya. After the initial registration, a confirmation e-mail is sent to the user, who must reply (either by hitting reply, or clicking on a URL contained within the e-mail) before you can add this person to your e-mail list.

Spam with Your SPAM?

It's been estimated that e-mail users spend roughly 52 hours each year—that's about one hour per week!—sorting and deleting spam (junk e-mail) messages from their inbox. Cox Communications, the seventh-largest e-mail provider in the United States, estimated that almost 3.6 *billion* spam messages were delivered in 2007 alone. Statistics like these prompted the CAN-SPAM Act.

The national CAN-SPAM Act went into effect in the United States on January 1, 2004. This law preempts all state laws governing commercial e-mail, and applies to both business-to-business and business-to-consumer marketers. (State laws are still in effect as they relate to fraud.) The law applies most specifically to commercial e-mail messages (the category into which most marketing messages fall), and not to transactional or relationship messages, which are those that are sent to complete a transaction; provide warranty, product updates, upgrades, or recall information; and notify users of changes in terms of subscription or service or account balance information.

The term *SPAM* originally comes from the meat produced by the Hormel Meat Packing Company in Austin, Minnesota, in 1937. Then-president J. C. Hormel created an amazing little recipe: a spicy ham packaged in a handy 12-ounce can. He held a contest to give the product a name as distinctive as its taste. The winner was SPAM, for SPiced hAM. During its very first year of production, SPAM grabbed 18 percent of the market. By 2002, more than six billion cans of SPAM have been sold with 44,000 cans per hour rolling out of Hormel. A can of SPAM is consumed in the United States every 3.1 seconds.

How does this translate to online clutter, though? Well, when it comes to the Internet, you've likely seen, heard, or even used the term *spam* and *spamming*, which refer to the act of sending unsolicited commercial e-mail (UCE), which implies that someone has sent a message that has no value or substance inside for the recipient.

FIGURE 4.4 SPAM

How might a company feel about its product being likened to something without value or substance? Hormel's official position on the term *spam* is as follows: "We do not object to use of this slang term to describe UCE, although we do object to the use of the word 'spam' as a trademark and to the use of our product image in association with that term. Also, if the term is to be used, it should be used in all lower-case letters to distinguish it from our trademark SPAM, which should be used with all uppercase letters."

The essence of the CAN-SPAM Act simply states that those sending e-mails have to be honest. It forbids the use of false header information, dictates that the "From" line must be real, demands that no use of deceptive or misleading subject lines occurs, mandates that all messages must give the recipient the ability to unsubscribe either through a link to a web site or a valid reply to an e-mail address, states that the opt-out links must be clear and conspicuous, and must work at the time the message is sent for 30 days thereafter. It orders that opt-outs must be processed within 10 business days, that each e-mail must include a valid physical postal address (while the original CAN-SPAM Act said that a post office box does not suffice, the 2007 revisions of the Act said it was legal), that an ADV[2] warning label must be in the subject line only if a company does not have express permission (affirmative consent) from the recipient, and that one's mail servers must not have an open relay or allow others to send e-mail through their servers without their permission.

An important technicality to note: The law defines the sender as the party providing the e-mail's content—not the one renting the list, and not the

---

2. ADV is a label that tells the recipient that an e-mail is an unsolicited *advertisement*.

list owner. Therefore, since any opt-outs are specific to the sender, you must obtain unsubscribe data from the list owner and add those names to your in-house suppression file. Remember: you have only 10 business days to process opt-outs.

The law also specifies that lists built with dictionary attacks, harvested e-mails, or randomly generated e-mail addresses are prohibited. A dictionary attack occurs when spammers connect to a server and ask to deliver mail to mailbox "A." If the server complies, then that address goes on their list. They then proceed to "AA," or "B," or any word or combination of letters that's in their automated dictionary. Randomly generated e-mails work the same way. Harvested e-mails require that someone search web sites—either manually or automatically—to collect all of the e-mails without the recipient's permission. Both of these techniques are illegal and can get you blacklisted.[3]

The Federal Trade Commission and states' attorneys general offices can enforce violations with civil action, which can include jail sentences along with fines ranging from $250 up to $2 million per message. Also, Internet Service Providers (ISPs) can enforce the law with a civil action for damages or for fines ranging from $250 to $1 million per message. In the case of fraud, there is no upper limit.

Spam Filters or Content Filters

Spam filters or content filters are online tools that are used to constantly survey and identify spam, and trigger spam blockers upon finding any. Some phrases that often trigger these spam filters include: "Free __," "$$$," "!!!," "Cash bonus," "ALL CAPS," "No Investment Necessary," "Satisfaction Guaranteed," "You Are a Winner," "No Purchase Necessary," "Social Security Number," and "No Strings Attached." How many times have you received an e-mail with one of these phrases in the subject line that actually offered any value? In fact, you're probably wondering why, if the laws in the United States are so tough, you still receive so much spam? Although the CAN-SPAM Act went into effect on January 1, 2004, most (if not all) of the spammers had moved offshore, mostly to Asian countries, in December 2003.

---

3. A blacklist, or blocklist, is a list of IP addresses or series of IP addresses that Internet service providers (ISPs) create to block or to prevent the sender of e-mail messages from a server that is suspected of transmitting spam. The term *blacklist* dates to 1619 and refers to a list of persons who are disapproved of or are to be punished or boycotted. More information regarding the Can-SPAM Act is available at www.ftc.gov/bcp/conline/pubs/buspubs/canspam.shtm.

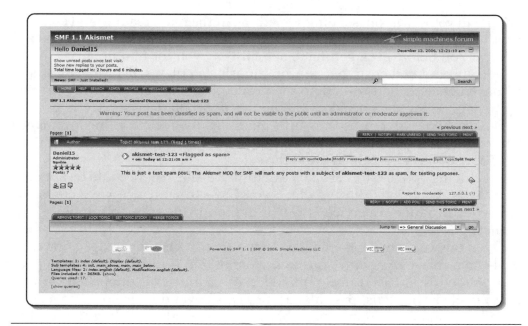

FIGURE 4.5 Spam Submit

There are resources available on different web sites; however, to spam check your e-mail subject lines before you send them, such as www .programmersheaven.com/webtools/Spam-Checker/spamchecker.aspx.

Content Really Is King

Just as it is in your web pages, your brochures, and your direct mailer, content is king—the most fundamental part of your e-mail. It therefore requires the most significant amount of attention. The most important rule in all of marketing is the question of "WIIFM": "What's In It for Me?" If you don't clearly and quickly convey the WIIFM in every marketing message, e-mail, and communication you have with your customers, then your work will be ineffective.

Think about how your customers perceive your corporate communications. Every time you want your customer to look at an e-mail, visit your web site, or open a piece of direct mail, there is a transaction. It is very much like a sale, in that you are asking your customer to give you some amount of money (or attention) in exchange for you providing a service or product. The customer evaluates your offer and compares your product or service to the total cost of the transaction, which might include your customer going to a web site,

driving to your location, sending something in the mail, reading and comprehending your offer, filling out a registration form, and completing credit card
information before even getting to actually pay you for that item.

Your potential customer subconsciously calculates all of these costs of
inconvenience and adds them to the product's dollar amount to determine
the overall cost—and decides whether your product or service is a good
value. To hook your prospects into investing their cost of inconvenience
before they actually decide to purchase, you have to convince them of their
WIIFM, or you've lost them—and the sale.

Enticing your customers isn't a one-time event. There could be as many
as a dozen occasions during which you have to convince your customer
that your product or service is worth the total cost of inconvenience and
money.

It's this very concept—the idea that attracting customers is a one-time
deal—that many companies too easily forget, and it therefore leads to poor
conversion rates. This frame of mind leaves your e-mails unopened without
ensuing click-throughs, pass-alongs, or visits beyond your home page, and
usually results in shopping cart abandonment. Understanding the need to
consistently woo your customers, however, will dramatically improve all of
your marketing—in addition to what you do with e-mail.

Tips, Techniques, and Tactics

The 1.54-Second Rule/5.0-Second Rule

To understand WIIFM more clearly, take a more concentrated look at how
people think, read, and evaluate these value propositions. Suppose, for
some reason, that you really wanted to read the newspaper advertisements
today. Your eyes are scanning over the pages of many ads, one of which
catches your eye. You decide to not turn the page, but to look at the heading
for that ad. How long do you think you are willing to spend to determine if
the WIIFM is worth your stopping to read further? A study showed that
people are only willing to invest or spend 1.54 seconds of time to make that
determination.

If that headline doesn't convince the reader—in those 1.54 seconds—
that there is a significant WIIFM and convey that value, then the reader is
likely to move on to another ad or another page. Think about it. Isn't that
true for you? If you are reading ads or flipping pages in a magazine, do you
spend any longer than a second or two before either stopping to read more or
turning the page? How about when you listen to an ad on the radio or are
watching television? Does 1.54 seconds sound about right? What about

when you are scanning down a list of Google Search results? Is 1.54 seconds still accurate? This emphasizes the great importance of that opening sentence—whether it's on television, radio, magazine, newspaper, search results, web page, or your e-mail message.

In a newspaper, it's called the headline; on your web site, it's the header; and in your e-mail, it's the subject line. Your subject line has to convince your customer in roughly 1.5 seconds whether he should move on to the next stage of time investment. This is why the subject line is so important, and why segmenting is important, as discussed in the next section.

Only if you experience success in the first part of this transaction or value proposition of the WIIFM can you go to the next critical step—reading the newspaper ads. If a headline catches your eye and you subconsciously agree to spend or invest again in this next part of this transaction, how much time do you now give the ad before you determine whether to continue or turn the page? The answer is now five seconds. And while that may sound like a lot, by comparison, five seconds isn't much time to convey a second-level WIIFM. In fact, it's only about enough time to read one sentence.

The second part of this transaction in e-mail marketing is the opening line of your message. Within the first second of reading, your message has to convey a strong enough WIIFM message to keep your customer engaged—and has to do so in five seconds or less. If you are successful in these first two parts of the WIIFM transaction, your customer will continue to read your message to fully understand your value proposition and convert to purchasing your product.

The third step is conversion. If you have successfully convinced your customer that there really is something in it for them, then he will follow your e-mail message's call to action. In nearly every case, an e-mail's primary goal is to convert that message to a click-through to a web page. You might also define your conversion as a pass-along, a sign-up, picking up the phone, or just simply informing your customer. And your e-mail message is *always* about maintaining or building your trusted network by providing a WIIFM. Even if the definition of conversion for your message is only to inform, be sure that the value of that information is at least equal to the time your customer will need to spend to get it.

Segment to Maximize Conversion

By now, you should understand the importance of the 1.54-second and 5-second rules. The underlying message is that there isn't much time to hook your customers and show them your value proposition. So to help with this important step, the experts do something called *segmenting*.

Segmenting is no more than splitting your overall e-mail list into segments and testing the success of each of your e-mail components with your clients. One approach is to divide your total list into equal segments; you can also just pull a random sample from your list to test your message.

Splitting the total group into equal segments allows you to test your entire group in a more homogenous random sampling. Consider the following scenario. Suppose you have a total mailing list of 5,000 customers, a group that you split into five equal 1,000-e-mail segments. For each segment, you are going to craft five different subject lines. The word *craft* is important, because you will want to spend time and effort designing these subject lines and paying close attention to the nouns, verbs, and adjectives you use. Take your time. Create these five subject lines deliberately.

Now, send out all five segments. The important concept is to keep the rest of the entire e-mail the same. Make no other changes. By keeping all of the other e-mail message components identical, you are testing the effectiveness of only the five different subject lines. Give the e-mail a week or more, depending upon how your customers have reacted historically to your e-mails, and then look at the metrics. If the third subject line showed a significant rise in conversion, then look at what you did there and do it again. Look at which one of the subject lines converted the most poorly and stop doing that. It's that simple.

Your next e-mail should test your opening sentences while you keep the subject line consistent. Wait an appropriate amount of time, and then look at your statistics. The next steps are to segment and test your call to action and your use of images. You would be surprised to see that a stock photo of a man instead of a woman—or vice versa—can often make as much as a 20 percent increase in your e-mail conversion rates.

If you follow these steps over a roughly six-month time frame, you will have tested and perfected your e-mail message WIIFMs, subject lines, opening sentences, calls to action, images, layout, color schemes, and even html versus text. You will be able to determine that your e-mail campaigns can have as high as a 30 percent conversion rate. How's that compared to a 0.1 percent conversion rate for conventional direct mail? And all the while you are building and reinforcing your trusted network.

Day Parting Will Get It Read

Another important component of e-mail marketing is a practice known as *day parting*. Most people have no idea of what that means, so if you don't either, don't feel bad.

The following example of day parting is one with which everybody is familiar. There is a time of day that is reserved for one particular type of television show on all the major networks. The time is Monday through Friday from 1:00 PM until 3:00 PM. What is it?

If you said "soap operas," then you answered correctly. Why are they called *soap operas?* You never see much soap (unless it's used during the gratuitous showering of a sexy star), and no one ever sings opera. These shows aren't really called soap operas by the TV networks; they are called daytime dramas. How did these shows come to be known by this name?

You're right: laundry soap. For nearly a half century, stay-at-home moms—and now dads—have been watching these shows. So what's the importance of 1:00 PM to 3:00 PM? That's when little Johnny and little Sally lie down for their naps—the first time during the workday that the stay-at-home parent can take an eye off the little darling to actually get some work done. And if you have ever had a child of your own, you quickly realize that laundry is a daily chore.

Can you think of any other hourly day parting on television—such as for news, prime time, and late night? Radio even has drive time, which is, of course, the time when the majority of listeners are traveling to and from work. These two time periods are traditionally from 6:00 AM to 10:00 AM and 2:00 PM to 6:00 PM, Monday through Friday, and represent the stations' highest listenership. Commercials cost significantly more during drive time.

Every media uses day parting for maximum marketing effect. Newspapers do it. What's Wednesday? Coupons and cooking (to sell more coupon products). This gives the reader Wednesday evening and Thursday to cut them out for Friday's shopping (most people get paid on Fridays, and therefore do their shopping that day). What about Thursday? Out on the town! Friday is too late to make plans, and Wednesday is too early. How about Saturday? Real estate and home repair. Sunday? Ads, ads, ads! This is the day during which the reader has the most time to read the advertising and to shop.

How about monthly day parting? Do you or your customers have more money in the beginning of the month or at the end? And what if you take day parting to the yearly interval, often called *seasonality.* Every company has seasonality. What do you think the slow time of year is for a construction company? It happens to be the same as the peak season for ski resorts.

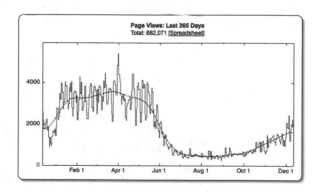

FIGURE 4.6 *Seasonality*

Understanding your customers' psychology, day parting, and seasonality will dramatically increase your conversion rate. Let's look at when you send your e-mails. Is it at night? Over the weekend? What are your customers doing when your e-mail arrives? When does the highest amount of Internet (e-mail) traffic occur? It's Monday through Friday, 8:00 AM until 5:00 PM, then 8:30 PM until midnight, and all day Saturday and Sunday. No surprise there, right?

If you sent your e-mail at night, your customer is most likely to receive it first thing in the morning. Is this good? Isn't this the time the mailbox is filled from the night before with spam? Isn't this the time she just came into work and is getting yelled at by six different people, preparing for meetings, and running around? How careful do you think your customer will be in determining whether she hits "delete" on your e-mail? Wouldn't around, say, 11:00 AM be better? Wouldn't she have had time to go to those early-morning meetings and deleted all of her spam and other unwanted e-mails?

How about that weekend send-off? Is first thing on Monday morning really the best time for your customers to get your value proposition that they will use just 1.54 seconds or less to determine if they will read or delete?

Statistically speaking, Tuesday through Thursday from 11:00 AM until 3:00 PM is the best time to send your message, although it might be different for your particular customer. You need to test it. Now that you know about segmenting, try dividing and sending your e-mail message at different times of the day and different days of the week. See which one works best—and keep doing that!

A conference attendee once asked, "What if I sold canoes? What would be the best time to send an e-mail for that?" The answer for that year was, "Thursday, March 21, at 9:00 PM." Why, you ask?

If you are selling canoes, you most likely have people's home e-mail addresses, as some companies are getting cranky about using the Internet at work for personal business. Customers for recreational items are often in front of their computers on a weeknight at around 8:30 PM. Allow 30 minutes to clean out their junk e-mails and have an empty inbox. So around 9:00 PM the canoe e-mail will arrive, and they will have plenty of time to look at it—and not simply dispose of it.

Thursday is the best day of the week, because a customer who is looking for a canoe is probably younger and possibly fit—and is therefore likely to be out of the house instead of in front of the computer on a Friday night. But the e-mail should arrive as close to the weekend as possible, so that the customer remembers to buy it on Saturday morning.

Considering seasonality, an e-mail for camping and other outdoor products should go out near the end of March. That's when people are thinking about spring and summer activities. In the fall, their thoughts go to, "Oh, man, how am I going to store all this stuff over the winter?"

See how a few rules and a little common sense can make e-mail marketing fun, challenging, and most important, rewarding? And by the way—it's almost completely free.

Providers

Deciding who is going to manage your e-mail list often leads to the decision, "Do I do it in-house or out-house?" This is a big decision. Do you have the resources to manage your own e-mail list? Can you be sure that every opt-out is removed within the 10-day period? Will you diligently keep a record of your opt-ins?

Outsourcing is usually less expensive than managing the human resources necessary to perform those duties in-house, and there's something to be said about an arm's-length relationship with a professional company whose only mission in life is to perform a given task to the best of their abilities.

While you can buy software packages and install them on your servers and PCs, and you can find several companies on the Internet, one good recommendation is Constant Contact. Based in Waltham, Massachusetts, Constant Contact has been managing e-mail campaigns for small businesses and organizations since 1998. (See Part III for more information on Constant Contact.)

This company has integrity, is respected in the industry, is whitelisted,[4] and even shut down yours truly for a week before writing this chapter because he had too many bounces from using a seven- to eight-year-old mailing list.

Constant Contact (and similar e-mail management companies such as RatePoint, VertitcalResponse, and Infusionsoft) automatically handles all of your requirements for you. They also have hundreds of premade templates, spell checking, incredible statistics and analysis, and duplicate e-mail elimination, and they are very reasonably priced. Set up an account and get discounts by clicking the link at www.theSocialMediaBible.com.

---

4. *Whitelisted* is the opposite of the definition of blacklisted. ISPs will list a sender as a legitimate e-mail marketer and not block those e-mails.

The ROI of Social Media

Atkins Taps Powered to Cultivate Brand Activists through Its Branded Online Community

Background

Up until the beginning of 2008, Atkins had supplied a simple forum solution that allowed some interaction between Atkins loyalists, but engagement was low. Without the brand truly engaging with the community, users were left with unanswered questions and would actually find other places on the Web to commune.

Strategy

Because users were not engaged directly with Atkins on the Web, the Company teamed with Powered, Inc., to launch an ambitious strategy to provide an open community for free (all of their competitors charged for online community access at the time) with expert content, including a blog by Atkins's vice president of nutrition.

As part of this strategy, Powered was tasked with building an online community that would activate Atkins users to the point that they become evangelists for the brand. Here are the first strategic steps that are considered the community's foundation:

- Audience acquisition and opt-in to the Atkins.com database
- Engagement to drive consideration of Atkins products
- Drive brand loyalty and retention
- Replace the Atkins.com message boards with a full-community solution

Implementation

Atkins and Powered started out by targeting current opt-ins to the Atkins newsletter and prospects who had indicated that they were interested in learning more about Atkins and how to get started with the nutritional plan. The developed online community features were built out in addition to the existing forums and provided the following engagement outlets:

- Community where visitors access advice, tools, resources, and support from other members
- Places for members to rate or review Atkins products, chart progress, and interact with a licensed nutritionist
- Professional, easy-to-navigate content, including courses, notebooks, checklists, and videos

- Encourage "Atkins Advocates" to reach out to new members and answer questions

Opportunity

The community has allowed members to come together to get advice from peers and Atkins nutritionists, share stories, and learn about the company's approach to weight loss and weight management. Community members have quickly learned that Atkins is committed to helping people succeed in their weight loss goals. As a result, Powered and Atkins have created a venue for loyalists to be supported and turned into advocates, driving acquisition, retention, and real-time consideration of Atkins products.

Conclusion

The impact of this richer community sent the number of registered members skyrocketing and engagement with the brand by other users has also been impressive. Here are initial stats coming out of the 2008 launch:

- Over half a million registered members to date
- 78 percent increase in community registrations versus message boards
- 70 percent increase in total posts to the message boards and forums

Atkins is now using Facebook (www.facebook.com/atkinsdiet) and Twitter (http://Twitter.com/atkinsinsider) as touch points to direct users to its community. Engaging with users through popular social media outlets is important, but these outlets can also be used as additional touch points and gateways to attract customers to the next level of engagement: A branded "home" community with the goal of creating relationships in which customers become an extension and voice of authority for a brand.

This approach has yielded impressive growth results and has continued to strengthen relationships between Atkins and its community members:

- Since the late 2008 launch, registrations for the first year of the community quadrupled by over 400 percent when compared to the same time period the year before
- Registrations for the community increased by 97 percent in 2009 when compared to 2008
- In January 2010, the community already achieved 80 percent of all 2009 registrations

Aaron Strout, CMO Powered, Inc.

http://community.atkins.com

Expert Insight

Neal Creighton, CEO, www.RatePoint.com

Neal Creighton

. . . I've been in Internet businesses for a while now. The first company I started was a company I called GeoTrust. I was the CEO there and it was a pretty proper company. It was securing like 30 percent of the transactions on the Internet. It was acquired in 2006 by VeriSign which is a well-known brand. But the GeoTrust brand is pretty well known as well.

And I got together with the founders and we really decided we wanted to do something bigger. And you know, securing 30 percent of Internet traffic is a good thing, but we thought there was a much bigger idea out there and that was really why we started RatePoint and why we got together. . . .

. . . You know RatePoint . . . you can tell by its name it has a variety of services and e-mail marketing is one of the services. You know we've combined e-mail marketing with a complete review platform so businesses can get reviews from their customers and republish those out in different places, and a lot of that is social. That's a big part of our services . . . surveys and e-mail marketing. But while e-mail marketing is an important area and people have been doing it for a very long time, and as you described it was one of the first places for having a dialogue with your customers where you were telling them what you were doing, it was much more personal. So it was the kind of the first phase of things but we've changed a lot recently with a lot of other places like Facebook and Twitter where you can have an ongoing dialogue.

But e-mail marketing is the base part of our service. A lot of businesses use it. The ROI on it is very, very clean; for every dollar you spend you get $43 back. So it's a very effective way to reach your customers and it's a big part of our service. . . .

. . . I mean we're right in the middle of a revolution on the Internet. A lot of it has to do with social media but the number-one thing people look out for before they transact with a business . . . you know it could be calling a landscaper or plumber . . . is do I buy from these businesses reviews. And they generally start at Google and they generally look up the business name and reviews can pop up; and 70 percent of people believe reviews or they trust reviews from people they don't know. But they see them on the Internet. They're looking for something; they pop up. If they are good they tend to believe it; if it's bad they tend to believe it. So we believe that business that participate with their customers solicit actively reviews from them, try to resolve negative issues before they get published. And you know they have to be transparent.

Social media is a good place to do that. But then we end up syndicating the concept back out to Google or Yahoo! or Bing, and a bunch of other places. So it really is . . . you know the name of the company is Great Point and it's all about reputation building. E-mail marketing is part of that but the reviews are the revolution that we're part of that is going to fundamentally change the way businesses and consumers interact as we go forward. . . .

. . . It's the most important thing that is happening on the Internet and it's happening on social networks and if you can get within social circles you could really be powerful if you're doing the right thing.

You know I tell people trying to make them understand a small business, "It's like you're walking on the street and you decided to go to a restaurant. And before you go in there are four people standing outside telling you they just got sick from eating the food there; you probably would not go in."

So if you started Google and you looked up a business and you see bad reviews you're going to tend to believe these versus positive ones. It's the same within your social circle. If you ask for advice there's a lot of statistics talking about how people will rely on that today. When they see things they actually will, within their social circle, believe it. So as a business if you can take advantage of that in a positive way and understand that you will have all the power if you can participate with your customers you can build a really strong competitive edge for yourself . . .

. . . I mean we believe that people are using e-mail marketing as, kind of, the first social area for all good candidates for reviews because anyone who wanted to communicate with their customers and tell them what they were doing certainly wanted to sell more and wanted to have a good quality business. So reviews are a big part of that so they were good candidates. So we find people coming in to use e-mail marketing and the converting to our review services every day because they understand, again, how powerful it is.

. . . You could compare it to other companies out there like Constant Contact and other folks. We have a very similar service. I think one of the things that we've done very differently is that we are very interested in the entry-level people in the market. Those are the people that are coming in and they want to do e-mail marketing for the first time. So we have this free-for-life product that gives you 550 free contacts that you can use and we hope that you will upgrade and then you'll see the benefit of our review service as you go through it and end up a paying customer. But we're really focusing on the entry-level market and we do have many large centers, many large

(continued)

(continued)

companies. It's a complete offering from end to end and fully integrated into social media. So it's pretty cool. . . .

. . . I think they were very early on this space and we had the advantage of coming later. And you know Constant Contact has been around for a while and with that comes advantages but also disadvantages. When we came around we could see the social media movement and the storm brewing and so we built everything in and we've been widely recognized and just recently got the My Text Award in New England for the best social media company in New England. And our customers love that.

It's not just e-mail marketing and a survey platform but a power in the review platform. So you may have a review that you get within the Facebook environment from our Facebook application that ends up being syndicated out to Google. So you're using your core group of people to help amplify your business and that's also ending up in a lot of different places. But it's integrated in social media from end to end. . . .

. . . I mean obviously Search Engine is a lot of fresh content. Review Content is like gold and Google has been doing a lot of work within Google Apps too, but generally our reviews show up extremely high next to the business and it's, you know more importantly the number-one tool. I think every business understands word of mouth and in the physical world if you tell . . . if you do a good job for a particular customer and they tell a few people and you get some money then it's great. But if you do it on the Web; like word of mouth of the Web is what I kind of like to say, and they tell people there they might tell a thousand people or more and the customer sees that. So SEO is a huge benefit when people see it and when they do see it, 70 percent of the people, or more every day . . . it's growing . . . believe what they see. This is because they are credible and people are looking for these reviews . . .

. . . Primarily if you ask anybody when they come into work what one of the first things they do is and they will say they check their e-mail. It's still the primary way we communicate with each other. We are certainly using social media in a major way but it's the starting point for basically everything on business nowadays, especially for small business. So they check their e-mail first thing in the morning, they look at it during the day. I think now what we have seen is that it's one of the tools in the toolbox and a very important one. You've got to use social media as well and you have to be cognizant of what's happening and integrate what you are doing with an e-mail with that environment and you've got a pretty good solution. But still, today, I bet we could talk 24 months from now . . . the first thing you would do when you get into the office is check your e-mail . . . and I don't think that's going to change. . . .

To listen to or read the entire Executive Conversation with Neal Creighton, go to www.theSocialMediaBible.com.

Commandments

1. **Thou shalt not spam.**

   You don't need to. As long as you're honest and understand the CAN-SPAM Act, you're good! If you are using your e-mail list to build and maintain your trusted network and your trusted community, then give them reason to trust you. Ask yourself this question: Are you informing your network that you really do have an offer that would benefit them if only they were aware of it? If the answer is yes, then send it.

2. **Thou shalt provide a significant WIIFM.**

   You always need to keep in mind that whether it's paper; electronic, e-mail, or web site text; or a brochure or cover letter, you have to convey a strong WIIFM to prove to your customer that there is a good rate of return on your value proposition.

3. **Thou shalt remember the 1.54-second and 5.0-second rules**

   Remember, you only have 1.54 seconds to hook your customers and convince them in the subject line that they should invest their time and effort in reading and comprehending your proposition. Remember, also, that even if you convince your prospect to keep reading, you only have 5.0 seconds in the first sentence to get them to read the rest and not hit the delete button. Your messages have to be clear, concise, and understandable in these two allotted time frames.

4. **Thou shalt segment to maximize conversion.**

   This is really about testing. You have to test your WIIFM, your 1.54, your 5.0, your images, and your layout to see what works for your customers and what doesn't. It's about understanding how your trusted network thinks, and figuring out what motivates them. Segmenting is about trial and error with a short cycle to find answers that only a few years ago marketers spent millions of their clients' dollars and years to understand.

5. **Thou shalt remember that day parting will get it read.**

   By understanding how your customer thinks, and what he is doing during the course of his day, week, month, and year, you can send very effective e-mails. Appreciating your customer's larger monthly and annual cycles allows you to better allocate your e-mail and search engine marketing budgets. Day parting means getting your message to your customers when the timing is most right for them to receive it.

Conclusion

So what does e-mail marketing have to do with social media? *Everything.* E-mail was the original social media. Before there was Facebook, Twitter, Flickr, YouTube, and all the other sites, people shared content with each other by sending it in e-mail messages. And in many cases, they still do.

Also, social media is about two-way communication between you and your customers. If you aren't communicating effectively—or at all because a spam filter is stopping your e-mail—then you're not marketing. Social media requires you to build trust in your network, listen to what your customers have to say, and provide value and a strong WIIFM. That's the same with e-mail.

The more you understand the most effective way to communicate through e-mail, the stronger your relationships will be with your customers. Remember, any time you send an e-mail to your customer and she doesn't opt out, she decides to remain part of your network. If you can consistently provide value in the form of knowledge, information, resources, discounts, leads, examples, white papers, or even entertainment, your customers will continue to correspond with you. And like any relationship, the more they agree to converse with you, the stronger the relationship becomes. Remember the old adage, "The best compliment a customer can give you is a referral." Customers who trust you and buy from you will recommend that others do the same.

To hear all of the Expert Interviews, go to www.theSocialMediaBible.com.

Readings and Resources

Arnold, John. *E-Mail Marketing For Dummies*. (Hoboken, NJ: John Wiley & Sons, Inc.)

Baggott, Chris, and Ali Sales. *E-Mail Marketing by the Numbers: How to Use the World's Greatest Marketing Tool to Take Any Organization to the Next Level*. (Hoboken, NJ: John Wiley & Sons, Inc.)

Bell, Arthur H., and Dayle M. Smith. *Management Communication*, 2nd ed. (Hoboken, NJ: John Wiley & Sons, Inc.)

Cavanagh, Christina. *Managing Your E-Mail: Thinking Outside the Inbox*. (Hoboken, NJ: John Wiley & Sons, Inc.)

Groves, Eric. *The Constant Contact Guide to E-mail Marketing*. (Hoboken, NJ: John Wiley & Sons, Inc.)

Liew, Mun Leong. *Building People: Sunday E-Mails from a CEO*. (Hoboken, NJ: John Wiley & Sons, Inc.)

Mask, Clate and Scott Martineau, *Conquer the Chaos* (Hoboken, NJ: John Wiley & Sons, Inc.)

Mullen, Jeanniey, and David J. Daniels. *E-Mail Marketing: An Hour a Day.* (Hoboken, NJ: John Wiley & Sons, Inc.)

Schneier, Bruce. *E-Mail Security: How to Keep Your Electronic Messages Private.* (Hoboken, NJ: John Wiley & Sons, Inc.)

Sterne, Jim, and Anthony Priore. *E-Mail Marketing: Using E-Mail to Reach Your Target Audience and Build Customer Relationships.* (Hoboken, NJ: John Wiley & Sons, Inc.)

Turner, Sean, and Russ Housley. *Implementing E-Mail and Security Tokens: Current Standards, Tools, and Practices.* (Hoboken, NJ: John Wiley & Sons, Inc.)

Downloads

For your free downloads associated with *The Social Media Bible,* go to www .theSocialMediaBible.com, select Downloads, and enter your ISBN number located on the back of the book above the bar code. Be sure to enter the dashes.

Credits

The ROI of Social Media was provided by:

Aaron Strout, CMO Powered, Inc., http://community.atkins.com

Expert Insight was provided by:

Neal Creighton, CEO, www.RatePoint.com

Technical edits were provided by:

Rosalind Morville, www.ConstantContact.com

CHAPTER 5

The World of Web Pages

What's in It for You?

According to Internet World Stats Miniwatts Marketing Group, there are an estimated 1,802,330,457 Internet users worldwide. This number breaks down as follows: Asia: 764,435,900; Europe: 425,773,571; North America: 259,561,000; Latin America/Caribbean: 186,922,050; Africa: 86,217,9000; Middle East: 58,309,546; and Oceanic Australia: 21,110,490. This is the reason companies are all participating in the World Wide Web. These numbers show the staggering number of people who are participating in the World Wide Web.

The Web became mainstream in 1995. It all began in 1989 with zero domain names (the name between the "www." and the ".com" for a web site), and grew to more than 206.6 million by March 2010. Domain names—or web sites, as they're more commonly known—have been growing at a rate of 1.3 million, each with an average of 239 pages per site. Even though no one knows for sure, or even can accurately guess, there were an estimated 29.7 billion web pages as of 2007 (see Figure 5.1).

The sheer magnitude of these numbers are the force that drives e-commerce, while also making competition difficult. If you have some basic understanding of how web pages work, then you have the ability to outsell your competition—and thereby realize revenues and ROI that cannot be attained offline.

Like any other process, once you realize some of the tactics, tools, and strategies, it's easier than you think to create highly visible, sticky web pages with a high conversion rate. *Sticky* refers to a web page that someone is willing to stay at for a higher-than-average amount of time before clicking

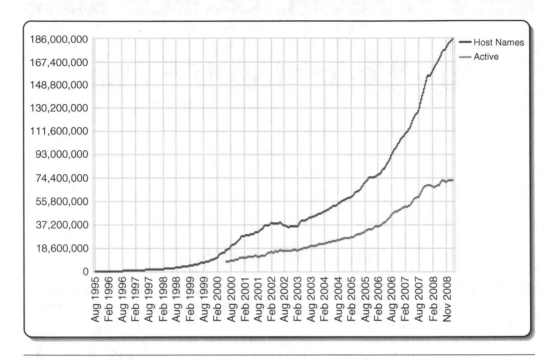

FIGURE 5.1 Total Sites across All Domains, August 1995 through November 2008

Source: www.netcraft.com.

"Back" or "Close." The tactics are easy to understand, the tools are easy to use, and the strategies are easy to implement. But before discussing these tools and strategies, consider a brief history of the Web.

Back to the Beginning

The very first web site, web page, and web server on the World Wide Web debuted in the latter part of 1990. The advent of global computer communication was physicist Sir Timothy John "Tim" Berners-Lee's dream. During March 1989, while working at the European Organization for Nuclear Research (CERN) in Geneva, Switzerland, Berners-Lee wrote a proposal blueprinting how computers could be connected to easily share information around the world by means of the Internet and the use of HTTP—or Hypertext Protocol, based on Vannevar Bush's work in 1945 and TCP/IP, Transmission Control Protocol/Internet Protocol (previously created by Vint Cerf). Both HTTP and TCP/IP are the systems used today to navigate across web sites and web pages.

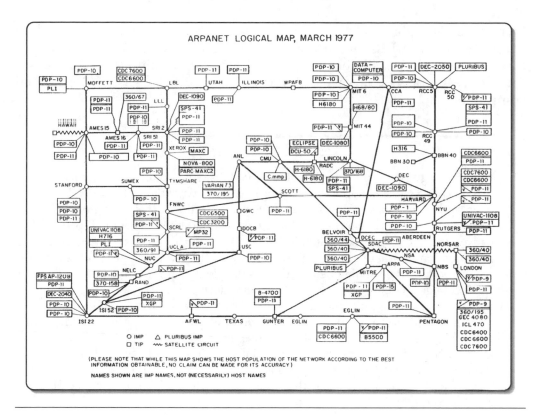

FIGURE 5.2 ARPAnet

For a complete explanation of HTTP, see Chapter 19, Spotlight on Search (Search Engine Optimization). For an interview between author Lon Safko and Vint Cerf, the inventor of TCP/IP, Transmission Control Protocol/Internet Protocol and codesigner of the Internet, go to www .theSocialMediaBible.com.

In 1990, Robert Cailliau[1] joined Berners-Lee and Cerf's team as a systems engineer. Soon, Cailliau became the staunchest supporter of connecting the Internet, HTTP, TCP/IP, and personal computers by means of creating the largest single information network on the planet. His goal was to

---

1. Robert Cailliau, who worked at CERN, had independently proposed a project to develop a hypertext system, and partnered with Berners-Lee in hopes of getting the Web off the ground. He rewrote his project proposal, lobbied management for funding, recruited programmers, and collaborated with Berners-Lee on papers and presentations. Cailliau helped run the first WWW conference and became president of the International World Wide Web Conference Committee (IW3C2).

help physicists share all of the information stored on each individual computer at the CERN laboratory, and hypertext would allow each user the opportunity to easily browse text on web pages using the HTTP links. The first examples of this were developed on Steve Jobs's NeXT personal computers.

NeXt Computer

After leaving Apple Computer in 1985, Steve Jobs went on to form a company that he called NeXT Computers—with products that were designed with all the bells and whistles available for computers at the time. This first prototype computer workstation was released in 1988, and had been developed specifically with the college student in mind (most likely due to Apple's early success in education—particularly in higher education). It was tested in 1989, after which NeXT started selling beta to universities. Jobs believed that if he could hook college students on his NeXT Computer during their college years, then they would want a similar model upon entering the workplace—and he would thereby be able to slowly push IBM and Windows out of the business market. However, the excessive amount of add-ons that were bundled with the base model at that time drove the price far too high ($6,500) for college students who didn't have that much extra cash on hand to afford one. Jobs sold NeXT to Apple in 1996 and he was soon back in the saddle again. Much of the current Mac OS X is based on the NeXTSTEP operating system.

Berners-Lee developed a browser-editor with the intent of creating a tool that would allow its users to build spaces to share information. The world's first URL address, web site, and web server was info.cern.ch. It ran on a NeXT Computer workstation at CERN on Christmas of 1990. Many names were considered for this newly created sharing tool, and in May 1990, the creators settled upon the *World Wide Web*, or *WWW*. At that moment, Robert Cailliau became the first person to ever surf the Web (*surf* having been derived from *Cerf*—a nod to cocreator Vinton Cerf's contributions).

The world's very first web address was info.cern.ch/hypertext/WWW/TheProject.html.

This page was set up to explain how this new Internet worked, what hypertext was, how to search the Internet, and even included technical data on how to create web pages. There is no record of how the very first pages looked, because they were being modified and updated daily.

The only available screen shot of the first web page/browser was taken three years later, in 1993. This image can be found at www.w3.org/People/

Berners-Lee/WorldWideWeb.html. The primary difference between the 1990 screen and the 1993 screen was color; the first web page was displayed in grayscale.

The largest problem that the team had in expanding the Web beyond their own personal computers was the existing state-of-the-art computers. To make their new Web work, they needed to create browser software that could run on the then-popular DOS-based IBM, Compaq, and Tandy computers, which paled in comparison to the sophisticated NeXT Computer. In early 1991, the team began testing the DOS-style browser to work with any personal computer or terminal. To operate on DOS, they needed the browser to eliminate all graphics and the mouse in exchange for just plain text, because Microsoft's DOS (Disk Operating System) could not recognize a graphic interface or the functions of a mouse.

By the end of 1991, Web servers began popping up in other institutions throughout Europe. The first Web server in the United States was at the Stanford Linear Accelerator Center (SLAC). Within one year of the Web's inception, there were a total of 26 servers worldwide. By the following year, the number had grown to more than 200.

By 1993, PC and Macintosh users were able to access the Web through Mosaic, a program released by the National Center for Supercomputing Applications (NCSA) at the University of Illinois at Urbana-Champaign. Within just two years, the Internet went mainstream with dial-up connections to companies like CompuServe and America Online (AOL). And now, with an estimated 1,802,330,457 Internet users surfing 206,675,938 web sites containing more than 29,700,000,000 (est.) web pages, the World Wide Web has come a long way.

What You Need to Know

To understand how and why a web page is effective, it is important to first discuss a few basic marketing and psychological concepts. Although *The Social Media Bible* is not intended to replace a book such as *Marketing For Dummies,* some fundamental understanding of the psychology of a sale is necessary to fully understand how to develop an effective web page. The first concept to discuss is called the *sales*, or *buying funnel* (see Figure 5.3).

The sales funnel is a metaphor that marketers use to imagine what prospects and customers are thinking as they move through their sales cycle—from the moment they realize they need your product or service to the time that they actually purchase. This cycle is especially critical with web

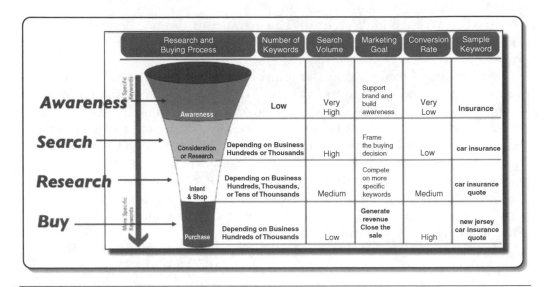

Table contents:

Research and Buying Process		Number of Keywords	Search Volume	Marketing Goal	Conversion Rate	Sample Keyword
Awareness		Low	Very High	Support brand and build awareness	Very Low	Insurance
Consideration or Research		Depending on Business Hundreds or Thousands	High	Frame the buying decision	Low	car insurance
Intent & Shop		Depending on Business Hundreds, Thousands, or Tens of Thousands	Medium	Compete on more specific keywords	Medium	car insurance quote
Purchase		Depending on Business Hundreds of Thousands	Low	Generate revenue Close the sale	High	new jersey car insurance quote

FIGURE 5.3 Sales Funnel

pages, because it doesn't simply dictate the design of your home page. It requires that you have a specific web page designed specifically to accept and address the types of questions that your prospects have at any given moment during the buying cycle.

The stages that your prospects move through in their sales funnel are Awareness, Search, Research, and Buy. Let's take a look at these steps, using the example of an auto insurance salesperson in Phoenix, Arizona.

Awareness

Your (potential) client realizes that she is in need of car insurance. She begins to consider how she might get more information about auto insurance in her area, what she might ask about it, and what to type in the search engines to start her search.

Search

Your client will then begin to search the Web, looking for information on car insurance. She's conducting a very general search at this point, since she doesn't yet know what companies offer it or even what type she is looking for. Her search would likely include only terms like "auto insurance" or "car insurance." Her frame of mind, however, is less general than it was during the Awareness stage, as she has already begun to think about what she is looking for by choosing her key search terms.

Research

Once your client gets the chance to poke around and identify the companies that provide auto insurance, she then may drill down to searching with a term like "auto insurance quotes." Your prospect is now more knowledgeable, and her searches are much less general.

Buy

The last part of this cycle is the point at which your prospect is ready to purchase. She knows what company she wants to go with, she knows the type of policy she is looking for, and her search becomes significantly different. Now she is searching for "Travelers auto insurance quote Phoenix." Makes sense, doesn't it? Don't all online consumers go through this process at one time or another—whether they're looking for insurance, shoes, or vacations?

The length of this particular buying cycle could last anywhere from one night to a year or more. If the buyer's insurance policy isn't due to be renewed until next year, then the client might begin looking now, wait to learn more details when she pays her next premium, and not complete her final research until the policy is due for renewal.

Now, let's put ourselves in the mind-set of the prospect. If you were in the Search mode—looking only at this point for companies that provided auto insurance—and were taken to a page for Allstate where you were asked to enter your personal information for a quote and a phone call from a salesperson—what would you do? You would probably leave that page, because the information provided therein wasn't appropriate for what you desired during your search mode of the cycle.

What if, on the other hand, the prospect was you, and you had completed all of the research necessary to choose an insurance company? You knew the type of policy you wanted, you studied the deductible, and you're ready to purchase. You search, you click, and you're taken to a specific insurance company's home page. Four clicks later, you still didn't find a place to get a quote; so what do you do? *You close the page.*

All that work the company did creating their site—optimizing their home page, paying for the pay-per-click just to get you there—and you leave. An ideal web page delivers the specific information your prospect is looking at during the appropriate time in their personal sales cycle. The lesson here: It's not about your home page; it's about everything that comes after.

Your Home Page Is Causing You Harm

People often judge a book by its cover. See: A Stanford study[2] involving 4,500 people over three years focused on how users determine the credibility of a web site. The research isn't new, but savvy consumers today are spending less time evaluating a web site than ever before.

Based on this research, here are some ideas you can use that still stand true:

Show you're real—a real organization, with real people, offering real benefits:

- Anyone can have a web site. While it's great that a small company's web site can appear alongside a big corporation's, this also pairs your legitimate company with less-than-reliable web sites that may not represent a real company at all. A web site doesn't provide any guarantee of an actual building, employees, or business experience. To single yourself out as a credible source, list your physical address prominently and include a picture of your office or feature memberships with local business organizations.

Explain why the real people at your real company should be trusted:

- Provide your credentials for visitors; this information can come in the form of business recognitions or awards, staff bios with experience listed, or testimonials from current clients.

Make it painfully easy for visitors to contact you:

- In addition to signaling that you're a real company, this tactic will help you get the leads you're looking for from your site. Give visitors several ways to contact you, so they can choose their preference—physical address, e-mail address, and phone number. If your company is larger, with several contacts, consider giving specific contacts for specific inquiries. Include this information throughout your site, not just in tiny text at the bottom of your pages or on a contact page.

---

2. Fogg, B. J. (May 2002). "Stanford Guidelines for Web Credibility." A Research Summary from the Stanford Persuasive Technology Lab., Stanford University.

Signal you're still there—often:

- Be sure to keep your site up to date. If you're not watching your site, why should anyone else be? Regular updates show your business is active and responsive. And, updates can help your search engine rankings.

And, possibly most important—an unbiased opinion, of course . . .

Create a captivating, appropriate visual site design:

- One of the main ideas this research found was that people quickly evaluate a site on visual design alone. Layout, content, and images, as well as a design that matches your company's purpose, were all main factors used to evaluate the credibility of a design.

Most people, however, erroneously believe that the home page is everything. They operate under the assumption that it's the only page that needs to be optimized and advertised, and the only place to which traffic should be driven. This is a misconception. Driving your prospects to your home page is causing you more harm than anything else you could be doing on the Web. Your home page is merely the cover of your book; it does not provide any of the information that your prospects are looking for.

Let's say a fellow worker who has read this book is holding it in her hand, and you ask her, "Where can I find the information in there about why home pages are bad?" Suppose that she responds by doing nothing but placing the book on the table in front of you, and pointing to the cover. How would you feel? Surprised? Confused? Angry? Wouldn't you expect her to open the book, find the chapter, turn to the page, and point to the paragraph? Well, that is akin to what your customers expect when they're looking for information on your web site. Don't simply point your prospects and customers to the cover. Your home page is meant for branding, because when you're advertising—whether online or off, and when all else fails—you still always need brand recognition.

However, you need to develop a plan that addresses your prospects' mind-sets, and unearths what they are searching for through each step of their buying cycle. Each of the pages is easy to create, and must be simple to understand. The Awareness page could very well be your home page. If you have more than one product, however, you might need a top-level page that must be generic and have general terminology along with high-level information. The Search page needs to be a little more specific, and perhaps mention all of your products with a description and some what's-in-it-for-me for each. Your Research page needs to describe the distinct qualities of your products or services, so that your prospects can compare the value of your offering against all of your competitors. And the last page—the Buy page—needs to only give your prospects the opportunity to review their order and, of course, to buy. Capture them when they are ready.

Designing a web page is unlike any other type of advertising you can do. Your web site captures your prospects and customers at the very moment in time when they actually desire that specific information. No other advertising can accomplish this. Another key difference is that your prospects are always asking for your specific help on a specific topic on a web page, and they are doing so voluntarily.

Your customers will engage with plenty of advertising involuntarily. For example, how do you feel when you open your mailbox and find it filled with junk, catalogs, and coupons? What is your reaction when telemarketers call you during dinner? Or survey people come up to you in the mall? Are you offended? Has your privacy been invaded? Are you annoyed? Now, compare that to how you feel when you seek out someone's advice on a question—and they are immediately happy to help you. Web pages provide the same kind of gratification—*if* you design them right.

Comparing web page design to direct mail advertising, a web page would be like a psychic mailman. The keywords that your prospect uses—based on where he is in the buying cycle—are like very precise mailing lists. The search engine result wording is like an envelope, and the exact web page you take your prospect to is the material inside. The web page contents have been designed specifically for what that prospect is looking for, and is delivered at the exact moment he asks for it. A well-designed array of web pages can convert your prospects into your customers.

This concept also applies directly and powerfully to your blog page, the photographs you share, video uploads, and podcasts as well. Be sure to have something for everyone at every stage or frame of mind.

There is one additional stage in this sales cycle funnel: Post-Sale. Your prospects may actually be in the Post-Sale stage of the customer life cycle and are seeking support, engaging in loyalty, participating in your blog, uploading videos about your product, and engaging in other related activities. Be sure that you have a mechanism to capture and retain your hard-earned customers, so that they will come back and, most important, refer their trusted network to you to become new customers. (Be sure to read the chapter on blogs, as this is the most effective way to keep your customers—and your company—in the loop.)

To broaden the appeal of your web pages, consider that your target audience's efforts may extend beyond the obvious. You need to consider your prospects, customers, resellers, distributors, the press, industry analysts, investors, and even employees who may use your web site as a resource or selling tool. Consider the needs and behaviors of all your important constituents. You may need to have specific web pages designed for each of them as they travel through their own sale (or thought) cycle.

Design Elements to Consider

The most basic concept to keep in mind when designing a web page is that this is where people tend to look *first* for information about your company or organization. Such design has essentially become a science. The *New York Times,* as well as many other major newspapers, are broken down into left and right pages, each of which contains six sections. The *Times* understands their customers' behavior so well that every story in their entire paper is specifically placed based on priority. The page split is designed to place important information where the eye looks first, and also takes into account how the newspaper will be folded by the reader when reading it on a train or other confined area.

(A great article about "How to Hold 'Em and How to Fold 'Em" can be found at query.nytimes.com/gst/fullpage.html?res=9F06E0D61738F935A 2575AC0A961958260.)

Madison Avenue advertisers never sleep (not a surprise, since Madison Avenue is in New York!). In their Landing Page Eyetracking Study of February 2005 (Figure 5.4), these advertisers showed that when bouncing low-wattage laser beams off the retinas of volunteers, people tend to look first at the *top left* of the page, time and time again. This comes as no surprise; after all, children are told to start at the top of the page on the left side. What does this say for web design? Put your most important message, image, or logo on the top left.

This study also showed that retailers who made their landing web page easy to read provided a strong what's-in-it-for-me, and favoring the top left section of the web page increased their conversion rate by as much as 64 percent.

Next, keep your message above the fold. While this term originated with newspapers, it refers to keeping your key message in the top window pane of your browsers; and don't expect your visitor to scroll down to find additional inspiration to stay on your page and hopefully convert. Keep in mind computer screen size. Your above-the-fold may not be the same as that of your prospects.

FIGURE 5.4   Eyetracking Study, February 2005

Source: Go to www.theSocialMediaBible.com for a clickable link.
www.google.com/url?sa=t&source=web&ct=res&cd=1&url=httppercent3Apercent2 Fpercent2Fwww
.marketingsherpa.com percent2Ftele percent2FLPET.pdf&ei=LqLBSN7wNKOmpA TR4OjoBg&usg=
AFQjCNEAMuKbC7U7qwiRAOqRuP3FvQ8HVQ&sig2=oVF8QcXCIUe1PlbY0blEZQ, and research.micro
soft.com/apps/pubs/default.aspx?id=77794

Psychological Marketing

Another effective tool in marketing on the Internet is psychological marketing, which requires that you go way beyond the traditional techniques of
studying the demographics of your customers and try to get into their heads.
You need to ask yourself, "What are they thinking when they reach my web
page? What are they doing *right now?* Which adjective should I use to

describe my product on this page? Which words will cause more conversions?"

As this isn't a psychology or marketing book, there is no room here to discuss this subject at length. However, if you go to www.theSocialMedia Bible.com, you can use your password to download the "Psychological Hot Buttons" document (yours free as the owner of this book).

It's All about Conversion

What are you planning to do with all of the traffic you get to come to each of your specific web pages? Don't let any of it go to waste. You've worked hard to get every eye. The most important design element you can consider is your conversion message. Now that you have your prospects' attention, what do you want them to do next? You want them to convert. (And no, even though this is called *The Social Media Bible, conversion* does not refer to religion.)

The term *conversion* actually has a lot of different definitions in the context of web design. In fact, every different page you design—based on the preceding rules—carries a different meaning of conversion. The most common and easiest to understand of these is "Click Here to Purchase." There are many others. Wikipedia defines *conversion* as: "In marketing, a conversion occurs when a prospective customer takes the marketer's intended action. If the prospect has visited a marketer's web site, the conversion action might be making an online purchase, or submitting a form to request additional information. The conversion rate is the percentage of visitors who take the conversion action."

If you have a pair of eyes on your home page, conversion means, "Read my message and click to another page." If your site visitor clicks to the next page that contains more detailed information and assists them through their sales funnel, you have a successful conversion. If you have someone land on a page that asks them to join your network and they sign up, you have a successful conversion. If they are asked to "pass this along to a friend" (referral) and they do, then your web page and call to action were effective and successful.

Accurately targeted traffic results in conversions—whether they are sales leads, large numbers of page views (visitors looking at pages), longer time on page or site (minutes spent interacting and reading: stickiness), brand awareness (due to immersion in the site and your marketing message), offline contact (often consumers change to offline contact through store visits or telephone calls), and pass-alongs (tell-a-friend referrals). Before you design the content of a web page, you must first consider its definition of conversion.

The most effective way to get someone to convert is to have a strong "What's In It for Me?" (WIIFM). Chapter 4, It's Not Your Father's E-Mail, went into detail on WIIFM. The first WIIFM's 1.54-second rule and the second with its 5-second rule will make the difference between your prospect converting and leaving. Be sure you've read and comprehend the section on the importance of selecting the right image to help convey that WIIFM message.

Each page should have only one definition of conversion stated by your WIIFM message. Once your prospect has found your page, you need to provide that person with the exact information they are looking for and capture them with a strong WIIFM message that conveys that conversion. This is why a home page is harmful and ineffective: It has many conversions—probably every conversion your site has to offer. It's therefore somewhat confusing to your prospects. Refer to early comments about home page.

Since Part I of this book is about tactics more than strategies (which are described in Part III), this section doesn't spend a lot of time on metrics. However, whatever your definition of conversion is for each page, be sure to design the page in a way that allows you to measure it. If you don't gauge your conversions, then you can't manage them. If you don't set up Google Analytics or another way to assess your web site's traffic, then you won't know if all of your hard work was successful. Determining what to measure is easy: How many visitors came to that page, how many converted (clicked through), and how many left.

If more people left your site than converted to the next step, then your conversion message was too weak, or it did not provide the call to action that your visitor was expecting. You need to constantly adjust and fine-tune your conversion message; test, measure, refine. Lather, rinse, repeat.

Here are a few other sample metrics to consider when quantifying your conversions:

- I want to increase the *number of orders* by 30 percent within one year.
- I want to increase the *click-throughs* on my page by 50 percent by next quarter.
- I want 25 percent more *visitors* who will look at *six pages* before leaving.
- I want the press to pick up our great *success stories,* resulting in *four trade articles* this year.
- I want to *reduce* the amount of tech *telephone support by 20 percent* this year by shifting it to *online support forums,* (YouTube how-to videos, tech support podcasts, and company blogs).

Some metrics will be difficult, and some even impossible to measure. There still is a great deal of benefit to gain from your efforts, however. An immediate order (e-commerce) is easy to track, but a lagged order (where your prospect comes back later to purchase) drives prospects to a retail store (which applies to both business-to-business and business-to-consumer) or converts to a telephone order (Dell Computer has 5,000 separate 800 numbers for tracking). These are called "blended success metrics," and one way to measure these is by incorporating extras like coupons, unique and trackable special offers, cashier questions, unique telephone numbers or extensions, promo codes, and unique URLs.

B2B Success Metrics

Business-to-business (B2B) marketers have an even more challenging time measuring their metrics. Consider tracking data like immediate lead generation, immediate order by phone, lead or other phone contact, lagged order long after the site visit (consider their buying cycle), faxed Request for Proposal (RFP) or Request for Quote (RFQ) based on information learned on the site, catalog or brochure request, white paper download or request, newsletter, e-mail, or other registration and sales meeting request.

Testing Different Landing Pages

Keep in mind that you aren't limited to only one landing page per sales funnel category or conversion definition page; in fact, you can create many different pages that can each test different images, colors, backgrounds, fonts, headings, font sizes, layout, and WIIFMs (Figure 5.5). By testing multiple pages intended for the same conversion, you can directly compare the pages and determine which is converting most effectively. This is a lot like the practice of segmenting described in detail in Chapter 4, It's Not Your Father's E-Mail.

Conversions

- *Man:* 33 sales, $72,795
- *No picture:* 32 sales, $67,435
- *Woman:* 25 sales, $54,120

The "man" picture sold 8 percent more than "no" picture and 35 percent more than the "woman" picture.

The remaining design element you must always consider is the content. Search engines love good content—as do your prospects and customers.

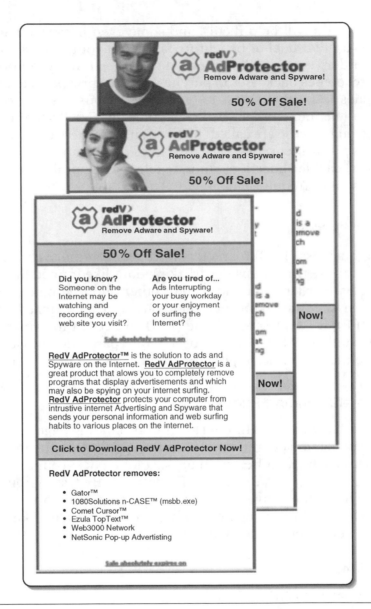

FIGURE 5.5 Landing Pages

Above all, be sure that your web pages address your prospects' needs and desires, and always provide a strong call to action along with satisfactory value. Many experts interviewed for one of the author's podcasts—all of which can be found at www.theSocialMediaBible.com—had the same advice. To quote 2007 SEO World Champion Benj Arriola, "Content is king."

Techniques and Tactics

The purpose of this book is not to teach you all you need to know about how to design an effective web page. It is more focused upon helping you understand the big picture, and imparting some of the little-known—and better-known—tips and tricks picked up along the way. If you really want to get into the technical side of web page programming, get books such as *Creating Web Pages For Dummies* by Bud E. Smith and Arthur Bebak.

Even so, some techniques and tactics help avoid many of the common errors that most people make. The first and most damaging relates to fonts. Never use serifs.

A *serif* is a term for characters that have a line crossing the free end of a stroke, sometimes referred to as *feet and hats* (see Figure 5.6). This style of typeface is thought to have been invented by the Romans. It is the most often used style of font and also one of the most legible styles in print, but *not* on the Web. The popularization of this font style emerged in newspapers, where the font size was nine points or smaller. Because this made large blocks of text difficult to read, adding the serifs—or the short line segments—created a sort of top and bottom line for the eye to follow when reading. Remember the faint blue lines that teachers taught writing with in first grade?

This aid became so helpful to the newspaper industry—particularly to the *New York Times*—that nearly all printed words are done with serifs. This is why the most common serif fonts have names like Times (designed for the *Times of London* newspaper) and Times New Roman. The only instances in which a newspaper doesn't use a serif font is when the text is designed large enough to be easily read, such as a title of an article (in which case they often use Helvetica).

Here's an interesting test: Take a page from the newspaper and look closely at the text. See how the serifs almost create a line across the top and bottom of the text? Now, slowly turn the newspaper page away from you so you are looking nearly on its edge, but can still see the text. The serifs almost join to create the definitive lines.

FIGURE 5.6   Serif and Sans Serif Fonts

This effect is fine if talking about print, which usually has dpi (dots per inch) greater than 300. Newspapers can be printed at 600-plus dpi, and many magazines can be printed at up to nearly 3,000 dpi. That's a lot of dots for every inch. However, reading a computer monitor is a completely different story.

The Internet is, by definition, viewed through a computer monitor (or worse, a mobile screen). No matter how much you pay for your high-resolution flat-panel monitor, the highest Internet resolution you are likely to see is . . . 72 dpi. This is a very poor quality compared to a printer. This is the case because the human eye can see only so many little bright lights—like those on your computer screen—per inch. At 72 dpi, serifs don't aid in reading; instead, they detract. The resolution of our monitors simply doesn't do justice to the fine detail of a serif. It just makes mud.

Web page and screen resolutions are rapidly getting better because of HD Video, ClearType fonts, and higher resolution monitors, but for now when designing a web page, be sure to always use nonserif, or what they call sans serif, fonts—like Arial, Geneva, Monaco, or Tahoma.

"Trademark Sucks"

Another effective technique is to use trademarks in your copy. This section is called "Trademark Sucks" because trademarks are a very effective tool for sucking or hijacking your competitor's traffic away from competitors and onto your web site.

You can usually use another company's registered trademarks in your copy if comparing or contrasting different products or services. Comparative pages are generally considered fair use in the United States; however, Europe views this differently. Trademark sharing is frowned upon outside of the United States, where content, editorial, and blog sites frequently leverage brands in content. Be careful when you do this, and always check which rules apply where—since there have been cases where trademarks in hidden copy or meta tags have been litigated.

Keyword Placement

Question: Who shows up when you search for your brand? Is it you or your competition? Do a search, and find out.

As explained in more detail in Chapter 19, Spotlight on Search (Search Engine Optimization), the placement of your keywords can help with search engine rankings, and make it clearer to your prospects exactly what you're offering them. Start your content's paragraphs with keywords that make sense both to your prospects and search engines. Use nouns that describe the product or service accurately, and use them early. Use phrases that might be searched, and weave them into the copy. Make your copy unique to every page. You need to have a unique WIIFM.

Frames

Frames are programming techniques that create a grid of pigeonholes called *framesets*, wherein blocks of text from other web pages are inserted to create one visually pleasing page. Don't do this! Frames compile text from multiple web pages, and links to internally framed pages lead to dead ends—or pages with no text of their own. Frames will kill your site's search engine friendliness; even if you get the site indexed, the searcher's experience is very poor. Remember: no frames! For more information on Frames, go to www.useit .com/alertbox/9612.html or visit www.theSocialMediaBible.com for clickable links.

Flash

Embedding Flash into your site is okay, as long as the navigation and content are also available elsewhere in the HTML code and on the page. Flash is an animated cartoon or film usually seen as a web site's home page introduction, created using Adobe Flash animation software as is a .swf file format. Full Flash sites are nearly unindexable (that is, they are practically invisible to search engines) because Flash isn't code that a search engine can read; it's compiled movie code with no HTML code of its own. Even Google and FAST, both of which claim to index Flash files, don't seem to rank them too highly. Flash may seem cool for your designers and marketers, but Flash misuse can kill your search engine optimization and anger your prospects. How many times have you been caught in a home page Flash demo and ran for the mouse to click "Skip Intro"? Your prospects feel the same way, too. Use Flash sparingly—and correctly.

Page Titles

Pick a page, any page . . . and look at your page title. It's even odds that your programmer never gave your page a title and that it's still called "untitled"— or it has the same name as all of your other web pages. Perhaps it's even just your company's name. You must have unique, descriptive titles on each page of your site; primarily for the search engines, and secondarily for your prospects. Be sure to use explanatory titles. These are the essence of each page, the WIIFM. Use titles that are unique and compelling for the searcher. Be sure to include phrases a searcher is likely to type (do some keyword research). Keywords in the title should be placed in web page copy as well. I would put the "keyword placement" section after "page titles" and explain there. An accurate description of the page's content is much better than engaging in keyword stuffing—in other words, just adding random keywords. Your title can be as long as 90 to 100 characters, but it's best to lead with your strongest keyword differentiator, not your site's or company's name. When titling your web pages, always consider plural and singular versions of a keyword.

Constructing Regional and Local Campaigns

It's important to understand the motivation behind the local searcher's query. If you are a local company, you must separate and differentiate your web pages by region or locale. Even if you are a national company, but sell and compete in different regions, localize your landing pages by using local state, town, city, county, and geographic names. This way, when your prospect is searching for a company in her area, your company will come up in her search—even if you are 1,000 miles away.

Offline Marketing Strategy

Before you had a web page, you likely had a conventional marketing strategy. What were the objectives of that strategy? And on an even more basic level, before you had this marketing strategy, what was the product or service that you wanted to sell? Your web page goals and objectives should align with your overall business goals and objectives. How close to your true goals and to your offline strategy can you get in online advertising and web page content? More about strategy is discussed in Part III of this book.

Affiliate Marketing

Many marketers rely on affiliates—or partners in branding and marketing—to generate sales on a commissioned basis. However, affiliate-marketing problems can and do arise. When you use this kind of sales program, you are essentially supporting someone else to compete with you for web page traffic. You need to ask yourself how your brand is portrayed, how much traffic you're giving away to your affiliates, whether you're fighting with an affiliate for your own traffic, whether your affiliates are escalating prices and costing everyone more—and, essentially, whether using affiliates at all is a good strategy. Affiliate marketing can be very successful for some companies; but it's not for everyone. Refer to the Readings and Resources at the end of this chapter for more information on affiliate marketing.

Web Site Platforms

The purpose of this book is to explain concepts relating to the Web and social media. It isn't the intent of this book to be a detailed teaching guide. The different varieties of platforms upon which your web site can be constructed are becoming more plentiful every day. The most popular include HTML-based—the old standby that's been used for more than a decade; Joomla, an easier-to-use, open-source platform; Ning, an easy-to-use, community-building platform; and WordPress, which is also a very easy-to-use, open-source, robust platform. You will have to research your options further as new ones are coming online every day. Find a web site developer whom you can trust, and ask him to explain the pros and cons of each platform so you can find what's right for you.

Providers

This section tries to give you a starting point on companies that provide services to support the subject matter of the chapter. In the field of web page developers, the list is limitless. To find a good provider in this field, solicit help from your trusted network. Speak with someone you rely on before hiring a developer. Unfortunately, far more companies are out there that don't know what they are doing as opposed to those that do.

One of the most important decisions you will need to make once you do find a trusted developer is the base platform on which you will develop: HTML, Joomla, WordPress, Java, or another technology altogether? Many developers aren't skilled in building on all of these platforms. They usually prefer only one, and they stick to it. Do a little research on how each kind of platform works, and have your developer explain the pros and cons of each. Many web sites are actually combinations of platforms. Remember that when all else fails, HTML is usually the most reliable method.

Alexa (alexa.com) is a web traffic information company founded in April 1996. Alexa Internet grew out of a vision that web navigation should be intelligent and constantly improving by way of user participation. Along the way, Alexa developed an installed base of millions of toolbars, one of the largest web crawls, and an infrastructure to process and serve massive amounts of data. For Alexa's toolbar and web site users, this has resulted in products that have revolutionized web navigation and intelligence. Developers are able to use a set of tools that are unprecedented in scope and that allow entirely new services to be created on the Alexa data and platform, including a free ratings toolbar.

In-House–Out-House

Unless you want to learn how to program a web site yourself, you should leave the programming to the web developers. If you choose what's called a high-level platform such as Joomla or WordPress, you should at least learn how to create and modify web pages and blogs. It's easier than you think; it could save you the time and money that it takes to go back to the developer each time you need a small change; and it can be fun to do.

The ROI of Social Media

Social Media Outreach Enhances Teen-Focused Cause Marketing Campaign

Background

In 2008, Staples, the world's largest office products retailer and an expert on back-to-school retailing, worked with DoSomething.org, a national not-for-profit organization that empowers teens to take action in their communities, to create "Do Something 101," a national school supply drive. The inaugural campaign raised more than $150,000 for local charities to purchase back-to-school supplies for students who need them and generated more than 211.8 million media impressions. For 2009, Staples aimed to make the second Annual Do Something 101 National School Supply Drive bigger and better than the inaugural campaign. Staples and DoSomething.org wanted to inspire more teens to "do something" by collecting new school supplies for underprivileged kids, connect with teens in a unique and meaningful way, and increase donations and impressions over the previous year.

Strategy

The strategy was to conduct ongoing conversations about the need for school supplies for underserved youth, and how the Do Something 101 campaign can help. In addition to the traditional marketing tactics of in-store signage, customer e-mails, public service announcements, and media relations, Staples launched a social media campaign to reach teens where they spend the most time: Facebook. Staples recently launched its own corporate

---

Facebook page geared toward its core audience of small business customers. Rather than trying to retrofit the Staples corporate page for teens, Staples developed a fan page focused entirely on the teen audience, as well as a new Facebook application, to raise awareness of the Do Something 101 school supply drive.

Implementation

Staples worked with a social media agency, Mr. Youth, to develop the Facebook fan page for Do Something 101, and create the new "Adopt-a-Pack" application. With Adopt a Pack, teens could tag their friends to fill virtual backpacks with school supplies to raise awareness for the cause and effort. With every backpack filled, teens could enter a sweepstakes for various prizes, including a trip to New York City to participate in a bag-stuffing event with the campaign's spokesperson, Grammy-winning Ciara. Staples spread the word about the fan page and application to cause-related and teen-focused blogs. It also worked with Mr. Youth's RepNation network to create a task force of students to spread the word through their existing online networks.

Opportunity

To connect with teens where they already lived online, allow them to show support for a worthy cause in a fun, unique manner, and build a foundation of teen engagement for future campaigns.

Conclusion

The Second Annual Do Something 101 national school supply drive raised more than $630,000 in customer cash donations, compared to $125,000 in 2008. Staples customers also donated thousands of items such as notebooks, calculators, and other supplies for students in need. The program received editorial coverage in outlets ranging from the *New York Times* to Seventeen .com, and resulted in 484.8 million media impressions, more than doubling 2008's results of 211.8 million media impressions. In addition, the Do Something 101 Facebook Fan page secured more than 6,000 fans who still continue to engage with the page well past the end of the 2009 campaign, and will serve as a base for the 2010 school supply drive. In addition, through the Facebook application, Staples achieved 211 million teen impressions (compared to 13 million teen impressions from a 2008 teen marketing program).

Staples, Inc., PR team
www.staples.com

Expert Insight

Vint Cerf, father of the Internet and futurist, www.google.com/corporate/execs.html

. . . Well, first of all labeling me the "Father of the Internet" is not fair to an awful lot of people, especially to Bob Kahn, because Bob started the Internetting program when he joined the Defense Department in 1972; and then he came to me when I was at Stanford in early 1973 and said, "You know, I have this problem. How do I hook all these different nets together?"

Vint Cerf

So the two of us did the basic Internet design, descriptions of the design of the TCP protocol. As the design evolved, we split out the Internet Protocol from the TCP, producing what is now called the TCP/IP protocol suite. But there are many, many people, both before and after that stage, that have contributed to make the Net what it is today.

So, I'm just happy that I participated in it because it has been a lot of fun. . . .

. . . It certainly has been something of a surprise to me that the users of the Internet, the consumers of information, have now become the primary producers of information on the network. It's very widespread. It shows up in a number of different forms. It shows up as blogs, it shows up as video uploads in YouTube, tweets on Twitter, Facebook, blog pages, and other similar services. It shows up at social game sites. Things like World of Warcraft. It's showing up as people populate their own web pages, send e-mail, use distribution lists, and so on.

Some of those things have been around for a while. E-mail, of course, was invented in 1971, so it's an old medium in some sense but still very heavily used, as are distribution lists. There's chat and there are other kinds of more real-time things, including video now.

So all of these different ways of interacting have been very rapidly absorbed by the public. Mobiles, which only recently have come on the scene, now account for over four billion users, not on the Internet but in the mobile world. But the Internet interfaces to many of the mobiles and so people are beginning to do texting in the mobile world, they are doing instant messaging, they are doing e-mail exchanges, and they are searching the Web from their mobiles.

What I'm seeing right now is a wide range of choices that people have in maintaining relationships and in interacting with people one on one, and in groups. I think this is likely to persist. Certainly, the sharing of information on the Internet has been dramatic. In the scientific world, equally so. Where scientists begin to build common databases that they can reference, such as the human genome database or astronomical information, or the geophysical information, we are finding that scientific results are achieved faster because people have reference to virtually everything that is known about some particular phenomenon because it's been codified in these shared databases.

So now we're seeing an increasing amount of collaborative work in the online environment and something, which Google, of course, is intensely interested in.

. . . [I]n these mediums, it's possible to be abusive, and I am very concerned about the side effect of cyber-bullying and things of that sort. Others have expressed a discomfort with the fact that anything and everything can be expressed on the Internet, including negative information . . . whether it's accurate or not, it sometimes has an impact.

So we have a potential for both positive and constructive and also rather negative kinds of interactions in this online environment; and I think we're still trying to discipline ourselves in how to treat these different media in a way that protects us from some of the abusive behaviors.

I am thinking not merely of the social media, but more generally speaking; things like viruses and worms and keyloggers that are looking for user names and passwords, or identifiers of account.

Those are all fairly pernicious abuses of this online medium, and I think we are still trying to learn how to cope with it socially and legally, as well as from the law enforcement point of view. . . .

. . . The FCC believes that it is responsible for all communications in the United States. It doesn't mean that it's responsible for communications outside the United States, but it has chosen to treat the Internet as a Title I Information Service. This is now in debate and the FCC has even suggested to move Internet services back into Title II (communication services). I think this might be beneficial if you are worried about the potential for anticompetitive behaviors among the broadband.

Internet service providers could abuse their control of the IP layer to ward off competing higher-level applications.

There are some side effects of that, which I think are not relevant to this discussion, although they're of concern to me; having a lot to do with "Common Carriage," and things like that; but the FCC has chosen to forebear to regulate, except in cases it considers to be anticompetitive practices. And you'll note that there was a recent decision by the FCC with regards to Comcast and its attempt to manage network use in the presence of BitTorrent and other kinds of peer-to-peer file sharing applications. That ruling is also in dispute at present.

(*continued*)

(continued)

The FCC censured Comcast for the way in which it undertook to do that management. There are other places in the world that are even more actively trying to control access to and use of the Internet. You're going to find that everywhere. The Internet is global in scope. It operates in virtually every country in varying degrees and countries have different views of what people should or shouldn't be able to do using this medium.

One of the biggest challenges, I think, is that no matter what position you take with regard to usage, you have the problem that if your position is different from some other countries' view, there is not much that you can do to enforce your view, and vice versa.

And so then you get into this question of, "Under my rules my citizen was attacked by a person in another country and I'm looking for some kind of compensation."

You will not be able to deal with those problems unless there are more common agreements about what is or is not acceptable behavior on the Internet. And since the social views vary from one country to another, I think it is going to be hard for us to come to global agreements; but I think we will come to some agreements commonly.

For example, as far as I know, every country in the world rejects child pornography as an unacceptable form of behavior, whether it's on the Internet or otherwise.

So, maybe there are other things that we can agree are commonly unacceptable and, therefore, should be either prevented or punished if they are detected. It's going to take a lot of international work to make that a reality. Social networking is so wrapped up in cultural norms that applications in this domain, taken on a global scale, is almost sure to run into societal issues . . . .

. . . And, by the way, I would like to say something about China. When you talk to Chinese people on the streets, you discover that some number of them actually appreciate the censorship. They claim to like it; they believe they are being protected; now whether that's true is independent of how they feel about it, or how they, at least, say they feel about it. So we shouldn't make the assumption that the First Amendment notion, which is powerful in our Constitution, is necessarily universally accepted as preferable.

There are cultures where, in fact, the citizens want this kind of control. . . .

. . . This reminds me of an interesting phenomenon that happened in the late 1980s. I had asked permission from the U.S. federal government to connect MCI, which is a commercial e-mail service, up to the Internet. And they reluctantly allowed me to do that. The reluctance came from the concern that we would be carrying, or using, government-sponsored backbones to carry commercial e-mail traffic.

After I put the MCI mail system up on the Internet, immediately the other e-mail service providers said, "Well, you know, the MCI Mail people shouldn't have an exclusive privilege." And so CompuServe came up and Ontyme came up and some of the other commercial servers also came up on the Net.

And the side effects of this was that they could suddenly interchange e-mail with each other through the Internet, which before they could not do. So it's this standardization that creates the possibility of interoperability. And this is why Google's OpenSocial, I think, is an important effort . . . because it potentially creates interoperability among those areas in social networks.

I think it will be very attractive for the users of those networks to be able to interact, regardless of which social networks systems you happen to be registered in. You know, we may see some interesting consequences of that interconnection as people begin to adopt it. There will be interactions that we might not have anticipated that are enabled by that standard. . . .

. . . I'm, of course, perhaps understandably, excited and feel positive about a lot of these new developments. The Internet was designed to be fairly insensitive to specific media, so it does not know if it is carrying a digital image or voice or video or some other digitized object . . . you know, part of a program or a piece of Web page. It just does not know, and that's very deliberate. It was intended to be a general-purpose transport mechanism, and the consequences of that is . . . every device that produces digital output potentially can be interfaced to the Internet and this output transfers around and delivers to other places. I think that we are going to see a very significant increase in the number of devices that are able to connect to and interact with other devices on the Internet.

There had been some discussion about the earlier phases of Internet being "Internet for everyone" and now it is becoming "Internet for everything?!" And I really do believe that. I think sensor networks, appliances, things at home, in the office, in the automobile, and that you carry around will all be Internet-enabled and this allows us to manage them better. These devices can report their status to us; they can accept, command, and control from third parties. You can imagine entertainment systems being managed over the Internet by third-party entertainment managers; you simply click here if you want this movie or that song, and it takes care of the details of getting it to the CD player in the car or the hard disc that replaced the CD player, or your iPod or some other DVR or whatever you have. All of these are possible once these devices become part of the Internet.

And, of course, mobiles are contributing to that because as they become more and more equipped with Internet capabilities, they too, will become remote controllers for many, many devices. . . .

To listen to or read the entire Executive Conversation with Vint Cerf, go to www .theSocialMediaBible.com.

Commandments

1. **Thou shalt understand your prospect or customer.**

    Have a firm grasp on what's important to them, what they are looking for, and what they expect to take away from your site. Only then will you understand how to create content that will really draw them in.

2. **Thou shalt understand the different sales funnel phases.**

    By recognizing the different phases that your prospect or client undergoes, you can develop specific web pages—and corresponding titles—that address their particular needs.

3. **Thou shalt implement metrics.**

    Really, if you can't measure it, you can't manage it. If you don't look at the numbers, you will never know if something you are doing is effective or a waste of your time. Once you have some analytics in place, test different ideas, layouts, taglines, headings, bullets, images, colors, and copy. Go with what works, and remember that this is a continuous process.

4. **Thou shalt understand the different conversion definitions.**

    Understand the different definitions of conversion you have for each and every page, and design each page specifically to attain that desired conversion.

5. **Thou shalt set specific measurable goals.**

    Set realistic and measurable goals for your web pages. This way, when you track these numbers, you will know when you are successful.

6. **Thou shalt remember that content is king.**

    Whether it's search engine optimization, stickiness of your page, or how well your page converts, it's all about content. If your content is valuable and meets the expectations of your prospects, then they will become engaged and most likely convert to purchasers.

7. **Thou shalt not use serif fonts.**

    Because of monitor resolution, fonts with serifs can become muddy and less appealing than a sans serif font.

8. **Thou shalt use frames and Flash cautiously.**

    Both frames and Flash make it difficult for search engines, and hence your prospects, to find you. Flash can also be annoying, so use it with caution.

Conclusion

Having a well-designed web page is probably the smartest thing you can do for your business. It certainly has the greatest return on investment. A cleverly designed site and page(s) will receive a high ranking on all of the search engines; be easy for your prospects and customers to find; provide valuable content for them; encourage them to stay longer on your site, thereby granting you a greater opportunity to convey your message; reduce customer service; expand your contact lists; build trust; and eventually convert them to a sale.

To hear all of the Expert Interviews, go to www.theSocialMediaBible .com.

Readings and Resources

Boudreaux, Toby. *PHP 5: Your Visual Blueprint for Creating Open Source, Server-Side Content.* (Hoboken, NJ: John Wiley & Sons, Inc.)

Buser, David, John Kauffman, Juan T. Llibre, Brian Francis, Dave Sussman, Chris Ullman, and Jon Duckett. *Beginning Active Server Pages 3.0.* (Hoboken, NJ: John Wiley & Sons, Inc.)

Butters, Keith. *Teach Yourself VISUALLY Flash CS4 Professional.* (Hoboken, NJ: John Wiley & Sons, Inc.)

Carey, Patrick. *New Perspectives on Creating Web Pages with HTML, XHTML, and XML.* (Boston, MA: Mariner Books)

Chapman, Nigel, and Jenny Chapman. *Web Design: A Complete Introduction.* (Hoboken, NJ: John Wiley & Sons, Inc.)

Chopra, Vivek, Jon Eaves, Rupert Jones, Sing Li, and John T. Bell. *Beginning Java Server Pages.* (Hoboken, NJ: John Wiley & Sons, Inc.)

Crowder, David A. *Building a Web Site For Dummies*, 3rd ed. (Hoboken, NJ: John Wiley & Sons, Inc.)

Crowder, Rhonda. *Cliffs Notes Creating Web Pages with HTML.* (Hoboken, NJ: John Wiley & Sons, Inc.)

Etheridge, Denise, and Janet Valade. *Master VISUALLY Dreamweaver 8 and Flash 8.* (Hoboken, NJ: John Wiley & Sons, Inc.)

Friedman, Shay, and Gaston Hillar. *ASP.NET 4 Programmer's Reference.* (Hoboken, NJ: John Wiley & Sons, Inc.)

Ganguli, Madhushree. *Making Use of JSP.* (Hoboken, NJ: John Wiley & Sons, Inc.)

Groh, Michael R. *Access 2010 Bible.* (Hoboken, NJ: John Wiley & Sons, Inc.)

Harris, Andy. *HTML, XHTML and CSS All-in-One For Dummies*, 2nd ed. (Hoboken, NJ: John Wiley & Sons, Inc.)

Hatfield, Bill. *Active Server Pages For Dummies*, 2nd ed. (Hoboken, NJ: John Wiley & Sons, Inc.)

Hiam, Alexander. *Marketing For Dummies.* (Hoboken, NJ: John Wiley & Sons, Inc.)

Holzner, Steve. *Ajax For Dummies.* (Hoboken, NJ: John Wiley & Sons, Inc.)

Huddleston, Rob. *HTML, XHTML, and CSS: Your Visual Blueprint for Designing Effective Web Pages.* (Hoboken, NJ: John Wiley & Sons, Inc.)

Jenkins, Sue, Michele E. Davis, and Jon A. Phillips. *Dreamweaver 8 All-in-One Desk Reference For Dummies.* (Hoboken, NJ: John Wiley & Sons, Inc.)

Jones, Bradley L. *Web 2.0 Heroes: Interviews with 20 Web 2.0 Influencers.* (Hoboken, NJ: John Wiley & Sons, Inc.)

Kinkoph, Sherry Willard. *Creating Web Pages with HTML Simplified.* (Hoboken, NJ: John Wiley & Sons, Inc.)

Kinkoph, Sherry Willard. *Creating Web Pages with HTML Simplified*, 3rd ed. (Hoboken, NJ: John Wiley & Sons, Inc.)

Kraynak, Joe. *Master VISUALLY Creating Web Pages.* (Hoboken, NJ: John Wiley & Sons, Inc.)

Leuf, Bo. *The Semantic Web: Crafting Infrastructure for Agency.* (Hoboken, NJ: John Wiley & Sons, Inc.)

Lowery, Joseph W. *Adobe CS3 Web Workflows: Building Websites with Adobe Creative Suite 3.* (Hoboken, NJ: John Wiley & Sons, Inc.)

Lowery, Joseph W. *Dreamweaver CS3 Bible.* (Hoboken, NJ: John Wiley & Sons, Inc.)

MacDonald, Matthew. *Creating Web Sites: The Missing Manual.* (Sebastopol, CA: O'Reilly Media, Inc.)

McFedries, Paul. *The Complete Idiot's Guide to Creating a Web Page & Blog.* (Royersford, PA: Alpha Publishing, Inc.)

McFedries, Paul, ed. *Windows XP Simplified Service Pack 2.* (Hoboken, NJ: John Wiley & Sons, Inc.)

Pascarello, Eric. *JavaScript: Your Visual Blueprint for Building Dynamic Web Pages*, 2nd ed. (Hoboken, NJ: John Wiley & Sons, Inc.)

Prussakov, Evgenii. *A Practical Guide to Affiliate Marketing: Quick Reference for Affiliate Managers & Merchants*. (Arlington, VA: AM Navigator, LLC.)

Ray, Deborah S., and Eric J. Ray. *HTML 4 For Dummies: Quick Reference*, 2nd ed. (Hoboken, NJ: John Wiley & Sons, Inc.)

Rinehart, Mac. *Java Server Pages For Dummies.* (Hoboken, NJ: John Wiley & Sons, Inc.)

Robinson, Mike, and Ellen Finkelstein. *Jakarta Struts For Dummies.* (Hoboken, NJ: John Wiley & Sons, Inc.)

Sanford, Jacob J. *Professional ASP.NET 2.0 Design: CSS, Themes, and Master Pages.* (Hoboken, NJ: John Wiley & Sons, Inc.)

Shreves, Ric. *Mambo: Your Visual Blueprint for Building and Maintaining Web Sites with the Mambo Open Source CMS.* (Hoboken, NJ: John Wiley & Sons, Inc.)

Simpson, Alan. *Cliffs Notes Creating Your First Web Page.* (Hoboken, NJ: John Wiley & Sons, Inc.)

Smith, Bud E. *Creating Web Pages For Dummies*, 9th ed. (Hoboken, NJ: John Wiley & Sons, Inc.)

Smith, Bud E., and Arthur Bebak. *Creating Web Pages For Dummies*, 6th ed. (Hoboken, NJ: John Wiley & Sons, Inc.)

Smith, Bud E., and Arthur Bebak. *Creating Web Pages For Dummies*, 7th ed. (Hoboken, NJ: John Wiley & Sons, Inc.)

Smith, Bud E., and Arthur Bebak. *Creating Web Pages For Dummies*, 8th ed. (Hoboken, NJ: John Wiley & Sons, Inc.)

Smith, Eric A. *Active Server Pages Bible*. (Hoboken, NJ: John Wiley & Sons, Inc.)

Spaanjaars, Imar. *Beginning ASP.NET 4: In C# and VB*. (Hoboken, NJ: John Wiley & Sons, Inc.)

Tittel, Ed, and Jeff Noble. *HTML, XHTML & CSS For Dummies*, 6th ed. (Hoboken, NJ: John Wiley & Sons, Inc.)

Tittel, Ed, and Mary Burmeister. *HTML 4 For Dummies*, 5th ed. (Hoboken, NJ: John Wiley & Sons, Inc.)

Wagner, Richard, and Richard Mansfield. *Creating Web Pages All-in-One Desk Reference for Dummies*. (Hoboken, NJ: John Wiley & Sons, Inc.)

Warner, Janine. *Teach Yourself VISUALLY Dreamweaver CS3*. (Hoboken, NJ: John Wiley & Sons, Inc.)

Warner, Janine. *Dreamweaver CS4 For Dummies*. (Hoboken, NJ: John Wiley & Sons, Inc.)

Warner, Janine. *Teach Yourself VISUALLY Macromedia Dreamweaver 8*. (Hoboken, NJ. John Wiley & Sons, Inc.)

Warner, Janine, and Susannah Gardner. *Dreamweaver MX 2004 For Dummies*. (Hoboken, NJ: John Wiley & Sons, Inc.)

Whitehead, Paul, and James H. Russell. *HTML: Your Visual Blueprint for Designing Web Pages with HTML, CSS, and XHTML*. (Hoboken, NJ: John Wiley & Sons, Inc.)

Wooldridge, Mike. *Creating Web Pages Simplified*. (Hoboken, NJ: John Wiley & Sons, Inc.)

York, Richard. *Beginning CSS: Cascading Style Sheets for Web Design*. (Hoboken, NJ: John Wiley & Sons, Inc.)

York, Richard. *Beginning JavaScript and CSS Development with jQuery*. (Hoboken, NJ: John Wiley & Sons, Inc.)

Downloads

For your free downloads associated with *The Social Media Bible,* go to www .theSocialMediaBible.com, and enter your ISBN number located on the back of the book above the bar code. Be sure to enter the dashes.

Credits

The ROI of Social Media was provided by:

Staples, Inc., PR team, www.Staples.com

Expert Insight was provided by:

Vint Cerf, father of the Internet and futurist, www.google.com/corporate/execs.html

Technical edits provided by:

Aaron Baer, Twitter: AaronMBaer

CHAPTER 6

The Internet Forum

What's in It for You?

The *forum* was the name for one of the first Internet-based networking and online communication tools—and still is a great way to engage people in an interactive ongoing conversation on a particular subject. If you want to start a debate, solicit advice, share an idea, run a poll, or just participate in a conversation on your favorite subject, this is where you go—to the forum (or chat room, as it's often called). A chat room differs slightly from a forum, however, because chat room participation requires the member to actively read and post to the conversation in real time, whereas in a forum, you can reply to responses days later. Either format allows you to log on, select a topic of interest, type your comments into a text box, and send them off so that others can see your thoughts—or *posts*—and have the opportunity to comment on your comment (which was a comment on a previous comment).

The forum builds strong community ties, loyalty, and really exemplifies the notion of a trusted network. You can easily apply this trend to your business and create a company forum, so that people from all around the world who care about your subject matter will read, participate, share ideas and concerns, and build a community of trust. By participating in other people's forums, you can develop your own credibility and strong ties with that community. As with all social media, it's about trust, participation, two-way communications, user-generated content—and it's free.

As an example, one forum web site—aptly named the Forum Site (www .theforumsite.com), which was created in 2004—put forth the following statistics as a snapshot of its activity: 3,210 Forums; 60,188 Members with 47 online, 96 new today; Topics 194,731; 2,971,801 Posts with 1,519 today; 37,748 Journals with 238,520 replies; 50,267 Pictures with 113,500 replies; and 97,272 Ratings, 565 Reviews, and 4,738 Polls.

theSocialMediaBible.com

Back to the Beginning

Forums—often referred to as chat rooms, message boards, or bulletin boards—go back to some of the very first uses of the private Usenet in the 1970s, and some of the early public Internet forums started at the beginning of the Web's first public uses in 1995.

The forum was the predecessor to the blog (see Chapter 7, The Ubiquitous Blog, for more information). One of the author's own first experiences participating in a forum was in 1986, when Apple announced eWorld—its own online service for communicating with its Value Added Resellers[1] (VARs; see Figure 6.1).

A VAR, or Value-Added Reseller, is a company that takes an existing product and adds its own value, usually in the form of a specific application for the product—for example, adding a special computer application and reselling it as a new product or package.

A strong sense of community or trusted network develops around forums, most of which have a theme or a conversation in which members share a common interest. Some of these include computers, cats, dogs, pets, sports, a particular team, religion, fashion, video games, politics, hobbies, cars, questions, comparisons, debates, polls of opinion—just about everything you can think of that people talk about. A forum is intended to promote an ongoing dialogue on a specific subject, which differs from the idea of a blog, since the owner of the blog is the one who posts a thought and allows comments—and then moves on to another thought.

What You Need to Know

A forum is a web site application that manages and provides a medium for ongoing online discussion on a particular subject (see Figure 6.2). The users are a group of contributors or members, along with a moderator, who participate in the conversation. The moderator monitors the conversation to be sure that it adheres to rules and regulations set up by the forum owner(s). A member can begin a topic, which will allow others to comment on and add discussion to the previous posts or comments. This two-way

---

1. Wikipedia defines a Value Added Reseller as: "A value-added reseller (VAR) is a company that adds some feature(s) to an existing product(s), then resells it (usually to end-users) as an integrated product or complete "turn-key" solution. This practice is common in the electronics industry, where, for example, a software application might be added to existing hardware."

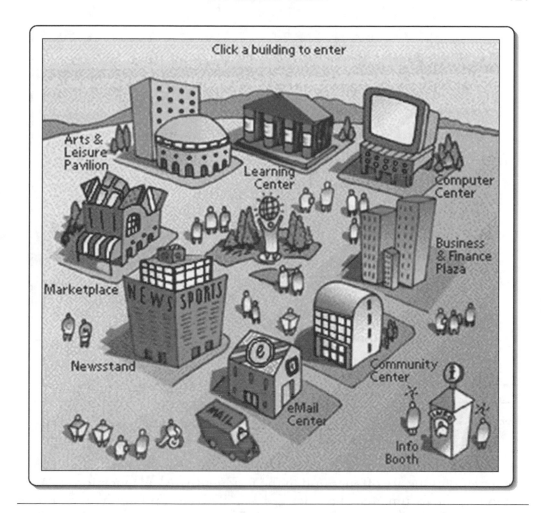

FIGURE 6.1 Apple eWorld Circa 1987

communication is called a *thread*. In most forums, participants are required to register and sign in to participate in a conversation or thread, whereas anyone is permitted to view them. However, anonymous visitors are usually prohibited from participating.

Forum Rules and Regulations

Forums are created, managed, and maintained by an individual or group of individuals who are referred to as *administrators*. Guidelines for all forums

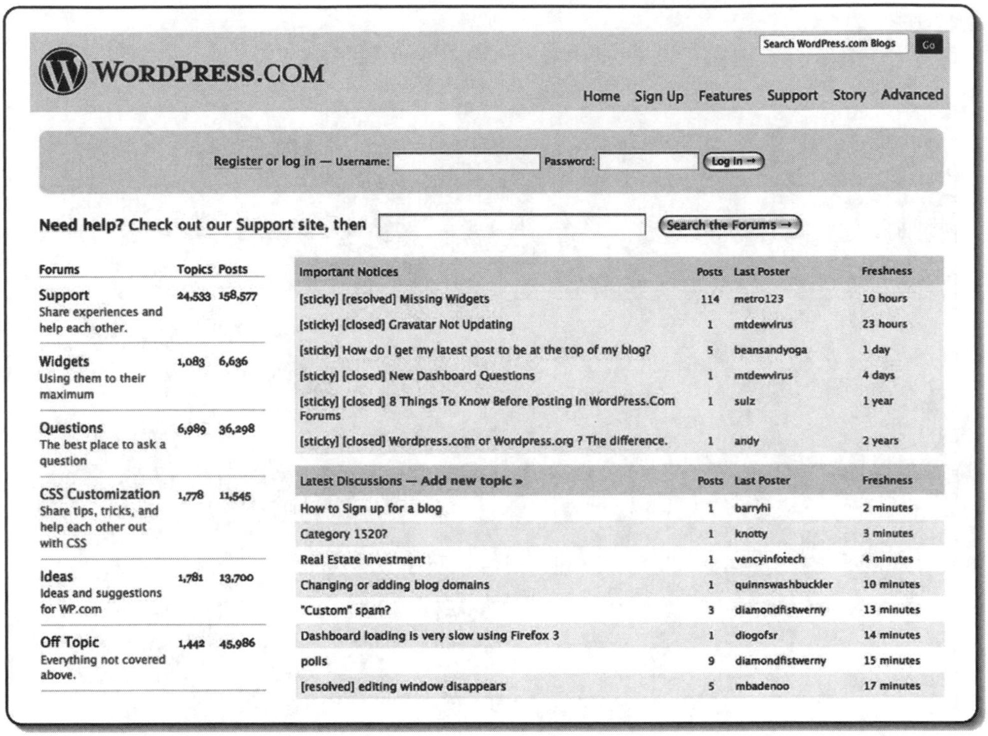

FIGURE 6.2   WordPress Forum

are created, and all participating members are required to follow them. These regulations are often found in the Frequently Asked Questions (FAQs) section of the forum, and the rules are usually basic and apply to common courtesy. Behavior that is prohibited includes insulting, swearing, harassing, inappropriate language, advertising, selling, spamming, personal information posting, sexual content, having more than one account, and warez or other copyright infringements. (*Warez* refers to works that are copyrighted and traded in violation of the copyright law, such as cracked or pirated versions of commercial software.)

Forum Moderator

Moderators—or mods—read and have editorial access to the posts and threads. Mods usually come to hold this position by being promoted from within the ranks of the members. A moderator can have control over banning and unbanning, splitting, renaming, closing, merging, and deleting threads.

The Mods referee members' conversations to keep them free from rule violations and spam. Mods may also receive reports of guideline infringement from members, and then notify the offender when a rule has been broken in order to enforce the rules and, often, administer punishment. It is then up to the moderator to implement an action against, warning to, or banning of that member. First-time offenders are usually warned, whereas repeat offenders can be banned or banished for days—or even permanently. The offending content is always deleted.

Forum Administrator

An administrator (or admin) manages the technical requirements of the forum web site. Administrators are responsible for promoting and demoting members to and from their positions as moderators, keeping the site running properly, and sometimes acting as moderators themselves. These are usually the owners of the forum or are appointed by the owners and have the ultimate say in the operation of the forum.

Forum Registration

To be able to participate in a forum, you most likely will need to register. Once you do so, you become a member of the forum and can participate in a thread, or start your own group or topic of discussion. Most forums require that a member be at least 13 years old; web sites that are collecting information from children under the age of 13 are required to comply with the Federal Trade Commission's (FTC) Children's Online Privacy Protection Act (COPPA; see coppa.org). Most forums allow you to create a user name and password, ask for a valid e-mail address, and ask the user to validate their registration through CAPTCHA Code (see Figure 6.3).[2]

You've seen these verification codes (sometimes including numbers, symbols, and letters) on many different logins and registration sites. Blogs have them to prevent the blogs from being automatically spammed.

---

2. CAPTCHA: Completely Automated Public Turing Test to Tell Computers and Humans Apart (see www.captcha.net) is a program that protects web sites against bots by generating and grading tests that humans can pass, but that current computer programs cannot. This term was coined in 2000 by Luis von Ahn, Manuel Blum, Nicholas Hopper, and John Langford of Carnegie Mellon University. At the time, they developed the first CAPTCHA to be used by Yahoo!. For example, humans can read distorted text like that shown in Figure 6.3, but current computer technology can't.

FIGURE 6.3   CAPTCHA

Forum Post

A post is a text message or a comment that a member types and submits. It is placed in a box that appears directly above the previous post box, and includes the member's user name, icon (or avatar), date and time submitted, and comment. In most forums, members can edit their own posts at any time after posting. This configuration of box upon box with more recent posts displayed in chronological order is called the *thread*. Once the original post has been made, subsequent posts will be placed on top of the previous one, continuing the conversation.

Most forum web sites limit both the minimum and maximum number of characters per post. These numbers are generally set at 10 characters for the minimum, and at either 10,000, 30,000, or 50,000 characters for the maximum, based on the administrator's decision.

Forum Member

Once you properly register to a forum, you become a member (or poster) and are recognized by a user name—or alias—that you choose. You can participate in posting threads to ongoing conversations, submit messages, and have access to all of the other features offered throughout the forum site. Members can use a signature (sig), photo, icon, avatar (see Chapter 16, Virtual Worlds—Real Impact), or other image that represents them and their posts (see Figure 6.4).

Forum Subscription

Members can subscribe to a forum, as they can with a blog. Subscription is an automated notification that alerts you when a new comment has been added to your favorite forum thread. This is done through RSS—Really

FIGURE 6.4 Avatars (left to right): Lon Safko, John Adam, Linh Tang, Chris Brogan, Jeremiah Owyang, and Jody Gnant

Simple Syndication—or Atom[3] feeds. (For more information on RSS, see Chapter 18, RSS—Really Simple Syndication Made Simple on how these feeds can be aggregated into one easy-to-read web page.) It's automatic, and every time there is a new post or comment, you see it without having to go to the forum web page to check.

Forum Troll

A member of a forum who repeatedly breaks etiquette—or *netiquette*—is referred to as a *troll*. This person deliberately posts inflammatory remarks in an attempt to incite irritated responses. When a troll posts a negative comment that engages other members to respond, it can create a flurry of angry comments, called a *flame war* or *flaming*. This activity happens often in forums, on Twitter (see Chapter 14, Thumbs Up for Microblogging), and even on social networking sites like MySpace and Facebook.

Flame wars take place when an ongoing dialogue becomes heated and its participants continue to post argumentative or inflammatory comments, which happens more often than you might think. It's especially frequent in

---

3. Atom is an XML-based document format that describes attributes of a file known as *feeds*. Feeds are composed of a number of items known as *entries*. Atom is used to syndicate web content such as blogs, podcasts, and news to web sites and aggregation pages.

forums that involve controversial groups and subjects like politics and religion. If a flame war breaks out, forum moderators will often warn the participants to stop the incendiary commenting. If this doesn't control the conversation and get it back on track, the moderator will then shut down the conversation thread—either for a finite period that is meant to give the participants ample time to cool off, or indefinitely. Excessive spamming can also cause flame wars and flaming.

Forum Spamming

Like flame wars, spamming is not appropriate or tolerated within the forum setting, and it's also considered a breach of netiquette. A spam message or post is defined as "any unsolicited communication that is not transactional, such as a message to complete a transaction, warranty, product updates, upgrades or recall information, change in terms of subscription or service, or account balance information" (see Chapter 4, It's Not Your Father's E-Mail, for a full history and explanation of spam). Forum spamming can also include any posting that is willful and malicious—such as repeating the same word or phrase over and over to provoke a negative or aggressive response.

Someone on LinkedIn once sent out an obvious spam message to everyone on the network. The message read something to the effect of, "Hello, my name is . . . and I do consulting for . . . so call me for a free quote." The community went insane. Hundreds of backlash e-mails went to her and to other members reprimanding her for her inappropriate message.

Forum User Groups

A *user group* is a group of forum members that grows out of a specific topic of discussion. The group keeps the conversation topic focused to what members of that group wish to discuss. By participating in this type of idea sharing and opinion sharing, the group members' passion on a specific subject forms a bond between them, and this bond is what makes the trusted network as effective and as loyal as it is.

For example, say you participate in an antique car collector's forum. After a while, the members will get to know you from the many posts and contributions you make to their forum. Then say someone wanted a recommendation on where to buy a hard-to-find part, and you suggested a resource; the members of that forum would trust you and your suggestion. You would have built their trust and friendship simply by participating. The same would hold true for a professional organization, a church group, or even a baseball league.

Forum Guest

A guest is an unregistered visitor to a forum site. Guests are generally allowed to access the entire site and read threads, but they are not permitted to participate and post comments in the discussions. To participate, they must be registered. A guest who visits a forum or group frequently without registering is referred to as a *lurker*. Lurking isn't necessarily bad; it's simply the way in which some people prefer to participate. It is somewhat like a blog; many people visit or subscribe to blogs and read them, but never comment on them.

Text Message Shortcuts

A lot of forum communication is done with text message slang or shortcuts. This is particularly popular in mobile text messaging, but is also used anytime you text in a manner that saves you keystrokes. (I'm no G9, but @TEOTD, ALCON, whether it's your BF or just K8T, BM&Y, there's always a BDN of people texting, but DQMOT.) For more about texting and text shortcuts—and to decipher this message—see Chapter 21, The Formidable Fourth Screen (Mobile), and the downloads from that chapter for the complete Text Shortcuts Language Guide.

Emoticons

You've seen them. They're the little smiley faces that show up in your e-mail, on a web page, or in the text of a comment. *Emoticons* are "emotional icons"—a single symbol or combination of symbols that are used to convey emotions within the text message. Forums allow you to type a series of characters and symbols and have them automatically replaced and displayed as a small graphic or icon. A ":-)" will automatically convert into a 😊, or a ":-(" will look like a 🙁. This also works in Microsoft Office programs like Word and Outlook. Microsoft's Messenger provides 70 different emoticons when you're messaging with friends to show them how you really feel. Emoticons are visual ways to express the way you feel when words alone just aren't enough. Try some emoticons in your next text message, e-mail, and Word document (see Figure 6.5).

Forum Social Networking

With the convergence of all things digital—photos, audio, music, and video—along with the popularity of social networking sites like LinkedIn and

	Smile	:-) or :)		Open-mouthed	:-D or :d
	Surprised	:-O or :o		Tongue out	:-P or :p
	Wink	;-) or ;)		Sad	:-(or :(
	Confused	:-S or :s		Disappointed	:-I or :I
	Crying	:'(		Embarrassed	:-$ or :$
	Hot	(H) or (h)		Angry	:-@ or :@
	Angel	(A) or (a)		Devil	(6)
	Don't tell anyone	:-#		Baring teeth	8ol
	Nerd	8-l		Sarcastic	^o)
	Secret telling	:-*		Sick	+o(
	I don't know	:^)		Thinking	*-)
	Party	<:o)		Eye-rolling	8-)
	Sleepy	l-)		Coffee cup	(C) or (c)
	Thumbs up	(Y) or (y)		Thumbs down	(N) or (n)
	Beer mug	(B) or (b)		Martini glass	(D) or (d)
	Girl	(X) or (x)		Boy	(Z) or (z)
	Left hug	({)		Right hug	(})
	Vampire bat	:-[or :[		Birthday cake	(^)
	Red heart	(L) or (l)		Broken heart	(U) or (u)
	Red lips	(K) or (k)		Gift with a bow	(G) or (g)
	Red rose	(F) or (f)		Wilted rose	(W) or (w)
	Camera	(P) or (p)		Filmstrip	(~)
	Cat face	(@)		Dog face	(&)
	Telephone receiver	(T) or (t)		Lightbulb	(I) or (i)
	Note	(8)		Sleeping half-moon	(S)
	Star	(*)		E-mail	(E) or (e)
	Clock	(O) or (o)		MSN Messenger icon	(M) or (m)
	Snail	(sn)		Black sheep	(bah)
	Plate	(pl)		Bowl	(ll)
	Pizza	(pi)		Soccer ball	(so)
	Auto	(au)		Airplane	(ap)
	Umbrella	(um)		Island with a palm tree	(ip)
	Computer	(co)		Mobile phone	(mp)
	Stormy cloud	(st)		Lightning	(li)
	Money	(mo)			

FIGURE 6.5   Emoticons

MySpace and photo sharing sites like Flickr and Photobucket—forums have become much more social. Many of the forum platforms now allow its members to include personal photo galleries, personal pages, and real-time member-to-member chat.

Providers

While blogging is somewhat easier than participating in forums, and equally as effective for community building, there are companies that provide software and Web-based solutions for setting up your own forum web site. You can create and manage the forum on your own server, setting it up on a provider's web site.

Create Your Own Forum Software

Ektron.com (*www.ektron.com*): Ektron CMS400.NET is a resource that provides a complete platform with all of the functionality necessary for developers and nontechnical business users alike to create, deploy, and manage your web site. Developers can take advantage of built-in Server Controls to launch a site out of the box, or customize this initiation using CMS400.NET's well-documented API. Businesses benefit from an intuitive user interface that is extremely helpful in managing their site's content and messaging. A comprehensive SEO (search engine optimization) Toolkit ensures that potential visitors are able to find your site. Memberships, personalization, subscriptions, geomapping, and Web alerts keep your site visitors coming back; and social networking and Web 2.0 tools (including wikis, blogging, polls, and forums) grow your online communities.

Forum Web Site

Yuku.com (*www.yuku.com*): Yuku (Part of *KickApps.com*)[4] is a site that allows users to create and participate in profiles, image sharing, blogs, and discussion boards all in one place. Your Yuku account can have up to five different profiles, because although you don't always want to use the same

---

4. The KickApps-hosted, white-label platform puts social media and online video functionality directly into the hands of every web publisher who aspires to be a media mogul and turns every web designer and developer into a social media rock star! With KickApps, it's now easier than ever for web publishers to leverage the power of social and rich media experiences on their web sites to drive audience growth and engagement.

profile, you *do* want only one account. Yuku's purpose is to help people connect and communicate online as easily and safely as possible. You don't need to download anything to use Yuku; all you need is an account, your profile, and your favorite Internet browser.

KickApps.com (*www.kickapps.com*): KickApps is a Web-based platform that makes it easy for you to add a wide array of social features to your web site. Whether you are a one-person shop or a global corporation, the Kickapps.com suite of applications are designed to integrate seamlessly with your web site and your brand.

The ROI of Social Media

Enabling Brand Advocates to Share Positive Brand Experiences with Their Friends on Facebook

Background

Multi-unit retailers are increasingly focused on driving "net promotions" or "intent to recommend" but are often at a loss on how to translate these customer intentions into actual brand recommendations. Empathica found that customers who frequented large retailers, restaurants, and financial institutions were willing to express their satisfaction with these brands online to their friends and family, but were not making recommendations because they lacked an easy and convenient process to do so. It is critical to not only understand the percentage of "net promotion" intenders of a brand, but also to marshall these customer voices into becoming active brand ambassadors.

As such, we recognized the need to create a tool to make it easy for brands to share their recommendations online. A Facebook application called Go-Recommend was developed to address these aligned consumer and business needs.

Strategy

Research has shown that consumers are increasingly turning to online reviews and recommendations when making a purchase decision. The advent of social networking sites such as Facebook allows users to easily share recommendations and reviews with friends, colleagues, and family through their social network. These relationships add greater value to the recommendation as it is coming from a reliable source. Anonymous reviews and recommendations, though abundant, hold less value than those obtained from someone the consumer trusts. The social nature of Facebook makes it an ideal platform for GoRecommend.

If one thousand satisfied customers were to recommend a brand experience using GoRecomend, and the average Facebook user has 130 friends, their personalized recommendations would be shared with 130,000 people.

Implementation

After a customer completes an Empathica retail experience survey, the GoRecommend engine prompts those who indicated a high intent to recommend their experience to share their recommendation with friends on Facebook.

The location-specific recommendation can be posted on the recommender's Facebook profile page, which exposes the personalized recommendation to all of the user's friends through the Facebook newsfeed. The recommendation can also be optionally posted to the brand's Facebook fan page.

These valuable recommendations can also include a coupon or an invitation for the recommender and his or her friends to join a brand's e-mail club or become a fan of the brand's Facebook fan page. These engagement tools easily turn the recommendation into an effective marketing tool that both drives traffic and extends the relationship between the brand and the consumer. By way of recent example, in just 60 days more than 15,000 satisfied customers recommended one large restaurant chain to their friends using GoRecommend. The program further generated over 10,000 e-mail club opt-ins and more than 1,000 Facebook fans for the brand.

Opportunity

GoRecommend is a true turnkey social marketing solution that fosters ongoing brand awareness by encouraging customers who have had a positive experience with the brand to make a recommendation. It is an automatic way the brand can utilize the social graph to generate positive, authentic, timely, and relevant communications about the brand.

It is cost effective and very easy to deploy, using an automated referral process that takes little to no effort from the brand itself.

Conclusion

Still in the early stages of deployment, to date GoRecommend has generated some 50,000 recommendations from satisfied customers that have been shared with over 7.7 million friends on Facebook.

Dr. Gary Edwards, EVP Client Services
Julia Staffen, Director Product Management, GoRecommend
Empathica, Inc.
Web: www.empathica.com
Twitter: @EmpathicaCEM
Facebook: www.facebook.com/EmpathicaCEM

Expert Insight

Stephanie Ichinose, director of communications, Yelp, www.yelp.com

Stephanie Ichinose

. . . I am the director of communications here so I manage a bunch of different functions. Primarily it is media relations, analysis relations, and the like. I work closely with our management team and I have been with the company since April 2006. Prior to that, I was managing a public relations team for Yahoo! that specifically sat right in the local space. . . .

. . . It is a great company, and . . . what started to happen was I, personally, started looking at the competitive landscape. I noticed (this is back in late 2005 to 2006) that user-generated content was gaining traction in a way that it had not before; and so when I came across Yelp and was looking at them, it just seemed like a really interesting opportunity. . . .

. . . The interesting thing about Yelp and its approach to local search was that we recognized that there was this old model of "word-of-mouth" that existed. It is not even a model; it has just existed since the beginning of time, basically. Individuals would share a lot of interesting and valuable information between each other with these person-to-person conversations. And so it was like, "Where can I find a great doctor? Who's the best mechanic in town for my small, little car that needs some work on it?" And the question at that point is how do we capture these conversations and bring them online?

Initially, we set out to solve that problem and were surprised to find that by building a community of individuals within a particular city we were able to really incite and encourage these conversations. On the back-end, users were really passionate about sharing that information. Yelp started out specifically only in San Francisco. And we focused our first year of operations to building up the site, supporting the community that existed in the Bay area, and tried to figure out what worked/what didn't; that sort of thing.

And then in 2006–2007, it was really a focus more on, "Okay, can we replicate this and push it out to other markets, with the same sort of conversation topics, in Chicago, in New York, in Boston?"

And we found, pretty quickly in 2006 that, in fact they do. We found that there was just something universal about people wanting to share all of their great hidden gems, or wanting to rave about specific businesses, the "Mom and Pops" that they want to support. And so there was a really interesting dynamic of community (and local community), that really resonated across the nation. . . .

. . . I think it is interesting that when we watch some of our most active Yelpers, there is this notion that they are contributing right to the bloggers (or this community in San Francisco, or in their particular area, whether it's Dallas, Austin, or Chicago, or wherever they may live); there's this notion of being able to support local businesses, help share that information so that others who are out there that might stumble across the information would find it helpful; and just sort of become a part of the local community of individuals who are passionate about sharing their experiences.

There is a network part of it, which is when you sign up on Yelp, you plug into a community of people who are like-minded, But then the broader effect is that information is then seen by so many more individuals. We have had 14 million unique visitors to the site in the past 30 days. And that number continues to grow and we are really excited about that. We currently have well north of 3.5 million reviews that have been written by Yelpers that contributed to the site.

Therefore, what that tells us is that there is a huge audience of people that are looking for this information and it is great that they are able to utilize this resource. In addition, we are then able to tap into the individual voices of the community, which is even better. . . .

. . . Actually, the cofounders really looked at the Craigslist model and figured out, "Okay, what did they do? What was part of their roll-out, and how did they achieve the success that they've achieved?" Therefore, there are some pages in this playbook; for instance, focusing and looking at individual markets and going deep, which is primarily what we did in 2005. . . .

. . . It has been interesting to watch the . . . part of that which is fueled by our growth in continuing markets. We currently have 21 actively managed communities in the major cities across the United States. But it has been fascinating to watch how each city ignites and how the communities are all very different and they all have their different cultural tones, and so on. But underneath it, all there is the same common thread; as in, "Wow, I am able to finally jump on my soapbox here and share all of my favorites." It is a little bit ego-driven, perhaps, but then the second part of that is about contributing back to the community in a meaningful way that is also heard by others. . . .

. . . I think what has been interesting to watch is that folks have made an analogy to Yelp as, "Oh, you are a social network?" And actually we see ourselves more as a local community site. And that's because when you log in to a social network, you're effectively creating your account and inviting your social network to participate and engage, and finding folks who may already exist on that particular platform.

Whereas in Yelp, it's really more about joining a community of like-minded individuals who (guess what!) happen to live within the parameters of

(*continued*)

(*continued*)

your geography, your city, and you all have a common interest. That is what Yelp is all about; that is, local businesses and services. And so, we are defining what that community discussion is about, and you plug in to that and meet with others. And so there have been questions like, "Do Yelpers meet offline?" and that sort of thing. And they absolutely do.

It's probably because wc all live within the same city; and very close people establish affinities, or interests. In particular are types of businesses, as in, say, Italian food or people who enjoy wines and a particular type of wine. And so often what we are finding is that Yelpers will organize groups and then meet offline and get together. So there is a really interesting social element there. All of these things speak very strongly to the notion of communities and we are designed to support that. . . .

. . . And that's what's illuminating. We've heard time and again that Yelpers are people who visit the site, perhaps more casually, just to find information. They may have lived in a particular city for all their life. Still they're finding new businesses that they never knew existed. In addition, Yelp (and the reviews they are finding on Yelp) is inspiring them to go out and try something that is outside of their comfort zone and perhaps go a little bit further than they would have driven for, say, a pasta dinner. But they are exploring and they are discovering new businesses because they have a bit of a preview into that. The Yelp community is really saying, "Wow, this place is absolutely worth the 30-minute drive to (the next town over). You should check it out, it would be worth your while."

So we are finding that Yelpers write back in and say, "Wow, it's been extremely powerful in helping me find great businesses, and spending my money and dollars with locally owned operations is something I enjoy doing, and I now have the confidence to be able to extend myself beyond what I normally would, to the businesses I would normally support, and try new things."

So that's been an interesting phenomenon. . . .

. . . I mean, you hit on this notion that being able to identify what, in broad strokes, the Yelp community thinks about a business is helpful. What I think you'll find over time, though, is that being able to then dive down in to the individual profiles of people who are talking about a business will even further refine those pick/sees.

Yelp is built entirely on this notion of community, and then individuals, as well, right? So my profile page has some general information about me, the light-hearted stuff (favorite movies, books, where I grew up, my interests in general). And so from there you immediately get a quick snapshot of what kind of person Stephanie is. And then you are able to look at all of my reviews, which serve in a way as lifestyle blogs. Like, as I go out to eat and that for the five or six restaurants that I may try this week, I'll write reviews of those and you get a sense of that. Everybody has different preferences and tastes, and so if you are following my blog and you decided at some point, "Hey, you know I have a lot in common with this type of person, and she's rating and reviewing things similar in nature to what I would." I would want to select what should be one of my favorites, and I could almost follow that individual over time.

So now, it's you building a small set of preferences on Yelp. And that way when you are doing searches, when you're logged in, you'll be able to refine enough to tell that these same voices are pointing you to the direction of the business that they've tried.

We believe that's important because understanding what a profile or a person is all about really helps instill an additional layer of trust and value in the information they are providing. . . .

. . . As for myself, for when I use the site in two different manners just for the purposes of keeping in touch, but I will use my "logged-in" profile when I am doing searches personally. When I want to find something like a great seamstress, or whatever; and I have all of my favorites set so that the reviews of folks that I have been following for a while will pop up if these are businesses that they have rated and reviewed.

So it definitely helps out quite a bit. . . .

. . . And the interesting thing is that even when we take a look at Yelp overall, we look at all of the reviews and we look at our category breakdowns. What we are finding is that less than 34 percent of businesses reviewed on Yelp are restaurants. And 34 percent is a number that is a lot smaller than a lot of people would have guessed. . . .

. . . It is followed by the shopping category, which comprised about 23 percent of the reviewed businesses. Then there is beauty and fitness, which drops off at around 8 percent, entertainment at 7 percent, and local services at around 7 percent.

So the distribution of this type of review is really various and spans a lot of different categories. Where most people think we just judge restaurants, we actually have a lot more to offer. . . .

. . . So we find that Yelpers are truly passionate about showing everything that they consume locally, and so therein follows all of the other local services, spas, salons, manicures, and pedicures . . . that sort of thing. Those are the other categories that round out nicely. . . .

. . . And that's our goal, really. It is all about connecting people with great local businesses. . . .

To listen to or read the entire Executive Conversation with Stephanie Ichinose, go to www.theSocialMediaBible.com.

Commandments

1. **Thou shalt search and participate.**

   Pick a topic of your liking and search for a forum that has a group with an ongoing discussion on that topic. Begin as a guest, if it makes you more comfortable, and then register and participate for a while to see what you can learn from it. Think about the trusted network and loyalty that this forum is providing for you, and how you might be able to build that same kind of trust around your company or brand.

2. **Thou shalt set up your own forum.**

   Once you've participated in a few forums and experienced what it is like to build these kinds of strong connections, you might want to next consider building this type of community around your company, product, or service. Give it a try. Using Yuku is a free and easy way to see if creating a forum is right for you.

Conclusion

While the forum is one of the oldest technologies on the Web, it still is a great way to easily create a trusted community around your company, product, brand, service, or subject matter. Try it! Set up your own forum, and invite a few friends, employees, customers, and prospects to engage in an ongoing conversation about your interests and what you do. It's free, and—as with many other social media tools—the ROI is unimaginable.

To hear all of the Expert Interviews, go to www.theSocialMediaBible .com.

Downloads

For your free downloads associated with *The Social Media Bible,* go to www .theSocialMediaBible.com, and enter your ISBN number located on the back of the book above the bar code. Be sure to enter the dashes.

Credits

The ROI of Social Media provided by:

Dr. Gary Edwards, EVP Client Services

Julia Staffen, director product management, GoRecommend Empathica, Inc., www .empathica.com

Expert Insight was provided by:

Stephanie Ichinose, director of communications, Yelp, www.yelp.com

Technical edits were provided by:

Lynne Johnson, www.lynnedjohnson.com
Stephanie Ichinose, director of communications, Yelp, www.yelp.com

CHAPTER 7

The Ubiquitous Blog

What's in It for You?

Scientists, psychiatrists, psychologists, and counselors have known for a long time of the therapeutic benefits that accompany writing about personal experiences in a diary or journal. Blogs provide a convenient tool for writing about your individual thoughts and activities. Research shows that journaling improves your memory, sleep—and now, maybe even your bottom line.

In the twentieth century, professional reporters and publishers decided what the news was and determined how the public saw it. Though we might still have some professionals making these decisions in the twenty-first century, we now have personal reporters and publishers—more than 50 million of them—who bring our news to us on a daily basis.

Although communication is—and always has been—a two-way process, the methods of communication to prospects and customers has changed dramatically over recent years. The use of social media digital tools have allowed for less reporting and more conversation. The web log, or blog, is the easiest and most effective way to provide a conduit for this type of communication. Blogs create communication, and communication builds trust—and blogs are completely free to build and access. In fact, in the year 2006, bloggers and other contributors to user-generated content were the reason that *Time* magazine named their "2006 Person of the Year" . . . "You."

Back to the Beginning

The term *blog* derives from *web log*, which is simply another word for an online journal. American blogger and author Jorn Barger was the first to coin the phase in December 1997, which prompted Peter Merholz to take the word *WeBLOG* and separate it into *We Blog* in a sidebar of his web page—www .Peterme.com—in May 1999. Entrepreneur Evan Williams first used the word *blog* as both a verb and a noun—in reference to posting to one's

FIGURE 7.1   Lon Safko Official CNN Reporter in Second Life

web log—and thus officially created the term *blogger*. Who better to do this than Williams—the developer for Pyra Labs' Blogger.com, the largest blogging platform in the world?

From 1983 through 1990—before HTTP was in common use—a service called Usenet was the primary medium for communicating over the World Wide Web. Usenet featured a moderated newsgroup, which was either group- or individually controlled. In fact, these newsgroups were no more than simple forums (see Chapter 6, The Internet Forum). Around this same time, Brian E. Redman—generally known as the first individual blogger—began posting summaries of other interesting information he found on the Internet, and thereby created his own blog called mod.ber (named for his initials, B.E.R.).

Back in the mid-1990s—before the personal blog became

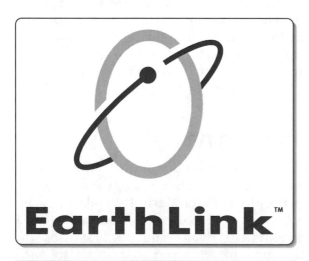

FIGURE 7.2   EarthLink

as popular as it is today—there were online communities such as GEnie, BiX, EarthLink, Prodigy, and CompuServe, all of which were the earliest ISPs (Internet Service Providers) and also provided bulletin board systems (BBS) and forums. Later, people would use this type of Internet

FIGURE 7.3 Prodigy

software to create online diaries or journals to document daily activities of their personal lives. They called themselves *diarists, journalers,* and *journalists.* In 1994, a student at Swarthmore College named Justin Hall became recognized as one of the first bloggers. Science fiction writer Jerry Pournelle and software engineer Dave Winer are credited with establishing one of the oldest and longest-running weblogs: "Scripting News" (scripting.com).

In 1994, an online diary called Wearable Wireless Webcam—which included text, photos, and video, broadcasting live using a wearable computer and EyeTap—was also credited with being one of the earliest blogs (see Chapter 15, Live from Anywhere—It's Livecasting). While this activity is referred to specifically as *livecasting* today, it was considered to be a form of the earliest semiautomated blogging of someone's personal life in the form of a video journal. This type of livecasting is also referred to as *sousveillance,* a term that describes the recording of an activity from the perspective of a participant experiencing that very event.

Other online journals began to pop up on the Internet in the mid-1990s. A computer programmer named John Carmack had his own widely read journal during this time on his "id Software" company web site. Video game developers Steve Gibson of Cary's video game Quakeholio (Shacknews), and Stephen Heaslip of Blue's News had been online since 1995. On February 8, 1997, Gibson was hired to blog full time for Ritual Entertainment—a turn of events that made him one of the—if not *the*—first paid bloggers.

Biologist and ecologist Dr. Glen Barry started his political blog back in January 1993, which became the oldest and largest political blog in history. Originally called Gaia's Forest Conservation Archives—and now operating under the name Forest Protection Blog (forests.org/blog)—Barry began his blog as both an outlet for his passion to protect the forests and as his PhD project. Forests.org has evolved into one of the largest environmental web site portals in the world.

The earliest blogs were simply continuous updates of a standard HTML web site—a process that was difficult, and which required a certain level of technical knowledge to maintain the HTML code. However, more recent

FIGURE 7.4   TSMB Dashboard

developments in browser-based blog platforms—enabling easy posting of articles in reverse chronological order and one-click editing features such as permalinks, blogrolls, and TrackBacks—made linking to other blogs and web pages easier (Figure 7.4). The ability to blog finally became accessible to the average nontechnical computer user.

Blogs can be used on a hosted service—such as Blogger.com or GoingOn.com—or can be hosted on your own server with software such as WordPress, Blogger, MovableType, or LiveJournal. (See Chapter 5, The World of Web Pages, for more information about WordPress. To hear the Executive Conversation interview with founder and developer of WordPress Matt Mullenweg, go to www.theSocialMediaBible.com.)

Nearly all web sites in the mid-1990s—personal and corporate—had a What's New or News section on them, which was usually sorted by date. This was essentially the earliest form of news-based blog. One such web page—the popular Drudge Report—was created by Matt Drudge and began simply enough: through Drudge's e-mails to his friends. In 1998, the Institute for

Public Accuracy posted one-paragraph news releases a few times per week. The use of blogs grew slowly until 1999, and expanded especially rapidly during 2006–2008. When this chapter was written, the number of blogs was approaching 200 million worldwide.

October 1998 brought the launch of Open Diary—a service that invented and introduced the reader comment, whereby readers could provide their own feedback to bloggers' posts. In August 1999, reporter Jonathan Dube of the *Charlotte Observer* published his own blog chronicling Hurricane Bonnie, which marked the creation of the first known use of a blog on a news site.

In March 1999, well-known blogger, programmer, and software author Brad Fitzpatrick began LiveJournal, a virtual community where users could go to blog or journal. In July of that same year, blogger Andrew Smales created Pitas.com—a version of the blog that was easier to maintain than a news page on a conventional web site. In August 1999, Evan Williams and Meg Hourihan of Pyra Labs launched blog publishing system Blogger.com, which was later purchased by Google in February 2003. In September 1999, a site called Diaryland—which focused more on the personal diary community— was started.

But people weren't just blogging about their personal lives and daily activities. In 2001, several popular political blogs emerged in the United States. British political commentator and speaker Andrew Sullivan created AndrewSullivan.com; attorney and journalist Ron Gunzburger launched his Politics1.com; political management essayist and author Taegan Goddard began Political Wire; University of Tennessee law professor and *Popular Mechanics* editor Glenn Reynold founded Instapundit; former jazz guitarist and software developer Charles Johnson established Little Green Footballs; and Democratic political strategist Jerome Armstrong started MyDD. Blogging was beginning to go mainstream, and was becoming so popular that there were how-to guides and established schools of journalism that began studying and comparing blogging to more conventional types of journalism.

In 2002, several comments made by U.S. Senate Majority Leader Trent Lott at a party honoring U.S. Senator Strom Thurmond proved to be appealing fodder for bloggers. Lott praised Thurmond by implying that the United States would have been better off had the longest-serving senator been elected president. Lott's critics interpreted these comments as approval of Thurmond's 1948 presidential campaign and his stand on racial segregation. This view was reinforced by documents and recorded interviews dug up by bloggers—such as Josh Marshall's Talking Points (www.talkingpointsmemo .com). The most interesting part about the event, however, is that even though Lott's comments were made at a public event attended by the media, no major media organizations reported on his controversial comments until *after* blogs broke the story. In essence, blogging helped to create a political crisis that forced Lott to step down as majority leader. The impact of this story gave greater credibility to blogs as a medium of news dissemination.

Blogging is often so timely that the mere term *blogging* has also come to mean *transcribed* or *editorialized*, as might occur during speeches or televised events. As an example, one could say, "I am blogging my reactions to speeches as they occur on television"—known as *liveblogging*. Many presentations are *tweeted* live using Twitter microblogging (see Chapter 14, Thumbs Up for Microblogging for more information on Twitter). These snippets of information can be tweeted to a presenter's followers or to the user's blog—using the freshest, most current information available.

In fact, during a recent presentation at a PodCamp weekend, a small giggle ran through the audience in the middle of a presentation about social media. The speaker stopped and asked what the chatter was about, and someone admitted that another audience member tweeted that there was a spelling error in the presentation. The speaker stopped the presentation, corrected the error, and thanked the blogging audience. How fresh is *this?*

The year 2004 saw blogs becoming increasingly widespread. News services, political consultants, and their candidates used blogs as outreach and opinion polls for their campaigns, and just to bond with their constituents. In the summer of 2004, blogs became a standard part of the publicity arsenal for the Democratic and Republican parties' conventions. Chris Matthews's MSNBC program *Hardball* and other mainstream television programs created their own blogs. And in that same year, *Merriam-Webster's Dictionary* declared *blog* as the word of the year.

Blogs were an especially important news source after the December 2004 tsunami. Sites such as Medecins Sans Frontieres used SMS text messaging to report from affected areas in Sri Lanka and southern India (for more on SMS, see Chapter 21, The Formidable Fourth Screen (Mobile)). And in August 2005, during Hurricane Katrina and its aftermath, a few bloggers located in New Orleans managed to maintain power and Internet connections, and blogged about the damage. Several blogs—including the Interdictor and Gulfsails—were able to disseminate information that the mainstream media did not cover.

In January 2005, *Fortune* magazine listed eight bloggers whom business-people "could not ignore": Peter Rojas (www.crunchbase.com/person/peter-rojas), Xeni Jardin (www.boingboing.net), Mena and Ben Trott (www.sixapart.com), Jonathan Schwartz (www.blogs.sun.com/jonathan), Jason Goldman (www.goldtoe.net), Robert Scoble (www.scobleizer.com), and Jason Calacanis (www.calacanis.com). Then, in September 2005, the British newspaper the *Guardian* launched a redesign that included a daily digest of blogs on page two. BBC News followed suit in June 2006 by instituting a blog for its editors.

In 2007, media mogul Tim O'Reilly proposed a Blogger's Code of Conduct to enforce civility on blogs by being calm and moderating comments. The code was proposed as a result of threats made to blogger Kathy Sierra. Tim O'Reilly stated, "I do think we need some code of conduct around what is acceptable behavior. I would hope that it doesn't come through any kind of regulation [but that] it would come through self-regulation" (www.radar.oreilly.com/archives/2007/04/draft-bloggers-1.html).

All of these clickable links can be accessed through www.theSocial MediaBible.com.

What You Need to Know

A *blog*—or *web log*—is a web site that is maintained by an individual with regular entries or posts that include commentary, thoughts, and ideas, and may contain photos, graphics, audio, or video. Posts are most often displayed in reverse chronological order. Most blogs provide news and content on a specific subject, while others operate as personal journals. Blogs usually have text, images, video, and links to other blogs and web sites that relate to the blog's subject matter. One of the most important features of a blog is the reader's ability to interact with the author through comments. While most blogs are made up of text, many bloggers prefer to add art (creating an artblog), photographs (a photoblog), sketches (for a sketchblog), music (or musicblog), audio (creating an audioblog—see Chapter 10, Talking about the Podcast (Audio Create)), or a podcast blog. And just like podcasting can mean either audio or video, blogging refers to anyone who writes an opinion about something.

A blog can be personal- or business-related. Business blogs can be used for internal communication to employees, or designed to be viewed by the public. Blogs used for sales, marketing, branding, PR, and communicating with customers and prospects are often referred to as *corporate blogs*.

Blogs can fall into a number of different categories. One kind provides a feature called a Question Blog—called *Qlogs*—where readers can submit a query through a comment, submission form, or e-mail. Blog writers and administrators are then responsible for answering these questions. A blog site that posts primarily video is called a *Vlog* (video blog web site); then there are blogs that only post links to other blogs, called *linklogs*. Blogs that post shorter posts and a lot of mixed rich media are referred to as *tumblogs*; and blogs about legal issues and information are called *blawgs*. And of course, the not-so-legitimate spamming blog is called a *Splog*. The entirety of all the blogs on the Internet is referred to as the *blogosphere*, while a collection of blogs located in the same geographical area is called a *bloghood*.

While most blogs are created and maintained just for fun, many are supported by advertising. Sites utilize resources such as automatic content-specific banners and other types of ad placements, like Google's AdSense. Most of the larger, more popular blogs that enjoy high monthly traffic are easily earning six figures in advertising income.

All of these different blogs spread out over the entire globe had to create the opportunity for blog-specific search engines. Besides the standard Google and Yahoo! search engines, other kinds each have a blog-specific option as well. There are online communities that help readers find the right blog for a particular topic or area of interest, such as BlogCatalog and MyBlogLog. In addition, there are blog-only search engines like Bloglines, BlogScope, and Technorati, which is the most popular blog search site at the time of this writing. Technorati (www.Technorati.com) actually provides lists of the most popular searches and tags used in posts (see Chapter 5, The World of Web Pages, for more information about tags).

A blog's popularity can be greatly enhanced by a high rating on Technorati, a site that was founded to help bloggers succeed by collecting, highlighting, and distributing information about the online global conversation. Technorati determines and assigns a ranking to each blog based on the number of incoming links (LinkLove), and Alexa user hits. As the leading blog search engine and most comprehensive source of information on the blogosphere, Technorati indexes more than 1.5 million new blog posts in real time and introduces millions of readers to blog and social media content. In August 2006, Technorati discovered that the most popular blog in the world was that of Chinese actress Xu Jinglei with a reported 50 million page views. They also cited the self-proclaimed "directory of wonderful things" blog Boing Boing, as the most-read group-written blog (www.boingboing.net).

Maintaining a blog requires work and a moderate amount of dedication and effort. (While working on writing *The Social Media Bible*, the author updated his blog only half a dozen times and did not tweet as frequently. One of his loyal readers scolded him.)

The Gartner Research Group expects that the novelty value of the blog will wear off eventually, since so many people who are interested in the phenomenon create a blog just to see what it's like. Gartner further expects that new bloggers will outnumber those bloggers who abandon their blogs out of boredom, and estimates that more than 200 million former bloggers have already ceased posting to their blogs, creating a huge rise in the amount of *dotsam and netsam* (a play on the terms *flotsam and jetsam*), or unwanted objects on the Web.

There are currently more than 300 mainstream journalists who write their own blogs, according to CyberJournalist.net's J-blog list. Many conventional bloggers have now moved over to more conventional media, including liberal media scholar Duncan Black (known by his pseudonym, Atrios; www.eschatonblog.com), Instapundit's aforementioned blogger Glenn Reynolds (www.pajamasmedia.com/instapundit), political analyst and current events reporter Markos Moulitsas Zúniga of the Daily Kos (www.dailykos.com), American writer and futurist Alex Steffen of Worldchanging (www.worldchanging.com), and Time.com editor and author Ana Marie Cox of Wonkette (www.wonkette.com), who have all appeared on radio and television.

Many bloggers have actually published books based on their original blog posts; these types of blog-based books are called *blooks*. Authors include Salam Pax, *The Clandestine Diary of an Ordinary Iraqi* from The Baghdad Blog; Ellen Simonetti, *Diary of a Dysfunctional Flight Attendant: The Queen of Sky Blog*; Jessica Cutler, *The Washingtonienne: A Novel* (washingtoniennearchive.blogspot.com); Scott Ott's *ScrappleFace* (www.scrappleface.com). In 2005, the Lulu Blooker Prize was created for the best blog-based book. So far, the only winner who has made it to the *New York Times* bestseller list with a book is Tucker Max, who wrote *I Hope They Serve Beer in Hell*, or, as Max puts it, "My name is Tucker Max, and I am an asshole." It's difficult to believe that his book was on the *New York Times* bestseller list for more than two weeks.

FIGURE 7.5 Blooker Award

Another example of a blogger, Julie Powell, becoming a book author is The Julie/Julia Project, which became the movie *Julie & Julia* in 2009. This American comedy/drama film was written and directed by Nora Ephron and starred Meryl Streep as Julia Child, Amy Adams as Julie Powell and Stanley Tucci as Paul Child, Julia Child's husband. This film won Meryl Streep an Academy Award nomination for Best Actress.

This film is based on the life of chef Julia Child and the life of Julie Powell, who cooks all 524 recipes from Child's cookbook over a one year period, while Powell describes her experiences on her 2004 blog (en.wikipedia.org/wiki/Julie%26Julia).

Providers

As with the other chapters' Providers section, there are far too many and different types of companies to list here, but a few to get started with are as follows:

- Search for blogs on Google, Yahoo!, BlogSearch, and Technorati.com.
- Start your own blog on WordPress.com, Blogger.com, and GoingOn .com.

The ROI of Social Media

Vistaprint Tweeting for Awareness, Reputation Management, and Revenue

Background

Toward the end of the 2008 calendar year, the Vistaprint public relations team began to notice buzz building around the company's brand in various social networks. While there was an overall positive tone, the team noticed that postings ran a gamut of emotions from truly positive to extremely negative and everything in between. Because social media was an apparently expanding marketing medium, the decision was made to research where it could have an impact, where to engage, and how.

Strategy

Knowing that the conversation about Vistaprint was happening with or without the company's involvement, the team decided that all mentions, positive or negative, warranted a response.

While the initial goal of interacting on Twitter was to increase the interaction level with customers and potential customers, the team also anticipated the impact the medium could have in terms of customer service and revenue generation. The approach toward revenue generation was to offer a soft sell rather than an aggressive offer (example: @jeffespo thanks for the plug @jaykeith; if you would like to give us a try, please visit www.vistaprint .com/twitter). The initial customer service queries would be fielded by the PR team to get a baseline and establish if there was a need for true customer service department involvement.

Implementation

Prior to entering the space, the Vistaprint team spent three months monitoring where the conversations were happening. By looking at the commentary coming from all neighborhoods of Twitterville, the team established a framework for responses. In certain situations, the team will use a standard message but the majority of the time tweets are unscripted. These responses bring personality to the brand and avoid the feeling that the account is run by an automated tool, or bot.

The company began interacting on Twitter from the @Vistaprint account. This was done exclusively by the PR team. After 12 months, the team noticed an increase in customer service issues and created a second account for the company. The new handle, @VistaprintHelp, is now manned by Vistaprint's customer service team and handles all customer service related questions.

The team selected Co-Tweet as a conversation monitoring tool. The Web-based application allows multiple users to log in to the company's accounts, assign workflow and see the lifetime conversation thread with users.

Opportunity

As an e-retailer, Vistaprint is very conscious of the ever-changing landscape of the Internet. Without a brick and mortar location, the company is constantly looking for new avenues to reach and expand its customer base. With the continual growth of Twitter and its integration with mainstream society, Vistaprint's interaction will increase awareness of the brand and attract new customers.

Conclusion

With just the investment of time, the PR team's strategy has hosted over 12,300 conversations through the company's main accounts (@vistaprint, @vista printhelp). During the 2009 fiscal year, the company generated over $25,000 in orders from the targeted soft-sell URL.

Jeff Esposito
www.vistaprint.com

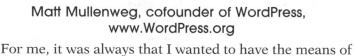

Expert Insight

Matt Mullenweg, cofounder of WordPress, www.WordPress.org

Matt Mullenweg

For me, it was always that I wanted to have the means of personal expression. I always enjoyed writing and, so, publishing. It was pretty exciting. And I would say that it was really the *interaction* from the readers. So, although blogging is great, I blog for the comments. Because I know if I say something that's wrong or anything like that, the readers will let me know. . . .

It [provides] access to people all over the world that you would never meet otherwise, so what's cool is

(*continued*)

(*continued*)

that sense; because my blog's very personal. It's people who are interested in the same things that I am. Maybe it's jazz or economics or photography or WordPress. So the answer to why I started blogging is I find it very, very rewarding. . . .

We probably do super-well on the search engines, and actually [they don't] try too many tricks or anything specific to target us at WordPress; [they] just create a really great user experience. Have the content well organized, have a permanent place for blogposts (which are often called a *permalink*). Just use proper HTML headings, tags, or the titles to the heading tags for the titles, for the posts. Some of these things get a little bit geeky, but if you create semantic, well-structured, frequently updated content, I think search engines . . . are just trying to serve their use by being one of the better resources on the Web. . . .

The development is, you know, 95 percent user-defined; so from release to release we have a time schedule that we plan on a year in advance. But in terms of features for release, it's really defined by what our users are asking for. So, for example, in the last release we had, sort of, a *wiki*-like tracking feature; so every version of every post is saved forever. So if you make a mistake or go off-edit approach, you can go and see exactly what changed. Things like that. . . . Some of our users don't even know it's there. It's a really powerful tool that your competitors haven't thought about yet. So we were able to get it early because we listened very closely to our community. . . .

I think what you really have to do if you're a leader of an open-source process is something that inspires people, something that people can coalesce around and get them excited to work on, even though they are not getting paid. On the carrot versus stick, all you really have is the carrot! So, (laughter) you really have to make it fun and engaging, and I think people will come, especially since they will control it in such an amazing way that has impact.

To listen to or read the entire Executive Conversation with Matt Mullenweg, go to www .theSocialMediaBible.com.

Commandments

While doing research for this chapter, the original intent was to take some items from David Risley's 50 Rapid Fire Tips for Power Blogging, paraphrase them, and turn them into "Commandments"—but David's list had just too much good information to choose from. So here are David Risley's 50 tips in their entirety. (*Thank you, David!*)

50 Rapid Fire Tips for Power Blogging

I have been blogging for a living for many years now. I've learned a lot and, today, I wanted to throw out a bunch of quick tips in rapid succession. The goals here are: (1) get lots of traffic to your blog, and (2) earn money with it. Okay, here we go (in no particular order):

1. *Use WordPress.* No other platform is as flexible with all the plug-ins, in my opinion.

2. *Post often.* I usually default to one post per day, when I'm asked. I try to do at least one per day on this blog, except for weekends.

3. *Use catchy blog post titles.* Put yourself in the shoes of a person who is casually surfing the Internet, seeing your post along with hundreds of others. Will your blog headline stand out? Copyblogger is an awesome source for information on writing.

4. *Ask open-ended questions.* One of the best ways to invite commentary on your posts is to ask for it. Ask your readers questions and tell them to answer in the form of a comment.

5. *Comment on other blogs—often.* I actually maintain a separate folder in Google Reader for relevant blogs I want to follow more closely than others. And, on those blogs, I comment regularly whenever I have something to say.

6. *Use Twitter.* You've got to be out there, being social. FriendFeed, too.

7. *Use Twitterfeed to pipe your latest posts into Twitter.* But, don't *only* use Twitterfeed. You've got to be a real person on Twitter, first and foremost. Twitter should not replace RSS.

8. *Make your RSS feed obvious*, above the fold, and preferably use the orange RSS icon.

9. *Provide an RSS-to-E-mail option* so people can subscribe to your latest posts without being forced to use an RSS reader. Many people still don't use RSS. FeedBurner provides a free RSS-to-E-mail service.

10. *Use images in your posts.* Images communicate on aesthetic wavelengths words cannot.

11. *Use header tags* to separate sections in your blog posts, where applicable: H1, H2, and H3 tags. And use good search engine keywords wherever possible in those headers.

12. *Structure your blog posts for easy scanning.* Use header tags, lists, and so on. Avoid long sentences and long paragraphs.

13. *Avoid MySpace-style blog designs.* What I mean by this is super *busy* designs with too much on screen, animated graphics, and so on. These things make your blog truly suck and makes your content too hard to pay attention to.

14. *If possible, use a custom WordPress theme.* It is getting to the point where people can recognize cookie-cutter themes. It is okay to use one, but at least modify it so that you have a unique header design.

15. *Start your blog's mailing list as early as possible.* The sooner you start, the longer you have to grow your list and, trust me, that list can be used to make money later. Jeremy Shoemoney made this mistake. John Reese used to hound him about building a list. When he finally got around to it, he realized how important it was.

16. *Research and choose your mailing list option correctly the first time.* I recommend Aweber. What you choose is up to you; however, moving a mailing list later can be a huge pain. I know from experience.

17. *When choosing a topic* to focus your blog on, two things should be considered: Your interest in the topic, and how marketable your topic is.

18. *Learn to sell.* The way to a full-time income by blogging is to learn how to *market* and sell things using your blog. Yaro Starak does a good job of selling via his blog, for example.

19. *Don't discount Facebook.* It is a powerful networking tool and you should take the time to build your network, just as you might on Twitter.

20. *Create a Facebook page.* On Facebook, create a page for your blog or yourself and invite your readers and Facebook friends to become fans. This page can be your blog's outpost on Facebook. Be sure to import your blog posts as notes.

21. *Don't be a me-too blogger.* You don't want to become a copycat news blog, where you type news-style posts about what is happening in a saturated market. In technology, this is common. Offer something unique that cannot be found everywhere else in your market.

22. *Learn to think about your blog as a business.* The blog is a promotional and delivery mechanism to your ultimate product or service.

23. *When writing your About Page, pay attention to what you write.* Don't just rattle off some dumb, cookie-cutter facts. Your About Page should tell a story of who you are and why your blog is worth reading.

24. *Do lots of videos.* Use TubeMogul to publish them in as many places as you can. And make sure your blog URL is not only in the video, but also in the text description that accompanies the video.

25. *When making videos, be* real *and be personable.* Your videos are an important component to your blog's brand. Don't waste the opportunity.

26. *Link to other, related blog posts regularly in your own posts.* Not only your *own* posts, but also the posts of others.

27. *Remember, blogging is a* social *business.* Be accessible to your readers and proactively get out there and talk with other people in your niche.

28. *If you can afford it, travel to blogging conferences.* Not only can you learn a lot, but also socializing with successful people often breeds so much motivation and success in yourself that it is simply beyond words.

29. *Write an e-book, create some videos*—whatever—but the idea is to create something which is of value to your readers on your subject, and have it available to *sell* to them on your blog.

30. *Get involved as an affiliate* and start linking to products relevant to your posts using your affiliate links. You are providing relevant links to your readers (valuable) while potentially making some money.

31. *Don't post low FeedBurner counts.* Do not show your RSS subscriber count unless you have a high enough number (at least a few hundred). A low number acts as social proof that your blog has no readers, and that's not good.

32. *Install Popularity Contest* or some similar plug-in which ranks your posts based on popularity. Whether you display this information in public on your blog or not, knowing which of your posts are most popular tells you that that particular subject material works and you should probably do more of it.

33. *Put relevant keywords into your blog's title.* Use All-In-One SEO to have more control over the titles across your blog.

34. *Use a photo gallery.* People dig photos, so a photo gallery can be a great component to your blog. If you use Flickr, check out the Flickr Photo Album plug-in for WordPress.

35. *Create an RSS widget* for your blog on WidgetBox and make it available for your readers to embed on their own blogs if they so choose.

36. *Spend some time creating some killer posts for your blog,* then link to them somewhere so that new arrivals can quickly see your best work. It is your best stuff, which is going to sell them into becoming a subscriber.

37. *Make sharing easy.* Put options on your blog for your readers to share your posts across social media. ShareThis is a great option for this.

38. *Share and share alike.* If you submit your own posts to sites like Digg or StumbleUpon, be sure to also submit other posts. I might even

recommend a 10-to-1 ratio of other people's posts to your own posts. You do not want to develop a reputation on these sites as somebody who only submits to their own content.

39. *When you write a post for your blog, aim to be helpful.* You want your visitors to come away with a solution to the problem they arrived with. Chris Brogan does so well because his posts are truly helpful.

40. *Read other blogs often.* When starving for ideas to write about, go to your RSS reader and read related blogs. Often, your own post can be a response to a post on another blog. In fact, this is usually a good idea.

41. *Train your readers to do what you want, if needed.* If you're in a market where the people will not know how to use social media, RSS, and some of these other things that help promote your blog, *train them.* Write posts or do videos which show your visitors how to Digg a post, use StumbleUpon, how to use RSS, and so on. Perhaps you can educate them and they'll become part of your promotion army for your own blog.

42. *When starting a blog, decide on its mission.* Your posts should, for the most part, center around a specific theme if you want your blog to really take off. If you run a personal diary kind of blog, where you write about anything that comes to mind, your blog traffic will always be limited because your blog will never attract any particular segment of people. Stay on topic. If you have no specific topic, that's fine, but realize your blog is going to be more a hobby than a business at that point.

43. *Don't overload your blog with JavaScript widgets.* These things slow down the load speed of your site. In fact, just recently I had to get rid of the MyBlogLog widget on [my] blog because it was having some effects on page loading time.

44. *Use Analytics.* I personally use Google Analytics as well as the Word Press.com Stats plug-in on [my] blog.

45. *Use Windows Live Writer.* It is the best blogging client program out there. Even though it is a Microsoft product and a Windows-only product, it is also better than any Mac blogging client I have tried. And it's free.

46. *Be yourself.* I believe it is a good thing to show personality on your blog. Don't be a fake. People can see right through it. Chris Pirillo draws people to his blog and Ustream feed almost solely on personality alone.

47. *Don't write like you're writing for Britannica.* You want your spelling and grammar to be correct, but be colloquial. Talk to people like you would normally talk to people, not as if you're writing a PhD dissertation.

48. *Link to your social profiles on your blog.* Link your various social media profiles right on your blog so that your readers can connect with you outside the confines of your blog.

49. *Go where your readers are.* Every market is different. When I blog about blogging, I know most of my readers are pretty adept online and probably hang out in the social media space frequently. If your readers are young, they might be on MySpace. If they're Linux nerds, they may be in the Ubuntu forums. Regardless, you need to maintain a consistent presence in the spaces your readers congregate. Be an authority and be helpful, and traffic will be drawn over to your blog.

50. *[Spend] equal time reading and writing.* You should probably spend just as much time reading and learning as you do writing for your blog. This is how you expand your knowledge, become a better blogger, and get new ideas for your own site. Blogging isn't all about you. Remember that.

(Original list appears at www.davidrisley.com/2008/11/28/50-rapid-fire-tips-for-power-blogging). Go to www.theSocialMediaBible.com for a clickable link.

Conclusion

Blogging is by far the easiest and most effective way to communicate with your customers and prospects. Starting your own blog is as simple as going to WordPress, creating an account, selecting the New Post button, typing your thoughts, and hitting Publish. That's really all there is to it. Please give blogging a try. It really only takes 15 to 20 minutes once a week, and is as easy as typing a half page in a standard word processor. By blogging, you create links by which your prospects can find you, you generate "Google Juice,"[1] you position yourself as an industry leader by providing the latest information in your field, you allow for a two-way conversation, and you build trust.

Once you have created a few posts, use all of your other forms of communication to promote your new source of information to your customers and prospects. Soon, the numbers will begin to grow, your LinkLove will increase—and the industry will be waiting to hear your next insights.

To hear all of the Expert Interviews, go to www.theSocialMediaBible.com.

---

1. Google Juice is a term used to describe the results that follow when you search for your name, your company's name, and your product or service's name in Google or other search engines. The more listings and the more pages that a search engine returns to the searcher, the more Google Juice you have. The goal of this book is to squeeze as much Google Juice as possible out of your social media marketing and communications.

Readings and Resources

Banks, Michael A. *Blogging Heroes: Interviews with 30 of the World's Top Bloggers*. (Hoboken, NJ: John Wiley & Sons, Inc.)

Bausch, Paul, Matthew Haughey, and Meg Hourihan. *We Blog: Publishing Online with Weblogs*. (Hoboken, NJ: John Wiley & Sons, Inc.)

Dean, Jodi. *Blog Theory: Feedback and Capture in the Circuits of Drive*. (Hoboken, NJ: John Wiley & Sons, Inc.)

Gardner, Susannah. *Buzz Marketing with Blogs For Dummies*. (Hoboken, NJ: John Wiley & Sons, Inc.)

Gardner, Susannah, and Shane Birley. *Blogging For Dummies*. (Hoboken, NJ: John Wiley & Sons, Inc.)

Gardner, Susannah, and Shane Birley. *Blogging For Dummies*, 2nd ed. (Hoboken, NJ: John Wiley & Sons, Inc.)

Gardner, Susannah, and Shane Birley. *Blogging For Dummies*, 3rd ed. (Hoboken, NJ: John Wiley & Sons, Inc.)

Getgood, Susan. *Professional Blogging For Dummies*. (Hoboken, NJ: John Wiley & Sons, Inc.)

Gunelius, Susan. *Blogging All-in-One For Dummies*. (Hoboken, NJ: John Wiley & Sons, Inc.)

Gunelius, Susan. *Google Blogger For Dummies*. (Hoboken, NJ: John Wiley & Sons, Inc.)

Harvey, Greg. *SharePoint 2007 Collaboration For Dummies*. (Hoboken, NJ: John Wiley & Sons, Inc.)

Hill, Brad. *Blogging For Dummies*. (Hoboken, NJ: John Wiley & Sons, Inc.)

Karr, Douglas, and Chantelle Flannery. *Corporate Blogging For Dummies*. (Hoboken, NJ: John Wiley & Sons, Inc.)

Kinkoph, Sherry Willard. *Teach Yourself VISUALLY Microsoft Office 2007*. (Hoboken, NJ: John Wiley & Sons, Inc.)

Reeder, Joelle, and Katherine Scoleri. *The IT Girl's Guide to Blogging with Moxie*. (Hoboken, NJ: John Wiley & Sons, Inc.)

Rettberg, Jill Walker. *Blogging*. (Hoboken, NJ: John Wiley & Sons, Inc., and Cambridge, UK: Polity Books.)

Rowse, Darren, and Chris Garrett. *ProBlogger: Secrets for Blogging Your Way to a Six-Figure Income*. (Hoboken, NJ: John Wiley & Sons, Inc.)

Rowse, Darren, and Chris Garrett. *ProBlogger: Secrets for Blogging Your Way to a Six-Figure Income*, 2nd ed. (Hoboken, NJ: John Wiley & Sons, Inc.)

Scoble, Robert, and Shel Israel. *Naked Conversations: How Blogs Are Changing the Way Businesses Talk with Customers*. (Hoboken, NJ: John Wiley & Sons, Inc.)

Utvich, Michael, Ken Milhous, and Yana Beylinson. *1 Hour Web Site: 120 Professional Templates and Skins.* (Hoboken, NJ: John Wiley & Sons, Inc.)

Wagner, Richard, and Richard Mansfield. *Creating Web Pages All-in-One Desk Reference For Dummies*, 3rd ed. (Hoboken, NJ: John Wiley & Sons, Inc.)

Downloads

For your free downloads associated with *The Social Media Bible,* go to www.theSocialMediaBible.com, and enter your ISBN number located on the back of the book above the bar code. Be sure to enter the dashes.

Credits

The ROI of Social Media was provided by:

Jeff Esposito, www.vistaprint.com

Expert Insight and technical edits were provided by:

Matt Mullenweg, cofounder, WordPress, www.WordPress.org

CHAPTER 8

The Wisdom of the Wiki

What's in It for You?

The word *wiki* comes from the Hawaiian word for "fast" or "quick," and it alludes to the pace at which wiki content can be created. While some say wiki is an acronym for "*What I Know Is*," this came after the original naming and is rarely used within the wiki community. Wikis are web sites that allow people to collect and edit their intelligence in one place at any time. These web sites truly represent the social media foundation of user-generated content and the wisdom of the crowds.

A wiki is a browser-based web platform that lets volunteers contribute information based on their expertise and knowledge, and permits them to edit content within articles on specific subjects. Together, this material creates an encyclopedia-type knowledge base that is founded on the integrity of the contributor's additions. Wikis can either be open to the public or restricted to members or employees. Many companies today, such as Pixar, are utilizing the wiki to create knowledge management systems for retaining corporate information for collaboration and for training. By incorporating a company wiki, many firms can gather the collective knowledge of their employees on subjects such as policies and procedures, manufacturing and sales, company history, products—and even how to fix the fax machine's paper jams.

As wiki inventor and computer programmer Ward Cunningham puts it, "The wiki concept has become a study in what's now called 'social software.' With a wiki, I write the seed of the idea and I come back in a week and see how the idea has grown."

The wiki has become an extremely valuable, easy-to-use, free resource tool. It is as simple as Edit, Write, and Save.

theSocialMediaBible.com

Back to the Beginning

Ward Cunningham came up with the concept for the wiki in 1994 and installed it on the Internet (domain c2.com) on March 25, 1995. Cunningham

wanted to create a unique online site for programmers involved in a type of software development known as object-oriented programming, which allowed the user to drag and drop, and just click to make easy edits. The first web site to be titled a *wiki* was Cunningham's own WikiWikiWeb (wikiwikiweb.com), originally described as "the simplest online database that could possibly work." Cunningham gave the site WikiWikiWeb this name upon recalling a Honolulu International Airport counter employee telling him to take the "Wiki-Wiki" shuttle bus in order to get

FIGURE 8.1   Wiki-Wiki Bus

from one airport terminal to another. Cunningham explained, "I chose wiki-wiki as an alliterative substitute for 'quick,' and thereby avoided naming this stuff quick-web."

Cunningham's initial design concept for his web site came from Apple's HyperCard, an easy-to-use programming language that the education industry had widely adopted for the Macintosh computer in the late 1980s and early 1990s. HyperCard was a graphic metaphor of a stack of index cards that contained links to other cards.

On March 15, 2007, the word *wiki* entered the online Oxford English Dictionary.

As Apple phased out HyperCard from its software library, software company Silicon Beach developed a programming alternative called the SuperCard. From the early to mid-1990s, Safko International Inc. was considered the largest SuperCard/HyperCard programming company in the country—with more than 150 programs and more than 1 million lines of code.

What You Need to Know

Cunningham and Bo Leuf—coauthors of *The Wiki Way: Quick Collaboration on the Web*—describe the wiki this way:

- A wiki invites all users to edit any page or to create new pages within the wiki web site, using a plain vanilla Web browser without any extra add-ons.
- Wiki promotes meaningful topic associations between different pages by making page link creation almost intuitively easy, and showing whether an intended target page exists or not.
- A wiki is *not* a carefully crafted site for casual visitors. Instead, it seeks to involve the visitor in an ongoing process of creation and collaboration that constantly changes the web site landscape.

A wiki's ease of use lies in the fact that it allows documents to be collaboratively written using a web browser. While the wiki web site is called the *wiki,* a single page is called a *wiki page*—which consists of user-generated content and hyperlinks to other articles, wiki pages, and external web sites.

Editing and Creating

Wikis allow the users to easily generate pages with the click of a button from any web browser. The name of the wiki is condensed into a page title where spaces and some special characters are removed. This type of titling is called *Camel Case.* To see the Camel Case title of the wiki page called Matt Mullenweg—cofounder of WordPress on *The Social Media Bible* web site, go to the clickable link on www.thesocialmediabible.com/2008/08/29/matt-mullenweg-founder-ceo-of-wordpress.

Simple Markup Language Tools

The system for creating and editing a wiki page is called SML (Simple Markup Language), or often simply called *wikitext.* If you have ever created a blog, then you know what this is. (If you haven't created a blog, you need to read Chapter 7, The Ubiquitous Blog, to find out why you should!) SMP is easy to use and has the "WYSIWYG" ("What You See Is What You Get") editing features of most common word processing software: bold, italic, underline, insert photo or video, center, right, left, and full justification, and so forth. Most wikis indicate who has made edits and when they've been made by keeping track of versions of the content, a feature that helps prevent mistakes and vandalism.

Security

Wikis are a very open set of documents, and are generally accessible to the public or an entire employee base—which only makes them all the more vulnerable to mistakes and vandalism. Wikis are designed to make it easy to correct errors, and they contain a useful Recent Changes page feature. This page lists all recent edits, when they were made, and by whom. In addition, wikis provide the previous unaltered version and what is called the "diff" feature—a tool that highlights the difference or changes between page revisions. This way, an editor can view the article before it was altered, compare it with the new page, and even restore the wiki page to its previous revision before the edit was made, if necessary.

While malicious vandalism can and does occur, a wiki's editors can easily catch it and revert to a previously stored edition to eliminate any unwelcome changes. Lars Erik Aronsson, a Swedish computer programmer, consultant, and founder of two Swedish web sites—the free electronic book archive Project Runeberg and the Swedish language wiki Susning.nu— summarizes the controversy as follows:

> [When] most people . . . first learn about the wiki concept, [they] assume that a web site that can be edited by anybody would soon be rendered useless by destructive input. It sounds like offering free spray cans next to a gray concrete wall. The only likely outcome would be ugly graffiti and simple tagging, and many artistic efforts would not be long lived. Still, it seems to work very well.

Depending upon how openly a wiki is designed, it can be susceptible to intentional disruption. This is why most open wikis require that you become a registered member or user before you are allowed to edit the contents of an article. Any intentional disruption is known as *trolling*. (For more information on trolls, see Chapter 6, The Internet Forum.)

Deciding whether to have an open or closed wiki presents one with pros and cons. While a closed wiki provides more security from vandalism, its content grows very slowly. An example of the difference would be Wikipedia versus Citizendium. Citizendium, another wiki encyclopedia project, requires the user to provide a real name and even a biography before being allowed to make edits. While this makes this wiki nearly vandalism free, it also hinders wiki growth. On the other hand, Wikipedia's open forum allows anyone with Internet access to edit capabilities to the articles—therefore permitting the site to grow quite rapidly. In fact, Wikipedia's English language version (en.Wikipedia.org) has the largest user base among all wikis on the Internet, and ranks in the Top 10 traffic of all web sites. (See further on for more information on Wikipedia.) Other popular wiki web sites include WikiWikiWeb, Wikitravel, Wiki Answers, wikiHow, Uncyclopedia, Memory Alpha, and Erik Aronsson's Susning.nu, the Swedish-language knowledge base.

Wikis have gained such popularity that there are now three well-known annual wiki conferences: The International Symposium on Wikis (WikiSym) conference, which is dedicated to general wiki research, the Wikimania conference, which focuses on research and practices of the Wikimedia Foundation's projects, such as Wikipedia and Recent Changes Camp, a barcamp-style Unconference focusing on wikis. In several cities worldwide, wiki aficionados attend Wiki Wednesday meet-ups on the first Wednesday of each month.

Wikipedia

Wikipedia is a nonprofit organization that provides a platform for the world's largest online user-generated content encyclopedia. The site contains roughly 15 million articles, has been visited by 59,123,362 visitors (at the time this chapter was written), and is by far the largest and most successful wiki there is.

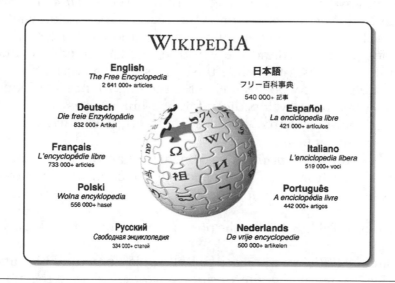

FIGURE 8.2 Wikipedia

The following was copied directly from the Wikipedia entry on Wikipedia.org:

> *Wikipedia* is a free, web-based, collaborative, multilingual encyclopedia project supported by the non-profit Wikimedia Foundation. *Wikipedia*'s 15 million articles (3.3 million in English) have been written collaboratively by volunteers around the world, and almost all of its articles can be edited by anyone with access to the site. *Wikipedia* was launched in 2001 by Jimmy Wales and Larry Sanger, and is currently the largest and most popular general reference work on the Internet. . . .
>
> . . . [C]ritics of Wikipedia accuse it of systemic bias and inconsistencies (including undue weight given to popular culture), and allege that it favors consensus over credentials in its editorial process. Its reliability and accuracy are also targeted. Other criticisms center on its susceptibility to vandalism and the addition of spurious or unverified information, though scholarly work suggests that vandalism is generally short-lived and an investigation in *Nature* found that the material they compared comes close to the level of accuracy of *Encyclopaedia Brittanica* and had a similar rate of "serious errors."
>
> Wikipedia's departure from the expert-driven style of the encyclopedia building mode and the large presence of unacademic content have been noted several times. When *Time* magazine recognized "You" as its Person of the Year for 2006, acknowledging the accelerating success of online collaboration and interaction by millions of users around the world, it cited Wikipedia as one of several examples of Web 2.0 services, along with YouTube, MySpace and Facebook. Some noted the importance of Wikipedia not only as an encyclopedic reference but also as a frequently updated news resource because of how quickly articles about recent events appear.
>
> The word *Wikipedia* was coined by Larry Sanger and is a portmanteau from *wiki* (a technology for creating collaborative web sites) . . . and *encyclopedia*.

Statistics in Table 8.1 show the phenomenal growth of wikis over the last nine years.

Despite the criticism in regard to Wikipedia's potential bias and factual inaccuracies, many of the site's critics have agreed that the information contained within Wikipedia is actually quite accurate. Even though the

Table 8.1

| Date | Article Count | Preceding Year | | |
		Increase	Percentage Increase	Average Increase/Day
2002-01-01	19,700	19,700	—	54
2003-01-01	96,500	76,800	390	210
2004-01-01	188,800	92,300	96	253
2005-01-01	438,500	249,700	132	682
2006-01-01	895,000	456,500	104	1,251
2007-01-01	1,560,000	665,000	74	1,822
2008-01-01	2,153,000	59,300	38	1,625
2009-01-01	2,679,000	526,000	24	1,437
2010-01-01	3,144,000	465,000	17	1,274
2010-08-02	3,367,661	223,661*	—	1,046*

*Calculated live, so far, as only for partial year.
Source: http://en.wikipedia.org/wiki/Wikipedia:sizeofWipedia#cite_ref_a_0=0.

Wikimedia Foundation repeatedly declined to participate directly in *The Social Media Bible,* the author agrees that web users should still be grateful for a resource like Wikipedia. This single site contains so much information on so many different aspects of the tools of social media. Wikipedia was an invaluable resource for the aggregation of information in this book.

MyGads

A great illustration of a very simple, easy-to-use, and free mini-wiki is a site called MyGads (MyGads.com). CommonCraft.com (commoncraft.com), a company that does great, simple, and easy-to-understand explanation videos, did one for MyGads on soccer team parents who need to keep track of which ones were responsible for bringing snacks to each game. The team coach created a page (mini-wiki) or a *Gad* on the MyGads web site, where team parents can add information to the page by just clicking and typing. The page contains information on all of the game dates, times, parents, and snacks. Because it is a MyGads page, the users can access the page through text message, instant message, or the MyGads web site. For example, soccer mom Sherrie is at the grocery store, and she needs to know if it's her turn to bring snacks. She sends a text message to MyGads that says, "June 26 Snacks." Within just a few seconds, she receives a message back that says

"Sherrie"; since she's in charge that week, she buys the snacks. It's as simple as that—and MyGads is secure, and always up to date.

Such a MyGads site would look like this:

Game Schedule		Snacks	
Date	**Time**	**Date**	**Snacks**
June 12	6:00 PM	June 12	Sheila
June 19	6:00 PM	June 19	Jenny
June 26	6:00 PM	June 26	Sherrie
July 3	6:00 PM	July 3	Vicki

MyGads is a useful resource for businesses as well; for example, let's say that you are a sales manager and need up-to-date inventory, price, and sales figures while on the road. MyGads works with most corporate databases, allowing you to keep the most up-to-date information on the MyGads page without any extra effort. You simply text message your MyGads page with "Medium Red Shirt," and instantly you get a message back: "247" in stock. And again, you can get all of this information through a text message or instant message, or from the web site. To watch the Common Craft demonstration video on YouTube, go to: youtube.com/watch?v=0S-WkhDygTA. Go to www.theSocialMediaBible.com for a clickable link.

Providers

While there are literally thousands of online wikis that contain millions of pages of information to choose from (the largest of which is Wikipedia), the easiest way to create your own wiki is to go to one of the following web sites that provide wiki platforms: www.wikia.com, PBWorks.com, WetPaint.com, or WikiSpaces.com. All of these wiki web sites allow you to create an account, so you can quickly begin building your very own wiki. Visiting Wiki Matrix can also help you find the wiki platform that's right for you.

The ROI of Social Media

Self-Service E-mail Marketing

Introduction

VerticalResponse, Inc., offers self-service e-mail marketing, online surveys, and direct mail service empowering small businesses to create, manage, and analyze their own direct marketing campaigns. Founded in 2001, VerticalResponse is aimed at small businesses, and enables anyone to get their e-mail marketing campaigns up and running within minutes, regardless of technical expertise.

Background

The target audience for VerticalResponse is small businesses with less than 100 employees. Due to the small staff size of their typical customers, often there is no dedicated e-mail marketing expert within the company. Additionally, small businesses may be fearful of social media tools, or be interested in implementing tools such as blogging, Twitter, and Facebook, if they only knew how.

Strategy

VerticalResponse believes that social media and e-mail marketing are complementary technologies and have similar fundamentals when it comes to using them for marketing purposes. By educating our customers on how to use social media with e-mail marketing, VerticalResponse can help make them more successful. Ultimately, when customers grow their business, this helps VerticalResponse, too.

After using webinars regularly to help educate small business customers, the company decided to create a Social Media Series webinar campaign. This webinar series would engage VerticalResponse customers and prospective sales leads by educating them about how they can use social media and e-mail marketing together.

Implementation

Given that VerticalResponse is an e-mail service provider, the company took the time to analyze its target customers and tailor the e-mail content to their specific needs. The seven separate e-mails in this series were sent to a total pool of several thousand people—however, this list was segmented for each e-mail according to their past social media preferences and which webinars customers had signed up for.

Opportunity

From a content perspective, the campaign was special because these e-mails introduced VerticalResponse customers to a free social media webinar series that they would not otherwise have access to. Small businesses are hungry for educational resources tailored to beginners that can teach them how to use other related tools such as social media to make them look like marketing gurus. VerticalResponse was positioned as a thought leader on e-mail marketing and social media.

(continued)

(*continued*)

Conclusion

The VerticalResponse Social Media Series webinar campaign highlighted the superior results that can be attained by integrating social media and e-mail marketing efforts. There were thousands of attendees and registrants for the seven-part series, made up of both customers and prospects. Of this group, approximately 50 percent were prospective customers—representing a huge sales and marketing opportunity for VerticalResponse. After listening to one or more of the social media webinars, these prospects were now "warm leads" for the company to advertise to.

The Series was also a key initiative for the retention of existing customers. By educating customers on the benefits of integrating social media and e-mail marketing, VerticalResponse is positioned as a thought leader within both spaces—and the go-to resource for small business marketing topics that matter most to customers.

Further validating the success of the VerticalResponse Social Media Series, the campaign won MarketingSherpa's fifth annual E-mail Marketing Awards—winning out against hundreds of competitive submissions. VerticalResponse took out Gold in the B2B category "Best Dynamic Content or Personalized E-mail." The e-mails sent as part of this campaign achieved double the open and click-through rates of VerticalResponse's standard customer newsletters. For example, one of the e-mails in the Social Media Series generated an open rate of 53.49 percent and a click-through rate of 51.16 percent. This is a high engagement rate for busy small business customers.

Janine Popick, CEO and founder, www.VerticalResponse.com

Expert Insight

Jack Herrick, founder of WikiHow, www.WikiHow.com

Jack Herrick

It's pretty interesting, isn't it? It's amazing—the variety, type, and quality of information we get using the wiki method. It's been really eye-opening for me. Like when I started WikiHow, I wasn't exactly sure what was going to happen. I wanted to build this how-to manual, and all its different topics. But the wiki method is really amazing . . . seeing what type of information people are writing about. It's definitely veered away from the traditional how-to manuals at this point.

We have things about relationships, about . . . all the how-to topics you'd expect to find . . . how to fix your car, how to solve problems in your computer. But we've got just totally different types of topics; really wild things. It's really expanding the definition of what a how-to manual can be. . . .

Well, I've always really been interested in building a really big how-to manual; and I'll give you the long story here. I owned e-How, which is sort of the Web One Point Zero version of the how-to manual. And e-How got started in nineteen ninety-nine during the dot-com boom, and they raised a ton of money from venture capitalists. They had two hundred employees, and they were writing this massive how-to manual; and at the time, I had nothing to do with that company. I was doing something totally different. [But] I knew the founder of e-How, and always admired the company. I thought it was a great idea. Unfortunately, when the first Internet downturn hit, [e-How] went into bankruptcy and had to lay off all two hundred employees; and basically, the company went into a deep freeze. It was bought out by another venture capital–funded company, called IT-Exchange, and they tried to nurse the site along and find a business model that would work; [but] they also failed to do that. They just . . . it wasn't profitable, and they couldn't get it working. They were about to shut the site off, and it was a company I had heard about and I really liked their site. I didn't want to see it go down. [Even though] I was working at another company, I hated to see e-How die. So a friend of mine and I got together and bought the site. We were both working full-time jobs . . . but we sort of brought the site back to life.

We hired a couple of writers and fixed lots of bugs on the old site—and it started to work; and on a very, very small cost basis we were able to get the site profitable and it was working quite well. We were pretty excited about it. But while I was doing that, I became a little disillusioned with the e-How business model. We hired writers; but . . . we found that you cannot hire writers to cover all the world's topics in all the world's languages. So, for example, I could hire someone to write about mutual funds, Viagra, you name any high cost-per-click (CPC) keyword and it was very profitable to have someone write about [topics like this]. But I wanted to have someone write about the really obscure things— there is no business model for that. It really wasn't my vision to have a how-to manual that was really only covering high-key CPC topics. I really wanted to have a how-to manual to cover every single imaginable how-to topic, and in multiple languages. And you just weren't going to get there with this professional writer model. At least you weren't going to get there with high quality. With e-How's business model, you either produce low amounts of quality work or high quantities of schlock, and I wasn't interested in doing either.

First, I was sort of puzzled about how we could accomplish this goal of producing high quality content across a broad range of topics. When I stumbled upon Wikipedia and was just amazed at the quality [and] the breadth

(continued)

(continued)

of information. . . . As I learned more and more about how it was written, I became even more impressed about what they were doing. So I started thinking if we could take the same wiki model and apply it to write a how-to manual. And so I tried that one. My engineer, Travis Derouin, and I sort of beavered away, and in late two-thousand four, [wc] tried to import the media wiki software and transform it to a how-to manual—something that would be better fitting for a how-to manual. And then we launched WikiHow on the anniversary of Wikipedia's birthday on January fifteenth, two-thousand five. . . .

I don't see my role as herding cats. I see my role as building a platform and enabling others to collaborate on a shared goal. I think there are a lot of people out there who want to do something, and a wiki allows you to put a certain [amount of information] together, and [give you] one place to do it. So, WikiHow attracts a group of people who are as passionate as [I am] about building a large, shared how-to manual; and it allows them to do that. So it works through its virtuous cycle. When I first started WikiHow, the very first month—we had it up in January two-thousand five—we had over two thousand people visit the site, and that was great.

And those two thousand people may [only] be five or ten people [who] actually wrote an article or edited something. And so there really wasn't much going on at the site in the very early days, but it works in a virtuous cycle where the next month you had these five articles, or ten articles and those brought some people in from search engine traffic, and what have you. And some of the people read the articles and said, "Hey, this article is not very good. I can do a better job." And they pressed "edit" and they improved the content; and then the content got better, and maybe moved up in the search engine rankings, [which] brought more people in . . . who've also said, "Wow, I can do better than this!" And *they* pressed "edit" and improved the content and the cycle keeps going . . . and is still running today on WikiHow. Synergy! I think that it definitely happened in the case of WikiHow. It definitely happened in the case of Wikipedia, and I've also talked to people who are working at Fortune Five Hundred companies and hearing those same sorts of stories you heard. People within the enterprise are turning on wikis and finding that the knowledge in the organization is far more than people at the top would have assumed. Allowing this sort of bottom-up collaboration can happen on a wiki; [it] produces [impressive] knowledge, and . . . I think more organizations are going to try and figure this out and protect it.

One organization that I've talked to is the U.S. State Department. They have a wiki internally called the Diplopedia which runs on Wikipedia software just like WikiHow and Wikipedia. So it's been a great resource for the State Department. . . .

In the wiki community there are thousands of people who contribute to WikiHow over any given month; and within that group there is a much smaller and tighter group of people that will number in the hundreds—people who I call the "Hard Core WikiHow Contributors"—and they are responsible for making sure the quality stays high. Every edit that goes to WikiHow is looked at by another human . . . a volunteer who looks at "edits" and says, "It is good" or "It is bad," or "I'm going to check this . . . am I going to send it out, or am I going to 'edit' this 'edit' to make it even better?" And so that's happening all the time, all day long in real time. Hundreds of people around the world are helping out. So that's our first line of defense. Then there's the reverse . . . if one of our "Hard Core Contributors" misses something, then our readers will often catch [it]; and since it is a wiki, they can edit the page and fix it on the spot.

And . . . one of the things that is getting pretty exciting about wikis is [that] we are finding more and more ways to improve quality. You may notice at the bottom of every wiki page now there is a "Is this article accurate? [Yes/no button]" [that] people vote on; so it percolates pages that might have accuracy problems—and we work on them and improve them. This really allows situations where you would think there would be complete chaos—where we allow anyone to edit. We do not even require people to log in or tell us any information about themselves whatsoever; and yet [by] allowing anyone to edit, wiki creates a high quality.

To listen to or read the entire Executive Conversation with Jack Herrick, go to www .theSocialMediaBible.com.

Commandments

1. **Thou shalt visit wikis.**

   Go look at the most popular wikis. Look at Wikipedia. Do some searching. Find a subject that you are passionate about. Read some of the articles . . . and comment on them. Add some facts. Correct some typos. Google other wikis, and check them out. Visit wikiindex.org to learn about the many different types of public wikis out there. Most importantly: Participate and contribute.

2. **Thou shalt create a company wiki.**

   Try to develop an internal company wiki. Go to one of the providers, sign up for an account, and create a wiki. Encourage other employees to participate; get them to create topic pages. Get others to contribute to the content. You will be surprised how fast your content and loyalty will grow within your trusted network.

Conclusion

Wikis are a great way to collect the wisdom of the crowd—whether it's a public wiki on a sport, hobby, or other area of interest, or a member-only company wiki that accumulates the collective knowledge of your employees. Wikis are a fun, easy, and free way to create your own information management system.

Without wikis like Wikipedia, the research and aggregation of the content in this book would have been significantly more difficult. Thank you to all of the contributors to Wikipedia, and the many wiki sites on the Internet!

To hear all of the Expert Interviews, go to www.theSocialMediaBible .com.

Readings and Resources

Blossom, John. *Content Nation: Surviving and Thriving as Social Media Technology Changes Our Lives and Our Future*. (Hoboken, NJ: John Wiley & Sons, Inc.)

Choate, Mark S. *Professional Wikis*. (Hoboken, NJ: John Wiley & Sons, Inc.)

Mader, Stewart. *Wikipatterns*. (Hoboken, NJ: John Wiley & Sons, Inc.)

Schwartz, Brendon, Matt Ranlett, and Stacy Draper. *Social Computing with Microsoft SharePoint 2007: Implementing Applications for SharePoint to Enable Collaboration and Interaction in the Enterprise*. (Hoboken, NJ: John Wiley & Sons, Inc.)

West, James A., and Margaret L. West. *Using Wikis for Online Collaboration: The Power of the Read-Write Web*. (Hoboken, NJ: John Wiley & Sons, Inc.)

White, Bruce A., and Andrew Pauxtis. *Web 2.0 for Business*. (Hoboken, NJ: John Wiley & Sons, Inc.)

Woods, Dan, and Peter Thoeny. *Wikis For Dummies*. (Hoboken, NJ: John Wiley & Sons, Inc.)

Downloads

For your free downloads associated with *The Social Media Bible*, go to www .theSocialMediaBible.com, and enter your ISBN number located on the back of the book above the bar code. Be sure to enter the dashes.

Credits

The ROI of Social Media was provided by:

Janine Popick, CEO and founder, www.VerticalResponse.com

Expert Insight was provided by:
Jack Herrick, cofounder, WikiHow, www.WikiHow.com

Technical edits were provided by:
Nicole Wilson, www.WikiHow.com

CHAPTER 9

A Picture Is Worth a Thousand Words (Photo Sharing)

What's in It for You?

The most important feature of photo sharing is that it's fun! Showing pictures to others is about sharing your memories with family members, friends, and colleagues. It's fun to display and remember your Christmas party guests, your coworkers at your promotion dinner, your child's school play, or the birth of your new son. It's also enjoyable to recall those moments

FIGURE 9.1 Sedona, Arizona

with your friends and family—wherever they are in the world. Additionally, there is something to be said about having all of your photographs organized into groups, sets, categories, events, and albums online where you can look at them anytime you wish—instead of having all of your memories stuffed in a shoebox in your closet or under your bed.

However, since this book focuses more heavily on utilizing social media for business than for fun, let's play "What if?" What if a prospect you were trying to land was doing some research on your product and went to Google Images, Flickr, or Photobucket and searched for either your trademarked name or a generic description of your product—and he found photo after photo? What if your prospect was preparing a budget presentation and needed photos of your type of product to secure funding, and his search consistently led him to your web site or photo sharing site? Wouldn't you or your company be perceived as the best-in-class expert in the field?

Now, imagine that your prospects were conducting just a general search—as they might do during the research phase of their sales funnel—and your company's product photos continued to appear. (See Chapter 5, The World of Web Pages, for more information about the sales funnel.) What would your prospect think about your company and your product? And now ask yourself: What if this type of marketing opportunity was completely free?

This high-quality and low-cost exposure is exactly what photo sharing brings to your business marketing and communications plan. By simply uploading your company's product photos for free, you are participating in an area of Internet marketing that is highly targeted, competitively advantageous—and completely free of charge.

When you are uploading your company's product or service snapshots to your photo sharing web site, be sure to remember the other items you have in your corporate shoebox. What if that same prospect also saw images of happy customers or your design or sales teams? How about some great shots of your company's headquarters, customer service installation, or repairs in progress? Take advantage of the resources that you already have, and use them frequently to provide visual proof of your business's dedication to its customers. After all, if only one prospect per quarter sees your photos and becomes a customer, isn't it worth the free posting?

Back to the Beginning

Photograph sharing dates back to the very first web page at CERN in early 1991. Whereas text was the most common information shared, photographs were easily second. The real rise of photo sharing web sites grew with the popularization of the digital camera in the late 1990s. Before the advent of digital cameras, the process of going from print to Web was a tedious one that required a flatbed scanner and software. Digital cameras allow you to go directly from your camera to the Web with only one step, and without any additional hardware or software. It is as easy as plugging your camera into your USB port and uploading your images.

Of course, the next natural application of photo sharing that came about was through e-mail. Sending your brother the photographs of graduation, or Grandma pictures of the kids, became increasingly popular—and increasingly demanding on the user to create e-mails for every viewer. The desire for a one-stop personal photo gallery—with your own personal photographs available 24/7 forever—became an ever-more appealing concept.

The other trend that quickly emerged—and added to the movement behind the photo sharing craze—was the incarnation of web sites such as KodakGallery.com (and others like it) that allowed customers to order prints made from their digitally uploaded photographs. As these sites developed greater capacity to store and view higher-quality (larger file size) photographs, thumbnails, and slideshows, the ability to classify them into albums amplified their popularity. And to assist digital photo sharing, many photo finishing stores—including local drugstores—could return photos in both print and digital CD formats.

With the advent of desktop photo management applications such as iPhoto—containing photo sharing features and integration that allow direct photo uploading, e-mail, and drag-and-drop through predesigned templates the task of organizing, uploading, and sharing photographs was more simplified than ever. There are currently a plethora of online photo sharing web sites that include online photo finishing, subscription-based sharing, peer-to-peer, peer-to-server-to-peer, peer-to-browser, and web photo album generators. Additionally, the process of sharing photographs has now grown beyond the digital camera and Internet to include camera cell phones, BlackBerrys, and PDAs (personal desktop assistants, such as the Palm Pilot). Today's standard camera phone allows you to take a picture, crop it, adjust the color, remove red eye, and e-mail it or immediately post that photograph to your web page or blog site—all with only a couple of simple clicks.

A Little about Digital Cameras

The cost of a good digital camera has dropped significantly over the past several years. You can actually buy a digital camera today for as little as $15 (for the Vkidz VGA Digital Camera); however, a larger investment in a good digital camera would be worthwhile. You can get a high-quality brand-name digital camera for $100 to $150.

Besides the standard options that accompany most cameras—such as auto-focus, auto-aperture, and digital display—the most common way to determine the quality of the camera is—unsurprisingly—by the quality of the picture. This is measured in megapixels, or the total number of pixels (picture elements)—or dots—the camera records in a single image. The higher the number of pixels, the better quality the image. While most cameras start at about 3mp (megapixels), some run at around 5mp—and a few consumer cameras are available as high as 10mp.

A 5mp camera is a camera that can record 5 megapixels per image. A megapixel is onc million pixels, or dots, per image. The total number of pixels is calculated by multiplying the total horizontal pixels by the total vertical pixels. Therefore, a 5mp camera will take a photo image with 5 million total pixels, or dots.

The importance in the number of pixels or image quality of a digital camera doesn't really count much for online viewing of your pictures, since the best quality that your monitor can display is 72 pixels per inch both horizontally and vertically. This number becomes important when you enlarge your image to print it as, say, an 8″ × 10″ photo. A lower-quality photograph will appear grainy or fuzzy if not taken at a high enough picture quality. Anything above a 3mp camera should print your photographs at adequate quality, and a 5mp or better will do a *great* job.

What You Need to Know

The first step in this process is fairly obvious: To actually *take* a photograph. The most popular way to do so today is using a digital camera. Most are point-and-click with fully automatic features and take incredibly accurate photos. And, because digital cameras don't use film, you can take as many photographs as you wish at no cost whatsoever. So go out and click away, practice, try different ideas, and take a lot of pictures. It's free!

There are other alternatives to using a digital camera, like your camera-enabled cell phone. Many of the newer camera phones—such as Apple's iPhone 3G —can rival the quality of a good digital camera, and have as high as 10 megapixels. (At that point, it essentially becomes a digital camera that you can use to make telephone calls!) You also have the option of using your digital video camera set to still photography.

The next step is to transfer your photographs from your camera to your computer. The cable (usually USB) and software, if you need it, will have been provided to you by the camera manufacturer. If you are using a camera that takes its pictures on film, then you can have your photograph developer process your photos in a digital format or store them on a CD. If your photos are older and have already been printed on photo paper, then you will need to digitize them through the use of a flatbed scanner and associated software. You can save time and effort if you still have the negatives for those photographs; then you can simply have your photo developer print them from the negative directly to a digital CD.

Once you've finished transferring, you can use a variety of software to crop, brighten or darken, sharpen, correct red eye, and otherwise enhance your photographs before uploading them to your photo sharing web site. The most popular photo editing application used today on both Windows and Macintosh computer platforms is Adobe's Photoshop. However, while Photoshop is one of the best and most versatile photo editing applications you can buy, it does cost over $200.

That's why you should be sure to check the original CD that came with your digital camera, since most camera manufacturers ship their merchandise with photo editing software. You can also download free photo editing software from the Internet—like Google's Picasa, for example—that will allow you to restore old photos with marks, water stains, and scratches to excellent condition, and even let you add text and watermarks. And most photo editing applications allow you to upload your photos directly to your web-based photo sharing site with the click of a button.

Now that you have all of your photographs edited to perfection, the next step is simply to upload them to your favorite photo sharing web site. Once you have created an account, just follow the directions on how to proceed. This usually is as simple as selecting Upload, then Browse, locating your image, and hitting OK. Many of these sites have their own uploader software applications that allow you to simply drag and drop your photos onto the application and automatically upload them to the web site. You can even transfer your photographs through your e-mail.

Once you've posted your images to a photo sharing web site, you can organize them into sets and albums, and add captions, titles, descriptions, and meta tags (keywords). These keywords are the ones you would use if you were searching the site for a photograph like yours. (For more information on metatags and keywords, please see Chapter 19, Spotlight on Search (Search Engine Optimization).) You can also have friends, family, prospects, and customers comment on your photographs, and you can comment on others' as well. Most photo sharing sites provide other services, like allowing you to order prints of your photographs, as well as create photo books or albums, and even custom calendars from your personal snapshots. And always remember to upload your photographs to the Flickr World Map or Google Earth. By selecting the user photograph layer, you can upload your photos and view those of others as well, based on geographic location.

Privacy versus Piracy

While some people believe that you should be less fearful of piracy than obscurity, others just don't want their photographs taken and used by the Internet community at large—especially for commercial purposes. Online photo theft and fraud have become critical issues with photo sharing web sites and their members. Nearly every one of these sites supports the Creative Commons License, which allows users to designate their photos by the level of copyright protection they wish to have. All the sites take theft seriously. (For more information on the Creative Commons License, see Chapter 10, Talking about the Podcast (Audio Create), or go to creativecommons.org.) The Creative Commons License allows many photo sharing web sites to grant those with copyrighted photographs access to use the site to sell licenses to their photographs. So, in addition to helping to protect the photographer, they are providing a system for the photographer to make money through their photographs.

Techniques and Tactics

Although this chapter acknowledges that uploading photos is largely focused on sharing with friends and family your images of birthday parties, bar mitzvahs, babies, and weddings, the purpose behind this book—and this chapter—is to show readers how to use photo sharing web sites to create additional revenue. Businesses are using these techniques to share images of their products, tech support, employees, assembly lines, inventory, and happy customers.

You can help this process along by uploading as many photographs as you can, and entering the best meta tags as possible. Be sure that you use product names, applications, and serial or part numbers. Also make sure that your company names, geographic areas, and service descriptions are part of the meta tags, captions, and even photo file names. Remember to approach this process from the mind-set of a prospect or customer who is searching the site for you and your product or service. What words would you use if you were them? What kind of images would you want to see, or would you find helpful?

Most photo sharing web sites allow you to create and participate in groups. Be sure to link your photos to the appropriate groups and communities on your photo sharing site. For example, the author presented with Matt Mullenweg, the cofounder of WordPress, at the Arizona Entrepreneurship Conference. Twenty-one press photos of the event were taken. These

FIGURE 9.2   Flickr

pictures appear at www.flickr.com/photos/lonsafko, with a group for these photos named #AZEC. The conference founders created a larger group named 2008 Arizona Entrepreneur Conference. This group pool combines 190 photographs from all of the other attendees. You can look at just one smaller group of photos of the event or all 190.

Remember to install a free widget, gadget, or plug-in to your company web site or blogging site so that it will pull your photographs from your photo sharing web site and place clickable thumbnail images on your web page. This step will introduce your prospects to the concept that you have photographs available for view on a photo sharing web site and allow them to hyperlink directly to your photo site.

Providers

Choices are plentiful when it comes to selecting a photo sharing web site. They include: Flickr, ShutterFly, KodakGallery, SnapFish, SmugMug, PhanFare, DropShots, Fotolog, Multiply, MyPhotoAlbum, Panoramio, PhotoBucket, Picasa, Pickle, PicMe, Pixamo, Slide, Tabblo, WebShots, WinkFlash, Zenfolio, Zooomr, and Zoto. To determine which of these is right for you, take a look at a few of them to better understand what features they offer in comparison to which are most important for you. It's also a good idea to maintain multiple photo sharing web sites; after all, the more places you are on the Internet, the more exposure you have. As with all of the chapters in Part I of this book, don't get overwhelmed; just start off with one site, see if you like it, create an account, and start uploading your photographs.

For providers of digital cameras and camera cell phones, spend a little time online looking at reviews, prices, and blogs. The same holds true for photo editing software. If you have Photoshop, then you have everything you need. If you don't, then check the box that your camera came in to see if the manufacturer provided software. If the answer is "no" to both, then do a search for free or reasonably priced software that best suits your needs.

The ROI of Social Media

Cross-Social Media Campaign to Build Awareness, User-Generated Content, Engagement, and Measurable Buzz

Background

Coach, the preeminent designer, producer, and marketer of fine accessories, sought to broaden its audience to reach a new, younger demographic, specifically females ages 17 to 22. Coach turned to Brickfish, The Social Media Solution, to produce a custom-designed program that would reach this new audience on the social Web across existing social media platforms like Facebook, Twitter, MySpace, and Tagged. Brickfish powers Cost Per Engagement–based cross-social media campaigns and tracks campaign reach, frequency, and viral activity in real time.

Strategy

- The Brickfish Solution for Coach was to launch a "Design a Coach Tote" social media program to engage consumers by creating unique and fresh designs for the classic Coach tote.

- Program entrants were able to download Coach tote templates, on which they would create original designs and then upload onto the Brickfish platform.
- The winning tote design would be turned into a special-edition item and sold in select Coach locations across the country.
- The program aimed to reintroduce young creatives and fashion lovers to Coach as a hip brand; savvy in the social media scene, with an open mind to new designs and directions.

Implementation

The "Design a Coach Tote" program was promoted on the Brickfish.com site as well as through an iFrame on the Coach site. Through PR and outreach, the program was featured on leading fashion blogs across the Internet, including Fab Sugar, Fashcentric, Nitrolicious, and dozens more driving traffic to the Coach.com site. Participants were encouraged to "click and share" their designs with their friends via their favorite social media platforms like Facebook, Twitter, MySpace, and Tagged.

Opportunity

In social media, engagement is the goal. Successful social media campaigns allow consumers to interact with their brand, which may include personalizing, tagging or rating content, sharing something new with friends, adding comments, and so on. The value of engagement depends on your business goals. If your goal is to build trust and credibility, then shifts in brand perception based on engagement activities should be considered. If your goal is to build consideration, then metrics such as registration, contributions, and other data are important to show how engagement is drawing the consumer closer to the brand.

Conclusion

- The "Design a Coach Tote" program received over 3,200 entries.
- The program resulted in more than six million consumer engagements.
- Each program participant spent an average of 8.5 minutes with the brand.
- The program reached over 8,000 unique URLs.
- Forty-eight percent of entries were virally shared across the Internet to sites such as MySpace, Tagged, Facebook, myYearbook, and more.
- OMMA acknowledged the campaign with a "Best Viral Program" Award.

Brickfish, www.brickfish.com

Expert Insight

Dharmesh Mehta, director of product management, Windows Live Instant Messenger, www.get.live.com/messenger/overview

Dharmesh Metha

Windows Live Messenger has been around about nine and a half years now. We originally launched it back in nineteen ninety-nine, and it was pretty much focused on just being an IM text solution. What you've seen over the years is, as we continue to grow, we've turned that from text chat and added voice and video. We then added photo sharing and games. We've added a ton of personal expressions so you can change your display pictures and record videos with your webcam. We allow you to have both those real-time conversations, but also a synchronous offline instant message. And today Windows Live Messages is actually used by more than three hundred twenty-five million people worldwide. So it's come a long way over the last nine and a half years, and we hope to see that growth continue. . . .

So you have your contacts in your Messenger's main window, and you can start a chat with them—and it's not just about chat. You can share files, just drag them right into there.

Actually one of the latest things we've just added is a really rich photo sharing. If you drag photos in, you can look at a set of photos with one of your buddies; or you can, at the same time, change what photo you are looking at while you're commenting and chatting about them. You can save them to Cloud and have them permanently shared out where others can see them.

Again, you can share that just with your contacts or you can open it up to the whole Internet. . . .

That's actually . . . for a while people felt like, you know, you had to have a side-load photo sharing application, or this side-load IM application, and their side-load e-mail application. But really, you're people and you have one set of people you want to interact with, some you might want to do some things with, and some another set of things; but whether you're in IM or you're up on the Web, or you're on your mobile phone, we want to make sure you can get your stuff. Whether that's photos or bios or being able to have real-time chat; we want to bring that context to you wherever you happen to be. . . .

So we offer a couple of different things on mobile phones. The first is for our PC users . . . when you're there chatting with someone and all of a sudden they go offline because they are no longer on their PC. The fact of the matter is many of those people are actually online on their phone and they can receive alerts. So we have connections from the PC and the web messaging experiences straight to your phone. And that's the first one.

But the one that I'm more excited about and continues to be growing really rapidly is about the fact that when you are on your mobile phone you now actually have far more phones that are data-capable. And so whether that's browse services for IM'ing or photo sharing; whether that's doing little micro-blogging and updating your status; or even on some of the higher-end phones, whether that's mobile or BlackBerry or Nokia and actually having rich client application.

Obviously you have to design those slightly differently; the context is different. There's different user experiences because of the fact that you're always reachable on your phone, but you may not always want to be reachable. But it's actually really exciting what's happening on the mobile phone, and it's really two things. It's bringing the things that people have been doing on PC and the Web and extending them to the phone. But then in some countries you just come online on the phone and you may never, ever get on a PC. They may never get download apps onto a Windows PC, but you want to make sure that you have as great a mobile experience that's served from their phone. . . .

And it's interesting that the different scenarios that you encounter in some of these countries, where your phone not only becomes SMS . . . and SMS on your phone not only becomes just a way to have short chats with people, but it's also a great way of getting little bits of information.

If you find a short SMS text message and you get the weather, you get your latest calendar appointment, or you do a web search. These are all things that are done slightly differently depending on the type of phone you have and the type of user you are. Mobile is actually a real exciting space for us, just for the amount of growth and the amount of different possibilities that are coming. . . .

On Windows Live Messenger today there are three hundred twenty-five million people who span the world, and so we are actually more of an international company than just being U.S.-focused, like some of the other instant messaging companies, and in terms of demographic, it spans everyone. So it's all the way from young teens to even younger than that, all the way up to adults and seniors.

We recently did some reports looking specifically at a fast-growing demographic of the seventy-plus population that's starting to come online and wanting to chat with their grandkids and share photos and talk to them. And it's actually really interesting how IM, which once upon a time was really just restricted to, almost, college students and very young age ranges, really brought in all people on the planet. It transected . . .

And I say more than 85 percent of those are actually outside the U.S. It's an interesting trend that you talked about. You know, often sitting here in the

(*continued*)

(*continued*)

United States we get very U.S.-focused and we often think that a lot of technology starts here in the U.S. and spreads to other parts of the world. But going back to that discussion that we had on mobile, some of the most interesting things in mobile are actually happening in Asia; whether that's Japan and South Korea or in India and China, where users are coming online on mobile and may never use a PC.

Think of this from a global perspective. We're learning and discovering from other players, other competitors, and companies, just around the world. . . .

To listen to or read the entire Executive Conversation with Dharmesh Mehta, go to www.theSocialMediaBible.com.

Commandments

1. **Thou shalt take a lot of photographs.**

   Get a digital camera or camera phone and start taking pictures. Because they are digital, there are no associated development costs. If you don't like the way the picture came out, you can simply hit Delete. If you are satisfied with it, then save it to your hard drive. Like anything else, the more you practice, the better you become.

2. **Thou shalt edit your photographs.**

   While many photo editing software applications have a one-click photo enhance feature, try using the manual adjustment sliders and effects. It's fun, and there's always an Undo function. To play it safe, always practice on a copy of the original photograph.

3. **Thou shalt upload.**

   Find as many photographs as possible that you already have. Combine them with the new photos you are taking, and upload them to the photo sharing site of your choice. Creating an account on a photo sharing site is easy, only takes about 10 minutes, and is free.

4. **Thou shalt use meta tags and descriptions.**

   Take a few minutes to think about the words that you will use to describe each photo, and the words that your prospects would use to search for your products and services.

5. **Thou shalt create and join groups.**

 Search your photo sharing web site for groups that are similar and appropriate to the type of product or service you sell. Often, the best way to become part of a group or community is not to sell; a trusted network works *because* of the trust. Observe, participate—and *then* sell.

6. **Thou shalt comment.**

 Participating means commenting. Comment on others' pictures, and encourage others to comment on yours. The more communication you have with one another, the more visibility your photographs will have.

Conclusion

Sharing your photographs with global communities, friends, family, co-workers, prospects, and customers and encouraging them to comment and communicate their feelings about your photos is the very essence of social media. Social media is all about two-way communication. Upload your photos, create communities, and start building credibility and trust with your clients and prospects.

 To hear all of the Expert Interviews, go to www.theSocialMediaBible .com.

Readings and Resources

Anderson, Todd. *Building a Photo Gallery with Adobe AIR.* (Hoboken, NJ: John Wiley & Sons, Inc.)

Busch, David D. *Digital Photography All-in-One Desk Reference For Dummies.* (Hoboken, NJ: John Wiley & Sons, Inc.)

Canfield, Jon, and Tim Grey. *Photo Finish: The Digital Photographer's Guide to Printing, Showing, and Selling Images.* (Hoboken, NJ: John Wiley & Sons, Inc.)

Chambers, Mark L., Tony Bove, David D. Busch, et al. *Digital Photos, Movies, & Music Gigabook For Dummies.* (Hoboken, NJ: John Wiley & Sons, Inc.)

Jamieson, Catherine. *Create Your Own Photo Blog.* (Hoboken, NJ: John Wiley & Sons, Inc.)

King, Julie Adair. *Shooting & Sharing Digital Photos For Dummies.* (Hoboken, NJ: John Wiley & Sons, Inc.)

Micheletti, Angelo. *iPhone Photography For Dummies.* (Hoboken, NJ: John Wiley & Sons, Inc.)

Micheletti, Angelo. *iPhoto '09 For Dummies.* (Hoboken, NJ: John Wiley & Sons, Inc.)

Sahlin, Doug. *Digital Photography Workbook For Dummies*. (Hoboken, NJ: John Wiley & Sons, Inc.)

Sammon, Rick. *Capturing Better Photos and Video with Your iPhone*. (Hoboken, NJ: John Wiley & Sons, Inc.)

Wilkinson, David A. *Flickr Mashups*. (Hoboken, NJ: John Wiley & Sons, Inc.)

Downloads

For your free downloads associated with *The Social Media Bible,* go to www .theSocialMediaBible.com, and enter your ISBN number located on the back of the book above the bar code. Be sure to enter the dashes.

Credits

The ROI of Social Media was provided by:

Brickfish, www.brickfish.com

Expert Insight was provided by:

Dharmesh Mehta, director of product management, Windows Live Instant Messenger, www.get.live.com/messenger/overview

Technical edits were provided by:

Stephen Farrington, owner, *OpusWorks Studio,* www.stephenfarrington.com

CHAPTER 10

Talking about the Podcast (Audio Create)

Automakers have been scrambling to make their cars iPod and iPhone compatible? Why do you suppose that is? Because so many people who drive—especially those who spend long periods behind the wheel—use that time to listen to music, news, sports, weather, and other forms of audio information. Historically, in-car audio programming has been the exclusive domain of radio, an industry that was built upon finding ways to entertain or inform, and then sell stuff to a captive audience of drivers during the highly lucrative drive-time hours.[1] But that was then.

Automakers today know that iPods (used synonymously here with iPhones and other MP3 players) have become so ubiquitous and indispensable that people routinely bring them into their cars. Now, you and your company can be there too, and in all of the other places people take their iPods. This is provided you know why, when, and how to make podcasting (producing audio for iPods) part of your business strategy.

After one of the authors of the first edition of this book began podcasting, he received an e-mail from a listener asking to make the podcasts available in MP3 format so the listener could more easily download them to his iPod. It turns out that every time a new podcast came out, the listener would transfer it to his iPod and listen to it at the gym. What an efficient way to use that time!

---

1. Drive time refers to 6:00 AM to 10:00 AM and 3:00 PM to 7:00 PM Monday through Friday when the majority of radio listeners travel to and from work and significantly more commercials are run.

 theSocialMediaBible.com

What's in It for You?

Podcasting is an effective way for you and your business to be heard—to capture the valuable mindshare of customers, prospects, and employees. And, like nearly all of the social media tools in the ecosystem, *it's free!* Podcasting is quite easy to do and produces a medium that is much more psychologically desirable—and frequently more accessible—to your customers and followers than mere text. A plethora of evidence supports this statement. One report states that 75 percent of all journalists prefer rich media (see Chapter 5, The World of Web Pages), and education studies show that rich media is more effective for teaching. Almost all Search Engine Optimization (SEO) people (see Chapter 19, Spotlight on Search) have known this for more than a decade. Even Confucius (551–479 BC) knew a picture was worth 1,000 words! A picture is worth a thousand words, an audio podcast is worth a thousand pictures, and a video is worth a thousand audios.

Back to the Beginning

The distribution of digitized audio recordings has been around—in one form or another—for nearly as long as the Internet has existed. In the early days, it was just called audio. The first audio files commonly appearing on the Internet were based on the Resource Interchange File Format (RIFF). These files included *Audio Interchange File Format (.aiff)* on Macintosh computers and later *Waveform Audio (.wav)* files on Windows PCs. RIFF-based files were big and clunky to download. A typical 3½-minute song at CD quality occupied an uncompressed file size of about 35 megabytes (MB). The size of these files made downloading audio time-consuming through a high-speed connection, and intolerable through a dial-up modem. Because of its smaller file size and faster download times, a highly compressed audio format called *MP3* emerged and soon became the de facto standard for Internet audio. *MP3* stands for the Motion Picture Experts Group standard MPEG-1 Audio Layer 3, and is able to fit that same 3½-minute song into roughly 3.5MB—a 10-fold reduction in size—with practically no discernible loss of quality. Podcasting, for the most part, is done in the MP3 format.

Note: Keep file size and download times in mind when creating your podcasts—a 20-minute session in CD-quality stereo could run more than 30MB. Fortunately, *bit rate* is a selectable parameter in most podcast recording software, and choosing a lower bit rate and monaural encoding can cut the size of a spoken language podcast by another factor of four while still sounding great.

The Birth of iPod

Apple CEO Steve Jobs introduced the first iPod to the world on October 23, 2001. The word *iPod* itself is also a combination of words: *Internet* plus *pod*— or small, self-contained gadget. The term was first proposed by Vinnie Chieco, a freelance copywriter who was commissioned by Apple to introduce the new device to the public. When Chieco saw the prototype, he was reminded of the conversation between Dave and Hal in the movie *2001: A Space Odyssey* to "Open the pod bay door, Hal!" Dave's "pod" comment referenced the white EVA Pods of their spaceship, the Discovery One.

While iPod was not the first portable digital music player—SaeHan Information Systems and Diamond Multimedia had both introduced models (*MPMan* and *Rio*) as early as 1998—with its sleek design and novel scroll wheel interface, the iPod quickly won the attention of consumers as the coolest MP3 player available. (A Diamond Multimedia marketing executive would later comment that he was too ashamed to reveal his newest *Rio* model to a fellow airline passenger en route to the product's introduction because the other guy's iPod, despite its use of (non-MP3) AAC encoding only and compatibility only with the iTunes music service, was still clearly a "cooler" product).

The iPod also benefitted from the use of a small hard drive, in contrast to the lower capacity flash memory systems of its competitors. And while the Recording Industry Association of America (RIAA) had been suing companies like Diamond Multimedia over their product offerings, Apple's iPod was tethered to Apple's legal downloading service, the iTunes Music Store (IMS), which to this day remains the world's top-selling digital music service (now offering untethered MP3 downloads). On February 25, 2010, Apple reported the 10-billionth song download from iTunes, and recent market reports have estimated its share of worldwide legal music downloads at 27 percent. According to Apple's CFO, Peter Oppenheimer, IMS accounts for about 85 percent of all digital music sales in the United States (at about $1 each).

iPod was the brainchild of former General Magic and Phillips employee Tony Fadell, who envisioned a small hard drive–based player that was linked with a content delivery system where users could legally obtain and download music. Fadell left Phillips in February 2001 to create his own firm, which he called "Fuse." He and his company developed a 5GB hard drive portable device that, as Tony would say, "Put a thousand songs in your pocket." After being turned down by RealNetworks, Tony went on to successfully cut a deal with Apple Computer, where he led a team that created the iPod based on a reference design by a company called PortalPlayer, which had been assisting other companies to develop MP3 players based on common software. When Steve Jobs introduced the first iPod in 2001, he repeated Tony's words exactly, "A thousand songs in your pocket," and this became the tagline of Apple's iPod marketing campaign.

Later generations of the iPod were developed to accommodate MP3, AAC/M4A, Protected AAC, AIFF, WAV, Audible audiobook, and Apple Lossless formats. The iPod photo model can display JPEG, BMP, GIF, TIFF, and PNG image file formats, and iPod video can play MPEG-4 (H.264/MPEG-4 AVC) and QuickTime video formats. With the introduction of Apple's third-generation video-playing iPods, Apple began selling video content through iTunes. By October 2008, Apple reported that over 200 million TV episodes had been sold. With the video on the scene, the term *podcast* began to apply to both audio and video recordings, but since *vodcasting* is becoming an increasingly popular term for video broadcasting, we will use the term *podcast* to refer only to audio.

The Birth of Podcasting

Podcasting is an equally accessible and entertaining application of the iPod. The word *podcasting* comes from combining the terms *iPod* and *broadcasting*. The first known public use of the word was in a Ben Hammersley article, "Why Online Radio Is Booming," which appeared on page 27 of *The Guardian*, on February 12, 2004.

Although systems that enabled downloading of serial episodic audio content onto portable devices for later playback had been around since 2000, the ability for anyone to produce and publish audio content as podcasts really took off after the first Bloggercon weblogger conference, organized by software developer Dave Winer and friends in October 2003. Winer is the author of RSS, a web-feed format used to publish frequently updated media, such as blog entries, and news headlines (see Chapter 18, RSS—Really Simple Syndication Made Simple).

At that first Bloggercon, Kevin Marks demonstrated a script to download RSS enclosures and pass them to iTunes for transfer to an iPod. Marks and early audioblogger Kevin Curry discussed collaborating, and following the conference Curry offered his blog readers an RSS-to-iPod script called iPodder. iPodder moved MP3 files from Winer's weblogging product, Radio Userland, to iTunes. Curry encouraged other developers to build on the idea, and thus podcasting became accessible to you and me.

Podcasting and You

Podcasting is both fun and fairly simple—because everything you need to be able to podcast is either already built into your computer (hardware) or free to download from the Internet (software). There is really no excuse *not* to give it a try.

Podcasts are ordinary MP3 audio files and aren't limited to the iPod or the iTunes Store. A podcast can be played on any MP3 player or right from your browser from any web site that offers podcasts. Go to www.theSocial MediaBible.com for nearly 50 Executive Conversations podcasts with social media industry leaders. You can listen to an audio recording live by streaming it into an audio player, or you can download and save the file to your PC. Once you have the file stored on your PC, you can transfer it to an MP3 portable player, or just listen to it at any time from your MP3 player or web browser.

Podcasts allow anyone, for the first time in history, to create one's own talk show, interview, educational or training seminar, sermon, speech, presentation, or music file that can be distributed worldwide to literally tens, hundreds, or even thousands of people who can play or download it and hear what you have to say . . . for *free*. You can create a following of colleagues, friends, and customers who care about what you have to say; and by podcasting, you've created a viral, entertaining, and informative medium through which you can be heard.

What You Need to Know

The more interesting you make your message, the more likely people are willing to hear it. Of all rich media—which includes video, audio, and animation such as Flash—audiences prefer video over audio, and audio over text. However, video—while the most desirable form—also requires the most effort and the greatest initial capital expenditure to create. For video, you need a computer, a digital video camera, and some video editing software at the very least.

On the other hand, audio podcasting is still a great and much simpler—expression of user-generated content, and all of the tools you need to create your own audio podcast are right there inside your computer. From the audience perspective, audio files are smaller and download faster than video, can be played on more existing portable players, and can be listened to while driving, walking to work, or working out at the gym. So, for many, podcasting audio content is the easiest and most effective way to broadcast their personal message.

To create an audio podcast, all you need is your computer, the built-in microphone (or an external one, if your computer does not have a microphone built in), the free audio recording and editing software that came with the computer—and a little bit of creativity. Just hit Record, announce your message, hit Save, and upload it to a web site like PodBean.com for Internet distribution, and you are podcasting.

Podcast Components

An audio podcast can range from less than a minute to more than an hour in total length, depending upon the content you wish to include. The podcast can sound slick, as though it was professionally produced, or have a rough-around-the-edges homemade flavor to it. It can start with an introduction to the content and speaker, and even have a musical intro. Many podcasters find the easiest way to sound natural is to have more than one person speaking, like a radio interview or discussion. Whatever your choice of content, podcasts are effective, portable, and fun.

The Value of Podcasting

Creating successful podcasts on a given subject will allow you to build a loyal following, and convey to your audience that you are an expert in your industry or subject field. Your audience may include people interested in your subject area or in following what you do. Most importantly, they may be both existing and potential customers of your product or service.

As with all of the other chapters in this book, a strong "What's in It for Me?" is imperative. If your podcasts contain valuable takeaways, your listeners will continue to come back for more. They will also be able to provide user feedback—yet another benefit of podcasting. By allowing your listener the opportunity to give comments on your podcast, you can hear directly from your audience what you are doing right—and what you can do better.

Podcasts are like blogs in that they can be RSS-fed (see Chapter 18, RSS—Really Simple Syndication Made Simple, for more about RSS). Essentially, your podcasts can be syndicated or distributed, and made available worldwide for free. People who like your podcasts and want to share them and be alerted when you've created more content can be informed every time you publish a new podcast. You can also set up Facebook, LinkedIn, and other free services to automatically publish when you have added a new podcast episode.

Tips, Techniques, and Tactics

How to Create Your Own Podcast

Creating your own podcasts is easy, so don't be afraid if you've never created one. The process follows four steps: planning, recording, editing, and publishing.

FIGURE 10.1 Podcasting For Dummies

A great resource for creating and distributing podcasts is *Podcasting For Dummies* by Tee Morris, Evo Terra, and Dawn Miceli (see Figure 10.1). Go to www .theSocialMediaBible.com to download the *Podcasting For Dummies* primer e-book. It's free!

Planning

It's best if you plan out your podcast ahead of time—gathering and importing information, and then writing the script. Although the goal of podcast production is to make it sound professional, it needn't be perfectly polished. What is right depends on your audience and your personal production style; many podcasters try to sound more relaxed and casual, while others go to great lengths to make their radio shows, audiobooks, and other recordings rival the production value of traditional media sources. Less than perfect is okay, even better. But be sure the audio quality is pleasing; your customers are more likely to listen to it all the way through.

The less-than-perfect maxim holds true for all social media you produce, and the reason is the audience's perception of the purpose for which the podcast was produced.

For the most part, when an audio or video has that polished, Madison Avenue, network production feel, it can safely be assumed that it cost a great deal to have it produced. It also stands to reason that if someone is writing a big check for the production, most likely there is an agenda for that media. And, other than public service announcements (PSAs), that usually means there is a commercial message behind all that professionally produced–sounding media.

With social media, the content is by the people, for the people. It's ad hoc, fresh, spontaneous, unbiased, and noncommercial. Most commercial products and companies wouldn't want to be represented by anything less than professional quality. So, with less of a focus on production quality comes a perception of homemade, honest, truthful, and trustworthy.

Keeping this concept in mind, it's better *not* to strive for perfection—and to be very careful how self-promoting and commercial your social media message may sound. This holds true for your blogs, vlogs, podcasts, and any other form of media you might produce (excepting only your corporate web page). You can mention your product, or even have a quick introduction to it at the beginning of your vlogs for your sponsor, company, or yourself; just do it tastefully and keep it at a minimum. Otherwise, you will lose your listener's trust.

Introducing Your Podcast

The next step of planning is to sketch out the type of introduction that you want to have. It can include a verbal opening explaining who you are, what your subject matter is, and what you will be talking about in this episode. It can also be saved for future use as the introduction for your next podcast. Remember: Your intro is your persona, your audio image, and your brand for you and your content.

Your introduction can also include a couple of riffs or a few bars of music. Get an idea ahead of time the feeling you want your podcast to convey: serious, businesslike, entertaining, educational, or something else. Then pick about five seconds of music that conveys that feeling to your listener. Apple's GarageBand (assuming you own a Macintosh computer) is a great tool for this. In just a couple of minutes, you can select a few instrumental riffs (several seconds, or chords), and lay down a track (create a piece of music) that will really get your listener's attention. If you aren't smart enough to own a Mac, then you can capture a few seconds of copyright-free music from any recording, or from the Internet.

The best part of working with GarageBand is that *anything* you create is copyright and royalty free. You always have to be sensitive about copyrights. Just because the music is on the Internet or a CD doesn't mean that it's free for you to use. Always keep in mind: *If someone else created it, it belongs to that creator.* You will need written permission from the copyright owner for you to use that music or sound. Otherwise, you could end up as Napster: The Sequel. And always keep in mind that if you (or anyone you know) play a musical instrument and can record it or play it directly into your PC through USB—you're good to go!

However—in terms of copyrighted music—there is the Creative Commons Project. Creative Commons (CC) is a nonprofit organization that has developed copyright licenses that grant certain rights to the public—rights that the owner of copyrighted material is willing to waive so that others may use those not-in-the-public domain materials. The Creative Commons licenses vary, and can include dedication of copyrighted material to public domain or open content. For more information on the Creative Commons Project, please visit http://creativecommons.org/. And, for more information on U.S. copyrights, you can visit www.uspto.gov and select "Copyrights," or www.theSocialMedia Bible.com for clickable links.

Recording

When making your podcast, use a few bullet points or a slide show to convey your main ideas. You can then simply read a bullet and just speak sponta- neously about that subject, without sounding too rehearsed or rigid. And if you don't want to plan out your podcast—then it's okay to just wing it!

Once you know what you want to say, it's time to record it. To begin, you will need to use your computer's built-in microphone or connect an external microphone for better quality. A number of high-quality USB-compatible micro- phones are available from online retailers for as little as $30 or less. You will also need audio recording and editing software. Use Audacity, Sound Studio, Garage- Band, or other inexpensive or free sound editing software. Some statistics sug- gest that nearly half of all of the creators of podcasts are either using or have used Audacity to record and edit their shows. It provides easy-to-use, high-quality tools—and it's free! Another new open-source—and *free*—recording and editing software is available from Koblo.com. Also, some of the USB microphones mentioned earlier come bundled with audio recording software, including podcasting-specific features. For straight-ahead no-frills recording, the latest release of Apple's Quicktime Player—a free download for Mac or Windows— will also record and save audio in the .mov, and .3gp formats. Of course, you're also welcome to use the more expensive and elaborate software.

Some audio editing software can import sound file formats such as .wav, .aiff, .wma, and MP3s, and record from a microphone as well as from the computer's sound card and auxiliary devices. For telephone interviews, VoIP (Voice over Internet Protocol) software, such as Vonage and Skype—both also *free*—can record both sides of the phone call directly though the use of add-ins like VoIP Recorder (for Vonage) and Pamela (for Skype). This is particularly handy if you want to have a talk-show format, and if you and your guest or cohost are working in different locations.

Starting with the release of the Leopard version of its operating system, Apple began shipping Mac OS X with an included utility called Podcast Capture. Snow Leopard includes version 2; it's in the Utilities folder inside the Applications folder. According to the introductory screen, "Podcast Capture 2 lets you easily capture high-quality audio and video from a camera or your Mac's screen and

(continued)

(*continued*)

send your content to a Podcast Producer Server for processing.'' Podcast Producer is a Mac OS X Server application that automates the publishing of podcasts to blogs, iTunes, and iTunes U. Podcast Capture requires you to enter the address of your Podcast Producer Server before it will let you do any recording, editing, and tagging, and most people I know don't have a Mac OS X Server lying around waiting to publish their podcasts, but if you are on a university campus or in another enterprise that runs one, this may be a viable option for you. And while no Podcast Producer hosting services have popped up as yet to fill this potential market niche, in the near future, you may find Podcast Producer services for hire on the Internet—maybe even for *free!*

Signing Off

The last part of podcast planning involves writing or rehearsing your close, or sign-off. During this part of the session, you should remind your audience of who you are and what your subject matter is, where they can find more of it, and perhaps mention your sponsor (if you have one). Your sign-off is perhaps the most important part of your podcast, because it is the last thing your listeners will hear each time they listen to you, and through repetition, it establishes your auditory brand identity. For a great example of a consistent sign-off, listen to podcasts from Talk of the Nation Science Friday (http://sciencefriday.com).

Editing

You will need to edit your podcast somewhat. In most software packages—even the free ones that came with your computer or that you downloaded from the Internet—it's as easy as copying, cutting, pasting, and deleting. At the very minimum, you will need to delete the dead air at the beginning and end of your recording; and in most cases, you will want to paste together the music and verbal intro and your sign-off content.

Most audio editing programs include basic editing tools such as the ability to cut segments, mix tracks, convert formats, and split tracks (see Figure 10.2). Some incorporate advanced tools like automatic gain controls and recording volume sliders. Many programs also feature a variety of filters and effects such as reverb (discussed in the following "Special Effects" section). This all might sound a little daunting at first, but after playing with the software for a mere 30 minutes, you might consider yourself an expert.

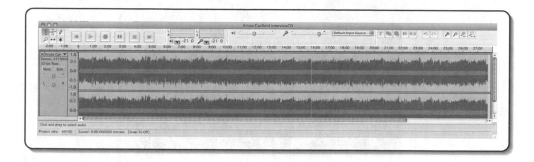

FIGURE 10.2 Audacity Sound Editing Software

Publishing

The final step in podcasting is publishing. Because of podcasting's growing popularity, a lot of new software now has podcast publishing wizards built right in. This software fully automates your podcast tags or keywords (see Chapter 19, Spotlight on Search (Search Engine Optimization) for more information on keywords), and RSS feed creation (see Chapter 18, RSS—Really Simple Syndication Made Simple). You simply click to publish, and you're immediately able to share your material. Podcasts are meant to be shared; the more people who share your podcasts, the more people who are sharing your thoughts and ideas—and the bigger the following you will have.

Liberated Syndication (www.Libsyn.com) is one of the largest media-hosting providers that podcasters use. For less than $10 a month, they'll give you all the bandwidth you need regardless of how popular your show becomes. Some people host their podcasts on their own server and have plug-ins to play the podcast directly from the web page, while most others upload it to podcast web sites—such as PodBean and iTunes (RSS)—where it is easily syndicated.

Special Effects

Special effects, properly used, can enhance your podcasts. By adding a little creativity and a special effect here and there, you can keep your content exciting and entertaining.

If your software has features that allow you to do so, you should first boost your volume and your bass. Most microphones—especially the inexpensive built-in types—can make your recording sound shallow and tinny.

FIGURE 10.3   Levelator

Boosting the volume and bass will add fullness and fidelity to your recording. Another (free!) piece of audio editing software called the Levelator does all that boosting for you automatically (see Figure 10.3).

Software

Podcast recording and editing programs include: GarageBand, Quicktime Player, WordPress PodPress Widget, Sound Studio, Soundtrack Pro, Audacity, Evoca, ePodcast Creator, Gabcast, Hipcast, Odeo Studio, Phone Blogz, Podcast Station, Propagan, WebPod Studio, and others. This may sound like a lot to think about, but remember, you only need one. Install a few editing applications, try them, and then stick with the one you like the best. It's that simple.

FIGURE 10.4   Digital Recorder

Hardware

Hardware can include your computer and accompanying microphone, desktop stand or lapel microphones, recording decks and mixers, telephone recorder interfaces (for recording directly off the telephone), headsets, and digital recorders. A $49 Overstock.com digital recorder was a great purchase. It is approximately one-half by one-half by four inches, fits in a breast pocket, works with a lavaliere or lapel microphone, and will record up to 12 hours of continuous stereo digital audio (see Figure 10.4). Whenever making a new or unique presentation, on it goes—and a podcast is recorded without any effort. All that's left to do is add the intro and the sign-off, and it's ready to go!

Web Sites and Podcast Distributors

You can find a variety of different types of podcasts on the Internet today on a variety of topics that range from subject-specific, to informative and educational, to entertaining, to commercial, to the occasional rant.

Podcasts are everywhere. When the term *podcast* is googled, almost 93 million results are returned for sites like PodCast.com, Digg, MSNBC, CNN, Yahoo!, *New York Times*, PodcastAlley, NPR (National Public Radio), PodBean, Grid7, iTunes, iTunes University, Scientific American, NASA, and CBS News.

For some great examples of podcasts and amazing content from 50 of the social media industry's founders, CEOs, and vice presidents, go to www .theSocialMediaBible.com menu item Insights.

Providers

Most of the tools that will help you create killer podcasts are free, and many even came out of the box with your PC. The first thing to do is to check your computer to see what types of audio recording and editing software were included. If you're not satisfied with what you have, go to www.theSocial MediaBible.com to download the free software for Audacity. Audacity is great for adding your intro or music bumper at the start and finish—and it's free.

The Levelator (available from www.conversationsnetwork.org/levelator) is a drag-and-drop software application that performs audio normalization— leveling out the volume of two people talking. This feature is very useful, since one person is usually a little closer to the microphone, or at the other end of the telephone. Other software applications include GarageBand, Quicktime Player, WordPress PodPress Widget, Sound Studio, Soundtrack Pro, Evoca, ePodcast Creator, Gabcast, Hipcast, Odeo Studio, Phone Blogz, Podcast Station, Propagan, and WebPod Studio.

A store like Radio Shack is a great resource for inexpensive hardware that allows you to connect a digital recorder to your telephone. When recording podcasts, you can use a portable office telephone or a cell phone from anywhere in the world. Plug in a $25 interface, an $8 earphone and mike, and a $60 digital recorder, and you're set to go with high-quality audio recording—everything you need to create professional podcasts for under

$100. In fact, while editing this chapter, the author recorded an interview with Kyle Ford, the director of product marketing for Ning, while surrounded by pine trees in a cabin in the mountains of northern Arizona.

The ROI of Social Media

Crisis Overnight: How We Raised 160K+ in Three Weeks with Social Media

Background

In early 2009, a beloved and trusted crisis community center helping hundreds of abused individuals in Elgin, Illinois, was in desperate economic straights. The center had completely exhausted its monetary resources and was waiting for a drawn-out decision from state lawmakers to approve a budget and release necessary funding.

Approximately three weeks before the center's funding and cash-on-hand was officially drained, the center's leadership made a desperate plea for help. They acknowledged a brutal fact—they might have to close their doors July 1, 2009.

Albeit impromptu, the right people came together at the right time, and the Crisis Center board and executive director trusted us to try something new. The decision to integrate social media and share the center's story publicly was agreed to unanimously.

Strategy

The idea for Crisis Overnight was born. In addition to traditional fund-raising efforts, an overnight awareness campaign would be held at the center, documented through social media with the call-to-action to encourage people to donate.

We had four days to develop a plan, create a donor web site, craft our messaging, and implement.

The truth of the situation became the primary messaging of the campaign: "The goal is simple. We raise $150,000 by July 1 and the Community Crisis Center stays open. We don't, and they close." However, because social media was an integrated part of the outreach, it meant reaching more than just a local constituency. The team developed separate messaging and tactics for the local community, and a broader message was used to appeal to a national audience who could relate to the causes of domestic violence, economic issues, and sexual assault.

Implementation

To communicate socially with the local community and world, we used the center's LinkedIn profile and amped up their social media toolbox by creating a blog, a Twitter account, and social bookmarking accounts.

Nevertheless, developing a community and building credibility via social media platforms takes time—something that was not available. To maximize the center's online visibility, I donated my entire online presence, a platform of more than 40,000 followers.

The online communities we used during the campaign included Twitter, Facebook, Seesmic, PRsarahevans.com, YouTube, and CrisisOvernight.org.

The campaign began as a one-night event and expanded into a three-week campaign, securing continuous donations, both in person and online. All online donors were populated on the Crisis Overnight Web site with their city and state to visually convey that people across the United States were fighting for one community's crisis center.

Opportunity

The opportunity was to generate local and national awareness of the crisis center's story, which would drive funding so that the institution could continue to support the abused individuals in the community.

Conclusion

As of July 30, 2009, all efforts related to Crisis Overnight raised $161,000, buying the center one month of payroll and the ability to pay off end-of-the-year bills.

Sarah Evans (@prsarahevans)
http://prsarahevans.com

Expert Insight

Evo Terra, coauthor, *Podcasting For Dummies*, www.podiobooks.com

Eva Terra

Well, there is a lot of information out there about starting a podcast, and the most common word that is given out is, "Just start, and figure it out as you go along." And that isn't bad advice for some hobbyist that just wants to play in the media. But for businesspeople—and for those who really want to get in to make a splash—I suggest they take a different route.

(continued)

(continued)

The very first thing I would suggest to people interested in podcasting is: do your homework. You know, find out if there are other people in the space that you are getting into. Most businesspeople are not going to say, "I want to open up an ice cream stand," without having some understanding of the ice cream market. You have to know what you are getting yourself into, even if you have no idea how to run an ice cream stand; you can, at least, know what the business is.

The same thing goes for podcasting. You can figure out what the competition is doing, if you want to think about it as competition. I don't. I use the word because we all understand it. But [you have to] at least understand what is competing with the topic of your podcast for people's time; and the other sorts of media that are doing the same thing, just not in a podcast form. Whether that's radio, or whether it's an audio book, you know, understand what your listeners are likely to want to listen to. Do your diligence. . . .

I could go on for days on what *not* to do. As I am often reminded myself, you know, there is no one right way to do things; but there are lots of wrong ways. There are lots of tip and advice books out there that will give you some suggestions; but one of the things I think I would caution people about is that, since we're talking about this user-generated content of podcasting, amateur people who have not had a lot of experience using the tools are getting into the space.

There are a lot of people out there advising that it's the content that's the most important, and I don't disagree with them. Content is *king*. You have to have something that is worth talking about and that is interesting to people. However, I think that oftentimes, this comes at the expense of quality. In fact, I have heard more than one person suggest that you ought to not worry about the quality of the show, because it's content that matters; and then discuss other reasons why quality does not matter. And I just . . . I have to disagree! And I have to disagree for one reason. I know how easy it is to make your podcast sound professional.

There are quite a few tools out there. I recommend that anyone starting out new in podcasting does not go out and spend crazy amounts of dollars. In fact, you should spend as little as possible. Download Audacity. It is a free software audio recording program. It works on both PCs and Macintosh systems, and it is, what I would estimate, 50 percent of [what] the podcasters still use today. I still use Audacity. It's free and it's simple and it does just about everything you are going to want to do at your level.

Now, if you're an audio engineer—then that's a different situation. You will want a different tool set from that; but Audacity is wonderful.

Let's see . . . that's your number one tool to do most of your work. There's another piece of equipment that I like to use called The Levelator. It is free software that you run your spoken-word audio through, and it magically (I don't mind using the word, because I have seen this tool work and I use it every day myself) brings up your audio level to a fantastic level. It is not a perfect tool; and there are plenty of engineers who don't like to use it. But my recommendation to all new people and all podcasters today is . . . if you are not using The Levelator and you don't have a good excuse why you're not using The Levelator . . . then you should be using The Levelator. It is amazing what it can do to your sound. . . .

Now there are some specialty tools which come into play if you want to record telephone conversations. Or maybe you want to buy a library of prelicensed music, so that you don't sound like everybody else discovering the free stuff. There are those investments to make. But if it is your first time doing it . . . don't! Don't invest any additional money. Your computer most likely already has set up what you need to do to get started, even with a cheap, $5 microphone that it came with. I know many people that started out that way, but once they figured out what they wanted to do, [they] eventually graduate to bigger and better equipment. But start off with spending next to nothing. . . .

You know, quality has become very important—even though people don't recognize or realize it. I think one thing that's becoming easier to discern from the podcast listeners—as they have matured over the last four years—is the issue of authenticity. And I think you may be right [about sounding *too* good]. Early on in the process, if something sounded really slick and polished, you started wondering, "What's the underlying agenda? What corporate underwriting sponsorship is happening here?"

But I think consumers are becoming a lot more educated in that now. They're a little more sophisticated, and they are really able to get down to the message. If your goal is to try and sound like the guy who does the ten o'clock news, then that's going to fail miserably. You know why? That's a terrible delivery. They have to do that in a certain way because they have a certain amount of time to get to people before they get to bed, and they drag you along and put the weather at the end. . . .

To listen to or read the entire Executive Conversation with Evo Terra, go to www .theSocial MediaBible.com or www.podiobooks.com.

Commandments

1. **Thou shalt podcast.**

   Go forth and podcast, often. Go and be creative! It's easy and free! Just try it. You will surprise yourself how good you are.

2. **Thou shalt not covet thy neighbor's copyrights.**

   Be careful not to take or use something that belongs to someone else. Creating a five-second song is really easy. There are even royalty-free sound bites and music you can use called "pod-safe" music.

3. **Thou shalt experience sound editing.**

   Sound editing sounds scary, but it is really easier than you think. Many good editing software packages either come free with your computer or can easily be downloaded from the Internet.

4. **Thou shalt not spend a lot of money.**

   Unless you really want to get into podcasting, don't spend a lot of money doing it. Remember in this one case that "good enough" might actually be *good enough*.

5. **Thou shalt RSS feed your podcasts.**

   By RSS feeding your podcasts, you are making them available to literally millions of potential listeners. You can learn more about RSS (Really Simple Syndication) in Chapter 18, RSS—Really Simple Syndication Made Simple.

6. **Thou shalt upload your podcasts to iTunes.**

   Be sure to upload your podcasts to iTunes. Tens of millions of people search iTunes every day looking for content that might be similar to yours. Be sure to follow their guidelines to ensure your podcast's success. And keep in mind that if your podcast falls under the "educational" category, you should upload it to the iTunes "iUniversity."

7. **Thou shalt keep your podcasts brief.**

   Most people only have about a seven-minute attention span for audio. Taking any more time than that will lose your listeners' interest. If you have a 30-minute interview or a 45-minute panel discussion, leave it at length. If your audio file can be broken into five- to seven-minute chapters, topics, or ideas, then break it up.

8. **Thou shalt produce in the right file format.**

   Be sure that when you link or upload your podcasts, they are in a usable file format. While QuickTime is great for Macintosh users to play, Windows and PowerPoint users have difficulties with it. Most people want your content in an MP3 format so that it is compatible with their digital music players.

9. **Thou shalt be conscious of file size.**

    While you may have a lot to say, a 53MB file is just too large for most people to download and install on their digital players. Most tunes run at about 3.5MB each, so try to keep your finished files in the single-digit MB range.

10. **Thou shalt be creative.**

    This, again, is the most important commandment. The more creative you are and the more "What's in It for Me?" you provide for your listener, the more people will download it, listen to it, pass it along to their friends, recommend it, and comment on it; and the more loyal listeners and followers and trusted network you will build. Remember to ask your customers to be collaborators of your content.

Conclusion

As long as your podcasts have a strong WIIFM, your listeners will keep coming back for more. The more you podcast, the more quality content and contributions you will provide to your followers, listeners, and customers. Keep podcasting, because it helps to build your trusted network; your customers and followers will perceive you as an industry and subject-matter expert; and when it's time to buy, you will be the one they think of first. It's free, it's easy, it's fun—so do it!

To hear all of the Expert Interviews, go to www.theSocialMediaBible .com.

Readings and Resources

Bove, Tony, and Cheryl Rhodes. *iPod & iTunes For Dummies*, 4th ed. (Hoboken, NJ: John Wiley & Sons, Inc.)

Cochrane, Todd. *Podcasting: Do-It-Yourself Guide*. (Hoboken, NJ: John Wiley & Sons, Inc.)

Frazer, J. D. *Money for Content and Your Clicks for Free: Turning Web Sites, Blogs, and Podcasts into Cash*. (Hoboken, NJ: John Wiley & Sons, Inc.)

Ihnatko, Andy. *iPod Fully Loaded: If You've Got It, You Can iPod It*. (Hoboken, NJ: John Wiley & Sons, Inc.)

Islam, Kaliym A. *Podcasting 101 for Training and Development: Challenges, Opportunities, and Solutions*. (Hoboken, NJ: John Wiley & Sons, Inc.)

Morris, Tee, Evo Terra, and Dawn Miceli. *Podcasting For Dummies*. (Hoboken, NJ: John Wiley & Sons, Inc.)

Morris, Tee, Chuck Tomasi, Evo Terra, and Kreg Steppe. *Podcasting For Dummies*, 2nd ed. (Hoboken, NJ: John Wiley & Sons, Inc.)

Morris, Tee, Evo Terra, and Ryan Williams. *Expert Podcasting Practices For Dummies*. (Hoboken, NJ: John Wiley & Sons, Inc.)

Ratcliffe, Mitch, and Steve Mack. *Podcasting Bible*. (Hoboken, NJ: John Wiley & Sons, Inc.)

Reeder, Joelle, and Katherine Scoleri. *The IT Girl's Guide to Blogging with Moxie*. (Hoboken, NJ: John Wiley & Sons, Inc.)

Scott, David Meerman. *The New Rules of Marketing and PR: How to Use News Releases, Blogs, Podcasting, Viral Marketing and Online Media to Reach Buyers Directly*. (Hoboken, NJ: John Wiley & Sons, Inc.)

Downloads

For your free downloads associated with *The Social Media Bible*, go to www .theSocialMediaBible.com, and enter your ISBN number located on the back of the book above the bar code. Be sure to enter the dashes.

Credits

The ROI of Social Media was provided by:

Sarah Evans (@prsarahevans), http://prsarahevans.com

Expert Insight was provided by:

Evo Terra, author, *Podcasting For Dummies*, www.podiobooks.com

Technical edits were provided by:

Evo Terra, author, *Podcasting For Dummies*, www.podiobooks.com

Stephen Farrington, owner, OpusWorks Studio,www.stephenfarrington.com

CHAPTER 11

Got Audio? (Audio Sharing)

What's in It for You?

Today, more than 30 million people subscribe to podcasts, and that number is growing exponentially. Podcasts are essentially a vehicle for the many other types of media that individuals and businesses can use in the realm of social networking. You can add music, digital photos, animated company logos, colorful videos—anything that it takes to get your message across.

Audio is by far the easiest of all rich media to create and share. All of the tools that you need are in your computer already, and those that aren't are available for free from the Internet. You probably already have a built-in microphone and the recording software (see Chapter 10, Talking about the Podcast (Audio Create)) in your PC. While audio isn't as appealing as video, it is a lot easier to record, edit, and share, so the trade-off between convenience and high-tech appearance is well worth it. Also, audio files make for a quicker download than video, and listeners can safely tune in to your content while driving or working out.

No one is an expert on everything, and when it comes to social media, it's hard to be an expert at all because the industry is simply changing faster than most people can keep up with. There are, however, a great number of people ahead of the pack, and hearing *their* insights is important. That's why this book and the associated web site present the collected wisdom of nearly 50 founders, CEOs, authors, and experts in the social media field. (See the many impressive and detailed Executive Conversations at www.theSocialMedia Bible.com.)

How does this apply to you and your business? Ask your customers and prospects what they would like to hear from you. The first step is to create some audio podcasts (see Chapter 10, Talking about the Podcast (Audio Create)) and share them. While *The Social Media Bible* is not intended to be a how-to book, an important topic is the basics of sharing audio. This chapter discusses two prime examples: iTunes and Podbean.

Back to the Beginning

Many of the "Back to the Beginning" sections in these chapters—such as networking, blogging, photo sharing, and e-mail—begin the same way. File sharing, for example, goes back to the original ARPAnet and UseNet, and audio is the same. As soon as a network became established, people began sharing the many different kinds of files that they had—text, photos, images, video, and audio. Most of these "Back to the Beginning" sections are the longest ones in each chapter. But since there is little new material to report on audio sharing that hasn't already been covered in another chapter, the focus here is on some of the tools that have made audio sharing such an easy and successful approach to business promotion (see the previous chapter's "Back to the Beginning" for more information on the history of audio creation and sharing).

What You Need to Know

Every single day, your customers, prospects, and employees are inundated with information from e-mail, voicemails, junk mail, and memos. The important question for you to ask is: How do you get your important messages across to them in a way that doesn't get lost in all of that noise? The answer is podcasts.

As explained earlier in the book, a *podcast* is an audio or video recording that a person can subscribe to, receive, download, listen to, or watch using a personal computer, iPod or iPhone, or other mobile device. Your customers and prospects can therefore listen to or watch this information whenever and wherever they wish—in their cars, during lunch, in the evening, at the office, at the gym, while jogging, or even on their day off.

A podcast is similar to a television program or radio show, but easier to create and distribute, and it's free to do so. The process of audio sharing requires that you first create an audio file, and then make it known and available. Chapter 10, Talking about the Podcast (Audio Create) describes in detail how to create an audio file podcast, while this chapter focuses more heavily on the process of sharing it with others. A great book to help with this topic is Tee Morris and Evo Terra's *Podcasting For Dummies*. For extremely helpful step-by-step instructions on how to publish your podcast using iTunes, go to www.mvldesign.com/itunespodcast.html.

Let's begin by discussing iTunes, the most popular audio and video solution for downloading, playing, aggregating, and publishing your podcasts.

iTunes

Apple Computer developed iTunes for both the Macintosh and Windows operating platforms and released it on January 9, 2001, at the Macworld Expo in San Francisco. iTunes is used for playing, organizing, downloading, and publishing audio and video files, and now iPhone, iPod, and iPad apps, through your desktop, laptop, mobile phone, and, of course, your iPod, iPad, or iPhone. iTunes enables users to connect to the iTunes Store through the Internet, where they can purchase and download music, music videos, television shows, iPod and iPad games, audio books, various podcasts, feature-length films, movie rentals, and ringtones. iTunes is available as a free download for Mac OS X, Windows 7, Windows Vista, and Windows XP from Apple's web site (Apple.com). iTunes also comes bundled with all Macs, and some HP and Dell computers, and can be accessed directly from iPhone and iPod Touch (through a Wi-Fi connection).

The original media player software that was iTunes's predecessor was developed in 1999 by Casady & Greene, a software publisher of shareware products, created primarily for the Macintosh and called SoundJam MP. Original developers Jeff Robbin and Bill Kincaid sold SoundJam to Apple in 2000, which gave it a facelift and the ability to burn CDs, and re-released it in January 2001 with its new name: iTunes. iTunes was available only for the Macintosh line of computers until March 2007, when Apple released its Windows version. iTunes 64-bit versions for Windows became available on January 16, 2008.

On September 9, 2008, Apple CEO Steve Jobs reported the following iTunes downloads and product statistics. In July 2008, Apple's iPod had 73.4 percent of the U.S. MP3 player market share. SanDisk had 8.6 percent, Microsoft had 2.6 percent, and 15.4 percent was distributed between all other brands of MP3 players. iTunes was the largest music distributor in the United States, topping big-name retail stores like Wal-Mart and Best Buy. iTunes had more than 8.5 million songs, 125,000 podcasts, 30,000 TV show episodes, and 2,600 Hollywood movies. Jobs also announced that the iTunes Store had sold over five billion songs, and set a new single-day record of more than 20 million song downloads on December 25, 2007. He informed potential users that the iTunes Store's movies for rent included content from industry giants 20th Century Fox, Warner Brothers, Walt Disney Pictures, Paramount Pictures, Universal Studios, and Sony Pictures Entertainment. Renting a standard-definition movie costs $2.99, while new releases cost $3.99. High-definition titles cost $1 more each, and these movies also work on all sixth-generation iPods.

Three thousand applications for the iPhone and iPod later: By April 2009, Apple's iTunes App Store had provided more than one billion downloads of

FIGURE 11.1 iTunes

apps and currently offers more than 160,000 titles. Ninety percent of the apps[1] are priced at less than $10, and thousands are available for free.

As an example of the astonishing apps available for the Apple iPhone, during a family dinner at the author's home, a song came over the radio that everyone liked but no one could identify. One member of the family stood up from the dinner table and held his iPhone up to the speaker for 10 seconds.

---

1. Applications, or apps, are small software applications that are designed to be installed in mobile telephones to increase the phone's utility and for fun. Applications include: Multi-Touch interface, accelerometer, GPS, real-time 3-D graphics, 3-D positional audio, Google Mobile Search, Maps, Gmail, YouTube, and hundreds more.

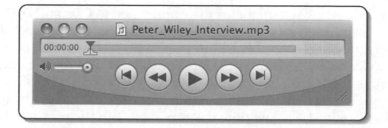

FIGURE 11.2 QuickTime Audio

The phone beeped, and the display showed the name of the song, the artist, and the album.

iTunes users can manage audio and video files on their personal PC, which is required for iPod operation and synchronization. Within the iTunes application, the user can engage in a variety of activities: Create playlists, edit file information, record CDs, copy files to digital audio or video players, purchase audio and video files from the iTunes Store, download free music

FIGURE 11.3 QuickTime Video

and audio podcasts, back up their music and video to CDs and DVDs, display a visualizer graphic effects screen, encode digital files in a myriad of formats, listen to any of a larger number of Internet radio stations, and publish audio files and podcasts to the iTunes Store. iTunes organizes music and video by creating virtual libraries wherein it stores and keeps track of each song's attributes such as artist, genre, album information and cover art, lyrics, how often it's been played, the last time it was played, and the personal rating that users can give it. iTunes users can view their music libraries in one of four ways; as a list of songs by title; by the music's cover artwork; in an application called Cover Flow, which is an Apple-style slide scrolling catalog of artwork; or a Grid View of the iTunes library that can sort music by artist, by album, and album by year.

iTunes can also rip or copy music from CDs, but not DVDs. Certain movie studios introduced iTunes Digital Copy in 2008—a bonus feature that is available on some DVDs, which provides an iTunes-compatible file for select films for otherwise copy-protected material.

iTunes can currently read, write, and convert between several types of files—including MP3, .aiff, .wav, MPEG-4, AAC, and Apple Lossless.

The application can also play any audio file and most video formats that QuickTime can play. QuickTime is a free application developed by Apple for both the Windows and Apple platform that allows the user to create and play videos in full screen, create movies for iPod, and download movies from the web. The $29.99 Pro version of QuickTime includes audio processing features such as equalization, sound enhancement, cross fade, and Sound Check, which automatically adjusts the playback volume of all songs to the same level. iTunes can produce static, party, and new Smart[2] playlists that can be played randomly or sequentially.

iTunes 4.8 added a video application on May 9, 2005. Users could choose to view movies in a small frame in the main iTunes display, in a separate window, or in full screen mode. On October 12, 2005, iTunes offered the ability to purchase and view video content from the iTunes Music Store. Video podcasts—or Vodcasts—and other downloadable video files are available in .mov, MP4, M4V, and .mpg formats.

On June 28, 2005, Apple announced that iTunes 4.9 would have built-in support for podcasting, which would allow its users to subscribe to podcasts for free in the iTunes Music Store or by entering the RSS feed URL. Once a

---

2. Smart playlists can be set to automatically filter your music library based on a customized list of selection criteria, similar to a database query. Apple recently introduced the Genius Feature as well, a tool that automatically generates a playlist of 25, 50, 75, or 100 songs from the user's library that are similar to a selected song.

user subscribes, any new podcasts would be automatically downloaded hourly, daily, or weekly, or manually. Users can listen to podcasts directly from the Podcast Directory, which is an index of user-generated content from commercial and independent podcasters. They can also browse podcasts based on their popularity, and even publish their own material through the iTunes Store. When this podcasting feature was added to such a mainstream and widely used application like iTunes, many podcasters reported that the number of downloads of their podcasts had tripled—and even quadrupled.

iTunes is now up to version 9.1 and has added the availability of CD song lyrics, liner notes, and photos, sharing of media libraries within a home network, movie special features, and has store categories dedicated specifically to Podcasts, Audio Books, Applications, Ringtones, Radio, TV Shows, Music, Movies, and iTunes U (educational podcast content).

Because iTunes takes full advantage of podcasts' RSS features—in other words, its role as a podcatching client—iTunes is now considered to be one of the best in its class of any of the other web sites that provide downloadable audio and video. iTunes has been rated higher than the audio file multiplatform distribution software Juice and Windows Doppler, and is superior to other podcatching web sites Amarok, Winamp, and MediaMonkey. iTunes is also closely integrated with Apple's iWork and iLife software packages—applications that directly interface with the iTunes Library and access the user's songs stored within iTunes. iTunes allows music files to be embedded directly into iWeb (Apple's web design software), Pages (Apple's word processing software); iMovie, which allows you to create and mix movies from video, music, and photographs; iDVD, which allows you to take those movies and create your own; Keynote (Apple's version of PowerPoint); and any song created and exported from GarageBand, Apple's music- and podcast-creating program. Any of these files are automatically added to the user's iTunes music library.

Ever since the first version of iTunes—aptly titled 1.0—Apple gave its users Internet radio service access to the most popular streaming radio available. As of February 2008, iTunes Radio provided users with access to nearly 1,800 streaming MP3-format Internet radio stations. These stations make up every genre from music to sports to talk radio to more traditional radio stations as well. Unfortunately, Apple's newer version of iTunes no longer directly supports the Internet radio feature. However, users can enter their own stream feed to listen under the Radio tab by selecting the menu option Advanced, then Open Stream. QuickTime, on the other hand, does support Internet radio, and you can find iTunes plug-ins from iRadioMast (www.iradiomast.com).

Now that you've read about the largest music sharing, upload, and download web service in the world, let's discuss another web site called Podbean—one that hosts, syndicates, and distributes your uploaded audio files for free.

Podbean

Podbean (www.podbean.com, Figures 11.4 and 11.5) opened in July 2006, providing podcast publishing tools for users to begin creating professional-caliber podcasts. Podbean allows them to do so in a very short amount of time, with an easy point-and-click, bloglike environment—and requires no

FIGURE 11.4 Podbean

FIGURE 11.5   Podbean Skin

technical knowledge. The web site gives users the chance to manage, publish, and promote podcasts with just a few clicks. Most importantly, Podbean hosts and serves up the actual media file that is your podcast's audio content (iTunes merely catalogs your podcasts—you still need to store them somewhere from which they can be downloaded). Podbean is used by a wide variety of podcasters—from education, religion, real estate, music, sports clubs, travel agents, government agencies, hobbyists, and entrepreneurs, to larger corporations.

Signing up for a Podbean account grants users a personalized podcast web site with one's own URL for banding. Users can even select themes or "skins" (see Figure 11.5) with different colors, fonts, and layout for their pages. Podbean also provides users with web site traffic reporting and analysis tools, so that they are able to measure their podcasts' success and know exactly how they're performing. Podbean provides an in-depth, multidimensional view of a site's visitors, subscribers, hits, and geographic location distribution, and even lets users download these data.

All of the Podbean pages have full RSS feed generation for RSS2, iTunes, and ATOM integrated right in. Podbean supports RSS 2.0 and ATOM feeds (see Chapter 18), as well as the extended Apple iTunes podcasting tags. Podbean also provides a Web 2.0–based podcast player that can be embedded directly into your web site, blog site, and other social networks. The more podcasts you create—and the more popular your podcasts become—the more regularly your files will be downloaded, the more storage and bandwidth you will require (see Chapter 12, Watch Out for Vlogs (Video Create), for more information on bandwidth). But no matter how popular your podcasts become, Podbean provides the storage and bandwidth you need for free. It also allows users to earn revenue through advertising, paid subscription, and merchandise sales. In fact, Podbean has a full-function online e-commerce tool provided to users for free.

Most of the social media tools covered in this book work on the free-mium business model—meaning that most of the service that the providers give to individual users is done completely free of charge, while enterprises or premium users pay a modest fee for additional services.

Providers

A list of podcasting, podcatching, and audio and music distribution sites appears here. iTunes is the largest for buying music and downloading audio podcasts, and Podbean is the podcast hosting and publishing web site. Visit the other web sites to find specific content and services that are designed for the creation and distribution of audio podcasts.

www.iTunes.com
www.Podbean.com
www.digitalpodcast.com
www.podcasting.net
www.ipodderx.com

www.penguinradio.com/podcasting

www.feed-directory.com

www.podcast411.com

www.sportpodcasts.com

www.podcastalley.com

www.podcastpickle.com

www.podcastingnews.com

www.podcasting-station.com

www.podrazor.com

www.podcasthost.com

www.juicereceiver.sourceforge.net

www.dopplerradio.net

www.amarok.kde.org

www.winamp.com

www.mediamonkey.com

www.tdscripts.com/webmaster_utilities/podcast-generator.php (podcast RSS feed generator)

www.softwaregarden.com/products/listgarden/index.html (software list garden)

The ROI of Social Media

Social Media in Focus

Introduction

Nicole Walker Photography is a small family portrait photography start-up based in Glendale, Arizona, that focuses on providing high-quality portraits to families that cannot afford to pay high studio prices.

Background

We consciously chose to leverage the power of Social Media to quickly create awareness to a targeted customer base without investing a significant amount of working capital on marketing-related expenses.

In an industry that is extremely competitive and with hundreds of direct competitors in a very small space, we needed to find a way to differentiate

(continued)

(*continued*)

ourselves and consistently keep the brand active and relevant in the eyes of consumers.

Strategy

Our strategy was to be active in a space where our customers already were. Our primary target consumer group is 21- to 40-year-old mothers and mothers-to-be within 25 miles of Glendale, Arizona. Many social media platforms allow for this specific level of search and filtering capability so we could easily create introductions, become visible, and interact with existing and potential customers.

Instead of being in constant sell mode, we chose to share our photos, start discussions, create content, and exchange ideas that add value to our communities of target customers that they would feel compelled to participate in and pass along to their friends and family.

Implementation

We created a blog using Blogger [a Google-owned blogging tool], as well as branded pages on Facebook, MySpace, and CafeMom. We have found that these are the spaces in which our target customers regularly interact with friends and family, and inserting ourselves into their daily interactions was extremely simple.

Opportunity

The opportunity is to showcase our talent to thousands of mothers and mothers-to-be by attaching the samples from each of our recent sessions to our various social media pages while discussing parenting and other family issues with a community of like-minded individuals.

Conclusion

Since launching our social media pages, we have generated thousands of unique visits to our web site with little push or hard selling. We have seen a consistent doubling to tripling month-over-month in new unique visitors (1360 percent total increase in the past 10 months). For many of our key search terms we are now found within the first five pages of Google, Yahoo!, and Bing. Additionally, we have improved our advanced booking pipeline from one to two weeks to two-plus months (even the slow summer season).

Chris Walker
www.NicoleWalkerPhotography.com

Expert Insight

Alan Levy, founder and CEO, BlogTalkRadio, www.blogtalkradio.com

Alan Levy

Well, we have two parts of the network. The main network is the network which we launched in October two-thousand six, which we launched from scratch. I mean, we created this idea. . . . I came up with the name, *BlogTalkRadio*. We had no content. We invented this technology which, essentially, incorporates using the phone, or any kind of phone, into the Web. And to date we've broadcasted about one hundred and ten thousand segments . . . maybe about a hundred and fifteen thousand. Each day, we broadcast five hundred new live shows. You can see them all at BlogTalkRadio .com. They all appear here in our programming guides.

We have had everyone on the network, from John McCain, who has been on three times, to Yoko Ono, Brad Pitt, Brian DePalma, Salman Rushdie, famous authors, actors, and of course, thousands and thousands of bloggers. Anybody, really, who is looking to communicate a message and promote an idea or promote a book can come on *BlogTalkRadio* for free. All they have to do is create a profile, set up a show on when they would like to broadcast, and they can dial in and be "on air" in a matter of minutes. . . .

We found that . . . I'm either very crazy or very smart; I don't know which one yet, but we realized that a lot of people that had been coming on *BlogTalk-Radio* were being asked to pay hundreds, if not thousands of dollars to have their own radio show. And we figured out a way to keep it at a very low-cost point by using the phone. That's my background, in phone technology. And by doing that, we are able to provide the service for free. And I think that when you create a platform that is open and available, you look into democratizing the medium, much like blogging did for bloggers and tech space communication.

BlogTalkRadio is doing the same for audio and, soon-to-be, video. . . .

Yeah, we are very pleased with the quality. You know, when I first came up with the idea, the podcasting . . . and this is, you know, podcasting was something that I really did not know much about . . . I did not set out to create or become another podcasting company. I set up BlogTalkRadio because I created a blog for my dad, who was ill with lymphoma and cancer, and I wanted to . . . and I learned about blogs, and I realized that there were seventy-five to eighty million of them. And everyone's talking about "conversation," and I could not hear any. So I created it. We created a platform that allows live, interactive conversation using the phone, of course, as I mentioned . . . and we achieve it. That's the easy part of it.

(continued)

(*continued*)

So, for us, I do think we're more like a broadcast medium as an alternative. If you look at our audience, the guests that are on, [there is] such diversity. It is incredible the type of content, and then it's archived for the long run, which we can then modify. . . .

We did build it from scratch, so we are . . . we have people looking at the site and our own internal customer service people and feature editors, and the like, and very often . . . you know . . . we'll get an e-mail from one of the hosts and it will say, "You know, we've got to call the FCC." And we say, "Fine, call the FCC."

I mean, they have no mandate here. This is a collection of conversations and it's all . . . it's monitored, it's run by us on our site. So there is no FCC. There is . . . but we do ensure that the quality is good, and we double up the best content, and the platform is not being used to facilitate hate or conversations like that, for example. . . .

Yeah, well, it is self-policing also, in a sense, because the hosts know that when they come on this network . . . they sign a form and they're responsible for content, and there's clearly terms and conditions; things they can and cannot do. And if they're in breach of those terms and conditions, I mean, they'll get a warning. But then, they'll be removed from the network. And there are no other places for them to go. . . .

So, you know, they're not going to go to Podcast, or they're not going to go to a podcasting platform because they don't even know how to create this podcast. We take care of everything from the broadcast, the live interaction, all the way through iTunes and the RSS feed. So, it is self-policing, and it's very exciting to see it grow and evolve. And many times the listeners become hosts. You know, they're getting involved and they say, "Why not! I could do one of these things."

To listen to or read the entire Executive Conversation with Alan Levy, go to www.theSocialMediaBible.com.

Commandments

1. **Thou shalt try iTunes.**

Go to www.Apple.com, and download iTunes for your Mac or Windows platform PC. Try it, even if you don't plan on buying and downloading music. See how the interface works. Refer to the previous chapter on podcasting, create a podcast, and try to upload your new podcast to iTunes. Get in the game. It really is here to stay, and the more you know, the more you can participate.

2. **Thou shalt try a podcast hosting site.**

Try using a podcast-hosting site such as Podbean. It really is easy to use; RSS syndication is just a one-click process, it's compatible with iTunes—and best of all—it's free! Just use your PC's built-in mike (or buy one for $8), open your sound editing software, and record your thoughts on your profession or other subject matter of interest to you. Think about the WIIFM (What's in It for Me?), from your customers' and prospects' point of view. What can you tell them in 10 minutes or less that is important to them? This way, they come away from listening to your podcast message with something of value. If you can give them that, then they will keep coming back, refer you to trusted colleagues, and perceive you as an industry expert. All this builds trust, loyalty, and revenue.

Conclusion

It's truly worth your effort to take some time to understand how easy and effective it is to download audio podcasts and music. You'll find that there is great ROI to uploading your podcasts, so that others are exposed to your professional thoughts, and can respond in kind.

Creating your new podcast is one thing, but making it available to your customers, prospects, and employees is quite another. It doesn't do you any good if you have captured your best ideas on audio but no one gets to hear them. So, share your ideas with the world. Upload your podcasts to iTunes and Podbean, and get your material out there. Embed your podcasts on your web site and blog site. Simply by creating a library of audio files with a great WIIFM content value will allow your customers and prospects to view you as an industry expert.

Consider your own reaction when you type an individual or company name into a search engine like Google, and see page after page of search results return. You immediately know that this person or firm has a widespread presence on the Web. Seeing these dozens of pages of results—including web pages, blog pages, photographs, audio podcasts, and YouTube videos—prompts you to view this party as an industry expert. Now, isn't that how you want your customers and prospects to see *you*?

To hear all of the Expert Interviews, go to www.theSocialMediaBible.com.

Readings and Resources

See Chapter 10, Talking about the Podcast (Audio Create), for readings and resources.

Downloads

For your free downloads associated with *The Social Media Bible*, go to www
.theSocialMediaBible.com, and enter your ISBN number located on the back
of the book above the bar code. Be sure to enter the dashes.

Credits

The ROI of Social Media was provided by:

Chris Walker, www.NicoleWalkerPhotography.com

Expert Insight was provided by:

Alan Levy, founder and CEO, BlogTalkRadio, www.blogtalkradio.com

Technical edits were provided by:

Stephen Farrington, owner, OpusWorks Studio, www.StephenFarrington.com

CHAPTER 12

Watch Out for Vlogs
(Video Create)

The audio podcast chapter mentioned that a video recording can also be considered a podcast since the iPod and other digital playback devices display photographs, audio, and video. This book differentiates audio recordings as a *podcast* and video recordings as just *video* or a *vlog*. As the word *blog* stands for weB LOG, *vlog,* comes from Video web LOG.

What's in It for You?

Human psychology is such that the more robust or stimulating the experience, the more engaging it is, and the better we comprehend and retain that experience. An engaging video also ensures that your viewer will watch it to its conclusion. This is why people often prefer watching a good movie at the end of the day as opposed to reading or even listening to an audio book. The more senses that are involved in gathering information, the more engaging the process becomes. This accounts for the overwhelming popularity of YouTube. Creating video, vlogging, and video posting are all about utilizing this human trait to better educate and communicate with your network and with your customers.

The human being evolved to communicate first through facial expressions, and then through speech. Verbal communication is a relatively new human trait, and the written word is even more recent. Writing can be traced back only a half dozen millennia, while communication using facial expressions and voice tones is the oldest method that any living being has used. Nearly every species on earth that can share information does so in this way.

 theSocialMediaBible.com

When two humans want to express an idea, thought, or concept, 55 percent of the communication comes from body language, 38 percent from voice, and only a mere 7 percent from the words. Letters and e-mails clearly don't contain inflection and body language, which is why writing can be so easily misinterpreted or misconstrued. Watching and listening to someone while he speaks allows us to study facial expressions and tone so as to help build trust and make it easier to recognize when someone isn't being sincere. For this reason, vlogs can be the most effective way to communicate with your customers.

All it takes to create a vlog is a digital video camera, some free editing software, and—most important—*creativity*. Companies such as BMW, Quiznos, and Nabisco are using video to grab huge audiences and increase their market share (see Figure 12.1). Even a blender company can get over a million views of its product video in just 24 hours by using off-the-shelf technology and a little creativity (see the "Will It Blend" example at www .theSocialMediaBible.com).

FIGURE 12.1 YouTube BMW

Back to the Beginning

Shortly after the introduction of the Internet, people were trying to push the limits of this new medium by providing more and more rich media: midi, music, audio, images, virtual reality images (QTVR), and video. The early constraints were CPU speed and bandwidth.

What Is Video?

The technical measure of video content is *frames per second*, which means the number of still images every second. For standard film, the frame rate can be 32 frames (or images) per second, while video frame rates can range from 25 to 30 and even 50 to 60 frames per second for high-definition (HD) video, which means that for a standard video that is running at 25 frames per second, there are 1,500 separate images every minute. Based on the dimensions of the video screen, that can add up to a lot of data per frame (image), and a huge amount of information every minute. Getting all of those data through the earliest 300-baud modem (300 bits per second), or even today's 56K-baud modem (56,000 bits per second) is a monumental task. This is why the earlier videos (and even some today) were small in size, short in length, low resolution, and often ran choppy (less than 32 frames per second) as the Internet tried to serve those data to the user. And as all those data came in, the CPU tried to assemble it into a continuously running, smooth video.

The *bit* is the most fundamental piece of data that a computer or any digital device uses to communicate, store, or display. A bit is a single 0 or 1, which represents either a charge or no charge. These digits of 0 and 1 are why today's electronics are called *digital*. Eight of these digits in a stream make up a single byte. Depending upon the computer, it takes as many as 4 bytes (32 bits) to represent a single pixel on your screen in a specific location—on, off, and color. So, if you have a 350K image, it would be 350,000 bytes (K stands for 1,000 in engineering, creating the term KB for kilobytes). That one image (frame) would consist of 350,000 bytes times 8 bits—or 2.8 million bits of information for a single image. Based on this, a 3-minute video would be 350K bits times 32 frames per second times 3 minutes (180 seconds), or more than 20 billion bits of information!

As the Internet grew, so did *bandwidth,* which is the size of the information conduit and the ability to push more bits through the wire or air—and, consequently, the amount of data that could be displayed. In the early days of the Internet, text was the first type of data because it could be transferred and displayed quickly because of the small number of bits (32 bits per character)

(*continued*)

(*continued*)

involved. A full page of single-spaced text can be as small as 2K (2,000 bytes). A standard color image can be 350K, a 3-minute small-size video can be 20MB (million bytes), and a full-length movie can be more than 4.5GB (4.5 billion bytes)!

With present cable technology, a residential cable Internet connection can provide you with download speeds as high as 4 to 6 Mbps (million bits per second; M stands for million). High-speed cable Internet compared to a 56K dial-up connection can run up to 70 times faster. For an additional fee—and assuming it is available in your area—most major cable providers, such as Cox Communication, Comcast, and Time Warner, also offer premium packages with speeds as high as 8 to 10 Mbps.

Yay for Apple QuickTime!

The first major breakthrough in video for the computer was Apple's release of QuickTime on December 2, 1991. For the first time, users were able to view reasonably good quality color videos on their computers. QuickTime was mostly about compression rate. The less information that needed to be sent out per frame, the more frames that could be transmitted, assembled, and played. Compression is about finding patterns in the data, creating a kind of shorthand for that pattern, and transmitting the shorthand data and rules, which represent much less overall information. Later versions of QuickTime maximized the video file size and allowed users to transmit very small videos through still-restricted bandwidth and play them on slow computers, but it worked!

With greater improvements in compression technology and increasingly faster transfer rates for modems, the video that the Internet was delivering became better and better.

Microsoft also released Windows 3.0 in 1991, along with their version of a video/audio player called Media Player. This eventually became Windows Media Player, which is now the Windows-based computer's standard file format for audio and video files.

The one other player that has had an influence on video players is

FIGURE 12.2 QuickTime

RealVideo. The RealVideo Player was developed by RealNetworks and was first released in 1997 with its own proprietary video format. Even though RealVideo is supported on many platforms—including Windows, Mac, Linux, Solaris, and several mobile phones—QuickTime and Windows Media Player still hold the largest market share.

With small-file-size compressed video available on the computer and distributed over the Internet, it was only a matter of time before people created web sites dedicated to sharing their thoughts through the use of video. On January 1, 2004, Steve Garfield launched his videoblog and announced that 2004 would be the "year of the video blog." In June of that year, Peter Van Dijck and Jay Dedman started the Yahoo! Videoblogging Group, which became the first—and to this day, most popular—community of vloggers.

The year 2004 also saw a growth in people interested in paying for vlogging. They had reached a critical mass and held their first conference the next year. Vloggercon was held in New York City in January 2005, and became the first videoblogger conference of its kind. On July 20, 2005, the Yahoo! Videoblogging Group expanded to more than 1,000 members. One year later, in July 2006, YouTube became the fifth-most-popular web destination, with over 100 million videos viewed, and more than 65,000 new video uploads every day. As of 2010, YouTube's members are uploading 13 hours of video every minute and more than 1 billion video downloads per day!

Bandwidth and Storage

Up until the advent of web sites like YouTube, video distribution was still somewhat of a problem. The video files were larger and longer, and with more and more people watching them, the total amount of data transmitted from one's web site could be quite huge. Most Internet service providers (ISPs) charge by the amount of data served on your behalf from your web site if you exceed a maximum.

Also, downloading all of the data before you watch a video is time consuming and impractical. No one wanted to wait until a file was completely downloaded to start watching a video. As a result, video streaming was introduced. Streaming takes place when the ISP spoon-feeds the data to the computer at a slightly faster rate than is needed, so that the modem downloads the video without interruption while the user begins to watch it. This was an efficient solution for distribution. However, video storage then became a problem. Since videos can be very large in size—and people can have a lot of videos—the amount of disk storage became very expensive.

FIGURE 12.3   YouTube

Along Comes YouTube

You can't discuss video creation without discussing video sharing; after all, it's what you do after you've created your video. (For additional information on sharing content, refer to Chapter 13, Got Video (Video Sharing).) With more people being connected to the Internet with broadband (high-speed transfer rate), such as DSL, Dish, and cable modems, the amount of data a person could download and view became less of an issue. CPUs became much faster, and the cost of disk storage plummeted. Then along came web sites such as Google's YouTube. YouTube, a video sharing web site allows users to upload, view, and share video clips. In February 2005, three former PayPal employees created YouTube. In November 2006, YouTube, LLC, was purchased by Google Inc. for US $1.65 billion and now operates as a subsidiary of Google.

In October 2006, the BBC launched its first official video blogging site for its children's television series *Blue Peter,* with video asking children to name a new puppy character on the show.

Early employees of PayPal Chad Hurley, Steve Chen, and Jawed Karim activated the domain name YouTube.com on February 15, 2005. They developed their web site over the next several months, and YouTube was presented to the public in May 2005.

For more information on video sharing and video examples, please read Chapter 13, Got Video (Video Sharing); and be sure to visit www.theSocialMediaBible.com.

FIGURE 12.4   Jody Gnant—Lifecaster

Lifecasting

Another extreme example of vlogs on steroids comes from Jody Gnant. She has created one of, if not the longest, video documentaries ever. Jody Gnant set up a web cam to her laptop and video streamed her life 24 hours per day for more than nine continuous months. For more information about Jody Gnant and on lifecasting, see Chapter 15, Live from Anywhere—It's Livecasting.

Vlogging is so appealing because it removes geographic boundaries and truly creates a global community through personal interaction. People in the United States are also fortunate to live in a country in which the government does not censor online videos. Because the FCC has opted to keep this information free of suppression (so far!), no restrictions have been placed on its content (except for child pornography).

The U.S. Constitution's First Amendment—related to freedom of expression, speech, and press—applies to this last stronghold of personal expression. Ever since the printed word was created, some faction of society has attempted to censor it—whether it was the church, the government, or just the one paying for the printing. A censor has nearly always monitored and controlled the expression of views on society, politics, religion, and opinions in one form or another. Ever since the FCC was established in 1934, it has regulated everything related to radio and television content, leading up to the advent of cable TV in the 1970s. Nowadays, with the Internet's popularity, vloggers, bloggers, and podcasters can say what they want—and, of course, accept personal responsibility for the good and the not-so-good content that they are creating and distributing. Although the FCC is still responsible for the Internet, they have thus far chosen not to censor or regulate its content. (As Will Rogers once said, "Thank God we don't get all of the government we pay for.")

What You Need to Know

Again, the most important thing to know is to *just do it!* The sooner you start vlogging, the sooner you will begin seeing results.

Uploading Your Videos

For more information on uploading video, please read Chapter 13, Got Video (Video Sharing), on video sharing.

Tips, Techniques, and Tactics

Creating Your Own Video

Vlogging can be as easy as using a cell phone with built-in video capabilities. However, while you can certainly use your cell phone, as famous blogger

Robert Scoble does occasionally, starting with this level of quality is not recommended.

Buy or borrow a video camera, and just start shooting some video. While shooting a comprehensive video is more involved than recording your voice in an audio podcast, getting something worth watching is not that hard, especially if there is good content—a valuable takeaway for your viewers.

Script Your Thoughts

It's always best to script your thoughts, or at least organize them as a list of bullet points. One suggestion for recording a video is to first create a Keynote presentation (PowerPoint, for non-Apple users). Position the monitor behind the camera or print the slides and tape them where you can speak to them while recording. Directly reading a script is the *worst* thing you can do.

Don't attempt to record too much at one time. If you can get through a slide, say "cut," take a deep breath, and start fresh with a new slide. If you are one of those people lucky enough to be able to just start talking, then by all means, do that. The bottom line is to do whatever you are the most comfortable with; you will come across as confident in the video.

Be sure to remember to record your introduction: who you are, your subject matter, and your web site address. Keep in mind that you must also record your conclusion, which will consist of a summary and a reiteration of who you are and your web site. The introduction and conclusion can also contain some music, and even titles.

Editing Your Video

Once you have created some raw digital video, it's time to edit. Select a video editing application such as Apple's iMovie and import your video (see Figure 12.5). Pick out some theme music, still photos, and other additional video clips you might want to include. You can also do a voice-over by recording directly from the microphone over your still photos or video clips.

Your video editing software will allow you to create tracks, which will enable you to place your video in as the main track, insert your introduction in front of it, and even lay down a separate music track that will play simultaneously. You can, of course, control the track volume, so that the background music remains in the background.

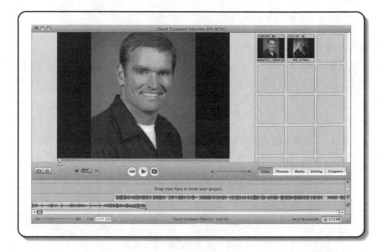

FIGURE 12.5 IMovie

There are many choices for video editing software; the one you use will depend on your computer's operating platform, be it Apple or Windows. Macintosh aficionados use iMovie to create and edit videos, benefitting from the drag-and-drop features of Macintosh software. You could also use Adobe Premiere or Final Cut Pro on the Mac OS. If you are a Windows user, you can use Adobe Premiere or ArcSoft's ShowBiz.

Once you have your video ready for prime-time viewing, it's time to decide how to distribute and otherwise make available your motion picture work of art. The easiest and most effective web site is, of course, YouTube. The process is simple: you set up an account, select Upload Video, enter a description, answer a few other questions about your video, and hit Upload. Wait a few minutes, and your video is now available for viewing anywhere in the world, 24/7, for free!

Keep in mind that just because your video is on YouTube doesn't automatically mean that others will watch it and you will become an overnight success. It is now your responsibility to drive traffic to your video. You do this through RSS, blogging, e-mails, commenting, and the use of other social media tools, so read on. See the chapters on RSS, blogs, and e-mails for more information.

Many open-source content management systems, like WordPress, Joomla, or Drupal, have integrated widgets and capabilities that allow you to post your video content. This permits vloggers to host and distribute their own video blogging, right from their own web sites.

Note

The convergence of mobile phones with built-in digital video cameras allows users to capture and publish video content to the Web almost as it is recorded.

Providers

FreeVlog.org is a great resource created by *Secrets of Videoblogging* authors Ryanne Hodson and Michael Verdi. This site has launched a thousand videoblogs, and is really helpful to new vloggers.

The ROI of Social Media

Tell a Friend Campaign

Background

Atlanta Children's Shelter has provided high-quality early child care and comprehensive social services for homeless families striving for self-sufficiency. Since 1986, ACS has stabilized over 5,100 families and cared for more than 7,800 children. On March 8, 2009, the Atlanta Children's Shelter held its first 5K Walk or Run fund-raiser with the goal of raising $10,000 in donations and attracting 250 runners and walkers to the event.

Strategy

The "Tell a Friend" social media campaign was launched as a means to reach new audiences by leveraging current relationships the shelter had with supporters as well as developing new relationships with online community members who shared a common interest with the goals of the shelter.

Implementation

- Concept Hub, Inc., researched the Metro Atlanta online community to identify people who were passionate about the Atlanta Children's Shelter or the cause that they support.
- Concept Hub, Inc., identified active 5K runners and walkers who would be interested in participating in the shelter's first 5K [run/walk] created an Online Street Team to build relationships with participants in other online communities and with influential Atlanta bloggers.

- Concept Hub, Inc., created a series of online assets, including a YouTube Channel, Flickr sites, Facebook Cause Page, Crowdvine Network, and widget to promote the 5K run/walk.
- Concept Hub, Inc., provided training to the staff and volunteers and work with the team to reach out to influential bloggers and supporters to request that they "tell a friend" about the upcoming 5K run/walk event.

Opportunity

The project enabled supporters of the shelter to raise awareness about the upcoming event by sharing information on their online profiles.

Conclusion

The Atlanta Children's Shelter set the goal of raising $10,000 in donations and attracting 250 runners and walkers to the event. They surpassed their goal, raising more than $26,000 and attracting 550 runners and walkers to the event.

Sherry Heyl
www.concepthubinc.com

Expert Insight

Patrizio Spagnoletto, senior director of marketing, Yahoo! Search Marketing, www.searchmarketing.yahoo.com

Patrizio Spagnoletto

. . . I have been with Yahoo! for about seven and a half years, and in my current role I manage the marketing team for the search-marketing product, which is basically the product where small and medium-sized businesses (or businesses of all sizes) can be listed in Yahoo! Search results. . . .

. . . To be more specific, it's the marketing part. So our team focuses on the awareness of the product, customer acquisition/retention, and just making sure that our customers, overall, are getting the most out of their investment with us once they start participating in this "sponsored-search world," and that happens through education, communication, and innovation of products that we provide for their products or features of the current search product. . . .

. . . When somebody goes to a search engine on Yahoo.com and searches for, let us say, cars (more specifically a used Honda), what the user has just

(continued)

(*continued*)

done is show an explicit intent that he is looking for and willing to purchase that specific product. Now if you flip that and put your advertiser hat on, that is probably the single most qualified lead that you will ever be able to receive. And that is because unlike other marketing media in Sponsored Search, it is the user that tells us that they are interested in buying our products and services. And this all happened because of the search engine results page. . . .

. . . And in fact when you think about it in context of direct response (meaning what a business wants to increase their sales), I really do not think there is any other marketing medium out there that is as effective as Sponsored Search. And we are doing a lot of research to justify a statement like that.

Having said that, marketers have multiple objectives. You know, whether it is "response" (and Sponsored Search does a great job there), or if it's "awareness" (or other mediums like television and the offline world; or graphical ad display, which I was a major player in), it is really the combination of the two that makes a business be really successful. Where the sum of the two is much greater than the individual parts.

Yahoo! is really in a unique position in that it is truly the only business that can offer the two products on an own-it–operate-it site. On the Yahoo! site, you can buy banners and you can buy sponsor search; and therefore, really create what we call a 360 Campaign where you can surround the user with both graphical and sponsor search. . . .

. . . Banner advertising is what most of us see when we go on pretty much any site. It is those graphical advertisements, sometimes they are video, or what we call "rich media," or sometimes they are just static images. But it is a graphical way for an advertiser to convey their message. And Yahoo!'s invention is a leader in this and has been since the inception of Yahoo!. And we are very good at targeting users through some of our own proprietary data on the back end. This is done in the way that we are able to target (whether it be demographic, behavioral, or graphic), or just some of the ways that we are able to match graphical advertisements with the users. Because online search is where you have the benefit of the user actually telling you what it is that they are looking for. With "graphical," it is really about the more general persona of a person that is visiting the site. . . .

. . . What we typically ask our small-business customer is, first and foremost, what is your objective? If their objective is really that they want *direct response,* that is a clear signal that they should really be investing at least their first trunk of money to Yahoo! Sponsored Search. And that is because it is by far the most effective medium to garner more sales. And for Sponsored Search, [it] is very easy to sign up for it on Yahoo!. You can do so online through a simple process, or you can, literally, just call in. We have reps that can help you go through this final process, the latter honestly being very unique to Yahoo!.

One of the things that we pride ourselves on is really helping our prospective customers by being, literally, just a phone call away from them. . . .

. . . And when you phone in for the sign-up process, what they will do is walk you through the actual online sign-up form, but with the advantage of just giving some of the "best practices" of thinking through. For example, what keywords to choose or how to write an effective description. So that is available right now. . . .

. . . We think it is extremely valuable because, as you probably know, small businesses are experts at what they do, but they are not necessarily experts at advertising, let alone Sponsored Search advertising. And so we feel it is almost *our* responsibility (and to be honest with you, it is in our best interest) to make sure that these customers get set up correctly the first time around so that they can start receiving the best results right off the bat. . . .

. . . Actually, you can trace it all the way back to a company that was called GoTo.com, which started in the late 1990s. That company that we branded to Overture, which subsequently was purchased by Yahoo!, and then rebranded to Yahoo! Search Market. So we are, quite honestly, the pioneers of paid search. We are the ones who invented the category that represents more than half of online spending. So it is something that is a good thing for us to think back on. . . .

. . . So our model is what we call a "pay-per-click model" frequently referred to as PPC. So the first comparison is to all other mediums, so let's say you are buying a newspaper ad or anything that is offline. There is a fixed cost to those purchases, which you may or may not recuperate, depending on how many people actually purchase your products. So in a newspaper, you will buy a half-page for, say a thousand dollars (I'm making up these numbers, of course), that is a stock cost, and you are going to try to make it up.

Whereas with Yahoo! Search Marketing, in a PPC model, you only pay when somebody actually clicks on your listing on the Yahoo! Search results. And the price is not set by us; it is actually set by the advertiser. And this is what you are referring to as a "bidding mall." If you think of every *keyword marketplace* as exactly that (a marketplace), advertisers will bid to be listed in those search results. It is important to know that it is not just how much you bid that determines your position. There are other factors in there, including the quality of the listing, and that is because we want to make sure that the experience for the users is optimal. So "quality of the listing" means we want to make sure that it creates a "relevant result" for our user. And we reward or we penalize if the listing is not good. . . .

. . . If all listings are created equal, meaning that the quality of each of the listings is exactly the same, then the amount you bid is really what will determine who shows off first, if you will, and second and so on and so forth. But I put that caveat of the listing quality because it is a really poignant one. So let me give an extreme example.

(continued)

(continued)

Let's go back to our used Honda car. If I was an advertiser and my listing says, "Buy the best car ever, at my site now" and by contract your listing said, "Quality used Honda cars at reasonable prices," my guess is that your listing is of a much higher quality than mine is because it speaks specifically to what the user was looking for. . . .

. . . And as a result, even if I am bidding, say sixty cents per click and you are bidding twenty cents per click, you may actually show up higher than I may because of the quality of your listing. And, again, all the numbers are completely fictitious. . . .

. . . It becomes even more important when you combine it with our display advertising because the user sees multiple impressions. So if you imagine a banner that talks about your used Honda car sale, and then actually apply it finally to a search query, and then a searcher sees your listing and recognizes the name of your company because they have seen it on a banner. That's what I was referencing, the two pieces really working hand-in-hand to increase not only the awareness of the brand, but ultimately in a product like that, the click-through rate and, obviously, the sales that follow. . . .

. . . Sure, so if you go to Yahoo.com, there are a couple of links that will take you to a sign-up process. The easiest one is at the bottom of the page. It is Search Marketing, so very descriptive. And at this place you will go through a couple of pages that will help you understand what the product is about, as I have done for you now. There are, at the core, really four steps.

The first one is *targeting*. So it is understandable whether you want your listing to appear to the entire nation or a specific geographical component, or area.

The second one is *choosing your keywords*. The used Honda is a perfect example of what we mean as a keyword.

The third is determining *how much you want to bid*. So back to your example of your pay-per-click, and we refer to that from the advertiser perspective "as your bid."

And then last but not least, obviously, is the usable budget, the marketing budget.

In addition, with Yahoo! Search Marketing, you can start your campaign for as little as $30. Although I will be honest with you, we encourage advertisers *not* to pay down at that limit, not because we want them to spend more, but quite honestly, it is because in many categories today they have become fairly competitive. So we want our advertisers to make sure that they have enough money in their accounts so that their listings appear and getting enough "click-through-ing" so that they start to get the returns that they are looking for.

So it is one of those models where you have a little bit of efficiency of scale, and if you spend a little bit more you actually see a lot more return. And by the way, when I say a little bit more, I do not mean in the thousands of dollars. For most advertisers, a couple hundred dollars is more than enough to get the feel of how this process works and then start deciding if they want to invest more in it. . . .

. . . So let us go back to our example. If somebody types in the keyword "car," that is an extremely broad word; and if I am selling used Honda cars where if I put my listing under the keyword "car," I am going to get all sorts of people and not necessarily all of them will be looking for what I have to sell.

However, if I choose as the keywords "used Honda cars" then almost by default I am limiting the queries (or the users) to the ones who are looking for exactly what I have to sell. Now there are two benefits in doing so.

The first is (what I just mentioned) a much more qualified prospect for you. And the second is, from the planning perspective, terms that have two or more words in a keyword phrase are, generally speaking, a little bit less expensive than what we call "head-turns to our cart."

Therefore, if you combine the two, you are getting better-qualified leads at a lower cost and that is really the best of both worlds for advertisers. . . .

. . . So if an advertiser knows what they are doing (and I really emphasize that) because there are a lot of advertisers who come in with the expectations that they can set up an account in 10 minutes, and then all of a sudden see sales fly. That is not going to happen, I will tell you that right now.

But if you know what you are doing (and by that I mean really taking the time to learn the account and the interfaces, and the teachers are there at your disposal) and take the time to manage it, then you will see the returns that you are designing. We have countless advertisers who see those on a daily basis, which is, quite honestly, why they stay with us.

And going back to the objectives of our team, this is to make sure our advertisers really do, clearly and simply, understand how to optimize their account. . . .

To listen to or read the entire Executive Conversation with Patrizio Spagnoletto, go to www.theSocialMediaBible.com.

Commandments

1. **Thou shalt look at some of the most popular videos shared.**

    Go look at the most popular videos posted on YouTube and other video sharing web sites. See what they have in common. Notice the strong entertainment value (entertainment is a very strong "What's in It for Me?").

2. **Thou shalt create a video.**

    Go out and create a video. Try it. Keep it light, and keep it short (three to five minutes). Try to have the highest WIIFM you can for your customers. Give them a takeaway in the form of information, such as an "I didn't know that," or a "You can use it that way"; or just plain have fun.

3. **Thou shalt not spend a lot of money.**

   If you have a digital video camera, start shooting. If you don't own one, borrow one first and try it to see if you like it. Download free software from the Internet, and have some fun editing.

4. **Thou shalt comment.**

   Start building a community around your videos, products, services, hobby, or other subject content. (See Chapter 2, Say Hello to Social Networking, for more information on how to build networks and communities.)

Conclusion

Creating your own video is a lot of fun. It is a little more technically challenging than an audio podcast or a simple blog, but the rewards are well worth it. Video is almost always the best medium for communicating with your customers. Being able to share your expressions, inflections, and body language builds much greater trust and conveys sincerity to your viewers. Watching someone deliver a message is powerful. Just look at how television influences lives.

Don't be afraid of trying to create your own video. Don't spend a lot of money to start out. Use your existing camera or borrow one from a friend and start videotaping. The best way to experience vlogging—to borrow a sport shoe slogan—is to "Just Do It!"

To hear all of the Expert Interviews, go to www.theSocialMediaBible.com.

Readings and Resources

Baig, Edward C., and Bob LeVitus. *iPhone For Dummies* (Hoboken, NJ: John Wiley & Sons, Inc.)

Blake, Bonnie, and Doug Sahlin. *50 Fast Digital Video Techniques*. (Hoboken, NJ: John Wiley & Sons, Inc.)

Bove, Tony. *iPod & iTunes For Dummies* (Hoboken, NJ: John Wiley & Sons, Inc.)

Bryant, Stephanie Cottrell. *Videoblogging For Dummies*. (Hoboken, NJ: John Wiley & Sons, Inc.)

Burgess, Jean, Joshua Green, Henry Jenkins, and John Hartley. *YouTube: Online Video and Participatory Culture*. (Hoboken, NJ: John Wiley & Sons, Inc.)

Dayley, Lisa DaNae. *Photoshop CS3 Extended Video and 3D Bible*. (Hoboken, NJ: John Wiley & Sons, Inc.)

Dedman, Jay, and Joshua Paul. *Videoblogging*. (Hoboken, NJ: John Wiley & Sons, Inc.)

Harvey, Greg. *Roxio Easy Media Creator 8 For Dummies*. (Hoboken, NJ: John Wiley & Sons, Inc.)

Hodson, Ryanne, and Michael Verdi. *Secrets of Videoblogging*. (Hoboken, NJ: John Wiley & Sons, Inc.)

Jarboe, Greg, and Suzie Reider. *YouTube and Video Marketing: An Hour a Day*. (Hoboken, NJ: John Wiley & Sons, Inc.)

Johnson, Brian, Duncan Mackenzie, and Harvey Chute. *Zune For Dummies*. (Hoboken, NJ: John Wiley & Sons, Inc.)

Kennedy, Pete, and Maura Kennedy. *Make Your Own Music Videos with Adobe Premiere*. (Hoboken, NJ: John Wiley & Sons, Inc.)

Kobler, Helmut, and Chad Fahs. *Final Cut Pro 4 For Dummies*. (Hoboken, NJ: John Wiley & Sons, Inc.)

Larson, Lisa, and Renee Costantini. *Flash Video for Professionals: Expert Techniques for Integrating*. (Hoboken, NJ: John Wiley & Sons, Inc.)

Larson, Lisa, and Renee Costantini. *Video on the Web* (Hoboken, NJ: John Wiley & Sons, Inc.)

Micheletti, Angelo. *iPhone Photography For Dummies*. (Hoboken, NJ: John Wiley & Sons, Inc.)

Richardson, Iain E. *The H.264 Advanced Video Compression Standard*, 2nd ed. (Hoboken, NJ: John Wiley & Sons, Inc.)

Sahlin, Dou, and Chris Botello. *YouTube For Dummies*. (Hoboken, NJ: John Wiley & Sons, Inc.)

Sadun, Erica. *Digital Photography Essentials: Point, Shoot, Enhance, Share*. (Hoboken, NJ: John Wiley & Sons, Inc.)

Sadun, Erica. *Digital Video Essentials: Shoot, Transfer, Edit, Share*. (Hoboken, NJ: John Wiley & Sons, Inc.)

Sammon, Rick. *Capturing Better Photos and Video with Your iPhone*. (Hoboken, NJ: John Wiley & Sons, Inc.)

Shaw, Russell, and David Merccr. *Caution! Music & Video Downloading: Your Guide to Legal, Safe, and Trouble-Free Downloads* (Hoboken, NJ: John Wiley & Sons, Inc.)

Stoller, Bryan Michael. *Filmmaking For Dummies*, 2nd ed. (Hoboken, NJ: John Wiley & Sons, Inc.)

Underdahl, Keith. *Digital Video For Dummies*. (Hoboken, NJ: John Wiley & Sons, Inc.)

Underdahl, Keith. *Digital Video For Dummies*, 4th ed. (Hoboken, NJ: John Wiley & Sons, Inc.)

Underdahl, Keith. *Premiere Elements 8 For Dummies*. (Hoboken, NJ: John Wiley & Sons, Inc.)

Watson, Lonzell. *Teach Yourself VISUALLY Digital Video*, 2nd ed. (Hoboken, NJ: John Wiley & Sons, Inc.)

Watson, Lonzell. *Final Cut Pro 6 for Digital Video Editors Only*. (Hoboken, NJ: John Wiley & Sons, Inc.)

Zink, Michael. *Scalable Video on Demand: Adaptive Internet-Based Distribution* (Hoboken, NJ: John Wiley & Sons, Inc.)

Downloads

For your free downloads associated with *The Social Media Bible,* go to www .theSocialMediaBible.com, and enter your ISBN number located on the back of the book above the bar code. Be sure to enter the dashes.

Credits

The ROI of Social Media was provided by:

Sherry Heyl, www.concepthubinc.com

Expert Insight was provided by:

Patrizio Spagnoletto, senior director of marketing, Yahoo! Search Marketing, www.searchmarketing.yahoo.com

Technical edits were provided by:

Lisa Von Bargen, www.beyondimplementation.com

CHAPTER 13

Got Video? (Video Sharing)

If you can get 43 million views of your video because of its entertainment value—as did a 23-year-old in Korea—or you can get 93 million views—as did one comedian who posted a six-minute segment of his comedy act—then wouldn't you? Especially if it was free?

Read on for more information.

Video sharing is the easiest and fastest way to start building your social media portfolio. You and your company already have a box of VHS tapes or video on a hard drive somewhere. You need to locate that video, identify the best representation of your company, and start uploading it to video sharing web sites. If you don't have good video, start making it. Uploading is free, it makes your message accessible to all of your prospects and customers, and it helps build your Google Juice![1]

As mentioned in the previous chapter, while video recordings can also be considered podcasts—since the iPod and other digital playback devices can display photographs, audio, and video—for the purpose of this book, audios are treated as *podcasts,* and videos are referred to as either *videos* or *vlogs*.

What's in It for You?

A blender company called Blendtec, which is located in Orem, Utah, uploaded a funny in-house product demonstration video to YouTube. Within the first 24 hours, more than one million viewers watched its video; within the same 24-hour period, the company sold out of its $600 Blendtec Blenders.

---

1. Google Juice is a term used to describe the results that follow when you search for your name, your company's name, and your product or service's name in Google or other search engines. The more listings and the more pages that a search engine returns to the searcher, the more Google Juice you have. The goal of this book is to squeeze as much Google Juice as possible out of your social media marketing and communications.

theSocialMediaBible.com

FIGURE 13.1 Blendtec

What would you pay to have your product or service's 90-second commercial viewed by more than one million potential customers in 24 hours? You most likely couldn't afford this kind of media exposure. The Blendtec video has now been viewed more than 3.5 million times (see Figure 13.1). (To watch Blendtec president Tom Dickson blend a brand-new iPhone on the day they came out—and other video examples—go to www .theSocialMediaBible.com; or go to YouTube and search for "Will It Blend.")

Can anyone guarantee that the phenomenal success that Blendtec has enjoyed will happen for you? No, but when you already have the video or can produce it easily as Blendtec did—and it's free to upload—then what do you have to lose?

Back to the Beginning

As with several of the other chapters that have both a Sharing and a Creation chapter (such as this chapter and Chapters 10 and 11 on Audio), the creation and sharing history of video sharing has been interwoven into the same story. And since video sharing's history is only a very small part of the larger video story, you can find this information later in this chapter.

What You Need to Know

The most important thing you need to know is to *just do it!* You have to start sometime, and the easiest way to do so is to gather all of the videos you currently have on hand and start uploading them to YouTube. It's actually

FIGURE 13.2 YouTube "Guitar"

simpler than you think. Set up your account (it's free), select Upload Video, follow the instructions, and there you have it. (For more information about creating your own video, see Chapter 12, Watch Out for Vlogs (Video Create).)

Examples are the best way to explain why uploading videos to a video sharing web site can give you such a great rate of return on this investment of your time. Three videos in particular discussed in this chapter have been extremely successful for their owners. One is a personal video, while the other two are business related. Remember, there's no guarantee that you will have the same success, but who knows?

The first example is one of the earlier and more popular videos on YouTube called "Guitar" (youtube.com/watch?v=QjA5faZF1A8; see Figure 13.2). This video of Pachelbel's *Canon* played on an electric guitar was created by a 23-year-old from Korea named Jeong-Hyun Lim who recorded his video himself in his bedroom in his mirror. The video "Guitar" has had more than 54 million views to date—simply because it's entertaining.

You can go to YouTube and type in "Guitar" or go to www.theSocial MediaBible.com to click on the link in the chapter section for a clickable link.

Another example of how popular a self-made posted video can become comes from the comedian Judson Laipply, who posted a six-minute portion of his comedy act, which he called "Evolution of Dance," on YouTube (youtube.com/watch?v=dMH0bHeiRNg; see Figure 13.3). To date, this video

FIGURE 13.3   YouTube "Evolution of Dance"

has had more than 109 million views—and has been the record holder for most-watched video on YouTube until recently, when a video for a music group has surpassed it.

You can go to YouTube and type in "Evolution of Dance" or go to www .theSocialMediaBible.com to click on the link in the chapter section for a clickable link.

Imagine having to invest nothing more than 10 minutes of your time uploading a video you already had in order to have 93 million people watch your six-minute commercial. While it doesn't happen often, there is an audience for a variety of works. How about that as an extraordinary ROI?

Uploading Your Videos

The only prerequisite for uploading videos is that they need to be in a digital format and not exceed the host's maximum file size. If you have made your videos relatively recently, they are probably already in a digital format. If your videos are still on VHS, then you will have to convert them.

You can buy some VHS-to-DVD recorders for under $100. Put the VHS video in, put in a blank DVD, hit Play, and when the video is at the end, you have a digital video on DVD. LG, Samsung, Sony, Toshiba, and Panasonic make some really good units. You can also find service providers that will convert your VHS videos inexpensively. Many services offer to accept your VHS tapes by mail and return them in a digital format recorded on a DVD. An example of this is Home Movie Depot, a company that charges anywhere from under $20 to more for damaged tapes.

You can also buy a VHS player made by Ion that connects directly to your computer via the USB port. Another alternative is to buy a converter box for about $250 that connects your VCR to your computer, such as the ADS PYRO A/V Link, Analog to Digital Video Converter that ships free with Adobe Premiere Elements 4.0 for around $160.

Once you have gathered all of your videos in a digital format, you can go to YouTube or another video sharing web site and start uploading. That's all there is to it. Make sure you have your tags picked out ahead of time. (See meta tags in Chapter 19, Spotlight on Search (Search Engine Optimization).)

Once you have a list of your tags or keywords and a short description, then you're ready to upload. And, like the shampoo bottle says, lather, rinse, repeat: load, tag, repeat.

Keep in mind that simply uploading your content to a video sharing web site doesn't create a post with an RSS feed. The video has to be included as an enclosure in an RSS feed, similar to a podcast, to allow your followers to subscribe to your chronological posts. This is a distinction that can be important if you are building a community and a following. By building your video into an RSS feed, it is easy for your video to become a viral one that is posted to the Web and passed around by word of mouth. Video posted to your blog is also video that isn't enclosed in the RSS Feed (see Chapter 18, RSS—Really Simple Syndication Made Simple).

Another advantage of posting a video to YouTube is the ability to comment back and forth and respond to comments the video posts have generated. In comment marketing, this kind of feedback is considered almost essential. Many videobloggers still feel that YouTube misses the main point, because their subscription model isn't RSS-based. So, although you can subscribe to favorite users in YouTube, that subscription can't be accessed in a video-enabled RSS reader such as FireAnt or iTunes. (For more information on RSS, see Chapter 18, RSS—Really Simple Syndication Made Simple. For more information on comment marketing, see the interview with Amanda Vega, from Amanda Vega Consultants.)

Peer-to-Peer

Another form of file sharing for music, video, e-books, movies, software, and other digital data is known as peer-to-peer (or P2P). P2P takes place when many computers on a network, connected through the Internet, all share digital data in the form of files. For example, if you want the latest music from your favorite band, you can download that copyrighted material by connecting to a peer-to-peer network, selecting the file, and downloading that file to your computer. All the while, your computer is being used to transfer digital bits of another file that someone else has requested. Once all of the bits have been downloaded to your computer, the file is put back together or assembled into the original working data file.

Napster

Peer-to-peer was made most famous—or perhaps infamous—when it was argued that 87 percent of all music available on Napster's download servers was copyrighted.

In June 1999, Shawn Fanning created an online music file-sharing service called Napster while he was attending Northeastern University in Boston. (Napster got its name from Fanning's nappy hair style.) Napster allowed people to easily copy and distribute MP3 files between one another for free. This led the music industry to accuse Napster of huge copyright violations. Napster was shut down in July 2001 by a court order, but it paved the way for decentralized peer-to-peer file-distribution programs. Services and products such as Kazaa, Gnutella, CAN, FastTrack, LimeWire, Bit Torrent, and Freenet came later on.

Napster changed the way university students used the Internet. Any piece of music could be taken (or *ripped*) from a CD and stored on your hard drive. Then, simply by performing a search for that song title, all of the computers around the world with that file turned up in the listing. All you had to do was select the file and wait a few minutes for it to be transferred from that computer to yours. That's it!

Peer-to-peer and Napster technology allowed music fans to easily share with each other song files in any format. This led to the music industry's accusations of massive copyright violations—and a $5.3 million lawsuit against Napster and a 14-year-old girl.

BitTorrent

BitTorrent is a type of peer-to-peer file-sharing protocol used to distribute data such as movies, music, photos, software, audio, and other digital data files. One computer starts as the initial distributor of the complete file. Each peer-to-peer (or individually connected) PC that downloads data also uploads data to other peers. This provides a significant reduction in the original PC's hardware and bandwidth costs. It provides redundancy against system errors and reduces dependence on an original distributor. BitTorrent also reduces the liability of the original computer's distribution of copyrighted materials, as the system actually passes around the data from machine to machine and compiles the completed files that have been transferred from many computers on the system.

Programmer Bram Cohen designed the BitTorrent protocol in April 2001, and it debuted on July 2 of that year. The original BitTorrent is now maintained by Cohen's company, BitTorrent Inc. This system is widely used to distribute copyrighted games, music, and movies that sometimes are still playing as first-run showings in theaters.

Providers

The following is a list of video sharing web sites that are listed on Wikipedia:

- Afreeca
- tvpakistan.com
- AniBOOM
- AtomUploads (part of AtomFilms)
- Blinkx
- Blip.tv
- BlogTV
- Break.com
- Buzznet
- Crackle
- Dailymotion
- EngageMedia
- ExpoTV
- Facebook
- Funnyordie.com
- Flickr
- Fotki
- Gawkk
- Gubb (Gubb.tv)
- Tangle.com (formerly Godtube)
- Google Video (no new uploads)

- Hulu
- imeem (ceased video hosting service)
- Indiavideo.org
- Kewego
- Liveleak
- Mail.ru
- Megaupload
- Metacafe
- Mevio
- Myspace
- MyVideo
- Nico Nico Douga (Japanese)
- OneWorldTV
- Ourmedia
- pandora tv
- Photobucket
- Pure Motorsport
- Rayzz
- Revver
- Rambler Vision (Russian)
- ReelTime.com

- RuTube
- Sapo Videos (only Portuguese)
- ScienceStage
- Sevenload
- The Video Bay
- Trilulilu (Romanian)
- TroopTube
- Truveo
- Tudou (Chinese)
- Vbox7 (Bulgarian)
- Viddler
- Videojug
- Vidoosh (Iranian)
- Vimeo
- Vuze
- Vzaar
- Yahoo! Video
- Youku (Chinese)
- YouTube
- Zoopy
- Veoh

Does this mean that you have to stay up all night uploading the same video to every one of these web sites? No! Just pick one or two, grab a video, and go for it. Look at some of the videos on only a few of these web sites. See which ones you like, and which are getting the highest number of hits. Then try to pick or create a video with the same kind of general content and upload it. Don't get overwhelmed; getting only whelmed is okay.

The ROI of Social Media

Chemistry Creates Mom-Pleazing Campaign for Steaz

Introduction

A $100K social media campaign created by Chemistry, Pittsburgh, for organic tea company Steaz, [in] Newtown, Pennsylvania, yielded a $500K monthly sales increase, and solidified and expanded retail distribution.

Background

Before October 2009, Steaz was sold in health food stores only. When Target's 1,500-plus stores began carrying the brand nationally, Steaz's total shopping audience quadrupled overnight—a huge opportunity for the fledgling brand, and also a challenge. The unfamiliar brand's shelf-presence within Target would be tiny, and if it didn't sell, it would soon be discontinued. Steaz needed a national promotion to generate awareness and trial, and quickly, within a two-month window.

Strategy

Chemistry estimated that, pre-social media, an outdoor and couponing campaign might have met those goals, at a $2M budget—far beyond Steaz's means. But because 72 percent of women online now learn about new products via social media, Chemistry figured a moms outreach program, focused on healthy ingredients and value pricing, could be implemented for $100K.

Implementation

Sample kits and e-mail went to 72 leading mom bloggers and 130 couponing bloggers. A real time, sample-supported, Twitter "tea party" generated 2,800 tweets in one hour. Ongoing Facebook and Twitter presences were developed, offering BoGo and free, one-per-computer couponing. The campaigns yielded 6,000 blog mentions/reviews, 30,000,000 total impressions, and most importantly, 250,000 COUPONS DOWNLOADED OVER 8 WEEKS.

Opportunity

Target sales were directly impacted, jumping 350 percent, from $6K to $21K, in one week. Three weeks in, the opportunity was nearly lost when sales matched total production and shelves emptied. (Production was ramped up.) At promotion's end, Steaz's $1M total December sales were DOUBLE ITS PREVIOUS BEST MONTH EVER.

Conclusion

Post-promotion, weekly sales settled at 200 percent of their pre-promotion level. Steaz remains in Target. And Kroger, with nearly double Target's locations, will soon carry the brand.

Rob Pizzica, Chemistry
www.visitthelab.com
Dan Barron, Conroy Barron Public Relations
db@conroybarronpr.com

Expert Insight

George Strompolos, content partnerships manager, YouTube, www.youtube.com

George Strompolos

I am the content partnerships manager here at YouTube, and that's really a fancy way of saying that I reach out to content creators and help them engage on YouTube and to distribute their content and connect with audiences around the world. And so YouTube being an open platform, those content creators can take on many shapes and sizes. They can be someone as small as a video blogger producing videos in their bedroom, up to what we call a "broadband studio" or a "digital studio," which creates original content just for Internet distribution. And this goes all the way up to traditional media companies and premium content providers that we are all familiar with: CBS and the National Basketball Association, Discovery, ESPN.

(continued)

(continued)

So, at its core, YouTube is a web site where people can upload videos to share them with the world. It's also a great place to watch videos. It's actually an interesting fact that YouTube currently receives twenty hours of video uploaded to the site every minute! In fact, more videos have been uploaded to YouTube in the past three months than ABC, NBC, and CBS have aired since 1948. It's staggering.

What you'll find is that people upload videos to YouTube for different reasons. Some of them just want to share pictures of their baby, or their vacation footage. We are certainly happy to support that. However, it's becoming more and more common for amateur and professional content creators to produce content for YouTube and make a living out of it.

The way that they do this is they become a "partner" through my team, or by applying online at YouTube.com/partners. They basically tell us, "Hey, we're producing original content and not only do we want to share it with the world through YouTube, but we want to give you the ability to run ads against that content." . . .

And then we will share the majority of that ad revenue back to the content creator. So I call it a *performance-based* model. In other words, you can become a content partner, and if you upload video and it gets zero views, well, there's clearly no ad revenue there, so nothing is being shared. But if you upload a video and it gets one million views, for instance, we put an ad on every single view. And so that ad revenue starts to accrue and, in many cases, can become significant for a lot of the Content Partners we have. . . .

The main format of advertising that you'll see on YouTube when you are watching a video (if you're watching a video from a partner) is what we call *in-video* advertising. And it is, essentially, a transparent overlay that shows up toward the bottom of the video window; and it's cool. It can be animated, and a cool example is when *The Simpsons* movie was premiering, the studio behind that movie ran an in-video overlay of Homer Simpson chasing a donut across the bottom of the screen. It goes pretty quick, you know, and it's usually relevant. I think they targeted that against comedy and animation content, so to that audience it was probably actually a nice surprise. And as a user, you can click on Homer Simpson and see, maybe, the movie trailer, or you can choose to close that overlay out, or just wait a few seconds and it will just disappear. We also run other industry standard ad formats such as pre-roll and companion banners.

So, creating original content and sharing in ad revenues is one way to approach YouTube, and that's more from an entertainment perspective. But from more a marketing perspective, I've just been amazed at the way that companies actually think of clever ways to use YouTube. "Will It Blend" is one of my favorite examples.

I should defer to them, of course, but I did read an article at one point that their sales actually went up 300 percent as a result of their presence on YouTube. . . .

This is from a marketing effort that essentially cost them nothing: Create a YouTube channel, no cost; set up a guy on camera with a blender (they make blenders so it cannot be that expensive for them), and blend a couple of cool things. And they were smart enough to blend things that are kind of hot and in the news. So the new iPhone comes out and they buy one on the first day and they blend it. And of course, people are searching for the iPhone video and things like that, and just the controversy of destroying something in a blender that is so sought-after is something that translates to a lot of video views. . . .

Here you have this tremendous marketing tool in YouTube, and for a company like Blendtec. What's interesting is that I read a blog post a few months ago from a well-known guy in Silicon Valley who said, "I see a future where your marketing can become a profit center." And if you look at "Will It Blend," that's a perfect example. So their marketing is clearly driving sales, but also they are providing original content.

So they are certainly welcome to join our partnership program, and if they are comfortable having other ads running against their videos, they can actually make money off those ads. So it's kind of an interesting situation there. . . .

You know, one of my favorite examples is a young guy named Lucas who has a character that he does on YouTube called "Fred." Lucas is about sixteen years old, and he plays this character named "Fred" who is a six-year-old, and the shtick is that he is a six-year-old with anger management problems.

YouTube "Fred Frigglehorn."

It's one of these things that are really made for kids—like a lot of Pixar Films, for instance—but it is also funny to adults. It's kind [of] a bizarre thing, and you can see it at YouTube.com/Fred; and it's really just taken off like a rocket.

I think it's actually the fastest-growing channel in YouTube history.

And Fred is a partner, so we traffic ads against his videos and we share the majority of that ad revenue with him. He's at a point where he'll post a video, and within a matter of days, that video will have at least three million views, I guarantee . . . sometimes as high as eight to ten million! So that is about one video every week, sometimes more. There are cable programs, even network television producers that would die for those numbers.

Absolutely an impressive feat, and if you look at someone like Fred who uploads a video and gets three million views at a minimum. All he has to do is post ten videos and he's going to achieve viewership on par with shows like *American Idol*. But don't forget that people are constantly watching Fred's older videos, too. It's really a powerful thing, and I won't get into the details of this partnership, but he's making decent money off of YouTube, substantial . . . and he's, naturally, being approached by all kinds of brands, because he's really hitting that tween audience. Fred actually has a feature-length movie coming out this year—talk about a YouTube success story!

To listen to or read the entire Executive Conversation with George Strompolos, go to www.theSocialMediaBible.com.

Commandments

1. **Thou shalt convert any VHS videos to digital format.**

   Take all of your useful VHS tapes and either convert them or have them converted to digital format. Get your product videos, your service videos, your company party video (use discretion!), your happy customer videos, and get them ready for posting.

2. **Thou shalt upload.**

   The highest ROI comes in finding all of the videos you currently have and getting them uploaded to a site. Your customers can't see them if they aren't there. Get any existing video you have, figure out its keywords, and upload. It's free!

3. **Thou shalt post everywhere.**

   Once you are comfortable with one video sharing site and have it loaded with all of your videos, consider posting your videos to a second or even a third video sharing web site.

   Post them on YouTube, and on several of the other free video sharing web sites. Don't forget to post to some of the lesser-known web sites such as Blip.tv, VideoEgg, and Daily Motion.

4. **Thou shalt comment.**

   Start building a community around your videos, products, services, hobby, or other subject content. (See Chapter 2, Say Hello to Social Networking, for more information on how to build networks and communities.)

5. **Thou shalt not post copyrighted material.**

   If you're going to post it, be sure you own the rights to it. Don't post something that belongs to someone else, *especially* if someone else owns the copyright.

6. **Thou shalt become familiar with the Creative Commons Act.**

   Go to www.theSocialMediaBible.com to find out more about the Creative Commons Act to find out what you can and cannot use when posting to the Internet.

7. **Thou shalt be sincere and have fun.**

   The most important step in this process is to be yourself, be sincere, and have fun. If you're not enjoying yourself when you are creating a video, it shows.

Conclusion

The common theme in this book is "Just Do It!" Video sharing is a great way to get your company and product names out there. The more "What's in It for Me?" value that the video has, the more it will be watched and passed along. Get your videos, pick out a few video sharing web sites, and start posting. Be sure to mention the videos in your blogs and e-mails. Be sure that you have chosen the proper meta tags, so that when someone is looking for your content, it can be found. And be sure to use RSS feeds whenever possible. Look at other people's videos and descriptions, and plagiarize (just kidding!). Be inspired by their style and content.

To hear all of the Expert Interviews, go to www.theSocialMediaBible.com.

Readings and Resources

Baig, Edward C., and Bob LeVitus. *iPhone For Dummies*. (Hoboken, NJ: John Wiley & Sons, Inc.)

Bove, Tony. *iPod & iTunes For Dummies*. (Hoboken, NJ: John Wiley & Sons, Inc.)

Larson, Lisa, and Renee Costantini. *Video on the Web*. (Hoboken, NJ: John Wiley & Sons, Inc.)

Shaw, Russell, and David Mercer. *Caution! Music & Video Downloading: Your Guide to Legal, Safe, and Trouble-Free Downloads*. (Hoboken, NJ: John Wiley & Sons, Inc.)

Zink, Michael. *Scalable Video on Demand: Adaptive Internet-Based Distribution*. (Hoboken, NJ: John Wiley & Sons, Inc.)

Downloads

For your free downloads associated with *The Social Media Bible*, go to www.theSocialMediaBible.com, and enter your ISBN number located on the back of the book above the bar code. Be sure to enter the dashes.

Credits

The ROI of Social Media was provided by:

Dan Barron, Conroy Barron Public Relations, db@conroybarronpr.com

Expert Insight and technical edits were provided by:

George Strompolos, content partnerships manager, YouTube, www.youtube.com

CHAPTER 14

Thumbs Up for Microblogging

What's in It for You?

American author Mark Twain once paraphrased French mathematician Blaise Pascal's famous comment by saying, "If I had more time, I would have written a shorter letter."[1] The character limitations on microblogging force us to communicate in a more succinct manner. The content of our text messages are written completely differently from our e-mails. This is why they are read.

If only Pascal or Twain had been writing during the dawn of microblogging. This increasingly prevalent trend's value lies in its portability, immediacy, and ease of use. It's simple to post a microblog for your friends, family, coworkers, clients, and prospects. Your complete thought must be conveyed in 140 characters or less!

Microblogging is text messaging and a little more. It can be as effortless as sending a text message from your cell phone to a select group of friends. Anyone can microblog as often as they like, and can promptly read posts from other like-minded bloggers. Microblogging includes the ability to send messages, audio, video, and even attached files; it empowers users to make friends; get directions; give and receive advice; review books, restaurants, and movies; obtain up-to-the-minute news; identify, research, and purchase products and services; update customers; inform clients; send calendar and event notices and news; and more. Or—in the particular case of *The Social Media Bible*—get advice on the book's chapters, the design, the content, interviews, and technical support.

Microblogging lets those who participate create small, intimate communities that are centered on topics such as politics, technology, or medical issues. You can read posts about cancer treatments and chemotherapy effects. You can send or read play-by-play updates from a conference or event happening at the moment you're reading. Microblogging lets your

---

1. Thanks to Ed Nusbaum for this quote.

 theSocialMediaBible.com

friends know where you are and what you are doing, and allows you to tell them things like, "I am at Twenty-fourth Street and Camelback Road. Anyone want to meet me for dinner?" With global and local, nearly real-time, mini-to-mini conversations; many-to-many IMs (Instant Messaging); two-way communication being sent and received on any computer, Black-Berry, PDA, or cell phone—microblogging is the epitome of social media two-way communication. For example, at a conference featuring musician, community marketer, and participant in the famed "One Red Paper Clip" story Jody Gnant (whose Executive Interview can be heard at www.the SocialMediaBible.com), she informed the audience that on the way to the presentation, she needed directions to find the venue. Within moments, she had 15 people microblogging her back with turn-by-turn directions. That's a powerful network, or, as Twitter puts it, "A global community of friends and strangers answering one simple question: What's happening?"

Back to the Beginning

Microblogging began with the advent of the web log, or blog. After some time spent writing lengthy, detailed accounts, people began to post more con-densed, convenient, portable, personal versions of their conventional blog posts into something that was termed a *microblog*. Microblogging was immediately hailed as conventional blogging's easier, faster, and more immediately accessible cousin. These benefits rapidly made microblogging an increasingly popular form of social interaction and communication, which people began using to seek and share information and daily activities.

One of the very first providers of the microblog was a company called Twitter, essentially providing technology that offered a simplified blogging service. Twitter was born in March 2006 as the result of an R&D project at the San Francisco–based start-up company Obvious. It was initially used by the company's own employees to communicate internally, and launched to the public seven months later in October 2006. On March 19, 2007, Twitter's official debut took place at the annual South by Southwest (SXSW) meeting in Austin, Texas—and it won the South by Southwest Web Award in the blog category. Jack Dorsey—Obvious CEO and the man behind the concept of Twitter—gave a humorous acceptance speech: "We'd like to thank you in 140 characters or less. And we just did!"

Twitter is a microblogging and social networking service that allows its users to send and receive brief (140 characters or less) text-based, micropost instant messages that are referred to as tweets. These text messages are displayed on the user's technology of choice—be it a text-messaging cell phone, web site, PDA, Twitter web site, RSS (see Chapter 18, RSS—Really Simple Syndication Made Simple), SMS,[2] e-mail, or an application such as Facebook, Hootsuite, Tweetdeck, or a web page aggregator. These messages are also delivered to anyone who has signed up and been accepted to "follow" your messages, and the same is true of any tweets that you have requested and been approved to follow.

What You Need to Know

While Twitter is the most popular microblogging platform, it certainly isn't the only one. Other platforms gaining recognition are Jaiku—which started in Europe and has since been acquired by Google—Pownce (now defunct),[3] and PlaceShout. (For a more comprehensive list, please see the Providers section later in this chapter.) However, for the purpose of this chapter, microblogging is discussed primarily in the context of Twitter, since the company had the first-to-market advantage at the time this chapter was written—with 75,000,000 users and more than 35 million tweets per day.

To give you an idea of how aggressive some twitterers (Twitter users) are, at the time this chapter was edited, twitterer and actor Ashton Kutcher was following 567 other twitterers, and had 4,965,723 people following him. In April of 2009, Ashton challenged CNN to a Twitter popularity contest, in which Kutcher edged out the news giant to become the first Twitter user to

FIGURE 14.1 Would It Kill You to Update Your Twitter Status if You're Going to Stay Out So Late?

---

2. SMS is the abbreviation for Systems Management Server, which is a communications protocol that allows the exchange of short text messages between mobile telephone devices. In different parts of the world, the acronym SMS is used as a synonym for a text message or the act of sending a text message even if SMS isn't actually being used. With 2.4 billion active users, or 74 percent of all mobile phone subscribers sending and receiving text messages on their cell phones, SMS text messaging is the most widely used data application on the planet. In spite of its wide use, as a cost-cutting effort, on August 14, 2008, Twitter removed SMS access to their U.K. service.

3. Pownce is a good example of the changing landscape of social media. Leah Culver was interviewed just a few months before her company closed its doors on December 15, 2008. Her interview and insights are still as valid as ever, so we left them. Technology will change, some existing player will go extinct, and many new companies will take their place.

reach one million followers. In May 2010, Kutcher was running a close second to Britney Spears, with almost five million followers each. President Obama was ranked fifth, behind Ellen DeGeneres and Lady Gaga.

Then there's the famous blogger, Robert Scoble—another Twitter fanatic. Robert is currently following 18,099 people and has 118,697 following his tweets.

As your presence on Twitter or any microblogging service grows, people you don't know will begin to follow you. This is kind of like people reading your blog or visiting your web site. The number of people whom you follow will be significantly less because there are only so many messages you can read, just as there is a finite number of blogs you read or web pages you visit. Some experts, such as Guy Kawasaki, suggest following every person who follows you. With more and more helpful platforms making their way to mainstream and the integration of Twitter lists, it's possible to follow hundreds of thousands and still stay apart of the conversation. While it's impossible to truly stay connected with each and every one of your followers, it's possible to follow many and stay connected.

Tweeting and following constitute the two-way communication and trusted network that drive the microblogging community. Any time someone you are following ceases to deliver relevant "What's in It for Me?" content, you can simply decide to "unfollow" that person. This is the power of permission-based marketing, whereby you choose who is allowed to market and communicate to you. Opting not to follow someone is like having your own built-in, user-controlled spam filter.

While microblogging started with the early adopters, it is currently a primary way that thought leaders, technophiles, Millenniums, Gen Y's, and technologically savvy users keep in touch with one another. It has moved into the mainstream and is now widely used throughout the United States. For example, Democratic presidential candidates Barack Obama and John Edwards both microposted details of their runs for office while actually on the campaign trail. Also, the *New York Times,* the BBC, and many other traditional media organizations have begun using microblogging to post headlines and links.

While many give credit to Twitter for being the first microblogging platform, some believe that the microcontent trend has been around for a while—depending upon your definition of the term. In fact, many think that regular blogging should be considered microcontent or user-generated content, while others contend that posting a small note or bookmark on del.icio.us.com, or typing some text on a photo posted on Flickr or Faccbook, or creating a review on Yelp is also considered microblogging. The purists of this movement still give Twitter credit for creating the first intentional interactive microblogging/micropost network.

The popularity of microblogging can be attributed in part to the ease of creating a micropost. While blogs are considered fairly simply to write and maintain, a two-sentence update is still easier. Microblogs are also significantly less complicated to digest than conventional blogs, especially when you are following several hundred or more twitterers. This makes the tweets more desirable, more current, and more likely to be read. Commenting on tweets spurs an entertaining rapid-fire exchange of conversational tweets from other twitterers. And—like so many other social media technologies discussed in this book—Twitter and other microblogging platforms are free.

Since microblogging requires much less effort than conventional blogging, many people find it more entertaining. You simply send out a tweet whenever you have a moment; there is much less pressure to regularly update your thoughts. Unlike your web page, blog page, Facebook, and other networks you can post on, there is no blog-roll showing visitors how frequently (or infrequently) you blog. Many people are using microblogging to supplement their main blog by publishing short descriptions of their latest blog post—along with a corresponding link to create attention and drive traffic to the web or blog site.

Twitter and microblogging aren't just U.S. phenomena; microblogging is widely popular around the world. Sysomos announced in January of 2010 that Twitter is still growing in popularity internationally. Growth in countries like Germany, Brazil, and Indonesia have led to the ever-increasing number of users around the world. While the popularity of the microblogging site has increased in the most recent past, countries like China continue to block the microblogging site from the entire country with the exception of 50,000 participants. Twitter creator Jack Dorsey stated in a recent New York panel discussion on social media, however, that in due time the Chinese should have access to Twitter.

The Microsphere Is Not All Good

Trivial Pursuit

The most common criticism of microblogging is the trivial nature of most posts (see Figure 14.2). Most people perusing the Internet really don't care if someone is about to eat their dinner or is currently waiting for a plane. The ease of use and the lack of cost encourage people to become tweeting maniacs, and people tend to lose a sense of responsibility by continuously tweeting about the most mundane occurrences in their day-to-day lives. When you are following 500, 1,000, or 5,000 twitterers—as well as receiving mobile telephone text messages, voicemails (home, office, and cell), news

FIGURE 14.2 Twitter Tweets

aggregators, snail mail, junk mail, and spam—it can create social media overload. Some people who thrive on social media are so fanatical that they've essentially overloaded themselves with too much data. They are receiving information as a steady stream of noise that has made it nearly impossible to contact or communicate with them. Their e-mail is full and won't accept any more memos; their outgoing cell phone message asks that you "please don't leave me a voice mail, because I don't retrieve them anymore" (and the recording is full anyway); and they no longer respond to their tweets.

In March of 2010, a study by Retrevo revealed our true social media obsession. *Retrevo* reported "We were not surprised to learn how many people appear to be, shall we say, obsessed with checking in with their social media circles throughout the day and even the night." The study reported that users under the age of 25 were more likely to interrupt activities such as eating, going to the bathroom, or even having sex to update microblogging sites such as Twitter. The trend, of late, is a growing obsession and dependency with microblogging and social media in general.

Microspam

When the first edition of this book was published, microblogging spam was not prevalent on microblogging networks. In August of 2009, Twitter reported to have seen a massive increase in spam, equivalent to 8 to 11 percent of overall tweets. On March 23, 2010, Twitter reported that the overall spam on the microblogging site had decreased significantly from its height in August of 2009, reportedly falling to as little as 1 percent. As discussed in Chapter 6, in forums there is flaming, or flame wars, in which other users will respond to a spammer with pretty nasty replies, which keeps spamming at a minimum in normal circumstances. This reaction also happens in professional networks such as LinkedIn. On Twitter, however, even flaming or flame wars have not kept spammers at bay. Experts suggest that while Twitter may claim to have as little as 1 percent spam, the level of spam is still high even if the proportion is small.

Microadvertising

The inevitable question often associated with microblogging sites comes back to "How can they make it profitable?" The developers at Twitter have been trying to figure that out for some time. Twitter, and many other microblogging sites, have little, if any, advertising. For sites that in essence are free, advertising is the largest way for them to generate income, for which Twitter has yet to release.

Twitter CEO Evan Williams announced at SXSW 2010 their plans for an advertising model. The "At Anywhere" platform will allow web sites to integrate Twitter deeply into their sites, giving users a seamless experience to use the service but not veer off the news site or web site they were on. Experts suggest Twitter's "At Anywhere" platform to be equivalent to Facebook Connect, allowing for better usability and accessibility on a given web site without taking the end user away. It seems that the team at Twitter, and at other microblogging sites, have given up on the idea of traditional advertising and are looking for alternative methods to create an income stream for their sites.

The Fail Whale

Only a year after Twitter was launched, it began experiencing outages with its user base. Because of its overwhelming popularity, the folks at Twitter still haven't been able to avoid server overload from the sheer volume of traffic to its site. The Twitter web site and service can sometimes be completely shut down for several hours. In August of 2009, the site experienced one of its longest outages because of a DDOS attack (distributed denial-of-service attack). While DDOS attacks are nothing new, the outage caused quite a stir online not only for Twitter, but also for Facebook, Live Journal, and others.

This isn't the first time a DDOS attack has affected hundreds of thousands or even millions of people. In the beginning of 2000 e-commerce sites like eBay, Amazon.com, and even Yahoo! were affected by a massive DDOS attack estimated to have cost a collective $8 million in damages and lost revenue.

On the occasions when the site is experiencing problems, twitterers' attempts to tweet or visit the web site are met with the all-too-familiar Fail Whale (see Figure 14.3). This character created by Yiying Lu—an image of a happy cartoon whale being lifted by a multitude of small red birds using nets to hoist him from the ocean—has become somewhat of an industry icon for monumental failure. Because of their high-pitched twitter, the Beluga whale is known as the "canary of the sea." Not surprisingly, the message on the image reads, "Too many tweets! Please wait a moment and try again."

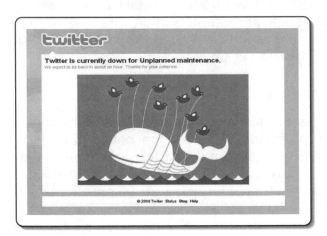

FIGURE 14.3　The Fail Whale

When people become dependent on a particular technology—like e-mail, BlackBerrys, or blogs—and that is taken away from them for even a short period, they become paralyzed. The social media industry as a whole has been too slow to sufficiently monetize its efforts. If this trend doesn't reverse, Fail Whales of all kinds will be appearing with more and more social media technology.

A good example of this is Pownce. Pownce is similar to Twitter without a really distinct competitive advantage. People in the social media world knew it didn't have a sustainable business model, either. Pownce didn't place unwanted advertising in your messages and didn't offer the industry fallback

FIGURE 14.4 Leah Culver, cofounder, Pownce

revenue model of freemium products that could be purchased in addition to all of the free services Pownce offered. As a result, Pownce and its whale went belly up.

During the writing of this book, Leah Culver, the cofounder of Pownce, spoke with the author of *The Social Media Bible* about her company, services, and business model. Then, without warning on December 15, 2008, came her e-mail that they were shutting down. Ironically, Leah Culver was on the cover of the July 2008 *MIT Technology Review,* where she was blowing a huge bubblegum bubble about to burst, accompanied by the headline, "The Next Bubble." The inside photo was her with the busted bubble.

To hear Leah Culver's interview, go to www.theSocialMediaBible.com. The interview remains on the web site to show how vulnerable this new industry is. More Pownce stories will occur as the industry matures.

How Safe Are Your Tweets?

On April 7, 2007, the well-known security researcher, author, and speaker Nitesh Dhanjani created the first Twitter security issue. Nitesh used SMS and FakeMyText.com to send phony messages (posts) to people's cell phones. Luckily, the only cell phones to which he was able to send the counterfeit messages were ones for which he already knew the telephone numbers. To counter this weakness in their system, Twitter initiated a PIN system for authenticating SMS originating messages. Since then, both Twitter and Jott have taken measures to prevent this security lapse

FIGURE 14.5

from happening again. You can read Dhanjani's article, "Twitter and Jott Vulnerable to SMS and Caller ID Spoofing," by going to www.oreillynet.com/onlamp/blog/2007/04/twitter_and_jott_vulnerable_to.html or go to www.theSocialMediaBible.com to just click on the link.

On the Lighter Side of Microblogging

Some Twitter Jargon

Twitter is the most prevalent microblogging technology used today.

- A *twitterer* is a person using Twitter to send out posts or *tweets*.
- A *tweet* is a post or text message sent from one twitterer to another.
- A *retweet* (RT) is reposting someone else's tweet
- The tweeting community is called the *twitosphere*.

Much like e-mail, once you hit Send, the tweet is out there. A regretted tweet is called a *Mistweet*. (Never tweet after a bottle of Chardonnay.)

Google Maps has a mash-up called *Twittervision*, which shows users the geographic location of twitterers. The list of Twitter jargon goes on and on.

Corporate Twitterers

Small, medium, and large companies alike are beginning to adopt social media tools into their marketing, public relations, communications, and customer service approaches. Like any early adopters, these companies will have a significant advantage over those who wait until social media becomes mainstream. Here are just a few of the many large companies that have incorporated microblogging into their corporate culture:

- Southwest Airlines regularly tweets as one of its standard customer service tools. The following is an actual tweet from Southwest Airlines: "twitpic.com/1bzrxh—Today, SW Employees donated these Easter Baskets to DAL Ronald McDonald House & Children's Medical Center Dallas 10:22 AM March 30, 2010" (a TwitPic is a clickable link to a posted picture on TwitPic.com).
- The somewhat controversial Dave Winer—who calls himself the "original blogger" and inventor of RSS—tweets his followers on a regular basis about his River project at the *New York Times*. The project is what Dave calls a "river-of-news format," wherein a stream of short text messages about the latest breaking news from the *Times* is sent to followers by cell phone, PDA, or web page aggregator to create a newsroll of top stories. Dave explains, "I created the site because I wasn't getting enough news about products. It's that simple. I'm interested in the other stuff too, the finance, trends, parties, puppets—the River Project allows readers to prioritize and aggregate their news in one web site."

- Frank Eliason is a Comcast corporate manager and blogosphere liaison in Philadelphia's Center City region. Frank has the daunting assignment of monitoring blogs and tweets for unfavorable posts aimed at Comcast. When Frank found a tweet that said, "My Internet goes out every day at 3:30. Why would that be?" he answered right away, "That should not be. We should have that looked at. Send an e-mail with account info to mailto:We_Can_Help@cable.comcast.com"; signed: @ComcastCares. This type of immediate and personal customer service sets companies like Comcast apart from their competitors.

- Chief blogger at Dell Computer Lionel Menchaca was immediately on top of things when Dell's laptop computer batteries began exploding. Lionel got tweets from customers and the media asking for information about the problem. He kept tweeting and blogging, and continuously updating his customers with the latest updates he had. The industry—as well as Dell's customers—were shocked to see a company that big taking such personal care of its customers. This provided a huge public relations advantage at a time when Dell needed it most.

- Large businesses such as Cisco Systems and Whole Foods Market use Twitter to provide product or service information to their customers through tweets.

- The Los Angeles Fire Department put the technology to use during California wildfires since 2007 to get up-to-the-second information of where the fires were breaking out, where people were trapped, and where their help was needed most.

- NASA used Twitter to break the news of discovery of what appeared to be water ice on Mars by the Phoenix Mars Lander. Other NASA projects, such as Space Shuttle missions and the International Space Station, also provide updates through Twitter.

- News outlets such as the BBC have also started using Twitter to disseminate breaking news or provide information feeds for sporting events.

- Several 2008 U.S. presidential candidates—including Democratic Party nominee Barack Obama—used Twitter as a publicity mechanism. The Nader/Gonzalez campaign used Twitter and Google Maps to show real-time updates of their ballot access teams across the country.

- The College of Golf at Keiser University is using Twitter to relay information to students such as school announcements, golf weather updates, and even encouraging students to ask questions through the online platform. They have also utilized Twitter to answer third-parties' questions about the sport of golf, and encourage the golf community to support each other through the platform.

- Westwinds Church in Jackson, Michigan, uses Twitter as a part of its weekend worship services, and actually introduced the concept of Twitter Church. Westwinds runs training classes for Twitter and encourages members to bring laptops and mobile devices to church. On occasion, the Twitter feed will be shown live on the screens in the auditorium, and everyone is encouraged to give their input, make observations, and ask questions to encourage an interactive worship format.

Microblogging clearly has widespread global appeal, and it can play a vital role in keeping people safe during disasters and tragedies. During the January 2010 earthquake in Haiti, Twitter users started flooding the Web with images and stories. The microblogging site was actually utilized to help a Doctors Without Borders cargo plane full of much-needed supplies and medicine land on the ground in Port-au-Prince. The Twitterverse bombarded the U.S. Air Force's account on Twitter, demanding they look into the issue Doctors Without Borders crew members were having on getting permission to land, after a crew member tweeted about it. The plane was on the ground within the hour. Twitter, and other networks, played a huge role in the outpouring of funds to the Red Cross and other nonprofit organizations raising money to help those affected by the massive earthquake.

Twitter has become the communication tool of choice by many emergency services around the world, and has been used by activists and journalists during other natural disasters.

Twitter is also credited with doing a better job of getting information out during emergencies than the traditional news media or government emergency services, as was the case with the Virginia Tech shootings in April 2007. In the Virginia Tech case, the news media and family members were getting real-time updates through Twitter while it was actually happening.

Tweets in the News

The Wall Street Journal Digital Network Twittering the US Airways Plane Crash

Shira Ovide

Notch Another Win for Citizen Journalism

Janis Krums, a guy with a camera and a penchant for social media tools, posted one of the first and most remarkable photos today of US Airways Flight 1549 after it crash landed in the Hudson River.

"There's a plane in the Hudson," the Sarasota native wrote on the microblogging site Twitter just as reports began to break of the plane hitting the water off Manhattan's west side. "I'm on the ferry going to pick up the people. Crazy."

The photo, which Mr. Krums posted online using a Twitter photo sharing site, has been viewed more than 43,000 times.

Social media tools like Twitter—which allows users to tap out 140-character status updates—have changed how breaking news events are recorded and covered. They made for on-the-ground reports from the Mumbai terror attacks in November [2008], for example.

After he documented the Hudson River crash, Mr. Krums then became a minor celebrity in traditional media, too. He conducted an interview on MSNBC and says on his Twitter profile that he's preparing for even more interviews this evening.

Source: http://blogs.wsj.com/digits/2009/01/15/twittering-the-usairways-plane-crash/tab/comments/#comment-346 For a clickable link, go to www.theSocialMediaBible.com.

Providers

Entire ecosystems of web sites and technologies have been created around Twitter. Twhirl, for example, is an authoring tool (or software package) based on the Adobe AIR platform that connects users to Twitter as well as other sites. Tweet Scan and Summize, which Twitter purchased on July 15, 2008, are tweet-specific search engines. Web site twitterholic.com tracks the most popular and active twitterers, and provides a list of Top 100 Twitterholics Based on Followers. And sites like dailyrt.com showcase the most retweeted posts of the day, supporting a large community of users and fans.

There are also sites that tag with what are known as *hashtags* and *mashups*, such as Twittervision.com. Hashtags are a community-driven convention for adding additional context and metadata to your tweets, so that they can be categorized and found easily by subject matter. Using a hashtag is similar to adding a tag to a Flickr photograph, or a meta-keyword to your web page. The main difference is that instead of adding the metadata behind the scenes—where the user doesn't see it—the hashtag is part of your tweet. Hashtags allow you to create Groupings on Twitter, by simply prefixing a word or phrase with a hash symbol or pound sign (#)—like #hashtag, or #thesocialmediabible. Hashtags became popular during the San Diego brush fires in 2007, when California resident Nate Ritter used his hashtag *#sandiegofire* to identify his personal Twitter updates related to the fires. Also, fund-raising efforts for the Haiti earthquake victims and information about the quake were preceded by #Haiti.

(For more information on hashtags, or to have your personal hashtags tracked in real time, go to hashtags.org.)

A mashup is a web application that combines data from more than one source into a single, integrated web site—as when real estate information is added to a Google Map. Another example is Travature (www.travature.com) a site that has integrated airfare metasearch engines, wiki travel guides, and hotel reviews, as well as applications that allow travelers to share photos and stories. A mashup creates a new and distinct web page and service that has not been provided by either source. It also includes rich media or a combination of text, blog post, tweets, images, audio, and video all in one place.

Microblogging beyond Twitter?

A number of services exist that have a similar concept to Twitter's, but have country-specific versions of their services, such as www.frazr.com. Other sites—such as Jaiku and Friendfeed—combine microblogging with other capabilities like file sharing and allow the Twitter user to attach a file to posts.

Plurk is another microblogging platform that has been gaining in popularity. This service launched in May 2008 and gained considerable acceptance in Silicon Valley during its first 30 days. While the number of Twitter users are far greater than Plurk's users, Plurk's horizontal time line and group conversations create a more robust interface and adds a spatial dimension to microblogging that make it a good alternative to Twitter.

Other services include Yammer, which launched on September 8, 2008, at the TechCrunch50 Conference and is marketed as an enterprise version of Twitter. Yammer asks, "What's happening at your company? With Yammer you can share status updates with your coworkers." The service is currently used at over 60,000 businesses worldwide.

Prologue is a microblogging tool created by Automatic—the makers of WordPress—that was released in January 2008 and allows its users to "post short messages about what they're doing" in a secured environment. Later in 2008, a new and improved version of Prologue, dubbed P2, was developed and made available to the public.

Then there's the Enterprise Social Messaging Experiment (ESME) created by Demo Jam at SAP Labs, which allows you to create new groups instantly by clicking on cloud tags or word frequency. For more information, see www.youtube.com/watch?v=y1dPAV8C0Tw or go to the www.theSocial MediaBible.com and click on the link.

SocialCast is a FriendFeed and Twitter tool for the enterprise, and Laconica is considered an Open Microblogging Tool—an open-source application (one in which software source code is available to the general public without a license that restricts or limits its use, modification, or redistribution) that can be installed on corporate servers and used behind the firewall.

And then there is OraTweet, created by Oracle—the world's largest enterprise software company—as a microblogging tool for internal employee and external client use. OraTweet allows companies, universities, and organizations to run their own in-house microblogs that keep their communications private and secure and that encourage the development of internal communities. OraTweet operates the same way as e-mail and instant messaging, but allows enterprises to broadcast messages safely within their own environments.

Some other sites include:

- *Status:* A lighter communication tool that displays an update of your team's progress on a single screen at one time.

- *Trillr:* A small group service intended for coworkers, partners, and customers to communicate. Trillr allows users to stay connected with quick, frequent exchanges of data, and answers the question, "What's on your mind?"

- *I Did Work:* A task-based update tool that provides teams with the ability to leave short status messages. This site creates a work log that keeps a history of your progress and shares it with your team.

- *Joint Contact:* A collaboration tool that incorporates microblogging features and connects Twitter to your project status to inform your followers of upcoming events. With JointContact, you can link your tweets to your project management system.

- *BlueTwit-IBM:* Launched in 2007, an internal Twitter client that has been providing IBM employees with an alternative to e-mail.

- *Present.ly:* A micro-update communication tool that gives employees the ability to instantly communicate their current status, ask questions, post media, and more.

- *Mixin:* A service that spans both internal and external corporate communications and "lets you share your daily activities and intentions to get together more often with your friends."

- *Spoink:* A multimedia microblogging service that integrates blogging, podcasting, telephony, and SMS text messaging. Spoink supports all major mobile audio, video, and picture formats.

And then there's identi.ca, Jaiku, FriendFeed, Dodgeball, tumblr, and TWiT Army—and all of the most popular social networking web sites such as Facebook, MySpace, and LinkedIn, which have their own microblogging feature called a *status update*.

The ROI of Social Media

Twitter for Business. You're kidding . . . Right?

Background

As an executive and entrepreneur, I don't have time for toys and fads. So back in March of 2006, when Robert Scoble stood on the stage of the First Arizona Social Media Conference and said that "TWITTER was the next BIG thing," I turned to Francine Hardaway in horror and whispered "You're kidding . . . Right?" Later, like many other new Twitter users, I signed up for an account and then promptly forgot about the whole thing. After all, it was just a fad. It wouldn't last.

Strategy

It was not until January of 2009, that I again took a serious look at Twitter as a business communication tool. And this time, I looked at it more strategically on the odd chance that maybe, just maybe, it was not a fad, after all. After checking in with the "experts" (it's in quotes since the people who know the most about this stuff HATE to be called experts), I got a few tips, tricks, and tools, and started to experiment. I started off slow. One Twitter ID (@joankw) and two blogs with the exact same content. (http://jkw.typepad.com and www .joankoerber-walker.com on WordPress) The test was simple. The TypePad blog would be promoted on Twitter. The WordPress blog would use standard SEO. I would try it for ninety days and see what impact Twitter had on traffic to the blog and for its acceptance by readers. We set the two up on FeedBurner and started gathering data.

Implementation

After 90 days, the results were not bad. We were running a traffic ratio of ten to one on the TypePad (Twitter-promoted) blog compared to the WordPress blog, according to FeedBurner statistics. With this small level of success, and due to a tweet frequency that was annoying to some, we moved to the next step and experimented with segmenting the company's potential Twitter audience into new categories through targeted profiles in the areas that were our corporate focus creating @CorePurpose for the company as well as @JKWleadership @JKWinnovation and @JKWgrowth, since as a company, we believe that Leadership plus Innovation equals Greater Growth. We were very transparent in our strategy, posting not only the twitter IDs but also our strategy AND the tools we were using right on each of our blogs (example: http://jkw.typepad .com/corepurpose_joan_koerberw/my-profiles-on-twitter.html).

Opportunity

CorePurpose is a thought leadership organization that provides solutions to BIG problems for large companies and organizations. We also publish, through our Core Purpose Publishing division, books for universities, trade associations, and business readers. Our advertising and marketing efforts target both potential customers and potential partners in key business areas of expertise. If Twitter, as a tool, would allow us to connect with that audience so that we could demonstrate our expertise and convert them to customers or partners, our business would increase.

Conclusion

And now for the big question. Was there a return on investment? One year later, I had on opportunity to speak to the Society of Women Engineers, and shared some results. You will find the video on You Tube here: www.youtube .com/joankw. By reinvesting marketing resources on Twitter, CorePurpose has had the opportunity to connect to both potential partners and customers on Twitter across FOUR continents. Relationships developed using Twitter as a business communication tool have allowed us to make connections, share and exchange information, and most importantly, convert contacts to customers and partners at a higher rate in one year than traditional marketing strategies did in our first seven years of operations. We have expanded our social media tool set to YouTube, LinkedIn, and numerous blogs. I sure hope Twitter is not a fad. You see it is working! And that ratio of RSS feeds is now 131:1!

Joan Koerber-Walker
www.corepurpose.com
Google Profile: www.google.com/profiles/jkoerberwalker

Expert Insight

Biz Stone, cofounder, Twitter, www.twitter.com

Biz Stone

I'm the cofounder of Twitter, and before that I helped start a service called Xanga.com, which is a social journaling service that we started in 1999 in New York City. They are still there, but I left and I ended up working at Google. I was specifically on the Blogger team for a couple of years before I left there, and sort of got back in to the start-up world with a project called Odeo. This is an audio on the Internet, a podcasting service, and it was actually when I was at Odeo that Twitter was actually a side project that we were working on that we fell in love with. This ultimately turned into its own company that just grew and grew and grew. That's where we're at today. . . .

Yeah, it's really just a short messaging service, at the simplest level, but a communication utility. What it becomes now that we have so many people using it, it really becomes the pulse of what's happening with the people and the organizations that you really care about most. So, on the one hand, you use it to just communicate; on the other hand, you look through it to find out what's going on. . . .

Twitter is the name of the service, and it comes from the idea of the word that you can look up in the dictionary which is a "short trill, chirp, or burst of information," referencing a bird call. People are tricked into calling it *individual updates*. Every time I give an individual update on Twitter, I actually get saved and achieved on Twitter. It becomes its own individual web page, and people have been referring to those individual updates as tweets. This is the axis of Twittering, or sometimes I say "tweeting," because they are fond of that word *tweet*.

It is nothing that we officially stated. People starting using it, so it works out well for us. . . .

Yes, it's a short message, a short text message. . . . One of the key things about Twitter is that it's agnostic when it comes to what sort of device you prefer to use to interact with the system. So if you prefer to use SMS and mobile texting on a mobile phone, Twitter will work that way for you. But it also works over the Web and it also works with several thousand right now (more in the future), third-party independent pieces of software that you can either download for Mac or a PC, or use with Slash. Basically we opened up our infrastructure; we created an API so that smart developers around the world can create custom interactive software to interact with Twitter. . . .

I mean we did it early on just to, sort of, scratch an itch. One of our very early developers wanted to be able to interact with Twitter a certain way, so we created a very simple HI; in fact what happened was the service is simple and the API was so simple that even a beginner API developer could jump in and build something on Twitter that worked very quickly. So it became popular to build on top of Twitter, and what it did for us is that it created so much variety out there (of ways of interacting with Twitter) that it ended up just creating a lot of traffic and creating a lot of opportunities and options for people, which is great. . . .

Yeah, and it's really that mobile aspect that we were trying to get at early. Twitter was basically inspired by the away messages on IM, so if you ever used an IM tool, you see that your coworkers or your friends are in a meeting, out for coffee, or whatever. You can look at a group of 12 people and get a sense of what everyone's doing, what everyone's up to; but that's related to the computer and what they are doing on the computer. So when we took that idea and we just broke it out and we made it more mobile by adding the ability to interact with SMS. We made it more social by building in more features.

Then we created, basically, new kinds of communications—a kind of real-time group communications that really didn't exist before. And it's something that turned out that can be very useful for people. . . .

To listen to or read the entire Executive Conversation with Biz Stone, go to www .theSocialMediaBible.com.

Commandments

1. **Thou shalt begin microblogging.**

    Don't be afraid of microblogging. It's easy, it's free, and it's fun. It's a great way to stay in direct and immediate contact with whomever you choose—whether it's friends, family, club members, church groups, coworkers, prospects, or customers.

2. **Thou shalt tweet.**

    Tweet! The technology isn't any good unless you use it. Tweets are only 140 characters, and are as easy to send as a text message. When you receive a relevant thought, text it out to your followers. And remember to always have that "What's in It for Me?" content value.

3. **Thou shalt follow twitterers.**

    Follow other twitterers. Find people with similar interests, good ideas—or just people you care about—and see what thoughts they share on a daily basis. Remember, if you don't like what they have to say, unfollow them and go find others who provide you with that WIIFM content.

4. **Thou shalt invite others to follow you.**

Be sure to invite others to follow you. They don't know that you are sharing so many pearls of wisdom unless you tell them. Send them your Twitter address, and tweet them often.

5. **Thou shalt set up groups.**

Set up groups in Twitter (or platform of your choice) using hashtags. Set up one group for your existing customers, another for your prospects, and yet another for your coworkers. Send different and appropriate tweets to each group.

6. **Thou shalt use news feed tweets.**

Set up a Twitter News Feed, so that you can get all of the breaking news as it happens—and only that which interests you—whether it's business, lifestyles, finance, gossip, sports, international, health . . . and so on!

7. **Thou shalt use tweets for internal communications.**

Try using Twitter for internal communications by setting up separate groups for your coworkers and employees. Send them status reports on the company's stock prices, new product developments, press releases, HR benefit updates, holiday information, or just an occasional atta-boy or pep talk.

Conclusion

Microblogging is a wonderful and interesting way to keep in touch with your family, friends, and coworkers. It's also an imaginative way to send quick updates on news, products, services, legislation, or any content that has a "What's in It for Me?" value to your customers and prospects. Keeping yourself and your company in the forefront of your prospects' minds—by giving them valuable information and updates—will likely convert prospects into customers.

Try it. Set up a free account, follow some like-minded twitterers; invite other twitterers to follow you. Monitor what they say. Evaluate the WIIFM value. Then begin tweeting yourself. Monitor the responses from that. After a short while, you will begin to see the most effective content you can deliver to your followers.

As has been written in almost every chapter thus far, the most important thing to remember is not to get overwhelmed; in fact, whelmed is the state of mind you are looking to achieve. Try using a microblogging platform. Send some tweets or posts. Read some tweets or posts. And enjoy it. If it becomes overwhelming or loses its appeal, back off and unfollow. Like any technology, the key is moderation.

To hear all of the Expert Interviews, go to www.theSocialMediaBible .com.

Readings and Resources

Banks, Michael A. *Blogging Heroes: Interviews with 30 of the World's Top Bloggers*. (Hoboken, NJ: John Wiley & Sons, Inc.)

Clapperton, Guy. *This Is Social Media: Tweet, Blog, Link and Post Your Way to Business Success*. (Hoboken, NJ: John Wiley & Sons, Inc.)

Collier, Marsha. *Facebook and Twitter For Seniors For Dummies*. (Hoboken, NJ: John Wiley & Sons, Inc.)

Comm, Joel, and Ken Burge. *Twitter Power: How to Dominate Your Market One Tweet at a Time*. (Hoboken, NJ: John Wiley & Sons, Inc.)

Comm, Joel. *Twitter Power 2.0: How to Dominate Your Market One Tweet at a Time*. (Hobokcn, NJ: John Wiley & Sons, Inc.)

Crenna, Daniel. *Professional Twitter Development: With Examples in .NET 3.5*. (Hoboken, NJ: John Wiley & Sons, Inc.)

Evans, Dave. *Social Media Marketing: The Next Generation of Business Engagement*. (Hoboken, NJ: John Wiley & Sons, Inc.)

Fitton, Laura, Michael Gruen, and Leslie Poston. *Twitter For Dummies*. (Hoboken, NJ: John Wiley & Sons, Inc.)

Fitton, Laura, Michael Gruen, and Leslic Poston. *Twitter For Dummies*, 2nd ed. (Hoboken, NJ: John Wiley & Sons, Inc.)

Gardner, Susannah. *Buzz Marketing with Blogs For Dummies*. (Hoboken, NJ: John Wiley & Sons, Inc.)

Gardner, Susannah, and Shane Birley. *Blogging For Dummies*. (Hoboken, NJ: John Wiley & Sons, Inc.)

Gunelius, Susan. *Google Blogger For Dummies*. (Hoboken, NJ: John Wiley & Sons, Inc.)

Harris, Jeanne. *The Celebrity Tweet Directory*. (Hoboken, NJ: John Wiley & Sons, Inc.)

Lacy, Kyle. *Twitter Marketing For Dummies*. (Hoboken, NJ: John Wiley & Sons, Inc.)

McFedries, Paul, and Pete Cashmore. *Twitter Tips, Tricks, and Tweets*. (Hoboken, NJ: John Wiley & Sons, Inc.)

McFedries, Paul. *Twitter Tips, Tricks, and Tweets*, 2nd ed. (Hoboken, NJ: John Wiley & Sons, Inc.)

Reagan, Dusty. *Twitter Application Development For Dummies.* (Hoboken, NJ: John Wiley & Sons, Inc.)

Reeder, Joelle, and Katherine Scoleri. *The IT Girl's Guide to Blogging with Moxie.* (Hoboken, NJ: John Wiley & Sons, Inc.)

Rettberg, Jill Walker. *Blogging.* (Hoboken, NJ: John Wiley & Sons, Inc.)

Rowse, Darren, and Chris Garrett. *ProBlogger: Secrets for Blogging Your Way to a Six-Figure Income.* (Hoboken, NJ: John Wiley & Sons, Inc.)

Sagolla, Dom. *140 Characters: A Style Guide for the Short Form.* (Hoboken, NJ: John Wiley & Sons, Inc.)

Scoble, Robert, and Shel Israel. *Naked Conversations: How Blogs Are Changing the Way Businesses Talk with Customers.* (Hoboken, NJ: John Wiley & Sons, Inc.)

Thomases, Hollis. *Twitter Marketing: An Hour a Day.* (Hoboken, NJ: John Wiley & Sons, Inc.)

Downloads

For your free downloads associated with *The Social Media Bible,* go to www.theSocialMediaBible.com, and enter your ISBN number located on the back of the book above the bar code. Be sure to enter the dashes.

Credits

The ROI of Social Media was provided by:

Joan Koerber-Walker, www.corepurpose.com

Expert Insight was provided by:

Biz Stone, cofounder of Twitter, www.twitter.com

Technical edits were provided by:

Kaila Strong, Social Media Architect, and Arnie Kuenn, CEO of Vertical Measures, www.VerticalMeasures.com

CHAPTER 15

Live from Anywhere—It's Livecasting

What's in It for You?

Whether you call it web radio, net radio, streaming radio, e-radio, talk radio, Internet radio, livecasting, lifecasting, webcasting, web conferencing, or webinars, broadcasting information online is all about creating live content that uses the Internet to distribute (or stream[1]) that content. All of these terms refer to the process of producing your own, current content, and then distributing that content live over the Internet. You can actually create your very own radio or television show that will only be as expensive as your production costs dictate. You are the host, the production manager, and the talent. You can speak about nearly anything you wish. You can broadcast your show each day, each week, or only when you feel like it. You can put on a live presentation, perform training, introduce or demonstrate a new product or service, create a preventative maintenance program for your customers, or just talk with a special guest about what's new in your industry. It's easy to do, it's a powerful medium, and there's no cost.

Think about that for a minute: For the very first time in history, you can actually produce your own radio or television show and distribute it to everyone around the world—live—for free!

---

1. Stream/streaming/multicast occurs when Internet-rich audio or video content is continuously uploaded and fed into your computer as you listen to or watch it. It is the opposite of the typical on-demand file downloading, wherein you have to wait for the entire file to be downloaded to your computer before you can play it. Streaming can deliver live, real-time content, or prerecorded podcast-type files (see Chapters 9 through 13 for more information on these topics). With livecasting, the audio and video content is broadcast live and is playing in real time; the listener/viewer has no control over the broadcast, as in traditional broadcast media.

 theSocialMediaBible.com

Back to the Beginning

As with the other kinds of rich media creation discussed in this book, livecasting falls into two major categories: audio (radio) and video (television). This chapter discusses how you can create your own radio show and broadcast it to your prospects, customers, coworkers, and fan base. In the video and television category, the chapter discusses how you can create your very own television show and broadcast that content for free.

Internet Radio

Technologist and author of eight books—including *Exploring the Internet* and *A World's Fair*—Carl Malamud first pioneered web radio in 1993. Each week, Malamud would interview a different computer expert during what he called the "first computer radio talk show." The show wasn't really livecasted, as it was prerecorded and distributed one by one to his listeners—who then had to download and play each audio file (an early version of podcasting). Malamud broke important ground, however, by introducing the concept of Internet radio.

The first groups to actually broadcast audio live over the Internet were existing commercial radio stations that were already producing audio content. The crossover from existing terrestrial radio stations or networks was logical and natural; all that the stations needed to do was take the existing content that they were already broadcasting over the AM and FM radio frequencies and broadcast it over the Internet. WXYC—89.3 FM in Chapel Hill, North Carolina— became the first traditional radio station to begin broadcasting over the Internet (not transmitted through wireless means) on November 7, 1994. WXYC had actually begun testing their broadcasts three months earlier, in August of that year. On that very same day in November, WREK—91.1 FM in Atlanta—also streamed their first radio show over the Internet; unlike WXYC, though, WREK did not advertise what they were doing until later.

That same month, the very first rock and roll concert was broadcast live, with the Rolling Stones becoming the "first cyberspace streamed concert." Mick Jagger welcomed his concert's listeners with, "I wanna say a special welcome to everyone that's, uh, climbed into the Internet tonight and, uh, has got into the M-bone. And I hope it doesn't all collapse."

Commercial Internet-Only Radio Stations

The next step in Internet broadcasting was for individuals—rather than traditional radio broadcasters—to take advantage of this new, effective, and free technology. People began creating their own radio show content and transmitting it over the Internet—from everywhere. A new industry was born.

In November 1995, the Minneapolis, Minnesota–based NetRadio Company founded by Scott Bourne and radio veteran Scot Combs began using RealAudio to stream music over the Internet. The company started with only four formats and had expanded to include more than a dozen formats within two years.

The logic of invention has always been intriguing. So many of the creations in places like the Smithsonian Institution were conceived by people who were merely taking "the next logical step in the evolution of technology." Seldom does someone create something out of nothing, or make major leaps ahead. They simply "take the next step."

For example, Alexander Graham Bell's March 10, 1876, invention of the telephone is often considered as a major breakthrough in communication technology by a genius of a man. But when looking at it in context, the telephone was simply an extension of the already-in-use telegraph. And Alex wasn't the only one taking the next logical step; on the very same day that Bell filed a patent for his device that could transmit speech electronically, Elisha Gray also filed his patent within hours of Bell. Bell simply got there first, and received the patent—which started a legal battle over the invention of the telephone that Bell eventually won.

At the time, most people weren't aware of the fact that so many others around the world were simultaneously working the "next logical step" in telecommunications. Nearly 16 years earlier, in 1860, Antonio Meucci invented *his* version of the telephone, which he called the *teletrofono*, or telectrophone. And twenty-two years before Bell, in 1854, a French telegraphist named Charles Bourseul published in the magazine *L'Illustration* his plan for transmitting sound—and even speech—over an electrical wire.

NetRadio became so popular that audio formatting company RealAudio made it a preset on their RealMedia audio players. NetRadio also received the first trial ASCAP (American Society of Composers, Authors and Publishers) license, which became the prototype for all Internet radio network licenses. The company is credited with another first: broadcasting, in July 1996, the first Internet-only, live weekly concert series. NetRadio—which at its peak of popularity hosted more than 125 music and talk radio channels—built its listener audience to more than 50 million listeners every month.

Radio audience research company Arbitron (which collects listener data about radio audiences similar to the way that Nielsen Media Research collects information about TV audiences) began rating Internet-based radio stations in 1997. They found that NetRadio continuously held 8 of the top 10 rankings. The Navarre Corporation purchased NetRadio and merged the company into one of its subsidiaries later that year, and NetRadio closed its doors in 2001. NetRadio played an important role in the development of Internet audio streaming and paved the way for other providers.

Livecasting

Livecasting as it is known today was made possible by the evolution of smaller, lighter, more energy-efficient (battery) hardware, which included more portable laptop computers, longer-life batteries, a video camera, and wireless Internet connections. As these technologies became more effective and widely used, more and more people began sharing their lives with the world through the Internet.

The first person to continuously broadcast his life live, in real time—with a first-person video from a wearable camera—was University of Toronto professor Steve Mann. Mann experimented with wearable computers and video cameras, and was streaming video as early as the beginning of the 1980s. His work eventually led to the Wearable Wireless Webcam.

In 1994, Mann transmitted his daily activities 24 hours a day, 7 days a week in a continuous stream of video that was truly the first livecast. While wearing a camera and display, Mann broadcasted, over the Internet for others to see, every event of his day-by-day goings-on, while inviting his viewers to communicate with him through text messaging in real time. Because of this early success and popularity, Mann grew his community of livecasters to more than 20,000 members.

The next livecasting phenomenon took place in 1996 with the emergence of the JenniCam—a video that followed the life of Jennifer Kaye Ringley until December 2003. This was followed by collegeboyslive.tv, a site that showed streaming live video of a group in their dorm room, and the University of Toronto's 1998 move to begin livecasting video streaming web sites. Then, in February 1999, the HereAndNow.net web site, founded by Lisa Batey—or Nekomimi Lisa, as her fans knew her—began livecasting 24/7. Batey and her roommates began to share their college life experiences in live, unedited 24/7 Internet video streams. Unlike JenniCam and other livecasting of their time, HereandNow.net broadcasted their video in higher quality and was the first to stream both full-motion video and audio. HereandNow.net stopped broadcasting in 2001, but Batey's community still exists in a chat room and Yahoo! Group.

In December 1999, Josh Harris (creator of the CBS television show *Big Brother*) introduced "We Live in Public," a formatted, conceptual art experiment in which he placed telephones, microphones, and 32 robotic cameras in the home that he and girlfriend Tanya Corrin shared. Viewers were able to text Harris and Corrin through their web site's chat room. Josh Harris is currently founder and CEO of Operator 11 Exchange (www.operator11 .com), a Hollywood-based company that is an Internet-based television studio and online web site.

In 2000, Mitch Maddox who was a former computing systems manager who called himself the "DotComGuy," hit the Web. Maddox's project goal was starting on January 1, 2000, to live for one year without leaving his home in Dallas, Texas. Maddox ordered-in and had delivered all of his food and other necessities off the Internet. His house was on camera 24/7 with several video feeds streamed online. The DotComGuy project had a large number of sponsors, including 3Com, Network Solutions, Peapod, Piper Jaffray, Travelocity, and, United Parcel Service. The DotComGuy project attracted a great deal of attention from the media, but public interest gradually faded away.

In early 2001, Mitch "Pud" Kaplan wrote on his web site that due to the dot-com crash the previous year, his investors were not going to pay him the $100,000 cash bonus for successfully living online in front of a camera for an entire year. Mitch later claimed that this was a mutual agreement between he and his investors and that the $100,000 was required to cover the expenses to keep the project online for that year. The phenomenon of livecasting simply continued to grow.

By 2007, software like Camtwist, Manycam, and WebcamMax allowed livecasts and live video streams to have overlays, commercials, effects, multiple cameras, and more. This expedited the look and perception of livestreams, which allowed a new level of professional-looking live journalism as well as fun shows to fit in.

As more shows joined, livestreaming wasn't solely for livecasting anymore. Walt Ribeiro became an online music instructor who livestreamed to a large virtual classroom. Playcafe became the "first online game show network," and there were presidential campaigns, bands performing live concerts, and even space shuttle launches. The technology was then not only used to broadcast people's lives and webinars, but was creating virtual worlds and businesses—in real time.

Justin.tv

The first person to significantly popularize the concept of livecasting was Californian Justin Kan. While living in San Francisco in early 2007, Justin

FIGURE 15.1　Justin Kan—Justin.tv

founded something he called "Justin.tv." While wearing a webcam attached to his baseball cap, Justin began streaming his life in a continuous, live video, beginning on March 19, 2007, at midnight. Justin is actually the person credited with giving this process the name *lifecasting*. He generated a lot of media attention when he announced he would wear his webcam 24 hours a day, 7 days a week and broadcast his life—nonstop. Justin's interview with NBC *Today* show reporter Ann Curry vaulted him into national attention in April 2007.

The credit for Kan's computer hardware goes to Kyle Vogt, one of the four founders of Justin.tv. Vogt created the portable live video streaming computer system that Justin used to broadcast, and he recalls,

I moved to San Francisco so I could be closer to the rest of the team. I mean *really* close. The four of us lived and worked out of a small two-bedroom apartment. I spent my time becoming an expert in Linux socket programming, cell phone data networks, and real-time data protocols. Four data modems in close proximity just don't work well together, so packet loss was as high as fifty percent. I fought with these modems for weeks but finally managed to wrestle them into a single one point two megabits per second video uplink. The new camera emerged from the pile of Radio Shack parts, computer guts, and hacked-up cell phones that had accumulated on my messy desk. It uses thousands of lines of Python code, a custom real-time protocol, connection load balancing, and several other funky hacks.

Enter Justine Ezarik

On May 29, 2007, designer Justine Ezarik became the second livecaster on Justin.tv with a livecast streaming from Pittsburgh, Pennsylvania, titled iJustine.tv. Justine changed the format a bit by aiming the webcam at herself, rather than using the host's point-of-view approach that was used before.

FIGURE 15.2   Justin.tv

Another major difference between Justine and Justin is that Justine spent considerably more time interacting with her viewers. Where Justin was more "this is what I am seeing," Justine was "here I am, interact with me." Justine was more conversational through text chat, and watching the feed was almost like being with her and talking face to face.

In the spring of 2007, Justin announced that he was going to make his technology available to the public through something he called "the big rollout." Justin.tv created more than 60 different channels to accommodate the continual flow of applicants wanting to create their own livecasts. Soon, there were a wide variety of participants—from college students to graphic designers, a Christian family radio station to a Subaru repair shop. By the summer of 2007, livecasting channels were being added to

FIGURE 15.3   Justine Ezarik—Justine.tv

Justin.tv at an average rate of two per day. The site expanded to nearly 700 channels by the fall of 2007.

Justin.tv generated more than 1,650 hours of daily programming that depicted characters like Australian shark hunter AussieBloke; 18-year-old "I'm a Plastic Princess" Meagan; culinary expert Justopia; San Francisco model Krystyl Baldwin; 22-year-old "Roxie," the San Luis Obispo, Silver Lining "Everyday Housewife"; and Jane, a 20-year-old Texas musician. Justin.tv became an open network on October 2, 2007, a move that enabled anyone to register and begin broadcasting their lives. Within only 11 days, Justin.tv had registered 3,200 broadcasting users.

On October 14, 2007, Randall Stross reported in the *New York Times:*

> This month, after seven months of beta-phase broadcasting, Justin.tv formally declared that it was open for business to one and all. In its first five days, the company said, it created 18,500 hours of video and pulled in 500,000 unique visitors. What those statistics do not show is how long anyone stuck around. In a sampling I did last week during a weekday, only 44 viewers, on average, could be found at each of the eight most heavily visited channels.

While Justin.tv catapulted livecasting to the public media forefront, there had actually been webcams livecasting for several years; however, these sites were offering content that was decidedly more adult in nature. Because of the staggering amount of revenue that adult pornography sites generate, most web-streaming technologies were actually developed to support them. A major provider of adult content reported that "with web sites generating as much as $52 million a month, companies like Sun Microsystems, Cisco, and Microsoft will certainly continue to advance streaming technology."

What You Need to Know

Do-It-Yourself Radio

Do-It-Yourself Radio is another form of livecasting. You are broadcasting live to an audience via the Internet. While more do-it-yourself Internet radio shows are limited to 1 hour and not 24 hours, it's still about communicating with your followers, live.

BlogTalkRadio is an Internet-based audio and radio platform that allows users to host their own, live Internet broadcast radio shows—needing only a telephone, Internet access, and a browser. BlogTalkRadio has been referred to as "a populist force in cyberspace,"[2] and "the dominant player in the latest media trend, one that allows anyone with a web connection to host a talk show on any topic at any time of day. It is the newest form of new media; the audio version of the Internet blog."[3]

Telecommunications executive and former accountant Alan Levy founded BlogTalkRadio, and is now its CEO. After creating a blog to update family members about his ill father, Alan launched BlogTalkRadio in August 2006. He wanted to create a way for bloggers to communicate more directly—and in real time—with their audiences.

Washington Post reporter Howard Kurtz has written many times about BlogTalkRadio in his "Media Notes" column, and claims, "The process is nearly idiot-proof. The host logs on to a Web page with a password, types in when he wants the show to air, and then—using a garden-variety phone—calls a special number. The computer screen lists the phone numbers of guests or listeners calling in, and the host can put as many as six on the air at once by clicking a mouse. Listeners can download a podcast version later."[4]

BlogTalkRadio allows up to five callers at any given time to participate in the Internet radio show itself, while the number of listeners is virtually unlimited. The user's radio shows are streamed directly from the host's web page during live broadcasts, and the shows are recorded, archived, and streamed as on-demand podcasts after the initial broadcasts. One can also subscribe to these shows through RSS feeds (see Chapter 18, RSS—Really Simple Syndication Made Simple, for more details on this process). You can post your BlogTalkRadio shows to your Facebook, MySpace, and other social networking web pages. And, since BlogTalkRadio is advertising supported, it's also free!

Before podcasting and Blog Talk Radio, there were Satellite Radio stations such as Sirius and XM. Founded in the early 1990s, they promoted a new wave and freedom in broadcasting. By the turn of the new millennium, they grew as fierce competitors to traditional radio stations. Although their talent wasn't DIY, they still managed to take many of traditional radio's personalities off the radio airwaves (which would have perhaps moved to the Internet) and onto a new medium.

---

2. Howard Kurtz, "With BlogTalkRadio, the Commentary Universe Expands," *Washington Post*, March 24, 2008; www.washingtonpost.com/wp-dyn/content/article/2008/03/23/AR2008032301719_pf.html

3. David Levine, "All Talk?" Condé Nast's Portfolio.com, February 26, 2008; www.portfolio.com?/?culture-lifestyle?/?goods?/?gadgets?/?2008?/02/26/Internet-Talk-Radio?page=0

4. Kurtz, "With BlogTalkRadio."

Conventional Radio Stations Weren't Happy

The ability to use inexpensive technology to webcast your own radio shows worldwide has allowed independent media to flourish. And as you might imagine, conventional radio broadcast stations weren't very happy with their new, free, global, Internet-based competition, which led to a series of controversial royalty legislation bills, congressional hearings, reforms, and appeals. As this book isn't intended to discuss historical legal aspects, you can learn more about this field by researching the following terms:

> The 2002 Copyright Arbitration Royalty Panel (CARP)
>
> The 2007 United States Copyright Royalty Board approval of a rate increase in the royalties payable to performers of recorded works broadcast on the Internet
>
> The 2007 Internet Radio Equality Act (HR 2060)

The good news is that even given the continuous controversy, in September 2008, the Copyright Royalty Board has decided to keep the royalty rate the music publishers must pay for each digital track they sell at nine cents per song for companies like Apple and Amazon. However, faced with an industry in transition, with new rules being written constantly, the three-judge panel opted to keep the royalty rate the same for the next five years. Many argue that instead of the per-track fee, the Copyright Royalty Board should have set the rates as a percentage of digital music revenues.

Webinar, Web Conferencing, and Webcasting

As discussed at the beginning of the chapter, the earliest form of webcasting or broadcasting video live over the Internet was called *web conferencing*. This particular method used conferencing software that connects two or more people or computers through the Internet, giving them the ability to speak and see one another simultaneously. People were able to conduct live meetings or presentations using this many-to-many two-way Internet video communication.

Webcast: A *webcast* takes place when a live broadcast or prerecorded media file is distributed over the Internet using streaming technology. It is broadcasted or distributed as a single-content source to many viewers simultaneously, or as a one-to-many one-way broadcast. Webcasting has many applications for commercial companies, including investor relations presentations, annual meetings, seminars, and e-learning. The largest web-casters today are existing radio and television stations that either simulcast their over-the-air (cable) broadcasts or provide their content in a prerecorded on-demand-type viewing.

Webinar: The word *webinar*[5] comes from the combination or concatenation of the words *web* and *seminar,* and is another form of one-to-many webcasting. Much like a presenter and audience at a live, on-ground seminar, a webinar usually entails one-way (occasionally two-way) communication. Text chat is often part of web conferencing; it allows the audience to communicate, ask questions, and interact with the presenter in real time. The audio portion of the webinar can be technically achieved by a conference call, wherein the presenter addresses the audience over a speakerphone while presenting visual information over the Internet.

State-of-the-art webinar software uses VoIP, or Voice over Internet Protocol (like Vonage telephone service), that allows the two-way audio conversation to also be transmitted over the Internet. This eliminates the need for conference telephone calling, and allows the software to capture both of the activities that are taking place on the screen (the video as well as the audio conversation). The complete webinar capture is able to be distributed and played again at a future date.

Videoblog

The videoblog is the same as the conventional blog, except that it uses short, prerecorded video in addition to text to convey your messages. (See Chapter 7, The Ubiquitous Blog, for extensive detail and explanation on the origin and use of videoblogs.)

Ustream.tv

Ustream.tv is a public platform that grants anyone the opportunity to lifecast through live streaming video for free. It was founded in March 2007 and currently has more than 320,000 registered users, who generate more than 350,000 hours of live video content per month. The Ustream site generates more than 10 million unique visitors per month and has received $11.1 million in funding for new product development.

Ustream also won some acclaim during some recent political campaigns for its usefulness in campaigning. While campaigning in the 2008 U.S. presidential election, former senator and presidential hopeful Mike Gravel

---

5. The term *webinar* was actually registered by Eric R. Korb in 1998 with the United States Patent and Trademark Office, but was too difficult to defend, so the term is in common use today.

became the first candidate ever to stream a debate using Ustream.tv. The site allowed Gravel to address a larger number of voters' political questions in real time.

Providers

So what does all of this livecasting have to do with you and your business? Well, people like Josh Harris, Jennifer Ringley, the DotComGuy, Jody Gnant, and Justin Kan moved what was a new and unfamiliar technology into the mainstream, thereby turning it into yet another possible way to get in touch with your employees, colleagues, customers, and prospects.

If you want to get started with your own Internet radio show, the best place to start is with BlogTalkRadio. It's easy to set up and simple to use, and because it's advertising-based, it's free. Other options for Internet radio and real-time audio communication are Skypecast.com, Waxxi.us, iChat, AOL AIM, and TalkShoe.com. Since the list is always changing, be sure to go to www.theSocialMediaBible.com for more up-to-date information on who's who in this space.

If you want to create your own television show or start your own livecast, be sure to check out Ustream.tv, blogtv, EveryScape, Fly on the Wall, Hasan M. Elahi, The Invention of More, Justin.tv, Social network service, Sophie Calle, Sousveillance, Stickam, and Tom Green Live. All of these web sites allow you to set up an account and begin your own livecast or radio show for free.

The ROI of Social Media

Social Media as an Effective Medium to Promote Off-Line Events

Background

Think Big Partners is a business incubation company created to help entrepreneurs find success more quickly. Located in Kansas City, the group was looking for a way to announce the launch of the incubation company and generate as much buzz in as short a period of time. With that purpose in mind, Think Big Partners created a local entrepreneurial conference called Think Big Kansas City.

Strategy

With the idea of "practice what you preach," Think Big Partners set out to establish the premier conference for Entrepreneurs, Investors, and Start-Ups.

The conference was a one-day event bringing over 30 expert speakers, including Chris Gardner, *New York Times* number one best-selling author of, *The Pursuit of Happyness*, the namesake for the blockbuster Hollywood movie with Will Smith and Joe Calhoon, Steven Covey's most requested speaker during the '90s, author of two books and the inventor of 1hour2plan.

The issue facing Think Big Partners was that they had just under 45 days to promote the event and get people to the venue. To that point, not a single shred of promotion had been done for this first-time event. And while the intention was to do the traditional mix of marketing, Think Big wanted to do just that . . . Think Big.

Implementation

Think Big turned to social media to help promote the event. On January 13th, Think Big launched a blog, Twitter profile, and Facebook Fan page for the March 3rd event. The idea was to generate brand awareness and help recruit attendees. Since attendees would have to pay for entrance, social media was being used as a lead generator to help with revenue and to sell out the show.

With nearly 30 speakers, Think Big had a tremendous pool of content to pull from. The blog was programatically tied to both Twitter and Facebook to allow all communication to be shared with each of the platforms. Participating speakers provided unique content for the Think Big Blog and helped with the link strategy developed for the event promotion. The partners at Think Big also committed to the effort providing for incentives to be used for recruitment. Signed books from Chris Gardner and scholarships were awarded through Twitter follow campaigns to help generate awareness and engagement. Additionally, a $10,000 business plan competition was created and promoted through a unique landing page developed for the Facebook fan page.

Opportunity

The opportunity was to show the tremendous reach of social media and just how much of an effect it could have on driving not only conversation, but actual people to the event. The viral nature of this medium provided a great chance to test the effectiveness of Word-of-Mouth advertising and Social Lead Generation.

Conclusion

Think Big KC was able to go from 0 to 1,540 Twitter followers on the day of the event, and just over 15 percent of the traffic to the blog and promotional pages for the event were attributed to social media efforts. Event planners attributed nearly 5 percent of ticket sales to the promotion. Secondary benefits were that

(continued)

(*continued*)

several published authors and professional speakers were introduced to Think Big Partners because of the social media campaigns and have requested the opportunity to engage with the Incubator as mentors and contributors.

Chad Herman
www.thinkbigkansascity.com

Expert Insight

Jody Gnant, singer, songwriter, and community marketer, www.jodygnant.com

Jody Gnant Laptop

Well, first and foremost I consider myself to be a singer/songwriter. That's what I've wanted to do since I was eleven years old; and I kind of always knew I was going to have to do it independently if I did not want to compromise who I wanted to be as an artist. Luckily, I was born and raised in a time when the Internet was being born and raised right around me, and so I kind of grew up with the Internet and the development of it.

I was chatting online at, you know, thirteen years old with the nickname of "Scooter," even before the Internet transitioned over to being more of a corporate arena for companies to put up these flashy web sites and wow the rest of us with their technical attributes. Now it is actually coming full circle. The Internet has been brought back to the people, so to speak, with social media, and it is really an exciting time to be an independent artist and to be able to promote what I do independently. So that is what I do. I sing, I write songs, and I put them out there for the world to see on the Internet.

Like I said, it seemed as if, when I was a little kid sitting on my dad's lap with the modem, with the rotary phone . . . it would just sit . . . . I don't know the technical term for what modem that was, but it was actually at that point about the people too. We would sit there and we would chat and we had the monochrome screens; you really could not do anything else. You could play Zork, which was like a great game. Love that game. However, other than Zork and chatting online, the Internet did not do much yet.

Then the companies took it over and I now feel like it is . . . it is being handed back to the people. That is kind of what I am all about as a musician; the entire reason I have decided to be a songwriter and a singer in the first place was to effect positive change. And I think that is why I like the Internet so much and why I like these tools—like blogging, livecasting—is because it allows us to continue to make that positive change in our own special way. Each of us has our own voice, and the Internet gives us the distribution channel for it. . . .

Lifecasting is. . . . I think it is awesome! Wikipedia explains it as a continual broadcast of a person's life through the general media. And basically a lot of lifecasters actually wear a camera and give the first-person perspective of what they see on a day-to-day basis, and so it's their lifecast. But I wanted it to be viewed as a promotional tool to launch the release of *Pivot*, which was the album that I had recorded and released as part of my "One Red Paper Clip" trade. And so we decided that we would just start broadcasting. And we broadcast the recording, mixing, mastering, and printing of the record . . . the rehearsing of the band for the CD release party; and then we would broadcast the CD release party . . . "Live . . . On the Internet!" with all these multicam systems and then . . . actually I was only going to do it for the six-week feed after the CD release party. But it dawned on me once I had had the CD release party, that really this was becoming the world's longest documentary *The Life and Times of an Independent Singer/Songwriter* (and the struggles that they go through).

So it actually became more of a journalistic process for me, and capturing for posterity what I was trying to accomplish as an artist. And . . . at some point, [it] became less of a promotional tool and more of something that was a personal mission for me to capture. The fact that there were other people along for the ride was just so cool, because people could actually choose to get involved in the process in real time. You know, if they wanted to affect how my music career was going, there was a chat right there; and they could do something about the fact that I was lost in L.A. And they would get on and Google and they would figure out where I was and they would say, "Go left down Wilshire!" So here I am having my own personal GPS through the Internet. Or—they could just sit back and watch the show.

And [something else that] dawned on me was that—even though I started using it as a promotional tool—without even knowing it, in just in the way that we were handling the situation, we had started to create a community. And so all of a sudden there were hundreds of people that would just come by on a daily basis to get a smile. People have told me that they were in the hospital coming out of a coma and they genuinely didn't know how they were going to survive the next seven weeks of a car accident; and then stumbled upon my lifecast. And the community is what helps them get through that time; and then they show me their scars and, you know, it is really humbling to know that what started out as a promotional tool ended up being a home and a community that still exists even without me.

(continued)

(*continued*)

Right now I am not lifecasting on the Internet, but there are 36 people on the chat befriending each other and talking about what they are going to be doing in their [lives]. It is very humbling; and it is not just broadcasting if you do it right . . . . [Then] it is actually community building, and probably the most enriching experience I've ever done for myself.

When you are doing a community marketing project, [you have to know] who you are focusing on, and which community you are trying to build. It is integral to know which [group] you are going after and how you want to affect them at the end of the day. What is interesting to me is that [there are] lives being affected. No longer am I just selling a product. You know when I was lifecasting, my response to every single thing that came across my plate was being broadcast and analyzed and, perhaps remixed and copied, or inspiring somebody else. And so as somebody who has—kind of—planned on being in the music business, the concept of living your life in the public eye was not completely foreign to me; but living it in such a way that every single thing you were doing could have an impact (whether it be negative or positive) on somebody's actual life all of a sudden became a huge responsibility . . . even above and beyond the content that I was putting out musically. . . .

Even if you think about trying a new product, you know . . . (laughter) and I was trying a new product live on the air, and somebody would see it either being really great or really bad. And I guarantee (and I'm not trying to jump around here) that what is really interesting is that . . . in, say, trying new coffeemakers in the lobby of my apartment complex, we would go out every morning and we would get this coffee. And because the lifecast also had a chat room attached to it, it was real-time feedback from people that were participating in the chat. And so you can actually count and monitor how many times a specific brand name is mentioned in the chat. And you can then monitor what types of questions are being asked about your brand. You can monitor every time somebody says, "Hey, I bought this specific product because you tried it in your lifecast and you said it was good." And so you become a brand ambassador of sorts, of every single brand that you pick up in your life. And the lifecasting, in that sense, is a really powerful brand-integration model in that sense . . . [something] you will see a lot more of in the coming years in terms of what's being put out there on the Internet.

And community marketing, in general—where the community is actually . . . I don't want to say "celebrities" . . . the community, the spokes-people, the brand ambassadors. And it becomes less about celebrities and more about trusted community members giving their thumbs up, too. We already see it now; but I think even more so as lifecasting and as citizen journalism become more of the valid form for the rest of the media world to pick up on and embrace, we will see a lot more of that kind of integration in the marketing in general. It's very powerful!

> I think if your friend told you to go see a movie because it was the best movie he had ever seen, you would go see that movie over and above and beyond Tom Cruise getting on the television and then saying, "It's the best movie I've ever seen!" Because you have a bond with your friend. . . .
>
> To listen to or read the entire Executive Conversation with Jody Gnant, go to www .theSocialMediaBible.com.

Commandments

1. **Thou shalt explore livecasting.**

   Go and explore some of the web sites mentioned in the chapter. Take a look at what Justin Kan has done with Justin.tv. Take a look at Alan Levy's BlogTalkRadio. Sign up for an account. Get to understand what options are out there for when you are ready to create your own radio or television show.

2. **Thou shalt get a webcam.**

   Go on, get a webcam and try it out. You can buy one for around $25. If nothing else, try a video chat with some friends or colleagues. Become comfortable with the technology. The next time you are on the road, try livecasting with your family, a friend, or a coworker. You will be surprised how different it is when you're able to see the person with whom you're speaking while away from your home or office.

3. **Thou shalt try a webinar or your own radio show.**

   Produce and perform a webinar. Create one for your prospects. Always keep the "What's in It for Me?" content in mind. Present your slides, have some real-time audio, and be sure to have some live text chat. You'll be surprised how differently your prospects will view you and your company.

4. **Thou shalt try a web conference.**

   Try setting up a web conference the next time you need to meet with colleagues—even if they are only on the other side of town. You can use iChat if you are a Macintosh aficionado, or AOL AIM on either platform. All you need is an inexpensive webcam and a free account. Again—like the sports shoe slogan says, "Just Do It!"

Conclusion

Whether you're someone like Justin, Justine, or Jody, or just someone who wants to build a community of trusted followers—or if you ever wished you had your own talk radio or television show—then you need to explore livecasting. A friend of one of the author's does a weekly show every Friday at noon, and over the past year, he has built a fan base of more than 5,000 people. While that number won't get the attention of the *New York Times*, it certainly is a great personal, loyal, trusted network of potential book buyers for his next novel.

What if you did a weekly radio show in which you interviewed industry experts (like the Expert Insights on www.theSocialMediaBible.com)? How would your customers and prospects perceive you and your company—even if you only did it a few times?

Invite your prospects to a webinar during which you talk about something important to them (always remember the WIIFM factor). Discuss new legislation, an innovative product or service, maintenance tips, installation, your development or manufacturing team, or a message from the president or CEO. This step will really humanize your company, and put a face on an otherwise faceless corporate entity. The best way to build trust is to talk with your customers and prospects.

And like the other social media tools, it only takes some time and creativity. To hear all of the Expert Interviews, go to www.theSocialMediaBible.com.

Readings and Resources

Novak, Jeannie, and Pete Markiewicz. *Web Guide to Producing Live Webcasts*. (Hoboken, NJ: John Wiley & Sons, Inc.)

Purcell, Lee. *Web Developer.com Guide to Creating Web Channels*. (Hoboken, NJ: John Wiley & Sons, Inc.)

Downloads

For your free downloads associated with *The Social Media Bible,* go to www .theSocialMediaBible.com, and enter your ISBN number located on the back of the book above the bar code. Be sure to enter the dashes.

Credits

The ROI of Social Media was provided by:
Chad Herman, www.thinkbigkansascity.com

Expert Insight was provided by:
Jody Gnant, singer, songwriter, and community marketer, www.jodygnant.com

Technical edits were provided by:
Walt Ribeiro, www.ForOrchestra.com

CHAPTER 16

Virtual Worlds—Real Impact

What's in It for You?

Any time you can become part of a "trusted network with a million-plus people in it," don't you want to be part of that—especially if you have similar interests?

In an interview, the CEO of Linden Labs, Mark Kingdon, said that Second Life—the 3-D virtual world created by Linden Research Inc.— experiences more than 1.2 million log-ins every 30 days, with more than two billion user-created items stored on the Linden servers. That sounds like the ultimate in *trusted network* and *user-generated content.* Second Life is only one of many three-dimensional gamelike virtual worlds or environments, but it is the largest virtual world without a gaming foundation. And according to Mark, when Google and its many resources create Lively, their own virtual environment—they are "validating the virtual world market." When these types of huge companies are inventing in this type of a social environment, there must be a reason.

In addition to being a fun, entertaining way to pass the time, virtual worlds give you the opportunity to browse new and unexplored domains, visualize and participate in imaginary communities, and do business in a virtual marketplace with real customers and colleagues. With companies like IBM, Coldwell Banker, Dell, Armani, Ben & Jerry's, BMW, CISCO, Coca-Cola, and Domino's Pizza doing business in Second Life, there is most likely good reason for *you* to be there as well.

Back to the Beginning

Virtual worlds began with simulators, which were three-dimensional graphic representations of a virtual, or simulated, environment. Then in 1968, Internet pioneer Ivan Sutherland developed the first computer-based virtual reality. Almost two decades later, in 1984, a NASA grant brought three incredible minds together: Jaron Lanier, Dr. Thomas Furness, and Dr. Sam Wise. These three men made significant improvements to the virtual world and its sensory input, despite the fact that they were far apart geographically and working in highly demanding fields. Lanier, a researcher at Atari Labs, became the CEO of VPL Research (first multiperson virtual reality [VR] and first commercial virtual reality products) and vastly enhanced the then-bulky VR goggles; Furness created an elegant VR environment while working at the Wright-Patterson Air Force Base in Mansfield, Ohio. He and a team of 16 PhDs had developed a closed-cockpit feedback system in which the inside of the F-15 fighter plane's cockpit was painted flat black and the pilots piloted their planes through television screens that showed a virtual representation of the actual world around them. Wise was the director of spinal cord injury for the Palo Alto Veterans Administration Hospital when he developed the sensory glove—which later became Mattel's data glove.

During the 1980s and 1990s, the author, Lon Safko, worked independently on his own, commercially available virtual environmental system called SoftVoice (later renamed SenSei when ported from the Apple II to the Macintosh Platform in 1986). While Lanier, Furness, and Wise's system was intended for F-15 fighter pilots and astronauts to perform complex repair without the need of dangerous spacewalks, SenSei was developed to help the physically disabled access computer technology and their environment (see SoftVoice/SenSei, discussed next).

    While developing this VR platform, Safko was lucky enough to spend a day brainstorming with Dr. Furness and William Gates Sr. at the University of Washington; as Dr. Furness put it, he "had to see a system nearly as elegant as my own . . . especially when mine cost 5 million dollars, and yours can be purchased for 2500 dollars." As a result of this meeting, Dr. Wise became a member of the corporate board of directors and advisors for Safko International Inc. in 1989 and provided a great deal of support and industry knowledge. He and John Williams, the author of the Americans with Disabilities Act, helped guide Safko International through the late 1980s and into the 1990s during the turbulent times of rights for the disabled and by advising on technology applications that helped the severely disabled.

The application of this three-dimensional virtual world was first implemented as an operating system for the Apple II, then Macintosh computers, and was intended to help the disabled and to teach individuals who had never used a computer before how to access its technology. It's hard to imagine today that during the early to mid-1980s most people had never used a computer before. And by definition, a disabled person had never used a computer because of physical disabilities.

The SenSei System was designed so that a user with no computer experience could sit down at a computer, look at the screen, and intuitively know what to do next. If she wanted to type, she selected the typewriter; to place a telephone call, she selected the telephone; to turn on the lights, select the light; to turn off the television, select the television; and so on.

The SenSei System included a collection of world's firsts, such as the fully graphic virtual environment operating system, first voice recognition, environmental control, telephone control, nurse call, all-in-one IR media control, electronic hospital bed control, software version user guides, and even ToolTips, the little window that pops up when you place your cursor over a button and get an explanation of what that button does.

The SenSei System later became the archetype for the Apple Newton (first PDA ever) and Microsoft's "Bob" operating system. The original SenSei operating system code and hardware now reside in the Computer History Museum, in Mountain View, California; Apple Computer Inc., Cupertino, California; the U.S. Library of Congress and the Museum of American History, Smithsonian Institution, Washington, DC; and is credited as the first computer to save a human life.

Figures 16.1 through 16.3 are examples of the SenSei System and the work done with the first commercially available three-dimensional virtual environment operating system.

Figures 16.4 and 16.5 are examples of Microsoft's "Bob" OS and the Apple Newton OS.

Figure 16.6 is the SenSei Library, 1987, and Figure 16.7 is the new Apple iPad.

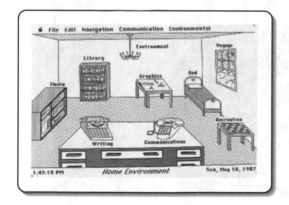

FIGURE 16.1 The SenSei Operating System, 1987

FIGURE 16.2 The SenSei Operating System, 1992

FIGURE 16.3 The SenSei Operating System, 1994

The first three-dimensional MMOG or MMORG (the acronyms for Massively Multiplayer Online Game or Massively Multiplayer Online Role-playing Game, coined by the developer of Ultimate Online Richard Garriott in 1997) virtual environment was created more than 35 years ago. In these MMOGs, participants would play the role of the main fictional character, and were challenged with obstacles that needed to be overcome in order to advance their status in the game. This first game was called the Maze Game, Maze War—or simply "The Maze" (see Figure 16.8). The avatars or representations of the player were eyeballs, and the environment was a three-dimensional wire-frame maze. The Maze was played on the original Internet—a network of computers

FIGURE 16.4 Microsoft's "Bob" Operating System, 1995

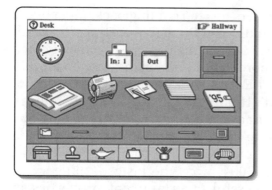

FIGURE 16.5 The Apple Newton Operating System, 1993

FIGURE 16.6 The SenSei Library, 1987

called ARPAnet—and could only be played on an Imlac computer, which was the first networked graphics workstation, which debuted in 1970.

During an MMOG, a large number of players interact with one another in a virtual world meant to resemble the real world. This game-culture social

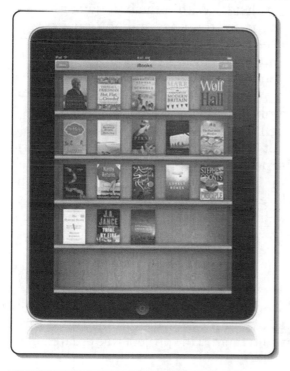

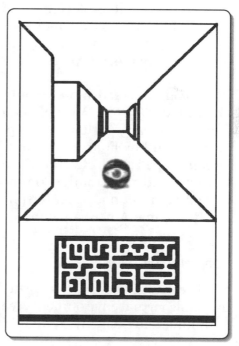

FIGURE 16.7 The Apple iPad Library

FIGURE 16.8 Maze War

interaction and competition motivates users to keep coming back. Most of the earlier games were similar to the more traditional Dungeons & Dragons, which remains the best-known and best-selling role-playing game, with an estimated 20 million people having played it and more than $1 billion in related book and equipment sales. The two most popular MMOGs today are Blizzard Entertainment's World of Warcraft and Microsoft's Halo 3 (designed by Bungie Studios).

On October 4, 2007, Microsoft announced that Halo 3 had officially become a global phenomenon, garnering more than $300 million in sales in the first week alone. The critically acclaimed Xbox 360 exclusive, which was released worldwide on September 25, 2004, was "the fastest-selling video game ever—and one of the most successful entertainment properties in history." Microsoft went on to claim,

> Halo 3 is quickly staking its place as the most popular Xbox LIVE game in history with members gathering in record numbers to play on the world's largest online gaming and entertainment network on TV. More than 2.7 million gamers have played Halo 3 on Xbox LIVE in the first week, representing nearly one-third of the seven million Xbox LIVE members worldwide. Within the first day of its launch, Halo 3 players racked up more than 3.6 million hours of online game play, which increased more than eleven-fold to more than 40 million hours by the end of the first week—representing more than 4,500 years of continuous game play.*

(You can read more about gaming in the next chapter, Chapter 17, Gaming the System: Virtual Gaming.)

Other early virtual-world prototypes emerged over the next several years, including Fujitsu Software Corporation's WorldsAway, CompuServe's Dreamscape, and educator Zane in 1987, becoming the first-ever online virtual world game for the Commodore 64 personal computer. The game was played using a modem, a telephone line, and Quantum Link, which eventually became America Online.

SoftVoice/SenSei

While certainly not the first virtual world, SenSei was the first commercially available virtual environment created to give the severely disabled access to a computer and their environment around them. This project was created back

---

* *Source*: HuliQ News, "Halo 3 Records More Than $300 Million in First-Week Sales Worldwide"; www.huliq.com/36851/halo-3-records-more-than-300-million-in-first-week-sales-worldwide.

in 1986 and was called SoftVoice, which stood for Voice Activated Software. It later became known as the SenSei System, and it was originally designed so that those with physical limitations could access a computer and other elements of their environment, such as lamps, telephones, and even electronic hospital bed controls. The first system ran on the most sophisticated and widely used computer at the time: the Apple II.

SenSei allowed its users to access all of its functions through voice commands. Once developed, the system was quickly redesigned for the new Macintosh computer. It used its distinctively different graphic operating system to navigate a virtual environment, which allowed access to the software functions of the computer by selecting, for example, a typewriter for word processing, a telephone to make a call, or a lamp or radio to turn on and off electric appliances. The user could control the computer navigation by moving one's head to activate a head-mouse, or simply by speaking the task they wished to perform. This gave the physically disabled—as well as any computer novice—the capacity to use a computer with little or no knowledge of how one operated, which was important in 1985.

Many original technologies spun off of SenSei's decade-long development, including the first fully graphic operating system, the first PDA, the Apple Newton OS, the Microsoft operating system "Bob," voice-activated environmental control, electronic hospital bed control, infrared television and media control (voice-activated all-in-one controller), the first-ever software user's guides, tool tips where you place your cursor over a button and a window pops up to tell you what that button does, and more.

The author personally had the pleasure of working with Steve Wozniak's post-Apple start-up, Cloud Nine, the company that developed the first All-in-One-Controller for infrared devices such as TVs, radios, VCRs, and stereos. Because the device had an RS-232 connection inside its case, crossover into the virtual world of the computer operating system was possible, using the real-life control of media equipment.

As with the wheelchair ramp and other disabled accommodations, many of these inventions—and their significant contribution to society— became mainstream. Eighteen of them are now housed in the permanent collection of the Museum of American History, Smithsonian Institution, in Washington, DC, along with 14 more inventions maintained by the Computer History Museum in Mountain View, California.

Second Life

Philip Rosedale founded Linden Research Inc. in 1999 after conducting some early tests with virtual worlds while studying physics at the University of

FIGURE 16.9   Lon Safko in the Virtual World, Second Life

California at San Diego. Many believe that Neal Stephenson's novel *Snow Crash* inspired Philip to create Second Life (even though Rosedale claims that he had imagined the concept before reading the book).

Rosedale set out to develop a VR system that would allow its users to become fully immersed in a 360-degree virtual world experience. He produced the Rig—a large, slow, expensive, and difficult to wear and use system. However, the Rig eventually evolved into the Internet software Linden World, which was designed to allow its users to play games and socialize with other users in a 3-D online environment. Linden World then grew into today's Second Life (SL) software experience.

The key to SL's success came as Rosedale observed participants at an investors' meeting gravitating toward the social, collaborative, and creative nature of Second Life. This caused Rosedale to see the importance of focusing more intently on the user-generated content and social networking aspects of his project—the very aspects that made Second Life such a success.

Second Life launched on June 23, 2003, and was closely followed by the unveiling of a 3-D virtual world intended for younger audiences, Teen Second Life. While Second Life caters to members over the age of 18, Teen Second Life is restricted to members between 13 and 18. With child online security as important as it is, the age restrictions are closely monitored.

What You Need to Know

A virtual world, or virtual environment, is usually an Internet-based simulated environment inhabited by avatars, or graphic representations, of its interactive users. An avatar can be represented textually, by a photograph, logo, image, or a 3-D cartoonlike person, animal, or object. While not all virtual worlds are 3-D, many began as forums, blogs, and chat rooms in which communities and trusted networks were created.

Figure 16.10 shows examples of two avatars used in Second Life—those of Mark Kingdon, CEO of Linden Labs, creator of Second Life, and the author. Mark's photo is on the left; his avatar is to the author's right.

Virtual worlds are often mistaken for user-immersed games in which players navigate their way through a simulated environment, shooting, fighting, and interacting with other players' avatars (that are controlled either by humans or

FIGURE 16.10 Kingdon Safko Avatars, Mark Kingdon, CEO Linden Labs (Second Life) and Lon Safko (author) avatars discussing social media

the game itself) with the goal of winning or overcoming a predetermined challenge. While virtual worlds may appear similar to and were inspired by these types of games, they are designed to serve a completely dissimilar purpose. There is no game-winning objective in a virtual world. Virtual worlds are designed for people from around the world—and their avatars—to enter into, navigate, and interrelate by engaging in personal, one-on-one communications. The intent of a virtual world is to encourage users to explore, learn, interact, do business, meet, and make friends

with new, multicultural people from around the world that they otherwise might never have had the opportunity to encounter. Virtual worlds may appear to be simulated versions of the real world, an accurate re-creation of part of the real world, or even an Alice-in-Wonderland-type fantasyland where reality has no place. Immersing oneself in this virtual world—or *metaverse*—environment is referred to as having a *telepresence*.

FIGURE 16.11 CNN in Second Life

Virtual Economy

Most of these worlds have even gone so far as to create and develop their own virtual economic systems. Second Life, for example, has a currency called the Linden Dollar (L$). While Lindens are fictitious and only negotiable within the confines of Second Life, the people at Linden Labs have made it possible to put real money into the virtual world and withdraw it as well; the Second Life economy does translate into real-world money. Not all virtual worlds have the same capability. By setting up an account with PayPal, the Second Life member can transact actual business. You can go to the mall and "buy" clothes, new hair, or even a car using Lindens (L$). Once the transactions have taken place, your credit card is charged (or credited), at the then going rate of Lindens per one U.S. dollar, and you don't need to be a vendor or own a shopping cart; you only need to be a resident with a credit card. Virtual products can include buildings, vehicles, animations, clothing, skin, hair, jewelry, plants, and furniture—almost anything that you can find in that environment. At the time this chapter was written, the exchange rate for buying Lindens was L$231.60 in real-world money and L$184 per dollar at the LindenX Exchange on the Second Life web site. Selling Lindens at the LindenX Exchange could be done at $1 for L$283 pulled out of Second Life. Linden Labs has even gone to the extent of recording and complying with a value-added tax (VAT) for many European countries.

While an exchange rate in which you can purchase a suit for $5 or new hair for 75 cents may seem small, many people have actually made money in this virtual world. In fact, at least one person became a millionaire. In November 2007, *BusinessWeek* ran an article by Rob Hof entitled "Second Life's First Millionaire," which told the story of Anshe Chung. Hof's article stated, "Anshe Chung's achievement is remarkable because the fortune was developed over a period of two and a half years from an initial investment of $9.95 for a Second Life. Chung (Ailin Graef, Second Life Persona) achieved her fortune by beginning with small-scale purchases of virtual real estate which she then subdivided and developed with landscaping and themed architecture for rental and resale. Her operations have since grown to include the development and sale of properties for large-scale real-world corporations, and have led to a real-life spinoff corporation called Anshe Chung Studios, which develops immersive 3-D environments for applications ranging from education to business conferencing and product prototyping." (To read the rest of this article, go to www.businessweek.com/the_thread/techbeat/archives/2006/11/second_lifes_fi.html.)

While stories like Chung's make for good press, few people have found this kind of fortune in a virtual world. However, it *is* possible. In Second Life

Mainland, prices run about $11.50 per square meter (at the time this chapter was written), and more for island and waterfront property. Properties are around 640,000 square meters on average, 410,000 of which are bought and sold by Groups each day—which equals roughly 1,050,000m or 16 regions of Mainland land that is bought and sold daily. Virtual Worlds Management—the leading virtual world's trade media company—estimates that commercial investments in the virtual worlds were in excess of $425 million in Q4 2007, and $184 million in Q1 2008.

Enterprise in Second Life

Many enterprises now have a presence in Second Life. Most people still don't completely understand how businesses can make money in a virtual world, but three things are clear: Some are doing it; some will figure it out; and merely having a presence in Second Life can give a company great brand recognition. As CEO of Linden Labs Mark Kingdon states, companies are using the Second Life platform for gauging customer reaction, receiving feedback, and testing prototypes; and—in the case of one of the author's own businesses—Paper Models Inc. has a storefront and 3-D displays showing the models adjacent to the

FIGURE 16.12 American Cancer Society's Memory Tree in Second Life

Social Media Bible Beach, www.slurl.com/secondlife/Pinastri/215/8/21, and selling some "first-life" products. This was an interesting transformation for Paper Models, which is now selling electron-based (PDF) items to real people through the Internet for real profits—versus selling virtual products in a virtual store to virtual avatars that simply represented real people. This kind of engagement in Second Life gives companies a significant competitive advantage. (To listen to the entire Mark Kingdon interview, go to www.theSocialMediaBible.com.)

Some businesses are also using the metaverse as a meeting place as well—for customers, prospects, and even employees. IBM has utilized Second Life on a regular basis as a forum for their engineers from around the globe to meet, exchange ideas, or see PowerPoint presentations—while never having to leave their respective offices. During a project in 2007, the author used Second Life to meet with paper model developers from Ukraine.

In fact, the first time in scheduling a call with developers—to discuss the American Cancer Society's Kiosk Design—it came as such a surprise to the author to actually hear the voice of Roman Vasilev, a developer with whom the author had been working for over two years through e-mail and the Internet. Up to that point, they had been able to "speak" with each other and exchange ideas and concepts in real time—and for free.

Sun Microsystems is another example of a company that has created its own island in Second Life dedicated solely to employee use. Their virtual island is a place where employees can go to seek help from colleagues, exchange new ideas, or advertise an innovative product. The American Cancer Society has its own in-world presence with its help island, which was established to raise awareness and provide support for this widespread, life-threatening illness. Paper Models was honored to sponsor and participate in ACS's Island Dedication in the fall of 2007 (www.slurl.com/secondlife/ Pinastri/246/4/22), an event that accompanied the free distribution of a 3-D model of its landmark in-world Memory Tree, a virtual tree that is surrounded by small flashes of light. Each flash of light represents the memory of someone who has passed away from cancer. While on the island, you can download a PDF, print it, and—with a little glue and scissors— re-create the virtual ACS Memory Tree in real life. (To download your free ACS Memory Tree, go to www.papermodelsonline.com/acstree.html.)

The author was also given the chance to work with ACS member Steven Groves (Estaban Graves in Second Life) and ACS in sponsoring an International ACS Donation Kiosk Design Contest. Second Life developers from around the world competed in creating the most imaginative freestanding kiosk through which residents within Second Life could pledge donations to help fight cancer. Dozens of entries were submitted; the winner was announced at the 2008 ACS's Second Life Relay For Life Launch Event. (Go to www.papermodelsonline .com/amcasodokiin.html to download your free copy of the ACS Kiosk winner paper model.) Two monumental events took place at this event, in addition to presenting the winner of this contest. First, in anticipating a good turnout for the event, Linden Labs agreed to assign additional servers to accommodate the high level of computation and distribution of data needed to bring so many avatars together at one

FIGURE 16.13 The ACS Kiosk Design Finalists in Second Life

time. Even with this precaution, so many avatars (residents) participated in this event that Linden Labs' servers were taken down and Second Life shut off until they were able to reboot. The second phenomenal occurrence was that the American Cancer Society raised more than $200,000 in real cash for its research at the 2008 Relay For Life in Second Life, up from $120,000 in 2007. (Be sure to visit the American Cancer Society's Island for this year's events.) Besides making some history and raising a significant amount in donations for a great cause, Paper Models had fun, garnered a great deal of publicity, and is now branded as having a presence in both first-life and Second Life.

At the time of this writing, other companies that are utilizing Second Life to conduct their business are 20th Century Fox, Armani, Avnet Inc., BBC Radio, Ben & Jerry's, Cisco, Coca-Cola, CNN, Coldwell Banker, Creative Commons, Dell, Disney, Domino's Pizza, IBM, ING Group, Mazda, MTV, Reuters, Starwood Hotels, Toyota, Wells Fargo, Paper Models Inc., and John Wiley & Sons, Inc. As an example, Wiley has a bookstore in Second Life in which you can go, sit, and meet other book lovers. Many of the companies mentioned here pay someone to represent them 24/7/365, so when you walk into their building, an avatar (with a real person operating them) will greet you and answer any questions you have about their product or service.

The Social Media Bible in Second Life

You guessed it. *The Social Media Bible* has a Garden in Second Life. Pinastri,158/205/21—www.slurl.com/secondlife/Pinastri/158/205/21—is what is referred to as a Second Life URL, or "SLURL." It can be typed/pasted into a standard web browser, and if you have a Second Life account, it will take you and your avatar there right away. This makes it easier to connect a Second Life location to the 2D web browser. *The Social Media Bible* gives away a virtual device here that is called a HUD (Heads Up Display) at the back of the garden, where you can take it and listen to any of the Executive Conversation podcasts while continuing to explore the garden—or anywhere else in Second Life. *The Social Media Bible* will continue to build the content of the Social Media Garden so it becomes a virtual world resource for all things social media. Just go to the SL address given earlier and select the SLurl; or go in-world in Second Life and look for the group "Social Media Bible Evangelists."

Your Own Second Life

Second Life appears as an example throughout this chapter since it is the most popular virtual world platform in use today. Many others are listed in the Providers section of this chapter; even Google has decided to compete in this space, as mentioned earlier, with their newest virtual world, Lively.

FIGURE 16.14 *The Social Media Bible* Headquarters in Second Life

Source: http://slurl.com/secondlife/pinastri/215/8/21.

To understand how a virtual world works, Second Life will remain as an example. See *The Social Media Bible* in Second Life (Figure 16.14).

To participate in Second Life, you can simply visit Second Life .com and download a program that allows you to enter this virtual world. This program, client, or viewer is free. Once you create your account (also free), you become a resident of Second Life. Now you are able to explore, interact with other residents, participate, learn, create, buy, socialize, and network.

Second Lifers refer to their world as *the grid*, which is divided into 2567 × 256-meter areas of land called *Regions* or *Sims* (short for Simulators). Each Region is created and housed on a single computer server and is assigned a unique name and content rating—either PG or Mature. While in SL or on the grid, your avatar can get around by walking, running, jumping, or riding in vehicles. Your avatar can also fly and quickly jump from one region of the grid or one place to another, or you can teleport—TP—directly to that location.

The ability to create virtual objects such as chairs, clothes, and even buildings from primitive shapes called *prims* is also built into Second Life. A scripting language called LSL (Linden Scripting Language) is similar to C++ programming language. LSL allows Second Lifers to add behaviors to these objects, like having avatars cross their legs when sitting on a chair. Other options to create more complex 3-D virtual objects are sculpties, textures, and animations. A *sculptie* is short for *sculpted prim*, which is a prim whose shape is created by an array of x, y, and z coordinates. Sculpties are used to create more complex, organic shapes for virtual goods.

Figure 16.15 shows an example of cows and horses created using sculpties.

FIGURE 16.15 Sculpties Design Elements in Second Life

The Avatar

The Second Life avatar often has a cartoonlike, yet slightly human appearance and may be male, female, or androgynous—in the case of an avatar being a boat, mythical creature, or even a pile of rocks. Avatars may be casually dressed, in a tuxedo, or wearing wildly ornate costumes that users can change at any time. You can even pay a service to take your photograph and create a skin that looks exactly like you do in real life, but many residents just choose to display themselves as their alter ego. An avatar's real identity is anonymous; you cannot access any personal details about an avatar's identity (a precaution that was implemented to provide age verification and to protect children).

Avatars can communicate through instant messaging (IM)–type text chat. They can alternately use a voice chat component that allows users to actually speak aloud to a computer's microphone using Voice over Internet Protocol (VoIP)[1] to transfer the two-way voice in real-time communications. Avatars are also able to send and receive e-mail, and their Instant Messages will roll over to an avatar's real-life e-mail when they log off if they choose to select this option. (See the Mark Kingdon Executive Conversation video at www.theSocialMediaBible.com.)

Expenses in Second Life

Even though this book continually touts the low- and no-cost benefits of social media, Linden Labs has adopted—as have most companies in the social media ecosphere—a freemium business model. (If you want to just browse and explore, however, your account is completely free.) Second Life offers a Premium Membership for $9.95 per month that entitles its users to own a small amount of land up to 512m without additional fees. It provides extra technical support and a salary or stipend of L$300 per week. If you own larger areas of land, you will incur additional rent or a Land Use Fee. Most members refer to this fee as a *tier*, since this is the manner in which it is charged—tiers that range from $5 per month or more depending upon the amount of land you own. As a member, you can choose to purchase land from another member or resident directly.

You can also purchase a different type of land that is known as a Private Estate. This usually consists of one or more Private Islands or Regions, and has a completely separate set of regulations and pricing policies. A Private Region is 65,536m (about 16 acres), and costs $1,000 to purchase with a

---

1. VoIP, or Voice over Internet Protocol, is the technology used to digitize voice into discrete packets of digital information and transfer or transmit that conversation over the Internet. Vonage is an example of a VoIP long-distance telephone service.

$295 per month maintenance fee. Included in the ownership of a Private Estate is the member's ability to alter the terrain of the land.

Second Life Stats

Second Life had a banner year in 2008. There were 16,785,531 registered Second Life residents spending more than US $100 million on virtual goods and services, and participating in more than 397 million hours in the world. The residents bought and sold more than 43,965,696 square meters of land with a total of 1.76 billion square meters of land owned by its residents, and as many as 76,000 residents logged on at any one time.

> www.blog.secondlife.com/2009/01/15/q42008/
> www.secondlife.com/whatis/economy_stats.php
> Or go to www.theSocialMediaBible.com for "clickable links."

The Viewer

You can browse SL using many browsers . . . the original one, the new viewer 2.0, the open-source official snowglobe, and the very popular Emerald. . . . It is hugely worthy of mention that Linden Labs has provided open source code and allowed developers to improve their viewer—and that they have implemented those improvements into the official viewer with regularity.

Providers

While Second Life is the most popular of the virtual worlds available, there are plenty of others to choose from, including:

- Active Worlds (a Second Life–like virtual world)
- Coke Studios (promotes music and bands)
- Cybertown (personal chat, inbox, message board, and free e-mail)
- Disney's Toontown (games, events, and contests to promote Disney)
- Dreamville (a virtual world that includes blogs, photo sharing, and customizable home pages)
- Dubit (online worlds and social networks for young people to engage, interact, communicate, and learn while having fun)
- Entropia (real people, real activities, and a real cash economy in a massive online universe)

- Habbo Hotel (a virtual world where you can meet and make friends)
- Blue Mars

Others are IMVU, Kaneva, Google's Lively, the Manor, Mokitown, Moove, Muse, the Palace, Playdo, the Sims Online, Sora City, There, TowerChat, Traveler, Universe, Virtual Ibiza, Virtual Magic Kingdom, Voodoo Chat, VPchat, VZones, whyrobbierocks, Whyville, Worlds.com, Yohoho! Puzzle Pirates, and the erotic-oriented Red Light Center.

The ROI of Social Media

Take It to the Social Media Streets: How Infusionsoft Builds Brand, Buzz, and Super-Sizes Serving Customers through Social Media

Background

Infusionsoft has a very robust combined e-mail marketing, CRM, and marketing automation application that nearly 20,000 users rely on to power their marketing activities. The Gilbert, Arizona–based company is poised to grow to support hundreds of thousands of small business users and desire to expand their footprint through social media. Key motives to leverage social media include brand awareness, participate in industry discussions, provide nonlinear support, and introduce lead-generation opportunities for the business.

As a growing business in a highly competitive small business market, we addressed the challenge of raising industry awareness on a lean marketing and communications operation. Social media has delivered results to yield serious merit and mojo to Infusionsoft's marketing, lead generation, and brand-building abilities.

Strategy

Infusionsoft's social media efforts began with its roots in community forums. After facilitating user forums that invoked many discussions across its user base and employees, the company in late 2008 decided to expand their efforts to outside social networking applications such as blogging, Twitter, LinkedIn, YouTube, and Facebook.

The company discovered the Infusionsoft blog experienced limited growth due to frequency of updates, lack of hard-hitting topics, and lack of variety of authors and content. Faced with the clear-cut opportunity to grow and utilize the blog as a communications hub that could engage customers, prospects, and market influencers in a dynamic way, the company's executive

(continued)

(continued)

leadership gave the Community Manager the green light to launch a focused and sustained social media–centric effort. This was the turning point for the company to focus on the merits of social media more seriously than before.

Foci of the social strategy included presence throughout industry conversations and emerging as a thought leader on the topics of e-mail marketing, customer follow-up, and marketing strategies. Target demographic included solo entrepreneurs, small businesses with 25 or fewer employees and who were already using the web to drive their marketing activities. Valuable content and unique perspective was a key component to its success. One requirement of the strategy is to give room for flexibility and agility to monitor and address topics prevalent in industry discussions and pertinent to the brand itself.

Implementation

We established our blog as the hub of our social media execution. Later, [we] expanded our Twitter and Facebook presence. We continued to identify social media outposts such as LinkedIn, Mahalo, YouTube, and other social network profiles.

To make our social media activities and practices known, we educated all employees about our social media program and have a very open policy for how employees engage in social media. We believe cross-division engagement is key to the level of participation the company has in social media.

Opportunity

Listening to and engaging in the conversation happening online around small business growth and e-mail marketing presents a huge opportunity for Infusionsoft, both internally and externally. Our activities in social networking enable market research, competitive intelligence, and lead generation just by listening to what people are talking about on key topics. We view Twitter and Facebook as key sites where the conversation is abundant and the opportunity to listen and engage is limitless. There's a real opportunity to showcase Infusionsoft's expertise and knowledge as thought leaders in e-mail marketing, CRM, and small business growth in an authentic way. Additionally, we leverage sites like Twitter and Facebook to enhance customer service and support so users receive killer service and have their needs met in ways other than simply phone support.

Conclusion

Social media has yielded impressive benefits for Infusionsoft, its users, and the industry at large. We have launched affordable brand-building activities that helped gain visibility and relevancy among top industry bloggers, including Anita Campbell, Starr Hall, and our industry competitors, including Aweber, 1ShoppingCart, MailChimp, and the popular marketing community at

Warrior Forums. This has positioned our company to be a viable candidate for the growing small business who doesn't have needs—or can afford—mid-size platforms like Netsuite or ExactTarget, but has outgrown their current separate e-mail marketing and CRM solution.

We've leveraged the live video streaming service, UStream on a number of occasions as a part of our annual user conferences and online educational sessions, attracting several thousand online viewers at our live events. These community engagements attract prospects and satisfy customers from across the globe, giving them a window into Infusionsoft—giving them a sense of exclusivity that recorded videos don't have.

Through continued focus on quality content and sustained quantity, our blog has grown from a Google PageRank of 2 to 5, attracting over 100,000 page views annually. We have tracked revenue from visitors who visited the blog first to becoming active paying subscribers to be over several thousand monthly. Content from the Infusionsoft blog has been featured by top bloggers [leading] to engagement with an ever-increasing amount of customers and prospects.

We monitor our brand 24/7 on Twitter and provide instantaneous support, rapid responses, and manage critical situations with the utmost of care and diligence. We attract more of our prospects toward our Twitter presence. In addition, our Facebook Fan Page has grown successfully and has a higher affinity with our users on it.

We listen and participate but not facilitate our user-driven groups on LinkedIn. We continue to have lively discussions on our community forum and frequently are mentioned frequently within our industry by thought leaders, analysts, and our loyal users.

Joseph Manna, community manager, Infusionsoft
www.infusionsoft.com

Expert Insight

Mark Kingdon, chief executive officer, Linden Labs, Creators of Second Life, www.SecondLife.com

Mark Kingdon

There's something like 2 billion items in the databases; you know, content and scripts that Second Life residents have created. It's really a powerful platform for cocreation, for collaboration, and just for [generating] amazing things. . . . We do a lot of our meetings *at* Linden Labs inside of

(continued)

(*continued*)

Second Life. I would say that I spend anywhere from one to four hours a day in Second Life and—as you can imagine because folks at Linden Labs are so involved in the Second Life experience—we have an amazing array of creative avatars. You can have jellyfish, tugboats, beagles, piles of rocks; it's just an endless array of crazy avatars. It's a blast!

Second Life is a platform and a set of content-creation and collaboration tools that members use to populate this incredible three-dimensional environment—this virtual reality—with immersive experiences. So Second Life is a destination, but it's [one] that's really created by the residents using the platform tools that we provide. And we have had—over the last sixty days, I think—1.2 million log-ins, as people come to Second Life. So it's a really rich and vibrant community with members from literally every country in the world. . . .

Well, the amazing thing about Second Life is, kind of, the breadth of the use-cases, right? Just like the real world, [Second Life] is incredibly diverse; [and] the audience—or the user base—is incredibly diverse [as well]. So the use-cases are as broad in Second Life as the experiences would be in the real world. People use Second Life to go to a live music venue and hear a concert in an intimate setting. They use it to go shopping with friends. They use it to create a personal space, like their own home, that they can enjoy in the virtual world. They use it to connect with other people around a common interest, a common concern, a common problem they share. Companies use it to work together to create products in a rapid-cycle product-development process, or for virtual meetings, for virtual learning. . . .

It's companies like IBM, Sun, Intel, Dell, Orange, British Telecom, Arcelor Mittal, CIGNA; lots and lots of companies around the world are using Second Life in their business. I saw Arcelor Mittal having a shareholders' meeting in SL. Whether it's CIGNA creating a help island where their customers can connect with health information in a unique way, [or] Cisco doing a developers' conference Q&A in Second Life—the use-cases are really, really broad. [And] it's an amazing way to experience a product before it's built. I think that we've only just started to scratch the surface on the "possible"—right? [Because] up until now I think that we were very much in [an] exploratory phase in the virtual world space. But what we're seeing now is companies who come back a second and third time, trying new ideas, and new approaches to doing business. . . .

One of the things that I can tell you is that we're really working hard to listen to our user base and to understand what our core customers are looking for in the platform. One of the really important customer segments that we want to develop further is the enterprise customer segment; so we've been listening to enterprise customers very closely to understand what their specific needs are. So, as we make adjustments and changes and improvements to the core Second Life platform, it's more supportive of enterprises and educational institutions. I think you should keep your eyes peeled, because as of next year [2009], there are going to be a lot of things that we do with and to the platform to enable business in a substantial way as we continue to support our core audience around the world.

To listen to or read the entire Executive Conversation with Mark Kingdon, go to www.theSocialMediaBible.com.

Commandments

1. **Thou shalt try out a virtual world.**

    Take a look at a few of the many available virtual world web sites, and become a member of one yourself. Sign up for a free membership and use it to explore. Don't be discouraged by the initial difficulty in navigating your way around. It isn't always intuitive, but you will become a pro in no time. The principal skills you need to focus on to have a satisfactory first experience is movement, communication, and how to find things to do that interest you.

2. **Thou shalt explore other company's successes.**

    Take a look around. Google some of the companies listed throughout this chapter and read about some of their successes. Get ideas about what has worked from them. After researching several companies, you will begin to formulate a plan about what will work for you and your company.

3. **Thou shalt explore selling.**

    Can you sell your products or services in a virtual world? Should you set up a virtual store? Can you partner with someone who already has a strong presence in a virtual world? Can you cross-promote between first-life and your virtual life? Think about how you might get started marketing and selling in a virtual world to see if it's right for you and your business.

4. **Thou shalt explore meetings and training.**

    Investigate the idea of holding your next design, sales, or marketing meeting in a virtual world. You must realize that there will be an initial learning curve for everyone, but once you bridge that curve, it's fairly easy from there on out. Maybe HR would like to present; maybe it's a new product or service you want your satellite offices to see. You can even do a PowerPoint-like slide presentation within the virtual world.

5. **Thou shalt join the community.**
   Take a look at the search menu options, and look for groups with whom you might have common interests within the virtual world of your choice. Find a group that shares a similar interest to yours and meet with them, share ideas, make friends.

Conclusion

The concept of doing business in a virtual world is still new. There is a tremendous opportunity for enterprises to participate in a huge trusted network of like-minded participants—in which many may be prospects. As with most technologies, it's the early adopters that get the home-team advantage. You won't know if marketing in a virtual world is right for you and your company until you explore the concept. Pick a virtual world, sign up for a membership, visit a few in-world businesses, talk to the business owners, talk with their customers, meet other avatars, follow and meet with groups within the community—and better understand how virtual worlds work.

To hear all of the Expert Interviews, go to www.theSocialMediaBible.com.

Readings and Resources

Aldrich, Clark. *Learning Online with Games, Simulations, and Virtual Worlds: Strategies for Online Instruction*. (Hoboken, NJ: John Wiley & Sons, Inc.)

Bertol, Daniela. *Designing Digital Space: An Architect's Guide to Virtual Reality*. (Hoboken, NJ: John Wiley & Sons, Inc.)

Cerling, Tim, and Jeffrey Buller. *Mastering Microsoft Virtualization*. (Hoboken, NJ: John Wiley & Sons, Inc.)

Golden, Bernard. *Virtualization For Dummies*. (Hoboken, NJ: John Wiley & Sons, Inc.)

Moore, Dana, Michael Thome, and Karen Haigh. *Scripting Your World: The Official Guide to Second Life Scripting*. (Hoboken, NJ: John Wiley & Sons, Inc.)

Perigo, Julie. *Winners in the Second Half: A Guide for Executives at the Top of Their Game*. (Hoboken, NJ: John Wiley & Sons, Inc.)

Porter, Lynnette R. *Creating the Virtual Classroom: Distance Learning with the Internet*. (Hoboken, NJ: John Wiley & Sons, Inc.)

Robbins, Sarah, and Mark Bell. *Second Life For Dummies*. (Hoboken, NJ: John Wiley & Sons, Inc.)

Rufer-Bach, Kimberly. *The Second Life Grid: The Official Guide to Communication, Collaboration, and Community Engagement*. (Hoboken, NJ: John Wiley & Sons, Inc.)

Rymaszewski, Michael, James Au Wagner, Mark Wallace, Catherine Winters, Cory Ondrejka, Benjamin Batstone-Cunningham, and Philip Rosedale. *Second Life: The Official Guide*. (Hoboken, NJ: John Wiley & Sons, Inc.)

Terdiman, Daniel. *The Entrepreneur's Guide to Second Life: Making Money in the Metaverse*. (Hoboken, NJ: John Wiley & Sons, Inc.)

Van Dusen, Gerald C. *The Virtual Campus: Technology and Reform in Higher Education*. (Hoboken, NJ: John Wiley & Sons, Inc.)

Vince, John, and Rae Earnshaw. *Virtual Worlds on the Internet*. (Hoboken, NJ: John Wiley & Sons, Inc.)

Weber, Aimee, Kimberly Rufer-Bach, and Richard Platel. *Creating Your World: The Official Guide to Advanced Content Creation for Second Life*. (Hoboken, NJ: John Wiley & Sons, Inc.)

Winder, Davey. *Being Virtual: Who You Really Are Online*. (Hoboken, NJ: John Wiley & Sons, Inc.)

Downloads

For your free downloads associated with *The Social Media Bible*, go to www.theSocialMediaBible.com, and enter your ISBN number located on the back of the book above the bar code. Be sure to enter the dashes.

Credits

The ROI of Social Media was provided by:

Joseph Manna, community manager, Infusionsoft, www.infusionsoft.com

Expert Insight was provided by:

Mark Kingdon, chief executive officer, Linden Labs, www.SecondLife.com

Technical edits were provided by:

Jeanie Sing, Jeaniesing Trilling, Second Life, slurl.com/secondlife/Pinastri/115/171/29

CHAPTER 17

Gaming the System: Virtual Gaming

What's in It for You?

Online gaming is another one of those Internet phenomena that just keeps gaining popularity. The trusted networks of the MMORPG—or Massively Multiplayer Online Role-Playing Game—communities are in many cases, in the millions. In fact, Blizzard Entertainment, creators of World of Warcraft (WoW, www.blizzard.com/us/press/081028.html), announced recently that the MMORPG game World of Warcraft "as of October, 2008 is played by more than 11 million gamers around the world. World of Warcraft has also achieved new regional subscriber milestones, with more than 2 million players in North America, more than 1.5 million players in Europe, and more than 3.5 million players in China." The developer of Ultima Online (the company that created a great deal of MMORPGs), Richard Garriott, first coined the term *MMORPG* in 1997.

As of January 2009, Xbox LIVE had more than 17 million subscribers: www.latimesblogs.latimes.com/technology/2009/01/microsoft-xbox.html, and even Barack Obama purchased advertising in the online racing game Burnout Paradise during his campaign: www.gamepolitics.com/2008/10/09/report-obama-ads-burnout-paradise.

Many people tend to view online video games as an activity with no business value—a waste of time in which only teenagers participate. However, any time you have 50,000 to 8 million people in the same place with the same interests in a trusted network, a business opportunity exists. In fact, only 25 percent of online gamers are teenagers; the average MMORPG player is approximately 26 years old. Fifty percent are employed full-time, 36 percent are married, and 22 percent have children. They include high school and college students, professionals, homemakers, and retired individuals.

On average, they spend 22 hours per week playing these games, and there is no correlation between hours spent playing and age. Sixty percent of all players report that they have played for 10 continuous hours at one time or another. Eighty percent of MMORPG players also play on a regular basis with someone they know in real life such as a romantic partner, family member, or friend. In fact, MMORPGs provide highly social environments where new relationships are forged and existing relationships are reinforced. Many players report feeling strong emotions while playing, and a recent statistical study showed that 8.7 percent of male and 23.2 percent of female players have even had online weddings. The average MMORPG player is by no means average.

(For more information about online gaming, be sure to also read Chapter 16, Virtual Worlds—Real Impact.)

What You Need to Know

An MMORPG is a genre of computer or Internet games in which a large number of players interact with one another in a virtual world on the Internet. In an MMORPG, players assume the role of a fictional character, often in a fantasy world. This first-person play allows the participant to control his or her character's actions in an ongoing virtual world—usually hosted by the game's publisher—that continues to exist and evolve. World-wide revenues for these types of games exceeded a half billion dollars in 2005, with U.S. revenues exceeding $1 billion in 2006.

Features that are common to all MMORPGs are themes, progression, social interaction, culture, and customization of the player's character. Most MMORPG's themes are based on fantasy and science fiction, such as the genre's two most popular games: Dungeons & Dragons, and World of Warcraft. Another subgenre of online games is called FPS, or First Person Shooter, such as Halo3.

All MMORPGs have some kind of progression for the main character's player, or avatar. You can earn points or capabilities, gain inventory or wealth, or be challenged with more difficult levels. The reverse is true as well; if the main character fails at the challenge—such as combat with another player's character, or with the character generated by the game itself—points are taken away, inventory is lost, and the main character is often forced to go back to the beginning or simplest level. This play/challenge/replay cycle is called the *level treadmill* or *grinding*.

In an MMORPG, characters are encouraged to communicate with one another, and often team up. By doing so, individual players can offer their

FIGURE 17.1   World of Warcraft

skills to other players, which results in many players becoming members—or even leaders—of that particular group. In many MMORPGs, a player's specialized abilities can be categorized as a *tank* (one who absorbs blows and protects members from the enemy), or a *healer* (who keeps the members of the team healthy). Then there's the *DPS—Damage per Second—*who inflicts damage; the *CC,* or *Crowd Control* character, who temporarily controls the opponent. There is also the *Buffer* or *Debuffer,* who use their abilities to affect opponents. Most players can have one, none, or many of these characteristics. All of these characters interact with the *NPC* (*Non-Player Character*), which is the computer-controlled entities that operate under limited Artificial Intelligence or scripts. Some are quest givers, others are Mobs (the enemies that players defeat). Most MMORPGs have a *Game Master* or *Moderator (GM)—* who is either a paid employee of the publisher or a volunteer from the game. The GM's job is to supervise and manage the game world.

Much like Second Life, MMORPGs run on the publisher's server 24/7/365, which means you can access and play any time of day or night. In order to play, participants download client software that's able to run on their PCs. The player then connects to the game's world by using the software and the Internet. This software can be made free—as with Second Life—or for purchase, as with World of Warcraft and EverQuest. Some MMORPGs require a monthly subscription, while others are moving to what is called a *thin client,* through which the game can be played without the use of client software, using only a web browser.

Back to the Beginning

As mentioned in the previous chapter on Virtual Worlds, a very fine line exists between participating in online gaming and a virtual environment (see Figure 17.2). Nearly every successful MMORPG today is a role-playing, full-immersion, three-dimensional virtual world scenario. This type of game play dates back to the early 1990s, while the earliest online game—called MazeWar or the Maze—which was much like the later PacMan, in which you maneuvered through a maze while being chased by objects that would harm you—began back in the 1970s (again, see Chapter 16, Virtual Worlds—Real Impact for more information). In 1984, Islands of Kesmai was released: "a semi-graphical, multiplayer, two-dimensional game interface that scrolled with turn-based play, where players moved in tiles on a grid utilizing short commands and key presses to find items on the floor of the dungeon."

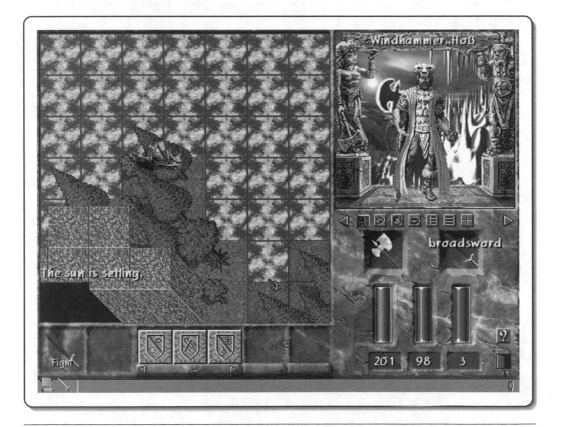

FIGURE 17.2 IOKesmai

FIGURE 17.3 NWNights

The first fully graphical multiplayer game, Neverwinter Nights, a role-playing game (RPG) set in a huge medieval fantasy world of Dungeons and Dragons, hit the Internet in 1991 and received promotion from then-president of America Online (AOL) Steve Case (Figure 17.3). Then there were MMORPGs from the Sierra Network—the first online multiplayer gaming system—that became popular in the early 1990s, like The Shadow of Yserbius (released in 1992), The Fates of Twinion (1993), and The Ruins of Cawdor (1995).

It took the National Science Foundation Network (NSFNET)—a major part of the early 1990s Internet backbone—until 1995 to remove their restrictions on the Internet. This relaxing of rules allowed developers to create more massively played titles such as Meridian 59—the typical 3-D, first-person game play. Then in 1996, the Korea-based company Origin Systems released Nexux: The Kingdom of the Winds in a pay-to-play MMORPG. The following September, the company launched the Ultima Online (UO), a game similar to D&D in which

there are lands to explore, houses to design and build, quests to complete, rare treasures to hunt for, exotic creatures to tame, and an almost infinite array of characters for building an MMORPG fantasy game. UO is similar to many of the other previous Ultima games (too many to list), and to this day is still being played on both the Internet and private consoles.

FIGURE 17.4 EverQuest

While both of these games really helped to create the MMORPG genre, EverQuest brought MMORPGs into the mainstream in the United States. EverQuest was designed by Brad McQuaid, Steve Clover, and Bill Trost, developed by Sony's 989 Studios and its spinoff, Verant Interactive, and was published by Sony Online Entertainment (SOE) in early 1999.

There are basically three MMORPG business revenue models: pay-to-play, free-to-play with in-game advertising and merchandising, and buy-to-play. Pay-to-play is when the player sets up an account and pays what is usually a monthly subscription to have access to the game. Free-to-play is when a player can log on and just play for free. And buy-to-play is when the player first buys the game, and can then play online for free. Holding the largest pay-to-play MMORPG market share is Blizzard Entertainment's World of Warcraft, followed by Final Fantasy XI and Phantasy Star Online. Titles with large market shares in the free-to-play category are MapleStory, Rohan, and Blood Feud, with the most popular buy-to-play game being Guild Wars.

Social Impact

Nick Yee (www.nickyee.com), a research scientist at the Palo Alto Research Center, studies online games and immersive virtual reality. Yee has created something called the Daedalus Project, which he explains as "an ongoing study of MMORPG players. MMORPGs are a video game genre that allows thousands of people to interact, compete, and collaborate in an online virtual environment. Over the past six years, more than 40,000 MMORPG players have participated in the project."

Yee's Daedalus Project has generated some interesting articles, such as "Superstitions: Exploring Superstitions in MMOs and How They Develop" and "Social Architectures in Virtual Worlds: How Do the Rules in Virtual Worlds Encourage Certain Social Behaviors?" Yee makes the following statement in his "Social Architectures" article:

> We tend to think of altruism and gregariousness as personality traits. Some people are more helpful; other people are more chatty. One reason why I'm fascinated with MMOs is because it seems that game mechanics also change how communities and individuals behave. For example, when people had to ask casters for "binds" (i.e., set their respawn point) in the original EQ, it seemed to help create a cultural norm of asking for help in general. In a way, altruism was not only an aspect of individual players; it was also partly fostered by the game mechanics. This "social architecture" of virtual environments is interesting because it hints at the possibility of shaping community and individual behavior via game mechanics.

Yee sees a potential for human behavior in the real world to change because of the types of behavior that are becoming more acceptable in virtual gaming worlds. By participating in an online world, players can more easily develop and embrace these particular traits and attributes once they've moved from their gaming interactions to those in their everyday lives.

British writer and game researcher Richard Bartle studied multiplayer RPG players and classified them into four primary psychological groups: explorer, socializer, killer, or achiever. Erwin Andreasen (www.andreasen .org) then expanded Bartle's classifications and developed this concept into the 30-question Bartle Test—which more than 521,112 gamers have taken and which is available on the Gamer DNA web site at www.gamerdna.com/quizzes/bartle-test-of-gamer-psychology.

Bartle's and Andreasen's data includes more than 200,000 of the original responses that Andreasen recorded between the years 1996 and 2006. Originally designed for MUD (multiuser dungeon) participants, it remains relevant to new virtual worlds and MMORPGs. Scoring is interesting and entertaining. The original wording of all questions has not been changed, except to modernize certain terms (such as replacing MUD with the more encompassing MMORPG).

The CDC in MMORPG WoW

Although MMORPG participants invent imaginary characters to play in what are usually considered make-believe games, one particular incident took place that proved to be great practice for a real-life disaster. On September 13, 2005, the Corrupted Blood epidemic hit (www.wowwiki.com/Corrupted_ Blood; see Figure 17.5). "Upon engaging the demon, players were stricken by a 'Corrupted Blood' which would periodically sap their life. It inflicted 250 to 300 points of damage (compared to the average health of 4,000 to 5,000 for a player of the highest level at that time) every few seconds to the afflicted player. The disease would also be passed on to other players who were simply standing in close proximity to an infected person. Originally this malady was confined within the Zul'Gurub instance, but made its way into the outside world by way of hunter pets that contracted the disease. Within hours, Corrupted Blood had infected entire cities because of their high player concentrations. Low-level players were killed in seconds by the

FIGURE 17.5 Corrupted Blood Screen

high-damage disease. For days, carpets of skeletons riddled the highest-populated towns and were rendered uninhabitable by the persistent plague."

This was a temporary programming error that created a virtual plague that infected and spread rapidly from character to character throughout Blizzard Entertainment's World of Warcraft—and resembled a real-life disease outbreak. This virtual plague attracted the attention of psychologists and epidemiologists across North America. The Centers for Disease Control and Prevention actually used this incident as a research model to study both the progression and transference of a disease and the potential human response to large-scale epidemic infection.

Virtual Economies

Like Second Life, MMORPGs also have thriving virtual economies. Virtual money can be earned through game play, items can be bought and sold, and wealth can be accumulated. And these virtual economies can have an impact on the economies of the real world, as demonstrated by Anshe Chung's ability to become the first real—or first first-life—millionaire generated from Second Life's virtual land. (See Chapter 16, Virtual Worlds—Real Impact, for Chung's full story.)

Edward Castronova (www.mypage.iu.edu/~castro/home.html)—one of the early researchers of MMORPGs—demonstrated that a supply-and-demand market that exists for virtual items often crosses over to the real world, or first life. This crossover assumes that the players have the ability to sell or barter items to each other for virtual currency, and that the currency translates—and exchanges—into real-world currency.

This real/virtual world currency connection is having a profound effect on players, the gaming industry, and the courts. When Castronova first studied the trend in 2002, he found that a highly liquid—and often-illegal—currency market existed. At one point, the value of EverQuest's in-game currency exceeded that of the Japanese yen. Some players—referred to as *gold farmers*—make a living by using these virtual economies. A few of the game publishers prohibit the exchange of real-world money for virtual items, whereas virtual worlds such as Second Life and Entropia Universe support and profit from this system. This link between currencies is common in virtual worlds, but rare in MMORPGs, where it is generally accepted that this kind of exchange is detrimental to game play. When real-world wealth can influence greater rewards than skillful game play, the incentive for strategic role-play and real game involvement can become diminished.

This blurred boundary between the various currencies has also led to the proliferation of in-world gambling. Because gambling is illegal or controlled in so many areas of the world, Second Life was forced to remove and prohibit gambling within its virtual world.

Raids

A fast-growing segment of the MMORPG is the *Raid*, which is an adventure or part of the parent game designed for specific groups of players—often 20 or more. Raids are copied from the parent game and allow that particular segment to be separated from the rest of the game world. This reduces competition, provides for faster game play downloads, and lessens screen-refresh lag times.

Single Player

Even though the MMORPG is designed for multiple players and social interaction, many games allow the user to interact solely with the game itself. As a result, many of the most popular MMORPGs have now developed single-player play options. Even the older Dungeons & Dragons Online was retrofitted to allow for single play. This change has increased the popularity of the MMORPG, because many of the gamers prefer to play while interacting with the computer only or offline. One of the authors recently tested an MMORPG car race game called FlatOut 2. While the racing interaction and competition with others from around the world is exciting, sometimes just taking the car out for a spin or against the computer can be a lot of fun as well.

User-Generated Content

More and more MMORPGs are encouraging user-generated content. Ultima Online provided a 30-page book that instructs players on how to collect, trade personal libraries, and build houses. In fact, any noncombat-type MMORPG relies on user-generated content—including textures, architecture, buildings, objects, and animations—much like the two billion user-generated items on the Linden Labs server. (Listen to the interview with Mark Kingdon, CEO, Linden Labs—Second Life, at www.theSocialMediaBible.com.)

Console-Based MMORPGs

Again—although the MMORPG is intended to be played on the Internet by large numbers of players at any given time—two major video game manufacturers are releasing console-based MMORPGs, including The Age of

Conan for the Xbox 360, which will allow the user to play these online games on their Xbox consoles or their PC while online.

The Largest MMORPG: World of Warcraft

World of Warcraft—commonly known as WoW—was designed by Rob Pardo, Jeff Kaplan, and Tom Chilton, developed by Blizzard Entertainment, published by Vivendi Universal, and released on November 23, 2004. WoW is considered a fantasy MMORPG, and is the fourth game released by Blizzard (the first was Warcraft: Orcs & Humans in 1994). World of Warcraft differs from other MMORPGs in many ways. Players complete quests and experience the world at their own pace, whether it be a few hours here and there or entire weeks at a time. Additionally, their quest system provides an enormous variety of captivating quests with

FIGURE 17.6 WoW (World of Warcraft)

story elements, dynamic events, and flexible reward systems. World of Warcraft also features a faster style of play, with less downtime and an emphasis on combat and tactics against multiple opponents. World of Warcraft is currently the world's largest MMORPG, with more than 11 million monthly subscribers, and holds the Guinness World Record for the most popular MMORPG ever with an estimated 62 percent of the MMORPG market in April 2008. While most online MMORPGs have peaked or flattened, WoW is really still "wow!"

The management of Blizzard Entertainment "didn't see the connection between WoW and social media's 'trusted networks'" and declined to participate in *The Social Media Bible*. To read their response, visit www .theSocialMediaBible.com.

Halo3

Halo3 is a first-person shooter, or FPS, video game. It was developed by Bungie software exclusively for the Xbox 360 video gaming console. Halo3 is the third edition in the Halo series, and concludes the trilogy story that

FIGURE 17.7 Halo3

began in the original Halo game. The game's themes are based on an interstellar war between twenty-sixth-century humanity—led by the United Nations Space Command—and a collection of alien races known as the Covenant. The MMORPG player assumes the role of the Master Chief, a cybernetically enhanced super-soldier, as he wages war in defense of humanity assisted by human Marines as well as an allied alien race called Elites, which is led by the Arbiter.

On September 25, 2007, Halo3 was released in Australia, Brazil, India, New Zealand, North America, and Singapore; in Europe one day later; and on the following day in Japan. There were 4.2 million copies of Halo3 in retail outlets on the day before its debut, and the game grossed more than $300 million during the first week following its release. Within the first 24 hours, more than one million people played Halo3 on Xbox Live. By January 3, 2008, Halo3 had sold more than 8.1 million copies and was the best-selling video game of 2007 in the United States.

FIGURE 17.8 Halo3

At the time this paragraph was being written, there were 68,064 Halo3 players online, with 604,821 unique players and 1,342,417 battles logged in the last 24 hours, and a UNSC Campaign Kill Count of 6,737,856,503.[1]

FIGURE 17.9 In-Game Ads

In-Game Advertising

As discussed in Chapter 16, Virtual Worlds—Real Impact, in-game advertising is growing in popularity. The following article from TechCrunch shows the level of interest of many of the Fortune 500 companies regarding in-game advertising.

Google to Buy Adscape for $23 Million

Nick Gonzalez, February 16, 2007

After some rumors of a deal earlier this month, Google has expanded its advertising reach by moving into video game advertising with their $23 million acquisition of Adscape. Adscape is a video game advertising company whose AdverPlay product lets developers place dynamic ads right inside the game and Real Virtual Gateway product enables two-way text, audio, and video communication via SMS Text or e-mail.

[In] May 2006, Microsoft had acquired a similar in-game advertiser, Massive, to run advertising across its Xbox Live and MSN gaming platform. The WSJ (subscription) placed the deal in the $200 to $400 million range. Massive claims they "can provide publishers and developers $1–$2 profit per unit shipped for their titles." AdverPlay and RVG are the product of five years of development and consist of one issued and 30 pending patents.

Source: www.techcrunch.com/2007/02/16/google-to-buy-adscape-for-23-million, or go to www.theSocialMediaBible.com for "clickable Links."

---

1. UNSC Campaign is the Brute Infantry Specialist Kill Count within the Halo3 game. At the time this chapter was written, according to the UNSC Campaign Report, the total number of Enemies KIA (Killed In Action) was 6,737,856,503. This in-game "killed" number is now higher than the world's estimated population at 6,704,845,726.

    Bungie, the developers of Halo3, monitors and reports statistics on the their game's usage. Bungie's servers record all manner of statistics when you play, all of which are used to track players across all of their Halo3 games, multiplayer and campaign alike.

Providers

There are currently over 225 different major MMORPGs available today—far too many to list here. The following is a link to MMORPG.com, which lists all of the current MMORPG games, genres, developers, fees, and a whole lot more: www.mmorpg.com/gamelist.cfm?bhcp=1.

The ROI of Social Media

Universal Studios Home Entertainment's *Public Enemies* Blockbuster Social Media Campaign

Background

The critically acclaimed gangster saga *Public Enemies* (www.publicenemies .net) has been described as "explosive . . . thrilling . . . suspenseful," "one of the best of the year," and "like no other." Those same descriptions accurately reflect the success of the wildly popular Facebook game, Zynga's Mafia Wars (www.zynga.com/games/index.php?game=mafiawars), that launched an unprecedented social media campaign to promote the film's high-profile December 2009 Blu-ray and DVD release. Mafia Wars enables social gamers to start a Mafia family with friends, run a criminal empire and fight to be the most powerful family in New York City, Cuba, and Moscow. For those who don't know, Mafia Wars is played by more than 25 million monthly active Facebook users!

Strategy

The campaign, led by appssavvy (www.appssavvy.com), a direct sales team for the social media space, in partnership with the Los Angeles office of Ignited (www.ignitedusa.com), a marketing innovations agency working on behalf of Universal Studios Home Entertainment (www.universalstudioshome entertainment.com), celebrated the home entertainment release by launching this first-of-its-kind integration reaching tens of millions of consumers.

The strategy was to maximize awareness of *Public Enemies* in the face of larger releases through unique opportunities that created viral buzz.

Implementation

During *"Public Enemies* Week" on Mafia Wars, players completed various jobs in order to unlock *Public Enemies* "Loot"—items such as John Dillinger's wooden gun, prison stripes, and *Public Enemy Number 1* Newspaper, among others.

Additionally, special *Public Enemies*–featured jobs were offered for a limited time. After completing jobs (playing the game), players were able to view clips from the movie and read John Dillinger factoids.

Opportunity

Mafia Wars was an incredibly dynamic environment to seamlessly integrate the *Public Enemies* property and to effectively engage a significant and relevant audience. The opportunities for marketers to engage with people in social media are vast and must be done in ways that are relevant to consumers—*Public Enemies* did just that.

Conclusion

To demonstrate the success of the campaign, *Public Enemies* Jobs were played nearly 45 million times by 19 million unique users and Loot garnered nearly 55 million interactions during the week-long campaign. Not only did the game reach millions of players, but it also over delivered by a multiple of 13, which ultimately supported the film's Blu-ray and DVD break-out during the busy holiday season.

Outside of Loot interacted with and Jobs completed, as one would expect, the integration was a viral success. Loot and Job interactions were posted to players' Facebook Newsfeed more than 7.6 million times delivering nearly a million (992,000-plus) viral impressions. Lastly, 1.5 million trailers were watched to completion. Meanwhile, the campaign generated nearly 25,000 "Likes" and more than 26,000 comments on the Mafia Wars Facebook Fan page.

Appssavvy
www.appssavvy.com/publicenemies

Expert Insight

Scott Clough, avid online gamer, www.myspace.com/brandrath

Scott Clough

Actually, I was playing a tabletop role-playing game, since probably the early 1980s. I started with games like Dungeons and Dragons, and honestly, as a teenager, I probably spent all of my free time doing so.

I then moved into playing computer games, especially ones that had elements of role-playing games in them. . . . Zork was a very early one; very simplistic. Then I moved up to playing games such as Ultima, Might and Magic, Bard's

(*continued*)

(*continued*)

Tale . . . and then they started making some of the Dungeons and Dragons into computer games. I got involved in the online role-playing at about 1996 when I went through a divorce and had suddenly lots of time, and in 1997 Ultima Online (the first of the genre) came out. And it gave me something to fill up my time.

I played Ultima Online until EverQuest was released, and that was probably the online game that probably really made the whole genre successful, because the numbers became staggering . . . how many people were playing.

It had graphics that were just amazing; it had a world that was in full realistic, and I think all the current big games owe a lot to EverQuest.

I used to play games with almost all my free time, but in later years I've learned to limit my playing. I also try to make sure it doesn't dominate my life, and I stopped playing particular ones when I realized I'm not being entertained. But I always look for something else to move on to.

So I've tried a lot of the games over the years. I wish I had tried the FlatOut one; I'll have to look that one up. . . .

It was interesting; I got really interested in fixing up computers for myself and then I was building bigger and badder machines for friends and family, even. One day I was online all over the games and I was looking for another job, and a guy who I was gaming with, never met, I had said to him I was seeking a new job. And he said, "Would you be willing to relocate?" And I said, "Yeah, sure, as long as it was Arizona."

The next day I had an interview set up, and since then I have been working in computer support and eventually ending up here at Hewlett-Packard. . . .

Well, [MMORPG] was a term coined by Richard Garrett, creator of Ultima Online. It means, "Massively multiplayer online role-playing game." Yeah . . . a mouthful! . . .

Well, yeah, it gives an explanation of it. The term was kind of coined to differentiate the different kinds of games that were out there at the time. You've got to realize, this kind of game was an evolution, and it's still in process. What had happened is back in the day, people were playing the very games I spoke of, such as Ultima, some of the Dungeons and Dragons games, and they were very active. The thing they kept saying they wanted to do was to be able to have a friend come over, like you with our brother, and play head-on-head or in the same world with it. And it was just a natural interest to say, "Hey, if we can make it so you can play with two, four friends, why not do it over the new medium called the Internet," back at that time. And as you know, Richard Garrett's Ultima . . . was the first one. And actually it was interesting because they had eight different versions of their stand-alone game before they came out with Ultima Online; and amazingly enough it's still out there! . . .

Yes, but it also has some drawbacks, because where as a bot or mob is going to react in a set mode based on the programming (and that has been developed more each year), some players that you get out there can be unethical. And they use cheats, hacks, exploits (as it's called out there) to get the edge on you rather than by skill. . . .

Well, it's really interesting. It's people in all the demographics, I would say. This is a hobby that has no separation by race, sex, religion. . . . You know a lot of the people out there try to classify the online player as a teenage boy, you know! But I've run into family groups that play, moms, dads, and the kids. I have met professionals who play everything, from computer engineers to lawyers to police officers, to soldiers sitting over in Iraq. . . .

You know the biggest appeal is the ability to be another person, or another entity. You can be a hero or a villain, just depending on how you want to play or the aspects of the game. There are some people out there who are dedicated to the role-playing aspects, and it's interesting because the games have started to have to modify to have to get there.

So they have dedicated role-playing servers, where everything you say or do is supposed to be in character. There are other servers who are dedicated to player versus player, and that's a real big growth area currently. And I would say most of the arguments in the games are about character balance in player versus player. In case you weren't aware, but that's where other players kill or defeat real players in the game, and usually you get some type of reward.

But I think the real attachment in the games is the community aspect. Usually, most of the games allow you to form up a group, usually called a guild. And the guild . . . you get to display your name over the name of the character; you get to solve a harder quest, kill the toughest monsters while working with people. And they do things such as raids, where they get fifty-plus people to go after a single creature.

And while you're doing this, you chat and you develop friendships. I've even known people to get married and divorced as a result of playing this game. . . .

It's something to watch because it's a new and developing technology, and games such as World of Warcraft have shown the worldwide appeal of such games. But you know, it's not just the game itself that is being sold. There's now a thriving industry on the items that are in the game . . . virtual items.

There's a third-party market on games guides, there's help web sites. There are even companies out there that are selling online money gold and characters for real-world cash. Now most of the games are like, trying to shut this down, this behavior. And most players do not like it. And also some of the games are based on the current entertainment industry. There's a Matrix game, Pirates of the Caribbean, Star Wars, and there's even a Star Trek game based on the recently released movie out there now. . . .

(continued)

(*continued*)

Yeah, there's online money. Actually, since most of the games are fantasy, it's gold, but there's also items in the game that people desire. Say for instance, a really powerful sword that's a very rare find. There's an organization out there that goes and they do what's called "camping." They sit there and wait for the mob that has it, they take it, and then when they get it, rather than using it for that character they turn it over to their company that sells it online. And I've seen back on some of the eBay-equivalent sites [they] are selling some of this stuff. I've seen items sell for hundreds of dollars. . . .

Actually if you're interested in statistics, there's a great site, mmorgchart .com, and they actually chart how many people are playing in certain games, the basic activities. And you can actually look at how the games have gone up and down in their numbers . . . fascinating numbers . . . and the runner of the site tries to put it all in scientific methods, and he tells you where his data comes from so you can make your own evaluations on the reliability.

If you're more casual and you just want to know what your kids are getting involved in, you can go on the Web and look for sites like wow.allakhazam.com; you can go to the manufacturer of World of Warcraft and get information off of those. You can also buy magazines such as *PC Gamer,* which is one example. And you can always tell them apart because they will have screen shots of the various games on their cover, usually.

But really, if you just want to know about the games, just go to any place that sells the software, such as Best Buy Electronics, and you'll see they have their own sections, their own shelves, and you can look at the game boxes and read what they're claiming that their world gives to you. You can actually buy even game guides that tell you how the game is played.

To listen to or read the entire Executive Conversation with Scott Clough, avid online gamer, go to www.theSocialMediaBible.com.

Commandments

1. **Thou shalt visit the occasional MMORPG site.**

    Go look at the most popular MMORPGs, and choose one to play. This is the perfect opportunity to buy an Xbox and Halo3 as a tax deduction under market research (see your tax professional for advice about this first, of course!). Experience it firsthand. Look for in-game advertising. See how it's used. Understand its application. Maybe it isn't right for you, your product, or your service, but what if it is?

2. **Thou shalt read MMORPG articles.**

   Read some articles about MMORPGs. MMORPGs are popular and have a very strong fan base, but the size and influence of the market can be staggering if you are unfamiliar with it. Study a few MMORPGs so that when the Fortune 500 companies have figured out how to effectively monetize in-game advertising to its huge loyal user base, you will be there.

3. **Thou shalt understand in-game advertising.**

   Read a few articles about in-game advertising. If all of the major online advertisers are buying and building companies that provide in-game advertising, maybe there is a reason. Encourage others to follow along until everyone understands the application and potential of this powerful new media.

Conclusion

The moral of the story is to remain open to all of what's going on around you in the world of social media and advertising. MMORPGs provide a huge base of trusted networks. When you have people with the same interest who participate in trusted social networks that are more than 600,000 members strong in any given 24-hour period—and eight million participants in one game alone—you might want to be aware of this as a businessperson. As you can see by the number of existing games, numbers of participants, and the rate at which this marketing opportunity is growing, companies like Microsoft and Google will figure out how to effectively monetize it. You need to be aware, informed, and there when it happens.

To hear all of the Expert Interviews, go to www.theSocialMediaBible.com.

Readings and Resources

Armitage, Grenville, Mark Claypool, and Philip Branch. *Networking and Online Games: Understanding and Engineering Multiplayer Internet Games*. (Hoboken, NJ: John Wiley & Sons, Inc.)

The Daedalus Project, The Psychology of MMORPGs, http://www.nickyee.com/daedalus

Incan Monkey God Studios Inc. *Asheron's Call 2—Fallen Kings: Sybex Official Strategies & Secrets*. (Hoboken, NJ: John Wiley & Sons, Inc.)

Jennings, Scott, and Alexander Macris. *Massively Multiplayer Games For Dummies*. (Hoboken, NJ: John Wiley & Sons, Inc.)

Johnson, Brian, and Duncan Mackenzie. *Xbox 360 For Dummies*. (Hoboken, NJ: John Wiley & Sons, Inc.)

Mileham, Rebecca. *Powering Up: Are Computer Games Changing Our Lives?* (Hoboken, NJ: John Wiley & Sons, Inc.)

Whitehead, James II, and Rick Roe. *World of Warcraft Programming: A Guide and Reference for Creating WoW Addons*, 2nd ed. (Hoboken, NJ: John Wiley & Sons, Inc.)

Downloads

For your free downloads associated with *The Social Media Bible*, go to www .theSocialMediaBible.com, and enter your ISBN number located on the back of the book above the bar code. Be sure to enter the dashes.

Credits

The ROI of Social Media was provided by:

Appssavvy, www.appssavvy.com/publicenemies

Expert Insight and technical edits were provided by:

Scott Clough, avid online gamer, www.facebook.com/sclough68

CHAPTER 18

RSS—Really Simple Syndication Made Simple

What's in It for You?

For the first time in Internet history, you can syndicate or distribute your original web site content worldwide for free. That's right. No longer do you have to subscribe to a news service or be part of a large media organization to send your news or receive news from any other web site from all around the world.

RSS—or Really Simple Syndication—is a one-click solution that allows all of your content to be sent to your followers the moment you publish it. The reverse is also the case; you can have each of your preferred blogs and news stories sent to you automatically without having to take the time to search all of your favorite web sites every day for new content and updates. Simply adding a syndication button to your blog site lets your followers click your Subscribe button and instantly receive your latest breaking blog.

But what exactly does RSS have to do with building an online following for your business? Let's start with some basic information, so that you can see how this really simple concept can be easily applied to your own company.

Back to the Beginning

The early RSS formats date back to 1995, when computer scientist Ramanathan V. Guha and several of his colleagues developed the Meta Content Framework (MCF)[1] at Apple Computer's Advanced Technology Group between 1995 and 1997. In July 1999, Guha developed the first version of RSS

---

1. Meta Content Framework (MCF) is a specific format for structuring metadata (behind-the-scenes information that the web browsers and search engines look at) about web sites and their data.

 theSocialMediaBible.com

FIGURE 18.1   RSS

(0.9) for My.Netscape.com. Guha's Netscape colleague Dan Libby is responsible for improving the first RSS by incorporating Dave Winer's "Scripting-News" format, which he dubbed "Rich Site Summary" (see more on Winer next). Winer is a pioneer of RSS as Really Simple Syndication, and his Scripting News is one of the oldest blogs on the Internet, having been established in 1997.

Dan Libby and Netscape abandoned the development of RSS for more than eight years when, in April 2001, new owner AOL restructured the company and eliminated that particular project. This allowed two new developers to pick up where Netscape left off—the first being the RSS-DEV Group, and the second being UserLand Software owner Dave Winer. Winer created software that could read and write in a modified version of RSS 0.91, which he made available on his UserLand web site. In December 2001, Winer applied for a U.S. trademark, but failed to respond to the United States Patent and Trademark Office, and his trademark application was rejected.

Winer continued to develop and release improvements to his RSS project, the most significant of which came in 2000 when he introduced a version that could enclose audio files. This technology made the still-new process of podcasting (see Chapter 10, Talking about the Podcast (Audio Create)) much easier and more user-friendly. Then, in December 2001, RSS-DEV Working Group—which by now included Guha and O'Reilly Media—developed RSS 1.0. Winer released his newest major revision of his RSS—2.0—in 2002, which then took on the name Really Simple Syndication.

With both developers working on the same technology at the same time—yet each on their own—there has always been controversy as to who should get credit for the development of RSS. Atom was born out of this controversy in June 2003. Atom was a ground-up redesign of the RSS delivery system that was adopted by the IETF, or Internet Engineering Task Force, Proposed Standard RFC 4287 (see the following for more details about Atom's creation and development). The Atom Syndication Format is similar to the RSS format and uses the XML language employed for web feeds. The Atom Publishing Protocol (AtomPub or APP) is a simple HTTP-based protocol for creating and updating web resources. Web feeds allow software programs to check for updates published on a web site.

In July 2003—the month following Atom's inception—Winer assigned his copyright for RSS 2.0 to the Berkman Center for the Internet and Society while starting a term as a visiting fellow at Harvard. Winer, Jon Udell, and Brent Simmins launched their group—which they titled the RSS Advisory

Board—to provide support to RSS 2.0. Mozilla Firefox was the first browser to adopt the familiar orange RSS subscribe (feed) icon with its radio broadcast waves, and within a few months, Opera Software, Microsoft Outlook, and Microsoft Explorer all recognized RSS as an industry standard. Computer book author and web publisher Rogers Cadenhead took over as head of the RSS Advisory Board in January 2006 upon Winer's departure. The RSS format was revised again in June 2007.

Atom

In June 2003, IBM software developer Sam Ruby created a wiki to discuss the deficiencies of RSS and to solicit ideas about syndication. Ruby wanted to come up with a better system than Blogger API or LiveJournal—the ones that were currently being used. More than 150 developers and prominent members of the online community came out to support the development of Atom, including Jeremy Zawodny of Yahoo!, Brad Fitzpatrick of LiveJournal, Glenn Otis Brown of Creative Commons, Timothy Appnel of O'Reilly Network, Mena Trott of Six Apart, David Sifry of Technorati, Jason Shellen of Blogger, and others. Even RSS originator Dave Winer gave Atom his full support. By July 2003, the project code names "Necho," "Pie," and "Echo" had become known as Atom 0.2. Google added Atom to its Google News and Google Blogger in December 2003—an event that marked the full support of the syndication community.

In June 2004, the Atompub Group was formed by Paul Hoffman and Tim Bray (codeveloper of the XML specification), which moved the Atom project to the Internet Engineering Task Force or IETF. In December 2005, the IETF accepted the Atom Syndication Format as the industry standard. Thanks to coeditors Robert Sayre and Mark Nottingham, the Atom Publishing Protocol was declared the standard in October 2007 in their IETF RFC 5023 (Internet Engineering Task Force Request for Comments #5023).

Even though Atom 1.0 is an IETF standard and widely supported by many podcasting applications such as iTunes and Google, RSS 2.0 still remains the most widely used and accepted format. Many web sites, such as those of the *New York Times*, CNN, and the BBC, will publish their feeds only in the RSS 2.0 format.

What You Need to Know

RSS is a way to feed (or web feed) your web pages, blogs, audio, video, and photographs automatically to people who subscribe to your content through a feed. In other words, every time you create something new on the Internet and hit Publish, a feed goes out to everyone who has asked for an update. Your followers are automatically notified through e-mail, mobile texting, or tweets (see Chapter 14, Thumbs Up for Microblogging), and your content is automatically added to their reader or aggregator page. You can also subscribe to this kind of material from others, and have news headlines, stock quotes, blogs, and other frequently updated information automatically sent to your reader page or feed reader—which can be either computer- or browser-based.

The only requirement for you to subscribe to a feed is to go to your favorite web site, blog, or news site, locate the Subscribe button or the familiar orange RSS Subscribe button, and select your feed reader (or paste the link into your Add Subscription box). That's it! Now each time that web or blog page publishes new content, your reader page will be notified and provided with a copy of that new content.

Reader or Aggregator

A reader, or aggregator, is a program or web site that will check and continuously search all of the blogs, news sites, or other web sites to which you have subscribed for new content (see Figure 18.2). If fresh material is identified, the reader page will show a summary of that information with a

FIGURE 18.2 iGoogle Reader

link to that page. This way—instead of having to visit all of your favorite web sites, news sites, and blogs—the newest content comes to you, and is aggregated—or summarized—in one reader page. Some web pages allow you to subscribe in RSS, Atom, or both formats.

iGoogle Reader (Aggregator): These reader pages or aggregators are designed as a stand-alone software program or as a web page (browser-based), such as iGoogle. Web-based or browser-based feed readers allow the user to access aggregated content from any Internet browser.

Social Bookmarks

FIGURE 18.3 Social Bookmark Chiclets

Social bookmarks are small icons found on nearly all blogs, web sites, news sites, sports sites, or any pages that provide fresh, updated content on a regular basis. By selecting your feed reader or aggregator icon, the content feed is automatically added to your specific reader page. Most of these social bookmarks are a one-click addition. Some feed readers might require you to copy and paste the URL of your favorite news or blog page into an Add Subscription text box. It's easy, and only requires one step.

Providers

Page readers or aggregators are free; the following is a list of the many readers you can choose from:

Aggregators

- Akregator
- AOL Explorer
- Avant Browser
- Blam!
- BlogBridge
- Bloglines
- BottomFeeder

- Camino
- Claws Mail
- Cooliris
- Epiphany
- FeedBeast
- FeedDemon
- FeedGhost

- Feedreader
- Feedview, a Firefox extension
- Flock
- FreeRange WebReader
- Gnus
- Google.com/Reader
- Hubdog
- IBM Lotus Notes
- iCab
- iGoogle
- Internet Explorer
- K-Meleon
- Liferea
- Apple Mail
- Maxthon
- mDigger
- Mercury Messenger
- Microsoft Office Outlook
- Mindity
- Mozilla Firefox
- Mozilla Thunderbird
- MyYahoo!
- NetNewsWire
- NewsAccess
- NewsBreak
- Newsbeuter
- NewsFire
- NewsFox, a Firefox extension
- Newsgator
- Omea
- OmniWeb
- Opera Mail
- Opera web browser
- Pegasus Mail
- RSS Bandit
- RSSOwl
- Safari
- Sage, a Firefox extension
- SeaMonkey Mail and Newsgroups
- Shiira
- Sleipnir
- Snarfer
- Tencent Traveler
- The Bat!
- Thinfeeder
- Vienna
- Windows Live Mail
- Zimbra

Web-Based Software

- aideRSS
- AmphetaDesk
- Bloglines
- Daylife
- Drupal Aggregator Module
- Fastladder
- Google News
- Google Reader
- Imooty.eu
- Live.com
- mDigger
- Netvibes
- Newsknowledge
- Pageflakes

- Planet
- Rojo.com
- Seeking Alpha

- Spokeo
- Yahoo!

Media Aggregators

- Akregator
- Amarok
- Canola
- Flock
- iTunes
- Juice
- Mediafly SyncClient

- MediaMonkey
- Miro
- Rhythmbox (GNOME)
- Songbird
- Winamp
- Zune

The ROI of Social Media

The Utility of B2B Twitter

Introduction

This chronicles the first three weeks of a successful experiment to evaluate the utility of Twitter as an adjunct to traditional B2B marketing and promotion.

Background

The company in this case is a medium-sized firm [that] provides products and services based on the technology of major partners, all of whom had well advanced social network strategies. Its normal methods for promotion are Web, newsletter, banner ad, trade show, purchased lists, press release, and published case study or white paper.

Strategy

Since the major partners all had an active Social Media presence, it seemed a strategy to follow and comment on these established social media blogs and tweets might give some early visibility.

Implementation

A Twitter account was opened in the company's name. The account followed one of the major partners and "re-tweeted" relevant messages. Where

(continued)

(*continued*)

appropriate, a Bit.ly URL was added to the tweet, which included Google Analytics tracking code to the company's web site. All other web and newsletter promotions were tracked with Google Analytics in this way, to allow comparisons of effectiveness over the period.

Opportunity

This program was timed to coincide with some major product releases from one of the major partners. This means potential customers were searching for just announced product names and following the major partners' social media tweets.

Conclusion

Since the nature of this B2B relationship is long term, the practical measurement ROI is difficult. We use ROO (Return on Objective), where Twitter can be compared to other media based on cost effectiveness for a specific objective. Objectives are *exposures*, meaning brand name exposed to target audience; and *access*, meaning audience follow-up—in this case, click thru to a web page.

Exposure of the company's name went way up. Exposures are the way magazines and banner ads are sold, and for a company seeking to build brand, exposures is a reasonable objective. By this measure, Twitter may mature to be a silver bullet.

By multiplying the company's tweets times the average number of followers, we calculate something like 10,000 exposures—to a fully opt-in audience. The cost for this is quite reasonable compared to exposures from banner ads or purchased e-mail lists, neither of which is opt-in.

Access to the company web site went up, too. In this case, Access means the number of times a person led by Twitter came to the company's web site.

Thirty-eight web visitors is not a lot, but it is more than could be expected from a typical 10,000-name e-mail distribution to a "blind" list, say, a list rented from a magazine.

What is most relevant is the comparison to other channels. During the test period, people were brought to the site by participation in a very popular sponsored blog site of a partner, and a mention in another partner's newsletter. Clearly, Twitter was more effective.

This effort was determined to be cost effective. Twitter was found as effective as the company newsletter, and more effective than other media.

Lawrence Ricci
www.EmbeddedInsider.com

Expert Insight

Krista Canfield, public relations manager, LinkedIn, www.linkedin.com

Krista Canfield

Basically, what LinkedIn does is [to] help professionals accelerate their success. They can do that in any number of different ways, whether it be looking for employees and trying to get a bit more background information on them, and what they've done in the past and who they've worked with in the past. We've even had companies that have acquired other companies through the web site. Small business owners are using the answers portion of LinkedIn to get advice on building their business and taking it to the next level. So, it really depends on what success means to you, but LinkedIn can definitely help in a variety of different ways. . . .

One company actually got acquired by the Weather Channel, and LinkedIn helped facilitate that whole process. There was [someone who] knew that his company was going to be the perfect fit for the Weather Channel. He just wasn't sure how to get in front of the right person. So what he did was actually search for the person on LinkedIn that might be the right contact at the Weather Channel, sent him an e-mail and began an e-mail dialogue; and within a few months his company ended up getting acquired by the Weather Channel. So this is a demonstration of how LinkedIn can get you in touch with the right people and to make sure you are getting your business ideas, your own personal brand in front of the right people. . . .

It's very cool! And, you know, it's all about leveraging your relationships. I think the whole idea of creating LinkedIn in the first place was to keep in contact with all the different people that you've worked with in the past: friends, family members, coworkers, all those sorts of things. You know, a lot of times if you get someone's business card and you want to get in touch with them three years later down the line, and you do need that reference or you need that recommendation . . . a lot of times that person has switched roles and they're at a different company . . . and that e-mail address and phone number may no longer be of use to you. So, first and foremost, [the site] was meant to be a way to stay in touch with all of the people that you have worked with in the past, even if they have changed positions or switched companies. But the other thing that it really enables you to do is to find the right person who is going to be the right contact for you, no matter *what* company they may be at.

If you're working on the relationship that you already have, you never know who your best friend may know. . . . Chances are that one of your contacts

(continued)

(*continued*)

already works at a totally different company in a totally different world from what you do; so they have a whole different network of people that you could probably utilize that might help you accomplish your goals. It's all about working off of those relationships. It gets things done . . . .

We do offer premium accounts for those members that are looking to reach out to more people outside of their network; but for the most part, that free version can actually help you get a lot done. Some people either jump in there with both feet and try it out, without having to worry about something you need to pay on a monthly basis, until you are ready for that level of commitment. . . .

The average user is around 41 years old, and has a household income of just over $110,000. But we also have everybody—from like high-level CEOs . . . Bill Gates is on LinkedIn. We have professional athletes, like Yao Ming, who has a profile on LinkedIn. Both presidential candidates have profiles on LinkedIn. But we also have over 600,000 small business owners. So there's really a wide range of people that are on the web site, and certainly professionally from every single industry. Yes—over 25 million people across the world!

Well, yeah, we do actually have an API[2] that a number of different sites use. So, if you go to, say, *Business Week*'s or the *New York Times's* web site—or if you go to CXO Media (which owns cio.com)—there is another site called "Simply Hired" that's using our API. What's really cool about the API is it will show you—if you are reading an article in *Business Week*—the first company that appears in the headline of the article. And if you give it permission to log in to your account simultaneously while you are looking at that article, it will show you—if, say, the article is about Volkswagens—who you know in your network that knows someone who works at Volkswagen. So it is very powerful to a professional who may be looking at an article and saying, "Wow, my company's a great fit for Volkswagen." Or, "I think Volkswagen would be the perfect client for us." Or, "Wow, gee, I'd love to work at Volkswagen." To be able to sit there and say, "Oh, my friend, Joe, is connected to Susan who works at Volkswagen." So, it definitely makes the world a smaller place, and it really helps you get business done much more efficiently. . . .

To listen to or read the entire Executive Conversation with Krista Canfield, go to www .theSocialMediaBible.com.

---

2. An API is the acronym for Application Programming Interface, or sometimes referred to as an "App." An App is a specific software application that allows one software application communicate and often exchange information with another.

Commandments

1. **Thou shalt sign up for a feed reader.**

   Go to one of the many web sites that provide a feed reader, such as iGoogle. This way, every time you open that page, all of the freshest content from the entire Web to which you subscribed will be there waiting for you.

2. **Thou shalt go forth and subscribe.**

   Go to your favorite web sites, blog sites, and news sites and hit the Subscribe button. Follow the directions, copy and paste the URL in the Add Subscription text box—and you're ready to go.

3. **Thou shalt be sure your site has social bookmarking.**

   Make sure that your company's web and blog pages have Subscribe and social bookmarking buttons, so that your customers and prospects can be easily, instantly, and automatically updated on all of your business's news.

Conclusion

The two most important items you need to know about RSS are as follows:

1. You can provide a one-click solution to any friend, family member, associate, customer, or prospect that will allow them to automatically view any new content the moment you hit your Publish button. You don't have to e-mail, call, or text message them; simply by hitting your Subscribe button, they are part of your syndication.

2. Be sure to subscribe to all of your favorite web, blog, and news sites. This way, all of the updates that you care about will be instantly sent to your reader page, and you'll never have to search the Web, site after site, to see if new content and updates have been published. It all comes to you!

   To hear all of the Expert Interviews, go to www.theSocialMediaBible .com.

Readings and Resources

RSS, or Really Simple Syndication, is a one-click process. If you wish to learn how to actually program RSS or Atom, you probably don't need to read the books suggested below. *Do*, however, read books such as *Social Media Marketing: An Hour a Day*, by Dave Evans and Susan Bratton. If you want to learn the programming aspect of RSS, here's a comprehensive list of resources.

Amiano, Mitch, Conrad D'Cruz, Kay Ethier, et al. *XML: Problem—Design—Solution*. (Hoboken, NJ: John Wiley & Sons, Inc.)

Ayers, Danny, and Andrew Watt. *Beginning RSS and Atom Programming*. (Hoboken, NJ: John Wiley & Sons, Inc.)

Crowder, Phillip, and David A. Crowder. *Creating Web Sites Bible*, 3rd ed. (Hoboken, NJ: John Wiley & Sons, Inc.)

Evans, Dave, and Susan Bratton. *Social Media Marketing: An Hour a Day*. (Hoboken, NJ: John Wiley & Sons, Inc.)

Evjen, Bill, Kent Sharkey, Thiru Thangarathinam, et al. *Professional XML*. (Hoboken, NJ: John Wiley & Sons, Inc.)

Finkelstein, Ellen. *Syndicating Web Sites with RSS Feeds For Dummies*. (Hoboken, NJ: John Wiley & Sons, Inc.)

Heaton, Jeff. *Programming Spiders, Bots, and Aggregators in Java* (Hoboken, NJ: John Wiley & Sons, Inc.)

Holzner, Steve, and Nancy Conner. *Joomla! For Dummies*. (Hoboken, NJ: John Wiley & Sons, Inc.)

Huddleston, Rob. *HTML, XHTML, and CSS: Your Visual Blueprint for Designing Effective Web Pages*. (Hoboken, NJ: John Wiley & Sons, Inc.)

Hunter, David, Andrew Watt, Jeff Rafter, et al. *Beginning XML*, 3rd ed. (Hoboken, NJ: John Wiley & Sons, Inc.)

Myer, Thomas. *Dashboard Widgets for iPhone*. (Hoboken, NJ: John Wiley & Sons, Inc.)

Orchard, Leslie M. *Hacking RSS and Atom*. (Hoboken, NJ: John Wiley & Sons, Inc.)

Reinheimer, Paul. *Professional Web APIs with PHP: eBay, Google, PayPal, Amazon, FedEx plus Web Feeds*. (Hoboken, NJ: John Wiley & Sons, Inc.)

Sabin-Wilson, Lisa. *WordPress For Dummies*, 2nd ed. (Hoboken, NJ: John Wiley & Sons, Inc.)

Downloads

For your free downloads associated with *The Social Media Bible*, go to www .theSocialMediaBible.com, and enter your ISBN number located on the back of the book above the bar code. Be sure to enter the dashes.

Credits

The ROI of Social Media was provided by:

Lawrence Ricci, www.EmbeddedInsider.com

Expert Insight was provided by:

Krista Canfield, public relations manager, LinkedIn, www.LinkedIn.com

Technical edits were provided by:

Lynne Johnson, www.lynnedjohnson.com

Spotlight on Search (Search Engine Optimization)

To some experienced members of the social networking community, Search Engine Optimization (SEO) may seem like an old-school process. However, it is still the very foundation of how search engines index all of your web site's pages—and therefore, how your customers eventually find you. SEO is incredibly important and relevant to any business. In fact, some people have only two pieces of information on their business cards: their name and their web address. At least one person has gone one step further: only the image of the Google Search Bar with his name in it printed on the face of the business card.

FIGURE 19.1 Google Search Bar

Web sites have become such an important marketing tool nowadays that they essentially serve as the foundation for everything that's done in business. The processes of SEO and Search Engine Marketing (SEM, the focus of the next chapter) are all about being sure that when people are trying to find you, your company, your product, or your service—they can.

What's in It for You

Search Engine Optimization (SEO) and Search Engine Marketing (SEM) are techniques by which you optimize your web pages, photos, blogs, social media profiles, and even videos to maximize search engine rankings. They are practices that almost everyone has heard of, but that few people understand. Search engine marketing requires implementing the optimization of your web pages and a Keyword-Sponsored Link Advertising program, or SEM. While SEO and SEM are two completely different functions, they are equally important; both refer to your web site's ability to be recognized by the major search engines. This chapter discusses search engine optimization.

More and more customers are searching on social media portals like Twitter, Facebook, and LinkedIn. When people are conducting an online search for the type of product or service you provide, they will use their favorite search engine—Google, Yahoo!, MSN, Bing, Ask, or some of the many others available today. They will type in one, two, or three words that they think best describe what you do, and hit Enter. How well you have completed your SEO will determine your position on the search engine results pages. If you did a good job, you will rank high—if not in the first position, then at least on the first page of results. Ensuring that your page appears on this first page is referred to as an *organic listing* or *organic search*, and in terms of SEO, it simply means that you are optimizing your web page (s) so you have the best ranking possible as determined by the search engines.

A plethora of books can teach you the specifics of all of the SEO techniques you can perform to guarantee you always have the highest ranking in the organic listings, but that's not what this chapter is about. Rather, this chapter explains the dozen or so techniques that anyone can perform that will probably attain 95 percent of everything you need to do to get your company's web pages or personal web pages listed in the top-10 search engine results for any given keywords.

Back to the Beginning

SEO has been around ever since the first search engine searched for the first computer file. Surprisingly, Google and Yahoo! were not the first search engines; Gerard Salton, a professor of computer science at Cornell University, beat them by nearly a half-century. His search engine, and the use of Hypertext (see the following), were actually developed in 1965 to locate and retrieve files from the earliest computers.

Salton worked in the field of information retrieval. He and his group developed the SMART (System for the Mechanical Analysis and Retrieval of Text) Information Retrieval System. As a result, Salton authored a 56-page book titled *A Theory of Indexing*, which explained his search theories—many of which are still used today.

Hypertext and the 1960s

In 1960, Ted Nelson developed Project Xanadu.[1] He coined the term *hypertext* in 1963 from *hyper* (meaning motion) and *text* meaning . . . well, text. This moving text then led to the development of the term *HTTP* (Hyper Text Transfer Protocol)—which are the first four characters of every web page address; and *HTML* (Hyper Text Markup Language), which is the language used today to create web pages. And of course, *WWW* stands for "World Wide Web."

Here's an example of how a typical web address would read if spelled out completely:

- Original: www.theSocialMediaBible.com/Index.html
- Spelled out: World Wide Web.theSocialMediaBible.Commercial/Index Page.Hyper Text Markup Language

(For a live interview with the inventor of the Hyper Text Protocol, Vint Cerf, go to www.theSocialMediaBible.com.)

Enter the Military and ARPAnet

Salton's and Nelson's work eventually led to the 1972 creation of ARPAnet (Advanced Research Projects Agency Network; see Figure 19.2), the predecessor to today's Internet. The very first official search engine emerged in 1990. It was called Archie—from the word *ARCHIvE*—and was created by McGill University student Alan Emtage in Montreal, Canada. By 1993, there were only a few hundred web sites to index, most of which were owned by colleges and universities.

Search capabilities allowed early Internet users to access a file; however, they didn't come with the ability to share files back and forth. For this application, Tim Berners-Lee developed FTP (File Transfer Protocol), a program used in place of HTTP for uploading and downloading files directly from a server.

The Internet has come a long way from the inception of HTTP, HTML, FTP, and Archie. SEO is an incredibly important element of Internet marketing that requires you to create a web page in the most efficient manner possible to facilitate its retrieval by a modern-day search engine.

---

1. Project Xanadu was the very first hypertext project, founded in 1960 by Ted Nelson. "Today's popular software simulates paper. The World Wide Web (another imitation of paper) trivializes our original hypertext model with one-way ever-breaking links and no management of version or contents."

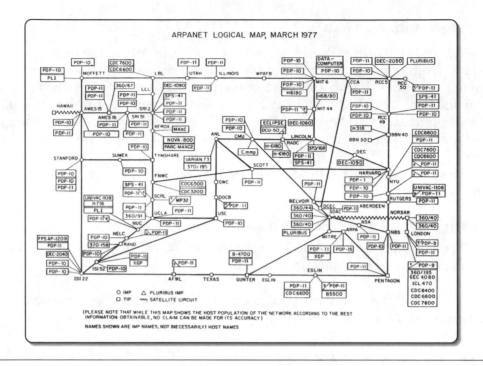

FIGURE 19.2 ARPAnet

What You Need to Know

A typical Internet search has three components to it. The first is a huge database that contains every word from every page from every web site in the world. This database can be searched and matched very quickly against any word(s) that you enter into a search engine. For example, at the time this chapter was written, a query of the term *social media bible* in Google (see Figure 19.3) returned "Results 1–10 of about 2.32 million for Social Media Bible. (0.21 seconds)."

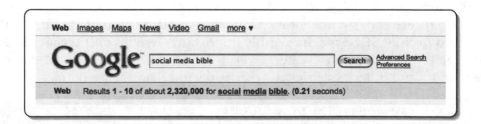

FIGURE 19.3 Google "Social Media Bible" Search

Thus, Google was showing the first 10 results—or matches—of 95.6 million possible matches; and it found all 95.6 million records in just about 0.27 seconds (see Figure 19.4). Pretty impressive!

The second component of a search engine is its spiders, robots, or just bots. These terms are metaphors for automated computer programs that go out and creep around on the Internet—find a web site, and crawl from page

FIGURE 19.4 "The Social Media Bible" Search

to page indexing and cataloging each page's content. Sound creepy? In reality, the search engine's computer simply opens a home page, captures the content, and goes onto the next page, and does the same thing. And the reason that that activity usually takes place at night is that Internet traffic is at its lowest.

James Burnes of MediaSauce describes it this way: "Because search engines are constantly indexing sites across the web, it is imperative that business's content be updated as soon as possible online to increase the relevancy and likelihood that your content will appear the next time someone searches for content. The reality is that bots and spiders run 24/7/365. The sooner you add content relevant to a user's search terms, the quicker you have a chance to be in front of them."

The third part of the process is your typical search interface, which is what you see when you go to Google or Yahoo! when you enter your query and see the results.

Search Engine Optimization

Let's first look at SEO, or organic listings. You can do many different things to your web site to achieve a high SEO ranking. While many are ethical, some are not. Most of them are fairly simple to execute, however, once you know how they work; nearly all of them are time-consuming. Everything you do in terms of SEO is meant to satisfy the search engine's algorithm (pronounced "Al-Gore-Rhythm"; you can insert the joke of your choice here).

The truth be told: Al Gore never actually meant to say that he invented the Internet. The joke was somewhat misleading and out of context, related to a statement Gore made during an interview with Wolf Blitzer on CNN's *Late Edition* in 1999. When asked to describe what distinguished him from his challenger for the Democratic presidential nomination, Senator Bill Bradley of New Jersey, Gore replied, "During my service in the United States Congress, I took the initiative in creating the Internet. I took the initiative in moving forward a whole range of initiatives that have proven to be important to our country's economic growth and environmental protection, improvements in our educational system."

Source: www.snopes.com/quotes/Internet.asp; CNN's transcript of that interview: www.cnn.com/ALLPOLITICS/stories/1999/03/09/president.2000/transcript.gore/index.html.

The Infamous Algorithm

An algorithm is just a mathematical formula that each search engine uses to determine how well your page matches against the user's query. Remember, Google or Yahoo!'s only real purpose is to return the most relevant match. The more sophisticated the algorithm, the more relevant the match is; the better the match, the more you will use that search engine. The incentive for a Google or Yahoo! is that a search engine will make more revenue from their advertisers every time it's used. When you consider Google's 2007 revenues were $17.91 billion, a lot is riding on the quality of its algorithm.

If you want to see how your web site is listed in the search engines, go to either Google or Yahoo! and type "site: www.yourdomain.com" (no spaces) into the search box. This will pull up all of the pages that have been indexed by that search engine. If an important page of yours isn't listed, it's not indexed—and you need to find out why.

Everyone—including the author of this book—wants to know exactly how each of the search engines work. But the fact is that no one except for the search engine developers knows. As you can imagine, anything that helps generate $18 billion in revenues is a closely guarded secret. So how do you find out what you can do to get that competitive edge? You test, test, test, and add a little common sense. The good news is that certain techniques will get your web page ranked top in the search engines. Don Schindler, digital strategist at MediaSauce, www.MediaSauce.com said:

> The search engine algorithms are based on "trust" and search engine language. They want to trust your web site, they want to trust that what you say you are is what you really are. They want to trust your relevance on the subject the searcher cares about. The search engine language is keywords, tags and text. Right now, it is all a search engine can read. If your web site is relevant but can't be properly understood, then it can't be ranked properly. When it comes to trust—the age of your site is important as well. If the URL is new to search engines, it is not trusted as much. If it is older and has had content on it for a long time, then the search engines trust the site more than new. This doesn't mean that site is put up and forgotten. Old content does not help drive SEO unless it is very meaningful to the audience.

The Key to Keywords

The most important criterion that a search engine examines are your keywords. These are the words that you (or your web programmer) have told the search engine are the best possible words to describe the content on your web page. These terms are placed into something called *meta tags,* which are the first thing you will see when you look at the code for your web page. Here is some of the HTML code text for *The Social Media Bible* web site:

<!DOCTYPE html PUBLIC "-//W3C//DTD XHTML 1.0 Transitional// EN" "www.w3.org/TR/xhtml1/DTD/xhtml1-transitional.dtd"> . . .

<title>The Social Media Bible</title>

<meta name="generator" content="WordPress 2.6.5"/> <!--leave this for stats--> . . .

. . . <link rel="alternate" type="application/rss+xml" title="The Social Media Bible RSS Feed" href="theSocialMediaBible.com/ feed/"/> . . .

. . . <meta name="description" content="The home of The Social Media Bible Published By John Wiley & Sons, Inc."/>

<meta name="keywords" content="social media, social media bible, lon safko, marketing, pr, sales, innovation"/>.

Take a thorough look at your meta tags. There is a chance that your web page is missing an important component in terms of your keywords, and this is where you look to find out. The missing components may have happened because the technical person programming your page didn't know what the meta tags should be and didn't bother to ask, whereas your marketing person knows your keywords, but might not be quite sure what a meta tag is. That's why you need to find out!

Content Is King

This industry has a saying: "Content Is King." The content of each of your web pages is critical. Evaluating that content—and choosing the most appropriate words to describe it—are an important part of SEO. You can read the page several times, or go to www.theSocialMediaBible.com and find the downloads for this chapter. A fun little macro there will help you. Copy the text from the page that you want to analyze, and paste it into a Word document. Run the Key Word macro, and it will tell you every word you used in that text and the exact number of times you used them. Look at the list, and disregard words like *at, is, a*, and *the*. Look at the main words, and determine which are the most important. This will help generate a list of keywords.

Once you've created your list, either place those words in your Meta Data line using a web page programming tool such as Dreamweaver, or give it to your technical person to do. It will take less than five minutes, so don't pay an exorbitant fee.

One of the most important pieces to SEO is the URL. Having proper keyword terms within the URL can really help your SERP position because of algorithm. Search engines put much emphasis on the URL. Not only is it good to have keywords in the main URL but also in the subdomains like www.businessnamekeyword.com/keyword-phrase-keyword.html and make sure you use dashes and not underscores as some search engines have problems reading underscores as separations.

Next is the Title Tags. Title tags should be your keywords but they should also match the content. If the Title Tags are not matched for the content or they are duplicated for multiple pages, the search engines will downgrade the Title Tag emphasis in indexing. Using less than 70 characters in the Title tags helps the search engines to focus on what the page means to the site.

Meta-Descriptions are important not for keywords but for users to understand what the page is. If you do not have a description for each page, the search engine may not know what to use for the description of the site and will either pull content from the page or pull a description from its database that can be written by a directory web editor. The main thing you should take from here is that it is important if you want users to hear your message. This shouldn't be longer than 150 characters.

Finally, you can add Meta-Keywords. Only use 7 to 10 keywords in this section. Any more are wasted and considered unnecessary by most SEO experts.

"MediaSauce frequently uses the free tools from Webconfs.com to analyze the keywords. We like them because it automatically disregards words that the search engines don't see and it picks up the title tags, keywords, navigation, and alt tags on the page," recommends Don Schindler, digital strategist for MediaSauce, www.webconfs.com/keyword-density-checker.php.

The Fresher, the Better

The next most important criterion is the notion of *content freshness*. Think about it. Many of our company's web pages haven't been changed since the year of the flood! If your job was to return only the most relevant results from a search, and two pages came up—one from 2003, and one that was updated yesterday—which page would you return to the customer?

The search engine assumes that the fresher the content, the more relevant the web page will be, which is where common sense comes in. You need to keep your content current. This is why all search engines put such a high priority on blogs, because blogs (see Chapter 7, The Ubiquitous Blog) by definition are new and fresh.

Don't ever try to fool the search engines into thinking that your content is fresh by changing a word or two and resaving. They know, and they penalize. Search engines actually compare, page for page, the difference between your new page and the one they last indexed. If it isn't considerably different, then you don't get the index points. "Some ideas for fresh content could be newsletters, latest customer success, product and/or your opinion on the latest news in your industry," says Sandy Rowley of Megastarmedia .com.

External Reputable Links

This crucial topic applies to web pages and blogs. An external reputable link is the place where another web site links back to yours. The more external web sites that link back to your web site, the better. Think about the logic behind this. Let's use two hypothetical web sites again—yours and your competitor's. Say that the search engine sees that 25 other web sites are linking to your competitor as a resource, and no one is linking to yours. Which one of you gets the higher ranking?

Of course, people have attempted to figure out how to try to beat the system. One group sold placement on a web site that consisted solely of web page links to other web sites. Sites like these are called *link farms*—don't use them! (This is where the word *reputable* comes in.) Search engines look at the content of the referring web sites to see if there is any similarity. If another web site is linking to yours, there is probably a reason; and there should be some similar words. If the referring web site is only a bunch of links . . . you get penalized. Again, think about the search engines' responsibility and interest in returning the best possible matches.

A very simple test can show you how many other web sites are linking back to yours. Go to Google and type "link:www.yourdomain.com," or go to Yahoo! and enter "linkdomain:www.yourdomain.com." You will immediately see how well you are doing. If you don't have at least 20 or so links to your site, you will need to consider setting up a link exchange campaign. This is when you search the Internet for complementing but not competing web sites, contact them, and pitch them on the notion that if they link to your site from their site, you will do the same for them. This tends to take a lot of time and follow-up, but it's worth it in the end. Sandy Rowley, social media marketer and developer, says, "It is also a good idea to perform this search on sites ranking for your keywords. Use this list to find out who is linking to them, helping their rankings."

When searching for relevant sites to have links to your site, do a search for "no follow" blogs. Some blogs have in their code a no follow, meaning they will not pass on points from the back link you post in your comment. So your link will not get SEO "credit," but you do get to share your opinions and build relationships with the community, which is very important for your online reputation.

One more tip: always check to be sure that each of your web pages has a unique page title, as discussed earlier in the chapter. All too often, web sites contain many untitled pages. This is a foolish oversight, and it's easily corrected. Name your pages, and ask your technical person to simply type the name in and save the page. That's all there is to it! It's a little bit of effort that can have a significant effect. A quick and free way to check which pages within your web site need unique title tags is to use xml-sitemaps.com. You have several options after your sitemap is completed. One is to use an html version to display on your web site to help your viewers find information they need. A second is to use an XML site map, which is automatically generated, which you should upload to your server. This will help search robots index the pages within your site. A third option is to scan through the site map to find any pages that have duplicate titles or worse, Untitled.

Last, read (or reread) Chapter 4, It's Not Your Father's E-Mail, and understand the importance of WIIFM (What's in It for Me?), because no matter how high your page ranking is—or how many potential customers you get to visit your web site—if they don't find something of value, they are out of there!

Don Schindler, digital strategist at www.MediaSauce.com, said:

> This is actually very, very important. External links mean more than almost all other pieces. This is also why black hat SEO guys can be successful quickly. They use unethical linking strategies to build networks and link sites together to push a site up to the top of a SERP for a specific keyword. But these sites quickly fail because search engines are getting better at discovering these sites and blacklist them.
>
> Every site has "voting" capability for any other site. If site A is linking to site B, then site A is passing along some of its PageRank to site B. If site A links to a lot of sites on the same page, then its voting relevance or link juice is degraded. If site A and site B are just

linking back and forth to each other, then both sites might be degraded.

The higher the site's PageRank the more voting power it has. You want quality links from sites with high PageRank but that are also relevant to your content. If the search engines see that the two sites do not have anything in common, then the link juice will be degraded.

Some of the highest ranking sites are sites where links cannot be purchased like .edu or .gov sites. There are many ways to link your site to other sites, especially through social media. Blog commenting is one of the most popular.

Practices to Avoid

Keyword Density: There is also an aspect of **SEO** known as *keyword density.* Search engine spiders check this by analyzing your list of important keywords and checking the number of times those words are actually used on your web page. This helps to prevent a process called *hijacking,* which occurs when someone lists important words such as "presidential election" for a web site that sells shoes so that it garners traffic for the site. Think about how much traffic you might generate with keywords that aren't true. It's actually *none,* because search engines check and penalize for this kind of dishonest keyword stuffing. Four to seven percent density is good for any given keyword. Go to the download section of www.theSocialMediaBible.com for your free Word Density Analyzer Macro.

A quick word of caution on web sites that have Flash web pages: because they don't have text content and keywords, getting a high ranking on such pages has been impossible in the past with a standard Flash design. Flash sites can now be optimized via web objects to showcase content. URL, title tags, description, and keywords are all available to use. Building an alternative HTML site specifically for the search engines is not only possible but is widely used and effective.

You Can't Hide Cloaking: A practice called *cloaking* is also worth mentioning. No, it doesn't have anything to do with *Star Trek*'s Klingons' ability to go invisible. It's about trying to hide your stuffing keywords—the ones that really have nothing to do with your content, and are only there to hijack web traffic—in plain sight. How might one do this? By loading your page's content with those unrelated words in a text color that is the same as the background. What would you see? Nothing!

However, the search engines are wise to this, and can spot it quickly— and if you get caught trying to cheat a search engine, you will be banned from that search engine for up to five years. Imagine learning that your web page will never be listed in a search again for the next half decade. Try explaining that to your supervisor or to your board of directors.

Tips, Techniques, and Tactics

Here is a quick list of some of the techniques mentioned in this chapter, and some that weren't addressed:

- Don't flood or stuff keywords with words not found in your pages' content.
- Don't bury or cloak text with the same color as the background or in margins.
- Don't participate in link farms.
- Don't use redirects, URLs, or web addresses that don't have pages, but only redirect the browser to another page unless you use a 301 redirect to permanently direct traffic to another site. Also you need to make sure you redirect your www.domain.com to domain.com—search engines see www and your domain.com as two separate sites. A permanent redirect on the www is a must. A quick call to your domain registrar can help you determine if this is set up correctly.
- Do have at least 25 reputable external links back to your site from other reputable and related content sites—it's a good start. Much more are required today to get significant SERP ranking movement. Remember, they must link from other high-traffic or high-impact sites within your industry.
- Do use vortals or Vertical Web Portal, directories (hubs), and blogs for link backs. See Chapter 5, The World of Web Pages, or search Google for more information.
- Do integrate a blog into your web site and add content to it regularly.
- Do rearrange your keywords to create keyword phrases.
- Do be sure that the keywords in your metas match your page content.
- Do create unique titles containing your most important keywords.
- Do include your keywords in your meta description.
- Do create good content (which contain your keywords).
- Do have at least eight keyword hyperlinks (internal, external, anchor).
- Do have at least eight keyword alt tags.

- Do place your keywords in your anchor code (see your programmer for this).

- Do research-related keywords and try to rank for them. This process never stops on successful SEO campaigns. You're either growing or you dying.

- Do place your keywords in your file names: .jpg, .gif, .asp, .php.

- Do link PDFs and text documents with keywords in actual content of those documents.

- Do create comprehensive site maps. There should be two site maps: one for users, which can be a straight HTML page, and one for Google, which should be XML. This is very helpful for search engines. www.xml-sitemaps.com is a free resource.

- Do place your keywords in captions and headings. H1 headings have the most emphasis, followed by H2, H3, then bold.

- Do use bullets, bold, and underlined (hyperlinked) text, for emphasis for both your viewers and the search engine spiders.

- Do keep your pages fresh, with at least 15 to 25 percent change. While there is no time limit on freshness, the fresher the better!

- Do use subdirectories: for example, with www.yourdomain.com/alligator/yourpage.html, the best solution is to use www.yourdomain.com/aligator/your-page and eliminate the ".html." Also, never go over four slashes total, and never use variables or "?" in the html.

- Do use subdomains: www.alligator.yourdomain.com, in which you create a folder with a keyword name. See your IT person to learn if and how you can do this.

- Never use Frames to build a web site. Search engines cannot read web sites that are inside frames.

- Keep navigation out of JavaScript with dropdowns. This is also harder for search engines to read.

- Do choose a handful of popular social media sites, join, be an active and helpful member.

- Do post comments on related blogs. Be honest, helpful, and follow the rules for that blog.

- Do post an update daily on your social media profiles. Need help finding content? Search for latest news in your industry and tweet, blog, or post about it. Share it with others.

- Do be patient. SEO is an ongoing process. Not something you try. This is vital to your company's success.

- Do integrate SEO into your daily routine. Set aside one hour a day to blog, post, comment, and share and add content to your web sites, social profiles, and online groups.

- Do be a friendly neighbor. Remember, everything you do online stays online forever. Customers will be reading your statements for years to come.

- Do keep up to date on what is considered White Hat SEO versus Black Hat. Visit www.theSocialMediaBible.com to keep up to date on what is now considered good SEO.

- Do share your resources. Volunteer for great online organizations like www.Kiva.org. One reason is you get a quality back link; a second is that you're helping your fellow man; and a third is that it is great public relations and something you can blog about.

- Do protect all of your company names online in the major social networks. Choose your company name as your user name on social sites to protect them from competitors and would-be fake employees.

- Also, if the keyword you are targeting is available as a user name, scoop it up. The future of search is in social media sites. So when someone searches in Twitter for social media, having your user name match this keyword will help you rank high.

- Do hold on to those old domain names. If you change your web site name, keep the old one and do a permanent redirect with all the pages within the site.

- Do keep the same URLs that are indexed. If you update your site, make sure to keep the same URLs for the pages.

- Do start a podcast and add to it at least monthly; weekly is best. You can rank quickly for keywords using free radio or podcast-like portals like www.blogtalkradio.com.

- Do write articles and submit to online PR sites linking back to your web sites, blogs, *and* your social media profiles.

- Do remember to post back links to your social media profiles.

Dozens and dozens of search engine criteria are used nowadays. Every time you score in a particular area, your web page gets points. Once the search engine's algorithm has tested everything and has awarded all of the possible points for each category, the algorithm then computes an overall *page rank*. You can see every page's ranking in the Google menu bar as a progressive green bar. The greener your page gets, the higher it's ranked.

(Side note: the term *page rank* was first used by one of the founders of Google, Larry Page. Perhaps it's more than a coincidence that it's called "page *rank*.")

Providers

SEO is a skill set that requires some technical understanding of HTML and how web pages function. The purpose of this chapter is to make you aware of the importance of SEO, to give you some tools that will allow you to check your existing web pages to see if they have been properly designed, and to begin setting up your SEM keyword campaign. The biggest question that you likely have at this juncture is whether you wish to take on these additional projects yourself, assign them to someone else internally, or hire a consultant to accomplish these tasks for you. It always comes down to in-house or out-house.

Literally thousands of companies can perform SEO (Search Engine Optimization), but there are few especially good ones. Now that you have read this chapter, you can much better determine which are superior. A simple question to ask a potential SEO contractor is how they feel about cloaking. If they support these practices, just ask them to leave. The best way to win at SEO is to be honest. If you do the right things, you will be listed highly on the search engines. If you try to trick them, it may work for a while; but you're likely to be caught eventually, and you'll suffer the consequences.

When interviewing someone to help with your internet marketing efforts, have in mind a set of specific goals to achieve for each quarter. For example, we would like to increase the number of sign-ups for a particular podcast, or increase the amount of white paper downloads on our site. Giving an SEO expert a goal to achieve helps her to gauge her success. Remember, a ton of traffic does not mean success. The most important ingredient is action. What did the person do once he landed on your site? Did he leave? Did he visit a couple of pages and bookmark any for later? Having strong web analytics integrated within your web site will help you gauge which keywords bring in the right clients. Services like www.ClickTale.com allow you to actually watch visitors while they are surfing through your web site and what actions they take. Other services, like www.FetchBack.com, goes as far as placing a cookie on the viewer's computer, so whenever that visitor is visiting large networks and sites like MySpace, About.com, and other large sites, they see your banner over and over again.

Organic SEO is life giving force for your company and cannot be ignored. Including a paid solution like PPC allows you to cover keyword sets multiple times on a web results page gains more coverage and exposure for your company. Integrating social networks only adds to this powerful marketing plan.

The ROI of Social Media

Blogging and BlogTalkRadio Really Made a Difference

Introduction

The PI Social Media network includes the Procurement Insights and PI Window on Business blogs, the PI Window on Business show on BlogTalk Radio and the PI Inquisitive Eye and TV2 Young Entrepreneurs Internet TV Channels. The PI Window on Business is a featured show on BlogTalk Radio.

The combined syndicated reach through affiliations with social media sites such as BlogTalkRadio (which has more than seven million listeners each month), [and] Evan Carmichael (500,000 visitors monthly) as well as various social networking groups and forums has enabled the PI Social Media to connect with an ever-expanding audience of readers, listeners, and now viewers.

Background

The PI Social Media network's origins began with the launch of the Procurement Insights blog in May 2007. The blog was created as a means of providing various magazines and publications with a single site access to our articles and reports.

Procurement Insights is today the top sponsored blog in its industry sector in terms of the number of total sponsors.

As a means of building upon and expanding the reach of the Procurement Insights blog, the PI Window on Business show was launched in March 2009. Within three months, it was a featured show across the entire BlogTalkRadio network.

In June 2009, the PI Window on Business blog was launched as an adjunct support for the show. Within the first six months, the total number of site visitors cracked the 10,000 mark on a monthly basis.

Based on the cross-pollination between venues both within and external to the PI Social Media network, the Procurement Insights blog realized an 1,100 percent increase in blog visitors in the past 30 days, while both the PI Window on Business show and blog have seen equally impressive growth.

The PI Social Media network recently launched two Internet TV Channels as well as corresponding blogs.

(continued)

(*continued*)

Strategy

The hive, or cross-pollination concept, or theory, is based on the observation that individuals will likely choose at most one or two primary social networks as their preferred platforms. That is, they will spend the majority of their social networking time interacting within these main "hives."

While they may venture out into the vast social media/social networking world visiting countless other networks, [just like] the honey bee, these forays are ultimately geared toward gathering information and insights to bring back to the hive to share with their established community of contacts.

Simply put, while static, single sites (blogs, web sites, etc.), that limit their cross-pollination activities to providing somewhat passive links to other similarly myopic single site blogs or web sites, have failed to recognize that market dynamics change, and that you have to connect with the audience through their preferred venue points.

Implementation

The PI Social Media and its service offerings provides our clients with an ability to transition from the traditional and largely ineffective broadcasting model of yesterday, to the relationship-centric conversational marketing world of social media.

Opportunity

The opportunity afforded the PI Social Media network, through its services both in the present as well as in the foreseeable future, has been proven by the steady and sustained growth in readership, listener, and viewer base.

Through this expanded and diverse reach that leverages venues such as blogs, Internet Radio, Internet TV, and social networks, the company's increasing revenue base reflects the model's effectiveness—even during a slow economic period.

Conclusion

The Company's revenue forecast for 2010 is $250K US. By the end of February, we had already hit 50 percent of the 2010 target. In June 2009 the PI Window on Business blog was launched, and by February 2010, the PI Window on Business blog's overall Alexa rank was 1,014,248 with a U.S. ranking of 627,904. In March 2010, the PI Window on Business blog's overall Alexa ranking was 855,686 (up 158,562 positions since the February numbers two weeks earlier). In terms of the new U.S. ranking, the March numbers showed that we are now at 328,775, which is a 299,129-position improvement over the 627,904 from two weeks previous.

The Procurement Insights blog took two and a half years to break the 100,000-reader mark while the PI Window on Business took only nine months to hit the 50,000 mark.

In its first year, the PI Window on Business show on BlogTalkRadio had more than 35,000 listens/downloads, and became a featured show within three and a half months of launching.

Jon W. Hansen
http://piwindowonbusiness.wordpress.com/book-resource-center/jon-hansen-host-pi-window-on-business-show

Expert Insight

Marc Canter, CEO of Broadband Mechanics, www.broadbandmechanics.com

Marc Canter

I'm the CEO of a company called *Broadband Mechanics*. The product enables any community to build and run their own social network. Most people use it to create their own "Facebook" kind of experience. But there are LOADS of other ways it can be utilized.

My past is that I have been in the software business for about 29 years. I started a company called *MarcoMind* that became *Macromedia*, so I'm a toolsmith by trade, and watched the blogging world and the world of what I call the "open mesh" evolve over the past few years; open social networking, and structured content, and what I call digital wide style aggregation.

It all leads to saying basically, "open" is the new black. . . .

. . . I mean, certainly in the world of expression and blogging that is kind of obvious. But the other thing is where the user's data, their profile record, their social graph, should be owned by them. We shouldn't be locked inside of *Facebook* or *MySpace*. So we are starting to see the standard, like *OpenID,* and a new effort from Google called *OpenSocial,* which they are using to build lots of great solutions with.

(continued)

(*continued*)

All these are standards that are emergent. We are even seeing Microsoft opening up, believe it or not! . . .

. . . Facebook's recent moves are showing that it very much wants to "take over the entire web." What people need to do is play along with those 400 million people and have a great time, while at the same time realize that THEY control their own destiny, not Facebook. So now—more than ever—open social networking is important. . . .

. . . I'm a tool smith and we've been trying to build some tools to help solve that. We call one of them a "persona editor," which helps to stay on top of managing all of your different persona. Okay?

The other thing is we are seeing a big trend going from giant, centralized social networks, these kinds of horizontal networks, to tens of thousands of niche vertical networks. Right? And a typical person will be in a membership of one or two horizontal networks, or maybe even five or ten niche networks. So whether that's the school you go to, or the after-school activities of you dealing with your friends and kids, the affinities like Reggae or Chocolates.

So the trick here is to have a world, have a blueprint, and a world within, that can practically adapt to the fact that Microsoft is going to do live mesh and Google is going to do this, and Yahoo! is going to have their own thing, and after a while we have to leave some crumbs on the table for a smaller-software guy. We want to get involved and we want to mesh into this huge world, and perhaps build our own eco-system.

All those poor people locked inside of Ning—need to get out—as soon as possible! . . .

. . . And we see more and more consolidation over the years. I mean, this is where us "old-timers" can tell you, "Back in the 80s, when it was between *Microsoft* and *Apple*," right.

That world has changed now. So, along the way the other thing we've seen the rise of is "international," and maybe the governments of Singapore or Dubai want to do some of this stuff and they do not want to use Yahoo! or Google, right! And maybe you see innovation coming out of Russia. I mean, this is no longer just a game that is played off of Silicon Valley or Lafayette, LA.

. . . Oh, by the way, needless to say both the Chinese and Russian governments are tightly coupled to these cyber-terrorists. Whether it's an attack on Google or an attack on Estonia or when they invaded Georgia, we're seeing the power of online technology being used in all sorts of ways. Right? So we are starting to see the realities of technology and politics, virtual economics. When the oil industry is attacked and they claim that they are making too much money, they can turn and say, "Well, look, the software business. They make even higher margins than we do." As if that matters. Right? This is somehow supposed to deflect the attention.

You know, we are finding the technology to be intrinsic and imbedded everywhere. It's no longer, "You can keep your head in the sand." And so, the issues of all software being about people and open standards, if users want to control the rights to this general notion of social media, as we move forward it will affect everything. . . .

. . . When I saw the Web first and it was simple HTML graphics, I felt as if we were going backward, because we did have graphics and video on our screens in the early 90s. They were coming over the wire; they were coming off of a CD-ROM. And it took about 10 or 15 years for the world to catch up.

Just now, with *Flickr* and *YouTube*, we now have a full media on our machines, right? And so we are seeing a number of different factors. One of them I call "persistent content." So, like the BBC or NPR, are going to put up all of this content into the clouds and it's going to be there, available, full time. And we've got *Hulu* and we've got *iTunes*, and it's all there and we are competing in all this knowledge and it's sitting there in the clouds waiting for us.

So whole new kinds of applications and services will be born that rely upon that stuff, you know, and then to be able to rely upon storage and computing grids and all this incredible stuff that, even five years ago, was only a dream and a glimmer in our eyes.

So if we jump forward four or five years in a natural helix, of course there will still be "normal" people who still just use e-mail. You know, it takes a long time for stuff to disseminate through society.

Checkout news regarding OAuth 2.0 and XAuth—timestamp—spring 2010. . . .

. . . Bell Canada is www.bellvideostore.ca. Another is a large media company called *Radio One*, so they have a site called www.radio-one.com. And they have a bunch of sister sites, because we also have an aggregation engine in the CMS publishing system. So, we have a bunch of sister sites that we also built for them.

GT Channel is a great kind of niche network for car enthusiasts, people who are into drifting. Then there is what we call a *Meta* network, called www.socialworld.com. These are for people who put on events, who produce concerts, and so they can get their own network and we built it for our customer called *Acteva*. So they sell tickets, and do ticketing online.

To listen to or read the entire Executive Conversation with Marc Canter, go to www .theSocialMediaBible.com.

Commandments

1. **Thou shalt understand your keywords for every page.**
   Be sure that every individual page is analyzed for its own keywords. You want to bring your customer to the exact page at the exact time they are ready to convert. (See Chapter 5, The World of Web Pages, for more on this.)

2. **Thou shalt check your page titles.**
   It's an easy thing to do, and to overlook. Open your pages and look in the Title Bar. Come up with a title that includes your most important keywords, and remember to do so for every page. Use free tools like www.xml-sitemaps.com to check for untitled pages.

3. **Thou shalt check your meta keywords.**
   Open your page, select View, then Page View, and look for your meta keywords. If they don't reflect your content, then you won't get ranked highly.

4. **Thou shalt build your external reputable links.**
   Type "site: www.yourdomain.com" into Google, and see how good you are doing. If you don't have 20 external reputable links, then go get some. When getting back links from sites, ask them to use one of your keywords to link to you.

5. **Thou shalt never try to trick a spider.**
   Never, ever, try to trick a search engine spider. It might work for a while, but they always will catch you. If they do, you could be banned from search engines for up to five years.

6. **Thou shalt always have a strong WIIFM.**
   This is always the most important commandment. Whether it's SEO, SEM, e-mail, web pages, or a hard copy brochure, your marketing message *always* has to have a strong "What's in It for Me?" (See Chapter 4, It's Not Your Father's E-Mail, for more information on this.)

Conclusion

What does SEO have to do with social media? A lot! It's all about having a presence on the Web. It's about being found exactly when your customers are looking for you. It's about being found before your customers find your competition. It's about always showing up in a listing no matter what your customer types in when they're trying to find your product or service—

despite where they are in the buying cycle, or whatever keyword they think is relevant. And it's about being part of the World Wide Web with integrity.

To hear all of the Expert Interviews, go to www.theSocialMediaBible.com.

Readings and Resources

Clay, Bruce, and Susan Esparza. *Search Engine Optimization All-in-One For Dummies*. (Hoboken, NJ: John Wiley & Sons, Inc.)

Cunningham, Court, and Stephanie Brown. *Local Online Advertising For Dummies*. (Hoboken, NJ: John Wiley & Sons, Inc.)

Darie, Cristian, and Jaimie Sirovich. *Professional Search Engine Optimization with PHP: A Developer's Guide to SEO*. (Hoboken, NJ: John Wiley & Sons, Inc.)

Darie, Cristian, and Jaimie Sirovich. *Professional Search Engine Optimization with ASP.NET: A Developer's Guide to SEO*. (Hoboken, NJ: John Wiley & Sons, Inc.)

Dover, Danny. *Search Engine Optimization (SEO) Secrets*. (Hoboken, NJ: John Wiley & Sons, Inc.)

Grappone, Jennifer, and Gradiva Couzin. *Search Engine Optimization: An Hour a Day*. 2nd ed. (Hoboken, NJ: John Wiley & Sons, Inc.)

Hedengren, Thord Daniel. *Smashing WordPress: Beyond the Blog*. (Hoboken, NJ: John Wiley & Sons, Inc.)

Hunt, Benjamin. *Web Design Optimization . . . from Scratch: Proven Methods for Creating More Compelling Web Sites*. (Hoboken, NJ: John Wiley & Sons, Inc.)

Jones, Kristopher B. *Search Engine Optimization: Your Visual Blueprint for Effective Internet Marketing*. (Hoboken, NJ: John Wiley & Sons, Inc.)

Jones, Kristopher B. *SEO Visual Blueprint: Your Visual Blueprint for Effective Internet Marketing*, 2nd ed. (Hoboken, NJ: John Wiley & Sons, Inc.)

Kent, Peter. *Search Engine Optimization For Dummies*, 3rd ed. (Hoboken, NJ: John Wiley & Sons, Inc.)

Ledford, Jerri L. *SEO: Search Engine Optimization Bible*. (Hoboken, NJ: John Wiley & Sons, Inc.)

Ledford, Jerri L. *SEO: Search Engine Optimization Bible*, 2nd ed. (Hoboken, NJ: John Wiley & Sons, Inc.)

Middleton, Simon. *Build a Brand in 30 Days: With Simon Middleton, the Brand Strategy Guru*. (Hoboken, NJ: John Wiley & Sons, Inc.)

Nelson, Melanie, and Shannon Lowe. *TypePad For Dummies*. (Hoboken, NJ: John Wiley & Sons, Inc.)

Downloads

For your free downloads associated with *The Social Media Bible,* go to www
.theSocialMediaBible.com, and enter your ISBN number located on the back
of the book above the bar code. Be sure to enter the dashes.

Credits

The ROI of Social Media was provided by:

Jon W. Hansen, http://piwindowonbusiness.wordpress.com/book-resource-center/
jon-hansen-host-pi-window-on-business-show

Expert Insight was provided by:

Marc Canter, CEO of Broadband Mechanics, www.broadbandmechanics.com

Technical edits were provided by:

Sandy Rowley, Webby Award–winning designer and marketer, www.megastarmedia
.com

CHAPTER 20

Marketing Yourself (Search Engine Marketing)

Search Engine Marketing (SEM) is one of the most effective ways you can market and advertise your web site on the Internet. There is nearly no financial risk; the costs are incredibly low when compared to any type of conventional advertising; and, unlike any other advertising, it's based on performance. There is, however, a great deal of risk involved if you don't understand that everything you say and do is part of your online brand.

People forget that you can't separate one from the other and it gets them in trouble. When was the last time you've heard a newspaper, radio, television, or magazine tell you that if your ad doesn't generate calls, you don't have to pay for it? Never.

Although it's possible for this chapter to be read and implemented without reading Chapter 19, Spotlight on Search (Search Engine Optimization), you are strongly recommended to also read that chapter. The two are complementary; one is the yin to the other's yang. And although either can be executed without the other, the synergy of doing both well can put you in the top of the rankings.

What's in It for You?

As discussed in Chapter 19, Spotlight on Search (Search Engine Optimization), when you take the time and follow the simple guidelines to making your web page appealing to the search engine spiders, you will rank the highest on the organic or nonpaid listings. When you add a well-thought-out SEM keyword advertising campaign, you will own the sponsored listings. When SEO and SEM are combined on one web page, the rankings are unstoppable.

theSocialMediaBible.com

SEM Stands for Search Engine Marketing

When someone is looking for the type of product or service you provide, he will use his favorite search engine—be it Google, Yahoo!, MSN, Ask, or one of the countless others available today. He will type in one to several words that he thinks best describe what you do or offer, and will then hit Enter.

SEM in part means marketing your web page(s) through a paid CPC (Cost-Per-Click) or PPC (Pay-Per-Click) marketing plan. You still have to consider your blog (see Chapter 7, The Ubiquitous Blog). If you are running an SEM campaign and are paying for PPC, the relevance of your online advertisements to the search query a user performed will determine where you show up on the Sponsored Links section of the search page, how much you are paying per click, and what you are spending each month for that campaign. This is referred to as a *paid listing*. When you use Yahoo!, Google, or other search engines to perform a search, you will usually see the organic listings in the left column, and the paid listings on the right column (or sometimes in the top several rows on the left above the organic listings).

Back to the Beginning

SEM Is Named and Introduced

The SEM advertising system first appeared in February 1998, when Jeffrey Brewer presented the Pay-Per-Click concept at the TED8 conference in California. Goto.com founder Bill Gross is given credit for conceiving of PPC while working at IdeaLab in Pasadena, California. Gross's 25-employee start-up became Yahoo!'s Overture, which is Yahoo!'s Search Engines' Pay-Per-Click system.

Google offered its own, impression-based form of search engine advertising in December 1999, based on CPM or Cost-Per-1,000 impressions (or views). They introduced AdWords in October 2000, which allowed their users to create their own ads for placement on the Google Search Engine result pages. In 2002, Google switched to PPC, the then-successful Yahoo! advertising model.

What You Need to Know

Assuming that you have read Chapter 7, The Ubiquitous Blog, and began blogging, and read Chapter 19, Spotlight on Search (Search Engine Optimization), and have performed your SEO, your pages are gradually being ranked higher in the organic listings. It's now time to work on your SEM—or simply, your Pay-Per-Click advertising.

PPC advertising requires that you decide which keywords or keyword phrases you used in your SEO campaign are most important—the ones that best match those that your customer will type into a search engine when trying to find your site. It's also the words and phrases that come directly from your web site's content—the words you will be able to pay for when a potential customer clicks on your link.

The definition of SEM used in this chapter is relatively generic, because the best way to experience the ease and excitement of creating and managing an SEM campaign is by actually *doing* it. Also, each search engine is a little different in terms of how you go about creating an account, adding funds to your budget, and reporting on its success.

While there are many providers of PPC, banner advertising, and other pay-for-performance advertisers, Google is by far the largest. According to VentureBeat Digital Media, the top five search engines in market share at the time this chapter was written were as follows: Google 61.6 percent; Yahoo! 20.4 percent; Microsoft 9.1 percent; AOL 4.6 percent; and Ask 4.3 percent. There is still a several-year trend of Google gaining market share (mostly from Yahoo!). What does this mean? That it's probably best to start your SEM campaigns with Google AdWords, as it already owns almost two-thirds of the market share or two-thirds of your potential customers.

Start Your SEM Campaign

To launch your SEM keyword campaign, you should begin with two- to four-word keyword phrases. These keyword combinations are significantly more specific than a single word and will help you connect with a more targeted and specific audience. Go to the SEM provider for your search engine of choice, such as Google AdWords, Yahoo! Search Engine Marketing (formerly Overture), or Microsoft's AdCenter, and sign up for an account; you can do this with a credit card or a PayPal account (Figure 20.1). Then follow the easy steps to complete your registration and set up a keyword campaign.

After you select your keyword, you'll want to see what others are willing to pay each time someone clicks on the word from the sponsored links section of that search engine. The more generic the word, the more expensive the CPC (Cost-Per-Click) is. Often, the keyword you like best is one that other advertisers desire most as well. This can drive the CPC up to a point where you may want to consider using a more specific—and less expensive—keyword.

While most keywords can cost under $1, many are as high as $5 per click, and they can even go as high as $80 for terms like "Austin DUI," for

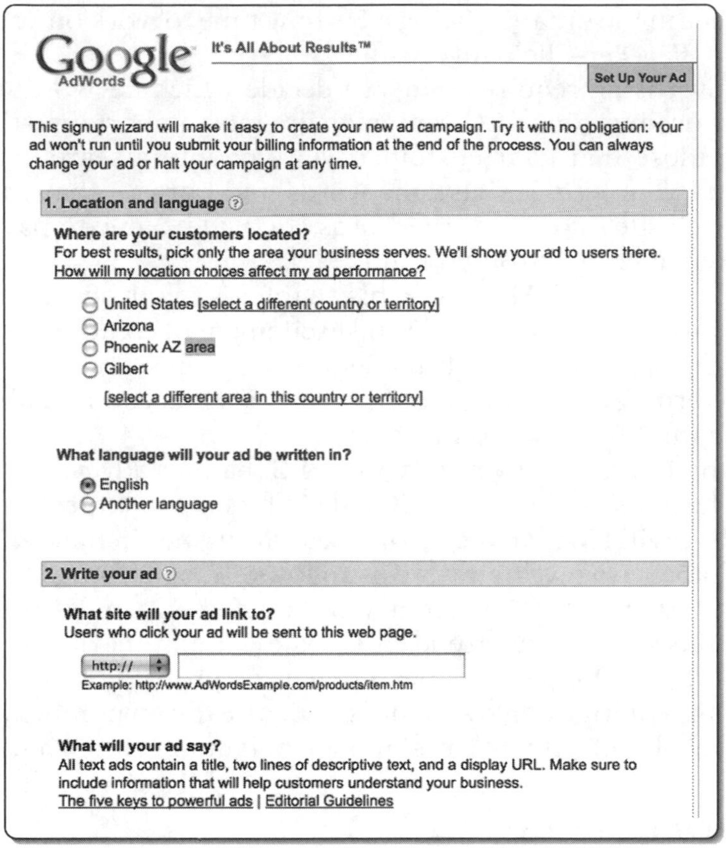

FIGURE 20.1 AdWords Wizard

example. Once you've done several keyword campaigns, you will find the *sweet spot*—the word that generates the most traffic at the lowest CPC.

What Are You Willing to Pay?

The next step is to indicate how much you are willing to spend on each click. It's a bidding system, and even though the last CPC was 50 cents, you may want to raise the stakes and claim that you're willing to pay $1 for that same click. By bidding higher, you have the opportunity to be placed higher on the search engine's list of paid sponsors. Remember: The reason and purpose in life for a search engine is the theory of relativity—that is, they must always return the most relative search results. The same is true for paid sponsors;

the victory doesn't always go to the highest bidder. Your relevance—and how often your sponsored ad has been clicked in the past—all determine your position.

Now that you have selected a keyword and know how much it will cost you each time someone clicks on it, the search engines will ask for your monthly budget: How much you are willing to spend each month on clicks for your entire advertising account. Start with a small amount—say, $100—and watch the keyword's progress over the next 30 days. That's all there is to it!

The next time you go to that search engine and type in your keyword or keyword phrase, you will be listed in the sponsored link section. If someone is listed above you, it means that they are willing to pay more than your maximum bid, or that they historically had a good click-through rate (which means that people clicked on them more often than the competing sponsors).

How the Search Engines Charge You

The good thing about the search engine's bids is that you don't have to pay your full bid Cost-Per-Click if someone picks you over the competition. The AdWords system automatically adjusts pricing so that you only pay the minimum amount necessary to maintain your position above the next ad—which may be less than the maximum cost-per-click you indicated you bid. This continues 24 hours a day, so at the end of the month, you may have a surplus of funds in your budget. If your funds become exhausted, you will receive a notice from your search engine partner that your money is about to run out, and you will be asked if you would like to add more money. If you do, everything continues normally. If you choose not to, you simply no longer appear in the sponsored listings.

Just as there is always someone trying to beat the SEO system with techniques like link farms, cloaking, and keyword stuffing, people try to beat the SEM system as well. Suppose, for example, that your competitor hires someone at minimum wage to sit and click on your sponsored link all day. Within a short amount of time, she would have cost you your entire SEM budget!

Things like this really did happen for a while. Then the search engines got wind of it and stopped it from happening. Now search engines track your Internet Protocol, or IP Address, which is a number assigned to your computer that looks like this: 74.213.164.71. An IP Address is unique and identifies each computer on a network. It can be for private use on a Local Area Network (LAN, like at work or your wireless network at home), or for public use on the Internet or other Wide Area Network (WAN, a network that interconnects geographically distributed computers, LANs, or the Internet).

The search engine checks the IP Address of the clicker, and if there are multiple clicks from the same user, it credits your account—and even bans that user from clicking in the future. (Don't you just love this stuff?)

Once you see the Return on Investment (ROI) on your SEM keyword campaign, you will want to go back to the search engine and create additional campaigns for new keywords and phrases. While teaching at a conference in Portland, Oregon, the author met someone who manages 165 keyword campaigns every month! He said that he spends a lot of money on them, but that they usually return 350 percent of what he spends in sales—and generates new customers. This alone is worth the cost of customer acquisition.

Tips, Techniques, and Tactics

To get started on your own SEM campaign, take the following steps:

1. Go to www.theSocialMediaBible.com and download your Key Word macro.
2. Use the macro to determine your most important keywords.
3. Use the keyword finder in Google or Yahoo! to gauge what others are paying for the keywords that you have selected.
4. Determine how much of an initial budget you are willing to spend on each of your keyword campaigns.
5. Consider two- and three-word keyword phrases, because they are often less expensive and significantly more specific—and can return more effective results.

Providers

SEO and SEM both represent skill sets that require some technical understanding of HTML and how web pages function. The purpose of this chapter is to make you aware of the importance of both of these processes; to give you some tools that will allow you to check your existing web pages to see if they have been properly designed; and to begin setting up your SEM keyword campaign.

The biggest question you probably have at this juncture is whether you wish to take on the SEM projects yourself, assign them to someone else internally, or hire a consultant to accomplish these tasks for you. As with SEO, the next decision you have to make is whether to complete these projects in- or out-of-house. Many companies can manage your SEM campaigns, but always keep in mind that someone else won't watch your money as carefully as you would watch it. Unless you have a dedicated person who can manage your campaigns, managing a consultant might be easier.

Considering the information presented earlier on the top five search engines by market share at the time this chapter was written, you'll probably want to start with Google, and then look at Yahoo!. Remember that even though Google and Yahoo! account for 82 percent of the total market, your particular customers might prefer using the Ask search engine. Experiment, and try different search engines to determine the most effective way to reach your customers.

The ROI of Social Media

Turning a Fun Hobby into an Internet Business

Background

Paul Petty, the creator of rcFoamFighters, dreamt of a way to escape the average everyday work routine. During a scheduled business conference in November 2008 in Miami, Paul attended a presentation by Lon Safko. The presentation and casual talks with Lon inspired Paul to try to turn his hobby of RC Airplanes into a part-time side business, with an eventual goal to free himself from the everyday cubicle work environment. rcFoamFighters was created on January 1st, 2009.

Strategy

Paul's strategy was to harness the power of social media to promote his new idea and spread word of his business, rcFoamFighters, across the globe. By using all the available free advertising via social media, there would be no substantial start-up costs.

Implementation

The primary method was to use YouTube to create a large viewer and fan base. This large fan base would eventually lead to large quantities of traffic [to] the independent rcFoamFighters blog site. The blog was set up with minimal costs for server space, and the freeware program Wordpress was used as the blog software. Other social media sites such as Facebook, Twitter, and MySpace were also utilized to get the message out. Social media ideas also included using the many RC forums that thousands of people use daily to share information about RC-related topics.

(continued)

(*continued*)

Opportunity

One opportunity was to become a YouTube partner, which allows for revenue sharing with YouTube. The blog site would host many affiliate ads to generate income from ad clicks and affiliate sales [and the] possible opportunity to land sponsors, which would provide free product and/or monetary compensation [and the] opportunity to sell actual products and digital products, such as PDF plans.

Conclusion

rcFoamFighters' level of current success has been all due to the use of social media to build a large fan base. Currently, the YouTube site has had nearly 500,000 views and 1,400 subscribers. rcFoamFighters is now a YouTube partner and receives monthly income from YouTube. The YouTube traffic is constantly growing and the revenue increasing. The independent blog site has been visited by over 30,000 unique visitors from 148 countries. Affiliate ad clicks and product sales are constantly increasing. rcFoamFighters is now associated with two sponsoring partners. One of them is one of the largest online hobby stores that provides compensation and free sponsored products. The original goal to be free from the typical cubicle work life is seen on the near horizon.

Paul Petty, founder of rcFoamFighters
www.rcFoamFighters.com

Expert Insight

Linh Tang, coauthor, *Launching Your Yahoo! Business* and *Succeeding at Your Yahoo! Business*, www.LinhTang.com

Linh Tang

Yeah, virtual-electronic-retailing—or V-E-Tailing—is about selling products that are digital. And what I mean by that is you could have [any kind of product]. Ours is paper models; and our Paper Model Inc. is three-dimensional advertising, creating corporate specialty products, and school projects. We specialize in replicas of buildings and monuments and even . . . cars. Our main customer is the education market; one model that made our site popular is "California Missions." We've had a lot of fourth-graders who have to come in and build that for their school projects; they come to our web site, download it, print it out on a computer, and within 30 minutes to an hour they have a replica of that particular model. . . .

That's the beauty of electronic retailing. Once you create the product, it's there! People continuously come and purchase your product—unlike eBay, [where] you continuously have to take pictures, upload to your store, and—once you've sold that particular item—go find new products.

Well, SEM marketing first started with optimizing your web site and doing link building. But with social media, it has taken . . . I believe it has taken the corner. What I mean by that is now it incorporates blogs, videos, RSS, social networks, alerts. Now, with the limited time people have, they don't want to come visit your site every day. But what you can do is feed out your information to all these other networks. I call it "The Mall." Why do you want to be at "The Mall"? Because everyone else is there. . . .

Now everybody can get traffic to their web site. You can do a little bit of Search Engine Marketing, but what happens when they're there? Now social media tools, such as video and blogs, give your potential customers added value, added information. For example, one of the web sites I'm working on is Office Chairs Outlet built on the highly recommended Volusion shopping cart platform. We did a product demo of one of the chairs, just as if you were walking into the showroom and getting a demo from a salesperson. Now, all the other web sites out there have a little description, which they all get from the manufacturers, anyway. But here, we are actually doing a demo for you. So you don't even have to sit and read the page of descriptions; you could actually just sit there and watch a thirty-second video of how that chair works, how that chair operates, how it's ergonomic, and why it's the best. . . .

You can now put your link, your URL, your web site information on YouTube. So, if anybody went to YouTube, [they could be sent] back to your site for further information. The beauty of YouTube is you can often embed that video onto your web site or blog. So you don't have any expensive streaming or hosting fees. . . .

The social media ecosphere is huge. There's a lot of tools out there, and what you should really do is sit down with a social media strategist to see, "What's your first step?" Is it doing video, or just doing a blog? We've seen success by just doing that. You can blog about anything. It doesn't have to be just about your product only—and that's what was going on with Search Engine Optimization, was that you were just optimizing using your web site for your information, your keywords.

To listen to or read the entire Executive Conversation with Linh Tang, go to www .theSocialMediaBible.com.

Commandments

1. **Thou shalt perform SEO.**

   The most effective way to win at SEM is to perform your SEO first. Even though you are paying to be placed in the sponsored links section, your position will depend on your page ranking (see Chapter 19, Spotlight on Search (Search Engine Optimization)), and how many times your link is clicked. If no one clicks your link, you will move lower and lower in the sponsored links until you disappear. You will be dropped, even if you are willing to pay the most.

2. **Thou shalt understand your keywords for every page.**

   Be sure that every individual page is analyzed for its own keywords. You want to bring your customer to the exact page at the exact time he is ready to convert. (See Chapter 5, The World of Web Pages, for more on this.)

3. **Thou shalt check your meta keywords.**

   Open your page, select View, then Page View, and look for your Meta Keywords. If they don't reflect your content, then you won't get ranked highly.

4. **Thou shalt always create good content.**

   Never, *ever* try to trick a search engine. It might work for a while, but they always will catch you, and possibly ban you from their sites for up to five years.

5. **Thou shalt focus on the WIIFM.**

   This is always the most important commandment. Whether it's SEO, SEM, e-mail, web pages, or a hard copy brochure, your marketing message *always* has to have a strong "What's in It for Me?" (See Chapter 4 for more information.) Even with paid or sponsored links, you have to have a strong WIIFM to hook your searcher to first read the subject line, and then to read your description. If each of these is written well, the searchers will click on you—and not your competition.

6. **Thou shalt search engine market through Pay-Per-Click.**

   Try it; it's fun. And while it's nearly the only place you need to spend any money while marketing on the Internet, it has the potential to return more than 300 percent of what you spend.

Conclusion

What does SEM have to do with social media? As much as SEO does—in other words, a good amount. Again, it's all about having a presence on the

Web, building community, and generating revenue. It's about being there when your prospect is in the buying phase of his or her cycle, ready to click on the Purchase button. You have to be found when someone is looking for you—whether it's on your web pages, in your photos and videos, on your podcasts, or on your blog. The combination of SEO and SEM is the most cost-effective way to achieve this goal.

To hear all of the Expert Interviews, go to www.theSocialMediaBible .com.

Readings and Resources

Arnold, John, Ian Lurie, Marty Dickinson, Elizabeth Marsten, and Michael Becker. *Web Marketing All-in-One Desk Reference For Dummies.* (Hoboken, NJ: John Wiley & Sons, Inc.)

Clay, Bruce, and Susan Esparza. *Search Engine Optimization All-in-One For Dummies.* (Hoboken, NJ: John Wiley & Sons, Inc.)

Darie, Cristian, and Jaimie Sirovich. *Professional Search Engine Optimization with ASP.NET: A Developer's Guide to SEO.* (Hoboken, NJ: John Wiley & Sons, Inc.)

Darie, Cristian, and Jaimie Sirovich. *Professional Search Engine Optimization with PHP: A Developer's Guide to SEO.* (Hoboken, NJ: John Wiley & Sons, Inc.)

Dover, Danny. *Search Engine Optimization (SEO) Secrets.* (Hoboken, NJ: John Wiley & Sons, Inc.)

Fox, Vanessa. *Marketing in the Age of Google: Your Online Strategy IS Your Business Strategy.* (Hoboken, NJ: John Wiley & Sons, Inc.)

Harwood, Martin, and Michael Harwood. *Landing Page Optimization For Dummies.* (Hoboken, NJ: John Wiley & Sons, Inc.)

Hiam, Alexander. *Marketing For Dummies*, 3rd ed. (Hoboken, NJ: John Wiley & Sons, Inc.)

Holden, Greg. *Starting an Online Business For Dummies*, 6th ed. (Hoboken, NJ: John Wiley & Sons, Inc.)

Gardner, Susannah. *Buzz Marketing with Blogs For Dummies.* (Hoboken, NJ: John Wiley & Sons, Inc.)

Jarboe, Greg, and Suzie Reider. *YouTube and Video Marketing: An Hour a Day.* (Hoboken, NJ: John Wiley & Sons, Inc.)

Jones, Kristopher B. *Internet Marketing.* (Hoboken, NJ: John Wiley & Sons, Inc.)

Jones, Kristopher B. *Search Engine Optimization: Your Visual Blueprint for Effective Internet Marketing.* (Hoboken, NJ: John Wiley & Sons, Inc.)

Joyner, Amy. *The Online Millionaire: Strategies for Building a Web-Based Empire on eBay and Beyond.* (Hoboken, NJ: John Wiley & Sons, Inc.)

Kent, Peter. *Pay Per Click Search Engine Marketing For Dummies*. (Hoboken, NJ: John Wiley & Sons, Inc.)

Ledford, Jerri L. *SEO: Search Engine Optimization Bible*. (Hoboken, NJ: John Wiley & Sons, Inc.)

Ledford, Jerri L. *SEO: Search Engine Optimization Bible*, 2nd ed. (Hoboken, NJ: John Wiley & Sons, Inc.)

Lindahl, David, and Jonathan Rozek. *The Six-Figure Second Income: How to Start and Grow a Successful Online Business Without Quitting Your Day Job*. (Hoboken, NJ: John Wiley & Sons, Inc.)

Lutze, Heather F. *The Findability Formula: The Easy, Non-Technical Approach to Search Engine Marketing*. (Hoboken, NJ: John Wiley & Sons, Inc.)

Miller, Michael. *Online Marketing Heroes: Interviews with 25 Successful Online Marketing Gurus*. (Hoboken, NJ: John Wiley & Sons, Inc.)

O'Keefe, Steve. *Complete Guide to Internet Publicity: Creating and Launching Successful Online Campaigns*. (Hoboken, NJ: John Wiley & Sons, Inc.)

Perlman, Corey. *eBoot Camp: Proven Internet Marketing Techniques to Grow Your Business*. (Hoboken, NJ: John Wiley & Sons, Inc.)

Rich, Jason R. *Unofficial Guide to Starting a Business Online*, 2nd ed. (Hoboken, NJ: John Wiley & Sons, Inc.)

Snell, Rob. *Starting a Yahoo! Business For Dummies*. (Hoboken, NJ: John Wiley & Sons, Inc.)

Szydlik, Sherry, and Lamont Wood. *E-trepreneur: A Radically Simple and Inexpensive Plan for a Profitable Internet Store in 7 Days*. (Hoboken, NJ: John Wiley & Sons, Inc.)

Szetela, David, Joseph Kerschbaum, and Michael Flores. *Pay-Per-Click Search Engine Marketing: An Hour a Day*. (Hoboken, NJ: John Wiley & Sons, Inc.)

Tang, Linh. *Launching Your Yahoo! Business*. (London, England: Que Publishing)

Tang, Linh. *Succeding at Your Yahoo! Business*. (London, England: Que Publishing)

Zimmerman, Jan. *Web Marketing For Dummies*. (Hoboken, NJ: John Wiley & Sons, Inc.)

Zimmerman, Jan. *Web Marketing For Dummies*, 2nd ed. (Hoboken, NJ: John Wiley & Sons, Inc.)

Downloads

For your free downloads associated with *The Social Media Bible,* go to www.theSocialMediaBible.com, and enter your ISBN number located on the back of the book above the bar code. Be sure to enter the dashes.

Credits

The ROI of Social Media was provided by:

Paul Petty, founder of rcFoamFighters, www.rcFoamFighters.com

Expert Insight was provided by:

Linh Tang, coauthor, *Launching Your Yahoo! Business* and *Succeeding at Your Yahoo! Business*, www.LinhTang.com

Technical edits were provided by:

Sarah Jew Lim, Global Communications & Public Affairs, Google.com

CHAPTER 21

The Formidable Fourth Screen (Mobile)

What's in It for You?

Mobile telephones are the epitome of both digital convergence and social media, and have probably done more to advance social media than any other single digital device. One of the first major breakthroughs after the Internet was created was cellular technology. Today's cell phones allow people to download music; read from and write to a blog; surf the Web; receive their e-mails; take and share photos and video; Jott speech-to-text messages to themselves and others; tweet to groups in excess of 6,000 followers; capture a photo of a billboard with an embedded link that takes the user to a product web site; have a five-star rating of all Italian restaurants within walking distance of your cell phone; get step-by-step directions on how to get from here to there; access maps, art, and encyclopedic information; watch a movie; take a high-quality photograph; post that photograph to a social, web, or blog site; text message; update your web site; listen to a podcast; organize your address book and calendar; record your notes . . . and, oh yeah—you can even make a telephone call.

According to a press release from the research firm IDC's Digital Marketplace Model and Forecast (www.idc.com/home.jhtml):

- Nearly a quarter of the world's population—roughly 1.4 billion people—was using the Internet regularly in 2008. This number is expected to surpass 1.9 billion unique users—or 30 percent of the world's population—in 2012.

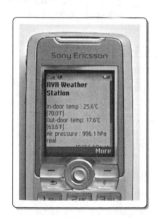

FIGURE 21.1 Mobile Weather on a Mobile Phone

theSocialMediaBible.com

- China passed the United States in 2007 to become the country with the largest number of Internet users, and the country's online population is predicted to grow from 275 million users in 2008 to 375 million users in 2012.

- Nearly half of all Internet users will make online purchases in 2010. By 2012, there will be more than one billion online buyers worldwide making business-to-consumer (B2C) transactions worth $1.2 trillion. Business-to-business (B2B) e-commerce will increase 10-fold, totaling $12.4 trillion worldwide in 2012.

- The global online ad spending will hit $81.1 billion by the year 2011, says a report released by the research firm Piper Jaffray & Co., more than 10 percent of all ad spending across all media. This share is expected to reach 13.6 percent by 2011.

- Roughly 40 percent of all Internet users worldwide currently have mobile Internet access. The number of mobile Internet users reached 546 million in 2008, nearly twice as many as in 2006, and is forecast to surpass 1.5 billion worldwide in 2012.

- The most popular online activities today are searching the Web, finding information for personal use, using Internet e-mail, accessing news and sports information, and accessing financial or credit information. In addition to these activities, more than 50 percent of online users worldwide are using instant messaging and playing online games. The fastest-growing online activities include accessing business applications, creating blogs, online gambling, accessing work-related e-mail, and participating in online communities.

- The most popular online activities among mobile Internet users include searching the Web; accessing news and sports information; downloading music, videos, and ringtones; using instant messaging; and using Internet e-mail. By 2012, downloading music, videos, and ringtones will become the number one activity among mobile Internet users worldwide.

According to John Gantz, chief research officer at IDC:

The Internet will have added its second billion users over a span of about eight years, a testament to both its universal appeal and its availability. In this time, the Internet has also become more deeply integrated into the fabric of many users' personal and professional lives, enabling them to work, play, and socialize anytime from anywhere. These trends will accelerate as the number of mobile users continues to soar and the Internet becomes truly ubiquitous.

Given the recent advances in mobile technology, the one tool that you must have to access this wealth of social media is a good cell phone. As Kakul Srivastava of Yahoo!'s Flickr said, "There are three cell phones for every human being on the planet. Get one, learn how to use it, and participate!"

Back to the Beginning

A mobile telephone, wireless phone, or cell phone (terms that are interchangeable) is a mobile, battery-operated electronic device used for voice or data communication over a network of cell sites, which is interconnected to the public switched telephone network (PSTN). Between 1880 and 1900, Nathan B. Stubblefield of Murray, Kentucky, invented the first "wireless telephone." Stubblefield's "Cave Radio," which later became known as his "Cave Phone," was the first U.S. patent for a wireless telephone and was issued in 1908 (Number 887,357). Stubblefield's phone was able to communicate without the use of wires using a radio signal similar to what we have today. The concept of creating a mobile telephone goes back to 1915, when an internal memo from American Telephone & Telegraph discussed the development of a wireless telephone as it is known today.

However, it wasn't until 1947 that AT&T's Bell Labs developed the first base stations (cells), upon which they continued to expand through the 1960s. Canadian inventor and electrical engineering professor Reginald Fessenden is credited with the development of the first radiophones and shore-to-ship communications during World War II. Later, during the 1950s, the military used radiotelephone links, which were radio-based wireless portable communication devices. By 1973, handheld cellular radios had become available.

The wireless phone with which people are familiar today was first patented in the United States (Number 3,449,750) on June 10, 1969, by George Sweigert of Euclid, Ohio. The first official mobile telephone call was placed on April 3, 1973, by Motorola executive and researcher Martin Cooper, from what has been accepted as the first practical mobile phone. His handset was portable and modern, but awkward and heavy.

Japanese company NTT launched the first commercial citywide cellular network—called 0 Generation, or 0G—for mobile telephone service in 1978. The first fully automatic cellular networks—1G, or 1st Generation—were introduced in the 1980s. And in 1981, the Nordic Mobile Telephone (NMT) system went online in Denmark, Finland, Norway, and Sweden. NMT first enabled the mobile phone for use internationally by creating "roaming" on other networks in other countries, a process that accelerated mobile phone use throughout northern Europe.

Motorola DynaTAC was the first mobile phone that the FCC approved in 1983; during the following year, Bell Labs developed modern cellular technology based on multiple base stations—or *cell sites*—each of which provided service to a small area, or cell, which partially overlapped and handed over the data transmission from cell to cell. This allowed a conversation to continue as the mobile phone traveled between cell sites.

The first modern digital cellular technology, or 2G (2nd Generation), was launched in 1991 in Finland by Radiolinja, a company that is now part of Elisa Group.[1] Mobile data services on mobile telephones first appeared in Finland in 1993, beginning with SMS,[2] person-to-person text messaging. The first commercial payment system for credit cards was launched in the Philippines by Mimick Banks in 1999 and by mobile operators Globe and Smart simultaneously.

The very first mobile phone content that was ever sold was ringtones in Finland in 1998. In 1999, the first mobile telephone designed to give wireless access to Internet e-mail was the Nokia Communicator. The new multi-use electronic devices created a new category of cellular telephone technology called the *smart phone*. In 1999, Japanese company NTT DoCoMo joined the conversation again by launching i-Mode, the first mobile Internet service—which is the world's largest mobile Internet service today and makes roughly the same amount as Google in annual revenues. NTT created the first commercial launch of the 3G (3rd Generation) mobile phone on the W-CDMA[3] standard in 2001. Today, more than 800 million people are accessing the Internet with their mobile phones.

1. Today, the Elisa Corporation is a leading Nordic communications services provider and a publicly listed Eurotop-500 company, with operations in the Nordic countries, the Baltics, and Russia. They serve some 2 million consumers regionally and around 15,000 enterprises internationally, offering a wide range of subscriptions with services. Their revenues for 2007 were €1.57 billion and they employ nearly 2,900 people. Elisa's global alliance partners are Vodafone and Telenor.
2. SMS—or Short Message Service—is a communications protocol that allows for the interchange of short text messages between mobile telephone devices. SMS text messaging is the most widely used data application on the planet, and in many parts of the world the term *SMS* has become synonymous for a text message or for sending a text message.
3. W-CDMA, or Wideband Code Division Multiple Access, is a type of 3G cellular network. W-CDMA is a higher-speed transmission protocol used in the Japanese FOMA and UMTS system, a third generation to the 2G GSM networks deployed worldwide.

It wasn't until the 1990s that the mobile phone truly became mobile. Before that time, mobile phones were large, heavy, bulky, and not easily carried in a jacket pocket or purse. Most mobile telephones had been installed as car phones until that time, but with the development of smaller digital components and better battery technology, mobile phones became small enough for us to carry.

By the end of 2007, the number of mobile telephones had surpassed 3.3 billion subscriptions worldwide—which represents more than half of the world's human population, and makes the mobile telephone the most common electronic device and most widely used technology in the world.

The Handset

According to GetJar.com (http://stats.getjar.com/statistics) the May 2010 mobile telephone manufacturer market share is as follows:

Nokia	47.22 percent
Samsung	10.82 percent
Sony-Ericsson	9.08 percent
BlackBerry	2.78 percent
LG	2.63 percent
Motorola	2.16 percent
Palm	0.88 percent
Apple	0.68 percent
T-Mobile	0.59 percent
Sanyo	0.34 percent
O2	0.27 percent
HTC	0.27 percent
Huawei	0.09 percent
Siemens	0.04 percent
Sagem	0.04 percent
Pantech	0.03 percent
UTStarcom	0.02 percent
NEC	0.02 percent
Lenovo	0.02 percent
BenQ-Siemens	0.02 percent
Sharp	0.01 percent
Alcatel	0.01 percent
Amoi	0.01 percent

FIGURE 21.2 Nokia Mobile Phone

All other manufacturers represent less than 0.01 percent market share.

Mobile telephone technology nowadays includes everything from the very basic mobile phone to the full-featured telephones with web access and multimedia capabilities, such as music phones (SonyEricsson Walkman), camera phones (Cybershot), video phones, the RIM BlackBerry, smart phones, LG Dare, PDA (Personal Desktop Assistants),[4] Nokia N-Series of multimedia phones, and the most recent addition to the bunch: the Apple iPhone and Google Android.

Phone Features

Today's mobile phones boast features beyond making a simple telephone call. Cell phones can now send text messages; perform Internet browsing; play back MP3-formatted music; record memos; organize personal information, contacts, and calendars; send and receive e-mail and instant messages; record, send, receive, and watch images and videos using built-in cameras and camcorders; play different ringtones, games, and radio; perform push-to-talk (PTT); use infrared and Bluetooth connectivity; perform video calling; and serve as a wireless modem for a PC. Nokia and the University of Cambridge have even introduced a bendable cell phone called "The Morph."[5]

To read Nokia's entire press release on "The Morph" go to www.nokia .com/A4136001?newsid=1194251, or visit www.theSocialMediaBible.com for all of the clickable links.

---

4. The Apple Newton was the first PDA released in 1992 and was sold until 1998. During the 1980s, while president and CEO of Safko International Inc., the author collaborated with the Advanced Technology Group at Apple. After demonstrating the fully graphic human interface (GHI) of the SenSei Operating System to Apple and General Magic, it quickly became the archetype for the Apple Newton Operating System.

5. Morph is a concept that demonstrates how future mobile devices might be stretchable and flexible, allowing the user to transform a mobile device into radically different shapes. It demonstrates the ultimate functionality that nanotechnology might be capable of delivering: flexible materials, transparent electronics, and self-cleaning surfaces. Dr. Bob Iannucci, chief technology officer for Nokia, commented, "Nokia Research Center is looking at ways to reinvent the form and function of mobile devices; the Morph concept shows what might be possible."

The mobile phone data services are most widely used for text messaging, music and picture downloads, video gaming, adult entertainment, gambling, and video or TV. Total revenues for paid mobile data services now exceed the revenues of paid services on the Internet—and is expected to grow to more than $300 billion by 2012 worldwide.

Mobile Applications

The most common data service used on mobile phones today is SMS text messaging.

More than 96 percent of the more than 270 million mobile phone users are actively using text messaging on a regular basis. We sent more than 84 billion text messages each month with more than 1 trillion SMS text messages sent in 2009 in the United States alone. Mobile telephone usage has surpassed cable TV, web access, and home PCs. More than 95 percent of all new mobile phones sold today are Web enabled and more than 70 million U.S. consumers use them regularly.

FIGURE 21.3 Mobile Music Download

Many companies have claimed to have sent the very first SMS text message. According to a former employee of NASA, Edward Lantz, the first message was sent by one simple Motorola beeper in 1989 by Raina Fortini from New York City to Melbourne Beach, Florida. Fortini used upside down numbers that could be read as words and sounds. The first commercial SMS message was sent over the Vodafone GSM network in the United Kingdom on December 3, 1992, from Neil Papworth of Sema Group using a personal computer, to Richard Jarvis of Vodafone using an Orbitel 901 handset. The text of the message was "Merry Christmas." The first SMS typed on a GSM phone is claimed to have been sent by Riku Pihkonen, an engineering student at Nokia, in 1993 (www.wapedia.mobi/en/Text_Messaging). Go to www.theSocialMediaBible.com for clickable links.

FIGURE 21.4 The Morph Mobile Phone

FIGURE 21.5 Text
Message

The next most common use of mobile data services is for music. Music file downloads generated more than $31 billion in revenue last year, with the next in line being ringtone downloads.

In the year 2000, Finnish telephone company Radiolinja (now Elisa) introduced the first mobile news service, delivered by SMS text messaging. After that came video games, jokes, horoscopes, TV content, advertising, and other content downloads. Mobile product sales for ringtones, games, and graphics are displacing the money that is spent on traditional youth products such as music, clothing, and movies.

Other mobile data services range from conducting a job search or seeking career advice from Monster.com; to transferring up to $1 million in cash from one mobile account in one country to another overseas; to paying your utility bills in one city and a parking ticket in another. Mobile devices and applications are seen as remote controls for the web, or, as Director of Strategy for Crayon Marketing Adam Broitman puts it, "The mobile phone is our remote control for our lives!" (See Broitman's Expert Insight later in this chapter, or listen to Adam Broitman's Executive Conversation by going to www.theSocialMediaBible.com.)

Rich Media

More and more content is being developed for the mobile telephone, as it has quickly become a mass media device—and even commonly called "the Fourth Screen" (with the other three being movie, television, and the PC). With the advent of the iPhone, Android, and other similar smart phones, movie distribution companies are taking new rich media distribution seriously and making it possible to download full-length movies from your PC and transfer them to your phone (in addition to downloading them directly from your mobile device).

Mobile technology is becoming so prevalent, in fact, that it has elicited the creation and inclusion of new words to our everyday vocabulary, one of which is the term *mobisodes*. A mobisode is a short episode of a popular television show that is specifically intended for mobile device viewing. Radio, television, and satellite TV broadcast media all require us to tune in at a very specific time (same time, same channel) in order to catch a given program or breaking news, unless you record it using a DVR or TiVo. If you aren't able to get to your TV set in time to view or record it, you either miss the program altogether, or you have to wait for the next broadcast time. Subscribing to a mobile news feed, however, enables you to receive this information anywhere, at any time.

What You Need to Know

Over the past several years, the mobile telephone has become increasingly more important to one's participation in social media. With popular networking sites such as MySpace, LinkedIn, and Facebook; photo-sharing sites like Flickr, SmugMug, and Photobucket; video sharing web sites such as YouTube; and information sites like Wikipedia, mobile telephone web access is more important than ever. Even personal publishing platform WordPress (see Chapter 5, The World of Web Pages) has plug-ins now that

FIGURE 21.6 MySpace Mobile App

give mobile phone users the ability to view their blog sites. (See Downloads at the end of this chapter.)

According to Brandon Lucas, senior director of mobile business development for social networking site myspace.com, MySpace Mobile United States had more than 1.4 billion impressions in one month. In fact, Lucas stated, "It wasn't until we rolled out m.myspace.com, a version of MySpace that displays on your mobile phone, that we got a sense of how powerful demand was for MySpace on cell phones." CEO of mobile community Mocospace Justin Siegel cites one billion visits to his site since its inception, and Facebook Mobile has surpassed both groups, claiming four million unique registrations.

Technology research group ABI Research conducted an online survey which found that nearly half (46 percent) of those who use social networks have visited these sites through their mobile phone. Of these, nearly 70 percent have visited MySpace, with another 67 percent also visiting Facebook.

Twitter

Twitter has also made a huge impact on texting, microblogging, and communicating through the use of a mobile phone. Please read Chapter 14,

Thumbs Up for Microblogging, for a more in-depth description of Twitter and "tweets."

Real-Time Social Engagement

The portability of the mobile telephone promotes real time, living in the moment, or life presence for its user. The device allows users to participate in an event and share their reactions and ideas with others instantly.

In 2000, this interaction might have been as simple as holding up a cell phone toward the stage at a concert and letting the person on the other end of the connection hear a song. Today, from a mobile telephone one could photograph the concert, videotape it, blog about it, and share it with friends, family, and colleagues even before the show ends! Being able to share these important experiences in real time creates strong social bonds.

In one case, a stolen mobile phone was even returned to its owner based on photographs that its camera took and automatically uploaded to the Web. And as far as sharing your experiences through text messaging, Twitter is a great way to post instant, up-to-the-minute news about what you are doing and thinking. (See Chapter 14, Thumbs Up for Microblogging, for more information on microblogging and Twitter.)

Reviews

Mobile user-generated content creates a powerful trusted network, whose recommendations can have a significant impact on your decision making. If a restaurant review comes from someone you know—whether it's a friend or just someone from your hometown—you're likely to receive that review with much more trust than one from a paid critic.

A great enterprise example of this is Yelp.com, a web site that you can access through your computer or through your mobile phone. Connecting to Yelp allows you to check out reviews for any kind of business just by typing in your zip code, or simply allowing your GPS-enabled mobile phone to tell Yelp where you are located. So, for example, if you are looking for a great pasta restaurant near the corner of Main and Broadway, Yelp will show you a half dozen or more restaurant reviews from people who live in that area and who have actually eaten at those restaurants. (To hear or read the Executive Conversation interview with Stephanie Ichinose, the director of communications for Yelp, go to www.theSocialMediaBible .com.)

Mobile Marketing

The popularity of marketing to mobile phone users has grown steadily since the rise of SMS in Europe and Asia in the early 2000s. During this time, businesses began collecting mobile phone numbers to send both wanted and unwanted (spam) advertising messages to their users. Due to global government regulations, SMS has become a legitimate form of advertising. Unlike the public domain in which the World Wide Web exists,

FIGURE 21.7 Mobile Gaming

mobile carriers control their own networks and have set guidelines and best practices for the entire mobile media industry.

The Mobile Marketing Association and the Interactive Advertising Bureau (IAB) have established strict guidelines and are evangelizing the use of mobile phones for advertisers. This initiative has been very successful in North America, Western Europe, and several other regions.

Another issue with which some countries are dealing is mobile spam advertising messages that are sent to mobile subscribers without an explicit opt-in (see Chapter 4, It's Not Your Father's E-Mail, for more information on opt-ins). This is due to mobile carriers' sales of subscribers' telephone numbers to third parties. Legislation often requires permission or an opt-in from the mobile subscriber to advertise to them, which has seriously delayed the growth of mobile advertising and marketing. The mobile carriers require a double opt-in from the subscriber and the ability for the consumer to opt out at any time by sending the word *STOP* by SMS or text messaging. These guidelines are very similar to the 2004 U.S. CAN-SPAM Act and are established in the MMA Consumer Best Practices Guidelines (see further on). All mobile carriers in the United States voluntarily follow these guidelines. (For more information on the CAN-SPAM Act, see Chapter 4, It's Not Your Father's E-Mail.)

In 2002, Labatt Brewing Company ran the first successful cross-carrier SMS advertising campaign. Since then, mobile SMS advertising has gained recognition as a new advertising channel and a way to communicate to the mobile consumer. Large consumer brands have accepted SMS advertising, and have created mobile domain names that allow their consumers to text message their brand name while in a store or at an event. Motorola's ongoing campaign at the House of Blues venues is another example of well-designed mobile advertising. The House of Blues allows their patrons to send their mobile photos to the LED display board and their online blog in real time.[6]

Mobile Web Marketing

For online mobile advertisers, the Mobile Marketing Association (MMA) provides a set of guidelines and standards that specify recommended formats for ads and mobile presentations. Google, Yahoo!, and other major mobile content providers are selling mobile advertising placement as part of their advertising services.

Bluetooth Connection

Bluetooth began in 2003 as a wireless radio protocol technology called *frequency hopping* or *spread spectrum* that chops up the data being sent and transmits chunks of it on up to 75 different frequencies. This allows data transmission utilizing short-range communications from fixed or mobile devices, creating a wireless personal area network or PAN. Bluetooth provides access and secure information exchange between devices such as mobile phones, digital cameras, telephones, personal computers, microphones and headsets, printers, GPS receivers, and video game consoles. Since Bluetooth provides secure high-speed transmission of data, it is an appropriate technology for mobile advertising and marketing. Companies like ProxiBlaster.com, bluetoothmagnet.com, and bluecasting.com are providing Bluetooth marketing solutions. Using Bluetooth, companies can automatically send media files to all Bluetooth-enabled devices, such as mobile phones, PDAs, and laptops within a range of around 100 meters. This is commonly referred to as bluecasting, bluetooth broadcasting, or proximity marketing.

---

6. . . . "Motorola is making mobile music access seamless for music lovers—in their homes, at work, on the road, and now at the premier live music venue—the House of Blues," said Kathleen Finato, senior director of marketing for North America Mobile Devices, Motorola, Inc. "It's a true marriage of entertainment and mobility as the music lifestyle fan receives the ultimate concert experience long before the first song is played. House of Blues is an innovator in the live music category. By combining our expertise with a mobile leader such as Motorola, we are able to create new interactive opportunities for our artists and customers," said Paul Sewell, senior vice president, sponsorship House of Blues Entertainment, Inc. "Together, Motorola and House of Blues will power the enjoyment for the growing tech savvy music generation." . . . www.motorola.com/mediacenter/news/detail.jsp?globalObjectId=5705_5683_23.

Location-Based Services

Location-based services (LBS) are a great way to send geographically specific advertising and SMS messages to a mobile phone subscriber based on GPS—or radiolocation—or trilateration location for those not equipped with GPS. Radiolocation and trilateration are methods by which a cell phone's location is determined based on its signal strength to the closest cell phone towers. You may have heard of the woman stuck in her car in a blizzard at night who was saved by rescuers who used radiolocation and trilateration to find her car in the snow bank. LBS can even be used to locate a stolen phone or kidnapped person.

Day-to-day uses for LBS might include locating the nearest type of business or service that a customer is looking for—such as an ATM, restaurant, or doctor; determining meeting room schedules; executing turn-by-turn navigation to a specific address; locating friends on a map displayed on your mobile phone; receiving personal alerts, such as notification of a sale on gas and traffic updates that can include warnings of traffic jams and bad weather; finding taxis, people, employees, or rental equipment location; fleet scheduling, identifying passive sensors or RF (radio frequency) tags for packages and railroad train boxcars; or using an E-ZPass, toll watch, or other geographically targeted mobile advertising.

Mobile LBS marketing has also been used for mobile coupons or discounts that are sent automatically to mobile subscribers who are near advertising retailers, restaurants, cafés, or movie theatres. In 2007, Singapore mobile carrier MobileOne initiated an LBS advertising campaign that involved many local marketers that was widely accepted by its subscribers. Companies offering location-based, geo-targeted advertising or geo-messaging include Loopt.com, Dodgeball.com, and GeoMe.com (in Spain).

Mobile Gaming

Mobile gaming takes place when a video game is played on a mobile phone, smart phone, PDA, or handheld computer. The first game that was factory-installed on a mobile phone was called Snake, which came equipped on certain Nokia models in 1997. Snake has actually become the most popular mobile video game on the planet, and is regularly played by more than one billion people worldwide.

Mobile games can be factory installed, installed via memory card or Bluetooth, or—in most cases—downloaded from the carrier for a fee. They can include both stand-alone and networked multiplayer games. (See Chapter 16, Virtual Worlds—Real Impact and Chapter 17, Gaming the System: Virtual Gaming, for more information on virtual worlds and gaming.)

One of the most popular gaming applications for mobile technology today is online mobile gambling. In 2005, PokerRoom, a poker software application, was developed by Ongame in which the player can play poker in a single-player or multiplayer mode for real or play money.

MMORPG

In addition to ordinary mobile gaming, MMORPG—or Massively Multi-player Online Role Playing Games—have become very popular with mobile phone users. (See Chapter 17, Gaming the System: Virtual Gaming, for a complete explanation of MMORPG.) The first of these for the mobile audience were called TibiaME and were developed by CipSoft SmartCell Technology. The company is also working on a gaming application for the first cross-platform MMORPG called Shadow of Legend, which is designed to be played on both PCs and mobile devices.

Location-Based Games

There are even games that one can play on mobile phones that use geo-graphic location technology such as GPS. These are called location-based games, and they integrate the player's position into the game play, making the player's coordinates and movement the main elements.

The most well-known example of a location-based game is a high-tech treasure hunt game called Geocaching, which is played throughout the world by adventure seekers equipped with GPS devices. The basic idea is to locate hidden containers—called geocaches—outdoors, exchange a hidden gift, and then share your experiences online. Geocaching has become popular with all age groups—especially for people who have a strong sense of community and support for the environment. (You can learn more at www.geocaching.com.)

Mobile In-Game Marketing

There are five popular categories of mobile gaming: interactive real-time, 3-D games, massive multiplayer, social networking, and casual games (the most popular kind). Casual games are single-player and very easy to play. In addition to many old favorite video games such as Space Invaders, Tetris, and Solitaire, many of the big video game companies have scaled down their computer and console games and have created mobile divisions such as PlayStation Portable and Nintendo DS. Many companies have developed their games directly for mobile phone play.

Large brands are now delivering advertising messages within those mobile games, and often even sponsoring an entire game to drive brand, sales, and consumer engagement. This type of advertising is known as mobile *advergaming* or *ad-funded mobile gaming*. Puma running shoe brand developed a comprehensive engagement marketing campaign by creating a racing game that coincided with the Shanghai F1 race. Their Advergame was called F-Wan, which sounds like F1 for Formula One racing and means "play" in Chinese. The racetrack was designed in the shape of their Puma logo, a jumping wild cat with its tail extended. F-Wan was a multiplayer game, allowing up to four gamers to race against each other. The top three best scores each week would win Puma merchandise.

Mobile Viral Marketing

Mobile viral marketing is similar to the e-mail and Internet variety. Its distribution and communication rely on customers to transmit a particular company's content—known as *mobile viral content*—by mobile SMS to other potential customers in their trusted network, and encourage these contacts to pass the content among themselves. To begin a viral marketing campaign, the enterprise *seeds* (or sends) content to first-generation key customers—also called *mavens* and *influencers*—who become *infected* with this information. These individuals, or *communicators,* then forward the message to recipients, who are encouraged to do the same and keep the message moving. The better the "What's in It for Me?" content, the more effective the viral spread of this message will be. In one case, the Italian Passa Parola (Spread of Mouth) [this is actually the "literal" translation. The correct translation is "word of mouth"] campaign reached 800,000 users solely by using viral marketing.

Mobile Marketing Future

A recent survey stated that approximately 89 percent of major brands are planning to market their products through SMS text and multimedia mobile messaging. One-third of those brands are planning to spend about 10 percent of their total annual marketing budgets on mobile marketing. Within five years, more than half of all major brands are expected to spend between 5 percent and 25 percent of their total annual marketing budgets on mobile marketing. Of the companies that responded to this survey, 40 percent of them have stated that they have already begun mobile marketing to their audiences because of their ability to reach a specific target audience, in a specific geographical location, with a very specific marketing message. For

more information, go to www.airwidesolutions.com/press2006/feb2106
.html.

Messaging Convergence

Multifunctional services are becoming more popular with mobile phone
users because of the ability of these services to integrate SMS text messaging
with voice—such as *voice SMS*, in which voice replaces text. One such
company is called Jott.

To sign up for Jott's service you simply create a free account with your
name, group names, and telephone numbers. Once this is complete, you call
an 800 number and talk to the answering machine, which asks, "Who do you
want to Jott?" You could give your own first name, and Jott replies with your
full name. After a confirmation and a tone, the user leaves a standard voice
message. Within moments, that message is transcribed from voice to text,
and sent to both the user's cell phone as a text message and to a designated
e-mail account.

Jott is a great service when you get an idea, remember something, or
need to be reminded of something. You can simply "Jott" yourself. This is
particularly good when you're driving 60 miles per hour on the freeway,
walking down the street, eating at a restaurant—any place where finding
paper and a pencil is inconvenient. It's also great to be able to Jott people to
tell them you are running 10 minutes late while driving in the car.

To listen to the Executive Conversation with John Pollard, the founder
of Jott, please go to www.theSocialMediaBible.com.

The Mobile Marketing Association

The Mobile Marketing Association (MMA; www.mmaglobal.com) is a global
nonprofit association that strives to stimulate the growth of mobile marketing
and its associated technology. The MMA has more than 600 global member
companies that include agencies, advertisers, handheld device manufacturers, carriers and wireless operators, retailers, software and service providers,
aggregators, technology enablers, market research firms—as well as any
company focused on the potential of marketing to mobile phones.

Mobile Phone Technology

The Apple iPhone: As a certified developer for Apple from the mid-1980s to the
mid-1990s, the author had a front-row seat to the advent of the many

innovations that paved the way in the world of technology. Twenty years later, Steve Jobs is still at it. This chapter would be incomplete without mentioning Apple's iPhone because of the impact this single product has had on social media (see Figure 21.8).

On January 9, 2007, Apple announced their version of the smart phone: the iPhone. The iPhone connects to the Internet, plays multimedia, and of course, is a fully

FIGURE 21.8   iPhone Mobile Phone

functioning mobile phone with text messaging and voicemail capabilities. The iPhone has a touch screen that replaces a mobile phone's conventional keyboard. It includes both still and video cameras, plays MP3-formatted music and other audio files, and proudly represents the fourth-screen category with a fully functioning video player similar to Apple's iPod. The iPhone allows its users to create, upload, share, and view audio, photographs, and video.

With the iPhone's ability to connect to the Internet, you can browse a web site, read a blog, access traffic reports, view your stock portfolio, or do anything that you can do with a standard PC and an Internet connection.

After repeated attempts to encourage Apple to participate in *The Social Media Bible*, it unfortunately declined.

Google Android: The Android is Google's answer to Apple's iPhone. It's a smart phone mobile device built on an open-system platform in cooperation with the Open Handset Alliance (OHA), which is a business alliance of 34 firms, including Google, HTC, Intel, Motorola, Qualcomm, Samsung, LG, T-Mobile, Nvidia, and Wind River Systems, which have joined together to develop open standards for mobile devices. The Android can function with any mobile carrier and features Google Search, Google Apps, Gmail (Google's e-mail system), and GTalk (Google's Instant Messaging application). Google's entry into the mobile advertising market is both welcomed and

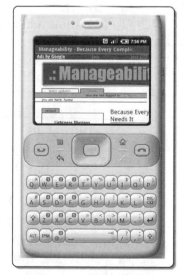

FIGURE 21.9   Android Mobile Phone

viewed as the company's intention to dominate the mobile-based advertising market as it did with the desktop.

As with all open platforms, a rush of high-quality developers are currently building the very best and most advanced applications possible. Similar to the advance in market share that computer technology has enjoyed over the past three decades, this open platform will create more applications, features, and benefits, and will dramatically increase Android's market share. With Google's dominance in Web-based advertising combined with the relatively untapped mobile advertising market, the company's revenue potential for dominating mobile marketing is huge.

Providers

Mobile social networks and communities are one of the fastest-growing sectors in social media. Founder and CEO of Amanda Vega Consulting and active blogger Amanda Vega points out that even in Third World countries where the average person cannot afford to own a computer or have access to high-speed broadband Internet, he can usually afford a cell phone. This is why there are currently more cell phones on the planet than there are people. (To listen to Amanda Vega's Executive Conversation, go to www.theSocial MediaBible.com.)

The following is a list of mobile social networking web sites that provide a type of mobile data service. As with the Providers sections of other chapters, don't get overwhelmed. Just pick out one or two, visit their sites, read their benefits, and try it for yourself.

- 3jam.com introduces SMS 2.0, which allows you to text message with your friends in a new way, and provides 3jam SuperText—your free text message inbox on the Web. You can send and receive text messages for free when you're online, achieve reliable message delivery to anyone with a mobile phone, and—unlike IM—reply to all group texting and other new tricks for your phone.
- Aki-aki.com is a German-based mobile social network web site.
- AirG.com is a mobile community with more than 20 million unique users worldwide, interconnected to more than 100 mobile operators in more than 40 countries.
- BrightKite.com allows you to see where your friends are and what they're up to in real time.

- Broadtexter.com is a mobile social community that lets you communicate with your audience, members, supporters, or patrons.

- Buddyping will manage all of your online social networks, locate friends who are nearby, manage your calendar, arrange a meeting, browse places in your area, and group message friends using your mobile.

- CallWave is another example of digital messaging crossover. This system allows you to forward your mobile phone voicemail messaging to transfer all of your recorded voicemails to your e-mail or the CallWave web site. With CallWave, you never have to retrieve your mobile phone messages again, since they've all been sent to your e-mail.

- Dodgeball.com alerts all of your friends to where you are at that moment so you can meet.

- Facebook Mobile is Facebook on your cell phone.

- Flagr.com shares cool places from online or right from your mobile phone.

- Friendstribe.com is a mobile social network specifically designed to be accessed through your mobile phone through text messaging.

- Funkysexycool.com is a fun, free, fast way to flirt and date with over 250,000 members from around the world using your mobile phone.

- Groovr.com helps users stay connected both online and offline by allowing them to move seamlessly from laptop to mobile phone to meet new friends in new places.

- Hobnobster is a web and mobile relationship service for singles to search and communicate with other connected singles online and through their mobile phone.

- Imity.com is a free application for your mobile phone that uses Bluetooth to sense other phones nearby and form a social network—online, offline, and all the other lines.

- Jaiku.com (now part of Google) users can create a microblog and connect with friends posting from the Web or by mobile SMS, or from desktop computers.

- JuiceCaster.com lets you instantly share your photos and videos with friends or directly to your MySpace, Facebook, or other social networking web sites from your mobile phone.

- Kiboze.com delivers interactive product information—such as print advertisements and billboards—to a user's cell phone on demand.

- Loopnote.com lets you create alerts that you can receive by e-mail, IM, text, or RSS.

- MeetMoi.com is a safe and easy-to-use dating service that uses ground-breaking technology to find people around your location and lets you browse pictures, send messages, and connect with members, all from your mobile phone.
- Mig33.com connects you to people from around the world through IM, chat rooms, e-mail, shared photos, SMS—and, of course, you can make cheap calls.
- Mobiluck.com lets you tell your friends where you are, receive alerts when they are nearby, and chat 24/7 for free.
- Moblabber is a group text messaging service, similar to a personalized message—only mass-produced and treated as if it's an ongoing conversation.
- Mocospace.com is a mobile-based social networking web site.
- myGamma.com is a phone and web community in which you can interact with people and showcase yourself by creating a private community with only invited friends with whom you can chat and share your blogs and photos.
- MySpace Mobile is MySpace on your cell phone.
- NowThen.com is a new way to capture the pulse of your life in mobile photos. Just snap, share, and store your moments for free.
- Placestodo.com helps you remember, share, and find new places and things to do.
- Rabble.com is a location-based social networking application you download to your mobile phone that allows you to combine all the things you love doing on the Web on your phone.
- Rader.net is an instant picture and video sharing site.
- ShoZu connects your mobile phone to the Internet and allows you to interact with a huge list of web sites and communities including Flickr, Facebook, YouTube, Blogger, and more.
- Socialight.com lets you create, share, and discover virtual sticky notes stuck to actual places all around you.
- The3gdatingagency.com is a mobile phone access dating web site that is a great way to find new friends or partners for fun, dating, and long-term relationships.
- Treemo.com is an online and mobile community for sharing digital media, empowering self-expression, and transforming creativity into

action by offering an ever-evolving gallery of video, audio, photography, words, and visual art, which inspires visitors to create their own digital expressions—and to share those creations with the world.

- Twitter.com is a service for friends, family, and coworkers to communicate and stay connected through the exchange of quick and frequent answers to one simple question: What are you doing? (See Chapter 14, Thumbs Up for Microblogging, for more information on Twitter. Be sure to also listen to the Executive Conversation with Biz Stone, the founder of Twitter, at www.theSocialMediaBible.com.)

- Veeker.com is video and picture messaging service for your mobile phone and the Web.

- Wadja.com is a mobile web, media, and social messaging service that manages your communication and interaction from your friends, family, and address book contacts.

- Yelp.com is a geographically based review web site that is accessible through your mobile phone. Just open your phone, access Yelp, and see what others have said about that restaurant, movie, or mechanic in your area. (See information earlier in the chapter, and listen to the Executive Conversation with Stephanie Ichinose, director of communications for Yelp, at www.theSocialMediaBible.com.)

- Zannel.com is a way for you to instantly share what you're doing, feeling, and seeing with your friends as it happens by allowing you to create your own mobile page where you can post videos, pictures, and text updates with your mobile phone.

- Zemble.com allows you to text message large groups of friends from your mobile phone by sending just one text message.

- Zinadoo.com allows you to set up your own voting, subscription, text in–text out SMS services, to promote your mobile web site, and to keep in touch with your community through SMS.

- Zingku.com is supercharged mobile text and picture messaging for you and your friends.

- Zyb.com is a mobile-based web site that lets you organize all of your personal information such as contacts, pictures, text messages, and calendar events online.

With a list like this, there's bound to be something that everyone can use!

The ROI of Social Media

Improving Online Visibility Using Social Media Properties

Background

Animation Mentor is an online animation school that specializes in advanced character animation. Students at Animation Mentor learn from professional animators from top animation companies including Dreamworks, Industrial Light & Magic, and Pixar. Anvil was tasked with improving online visibility for Animation Mentor for targeted keywords such as "animation school" and "character animation," but Animation Mentor's web site was built entirely in Flash, leaving little room for search engine optimization efforts.

Strategy

Anvil developed an optimization and promotion strategy for Animation Mentor's social media properties that would both drive traffic to the properties and rank well in search engines.

Implementation

Anvil collaborated with Animation Mentor to pursue the following tactics:

- Created multiple social media profiles on top tier social media sites Facebook, MySpace, YouTube, and Twitter.
- Launched Animation Tips and Tricks ebook and advised on the development and promotion of Animation Mentor's blog.
- Created a StumbleUpon campaign to direct traffic to the blog, home page, and social media properties; directed paid search traffic to blog, site-hosted webinars, and social media properties.
- Anvil interlinked all social media properties, directing new friends and fans from Facebook and MySpace to the blog and webinars. Anvil also created a blog roll of social media sites for www.animationtipsandtricks.com and directed users to various social media properties with Twitter.

Opportunity

The opportunity was to capitalize on social media properties created to reach users in the communities in which they feel comfortable.

Conclusion

Animation Mentor's Facebook fan page rose quickly in the rankings, ranking in the top ten for "character animation," "best animation school," and "online animation school" and ranked 12th for "animation school" queries when tested in September 2008. In August 2008, social media accounted for over 4,000 visitors to www.animationmentor.com. Since Anvil has started working on social media with Animation Mentor, Animation Mentor has witnessed a substantial increase in accepted students:

- 60 percent YTD increase in enrollment
- 40 percent increase in enrollment since last quarter
- 700 percent increase following term YTD enrollment
- Increased conversion rate by 315 percent

Mike Nierengarten, account executive, Anvil Media, Inc.
www.anvilmediainc.com.

Expert Insight

Angela Courtin, senior vice president of marketing entertainment and content, MySpace, www.myspace.com

Angela Courtin

You know, I think the beautiful thing about MySpace is that it's different things to different people. We consider ourselves a premier lifestyle portal that connects friends discovering popular culture, and making a positive impact on the world. We really look at it through a different lens. It really is about the experience . . . your personal experience on the space.

We also have a global community, so we are connecting people both domestically as well as internationally. We are in over 30 territories now; and again, I go back to the idea that it is about the fabric of what social media is: the profile of blogging, instant messaging, e-mailing. And then you also get to stream music and watch videos. You get to upload your own photos. At MySpace, you can go into classified listings. We've just created a new business for small businesses

(continued)

(*continued*)

in order to advertise their own wares. You can check out events in your neighborhood, in the state, or in the country. You can join groups. You can blog on forums and communities. You can search and befriend celebrities as well as bands, TV shows, your high-school and college friends, your fellow mommies—anyone in your network. So it really is what you want it to be and what you make it. . . .

There's really no typical demographic on our site. Our user base is expanding every month, and I think it's a misconception (as you say) that this is a young person's site. We're more than 85 percent over the age of 18, in terms of our user base. And there are 70 million users in the United States alone that have a profile. And if you think . . . one of my most favorite demographic nuggets to share with people is that 40 percent of all moms that are online are on MySpace. . . . That's a huge number, and they are not going there to spy on their kids; they are actually going there to engage in the tools that make social networking so powerful, as well as the discovery of content. . . .

I [always] go back to this: You can personalize it the way you want. If you want to have a very robust page, you can. If you want to keep it simple, you can do that as well. If you want to build a playlist of your favorite music that you like to listen to, or you just want to have a single track, there's that capability to expand and contract. It's really up to the user. . . . First and foremost, I think it's all about connecting and communicating—regardless of whether you are contacting your friends or community, or your favorite band or celebrity; but it also takes the next step. So it's *how* we communicate through e-mailing and instant messaging, connecting with people of similar interests, uploading photographs, commenting on photographs, sharing photographs. We make it very easy to stay in touch and maintain connection with your family or community of friends. And so this goes back to the analogy of scrapbooking. . . . It is a way to have a one-to-many conversation if you want to keep it that way . . . like, if you want to upload your baby's photos and send those to your friends and family, you can do that with the touch of a button.

So you can blog and you can share on a daily basis what your musings are on everything from politics to music, to your favorite cupcake joint in the neighborhood, or just whom you connected with. It may be an old high-school friend and you want to share that with your other high-school friends.

And then, of course, we're now creating a portable experience; and now you can take that online experience in MySpace and take it directly to your mobile phone. So you can connect whenever you want to, wherever you are, as long as you have your mobile phone . . . which is incredible for someone who is just an average user, connecting with their friends; but even extrapolating beyond that . . . for a band (whether you're signed or independent) the ability to be able to push out communication to 1,000, 14,000, 140,000, 1.4 million, now became very acceptable.

To listen to or read the entire Executive Conversation with Angela Courtin, go to www.theSocialMediaBible.com.

Commandments

1. **Thou shalt learn more about mobile marketing.**

   Read some mobile marketing blogs. Watch how some of the big players are branding, selling, and interacting with their customers and prospects through mobile marketing. Give this commandment 15 minutes, two or three times a month. Follow mobile marketing to see when it's the right time for you to jump in.

2. **Thou shalt understand the technology.**

   Understand the technology's capabilities. No need to go totally geek, but just understand the main features and benefits of the major players. Before reading this chapter, did you know you could do that much with a simple smart phone? Spend a few minutes to see how the iPhone and Android work. The more you understand about how the technology functions, the better you will understand how to apply it to your own marketing and advertising concepts and campaigns.

3. **Thou shalt set Google Alerts.**

   Set some Google Alerts for the terms "mobile marketing," "mobile advertising," "mobile marketing [fill in your industry terms]." See what others are doing in your industry with mobile marketing. Most important, remember to keep an eye out for the competition by including their company, product, and service names in your alerts.

4. **Thou shalt try mobile applications.**

   Set up a Jott account and see how you quickly cannot live without it. Get a few of your customers and prospects to opt-in on receiving your company updates in their e-mails and their mobile phones. Try Twitter for communicating with your employees. Capture a photo or, better yet, a two-minute video at your next conference and send it to a few key prospects who could benefit from that "What's in It for Me?" content.

5. **Thou shalt try the mobile Web.**

   Try accessing your favorite sites with your mobile phone. Go to Yelp the next time you're out and want a good restaurant recommendation in your area. If you are GPS-enhanced, try getting directions the next time you're lost (especially you guys out there). Important: See what it takes to get your web site mobile ready. If it's WordPress, you need only a plug-in (see the following Downloads).

Conclusion

Wow! Mobile phone technology is advancing at breakneck speeds while new features are being added every day. The mobile telephone is truly social media in a box that includes nearly every social media tool in one device. Today's smart phone lets you take pictures; upload them to your blog or photo sharing site; send them to friends, colleagues, and customers; or view others' photographs. And you can do the same with audio, music, and video.

You can surf a web site, get tweets, and send and receive text messages. You can receive up-to-the-minute news and stock quotes, traffic reports, and weather. You can listen to music, watch a full-length video, have it wake you on time in the morning, give you turn-by-turn directions, let you know the best pasta restaurant closest to you . . . and even make a call.

As the smart phone continues to develop and become part of everyone's "remote controls for life," more and more companies will understand how to better serve you with demographically specific, geo-targeted, trusted network, permission-based information and advertising.

Mobile marketing is expensive, and companies and providers have only begun to understand how to best serve information to trusted customers using this technology. While mobile marketing might not be a viable solution for every business right now, it likely will be soon. You owe it to yourself and your company to monitor this industry. Watch the technology, and follow the players in this field so that when it is the right time for you to begin mobile marketing, you will recognize the opportunity.

To hear all of the Expert Interviews, go to www.theSocialMediaBible .com.

Readings and Resources

Ahonen, Tomi T., Timo Kasper, and Sara Melkko. *3G Marketing: Communities and Strategic Partnerships*. (Hoboken, NJ: John Wiley & Sons, Inc.)

Andersson, Christoffer, Daniel Freeman, Ian James, et al. *Mobile Media and Applications, From Concept to Cash: Successful Service Creation and Launch*. (Hoboken, NJ: John Wiley & Sons, Inc.)

Ballard, Barbara. *Designing the Mobile User Experience*. (Hoboken, NJ: John Wiley & Sons, Inc.)

Brenner, Michael, and Musa Unmehopa. *The Open Mobile Alliance: Delivering Service Enablers for Next-Generation Applications*. (Hoboken, NJ: John Wiley & Sons, Inc.)

Chehimi, Fadi, Leon Clarke, Michael Coffey, et al. *Games on Symbian OS: A Handbook for Mobile Development*. (Hoboken, NJ: John Wiley & Sons, Inc.)

Eylert, Bernd. *The Mobile Multimedia Business: Requirements and Solutions*. (Hoboken, NJ: John Wiley & Sons, Inc.)

Hirsch, Frederick, John Kemp, and Jani Ilkka. *Mobile Web Services: Architecture and Implementation*. (Hoboken, NJ: John Wiley & Sons, Inc.)

Iwacz, Grzegorz, Andrzej Jajszczyk, and Michal Zajaczkowski. *Multimedia Broadcasting and Multicasting in Mobile Networks*. (Hoboken, NJ: John Wiley & Sons, Inc.)

Karlson, Bo, Aurelian Bria, Jonas Lind, et al. *Wireless Foresight: Scenarios of the Mobile World in 2015*. (Hoboken, NJ: John Wiley & Sons, Inc.)

Klemettinen, Mika. *Enabling Technologies for Mobile Services: The MobiLife Book*. (Hoboken, NJ: John Wiley & Sons, Inc.)

Niebert, Norbert, Andreas Schieder, Jens Zander, and Robert Hancock, eds. *Ambient Networks: Co-Operative Mobile Networking for the Wireless World*. (Hoboken, NJ: John Wiley & Sons, Inc.)

O'Farrell, Michael J., John R. Levine, Jostein Algroy, James Pearce, and Daniel Appelquist. *Mobile Internet For Dummies*. (Hoboken, NJ: John Wiley & Sons, Inc.)

Sauter, Martin. *Communication Systems for the Mobile Information Society*. (Hoboken, NJ: John Wiley & Sons, Inc.)

Sharma, Chetan, Joe Herzog, and Victor Melfi. *Mobile Advertising: Supercharge Your Brand in the Exploding Wireless Market*. (Hoboken, NJ: John Wiley & Sons, Inc.)

Shorey, Rajeev, A. Ananda, Mun Choon Chan, and Wei Tsang Ooi. *Mobile, Wireless, and Sensor Networks: Technology, Applications, and Future Directions*. (Hoboken, NJ: John Wiley & Sons, Inc.)

Downloads

For your free downloads associated with *The Social Media Bible*, go to www.theSocialMediaBible.com, and enter your ISBN number located on the back of the book above the bar code. Be sure to enter the dashes.

Credits

The ROI of Social Media was provided by:

Mike Nierengarten, account executive, Anvil Media, Inc., www.anvilmediainc.com

Expert Insight was provided by:

Angela Courtin, senior vice president of marketing entertainment and content, MySpace, www.myspace.com

Technical edits were provided by:

Lisa J Von Bargen, www.BeyondImplementation.com

FIGURE 21.10   Couple Sharing an iPhone

CHAPTER 22

Let the Conversation Begin (Interpersonal)

What's in It for You?

Interpersonal refers to the many applications and web sites in the social media ecosphere that allow us to communicate live and in real time on one-to-one, one-to-many, many-to-one, and many-to-many bases. Examples of one-to-one exchange are tools such as Skype, AOL AIM, GTalk, Apple's iChat, or something like Jott—with which you can leave notes and messages for yourself through the phone. One-to-many social media tools include Jott, Twitter (see Chapter 14, Thumbs Up for Microblogging), Yahoo! Messenger, Microsoft Live Messenger, and Doodle. Many-to-many examples are applications like GoToMeeting, WebEx, and Adobe Connect. So many of these tools are free and can significantly reduce or even eliminate expenses like long-distance telephone calls. Using IM and web conferencing eradicated the cost of airfare and hotels for many companies. Many-to-one could be considered page aggregators, with which the conversations of many different bloggers are compiled into your web page, or even Google Alerts, with which alerts about many different mentions of your search terms are sent directly to your personal e-mail.

Of course, this list is by no means complete; it's simply intended to provide a sampling of some of the wide variety and broad range of social media interpersonal tools. As with all of the other chapters' content, useful tools, and applications, the players are continuously changing. Many are being added, and some are becoming extinct. For example: When work on this book began, Pownce (a free message and file sharing site) was a viable company with growing numbers and a useful service. But on December 15, 2008—as the first edition of this book was wrapping up—Pownce announced that it was shutting down. And by the time this book, the second edition, actually hits the bookstore, countless other changes will have taken place in the social media tool roster. To help with the constantly changing nature of this field, the web site accompanying this book will be constantly updated with the latest information on social media techniques, tools, and strategies, and updates to *The Social Media Bible*. So visit www.theSocialMediaBible .com often, and contribute to the future of social media.

One impact of social media on the present way of doing business relates to training presentations, which can now be delivered without the speaker leaving his hometown. Before all the social media tools came into place, companies might fly anywhere from 200 to 800 employees in from around the United States; put them up in a hotel; pay for the ballroom, food, and other expenses; and incur the expense of four days of down time for 800 employees (3,200 lost days!). Now a speaker can set up a camera, a web conferencing application, and IM chat, and present to locations around the world in real time, and even answer audience questions live! And then everyone goes back to work with no expenses whatsoever incurred (except, of course, for the speaker's time). Imagine what that is worth to a company! This type of *webinar* can be done in place of telephone calls; for remote training of employees; for state-of-the-company addresses by the CEO; and for announcements to employees that include new products, HR policy changes, public relations issues, sales meetings—and more. All for free (or nearly)!

What You Need to Know

As you might suspect, this chapter's format needs to be a little different. Sections like *Back to the Beginning* and *Providers* really aren't appropriate. Instead, this chapter provides you with some facts about the features and benefits based on a few hand-selected, highlighted companies, and introduces you to some extraordinary tools in the social media ecosphere. You will also see that many of these selected companies and services—although listed in the "one-to-one" section—can be used for one-to-many, or even many-to-many communications. A good number of the sites actually fit into more than one category.

One-to-One

Skype: Low-cost calls are what Skype (www.skype.com, see Figure 22.1) is made for. You can use this service to call another person who also has Skype to anywhere in the world and at any time, day or night, morning or weekends, and it is totally free. Yep—it costs absolutely nothing. Zip. Zero. Zilch.

Once you and your friend, family member, or colleague have downloaded Skype, you can get started on the really cool stuff, such as making completely free and great quality calls from your computer. That's the impressive thing about Skype besides its price tag of zero dollars: You can use tools that you already have—your Internet connection and your computer—and make Skype-to-Skype calls. You and the person you are speaking with will need to have a headset (or use your computer's built-in microphone and speakers) to talk to each other. A headset will really improve the sound quality of your calls; or, you can take it to the next level with free video calls.

You can also use Skype to make pretty cheap calls to landline telephones and mobile phones. Just locate the person you want to call in your contact list and click her name. To call her for free, simply click the green button. This will start the call, and you can talk for as long as you want, whenever you want.

FIGURE 22.1 Skype

Skype provides more than just free Skype-to-Skype calls; it's about inexpensive local, national, and international calls to phones and mobiles. For example, why not send a text message directly from Skype; forward a call to your mobile; or set up an online number for friends, family, and colleagues to make a local call from their old-fashioned phone to your Skype, wherever in the world you are? All you need to get going with these products is a pay-as-you-go Skype Credit. Alternatively, you can get unlimited calls to landlines and a great bundle of useful features with a subscription package for a low monthly fee.

There are two ways to start using Skype products. One involves a pay-monthly subscription; the other is a pay-as-you-go option with Skype Credit. This second option simply allows you to use it as you need it. Skype Credit allows you to add money to your account and start calling locally, nationally, or internationally. The pay-monthly option lets you make unlimited calls to a country or region, and also includes an online number and voicemail. There's no long-term contract needed.

AOL Instant Messenger: AOL Instant Messenger (AIM, www.AIM.com; see Figure 22.2) is a free online service that lets you communicate in real time. Using the AIM Buddy List window lets you see when your buddies are online and chat with them. Chatting and sharing with your friends, family, and colleagues is more

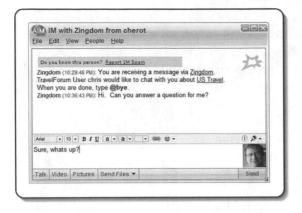

FIGURE 22.2 AOL Instant Messenger

fun than ever using this application. You can send text messages, share photos and URLs, make a PC-to-PC voice call, create an online personality, and more.

The AIM software includes many new and improved features that increase the compatibility and flexibility of your instant messaging experience. The service is now compatible with Windows Vista and Windows XP 64-bit, and the free software includes Instant Messaging, Talk and Voice chat, Video IM, e-mail, and Text Messaging. Additional features of the AIM software include AOL Radio; file transfer for pictures and documents; Buddy List; Address Book; integration of Address Book with Plaxo, the industry leader in Web-based contact management; IM forwarding to mobile phone; AOL Alerts and Reminders; and browse or search the Web through AOL Explorer.

Anyone with a computer and an Internet connection can use the AIM service—completely free. However, you are responsible for purchasing a connection to the Internet, any associated telephone charges, or any premium services that you choose. You can download the AIM software by visiting www.aim.com, then clicking either the Install Now button or the link for the correct version for the operating system on your computer.

There is also a service called AIM Express, which is a convenient, travel version of the AIM service. This application lets you view your Buddy List window and send instant messages from any computer with a Web browser and an Internet connection without having to download the software. Just like the AIM service, the AIM Express service is also free.

Google Talk: Google Talk (GTalk, www.google.com/talk; see Figure 22.3) is search-engine giant Google's approach to instant communication. Google Talk can either be downloaded to your computer or launched through a browser.

FIGURE 22.3 Google Talk

Google Talk allows you to communicate for free with your friends, family, and colleagues—anyone with whom you want to chat online. Google Talk features include instant messaging, which—like AIM—allows you to chat with all of your Google Talk and Gmail contacts in real time, free PC-to-PC voice calls, which lets you talk for free to anyone else who is online and is equipped with the Google Talk client. GTalk allows you to send and receive voicemails and provides unlimited file transfers that lets you send and receive files to your contacts without file size or bandwidth restrictions. Even if the person you are calling isn't available, you can leave a voicemail. Gmail notifications on your desktop appear when you're signed into Google Talk, so you'll be notified of new messages in your Gmail inbox.

The Google Talk gadget does not require any download; you can start chatting immediately from any computer. You can also create a group chat and invite multiple people to join an online conversation. Google Talk also has media previews that allow users to cut and paste video and slideshow URLs from sites like YouTube, Google Video, Picasa Web Albums, and Flickr into your chats, and view them in your chat window.

You can also add the Google Talk gadget to your iGoogle homepage to put chat alongside other useful and entertaining gadgets, and you can add Google Talk to your own web page; just cut and paste the code into your own web page or blog to embed the Google Talk gadget.

iChat: With Apple's iChat (www.apple.com/macosx/features/ichat.html; see Figure 22.4) feature, you can chat from anywhere—as long as you are

FIGURE 22.4 iChat

using a Mac. iChat offers crystal-clear audio quality that delivers the clearest possible sound during audio chats. Apple's wideband codec AAC-LD—which samples a full range of vocal frequencies—sounds great with any voice. iChat also offers text messaging that includes Tabbed Chats, Multiple Logins, Invisibility, Animated Buddy Icons, SMS Forwarding, Custom Buddy List Order, File Transfer Manager, and Space-Efficient Views.

The iChat Tabbed Window AIM Icon works with AIM, the largest instant messaging community in the United States (see the earlier description). You and the people with whom you chat can be either AIM or Mac users. You're able to text, audio, and video chat whether your buddies use a Mac or a PC. Sign in with your AIM account, and all your buddies appear in your iChat buddy list.

New video backdrops built into iChat can make it look like users are chatting from the Eiffel Tower, under the sea, or the surface of the moon. They can also create their own custom backdrops by dragging a picture or video from iPhoto or the Finder into the video effects window. Backdrops even show up on the screens of buddies who don't have the Mac operating system.

Users can also transform video chats using new Photo Booth effects, with which they can add a special twist to a chat with the comic book effect. They can alternatively soften images with glow, or just choose any effect that changes the video instantly.

With iChat, you don't have to wait for a darkened room and a projector to present vacation photos or Keynote slides. iChat's Theater Now application lets you do it all remotely. Simply put on a photo slideshow, click through a Keynote presentation, or play a full-screen movie—accompanied by a video feed of you hosting—while your audience watches. In fact, you can show any file on your system that works with Quick Look (see Figure 22.5), which is Apple's file contents preview window.

Thanks to iChat screen sharing, you and your buddy can also observe and control a single desktop—a feature that makes it a cinch to collaborate with a colleague, browse the Web with a friend, or pick plane seats with a family member. Share your own desktop—or your buddy's—and you both have control at all times. And iChat automatically initiates an audio chat when you start a screen-sharing session, so you can talk things through while you're at it.

iChat also allows users to save audio and video chats for posterity with iChat recording. Before recording starts, iChat notifies buddies and asks for their permission to record. When the chat is done, iChat stores the audio chats as AAC files and video chats as MPEG-4 files—so that users can play them in iTunes or QuickTime. Share them with friends, family, and colleagues, or sync them to your iPod and play on the go.

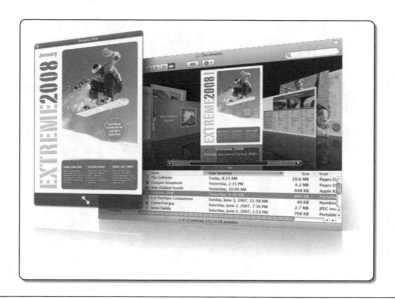

FIGURE 22.5 QuickLook

Jott: Jott (Jott.com; see Figure 22.6) is a web application that makes sure that users stay on top of everything in their lives. With a simple phone call to 866-JOTT-123, you can capture notes, set reminders and calendar appointments, and stay in touch with friends, family, and colleagues while you interact with your favorite web sites and services—all with the sound of your voice!

Jott's technology joins cell phone voice and text messaging, your blog, Twitter, groups, and e-mail. By entering the Jott toll-free number into your speed dial, you can access all of Jott's capabilities with the touch of a single button. Jott works on any phone—cell or landline—independent of carrier, and requires no downloads or training. While your cell phone might be your first choice, you're not limited to just one telephone. You can Jott from your house or office phone, too. Just add those numbers to your Jott account.

Jott Links are essentially web pages that can receive HTTP posts and write out a text response. They're called Jott Links because you use them to "link" Jott messages with other services, such as blogging and social networking sites—including Twitter and Zillo. At the time this chapter was written, Jott was compatible with Jaiku, Blogger, TypePad, WordPress, Twitter, Yahoo!, Zillo, LiveJournal, Tumblr, Amazon, 30Boxes, and Sandy.

Jott uses your mobile phone to convert your voice into text messages that are sent directly to e-mail, cell text messages, blogging sites, groups, and even content management–enhanced web sites that are driven by such platforms as WordPress and Joomla. In its first 12 months, Jott had already

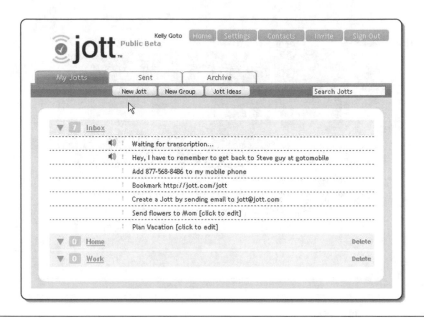

FIGURE 22.6   Jott

sent more than a million messages for business travelers reporting expenses, as well as personal applications such as status messages to coaches, parents, students, and teachers.

Jott can be used as an alarm or reminder of timed events. After calling in to Jott's toll-free telephone number, you will be asked whom you would like to Jott. You say "Reminder," list the day and the time that you would like to receive your reminder, and then leave your reminder message. When you hang up, your reminder will be sent 15 minutes before the scheduled event to your cell phone, e-mail, blog, or Twitter account. You can also use the service to send your translated messages to coworkers, friends, or family members with instructions, updates, or action items. Just call Jott and record the name of the person or people whom you want to receive your text message—and Jott instantly translates and sends your instructions to the appropriate contacts. You can even send these to your cell phone or e-mail as well.

Teams or groups of coworkers, friends, or family use Jott's services to alert one another of impending or recent events. When that new baby is born, a meeting is about to begin, or there's a change in travel plans, Jott will send the same message to any group you create. You can even just send it to your Yahoo! Groups using Jott Links (www.jott.com).

Jott also allows you to keep track of your expenses in a straightforward and organized manner. Just call the 1-800 number, and you can message your costs as they happen. With simple rules set up in your e-mail, Jott expenses can go from your voice message directly into your expense or accounting folder in your e-mail. Do you bill by the hour? Just phone Jott at the end of each session, and your billable hours—along with any special message—will be delivered to your e-mail's Hours folder for easy accounting.

Do you think that blogging is a time-consuming chore? Not anymore! You can use Jott to record your voice message and have it instantly converted and added to your personal blog. You can also send a group e-mail or text message to all of your contacts, and let them know that you have a new blog waiting for them.

Do you sometimes just want to inform someone of important news immediately, without having to engage in a half-hour conversation about what she did the night before? Jott her! This way your message goes directly to her cell phone without having to keep saying, "I gotta go!"

Jott is especially convenient when you're driving. In more and more states, it is illegal to text message and drive. Jott provides a reliable, safer alternative to texting while behind the wheel. Because 40 percent of cell phone usage occurs while driving your car, Jott is a more prudent way to record information than, for example, scribbling information on a piece of scratch paper or fast food napkin. Jott is voice-activated, so you will no longer have to try to write notes, reminders, telephone numbers, or driving directions on scraps of paper. Just say it, and display it.

One-to-Many

Twitter: The most popular one-to-many communication tool today by far is Twitter (www.Twitter.com), the microblogging platform. Twitter is a micro-blogging and social networking service that allows its users to send and receive brief (140 characters or less) text-based, micropost instant messages that are called tweets. These text messages are displayed on the user's technology of choice—be it a text messaging cell phone, web site, PDA, Twitter web site, RSS (see Chapter 18, RSS—Really Simple Syndication Made Simple), SMS,[1] e-mail, or an application such as Facebook,

---

1. Wikipedia defines SMS as "Short Message Service (SMS) is a communications protocol allowing the interchange of short text messages between mobile telephone devices. **SMS** text messaging is the most widely used data application on the planet, with 2.4 billion active users, or 74 percent of all mobile phone subscribers sending and receiving text messages on their phones. The **SMS** technology has facilitated the development and growth of text messaging. The connection between the phenomenon of text messaging and the underlying technology is so great that in parts of the world the term 'SMS' is used as a synonym for a text message or the act of sending a text message, even when a different protocol is being used."

Twitterrific, or web page aggregator (see Chapter 18, RSS—Really Simple Syndication Made Simple). These messages are also delivered to anyone who has signed up and been accepted to follow your messages, and the same is true of any Tweets that you have requested and been approved to follow.

For a complete discussion on Twitter, please see Chapter 14, Thumbs Up for Microblogging.

Yahoo! Messenger: Friends are only an instant away on Yahoo! Messenger (www.messenger.yahoo.com; see Figure 22.7). With this tool, you can send text messages in real time to your friends, family, and colleagues on Yahoo! or Windows Live Messenger; decide who sees you online with stealth settings; swap photos and monster files (up to 2 GB) in real-time; enjoy voice calls and webcam video; join a chat room to meet new friends while you discuss your favorite topics; share photos from your desktop or Flickr, then discuss them over IM while you and a friend view them together; make a voice call to another Yahoo! Messenger user for free (microphone and speakers or a headset are required); or even call others on their regular or mobile phones from Messenger for as low as one cent a minute (a Phone Out account is required). Yahoo! Messenger provides a Phone In feature to get a phone number for Messenger. This application provides a new phone number that allows you to receive calls in Yahoo! Messenger (Phone In account required). Yahoo! Messenger also offers SMS, or text messaging,

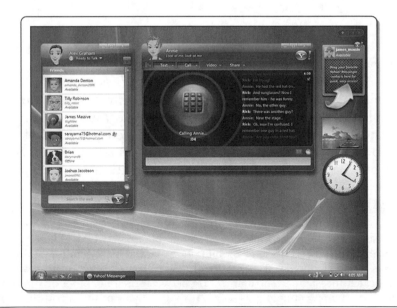

FIGURE 22.7 *Yahoo! Messenger*

wherein you can send text messages from Messenger to your colleague's mobile phones for free. You can also plug in your webcam to share live video on Yahoo! Messenger.

Another feature of this service is IM Conferencing, with which you can Instant Message with many colleagues at once and use voice capabilities where available. You can IM with colleagues on other networks—such as Windows Live Messenger, Reuters Messaging, and Lotus Sametime—as well. The File Transfer option lets users instantly send files (with a 2 GB limit) to a friend while you IM. There is also IM Forwarding to Mobile that sends IMs to your phone as text messages when you sign out of Messenger. You can use Yahoo!'s Contact Search Bar to quickly find a contact to IM, call, SMS, or more. Yahoo! Search lets users begin a web search directly from their Yahoo! Messenger window. The Yahoo! Address Book provides the chance to view and edit any Yahoo! Address Book information for contacts right from Messenger. There is also a Stealth/Privacy Settings, with which users can make themselves appear online to some friends and offline to others.

Yahoo! Mail alerts notify users when a new Yahoo! Mail message arrives. The included voicemail service allows colleagues to call you on Yahoo! Messenger and leave a voicemail if a user is unavailable. This also includes Message Archiving, which maintains a private archive of IM conversations. There's also Tabbed IM Windows that reduce desktop clutter by organizing multiple conversations into a single window.

Yahoo! Messenger gives you Buzz Alert to get your colleague's attention with a click of the Buzz button. There are also Yahoo! Updates that get you real-time alerts in Yahoo! Messenger about what your colleagues are posting online, reviewing, and generally buzzing about. You can also get their plug-ins that add content, services, and games to Messenger that you can enjoy on your own, or with colleagues while you IM.

Then there's Yahoo! Messenger Audibles, a service that sends an animated, talking character to a friend to liven up your IM conversation. And, of course, emoticons to express your feelings with animated, smiling faces. There are also avatars, which represent your likeness with a stylized, graphic image where you can choose the hair, clothing, and more. You can display images to represent yourself to your friends.

Yahoo! Messenger even has different skins that allow you to give your IM world a new look. It also includes IMVironments to liven things up with interactive, themed backgrounds in the IM window. Yahoo! Games allows you to play a game of pool, backgammon, checkers, and more with a friend while you IM. Custom Status Messages will tell your friends what you're doing, seeing, or feeling by customizing your online status message. There are even Custom Ringtones that you can assign to different callers, or upload your own audio files to use. And if all of that wasn't enough, Yahoo! Messenger also has Customizable Fonts and Colors that allow you to IM with a font, color, and style that suits your personality. Sound Effects and Soundtrack (during voice calls) can throw a sound effect in while you're on a call or upload a music file to play as a soundtrack in the background. Wow!

Microsoft Live Messenger: Much like AIM, GTalk, iChat, and Yahoo! Messenger, Microsoft Live Messenger (www.WindowsLive.com; see Figure 22.8) allows you to connect and share with contacts—anywhere. This service provides a Hotmail account, which allows you to stay connected anywhere with your Web e-mail account; access to your multiple e-mail accounts in one place; a Messenger tool that lets you connect, share, and make your conversations count; and a Toolbar that makes it easy to access Windows Live services from any Web page.

Microsoft Live Messenger Share provides SkyDrive, which is a password-protected online file storage feature; Spaces, the best place to share your world online; Photo Gallery, where you can get creative and share your photos and videos; Writer, where you can easily publish pictures, videos,

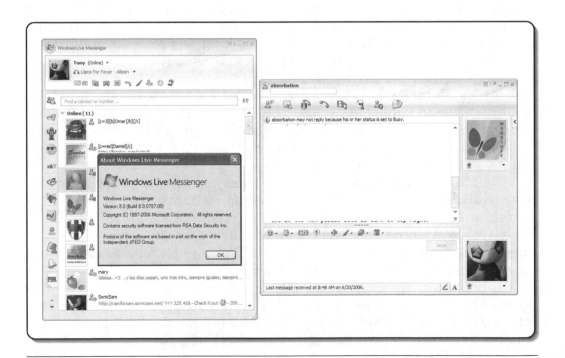

FIGURE 22.8 Microsoft Live Messenger

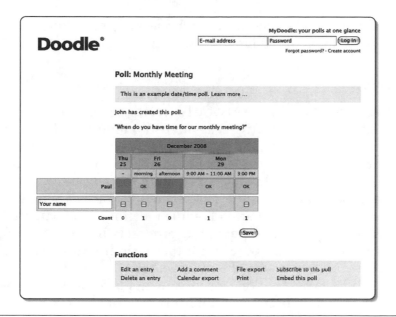

FIGURE 22.9   Doodle

and other rich content to your blog; and Events, where you can plan your next meeting or gathering, send invitations, and share photos.

Doodle: Doodle (www.doodle.com; see Figure 22.9) is an online coordination tool that makes it easy to find a date and time for a group event by helping to determine common availabilities among all parties involved. The basic services are free, requires neither registration nor software installation, and allows users to schedule events like board meetings, business lunches, conference calls, family reunions, or movie nights. Its name is short and simple to remember, and while Doodle is not a drawing service, it indeed makes scheduling events so simple that it becomes a casual task. This service is particularly easy to use, and even passes the "grandma test"—so easy your grandma can do it! That's the main reason why the user base of several million per month is still growing rapidly.

As the pioneer in online scheduling, Doodle has set standards concerning the ways people communicate when they plan a meeting: transparent, democratic—and simple. A tabular display shows the time slots and the availabilities of all participants. The meeting organizer can immediately spot a suitable time as soon as all participants have casted their votes.

Doodle also offers a one-click reminder feature for the organizer to further accelerate the voting process. The tool integrates into all major calendar systems like Outlook, Google Calendar, or Notes. Doodle also features a mobile-ready version, an iPhone app, scheduling across time zones, and is available in 30 languages.

Many-to-Many

GoToMeeting: GoToMeeting (www.GoToMeeting.com; see Figure 22.10) is for any business a cost-effective, easy-to-use online meeting solution that vastly improves productivity and sales. This service is to use on the fly or for scheduled presentations; to perform live demos; or to collaborate on documents in real time. GoToMeeting's web conferencing tool allows users to meet online rather than in a conference room. It's the easiest and most cost-effective way to organize and attend online meetings. The patented technology enables colleagues, customers, and prospects to view any application running on your PC in real time. With the flexibility to meet in person or online, you'll be able to do more and travel less.

Clients and coworkers don't need your application to view your files; even files created with specialized applications, such as CAD drawings, are

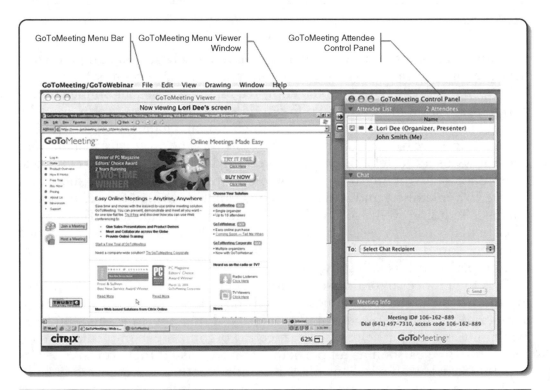

FIGURE 22.10 GoToMeeting

viewable. Just use the GoToMeeting icon in your system tray, an e-mail, or an instant message for logins or setups. It takes about two minutes to set up, and a few more seconds to start a meeting. That's it! With GoToMeeting, you can meet as often as you want, for as long as you want—for one low rate.

GoToMeeting allows users to turn calls into instant online meetings, and also has a cost-effective online meeting product called All You Can Meet—which allows users to host unlimited meetings for an unlimited duration with up to 15 attendees per meeting—all for one flat fee! GoTo-Meeting is also a secure online meeting tool. Industry-standard security features ensure that your confidential meeting information remains private. If you need to reach a larger audience or want additional marketing tools such as polls, surveys, and reports, GoToWebinar offers unlimited webinars with up to 1,000 attendees, plus the collaborative online meeting capabilities.

WebEx: WebEx (www.WebEx.com; see Figure 22.11) provides the benefit of on-demand web meetings with no significant up-front costs, no servers to maintain, and no software to install or support. With just a web browser and a telephone, you can use WebEx. Users can integrate WebEx into daily business workflow, and use online meetings to get together with anyone at any time. Coworkers and associates can demonstrate products and services, share presentations in any format, and resolve open issues in real time with secure and reliable technology. WebEx allows the impact of live events by holding large, scalable online proceedings—such as all-hands meetings,

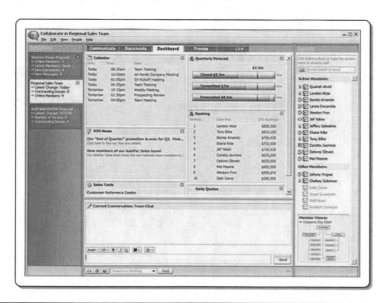

FIGURE 22.11   WebEx

shareholder presentations, and webinars—with interactive and dynamic multimedia presentations.

Professionals can use WebEx to deliver interactive world-class training and reach more people than they ever thought possible by offering on-demand and live, online classrooms. Technical issues are resolved more quickly and productivity is increased while you reduce support costs; increase client satisfaction with both unattended and attended remote support; shorten the sales cycle by connecting with anyone, anywhere with dynamic online sales presentations; and close deals faster.

On-demand web conferencing has become the preferred communication medium for businesses today. By combining the ease of audioconferencing with the interactivity of videoconferencing directly from your desktop, you create a truly personalized interactive experience.

Adobe Connect: Adobe Connect (www.adobe.com/products/acrobat connectpro; see Figure 22.12) is the next best thing to an in-person meeting. With Adobe Acrobat Connect Pro software, you can provide instant access to engaging, collaborative meetings with just a web browser and the Adobe Flash Player runtime. You can enable attendees to jump into always-available personal meeting rooms with no scheduling or registration required. They're able to share screens, use a whiteboard, chat, videoconference, and enjoy real-time interactions without the hassle of travel. They can control meetings and related assets with robust management and reporting tools, and protect

FIGURE 22.12 Adobe Connect

sensitive business data and meeting content with tight security and strong access controls.

With the Adobe Acrobat Connect Pro software, marketing and sales departments can increase leads, boost response rates, and close deals faster through high-impact web conferencing. Forget specialized software; all it takes is a web browser and the Adobe Flash Player runtime. You can boost audience attendance and participation, generate more qualified leads at a lower cost, and save time with expert assistance.

Adobe Connect requires no plug-in downloads, which eliminates technical barriers to instant access. Even the best online seminar is useless if your audience can't participate. You can reach your participants right away and eradicate any obstacles to attendance with Acrobat Connect Pro. Because the tool is based on Adobe Flash Player—which is already installed on more than 98 percent of Internet-connected desktops worldwide—you essentially have everything you need already. This means your audience can join Acrobat Connect Pro seminars and access Adobe Presenter presentations just by clicking a URL—without cumbersome software downloads.

Adobe Connect allows you to play videos of corporate executives during Acrobat Connect Pro seminars, to communicate high-level messages, and to use customer testimonial videos to enhance credibility. You can share high-impact multimedia content, including streaming audio, video, and software simulations, to make your seminars and on-demand presentations both compelling and persuasive, and can easily conduct breakout discussions for increased interactivity and participation. You can even record web seminars—including those using synchronized audio—from either Internet (VoIP) or telephone audioconferencing, and make them available to people who can't attend. You just use simple mark-in and mark-out tools to edit out unwanted sections, and make recordings available for download on a web site or for offline viewing and distribution.

Adobe Connect also allows users to host lively and informative web seminars to engage prospects and respond to questions in real time. Take advantage of multiperson video in Acrobat Connect Pro, your choice of Internet (VoIP) or telephone audioconferencing, and unparalleled support for rich multimedia content to deliver web seminars that are the next best thing to being there. You can increase the success of your e-mail and online ad campaigns by driving prospects to engaging, narrated Adobe Presenter presentations instead of simply linking to static landing pages. Get feedback instantly through embedded surveys. Respondents simply click an embedded URL to view a multimedia presentation, fully branded with your corporate logo and colors. You can also automate attendee registration, notifications, reminders, and postevent thank-you e-mails. Customize registration pages and the look and feel of your online seminar rooms to reflect your corporate branding.

Within your meeting, you can create multiple breakout rooms—each with its own private VoIP or telephone conference call. Use a default template or create custom layouts for each meeting room, and provide specific content appropriate for each breakout. Hosts can monitor all breakouts, move between them, and broadcast messages to all participants across room boundaries. When it's time to bring the groups back together, hosts can review breakout room content with the entire group in the main room.

Within a meeting or virtual classroom, hosts can see a list of invitees and their presence through your corporate instant messaging server. Hosts can initiate chat conversations with IM users from directly within Acrobat Connect Pro. Acrobat Connect Pro and Adobe Presenter software provide an intuitive Web-based interface that enables users to customize the entire web conferencing experience to reflect their organization's brand. Color schemes and logos can be easily applied to login screens, web applications, live meeting rooms, presentations, and training modules.

The ROI of Social Media

Generating Brand Awareness and Lead Nurturing through Comprehensive, Company-Wide Training and Programs Using Facebook, LinkedIn, Blogging, Twitter, and YouTube

Background

The largest family-owned-and-operated real estate company in the Northeast, a private company with 67 offices and 2,000 agents, wanted to implement social media into their marketing efforts to help agents and increase corporate sales. Owner asked us to determine which tools were most appropriate for their business and to educate staff on social media concepts, strategy, and tactics.

Strategy

Assessment and Recommendations: We started by monitoring and evaluating competitor activities and best practices in the marketplace. We presented data on what was happening in real estate in the Northeast, as well as nationally, what the best tools are to use, and a preliminary strategy for the company.

Our research showed that very few, if any, RE firms in the Northeast had integrated, systematic programs in place companywide, which provided excellent opportunities for the company to make a mark and stand out from their competition.

Implementation

Executive Education: Presented social media primer to top leadership (120 managers) at monthly sales meeting.

After manager buy-in, we developed Social Media Guidelines, which spell out the company's expectations for agent behavior online.

Social Media Primer Webinars: Delivered webinars for all sales agents to educate them on the value of social media and to walk them through the guidelines.

Train the Trainer Program: Recruited Social Media Consultants from each office (67 people). Delivered Train the Trainer Program in two locations (CT and MA) to train them and support them in training others. Topics: Facebook, Twitter, YouTube, LinkedIn, and blogging with specific industry tie-ins and how to [manage] information.

Agent Blog Program: Developed turnkey WordPress MU back-end system that allows agents to set up a blog with the "click of a button" on their intranet site. With our Wordpress template, the agent's data is pulled in with pre-loaded blogroll and SEO tools. The blog is set up within minutes.

Agent Social Community: Set up a private social media resource center community on Ning to post educational information and field questions, provide support to agents companywide.

Corporate Blog Program: Redesigned, optimized, and created content strategy for company.

Social Networks: Set up Twitter, Facebook Business Page, YouTube Channel, and audio feeds from Blog. Trained internal staff to manage them.

Opportunity

The opportunity is to show the company's expertise and knowledge in the Real Estate marketplace and provide multiple communication channels via posts, photos, audio, and video, for agents to interact with prospects and clients.

Conclusion

Metrics to Date:

Program started: July 2009, completion: April 2010

To date, there are over 1,000 Facebook fans on company business pages; 200 agent fan pages; 1,100 sales agents have profiles on LinkedIn; [and] more than 200 have a feed from the company blog on their profile.

(continued)

(*continued*)

More than 60 agents have set up blogs and received blog training as part of the Agent blog program. Second wave to be implemented in April 2010.

Since the program's inception, agents and corporate officers report the company's social media strategy along with their presences in the social sphere, have made a significant impact on netting new customers, and increasing close rates.

Catherine Weber
Web site: www.webermediapartners.com
Blog: www.impressionsthroughmedia.com

Expert Insight

John Pollard, CEO and founder, Jott, www.Jott.com

John Pollard

[Jott] is an alternative way of accessing the Internet. In some ways, the cellular infrastructure is completely bypassing the need to build out landline infrastructure. Landline infrastructure—you know, the back haul that was done in the developed world for so many years—has not really been done in the developing world, in some places. It has really been remarkable, and it's a great thing in general. . . .

You know I am a firm believer that there are going to be different ways of accessing the Internet, and that in some populations, it's going to be primarily mobile-driven. In [certain] economies and geographical areas, it's going to be a healthy mix of a desktop and a mobile phone. But I am a big believer in mobile, and I think sometimes things are over-hyped and people overestimate what's going to happen to one degree or another. However, we think it is here to stay. I know one of the essential things behind Jott is that people look at their mobile phones—whether it is an iPhone or it is just your humble average phone—as a trusted appliance, this thing that they have with them all the time. . . .

Let me try to put it this way. I sort of ask questions, which are, "Would you hire the following kind of person—someone who always picked up the phone for you? Took dictation? Sent e-mail and text messages for you (hands-free so you did not have to take your eyes off the road)? Posted messages or calendar items to Google Calendar just using your voice? Would help you retrieve information from your favorite sources (like the *New York Times* or Tech-Crunch, or what have you) with just their voice? Would never sleep, does not complain, does not whine, and does some of this for free?"

Would you hire this person? . . . And, of course, the answer is yes!

Really . . . Jott is a mobile-productivity tool that works on any phone. It does not require any downloads or a particular carrier or contract; it does not require anything but what you already have. You simply call a number—1-866-J-O-T-T-123—and you will be asked a simple question which has many answers—"Who do you want to Jott?" And if you say, "Yourself" or if you say "Notes," you will hear a beep and you can say something and hang up; and we will take your voice and convert it to text automatically and then give it to you on your desktop.

And it is really as simple as that. You call a number, you say something, and you hang up. Everybody in the world knows how to make a phone call; and so everybody in the world already knows how to use Jott automatically. The beauty of [this service] is that that simple sequence of things allows you to capture thoughts, be more organized, and communicate with people hands-free. So in response to the question, "Who do you want to Jott?" I could say, "Lon Safko," and you would hear "beep," and then I could record a message to you and Jott would deliver that text message and an e-mail message to Lon Safko. So, if I was in traffic and I really needed to contact you, I could Jott you. It is really quite remarkable that something so simple with such an easy-to-use user experience does so many things and is so powerful. I think we have really struck a nerve. . . .

What we decided at the beginning of the company was that what mattered to people most was simplicity and quality. It would not make any sense to build a product where what came out the other end was gobbledygook. We really needed . . . a super-simple front-end that works the way people work, and then deliver quality results in the back-end. The reality is that people are using Jott in real places. They use it in their car, and they use it between meetings. They use it in places where there is background noise; they speak normally, they say names, and they speak the way you and I typically speak. They have some "umm's" and "ahh's" and they repeat themselves. . . .

To have the speech-recognition engine all by itself—to take out the noise, the pops, and the poor cellular activity issues and turn out 100 percent accurate transcription . . . really is quite impossible. So what we have done is to take the voice and run it through a couple of different speech recognition engines. We have gotten very, very smart about this and . . . we sort of preprocess as much as we can. We are automating so much more than we used to, and many messages are completely automated. As that ratio improves, so will our business.

(continued)

(*continued*)

And then we have people, frankly, on the other side of the planet (thank God for the speed of light!) that clean up pieces of this when necessary. You know, it is very much like people who work in call centers overseas, who process information; or people who are in the medical transcription business where they write up doctor's notes and things like that. It is very highly organized; it's highly, highly secure; it's very controlled.

And it is a real challenge to get it right for a lot of reasons. . . . One: because a bunch of people are spread all over the place, and two: we have to keep the quality high, and three: we need to do it at a price that will translate, or at a cost that will translate to an affordable product here in the United States. That is not easy to do; and I am happy to say that because that is not easy to do, it makes it very difficult to replicate what we have done. You know, speech recognition is going to get better and better and better, and I am excited about the prospects there, because every time there is an evolution in the state of the art there, we benefit from them and so do our customers. . . .

Yeah, it is interesting. We have decided that we are not a real-time business. We don't need to be real-time, because the case [around which] we are modeling in most of our design is the person sitting in a car who really needs to capture that thought, that action-item or that idea that they had, or that promise that they made to a customer. They need to seize it, so that they do not forget it. And it is not critical that they get it immediately, or real time. What's important is that it is safe and secure and captured. Therefore, it can be a couple of minutes delayed; no problem. So that's what we model that on, and we usually achieve that pretty well. You know, there are times when we have super-fast turnaround times and sometimes when it takes a little bit longer, but overall we get the turnaround done very quickly. . . .

And we designed it so that it could be useful for anybody. We really believe it, and we have this mantra inside the company—you know, in our little office here—that says, "Everybody should have Jott One-Two-Three on speed dial." And we mean that; whether you are a casual user who uses it a couple times a week, or if you are a super hard-core Jotter who uses it many times a day. It is almost like insurance. It's almost like having AAA on your phone. It's just there; you should have it there.

It is so simple that it scales well; from the grandmother who is trying to text to her grandchildren . . . (laughter) to the road warrior who is reeling off expenses as he gets out of his cab. And it is broad-set, [which doesn't] mean that we are sloppy, or that we're not targeting people. However, I think everybody has too much going on these days. Everybody could use a little bit of help, and happily Jott morphs itself to whatever need you might have. If you need casual usage of it, great. If you need really heavy usage of it, we also scale for that. So it works out well for everyone.

To listen to or read the entire Executive Conversation with John Pollard, go to www.theSocialMediaBible.com.

Commandments

1. **Thou shalt explore.**

    This is the only commandment for this chapter, because it is so incredibly important. Go look at a few of the applications discussed in this book. Read some of their online literature, download their trials, and try them out to see if they are right for you and your business. Decide which ones work the best for your purposes, and really hone in on your use of those applications. Knowledge really is power; and we are in the midst of the Age of Knowledge. For the first time in human history, nearly the entire accumulation of human knowledge is at our fingertips and accessible in an instant. The more you know about social media and its tools, the more capabilities you will be able to access; the more you can reduce expenses; and the more competitive you can be. And isn't that what everyone is looking to do for our businesses: Reduce expenses and increase revenue?

Conclusion

As with all of the other chapters, the advice is to go explore. A lot of great social media applications allow you to better communicate with your customers and prospects, which is really the essence of social media. And surprising as it may be, nearly every tool mentioned in *The Social Media Bible* is either free or almost free. Unless you investigate and try out the various services that you've read about here, you won't know what incredible tools are available to help grow your business, build your community, and develop trust within that community.

To hear all of the Expert Interviews, go to www.theSocialMediaBible .com.

Readings and Resources

Abdulezer, Loren, Susan Abdulezer, Howard Dammond, and Niklas Zennstrom. *Skype For Dummies.* (Hoboken, NJ: John Wiley & Sons, Inc.)

Camarillo, Gonzalo, and Miguel-Angel García-Martín. *The 3G IP Multimedia Subsystem (IMS): Merging the Internet and the Cellular Worlds.* (Hoboken, NJ: John Wiley & Sons, Inc.)

Dreamtech Software Team. *Instant Messaging Systems: Cracking the Code.* (Hoboken, NJ: John Wiley & Sons, Inc.)

Kao, Robert, and Dante Sarigumba. *BlackBerry Storm For Dummies*. (Hoboken, NJ: John Wiley & Sons, Inc.)

Smith, Bud E., and Chris Dannen. *Google Voice For Dummies*. (Hoboken, NJ: John Wiley & Sons, Inc.)

Stevenson, Nancy. *WebEx Web Meetings For Dummies*. (Hoboken, NJ: John Wiley & Sons, Inc.)

Downloads

For your free downloads associated with *The Social Media Bible,* go to www
.theSocialMediaBible.com, and enter your ISBN number located on the back
of the book above the bar code. Be sure to enter the dashes.

Credits

The ROI of Social Media was provided by:

Catherine Weber, www.webermediapartners.com

Expert Insight was provided by:

John Pollard, CEO and founder, Jott, www.jott.com

Technical edits were provided by:

Zen Benefiel, possibilities coagulator, Be The Dream, LLC, www.BeTheDream.com

PART II

TOOLS

In the first section of this book we introduced you to hundreds of different concepts and different tools; everything from microblogging and social networks to gaming and virtual worlds, to the old standards of e-mail, SEO, and SEM. The purpose of Part II is to show you where to go to find the companies providing those tools.

The most difficult part about updating this book was who to include and who to leave out. As you can already see, it's a big book as it is. You will find included in this section, a guide to the major players in each of 15 major categories of social media platforms.

I realize there are many good tools and companies that were not included in this section. I had addressed more than 100 of these top companies and had to draw the line somewhere. If there is a particular tool that you have been using that is worthy of mention, please contact me and let me know. I will be happy to include it in the next edition and on our web site www.theSocialMediaBible.com or www.TSMB2.com.

What's Included

In each of the next 15 chapters, I will first describe the category so you will better understand the need or niche the following companies are filling. Then for each company included I will list the Company Name, URL, Location, Founded, Revenue Model, Fees, How It Can Be Used, What Other Applications It Works With, Who Uses It, Should You Use It, and Who Started It.

When we tried to interview many of the companies included in this guide, I was told that they were just too busy to comment. As a result much of the information has been gathered from their own web sites, from EDGAR, and from reporting agencies. Some of the information is changing quickly, especially after the economic downturn and now upswing. If specific and highly accurate information is required, I encourage you to contact the company directly to attain the most up-to-date information possible.

CHAPTER 23

Social Networks

Social networking is as old as humans have been around. Just as in nearly every other species, humans have an instinctual need to be with, communicate with, and share thoughts, ideas, and feelings about their daily lives. Only the tools in which we communicate have changed over the millennium.

The earliest recorded human conversation goes back to before history itself (prehistoric), even before the spoken and the written word. We see evidence of this early communication in cave paintings on the walls and ceilings that shared the most important stories of their times; the hunt with their tribe or clan. These earliest European cave paintings date back some 32,000 years. The oldest of these paleolithic cave paintings were found in Lascaux, France.

As time passed, technology improved. Over the last 6,000 years, we used drums to communicate with other like-minded people, then it was bells in towers, and the written word in books, newspapers, and letters. Over our grandparents' lifetimes we have seen the invention of the telegraph, telephone, radio, television, mobile phones, Internet, and now social media. The basic need to connect hasn't changed in thousands of years, only the technology we use to make that connection.

The following companies are carrying on this 40 millennium tradition with new and innovative ways for us to connect, gather, share, and document those conversations. As you read each profile, keep in mind that its features and functions may or may not be right for your particular business. Use the **Tool Scorecard** at the end of the chapter to help you determine which of these tools qualify for further consideration when you begin creating your social media strategy in Part III of the book.

Bebo

Company Name:	Bebo Inc.
URL:	www.bebo.com
Location:	San Francisco, California, United States
Founded:	2005
Revenue Model:	Advertising

What Is It?

Bebo is a mediacentric online social networking application. Bebo users create profiles and then interact with other users through actions such as sharing photographs and videos, communicating through messages and blog posts, and taking polls and quizzes. Bebo also allows for the creation of Groups, which are collections of users who share a common interest or characteristic. The content on Bebo is not just driven by individual users; large media corporations and amateur artists alike use Bebo for marketing and networking purposes.

How Can It Be Used?

Bebo can be used as a social networking tool as well as an engaging marketing vehicle. With Bebo Music, artists and bands can create a profile to advertise directly to fans and sell their music online. With Bebo Authors, authors of a book can upload select chapters to receive feedback and give potential readers the ability to preview the author's work. Bebo can also be used to upload and share videos—anything from a movie trailer to a clip from an online comedy show.

What Other Applications Does It Work With?

Bebo integrates with several other applications to enhance the user experience. Through Bebo Music, users can include iTunes links alongside their albums or songs, making it easy for other users to purchase their music through the iTunes Store. Users can also showcase videos from YouTube and VideoEgg.

Who Uses It?

Consumers and producers of media both use Bebo. Miley Cyrus, Slipknot, and AC/DC are just some of the musical artists who are using Bebo Music to market directly to fans and interact with them. Authors such as Michael Largo, who wrote *Final Exits*, and Anastasia Goodstein, author of *Totally Wired*, use Bebo Authors to reach new audiences. Popular media companies like Comedy Central, ESPN, and CBS provide content for Bebo users and gain publicity in the process.

Should You Use It?

You should use Bebo if you are looking for an online social networking application that places an emphasis on engaging media that is aimed toward consumers. With Bebo you can go beyond just creating an online profile that other users will see; you can actually upload content that customers will access directly, providing you with the potential for valuable feedback and advertising exposure.

Who Started It?

Michael and Xochi Birch started Bebo in January 2005. In July 2005, Bebo underwent a complete relaunch. The two of them, along with Paul Birch, also founded BirthdayAlarm.com. On March 13, 2008, AOL purchased Bebo for approximately $850 million.

Facebook

Company Name:	Facebook
URL:	www.facebook.com
Location:	Palo Alto, California, and New York, New York, United States; Dublin (headquarters for Europe, Middle East, and Africa), Seoul, South Korea (Asia headquarters)
Founded:	2004
Employees:	500+
Revenue Model:	Advertising, banner ads
Fees:	Free

What Is It?

Facebook provides a platform for users to quickly connect with friends, family, coworkers, and acquaintances in various network groups. Facebook promotes communication within various social networks via a customizable user interface and a variety of compatible applications to further personalize the experience. Depending on the setup, users are notified when someone in their network updates their page or status. Users create their pages based on their personal preferences; add others to their network categories; and share events, pictures, videos, or experiences.

How Can It Be Used?

Facebook can be used in business environments for networking, locating business leads, as a method of intercompany communication, as a platform to organize and track events, and as a medium to provide updates between organizations and departments. Due to its popularity, Facebook could be used to promote a new product, service, or performer by word of mouth through "friends" within a social network. In academic environments, Facebook can be used to promote or enhance course communication, organize school functions, and as a platform to organize and track intramural and extracurricular events.

What Other Applications Does It Work With?

Facebook works with numerous applications: Owned, Lil Green Patch, YouTube, Poked, Cheers, Bumper Stickers, Top Friends, Karma, Wall, Super Wall, a variety of prime-time media applications, iPhone, Chat, Translations, Twitter, Causes, Graffiti, Windows Interactive, Trip Advisor and others. A unique feature of Facebook is that it enables developers to create their own applications, which provides an ever-growing list of applications to use with it.

Who Uses It?

Facebook started as a networking tool to meet others and learn about communities and organizations on college campuses. Its popularity with the high school crowd promoted the impression that Facebook is primarily used as a communication tool between friends. However, recent data shows Facebook is increasing in popularity for users over the age of 30. Many in this demographic utilize the add-ons as a means of expressing their social and political affiliations, for organizing and tracking events, and as a purchasing/advertising tool, in addition to networking.

Should You Use It?

If you are looking for a quick and convenient way to update a multitude of friends, family, coworkers, or acquaintances on what you are doing, Facebook would be an appropriate platform. Many users send invitations via Facebook for gatherings, meetings, movie premieres, and other events. Some businesses use Facebook advertising as a way to reach consumers in specific demographic populations.

Who Started It?

Mark Zuckerberg founded Facebook in 2004 in his sophomore year at Harvard as a social medium for students to get acquainted. In less than a month, more than half of the student body registered. Dustin Moskovitz, Eduardo Saverin and Chris Hughes joined to help promote the site.

Facebook's founders relocated to Palo Alto, California, in 2004, where they received an introduction to their first investor, Peter Thiel, cofounder of PayPal.

Fast Pitch!

Company Name:	Fast Pitch!
URL:	www.fastpitchnetworking.com
Location:	Sarasota, Florida
Founded:	2006
Revenue Model:	Subscriptions
Tagline:	Are you ready to make your pitch?

What Is It?

Unlike most networking sites that focus on the social aspect of networking, Fast Pitch! is geared toward the business professional. As one of the fastest growing social networks for professionals, Fast Pitch! has connected businesses across the world and provided a simple way for users to enhance their online presence using networking to market their business.

How Can It Be Used?

Fast Pitch! makes it easier for professionals to network using a profile displaying what they do, what they sell, and what makes their company unique. Profiles are interactive with the ability to imbed video, photos, blog, and podcasts. Users can network with other professionals based on industry, education, location, affiliations, and so on. "Virtual" trade shows let members connect via live chat or two-way streaming video.

Users can distribute content to others such as press releases, news, letters, event announcements, videos, classifieds, live chat feature, imbed videos, podcasts, e-mail campaigns. Fast Pitch!'s distribution system automatically targets the audience the user is trying to reach ensuring that their posts are viewed by the target audience.

Users can evaluate their success on Fast Pitch! by using account statistics to view the number of views on their profile, advertisements, press releases, and events.

What Other Applications Does It Work With?

Fast Pitch! has many of the same applications that a regular social networking site would have such as blog, video, live chat, podcasts, and so forth. The difference is that Fast Pitch! is geared toward marketing so the newsfeed, classifieds, press releases, and other applications are geared toward the marketing aspect of networking. Fast Pitch! also has applications on other sites like Facebook, Foursquare, Blogger, and Twitter that link the sites together.

Who Uses It?

Fast Pitch!'s main customers are small business professionals, sales and marketing executives, and business owners who are involved in promoting their businesses by networking and marketing. Fast Pitch! is also used as a tool for finding more career opportunities. Fast Pitch! prides itself on not being a "monster network" with 50 million users, many who are inactive. Instead, Fast Pitch! deletes inactive accounts so that the network is full of active members who can be contacted. Therefore, all users are active members.

Should You Use It?

If you are a business professional who is looking to enhance your web presence and to make connections with other professionals, then Fast Pitch! may be for you. Take advantage of the different applications Fast Pitch! has to offer to benefit your own professional needs.

Who Started It?

Before becoming CEO and founder of Fast Pitch! Bill Jula worked as director of Business and Development at Backsoft Corporation, was executive campus director of the University of South Florida, and a regional representative for the Tampa Bay Devil Rays. Using his interest in technology, as well as his background in sales and marketing, Bill developed Fast Pitch! It initially began as a networking event company that did "Speed Networking Events" that has since grown into Fast Pitch! The experience he had with the different people he connected with led to what Fast Pitch! is today.

Friendster

Company Name:	Friendster
URL:	www.friendster.com
Location:	San Francisco, California, United States
Founded:	2002
Employees:	57
Revenue Model:	Advertising

What Is It?

Friendster is an online social networking service that places an emphasis on the network between individuals. By utilizing a patented technology that is described as "a method and apparatus for calculating, displaying and acting upon relationships in a social network," Friendster acts as a virtual hub that can connect people based on commonalities. Friendster is also an entertainment and communication vehicle with features like Friendster Video, Reviews, and Forums (which are currently in the beta stage).

How Can It Be Used?

Friendster can be used to stay in contact with old relationships and create new ones. Like most social network services, users on Friendster are able to browse other profiles, send messages, and add new friends. Friendster allows users to search for people based on information that they have entered, such as current and past schools and colleges, which makes it easier to connect with old classmates and friends. Additionally, Friendster allows for a unique profile privacy setting, Two Degrees. When Two Degrees is selected, your full profile view is restricted to only your friends (One Degree away from you) and the friends in their network (Two Degrees away from you). This approach allows you to meet new people through the filter of your friends, while still keeping your profile private from the majority of users.

What Other Applications Does It Work With?

Friendster works with several online video applications. Inside Friendster Video, you can view videos from YouTube, Crackle, Metacafe, Break, Video Detective, and SingingFool. Additionally, you can put a Friendster Badge on a variety of web sites, including blogs and other social networking sites. Friendster also includes mini-applications that can be added to customize your profile.

Who Uses It?

Many different individuals use Friendster to network and meet new people. One major aspect of Friendster is the use of Official Profiles, which are the Friendster-sanctioned profiles of users like celebrities, athletes, and musicians. Other users can then become Fans of these Official Profiles. People with Official Profiles on Friendster include basketball player Allen Iverson, wrestler Chris Jericho, and musician Avril Lavigne. The largest segment of Friendster visitors are between the ages of 18 and 34, and most of the web site's traffic comes from the Philippines.

Should You Use It?

You should use Friendster if you are looking for a social network service that has a structured approach for meeting new people online. With Friendster, you are able to see what connects you to another user, whether that link is a common friend or a shared university. You should use Friendster if you would want features like Reviews, Forums, and Games to be a part of your social network. You should also use Friendster if you are looking to promote yourself or something else, as a Friendster Official Profile could help you gain exposure.

Who Started It?

Jonathan Abrams started Friendster on March 22, 2002. The company is currently privately owned and continues to receive investments from multiple companies and individual investors.

Gather.com

Company Name:	Gather.com
URL:	www.gather.com
Location:	Boston, Massachusetts, United States
Founded:	2005
Revenue Model:	Advertising and branded communities
Fees:	Free
Tagline:	Keep up with the people, conversations, and moments that matter.

What Is It?

Gather.com is a social media platform that provides forum communities of users with similar interests and is promoted as a means for the over-thirty crowd to discuss topics relevant to their lives. According to the *Boston Globe*, "Executives from Gather Inc. are recruiting bloggers by offering them a share of the company's advertising revenue."

How Can It Be Used?

Gather.com is used as a platform to communicate, educate, engage, and inform on a variety of subject matters. These forums are categorized by topics and ranked "based on how many readers they attract, how readers assess their quality, and how much online discussion they generate." Gather .com is an effective tool for publishing individual perspectives on a vast number of subjects.

Gather.com can also be used to earn money and gift cards. When people share content that becomes popular, Gather rewards them with Gather Points. Gather Points can be cashed in for gift cards at places like Starbucks, Target, and Amazon.com—or even for cash through PayPal.

What Other Applications Does It Work With?

Gather.com is a community web site and works with most Internet browsers.

Who Uses It?

Individuals use Gather.com to express their ideas, concerns, and viewpoints. Users can find information about topics ranging from crafts and home improvement to politics and business. This platform allows users to interact with a larger community than might be possible with face-to-face communication. Several users have gained interest in their writing projects and promoted books through Gather.com.

Should You Use It?

If you are looking for a way to express your interests and viewpoints to a vast audience with minimal investment, or to engage your readers, Gather.com provides an effective platform. This forum provides a community for otherwise unconnected users to meet and discuss topics of importance to them and that impact their daily lives.

Who Started It?

Gather.com was founded in 2005 by Tom Gerace and the American Public Media Group (APMG); Gather's chairman is William H. Kling, the APMG CEO and president. Gerace is also the founding committee chair of SMAC, the Social Media Ad Council, an industry community launched in September 2008. SMAC is, by its own definition, "A group of advertising, communications, brand management and social media executives coming together to create a common vocabulary, standard buying units, and uniform measurement methods for social media."

KickApps

Company Name:	KickApps
URL:	www.KickApps.com
Location:	New York, New York; Los Angeles; San Francisco; Orlando; London; and Mumbai
Founded:	2005
Revenue Model:	Ads and user fees
Fees:	Fees are based on CPM usage

What Is It?

KickApps is a web-based platform that enables users to grow and engage their audiences and create new revenue opportunities by adding social features, user-generated content, video players, and widgets to their web sites. KickApps connects editorial content, user content, applications, media and advertising experiences enabling users to grow and cater to their audiences. The result is more intelligent ad serving, viral audience growth, and an overall better user experience.

How Can It Be Used?

Social networking features enable users to build a community and connect with others. Each member gets a customizable profile where they can add friends, participate in groups, and send messages.

UGC video, photo, audio and blogging features enable the user's members to upload, share, rate, and comment on the user's media. Customizable players give users the ability to program and customize online videos on their sites. Message boards and blogs are all video-enabled as well. The Widget Builder allows users to create and deploy customized, viral Widgets that match the user's brand.

The KickApps Social Graph Engine for Publishers collects contextual data about the web site's audience, content, and activities. The information on the social graph can be used to enhance the web site's applications and advertising opportunities.

What Other Applications Does It Work With?

KickApps uses a range of other applications including social networking, user-generated content, online video players, and viral Widgets. These applications are designed to integrate with each client's web site and brand. KickApps can be customized with any web site using HTML, CSS, Java-Script, and APIs.

Who Uses It?

KickApps provides services to more than 40,000 sites. Their broad range of clients include universities, magazines, newspapers, political candidates, large corporations, small businesses, and bloggers. Some of KickApps high-profile clients include Budget Travel, HBO, ABC Family, BBC, the Phoenix Suns, the San Francisco 49ers, CW's VIP Lounge Community, and Rachel Ray.

Should You Use It?

If you are looking to build, manage, and deploy social media services while growing your audience then KickApps may be for you. Small businesses or global corporations can benefit from the publishing capabilities of KickApps by adding rich media experiences and more revenue opportunities to their web sites.

Who Started It?

Kickapps was founded by Eric Alterman and Pete Clark. In addition to being one of the founders and chairman of KickApps, Eric Alterman is the founder of MeshNetworks, Military Commercial Technologies, TeraNex, SkyCross, Jed Broadcasting, Quadfore, Centerpoint, and Triton Network Systems.

LinkedIn

Company Name:	LinkedIn
URL:	www.linkedin.com
Location:	Mountain View, California, United States
Founded:	2003
Employees:	24
Revenue Model:	Advertising and premium subscriptions
Fees:	Business level: $299.40/year; Business Plus: $599.40/year, Pro: $5,999.40
Tagline:	Relationships matter.

What Is It?

LinkedIn's philosophy is "Relationships matter." LinkedIn describes itself as an online network of more than 24 million experienced professionals from around the world, representing 150 industries. LinkedIn can be used to maintain professional relationships (as opposed to "just exchanging business cards"), search for jobs as well as recruit candidates, exchange solutions for problems, and find high-quality passive (employed) candidates.

How Can It Be Used?

Users create accounts and invite other users to become connections. Connections are rated in "degrees," meaning direct connections are first-degree connections, users listed as connections on that user's profile are second-degree connections, and so forth. Introductions are made through these degrees of connections, as it is assumed there is a level of trust inherited by having a first-degree connection in common. By posting a well-written resume, a user can search for jobs, or conversely a user can search for candidates. LinkedIn also has a feature called Linked Answers, in which users can post questions and receive suggestions/solutions related to those questions.

What Other Applications Does It Work With?

Aside from the obvious feature of being accessible from any device with an Internet browser, LinkedIn works with various applications that include WordPress, Amazon Reading List, Google Presentation, My Travel, Box.net, Tweets, Blog Link, Huddle Workspaces, Company Buzz, SAP Community Bio, SlideShare Presentations, Polls, and Events. If you have an AOL account, you can use that to log into LinkedIn as well as search for contacts through your e-mail account that are already on LinkedIn. If you don't have an AOL account, once you establish your rudimentary profile, you can have LinkedIn search your Outlook, Hotmail, or other e-mail address lists. Linked-In will also search alumni networks as indicated by your profile information to lead you to college connections.

Who Uses It?

Professionals in all industries use it to establish and maintain relationships. There are recruiter success stories, such as the recruiter who spends $7,000 annually to search LinkedIn, and nets $100,000 annually in commission for his successful headhunting of passive candidates. LinkedIn is also working in the way of sales leads. One success story is that of a CEO of an online advertising company who used an introduction from a connection to contact the COO of a potential client. He invited him to lunch. The COO responded that he didn't have time for lunch but that he did need a new ad server. The two signed a contract two weeks later.

Should You Use It?

As stated previously, this web site is geared toward professionals in any industry. Whether you are looking for business contacts, a new job, or a new candidate to come work for your company, LinkedIn provides you with the social networking mechanisms to do so without all the extraneous negative personal data that would otherwise turn off employers or professional contacts. Confidentiality is also a major attraction for using LinkedIn. As a professional, you can set your privacy settings, ranging from receiving no requests at all from unknown users to being completely open to receiving connection requests.

Who Started It?

Founder Reid Hoffman and some college friends created LinkedIn following Hoffman's success in establishing and selling PayPal to eBay Inc. Hoffman is a true entrepreneur, with a talent for scouting successful Internet start-up ventures, according to a January 2008 article by the Associated Press. With the assistance of fellow Stanford graduate Constantin Geuricke, LinkedIn was created. Dan Nye, current CEO of LinkedIn, previously filled a number of senior management positions at Intuit.

MOLI

Company Name:	MOLI, LLC (owned by Mainstream Holdings Inc.)
URL:	www.moli.com
Location:	West Palm Beach, Florida, United States
Founded:	2008
Revenue Model:	Advertising and premium tools
Tagline:	Control your privacy.

What Is It?

MOLI is an online social networking service that is designed to fix one of the biggest concerns with other social networking services—namely, the lack of privacy that can occur. MOLI seeks to accomplish this by allowing users the ability to create multiple profile pages, each with their own privacy settings, from one user account. According to the MOLI web site, "MOLI provides an easy to use, content-rich, multimedia interactive platform ideal for both community collaboration and e-commerce." MOLI also provides premium tools, such as an online store and ad removal, which users can buy to enhance their experience.

How Can It Be Used?

MOLI can be used to network and interact with all your online relationships from one spot. For example, a person could create an account on MOLI and create three separate profiles—one for friends, one for family, and one for professional purposes. The friends profile could contain personal pictures or comments that the user's coworkers would never see. On the family profile, the user could put up pictures from the last reunion and give only other family members permission to look at that profile. On the professional profile, the user could network with coworkers freely and never have to worry about what other content is available to them. With the addition of an online store to a MOLI account, a user could also sell commodities through their profile. Along with the networking aspect, MOLI focuses on adding content for users. MOLI Video allows users to view a variety of videos including MOLI Rollers ("a magazine article in video form"), and MOLI View provides information on subjects such as sports, entertainment, and travel.

What Other Applications Does It Work With?

MOLI allows the embedding of photographs and videos in certain areas of your profile page so it works with photo applications such as Flickr and Photobucket and video applications like YouTube. Additionally, if you add the online store to your MOLI account, the store is compatible with PayPal and Google Checkout.

Who Uses It?

The target audience base that the MOLI web site claims to aim for is "enterprising individuals above the age of 18 and small business owners." Small business owners and individuals who have items to sell use MOLI because of the ability to add online stores to their profile. Another audience base is students and young professionals who enjoy using online social networking services to correspond with friends, but are concerned about unintended viewers seeing that content.

Should You Use It?

You should use MOLI if you are interested in a social networking web site that is concerned with your privacy and also provides some entertaining and useful features. MOLI is also a good choice if you want to handle the majority of your networking, whether it is recreational or commercial, in one location. With other facets available such as MOLI Video, blogs, and MOLI View, you should use MOLI if you are looking for entertainment and information from your social networking service.

Who Started It?

Dr. Christos M. Cotsakos, the founder, chairman of the board, CEO, and president of Mainstream Holdings, founded MOLI. Cotsakos is also the former CEO of E*TRADE. MOLI received funding from several contributors to help its launch, the total of which has been estimated to be more than $55.5 million as of January 2008.

MySpace

Company Name:	News Corp. Digital Media
URL:	www.myspace.com
Location:	Beverly Hills, California, United States
Founded:	2003
Employees:	1,000
Revenue Model:	Advertising
Tagline:	A place for friends

What Is It?

MySpace is an online social networking application. Users create a MySpace profile and then interact with other users while developing existing relationships and creating new ones. It is one of the more popular social networking applications and is available in 15 different languages. MySpace offers its users numerous features, including blogs, groups, bulletins, widgets, and instant messaging. It also allows users to customize their profile pages through HTML coding or the MySpace profile customizer.

How Can It Be Used?

MySpace offers a tool called MySpace MyAds that offers users the capability to run an effective online marketing campaign within their social network. With MySpace MyAds, anyone can design their own advertisement, choose which users will see it displayed throughout MySpace dependent on characteristics like listed gender and location, and then pay based upon the number of clicks the advertisement receives. For example, a web site that is based in Arizona can design an advertisement that appears only to users who have selected Arizona as their current location.

What Other Applications Does It Work With?

Various applications and web sites can add functionality, entertainment, and features to a MySpace profile page. YouTube, Slide.com, RockYou!, Quizazz, Poker Palace, Flixster, and Playlist.com are just some of the MySpace-compatible entities available. MySpace also has a MySpace Developer Platform that allows users to design their own applications that can then be made available for other MySpace users.

Who Uses It?

A very large and diverse audience uses MySpace. It is estimated that MySpace attracts 230,000 new users a day from all over the world. Numerous notable users on MySpace include organizations like Operation Blessing International and Planet Aid. The presidential campaigns of Barack Obama and John McCain were on MySpace as well. Those who are looking to market directly to an audience also use MySpace, whether through the creation of a profile or purchasing MySpace MyAds.

Should You Use It?

You should use MySpace if you are looking to network or advertise within one of the largest social networking communities online. By creating a profile, you can be selective about who you communicate with, or you can interact with as many people as possible. You should also use MySpace if you are interested in marketing directly to a targeted audience, and then tracking how effective that advertising is. With the introduction of MySpace Developer Platform, you should consider using MySpace if you would like to create a MySpace application that can promote your web site or services.

Who Started It?

Brad Greenspan (founder of eUniverse), Chris DeWolfe (MySpace CEO), Josh Berman, Tom Anderson (MySpace president), and a team of programmers from eUniverse started MySpace in August 2003. The company eUniverse eventually became Intermix Media Inc. Intermix was acquired by News Corporation, the parent company of Fox Interactive Media, in July 2005 for an estimated $580 million.

Ning

Company Name:	Ning
URL:	www.ning.com
Location:	Palo Alto, California, United States
Founded:	2004
Employees:	41
Revenue Model:	Advertising and premium subscriptions
Tagline:	Create your own social network for anything.

What Is It?

Ning is an online social networking service. Ning, however, is different in its design from other networking services like Facebook and MySpace. Rather than having users join one giant social network, Ning allows users to create their own social network web sites that other Ning members can then join. Once a member joins your community, he or she can then create a profile page for that network. Additionally, Ning operates on a platform that allows users to customize their social network if they have the inclination. As the Ning web site puts it, the Ning platform is "the software equivalent of Home Depot. Unlike other services that offer a 'one-size-fits-all' offering, your social network on Ning runs on a programmable platform."

How Can It Be Used?

Ning can be used in a large number of ways, depending on the user's needs and intentions. An artist could use Ning to create a social network based around one's art and then use Ning to answer questions from fans, keep the audience posted on important upcoming dates, and post images of the artist or the artwork. Another potential use is a social network centered on aquarium enthusiasts, wherein a community of users could post meeting dates, post articles on caring for fish, and discuss the hobby with other like-minded individuals.

What Other Applications Does It Work With?

Ning works with several online applications to make the creation of a social community easier. For example, you can import photographs from Flickr and embed videos from YouTube. Additionally, Ning has widgets that you can add to MySpace, Facebook, or your own personal web site. Ning also works with Google Gadgets.

Who Uses It?

Ning could potentially be used by anyone, provided the interest in creating a social web site exists. Currently, everyone from political activists to urban improv groups have social networks that are built with the Ning platform. Celebrities such as the musician 50 Cent and the mixed martial arts fighter B. J. Penn are among the people using Ning. Educators are another rapidly growing subset of Ning users, with social networks being created to discuss teaching methods globally.

Should You Use It?

You should use Ning if you are interested in creating a social network for any subject or purpose. Ning is attractive because it allows for the creation of features like memberships and discussion forums on your social web site, with less technical knowledge required than if you were to try and build one from scratch. As Ning says, you can use it for nearly anything, and you have the option to do so for free. Some of Ning's suggested uses range from a personal wedding site to a high school alumni community to a local neighborhood block web site.

Who Started It?

Marc Andreessen and Gina Bianchini created Ning in October 2004. Andreessen is an entrepreneur and software engineer who cofounded Netscape Communications Corporation and Loudcloud, which later became Opsware. Bianchini was the cofounder and former CEO of Harmonic Communications prior to becoming the CEO for Ning.

Orkut

Company Name:	Orkut (owned by Google)
URL:	www.orkut.com
Location:	Originally hosted in California, Google announced in August 2008 that the Orkut operation will be moving to Brazil.
Founded:	2004
Employees:	20,000 (Google)
Revenue Model:	Google advertisements
Tagline:	Who do you know?

What Is It?

Orkut is an online social networking service owned by Google. Its purpose is to allow users to network, socialize, and create new relationships with other Orkut members. In order to utilize Orkut, you must have a Google account, which then also becomes your Orkut account. Orkut has several primary features available for users, including Scrapbooks, Communities, and Applications. Orkut, according to the web site, "is an online community designed to make your social life more active and stimulating."

How Can It Be Used?

Orkut can be used as a supplemental tool for any stage in a relationship between members. For example, someone who was interested in meeting area bicycle riders could use the search engine to find members who listed cycling as one of their interests and then interact with them by sending a Message, adding them as a Friend, or adding them as a Crush. If you are already friends with someone on Orkut, you can communicate through features like Testimonials and Scrapbooks. Orkut also allows for the creation of Communities, a mechanism to bring users together under common interests.

What Other Applications Does It Work With?

Google Talk can be integrated with Orkut so any Orkut members who are listed as your friends can contact you via Google Talk without having to add you manually. Members can upload videos to their profiles using YouTube and Google Video. Orkut also has numerous third-party applications that you can add to your Orkut account. These applications vary greatly and add quite a bit of character to Orkut. Some uses of these applications are games, matchmaking tools, chat rooms, and competitions.

Who Uses It?

The Orkut community comprises a wide variety of audiences and users. These can range from high school students to business consultants to war veterans. According to Orkut demographics, 73.43 percent of the user base are between the ages of eighteen and thirty, and 71 percent of the members are based in Brazil and India, with 15.14 percent of the users coming from the United States. Orkut is not very popular in North America when compared to other social networking services.

Should You Use It?

You should use Orkut if you are looking to join a social networking service, especially if you already have a Google account. If you use Orkut, it will give you a new way of initiating and maintaining relationships, along with some entertaining tools to interact with others. Additionally, you should use Orkut if you are primarily interested in communicating with users who are under thirty years old and live in either Brazil or India.

Who Started It?

Orkut gained its name from the Google employee who designed it, Orkut Büyükkökten. Büyükkökten, a software engineer from Turkey, designed Orkut independently while working at Google. Shortly after Orkut's launch, there were some complications as Büyükkökten's previous employer, Affinity Engines, claimed that the Orkut code was based on one of its own projects called InCircle. In June 2004, Affinity Engines filed a lawsuit against Google based on this claim. The lawsuit has since been settled on terms that have not been released.

Plaxo

Company Name:	Plaxo Inc.
URL:	www.plaxo.com
Location:	Mountain View, California, United States
Founded:	2006
Revenue Model:	Premium subscriptions

What Is It?

Plaxo is a social network application that is focused on staying in touch with your contacts better. Through Plaxo, you can synchronize contact information from several different sources—for example, Google address book and Outlook contacts—and then store that information in your Plaxo Address Book. In addition, when one of your contacts changes his or her own information in Plaxo, that change is reflected in your own address book. With Plaxo you can also use Pulse, a feature that acts as a sort of personal news page by displaying information that your Plaxo Connections choose to share.

How Can It Be Used?

A business could use Plaxo to keep all employees up-to-date with each other's contact information. For example, if one employee changed a phone number on her Plaxo profile, all the employees who are connected to her on Plaxo would have that change automatically updated in their own address book. This function makes it easier for employees to communicate and collaborate, and it simplifies company cohesion as people don't have to be notified independently of changes.

What Other Applications Does It Work With?

Plaxo Pulse allows users to consolidate their content from multiple web sites in one area for other Plaxo users to view. For example, if you add Flickr to your Pulse account, every time you upload a photograph to Flickr you can also share that photograph with the Plaxo connections that you allow to see it. Plaxo Pulse also works with Open Social. Some of the web sites that Plaxo works with are MySpace, LiveJournal, Picasa, Bebo, YouTube, and Amazon. Additionally, Plaxo works with numerous applications to synchronize contact information, including AOL, Outlook, Google Address Book, LinkedIn, and Hotmail.

Who Uses It?

Organizations and individual users both use Plaxo. Businesses and organizations use Plaxo to stay in touch with other businesses and organizations, clients, and employees. Individuals use Plaxo to keep track of their connections' presence on multiple web sites. As of May 2008, Plaxo is reported to have over 20 million users, a number that is expected to continue growing.

Should You Use It?

You should use Plaxo if you are looking for a social media application that allows you to maintain contacts and discover more about them. If you need a way to synchronize contact information in one place from multiple sources, or if you are having trouble keeping track of the various places your connections update online, consider Plaxo to consolidate it all in one place. You should also use Plaxo if you are looking to network with past and new contacts, as Plaxo allows you to search for other Plaxo users, and then connect with their permission.

Who Started It?

Sean Parker (a cofounder of Napster), Minh Nguyen, Todd Masonis, and Cameron Ring started Plaxo. Plaxo announced on May 14, 2008, that it had signed a deal with Comcast for terms that were not disclosed. Plaxo is currently a subsidiary of Comcast Interactive Media.

Tool Scorecard for Chapter 23: Social Networks

Instructions: Using the following five-point (0 to 4) scale, rate each tool in this chapter on the basis of how valuable it *might be* to the internal and external operations of your company. Make notes about which tools appeal to you the most.

4 = Extremely Valuable

3 = Very Valuable

2 = Somewhat Valuable

1 = Not Very Valuable

0 = No Value

Tool	Internal Value	External Value
Bebo	4 3 2 1 0	4 3 2 1 0
Facebook	4 3 2 1 0	4 3 2 1 0
Fast Pitch!	4 3 2 1 0	4 3 2 1 0
Friendster	4 3 2 1 0	4 3 2 1 0
Gather.com	4 3 2 1 0	4 3 2 1 0
KickApps	4 3 2 1 0	4 3 2 1 0
LinkedIn	4 3 2 1 0	4 3 2 1 0
MOLI	4 3 2 1 0	4 3 2 1 0
MySpace	4 3 2 1 0	4 3 2 1 0
Ning	4 3 2 1 0	4 3 2 1 0
Orkut	4 3 2 1 0	4 3 2 1 0
Plaxo	4 3 2 1 0	4 3 2 1 0

CHAPTER 24

Publish

The ability to accurately publish or record our conversations to pass on to future generations is a relatively new concept. For thousands of years, stories containing myths, legends, laws, and mores of a group or society have been passed down through oral reiteration, that is, storytelling. There have been clay tablets, papyrus, hieroglyphs, handwriting, the printing press, movable type, lithography, computers, desktop publishing, print-on-demand, forums, e-mail, web pages, blogs and comments, text messaging, photo and video sharing, voicemail, and Twitter. What could be next?

It's all about saving and distributing content, some valuable, some conversational, but all a necessity of human nature. The following chapters list some of the cutting-edge companies that are providing publishing technology right now. For the first time in human history, we have an easy and free means to collect and save our thoughts and ideas, and for the first time ever, we can distribute those ideas to the global tribe instantly, also for free. It's "Word of Mouth at the Speed of Light."

As you read each profile, keep in mind that its features and functions may or may not be right for your particular business. Use the Tool Scorecard at the end of the chapter to help you determine which of these tools qualify for further consideration when you begin creating your social media strategy in Part III of this book.

theSocialMediaBible.com

Blogger

Company Name:	Blogger (owned by Google)
URL:	www.blogger.com
Location:	Mountain View, California
Founded:	1999
Employees:	5 (Google 20,000)
Revenue Model:	Advertising
Fees:	Free
Tagline:	Push-button publishing

What Is It?

Blogger enables writers of all skill levels to become their own publishers, through the Internet. Users can blog about their professional interests, personal hobbies, sports, family life, or any topic at all. Blogger is available in 41 languages, and a variety of third-party applications are available to enhance Blogger blogs. These applications vary by the type of computer operating system being used. Blogger users can even blog on the go from a smart phone like a BlackBerry, iPhone, or other handheld device for instantaneous information sharing.

How Can It Be Used?

Blogger's self-publishing capability allows a user to write and publish instantaneously, with the ability to post pictures and videos. Companies, educators, and nonprofits can use Blogger to share information with their user audience, receive feedback and ideas, track the number and location of readers, network with other entities in the same field, or initiate collaboration. Blogger allows for group blogging, so blogging responsibilities for a company or other entity would not necessarily have to fall on one person. A side benefit is that multiple people posting to one blog provides for a well-rounded view of the company.

What Other Applications Does It Work With?

Blogger works with a number of applications, some dependent on the type of computer operating system being used. Web applications that can be used with Blogger include Audioblog, batBack, BlogAmp, BloggerBox and

WikyBloggerBox, Blogger to FOAF, Buzznet, FeedBlitz, FeedBurner, Flickr, FotoFlix, Gabcast, Lovento, Photobucket, and Wikispaces.

Who Uses It?

It would be easier to ask, "Who doesn't use Blogger?" Name it, and you can find the topic available on Blogger. You can find tax advice from blogger Roni Deutch, small business marketing strategies from Rikki Arundel, or information about rehabilitation efforts of a small town in the Philippines with the aid of the Southern Leyte Rehabilitation Program. What's great about starting a Blogger blog is that once you begin, you find yourself embedded in a social community, collaborating and communicating with others who are interested in the same topic you are writing about.

Should You Use It?

Blogger is easy to use, free, and one of the largest blogging sites on the Internet. With the advent of Google, it is now easier than ever to search for Blogger blogs on specific topics. Blogging can be a great marketing tool for your business or group, and it gives you a more personal way to reach out to your audience.

Who Started It?

Pyra Labs, which consisted of Evan Williams and Meg Hourihan, started Blogger in August 1999. Evan and Meg created a weblog for their use, and the code for that weblog became the foundation for the initial version of Blogger. Blogger was bought out by Google in 2003, after which general Blogger service became enhanced with the use of Google server technology. Blogger replaced Google Blog.

Infusionsoft

Company Name:	Infusionsoft
URL:	www.infusionsoft.com
Location:	Gilbert, Arizona, United States
Founded:	2001
Employees:	140
Revenue Model:	Subscription
Fees:	Free trial; monthly subscription
Tagline:	E-mail Marketing 2.0

What Is It?

Infusionsoft is the solution to automate marketing in a small business. Infusionsoft markets its product as software that "is the first to marry e-mail marketing and CRM into a single application that is driven by a powerful automation engine." By providing advanced e-mail marketing, customer relationship management (CRM), e-commerce and a unique approach on marketing automation, Infusionsoft improves response from customers and prospects, consolidates multiple marketing applications and increases productivity. Through what the company calls e-mail marketing 2.0, Infusionsoft allows small businesses to send more than just e-mail so that they can follow up effectively and grow their small business (2–25 employees) enabling them to deliver the right message to the right person at the right time and increase sales. Through the combination of powerful tools Infusionsoft delivers a true small business growth suite.

How Can It Be Used?

Infusionsoft is used to automate marketing activities via web-based application. It features the ability to host multiple users and allows fine-grain customization to the lead-generation process for small businesses. This functionality allows users to scale their efforts and grow their footprint without necessarily growing their staff through efficient automation. Examples include follow-up on generated leads, ability to systematically enable or disable campaigns, execute billing operations including invoicing and running an online shopping cart.

For the individual, Infusionsoft is a useful tool to utilize their Automation Links in e-mail marketing to capture responses through e-mail marketing. Segmentation and customer targeting are strengths of Infusionsoft.

What Other Applications Does It Work With?

As a web-based application, Infusionsoft can be used from a powerful web browser such as Mozilla Firefox. This capability is helpful because not all users use a specific operating system and Firefox is a platform-agnostic. Infusionsoft recently released Infusionsoft for Outlook, a plug-in that allows users of the most popular e-mail client to find contacts, start and stop campaigns and add contacts to their CRM all without ever leaving Outlook.

Additional add-ons can be utilized through their open Application Programming Interface (API). Such implementations are offered via a community of certified developers. This empowers business owners to leverage Infusionsoft for many additional aspects in their business.

Who Uses It?

Small businesses and entrepreneurs use Infusionsoft to elevate their marketing and improve productivity. According to Perry Marshall, respected thought leader on search engine advertising on the web, "One of the most important aspects of Infusionsoft is the ability to do automated marketing sequences. I just used auto-responders before, but now I can do a lot more. It's one thing to have auto-responder sequences, it's another thing to be able to take people on and off of lists, to segment them when they take a certain action, to make different triggers cause sequences to start and stop, so that customers and prospects are treated according to their individual interests and preferences."

Should You Use It?

Infusionsoft is an effective application for automating, growing, and improving marketing activities in a small business. If you are looking for a way to follow up on prospects, leads, and customers and don't want people to fall through the cracks, Infusionsoft would be a viable option. As many businesses are taking their business online, Infusionsoft reigns superior as the ideal application to capture and segment visitors to a small business's web site. Considering the continued growth of telecommuting, Infusionsoft would be a beneficial application to keep the business running smoothly and sustainably between on-site and remote employees, and to operate efficiently. In a sales environment, Infusionsoft offers a total solution for managing a sales pipeline and intelligently routing prospects to a sales team at the right time, optimizing every contact with every lead.

Who Started It?

What began as a software start-up dream in an Arizona strip mall has evolved into a fast-growth, venture-backed technology company with a product that directly addresses a deep, widespread problem for small businesses. Infusionsoft helps small businesses grow fast with targeted e-mail marketing (they call it e-mail marketing 2.0) that responds and adapts to customer behavior. Infusionsoft was founded in 2001 by Scott Martineau and Eric Martineau, and later joined by CEO Clate Mask, as a custom software development company. By introducing software application named

"ManagePro CRM," they ignited their path to building a powerful CRM application tailored for small businesses. In 2007, the company was named "Infusionsoft," and after continued growth, the company attracted private investor, Mohr Davidow Ventures and later vSpring. Built on a core of CRM technology, its e-mail marketing features continue to propel the company into meteoric growth.

Joomla

Company Name:	Joomla Project (Open Source Matters)
URL:	www.joomla.org
Location:	New York, New York
Founded:	2000
Employees:	12 (There are 12 Core Members of the Joomla Project, but it is not known if they are paid, as Joomla claims it is a volunteer-run organization.)
Revenue Model:	Donations
Fees:	Free
Tagline:	. . . because open source matters.

What Is It?

According to Joomla's web site, it is an award-winning content management system (CMS) that allows users to build web sites and applications. Joomla is free for anyone to use under the General Public License (GPL), a license that allows free software to avoid becoming copyrighted. The selling point for using Joomla is that the CMS capability makes it easy to manage your content, whether it's text, photos, videos, or music. Joomla claims that its software requires almost no technical skills or knowledge. Joomla 1.0 was a derivative of the Mambo 4.5 code base. Joomla translation is also available in 20 languages, plus users can contact Joomla for additional translation needs.

How Can It Be Used?

Joomla is usable by anyone in just about any industry. Joomla's web site provides a list of ideas for the creation and management of content:

- Corporate web sites or portals
- Corporate intranets and extranets
- Online magazines, newspapers, and publications

- E-commerce and online reservations
- Government applications
- Small business web sites
- Nonprofit and organizational web sites
- Community-based portals
- School and church web sites
- Personal or family home pages

What Other Applications Does It Work With?

Joomla developers can pair with any number of applications. The whole idea behind Joomla is that because it's open source, the possibilities for application development and usage are endless. Joomla refers to applications as "extensions" because these are plug-ins to add to your web site to enhance the user's interaction experience. Nearly 4,000 extensions are available on Joomla's web site, as well as other web sites that claim to specialize in Joomla application/extension development for customers.

Who Uses It?

A variety of businesses and organizations use Joomla to develop their web sites. Joomla lists the following on its web site as examples of users:

- MTV Networks Quizilla (social networking, quizilla.com)
- IHOP (restaurant chain, ihop.com)
- Harvard University (educational, gsas.harvard.edu)
- Citibank (financial institution intranet, not publicly accessible)
- The Green Maven (eco-resources, greenmaven.com)
- *Outdoor Photographer* (magazine, outdoorphotographer.com)
- PlayShakespeare.com (cultural, playshakespeare.com)
- Senso Interiors (furniture design, sensointeriors.co.za)

On the Joomla forum, Web Site Showcase, a wide variety of users appear: used car dealers, real estate agents, gamers, and historians are just a sample.

Should You Use It?

If you are looking for a free, open-source tool to develop your own web site, Joomla seems to have provided the answer. The added content management capability is also valuable, as the amount of information and content that stockpiles on a web site sometimes creates a problem for businesses and organizations.

Who Started It?

Michelle Bisson is one of the Joomla cofounders. She is also a member of the Mambo core team. There are 11 other Core Team Members of the Joomla Project from different areas around the world and different experiences. Several of the Core Team Members also belong to Mambo, such as Mitch Pirtle, Andy Miller, and Louis Landry. They were instrumental in taking Mambo 4.5 code and turning it into Joomla 1.0.

Knol

Company Name:	Knol
URL:	knol.google.com/k
Location:	Mountain View, California
Founded:	2008
Employees:	20,000 (Google)
Revenue Model:	Advertising
Fees:	Free

What Is It?

Google has defined Knol as a unit of knowledge and has launched this concept into a platform for authors to publish their knowledge on a variety of subjects. Each subject can have content published by many different authors with myriad levels of authority on the subject. Google developed this platform as a means to help people share their knowledge. According to the Google blog, "There are millions of people who possess useful knowledge that they would love to share, and there are billions of people who can benefit from it. We believe that many do not share that knowledge today simply because it is not easy enough to do that."

How Can It Be Used?

Knol contributors must have a Google account, and it is highly recommended that real names are used to highlight the authors of the content.

Google hopes that "Knol will include the opinions and points of view of the authors who will put their reputation on the line." Knol allows users to contribute, submit comments and questions, and edit, rate, or review the content. The author of the content is able to determine whether ads will be included.

What Other Applications Does It Work With?

Knol is currently in beta testing phase, which limits the accessibility of this service, but it is presently used with most Internet browsers.

Who Uses It?

In its current beta testing phase, Knol initially invited authors to contribute content, but the service is expanding to allow those with Google accounts to contribute material for publication. The general purpose of Knol is for those with authoritative information to share it with those looking for that information. However, anyone with a Google account and information to share can create a Knol. Users looking for information enter a topic in the search field, which returns results for all content containing that subject matter.

Should You Use It?

If you have information you believe should be made public, Google's Knol is an effective platform. If you are searching for information, Knol may be a resource to consider, but it is necessary to recognize that Google does not verify or edit the content published. With that in mind, users must accept responsibility to verify for themselves that the information is accurate and use caution when applying the information received through Knol.

Who Started It?

The engineering team at Google, headed by Udi Manber, vice president of engineering, created Knol to build a platform to "help people share their knowledge."

RatePoint

Company Name:	RatePoint, Inc.
URL:	www.ratepoint.com
Location:	Needham, Massachusetts, United States
Founded:	2006
Revenue Model:	Subscription-based pricing
Fees:	RatePoint offers a free for life product for up to a 550 contact list. Paid accounts start at only $10.00 per month

What Is It?

RatePoint Inc., the leading provider of customer reviews, testimonials, and online reputation management services, helps small businesses protect and build their online reputation, allowing them to harness the power of credible customer feedback and leverage it into a sales, marketing, and customer service asset.

RatePoint was created to promote online and offline business quality while enhancing the relationship between businesses and consumers. Launched in 2006, RatePoint champions the needs of businesses worldwide by providing them with an easy and affordable way to build successful, lasting customer relationships, manage their online reputation, grow their business, and increase consumer confidence. For consumers, we provide an easy way to reach out to businesses and improve communications.

How Can It Be Used?

RatePoint is an easy-to-use, Web-based communication service which includes customer feedback tools to collect business reviews and product reviews as well as e-mail marketing, survey, and dispute resolution capabilities to provide small- and medium-sized businesses with the ability to collect, manage, and promote customer feedback directly from its web site.

RatePoint automatically integrates social media with its services, providing small businesses with the ability to promote content in the form of news, information and reviews online and integrated with Twitter and Facebook, seamlessly bringing a business's message to potential customers.

Through RatePoint, businesses can create an instant Web version of an e-mail newsletter and link it to Twitter and Facebook with one click. Not only do these social networks provide updates to friends and followers, but the keywords used in the social network updates also serve to enhance search engine optimization. That means that countless consumers who are starting purchase decision research with a search engine can find the link to your e-mail newsletter when their search terms match that of your update.

What Other Applications Does It Work With?

RatePoint works with many applications that support HTML templates, and supports "e-mail addresses in 3 file formats; .txt (text file), .csv (Comma Separated Values) and .xls (Microsoft Excel Spreadsheet)."

Additionally, RatePoint is integrated with Twitter and Facebook with one click social sharing.

Who Uses It?

RatePoint was created to promote online and offline business quality while enhancing the relationship between businesses and consumers. Launched in 2006, RatePoint champions the needs of worldwide businesses by providing them with an easy and affordable way to build successful, lasting customer relationships, manage their online reputation, grow their business, and increase consumer confidence. For consumers, we provide an easy way to reach out to businesses and improve communications.

RatePoint is ideal for the very small business and small-business community—including associations, nonprofits, businesses, professional and personal services providers, recreation and entertainment firms, religious organizations, restaurants, retail outlets, and travel and tourism organizations.

Who Started It?

RatePoint is a private company and was founded in 2006 by a team of five innovative entrepreneurs:

1. Neal Creighton, cofounder and CEO
2. Chris Bailey, cofounder and EVP of Business Development
3. Mike Rowan, cofounder and CTO
4. Kefeng Chen, cofounder and vice president of R&D
5. Tom Serani, cofounder and vice president of Sales

SlideShare

Company Name:	SlideShare
URL:	www.slideshare.net
Location:	San Francisco, California; New Delhi, India
Founded:	2006
Employees:	10
Revenue Model:	Advertising
Fees:	Free

What Is It?

SlideShare describes itself as a community for sharing presentations (publicly or privately) in PowerPoint, PDF, or Open Office (Mac users should use PDF to post their Keynote presentations). Anyone can find presentations on their topic of interest. Presentations can be tagged, downloaded, or embedded in web sites or blogs. Users can join groups to share common interests with other users. The maximum allowed space per user account is 100 megabytes. SlideShare is available in 11 languages.

How Can It Be Used?

SlideShare provides a number of ideas for using its web site. In addition to sharing your presentations either publicly or privately, you can add audio to your presentation, market your event, join groups of people who share your interests or occupational field, and download presentations and PDFs. SlideShare is even usable with your company's intranet. You can also embed your SlideShare presentation into blogs, wikis, and other web sites. SlideShare also provides for users to use creative commons licensing. You can create a *Slidecast*—a presentation that is combined with your podcast for an *MP3 mashup.* In 2007, a creative project called Freesouls was started by Joi Ito, who sees himself not as a photographer but as a "professional elsewhere." The project was created to allow anyone access to and use of these photographs, with the single caveat that they be attributed to Joi Ito.

What Other Applications Does It Work With?

SlideShare works well with Facebook, Twitter, Blogger, MediaWiki, Joomla, Altassian Wiki, Tumblr, Wikispaces, and WordPress. The main feature behind SlideShare being usable with these applications and web sites is the ability to embed SlideShare material in third-party web sites.

Who Uses It?

There are a variety of SlideShare users. Businesses, private individuals, and those in the education field use it—any groups of users who have a common interest and share their information and ideas with one another. Consultants, religious patrons, entrepreneurs, and professional speakers use SlideShare to convey their messages. Teachers and students alike use SlideShare for courseware presentations.

Should You Use It?

Giving presentations is nearly obligatory in running a business or organizational entity. Being able to share presentations either publicly or privately can have distinct advantages. SlideShare provides an easy online repository for storing the data, reducing either the need for carrying a laptop or irritating issues such as network connection and synchronization during travel. Your audience can learn more about your product or service from anywhere in the world. Businesses and organizations can share information and compare data. Educators and trainers can use SlideShare to post PowerPoint lectures for students or employees, a valuable asset for online courses. Students can also post project presentations, essays, and electronic portfolios.

Who Started It?

Jonathan Boutelle, one of the founders, stated in a 2006 Indezine.com interview that the idea for SlideShare came about because he was trying to put together a presentation for a conference and was being sent different pages of the presentation to upload to the Web. He worked with the other two founders, Rashmi Sina and Amit Ranjan, on their first creation, Mind-Canvas, a web-based market research platform.

TypePad

Company Name:	TypePad (a product of Six Apart)
URL:	www.typepad.com
Location:	San Francisco, California
Founded:	2003
Employees:	150 (Six Apart)
Revenue Model:	Blog and host services fees
Fees:	$107.40–$1,079.40/year
Tagline:	Inform. Influence. Inspire.

What Is It?

According to a press release from Six Apart, "TypePad is the award-winning hosted blogging service preferred by professionals, small businesses, and enthusiasts. TypePad provides a rich set of features for publishing, updating, and sharing information on the Web. No installation or configuration is required. TypePad blogs are fully hosted and managed by Six Apart." Five different levels of user fees address different needs of users.

How Can It Be Used?

TypePad can be used to share personal thoughts, experiences, and stories. Businesses can use TypePad to create the human element, to communicate a behind-the-scenes look at a reader's favorite business or industry. Another business application of TypePad is to network and develop new business leads and customer bases. With the advent of using the TypePad application (or app) with the iPhone and iPod Touch, mobile blogging has been taken to the next level of convenience, ease, and instantaneous communication.

What Other Applications Does It Work With?

TypePad works with Twitter, LinkedIn, Google Chrome, FeedBurner, Facebook, BlackBerry, iPhone and iPod Touch, and numerous other smart phones that have an Internet browser capability. There are also numerous widgets (applications you can use with a certain program to give it additional features and uses) listed on sixapart.com/typepad/widgets to add to the TypePad experience.

Who Uses It?

There are numerous users of TypePad. Testimonials on the TypePad web site include those from the food industry, accessory and handbag design businesses, news media such as MSNBC and the *Los Angeles Times*, entertainment blogs such as Celebrity Baby Blog and coporations like Coca-Cola and Roxy. Businesses that want to reach their audience in a more personal, direct way can do so using TypePad blogging.

Should You Use It?

Blogging has become the next marketing must-do for businesses. According to TypePad, businesses should blog because a blog:

- Is a simple, cost-effective way to create a professional online presence.
- Creates a conversation between you and the people who matter to you.

- Is a tremendous way to boost your search engine rankings.
- Delivers a huge impact for very little money.
- Allows you to take control of what you publish.
- Allows you to develop a position of thought leadership.
- Is a valuable business tool for collecting customer feedback.
- Creates a historical record of your content.

All of these reasons are valid for blogging in general, not just in using the TypePad product. The main issue at stake in using TypePad is whether the user wishes to pay for services. The most inexpensive subscription fee is $4.95 a month. Numerous other blogging programs are available for free, which may be the biggest draw for the new blogger. A search query of "TypePad comparison" nets a number of blog reviews of TypePad against other blogging programs such as Blogger, and each one is different in its opinion. Perhaps the biggest reason to pay for TypePad is the customer service you receive for the monthly fee.

Who Started It?

Ben and Mena Trott are the married cofounders of Six Apart Ltd. The name of the company refers to the six days' difference between their birthdays. During a period of unemployment in September 2001, Ben wrote a weblog program to suit his wife's needs, and that program became Movable Type. When Movable Type 1.0 was released, it was downloaded 100 times in the first hour. This development led to the creation of Six Apart and its ensuing products and services.

VerticalResponse

Company Name:	VerticalResponse, Inc.
URL:	www.VerticalResponse.com
Location:	San Francisco, California, United States
Founded:	2001
Employees:	100
Revenue Model:	Pay as you go or monthly subscription pricing for small businesses; free e-mails for nonprofit groups and business/associations
Fees:	Pay as you go pricing from $10.00/month or 1.5¢ per e-mail.

What Is It?

VerticalResponse, Inc., offers self-service e-mail marketing, online surveys and direct mail service empowering small businesses to create, manage and analyze their own direct marketing campaigns. Founded in 2001, Vertical-Response is an online solution that enables anyone to get their e-mail marketing campaigns up and running within minutes, regardless of technical expertise.

How Can It Be Used?

VerticalResponse's flagship product is an online e-mail marketing solution that can easily be used by small businesses, without breaking the bank. Small businesses and nonprofit customers benefit from a host of features and tools, including hundreds of e-mail templates, easy list management, and analytics that enable them to see how their campaigns are working.

What Other Applications Does It Work With?

VerticalResponse integrates with Google Analytics for advanced tracking and reporting of e-mail campaign performance, and it was recently added to the Google Apps Marketplace. In addition, VerticalResponse is offered on the Salesforce AppExchange. VerticalResponse has a social media sharing functionality, which enables customers to easily share their e-mail marketing content with popular social networks such as Twitter and Facebook.

Who Uses It?

VerticalResponse has a customer base of just over 75,000, which spans across industries including wineries, retail, ad agencies, real estate agents, software, and hardware vendors. Another key audience segment is the nearly thousands of nonprofit organizations that take advantage of the 10,000 free e-mails VerticalResponse offers to those with 501(c)(3) status. The one aspect that all its customers have in common is that they need to continue to evolve their business knowledge and e-mail marketing expertise through new media.

Should You Use It?

VerticalResponse is tailored to the small business market, and is ideal for anyone who is either starting e-mail marketing programs for the first time or who understands the medium. It is the only leading E-mail Service Provider

(ESP) to bundle self-service e-mail marketing, online surveys and direct mail services in one package.

Small business customers can rely on VerticalResponse for their newsletters, customer loyalty programs, sales and promotions, and many more programs essential to keeping their businesses growing and profitable.

For the budget-conscious small business, VerticalResponse offers two pay models for maximum flexibility, pay-as-you-go or monthly subscriptions. There are no initial sign-up fees or minimum fees to use the product. If a user wants to create an e-mail and send it to 1,000 contacts it costs just $15.00 on his or her credit card.

Who Started It?

VerticalResponse was started by CEO and cofounder Janine Popick in 2001, just after the challenging dot-com era. Nine years later she has not strayed from what she first set out to do: make small businesses look like giants through the help of e-mail marketing. With Janine's years of direct marketing and entrepreneurial experience, she has successfully built a company that provides an essential service to over 75,000 customers

Volusion

Company Name:	Volusion
URL:	www.volusion.com
Location:	Austin, Texas; Simi Valley, California, United States
Founded:	1999
Employees:	150
Revenue Model:	User fees
Fees:	Monthly plans starting at $24.99 and up depending on package
Tagline:	Succeed online.

What Is It?

Volusion offers an all-in-one e-commerce solution so anyone can open an online store. The solution includes comprehensive shopping cart software and web site hosting, which means that sites are stored on the company's secure servers. The shopping cart software includes hundreds of features, allowing merchants to manage their entire business from one web-based administration area. Software highlights include: a full customer relationship management system, built-in e-mail and newsletter programs, inventory control tools and a robust marketing and social sharing suite. As one of the only PCI/CISP certified e-commerce solutions on the market, merchants look to Volusion to successfully and securely sell online.

Volusion provides additional services to help merchants manage and grow their online business. Storeowners can purchase domain names, security certificates, and fraud protection services. Additionally, the company provides credit card processing solutions to all customers, along with custom design services. To help customers market their online store to the masses, Volusion also offers professional pay-per-click (PPC) and Search Engine Optimization (SEO) services.

How Can It Be Used?

Volusion gives those wanting to establish an online retail presence the opportunity to build and manage a successful online business. Whether it is a merchant's first time selling online or an experienced brick-and-mortar operation moving to the Web, the integrated e-commerce solution provides a full suite of tools for business growth. Storeowners can handle all aspects of operations, including marketing and promotions, customer interactions and complete inventory management within the software. Additionally, merchants have full control over the design and branding of their store, with access to both HTML and CSS code.

Users of the Volusion system can also use the software to fully process all of their orders, as opposed to logging in to various gateway sites. Merchants can process returns, handle incoming phone orders and provide various pricing levels to specified customers. All of these tools can be utilized by multiple workers, with access to various data points fully designated by the business owner.

What Other Applications Does It Work With?

Volusion has built-in integrations with PayPal, Google Checkout and Quick-Books accounting software. With its open application programming interface (API), integrations are possible with any other application with an API. Some popular integrations include Endicia and eBridge.

Volusion also integrates with all major shipping providers, including UPS, USPS and FedEx. Volusion's partner WishPot provides an application for customers to list products within a gift registry. There are also social media integrations with Facebook, Twitter, and several others with an AddThis integration, which allows merchants to share their products across hundreds of social media sites.

The company was the first to introduce direct social shopping by introducing its Social Store Builder, which allows users to sell products directly on their Facebook profiles and fan pages.

Who Uses It?

Over 100,000 entrepreneurs have trusted their online business to Volusion. This number includes a wide variety of retailers, crossing the spectrum from small businesses to enterprise clients selling thousands of products. In addition to its base of small to medium-sized businesses, some of Volusion's larger clients include Disney, Motorola, 3M, Michigan State University, and the *Chicago Tribune*.

Regardless of size, all customers are provided with free, 24/7 live phone support for any technical questions. Apparel customer Repeat Possessions shares the following, "There are many features that Volusion offers that can increase my sales, and *I learn something new almost daily*. My site has grown so much since conception. I continue to learn about blogs and SEO, and with Volusion's support, I have been able to further market my store."

Volusion continues to grow its customer list while continuously improving its platform to meet emerging trends from the e-commerce industry.

Should You Use It?

Anyone who is looking to sell online with a credible and long-standing presence can easily use Volusion's e-commerce solution to handle all aspects of their webstore. Regardless of technical experience, users of all levels have launched their online business with Volusion. The company's 24/7 free phone support and extensive online training materials make the process easy and convenient.

Many business owners are wary of processing payments online due to growing security and privacy concerns. Volusion has addressed this issue by investing millions into its infrastructure to become PCI/CISP Certified. This means that the company has exceeded industry standards in providing secure credit card processing for its customers.

Pet supply retailer Organic Pet Boutique sums up its Volusion experience with the following, "We couldn't be happier with the amount of control we have over the web site. From viewing orders, checking inventory, shipping options, and controlling the web design, everything is at our fingertips and offered at lightning speed."

To ensure that Volusion is the best solution for one's business, interested parties can enter a free 14-day trial to test drive the software.

Who Started It?

Founder and CEO, Kevin Sproles, started Volusion in his bedroom as a web site coder. As his client list grew, he quickly began to see an emerging trend in customer requests—a shopping cart. At this point in time, e-commerce was in its infancy and was only available to major players with deep pockets. Always up for a challenge, Kevin began programming shopping cart software that could be used by any entrepreneur.

One of Kevin's early clients soon became a driving force in growing the company. Current COO and CMO, Clay Olivier, left a successful career at Dell and wanted to launch an environmentally friendly online store. After conducting significant research, he chose Volusion to build his new online business. Kevin and Clay spent countless hours on the phone discussing the software and its potential. Eventually they met in person and the rest is history—or as they say, the present and the future of e-commerce.

Now, after several software versions and the addition of over 150 employees, Volusion continues to create simple and innovative experiences to help their clients succeed online.

Wikia

Company Name:	Wikia
URL:	www.wikia.com/Wikia
Location:	San Francisco, California; Poznan, Poland
Founded:	2004
Employees:	50
Revenue Model:	Series A & B funding and advertising
Fees:	Free
Tagline:	Find and collaborate with guys who love what you love.

What Is It?

Wikia, a company started by Wikipedia cofounder Max Levchin, is different from Wikipedia in that it is not a wiki-styled encyclopedia of information. It is rather a conglomeration of specialized topics (called content hubs), such as gaming, hobbies, and sports. Wikia's intent is to contain information that is community-based with broad generalized topics.

How Can It Be Used?

Wikia contains information that is less formal and could even be labeled entertainment. Sports, health, politics, philosophy, comics, and the performing arts are just some of the topics that make up the content hubs of Wikia. The content focuses more on the personal and entertainment side of information as opposed to the academic and professional aspect.

What Other Applications Does It Work With?

Wikia works with a number of popular social networking applications: Twitter, Facebook, Flickr, YouTube, Google Maps, and RSS2Wiki are all compatible with Wikia. A Google map can be inserted into a Wikia page, blogs or other web site content can be fed into Wikia pages, and YouTube videos can be added to enhance content on Wikia. Additional Wikia features include calendars, e-mail, polls, image tagging, and WidgetTag. WidgetTag allows wiki creators to insert a special symbol to designate the inclusion of a widget into their wiki page.

Who Uses It?

Just like Wikipedia, Wikia reaches an extensive audience. According to Compete.com, Wikia had 3.9 million unique visitors in February 2010. A number of wikis serve as unofficial guides, manuals, or how-tos on certain topics. As an example, there is an unofficial Applepedia on Wikia, whose primary contributors are three individuals from Adelaide, Australia. Another example is a Wikia page on the CHDK firmware for the Canon Digic II and Digic III cameras. There are a number of contributing users to this page, including Wikia cofounder Angela Beesley.

Should You Use It?

There is opportunity for businesses within Wikia besides advertisements, although advertising should not be ignored. Because Wikia has more of an entertainment purpose, businesses have an opportunity to be listed or associated with topics. As an example, under the content hub of "Special FX" there is a subtopic of "Cosmetics." Under "Cosmetics," there is another subtopic of "Alcohol-activated Makeup." The content for Alcohol-activated Makeup includes the names of companies that are well known for providing this type of makeup to the film industry. Such a reference does as much for leading users to investigate those businesses as if they paid for advertisements on Wikia. Should a business choose to, a business could use Wikia to post consumer-oriented information such as manuals or user tips for its product or service.

Who Started It?

Wikia was created by Wikipedia/PayPal founder Jimmy Wales and Angela Beesley. A British Internet entrepreneur according to his Wikipedia bio page, Wales first created Nupedia, an extensive peer-reviewed, open-content encyclopedia, in March 2000. He hired Larry Sanger to be the editor-in-chief, and in 2001 Sanger suggested that a wiki could be used to create an encyclopedia. Wales loaded wiki software and gave Sanger permission to begin creating the web site. Wikia's creation followed Wikipedia's, but the companies have different concepts and audiences.

Wikipedia

Company Name:	Wikipedia
URL:	www.wikipedia.org
Location:	San Francisco, California
Founded:	2001
Employees:	15
Revenue Model:	Donations and grants
Fees:	Free
Tagline:	The free encyclopedia that anyone can edit

What Is It?

The mission of the Wikimedia Foundation, according to its web site, is "to empower and engage people around the world to collect and develop educational content under a free license or in the public domain, and to disseminate it effectively and globally." Wikipedia is one of the largest online reference web sites on the Internet. It is written collaboratively by volunteers, and is available in multiple languages. Anyone can add content, citations, or cross-references as long as they adhere to Wikipedia's editing policies.

Because content is always being added, Wikipedia advises that older content tends to be more balanced and substantiated, while new content tends to have inaccuracies.

How Can It Be Used?

Wikipedia is used primarily as a research tool, but even Wikipedia presents disclaimers against using its content, particularly new content, as a sole reliable reference for an item of information. Wikipedia's layout is simple but powerful, allowing for contributors and editors to focus on the content, not on the page layout. Users can also edit previously contributed content, which aids in the improvement and accuracy of the content. Content is not limited to text: Images, maps, and statistical data are also highly encouraged.

What Other Applications Does It Work With?

Wikipedia is not made to be used with a lot of other application tools. It is available as an application for iPhones and iPod Touches. Wikipedia offers a language translation capability through the use of Transbabel. It also has a meta-tool known as Sandbox. It is intended for experimental pages, and the information is not retained. Wikipedia also offers a meet-up capability for those who are involved in Wikipedia projects.

Who Uses It?

Wikipedia states it has nearly 68 million visitors monthly, and over 91,000 contributing writers. With Wikipedia's focus on collection of all known information, its attraction is just that: users typically access Wikipedia to find information. It's become a popular starting point for research papers as well as answers to homework questions or trivia.

Should You Use It?

Users who want a starting point for an item of information typically use Wikipedia. Businesses that wish to add or edit information purely for the educational benefit of the audience can use Wikipedia. There really aren't any other ways for businesses to use Wikipedia; there are no advertising opportunities, and information that has a promotional slant to it is usually identified and marked with a banner until someone else can verify or dispute the information.

Who Started It?

According to the Wikipedia bio page of founder Jimmy Wales, he first created Nupedia, an extensive peer-reviewed, open-content encyclopedia, in March 2000. He hired Larry Sanger to be the editor-in-chief, and in 2001, Sanger suggested that a wiki could be used to create an encyclopedia. Wales loaded wiki software and gave Sanger permission to begin creating the web site. Sanger coined the term *Wikipedia*. Wikipedia was originally intended to be the information feed for Unpaid, but it grew so rapidly in popularity that it became the web site's focal point. Wales described his plan for Wikipedia as follows: "Imagine a world in which every single person on the planet is given free access to the sum of all human knowledge. That's what we're doing."

WordPress

Company Name:	WordPress.com (associated with Automattic)
URL:	wordpress.com
Location:	San Francisco, California
Founded:	2005
Employees:	55
Revenue Model:	Advertising, premium subscriptions, and limited VIP hosting
Fees:	Ranges from free to $12,500 (top-level VIP hosting) per month (requiring a $600 set-up fee)
Motto:	Express yourself. Start a blog.

What Is It?

WordPress.com is a product of Automattic (also the company behind Wordpress.org, the actual blog software). It provides blog hosting services ranging from free blog accounts to premium paid blog accounts to limited VIP hosting. WordPress is open source and has a robust plug-in architecture that allows for the inclusion of third-party applications to enhance the WordPress user experience.

How Can It Be Used?

WordPress has a variety of features, to include multiple author–multiple blog capability, tagging, photo use through Flickr or Photobucket, Akismet for comment tracking and blocking spammers, and for free accounts, 3 giga-bytes of storage. WordPress also provides excellent customer service, with feedback provided within 24 hours of requested assistance. For premium paid accounts, there are no advertisements as well as additional storage options ranging from 5 gigabytes to 25 gigabytes ($20 to $90 annually). A variety of additional features are available for the premium accounts, each with their own annual costs. WordPress also offers 60 templates for account holders to choose from, in case they don't want to make their own template or don't have the technical knowledge to create their own.

What Other Applications Does It Work With?

The beauty and power of WordPress is that by being open source, and built on open standards with a very robust plug-in architecture, WordPress allows for any outside service to work seamlessly with it. Examples include Twitter, Flickr, Facebook, BlackBerry, Dopplr, del.icio.us, Meebo, iPhone, Gravatar, and more. A good example is Robert Scoble's blog, hosted on WordPress.com at scobleizer.com. He's embedded Twitter, Flickr, Friend-Feed, and more.

Who Uses It?

WordPress has a substantial list of users that are well-known to the U.S. public: CNN's Political Ticker; Dow Jones's All Things Digital; Fox's Greta-Wire; the *New York Times*'s The Moment; Time-Warner's The Page; *People* magazine's StyleWatch Off the Rack; and famous bloggers like Dan Lyons (formerly known as Fake Steve Jobs), and Robert Scoble. Other interesting WordPress users include the virtual online game Second Life.

Should You Use It?

WordPress is a popular blog service used by millions of people. With its open-source software backbone, it encourages users to create, develop, and publish their own blogs or web sites. Conversely, you don't have to be a web design guru to use it; you can keep your blog as simple as you choose. For larger companies or prominent individuals (you have to apply and be accepted), the VIP hosting service is a valuable tool, as it allows those users to piggyback off the WordPress infrastructure. Well-known entities such as the virtual online game Second Life and Flickr use the VIP hosting services for their community blogs.

Who Started It?

The company was cofounded by twentysomething Matt Mullenweg and Mike Little. Matt continues to be the primary developer and spokesperson for the company. WordPress's predecessor was called b2/cafelog. B2/cafelog was written by Michel Valdrighi, a current contributing developer for WordPress. One unique fact about WordPress releases is that each one is named for a jazz musician: WordPress 1.2 was named Mingus after Charles Mingus.

Tool Scorecard for Chapter 24: Publish

Instructions: Using the following five-point (0 to 4) scale, rate each tool in this chapter on the basis of how valuable it *might be* to the internal and external operations of your company. Make notes about which tools appeal to you the most.

4 = Extremely Valuable

3 = Very Valuable

2 = Somewhat Valuable

1 = Not Very Valuable

0 = No Value

Tool	Internal Value	External Value
Blogger	4 3 2 1 0	4 3 2 1 0
Infusionsoft	4 3 2 1 0	4 3 2 1 0
Knol	4 3 2 1 0	4 3 2 1 0
RatePoint	4 3 2 1 0	4 3 2 1 0
SlideShare	4 3 2 1 0	4 3 2 1 0
TypePad	4 3 2 1 0	4 3 2 1 0
Volusion	4 3 2 1 0	4 3 2 1 0
Wikia	4 3 2 1 0	4 3 2 1 0
Wikipedia	4 3 2 1 0	4 3 2 1 0
WordPress	4 3 2 1 0	4 3 2 1 0

CHAPTER 25

Photo

Napoleon Bonaparte has been credited with the idea that "a picture is worth a thousand words" and if that's true, then Flickr's photographs are worth, well 4,000,000,000 × 1,000. . . . Way too many zeros for me! Flickr now houses more than four billion photographs, which doesn't count Picasa, SmugMug, PhotoSwarm, or the many other photo sharing sites.

Ever since there were photos, people were sharing them with one another. Taking pictures is a way of capturing moments in time, which captures the emotions that we can share with others. Simply by looking at a photograph we get a rush of emotions, memories, and a recollection of that very moment that we can share.

Photos really are worth a thousand words, and some even more. One photograph of a happy customer using your product with a big successful smile on her face will sell your product a thousand times faster than a salesperson droning on for 15 minutes about its features and benefits. There's another old adage, "Seeing is believing!" Let your customers and prospects see with their own eyes that buying from you will create a successful experience. All those people in your photos can't be wrong.

I show in this chapter some of the many larger photo sharing web sites available to you. Most of these sites use the *fermium* business model as described in an earlier chapter. Nearly all are completely free for the basic service with small incremental charges for upgraded services. While every photo sharing site might not be listed here, all of the major players are. If you have a photo sharing site you like and it's not in this book, e-mail me and I will try to include it in the next edition. As you read each profile, keep in mind that its features and functions may or may not be right for your particular business. Use the Tool Scorecard at the end of the chapter to help you determine which of these tools qualify for further consideration when you begin creating your social media strategy in Part III of the book.

Flickr

Company Name:	Flickr (associated with Yahoo!)
URL:	www.flickr.com
Location:	Sunnyvale, California
Founded:	2004
Employees:	50
Revenue Model:	Advertising and pro accounts
Fees:	Free; pro accounts: $24.95 per year
Tagline:	Share your photos. Watch the world.

What Is It?

Flickr's mission is to help users get their visual content out to their intended audience through the Web, mobile devices, e-mail, the Flickr web site, RSS feeds, outside blogs, or any other technological method that may be developed. One of the social features that Flickr considers so important to its product is the ability for a user to allow family and friends to participate in the organization of posted photos and videos. Flickr's site is usable in eight languages, including English.

How Can It Be Used?

Free Flickr accounts are allowed for 100 megabytes of uploads a month; pro accounts are unlimited. As another incentive, pro accounts are ad-free. You can post to blogs easily once you authenticate their blog the first time they post photos or videos. You can also post photos to Flickr by e-mail, which is great for photos taken with camera phones. Photos can be shared publicly and privately, but it is estimated that 80 percent of Flickr photos are shared publicly. Photos can be tracked by location and date of creation. Photos can be tagged and viewers can leave comments. A new feature is the ability to print pictures, and products such as postcards can be created. For pro accounts, videos can be uploaded with a maximum of 90 seconds and up to 150 megabytes in size.

Photo   499

What Other Applications Does It Work With?

Apple TV2 works with Flickr, as well as blog applications, Facebook, and MySpace.

Who Uses It?

With more than three million users, there are many types. Personal users want to share special moments, while those engaged in some type of artistic endeavor can share their art, such as photography, jewelry, crafts, music, and more. Besides personal users, the largest group by far appears to be those in the photography field, whether they are using Flickr to test audience response to their work or to offer their work for use under creative commons licensing.

Should You Use It?

If you are looking for a way to share and organize your photos, or collaborate with others using pictures, Flickr is a popular tool that will easily facilitate your needs. Using Flickr to share photos or video related to your business or organization is an excellent way to reach a large audience, but also facilitate posting, tagging, and organization of your visual content. Another benefit of Flickr is that if you are looking for a photo to use, many users allow usage of their material through creative commons licensing; in essence, you may use someone's visual creation as long as you give proper credit and attribution. It also works the other way; if you wish to allow use of your material, you can establish by what four means it becomes available: attribution, noncommercial, no derivative, or share alike. Educators in the photography field might find it valuable as a learning tool or a method to share projects. Schools might find it valuable for sharing material about school events, but proper copyright and legal permissions would have to be taken into consideration.

Who Started It?

Gaming entrepreneurs Caterina Fake and husband Steward Butterfield initially developed a hack that allowed users to post photos to the Web, and subsequently developed tagging capabilities for those photos. These designs, in turn, became Flickr in 2004. Sixteen months later, Yahoo! bought Flickr for $30 million.

Photobucket

Company Name:	Photobucket (Fox Interactive Media)
URL:	photobucket.com
Location:	Denver, Colorado; Seattle Washington; San Francisco, California
Founded:	2003
Employees:	60
Revenue Model:	Advertising and premium subscriptions
Fees:	Free; pro account: $24.95 per year
Tagline:	Where millions upload and share their photos and videos

What Is It?

Photobucket allows users to upload, share, link, and find photos, videos, and graphics. Photobucket offers free tools for making slideshows of photos and videos with music. Users can share photos and videos with friends by e-mail, instant messaging, and mobile phone. Photobucket also maintains a substantial online library of photos and videos. In addition, Photobucket provides an online printing service that allows users to print pictures (now in conjunction with Target stores) and add pictures to products such as T-shirts, mugs, calendars, stickers, and more. Users can also create online scrapbook collages. Photobucket is used to upload photos to sites such as MySpace.

How Can It Be Used?

Photobucket is used for editing and sharing photos and videos with family, friends, and associates. There are group albums that focus on a certain topic, such as "cute puppies," and group members contribute photos to that specific group. Users can now create scrapbook collages to enhance their photo presentations, make slides of their photos, or upload their videos and add music as background. Users can also share graphics such as MySpace icons and backgrounds as well as add other graphics. Photobucket sponsors image-related contests for releases of new films—as it did with *Quarantine*, in which users searched for five *Quarantine* images on the site to make themselves eligible for prizes.

What Other Applications Does It Work With?

Photobucket works with Adobe Premier Express, Digg, Doodle, Friendster, Live Journal, Rock You!, MySpace, JuiceCaster, iPhone, Morpheus software,

Photo   501

Albelli Photo Books, Blogger, Facebook, Chumby, TiVo, and the Flock web browser.

Who Uses It?

Photobucket is used primarily by teens, young adults, and hobbyists. There doesn't seem to be an extensive professional audience present on Photobucket. A large demographic focuses on graphics, celebrities, models, and special personal events.

Should You Use It?

Photobucket usage seems to be more oriented toward personal and hobby interests. The best business-oriented reason for using Photobucket would be the ability to advertise to more than 41 million members. Like Flickr, many involved in the photography industry do post their photos on Photobucket to gain exposure and passively acquire a customer and fan base. There are pictures of events like political conventions, conferences, and other venues.

Who Started It?

Photobucket was founded in 2003 by Alex Welch and Darren Crystal and bought by Fox Interactive Media in 2005. The two observed that the users of e-commerce and social networking needed a main hub from which to post and share their photos and videos. According to a 2007 *USA Today* interview, Alex Welch "wanted Photobucket to serve as a photo depot for simple uploads across a wide swath of the Web."

Picasa

Company Name:	Picasa
URL:	picasa.google.com
Location:	Mountain View, California
Founded:	2001
Employees:	20,000
Fees:	Free
Tagline:	The easy way to find, edit, and share your photos

What Is It?

Picasa is an application for organizing and editing digital photos that specifically targets the most novice users. Picasa is acclaimed for being extremely user friendly by simplifying digital editing with many one-touch edit buttons, and for providing additional editing features previously only available through more expensive software products with a higher learning curve. Users can create movies, collages, and slideshows from their photographs, as well as upload photos to share with friends and family. Picasa interacts with the images on your computer by organizing and sorting images by date.

How Can It Be Used?

Picasa offers the ability to organize and sort images by date, to move and rename images on your computer's hard drive, add star ratings to your favorite pictures, or password-protect specific collections. Users can create an album with the ability to keep one picture in multiple albums without taking up extra hard drive space, edit photos, and create visual effects and captions. Picasa automatically attaches and resizes images to e-mail messages to make them easy to open and be closer to standard sizes.

What Other Applications Does It Work With?

Picasa works with most e-mail programs and all of the newest compact flash devices for ease of transferability. Photos from Picasa can be uploaded to most photo processing web sites to order prints and other products. The "Blog This!" button transfers selected photos directly to Blogger, and the "Web Album" button publishes images onto the web page you designate. Picasa states that an "iPhoto plugin or stand-alone program for uploading photos is available for Mac OS X 10.4 and later, Windows and Linux."

Who Uses It?

Many of Picasa's users are pleasure photographers using the software to enhance their images, create slideshows and movies, or share their images with friends and family. The functionality available through Picasa could easily fit the needs of many novice or intermediate photographers, and depending on the type of photography, could be effective for some professional photographers. This software could be used in various organizations for touch-ups or enhancement of photographs taken at business functions or events in which a professional photography service was not used.

Should You Use It?

If you are looking for a photograph-editing program without a significant learning curve, Picasa may be an effective solution. Some of the primary

Photo 503

complaints regarding many photo-editing programs lie in the lack of usability, which Picasa solves with many one-touch editing buttons and the diversity of features available.

Who Started It?

Picasa—a blend of "Pablo Picasso, the phrase *mi casa* for 'my house,' and 'pic' for pictures"—was originally created by Idealab. Google acquired Picasa in July 2004 and offers the software in free and paid subscriptions.

Slide

Company Name:	Slide
URL:	www.slide.com
Location:	San Francisco, California
Founded:	2005
Employees:	64
Revenue Model:	Advertising
Fees:	Free
Tagline:	The world's largest publisher of social entertainment applications

What Is It?

Slide's concept is to give users creative capability to tell their stories through pictures and video. Slide claims to be the largest publisher of social entertainment applications. Users can share photos in the form of a slideshow, share favorite videos, skin their YouTube videos, or use widgets and applications as entertainment, such as sharing a virtual latte with a friend.

How Can It Be Used?

Slide is primarily used for entertainment purposes. Slide is also used by those who are involved in the entertainment industry. Models, photographers, videographers, and musicians use Slide to post promotional material. You can have lists of fans and friends—the difference being that when you create something new, your fans and friends are notified. You are notified in return only when your friends create something, though, not when your fans create something. Users can choose to become fans when they want to be notified of your new creation, but you can add a fan as a friend.

What Other Applications Does It Work With?

Slide works with a number of applications such as MySpace, Facebook, eBay, Bebo, Hi5, Xanga, Tagged, Orkut, Friendster, and Blogger. Music can be added to slideshows on Slide, and there is also a Slide screensaver and desktop application.

Who Uses It?

Slide users primarily appear to be those who want to share pictures and videos for personal enjoyment. There are also users who are active in the entertainment industry at all levels of success who post their promotional items on Slide.

Should You Use It?

For corporate businesses, it is best used primarily for advertising purposes. Slide reaches 134 million viewers. Companies such as McDonald's, AT&T Wireless, and Paramount Pictures advertise on Slide. It would be feasible to use Slide to post event photos and videos to reach the large audience, but Slide's focus is primarily social entertainment. If a company is prepared to use Slide to entertain its audience as it markets its product or service, then Slide is a valuable social marketing tool.

Who Started It?

Max Levchin is not only the cofounder of Slide, but also PayPal. Levchin is behind Slide's biggest risk, using its capability to auto-insert in MySpace profiles, which was against MySpace guidelines. MySpace didn't react, and Slide became an instant hit among users of social networking sites.

SmugMug

Company Name:	SmugMug
URL:	www.smugmug.com
Location:	Mountain View, California
Founded:	2002
Employees:	50
Revenue Model:	Paid membership levels
Fees:	Free trial version; membership accounts: $39.95 to $149.95

Photo 505

What Is It?

SmugMug is an independent photo sharing site that targets professional photographers. Professional photographers can access features such as "watermarking, selling downloads, prints, gifts, and creating galleries of photos" with the ability to use their own domain names. SmugMug offers the functionality of most photo sharing sites accessible to the common user, but is geared more toward the professional photographer.

How Can It Be Used?

SmugMug can be used as a photo sharing site for individuals to upload their digital images and share with others. The account membership levels offer varying tiers of options: the basic account provides users with a custom web site and address; the upgraded account offers customization of site design and layout; and the highest account level allows users to remove SmugMug from the address for a more tailored experience.

What Other Applications Does It Work With?

SmugMug offers functionality to upload images from Picasa, iPhoto, and iTunes. SmugMug also offers a published application programming interface (API) for developers and programmers to create functionality for new applications.

Who Uses It?

The modality of SmugMug as a photo sharing web site is such that anyone can use it, but the features and pricing options are designed for the intermediate or professional photographer.

SmugMug can be used by many organizations as a photo sharing site or as a photo hosting and sales site. The highest account level was designed at the request of the Howard Dean presidential campaign in 2004 to use the service without the SmugMug name in the URL.

Should You Use It?

With features such as watermarking; selling downloads, prints, and gift products; and creating photo galleries, SmugMug is designed with the professional or aspiring professional photographer in mind. The various options and functionality provided by SmugMug could be beneficial for organizations or sole proprietors as a platform to showcase commodities. For the aspiring or professional photographer, SmugMug offers an accessible virtual gallery to display their work, and for a percentage, the ability to sell their prints. The download, print, and gift products could be used by a wide variety of organizations as a way for participants to commemorate a special event or ceremony.

Who Started It?

SmugMug was started in 2002 by Chris and Don MacAskill and was the unintended offshoot of a start-up video game–oriented web service. As the company progressed, more family members joined the staff at SmugMug to carry on their vision to offer an ad-free and spam-free photo sharing site.

Twitxr

Company Name:	Twitxr
URL:	twitxr.com
Location:	Girona, Spain
Founded:	2008

What Is It?

Twitxr is a photoblog service created to enhance communication with your friends and family. Using your mobile phone, you can share pictures and ideas in one message that automatically adds location information to your photos and updates. According to Martin Varsavsky, Twitxr was "specifically designed for iPhone" but "as a third party application . . . it isn't officially available for the iPhone." You can automatically add your location, update your status, and publish your photos and messages on social networks and photo sharing sites in a single message.

How Can It Be Used?

The majority of users of Twitxr send pictures and updates on their daily activities to friends, family, and coworkers. Twitxr claims it works with any mobile phone and all major social networks. Updates can be shown on blogs and personal web sites also with minor customization. "Twitxr has a public API"; this enables developers to integrate Twitxr with their applications.

Photo 507

What Other Applications Does It Work With?

Twitxr claims it works with iPhone and major social media applications, but specifically states on its web site that it supports Twitter, Facebook, Picasa, and Flickr; blogs and personal web pages; and customized applications.

Who Uses It?

Currently Twitxr is used by private individuals providing updates on their daily activities to communicate with friends, family, and coworkers. If the functionality improves, Twitxr may have the potential for expanded business use as a marketing research service or for feedback on products and services.

Should You Use It?

The potential exists for Twitxr as a beneficial business tool for real-time updates for time-sensitive information. Founder Martin Varsavsky claims Twitxr "makes uploading text and a photo from the iPhone very easy," but "you have to 'jailbreak' the phone before you can install their application."

Who Started It?

Twitxr is a product released in 2008 by FON Labs group. "FON founder Martin Varsavsky announced the product on his blog."

Zooomr

Company Name:	ZooomR
URL:	www.zooomr.com
Location:	San Francisco, California
Founded:	2005
Employees:	10
Fees:	Free to $19.95 per year upgraded pro feature

What Is It?

Zooomr is a start-up photo sharing application that incorporates Geo-Tagging, Ajax, and RSS features and currently supports 16 locales. While similar to many of the other photo sharing sites, Zooomr sets itself apart with the OpenID multilogin capability; LightBox, which is similar to a slideshow; SmartSets, "which are dynamically generated albums; PeopleTags, which allows users to add themselves inside photos and search for people inside photos"; and Zipline, which "adds a social networking aspect to the site allowing users to send a message to one of their 'contacts' or to see when a contact uploads photos."

How Can It Be Used?

Zooomr is used like many other photo and image sharing sites. Users can upload photos or other digital images to share with friends and family. The unique GeoTagging feature can assist users in finding location-specific information, location-based news, web sites, and other geographical identifiers. With people tags, users can find themselves and others in images. Zooomr is available in more than 15 languages.

What Other Applications Does It Work With?

Zooomr integrates with most social networking applications, including Facebook and MySpace.

Who Uses It?

Zooomr is available for use by anyone wishing to share photos or other digital images and is significantly useful for non-English speakers because of its availability in a variety of languages. A beneficial aspect of using Zooomr includes unlimited uploading, storing, and archiving of photos. Users of Zooomr are those interested in interacting with others while sharing memories, special moments, important events, and key locations.

Should You Use It?

If you are looking for a way to share photos in an interactive environment, Zooomr may be the solution. If you've ever looked at a picture and wondered where it was taken, the GeoTagging feature provides the answer. Viewing photos from friends and family has become more informative. Users can obtain the answers to the questions: "who?" "what?" and "where?" with PeopleTags, Notes, and GeoTagging features.

Who Started It?

Kristopher Tate and Michael Van Veen started Zooomr in 2005 as a platform to "share photos with his friends in Japan. The site was made so it could be

Photo 509

viewed in both English and Japanese." Zooomr recruited Thomas Hawk as its "chief evangelist" and was relaunched in 2006.

Tool Scorecard for Chapter 25: Photo

Instructions: Using the following five-point (0 to 4) scale, rate each tool in this chapter on the basis of how valuable it *might be* to the internal and external operations of your company. Make notes about which tools appeal to you the most.

4 = Extremely Valuable
3 = Very Valuable
2 = Somewhat Valuable
1 = Not Very Valuable
0 = No Value

Tool	Internal Value	External Value
Flickr	4 3 2 1 0	4 3 2 1 0
Photobucket	4 3 2 1 0	4 3 2 1 0
Picasa	4 3 2 1 0	4 3 2 1 0
Slide	4 3 2 1 0	4 3 2 1 0
SmugMug	4 3 2 1 0	4 3 2 1 0
Twitxr	4 3 2 1 0	4 3 2 1 0
Zooomr	4 3 2 1 0	4 3 2 1 0

CHAPTER 26

Audio

Audio is a very powerful medium. It's easier to digest than text and evoke mental images that video doesn't allow. Do you listen to the radio? Had you ever heard a book on CD? Have you ever heard Edgar Allan Poe read aloud?

Audio allows us to sit back and allow the author or orator to slowly spoonfeed us content with inflection, dramatic pauses, and human nuances of them being right there in the room speaking to us. While we listen to the cadence of the words being formed into sentences and thoughts, we can imagine the associated images and watch them play out in our minds to form the story the author is trying to portray.

Audio is also the easiest to create and edit short of using text. Most PCs have a built-in microphone and recording software already on the hard drive. All you need to do is click record, speak, stop, and share.

I list in this chapter some of the many companies providing recording and editing software and web sites where you can share your story, your emotions, your imagery, and your audio with your customers and prospects.

As you read each profile, keep in mind that its features and functions may or may not be right for your particular business. Use the Tool Scorecard at the end of the chapter to help you determine which of these tools qualify for further consideration when you begin creating your social media strategy in Part III of the book.

theSocialMediaBible.com

iTunes

Company Name:	Apple Inc.
URL:	www.apple.com/itunes
Location:	Cupertino, California
Founded:	2001 (Apple 1976)
Revenue Model:	Advertising and merchandise
Tagline:	The entertainment capital of your world

What Is It?

iTunes is a digital media application that works on both Macintosh and Windows operating systems. iTunes allows users to access, organize, and play video and music files. Another big aspect of iTunes is the ability to buy songs, albums, movies, television shows, podcasts, audio books, and other digital media through the iTunes store, provided you are connected to the Internet. (A podcast is generally defined as a series of audio or video files available on the Internet for users to listen to or watch on their computer or portable multimedia device.) iTunes is also the interface software that is used to interact with products like the iPhone and the iPod.

How Can It Be Used?

iTunes can be used in many different ways. The primary function is to act as a player and library for your digital media files. Through it you can download, structure, and play your videos and music. iTunes can also be used as a means of disseminating information widely since it allows users the ability to subscribe, receive, and listen to podcasts. It also gives users the ability to submit their podcasts to the iTunes podcast directory.

What Other Applications Does It Work With?

iTunes is very closely integrated with other Apple applications, especially GarageBand and the iWork and iLife suites. The applications in both of the suites allow users to access the iTunes library and import them into their respective projects. Any song created in GarageBand can be exported to iTunes. Scripting is also possible in iTunes, which gives users the ability to coordinate it with additional applications.

Who Uses It?

iTunes is used by a very large number of digital media users. This popularity can probably be attributed to several factors, such as the advent of the iPod, the fact that iTunes software is free to download; and the high number of podcasts and songs available for download and purchase through the iTunes store. For this reason, many podcasters use iTunes in an attempt to reach as many listeners as possible. The vast majority of Mac computer customers use iTunes since the application comes bundled with all Macintosh computers.

Should You Use It?

You should use iTunes if you are interested in a free, user-friendly digital media application. You should also use iTunes if you would like to buy a variety of different digital media files, download them, and then play them within the same application. iTunes is a good media player to use if you are interested in podcasting, either as a subscriber or as a creator, since it provides access to numerous podcasts and potential listeners.

Who Started It?

iTunes is based on an old software application called SoundJam MP, which was created in 1999 by Jeff Robbin and Bill Kincaid, and then purchased by Apple in 2000. After Apple adjusted the interface, skins, and feature set, the program was released as iTunes in January 2001.

Podbean

Company Name:	Podbean
URL:	www.podbean.com
Location:	Wilmington, Delaware
Founded:	2006
Employees:	10
Revenue Model:	Advertising and premium subscriptions
Motto:	Podcast hosting, social subscribing
Fees:	Free to $19.95 per year

What Is It?

Podbean is a podcast service provider that was created to allow individuals and businesses the ability to publish podcasts easily without any prior technical knowledge in web site design or podcasting. Podbean consolidates publishing, management, syndication, and analysis podcasting tools in a user-friendly, point-and-click interface that is similar to a blog environment. Podbean also allows users the ability to browse, listen, and subscribe to podcasts, Podbean hosted or otherwise, all in one location.

How Can It Be Used?

Podbean can be used in two primary ways: as a podcast archiving tool and as a means to disseminate podcasts easily. Users can collect their podcast subscriptions from all over the Internet, as well as browse all podcasts delivered through Podbean, and store them in one spot on their Podbean account. Podbean also functions as a podcast delivery mechanism by allowing subscribers the ability to post and deliver podcasts in an effective and simple manner. Additional tools such as scheduled podcasts and subscriber stats are available for upgraded account packages.

What Other Applications Does It Work With?

Podbean is compatible with several applications to increase the exposure and flexibility of a user's podcasts. Among the more highly visible applications are iTunes, social networking web sites such as MySpace and Facebook, blogging web sites like LiveJournal and Blogger, and PayPal. Podbean also allows a multitude of file types to be uploaded, ranging from different audio formats to Microsoft PowerPoint documents.

Who Uses It?

A wide variety of users, in professional and recreational contexts, employ Podbean. Individual listeners use Podbean by searching through a large catalog of subjects to discover new podcasts to listen to, along with gathering their other podcast subscriptions in one place. Podcasters of all types also make use of Podbean. Individuals can publish podcasts on a desired subject so audiences with similar tastes can listen to their thoughts. Educators also make use of Podbean, whether to share research with colleagues or to teach lessons to students. The last core segment of Podbean users are commercial podcasters, who either sell their podcasts or use their podcasts to market a commodity.

Should You Use It?

You should use Podbean if you are currently, or desire to be, involved with podcasting as either a listener or a publisher. From a listener's perspective, Podbean makes it easy and efficient to become a consumer of podcasts. The ability to search through the large podcast catalog makes it simple to find new podcasts, and the embedded player gives you the option of listening to them right in your web browser. Also, the capability to gather all your podcast subscriptions in one spot means you can access your podcasts from any computer with Internet access. From a podcast creator's perspective, Podbean gives you several tools to publish and share your podcast. The included personalized podcast site, along with the point-and-click interface handles the majority of the technical issues, so someone who is new to publishing podcasts can become acclimated rather quickly. The large array of compatible technologies is also a benefit to Podbean users. Through Podbean and entities such as iTunes, social web sites, and other blogs, your podcast could quickly market itself to new audiences. Lastly, Podbean is friendly toward commercial podcasting, so if you are a business or an entrepreneur looking to make podcasting a potential asset, Podbean is a good podcast service provider to consider.

Who Started It?

Podbean was created in February 2006. On April 10, 2007, it was incorporated as a limited liability company according to the Division of Corporations of the state of Delaware.

Podcast.com

Company Name:	Podcast.com
URL:	podcast.com
Location:	Cambridge, Massachusetts
Employees:	15
Revenue Model:	Advertising and sponsorship

What Is It?

Podcast.com is a platform created by Treedia Labs on which to view or listen to podcasts without additional software or devices, and "provides access to a growing list of over 85,000 curated and constantly updated podcast feeds." Treedia Labs promotes Podcast.com as a "unique value proposition to content consumers" that "presents an unsurpassed way for content providers to reach an audience that consumes podcasts via the Web, multimedia devices and Internet radio."

How Can It Be Used?

Podcast.com can be used to reach niche audiences and those consumers who are too busy or who are unable to view traditional media outlets for information or entertainment. Treedia claims Podcast.com "is the only podcast consumption site to incorporate directory, social media, viral sharing, and personal directory management functionality." Businesses can use podcasting to communicate with consumers or clients, and market products or services. Users can subscribe to the feed and enable a notification feature to indicate when a new podcast is available.

What Other Applications Does It Work With?

Podcast.com is a platform that enables the user to listen to or watch content on a computer or mobile device without any additional applications, services, or hardware. Users can view or share podcasts through their mobile device.

Who Uses It?

Individuals use Podcast.com to keep current on local, national, and international news; to watch programs; or to listen to music or other audio files. Businesses can use podcasts as a means to communicate with employees, clients, or constituents; make product or service announcements; provide information on news and events; or educate others on a particular subject or process. Educators can use podcasts to supplement text, provide a demonstration, or interact with students.

Should You Use It?

Podcast.com offers a wide range of available topics that appeal to a diverse audience. To enhance media relations, organizations can "incorporate quotes from product specialists or senior executives" for distribution to "key journalists." Podcasts can be an informative tool when programs are created to provide advice or direction from subject-matter experts on essential industry topics. Podcasting is a valuable tool for professionals unable to attend conferences as a means of obtaining the pertinent information. If you are looking for a means to communicate more effectively with your audience, Podcast.com is a useful platform.

Who Started It?

Podcast.com was started by Treedia Labs, which "enables a rich user experience that promotes sharing."

Rhapsody

Company Name:	Rhapsody (subsidiary of RealNetworks Inc.)
URL:	www.rhapsody.com
Location:	Seattle, Washington
Founded:	2001
Revenue Model:	Advertising and premium subscriptions
Fees:	Free: Up to 25 songs per month
Rhapsody Unlimited:	$12.99; unlimited music any time through any web browser
Rhapsody To Go:	$14.99; unlimited music any time through any web browser and on a compatible MP3 player
Tagline:	Listen all you want. Whenever you want.

What Is It?

Rhapsody is an online music library that allows you to experience full-length, high-quality digital music and music videos. As they say at Rhapsody, "Listen to whatever you want, wherever you are." Rhapsody offers music from thousands of artists—new, old, and everywhere in between. Using Rhapsody, you can share music, playlists, and music videos with anyone in the world. With Rhapsody's monthly membership services, you can listen to unlimited amounts of music from any web browser, transfer your music to a compatible MP3 player, or enjoy it using a compatible home audio device.

How Can It Be Used?

Rhapsody is an effective tool for music research, acquisition, and sharing. With over four million tracks to choose from, Rhapsody covers even the most obscure musical tastes. The playlist function helps to separate like genres of music for certain dedicated situations. They also have an affiliate program that offers the use of Rhapsody's RealPlayer to bloggers and developers for use on their personal web sites. Many leading companies have paired with Rhapsody for live event sponsorship, special events, or promotions to engage their target audience and strengthen brand initiatives. MINI Cooper teamed up with Rhapsody for a concert at the House of Blues in Las Vegas to support the participants in the "MINI Takes the States" cross-country road rally. In addition to the live event, a customized MINI Cooper RealPlayer skin and rich media campaign were integrated on Rhapsody for added exposure online.

What Other Applications Does It Work With?

Rhapsody works with Twitter, Facebook, and MySpace in adding music to profiles. The Rhapsody MP3 store offers music downloads compatible with iPod. Rhapsody works with Slide.com in creating an appropriate soundtrack for your slideshows. TiVo's broadband-connected DVR can play music from Rhapsody. Rhapsody can sync with your Last.fm page to show all recently played tracks from Rhapsody. Verizon Wireless VCast customers can upload their music to their mobile phone library using Rhapsody.

Who Uses It?

Rhapsody can be used to pair a brand side by side with popular music talent to increase brand awareness with a desired demographic. Companies that want to promote events and celebrities would do well with Rhapsody's sponsored playlists and dedicated RealPlayer skins. RealNetworks can develop a complete custom advertising campaign that encompasses desired media, promotion, and live events. Bloggers have also found Rhapsody helpful in using it for music playback and music reference on their blogs and web sites.

Should You Use It?

Rhapsody has paired many brands alongside special concerts and music festivals. Hyundai sponsored the first Rhapsody Independent Music Event in San Francisco, using Rhapsody's editors to combine its brand with cutting-edge music, and RealNetworks produced successful performances. The option of playing short advertisements before music videos on Rhapsody grabs the attention of your target audience. If you want to boost interest on your company's blog, Rhapsody can help by adding a media player and music playlist to your blog. If you want to reach a younger demographic effectively through artists and concerts, Rhapsody is an avenue to explore.

Who Started It?

Tim Bratton, Alexandre Brouaux, Dave Lampton, J. P. Lester, Sylvain Rebaud, and Nick Sincaglia were developing a revolutionary streaming audio engine in 1999 first launched as TuneTo.com. This customized radio service was acquired by Listen.com in 2001 to add the streaming audio to their already comprehensive online music directory. Rhapsody was born in December 2001. Rhapsody was the first online music subscription service to offer its customers unlimited music for a low monthly fee. In 2003, Listen .com was acquired by RealNetworks to extend its reign in the digital music revolution.

Tool Scorecard for Chapter 26: Audio

Instructions: Using the following five-point (0 to 4) scale, rate each tool in this chapter on the basis of how valuable it *might be* to the internal and external operations of your company. Make notes about which tools appeal to you the most.

4 = Extremely Valuable

3 = Very Valuable

2 = Somewhat Valuable

1 = Not Very Valuable

0 = No Value

Tool	Internal Value	External Value
iTunes	4 3 2 1 0	4 3 2 1 0
Podbean	4 3 2 1 0	4 3 2 1 0
Podcast.com	4 3 2 1 0	4 3 2 1 0
Rhapsody	4 3 2 1 0	4 3 2 1 0

CHAPTER 27

Video

If a picture is worth 1,000 words, then at 25 frames (pictures) per second, video adds up to 1.5 million words per minute! That's why everyone loves video!

Video is the overall preferred medium of choice for relaying information. After a hard day at work, do you pick up a book, turn on the radio, or settle down in front of the television for a good movie or uplifting sitcom? Most likely we turn to the television to coast through some nightly brain candy.

People love video because it's the next best thing to being in the same room with the person sharing their knowledge and experiences. You can hear the words, see the images they convey, and also watch and become involved in the scene that is taking place at that moment. We can see what the author is explaining, and become emotionally involved in the scene. We can hear the actors' inflections while experiencing their facial expressions and body language. It is estimated that 55 percent of all communication comes from body language, while 38 percent from voice, and only 7 percent from the words themselves.

YouTube currently hosts more than 120,000,000 videos with 200,000 more being added every day. If you were to view all of the videos that YouTube had to offer, it would take you more than 600 years. More than 200,000,000 are viewed every day. YouTube has officially become the second-largest search engine on the planet. There is good reason for that. People, your customers, and prospects all love video.

I list in this chapter some of the key players in the business of recording and sharing video.

As you read each profile, keep in mind that its features and functions may or may not be right for your particular business. Use the Tool Scorecard at the end of the chapter to help you determine which of these tools qualify for further consideration when you begin creating your social media strategy in Part III of the book.

Brightcove

Company Name:	Brightcove
URL:	www.brightcove.com
Location:	Cambridge, Massachusetts; Seattle, Washington; New York; London; Tokyo; Beijing; Barcelona; Hamburg
Founded:	2004
Employees:	110
Revenue Model:	Sales of service packages
Fees:	Must contact for quote

What Is It?

"Brightcove is an online video publishing company" that serves as a platform for content owners to reach their audience directly through the Internet, enables web publishers the functionality to "enrich their sites with syndicated video programming," and provides "marketers more ways to communicate and engage with their consumers." Brightcove promotes its services as "flexible, yet comprehensive" and claims to "maximize your Internet video presence by integrating Brightcove directly with your existing media solutions such as content management systems, ad servers and analytics platforms."

How Can It Be Used?

Several options for use of Brightcove are available. Networks, broadcasters, newspapers, and magazines can reach new audiences, expand advertising options, and reach "niche audiences through managed and tracked viral sharing options." Music labels and artists can use "online video to create revenue streams and drive music sales." Web sites can integrate online video to increase page views and time spent on a page and increase traffic "through syndication and viral distribution." Business-to-consumer marketers can build brand recognition through online content and video campaigns, and increase online sales through in-depth product coverage. Government agencies and educational organizations can use Brightcove online video solutions for meeting and speech coverage, and by offering distance-learning modules.

Any organization can use the video production services provided by Brightcove to create recruitment videos, testimonials, and documentaries.

What Other Applications Does It Work With?

Brightcove videos use Adobe Flash technology to stream Flash video to widgets, which enables compatibility with applications supporting Flash Video. Brightcove also established a "distribution partnership with TiVo" and a "content delivery partnership with Limelight Networks," and "partnered with Reuters to create a program to syndicate customized news video players." Some additional technology partners include: Google AdSense, Tremor Media, Ad Tube, and Livestream.

Who Uses It?

With the development of magazine and newspaper publishers expanding to online video, Brightcove capitalized on this movement and signed deals with companies such as Time Inc., TV Guide, Discovery Communications (Discovery Channel, Travel Channel, TLC, and Animal Planet), the Washington Post, Newsweek Interactive, the Meredith Corporation, the Hearst Corporation, Nielsen Business Media, Crain Communications, Reed Business Information, Wine Spectator, and the National Geographic Society.

According to Chris Lucas, vice president and executive producer of digital media for Showtime, "Showtime is a content company, not a technology company. The Brightcove Platform allows us to focus on what we do best."

Should You Use It?

Brightcove offers numerous solutions for video publishing that integrate directly with existing media solutions for a variety of organizations. If your organization is working on expanding into online video services, Brightcove may be an appropriate solution to reach new audiences. Existing news media publications can "syndicate to and from related publications and affiliates" and "drive revenue with a wide range of ad formats and targeting options." Brightcove also supports content such as slideshows, podcasts, and audio for added flexibility for users.

Who Started It?

Jeremy Allaire initially cofounded Allaire Corporation with his brother, J. J. Allaire, in 1995 when they created the web development tool ColdFusion.

"When Macromedia acquired Allaire in March 2001, Jeremy became Chief Technology Officer" and "helped develop the Macromedia MX (Flash) platform." He left Macromedia in 2003 to join venture capital firm General Catalyst. Jeremy founded Brightcove in 2004 and currently serves as CEO. Brightcove is a venture-backed private company.

Google Video

This can no longer be used to upload videos. The videos already on there before January 2009 will remain, but no more can be uploaded. Google now uses it to find technology to help its users find videos on the Web.

Company Name:	Google Video
URL:	video.google.com
Location:	Mountain View, California
Founded:	1998
Employees:	20,000 (Google)
Revenue Model:	Advertising and revenue-generating search engines
Fees:	Basic: Free; Premier version: $50 per year per user
Tagline:	Organizing the world's information and making it universally accessible and useful.

What Is It?

Google Video is a video sharing web site that offers premium services for a small annual fee. Its primary focus is on providing freely searchable videos featuring amateur media, Internet videos, viral ads, movie trailers, and commercial professional media. A beneficial feature of Google Video includes a reporting tool that logs and stores details on the number of times each of the user's videos has been viewed and downloaded within a specific time frame, which can be downloaded into a spreadsheet or be printed.

How Can It Be Used?

Google Video can be used to share videos such as internal training videos, corporate announcements, e-learning modules, and presentations. Videos can be kept secure and private without the necessity of e-mailing or downloading large files. These uploaded videos can be connected to personal or corporate web sites and sorted by date or popularity. Users can also download videos and save them on their cell phones.

What Other Applications Does It Work With?

The Google Video search database includes video from YouTube, GoFish, ExposureRoom, Vimeo, MySpace, Biku, and Yahoo! Video. Google Video runs on Windows and Mac OSX, and is compatible with VirtualDub and GVideo Fix, which can read the .gvi files and convert them into different formats. Linux versions of VLC Media Player and Kaffeine are also compatible with Google's .avi format.

Who Uses It?

Business and educational organizations can use Google Video for internal training videos, corporate presentations and announcements, product demonstrations, and e-learning modules.

According to Manesh Patel, chief information officer, "Cost and complexity have until now limited the effective use of video to improve business functions. The integration of video into Google Apps, combined with continuing improvements in video devices and network infrastructure, provides significant opportunities for innovation and saving throughout our global teams."

Should You Use It?

If your business or organization is looking to implement video training, e-learning modules, product demonstrations, or corporate announcements, but does not have the staff or available funds in the IT department, Google Video may be an appropriate solution. Since Google Video requires just a standard browser, virtually any department with Internet access can use it. "Google securely hosts and streams your videos, so employees don't need to share videos over e-mail, or burden IT for a video solution."

Who Started It?

Larry Page is cofounder and currently serves as president of products. His love for computers began at the early age of six, and he later graduated from the University of Michigan with a bachelor's degree in engineering, with a concentration on computer engineering. While in the PhD program in computer science at Stanford University, Larry met Sergey Brin. Together they developed Google, which began operating in 1998.

Sergey Brin is cofounder and currently serves as president of technology. He received his bachelor's of science degree with honors in mathematics and computer science from the University of Maryland at College Park. While pursuing his PhD in computer science at Stanford University, he met Larry Page and developed Google.

Hulu

Company Name:	Hulu LLC
URL:	www.hulu.com
Location:	Los Angeles, New York, Chicago, and Beijing
Founded:	2007
Revenue Model:	Advertising
Tagline:	Watch your favorites. Anytime. For free.

What Is It?

Hulu is a service that provides free streaming videos on demand to users through a web browser. The company is supported entirely through limited commercial interruption, with the advertising playing either periodically throughout a video, or at the beginning of the selected content. Full versions and clips of television shows, movies, news programs, and sports games are just part of the video offerings at Hulu. Numerous content providers constantly add media, both old and current, to Hulu. Hulu also provides web syndication services for other web sites.

How Can It Be Used?

Hulu can be used to view and share videos online. If a user wanted to share a video, Hulu provides an embedding code that a user can add to a blog, social networking site, or personal web page. Hulu also allows users to create a queue, which acts as a playlist for their selected videos, as well as subscribe to specific shows, which automatically adds new clips and episodes of that show to their queue as they are uploaded.

What Other Applications Does It Work With?

In addition to embedding videos in other web sites, Hulu also allows users to create widgets from which Hulu videos can be viewed. These widgets work with a variety of other applications such as iGoogle, Windows Vista, Macintosh OS X, and HoverSpot. Some of the web sites Hulu provides syndication for are Facebook, MSN, Comcast's fancast.com, Yahoo!, AOL, and MySpace.

Who Uses It?

Hulu is used by a large audience throughout the United States. It is not currently offered internationally, as there are business and legal issues involved with streaming the content outside of the United States. There are numerous content providers contributing to Hulu; among them are Warner Bros, NBC Universal, FX, Comedy Central, National Geographic, FOX, MGM, and Sony Pictures Television.

Should You Use It?

You should use Hulu if you are interested in using online video advertising to reach a user base that exists within the United States. Hulu is unique in that it is supported by a large number of popular content providers, so you can target an already established and varied audience. Advertisers who work with Hulu are offered several benefits, such as the ability to customize sponsorships, exposure through syndication partners, and marketing through additional sites with embedded and shared videos.

Who Started It?

NBC Universal and News Corporation founded Hulu in March 2007. It is operated by a dedicated, independent management team. A private equity firm, Providence Equity Partners, invested $100 million in October 2007. Jason Kilar, formerly of Amazon.com, was named the CEO in June 2007.

Metacafe

Company Name:	Metacafe
URL:	www.metacafe.com
Location:	Palo Alto, California, headquarters; New York, New York; Tel Aviv, Israel
Founded:	2003
Employees:	60
Revenue Model:	Advertising
Fees:	Free: web site, application, and services
Tagline:	Serving the world's best videos

What Is It?

Metacafe proudly markets itself as "the world's largest independent video sharing web site." This site provides opportunity for a broad spectrum of video producers to showcase their creations. Short-form videos from independent creators, small to mid-sized production groups, and major media companies are available for viewing. Metacafe emphasizes the quality, not the quantity, of the videos and prides itself on entertainment value. In a recent partnership with Nareos and Zed, Metacafe video enthusiasts have the capability to stream and download content to their mobile devices, allowing instant access to video entertainment. With more than 40 million viewers each month, Metacafe has a stronghold in the short-form virtual video entertainment market.

How Can It Be Used?

Metacafe offers a video entertainment platform that hosts audience-driven, short-form original video entertainment for a large audience. As such, it can be used to inform with how-to videos, to entertain with a vast array of video categories, or to market a new concept or product. This is a beneficial medium for private individuals, small production companies, and independent filmmakers to showcase their talents and gain exposure. Metacafe offers a Producer Rewards program that generates revenue for creators of original content that crosses a specific threshold of total views and VideoRank score.

What Other Applications Does It Work With?

Several applications can be used in conjunction with Metacafe. Skype is one application that allows users to share videos found on Metacafe. Nareos and Zed offer a downloadable mobile application that allows users to instantly view entertainment-grade videos from Metacafe. Nareos is enabling this capability in Germany, the Netherlands, Italy, England, India, and Sweden, and Zed is enabling this capability in Spain and the United States.

Who Uses It?

Entry-level producers use Metacafe to gain exposure, production companies use Metacafe to find new talent or showcase a pet project, and numerous private individuals use it for a quick entertainment break. Videos uploaded to Metacafe could also be used as an advertising tool by creating an entertaining video featuring a product or service. If your company provides a technique or service, a video on Metacafe could demonstrate how your offerings meet the needs of your target demographic. If you are looking for a means of providing in-house training for employees, the how-to section may be a cost-effective resource to consider.

Should You Use It?

Many current viewers of videos on Metacafe do so for personal enjoyment. Independent video producers and production companies use Metacafe to increase exposure to their work, leading to name recognition and the potential for future project offers.

Metacafe was the platform used by Brandon McConnell for his video creations. He is a zoo groundskeeper by day and spray paint artist by night. Brandon posted two videos of himself creating a painting in minutes. "More than one million people have viewed his *Amazing Spray Painting* and *Amazing Sprayer!* videos, netting Brandon about $5,300 during the Producer Rewards beta program."

Who Started It?

Eyal Herzog founded Metacafe Inc. in July 2003 and serves as its chief technology officer and chief product officer.

Ofer Adler has been chief product officer of IncrediMail Ltd. since November 1999. Mr. Adler cofounded IncrediMail Ltd. and Metacafe Inc. in July 2003. He serves as a director of Mctacafe Inc.

Arik Czerniak cofounded Metacafe Inc. in July 2003 and served as its chief executive officer until February 7, 2007. Czerniak now serves as a director of Metacafe Inc. Trained in physics, computer science, and math, Czerniak also was part of the Israeli military research and development team.

Viddler

Company Name:	Viddler
URL:	www.viddler.com
Location:	Arizona, Pennsylvania, and Florida, United States; Poland
Founded:	2005
Employees:	17
Revenue Model:	Advertising and premium fees
Fees:	Free for noncommercial users with premium fees for commercial users who want upgraded features. The price is based on bandwidth and starts at $100 per month.
Tagline:	The best way to watch and publish your videos.

What Is It?

Viddler is a video sharing entertainment site that provides a platform for users to upload, enhance, and share their videos from their browser to showcase their work. Viddler offers a unique feature to tag or comment on portions of the video rather than the whole video. Through streaming capability, users can view and search without waiting for the entire video to download.

How Can It Be Used?

Rob Sandie, founder of Viddler, was looking for a way to share football video reels with his family and key in on specific moments, which spurred the creation of Viddler. Using the Viddler ad system, advertisers can "bid on videos with relevant keyword tags about the whole video or a specific point in time during the video." "Uploaders can also sign up to partner in a revenue share with Viddler for advertising served during their videos."

What Other Applications Does It Work With?

Viddler works with Facebook, WordPress, iTunes, and several other podcast services. You can also create Digg button tags for your videos.

Who Uses It?

Viddler is currently used primarily by private individuals looking for an entertainment break, but entry-level producers could use Viddler to gain exposure. Videos uploaded to Viddler can be used as an advertising tool by embedding ads within the videos, or creating an entertaining video featuring a product or service. If your company provides a technique or service, a video or ads within videos on Viddler could demonstrate how your offerings meet the needs of your target demographic.

Should You Use It?

With the streaming technology offered by Viddler, consumers no longer have to wait for the video to download for them to view it and search within the content of videos for objects, people, or places. Timed commenting allows users to discuss specific moments in the video, which would be beneficial in an academic environment for dissection of specific themes. This is a beneficial medium for students and educators in the fields of cinematography and videography and the graphic or visual arts, or those in marketing for a hands-on experience. If companies are looking for a way to market their products through ad placement within videos, Viddler is an effective platform because of the tagging feature provided.

Who Started It?

Robert Sandie, president, cofounded Viddler in 2005, along with Donna DeMarco, vice president. Sandie was looking for a way to share his college football highlights with his family and came up with the concept for Viddler.

YouTube

Company Name:	YouTube (Google)
URL:	www.youtube.com
Location:	Mountain View, California, (Worldwide)
Founded:	2005
Employees:	67
Revenue Model:	Advertising
Fees:	Free
Tagline:	Broadcast yourself.

What Is It?

YouTube is an online video sharing site that allows users to upload and share video clips on the Internet through web sites, mobile devices, blogs, and e-mail. The videos on YouTube range from amateur to professional levels of media, television show clips, movie trailers, newscasts, sporting event highlights, and homemade movies. Users can comment on videos, join communities, and use copy/paste code for e-mailing and posting on a web site.

How Can It Be Used?

YouTube can be used to share personal videos, provide exposure for amateur videos, promote performers, and stay current on local, national, and international events. Users can tag videos, comment, join communities, e-mail, and post videos on web sites. YouTube claims to provide ease of use; through "simple video embeds to our full-powered APIs, you can integrate video at all levels of technical expertise." Additional features include personal profile pages, search capabilities, categories, and specialized sections. Users can also "sample new features before they are released on the site through Test Tube."

What Other Applications Does It Work With?

YouTube has an application for Apple's iPhone and states it has a "full-powered API," allowing users to create tools for their own applications or to integrate it into existing applications.

Who Uses It?

The success of YouTube is credited with the idea that "uploading, viewing and sharing videos . . . appeals to nearly every age, race, and nationality." With millions of users every day, YouTube has captured the attention of a significant portion of the population. According to YouTube from May 2010, in the United States the YouTube demographic of users are evenly distributed between male and female at 50 percent each and the age groups as follows: 3–12 at 5 percent, 13–17 at 21 percent, 18–34 at 36 percent, 35–49 at 27 percent, and the 50+ age group at 16 percent.

Should You Use It?

YouTube is an entertainment site that appeals to a broad range of users. For business purposes, YouTube strives to revolutionize the way media companies do business through its YouTube Video Identification program, which uses the Claim Your Content platform. This is a means to "identify content and attribute it to its owner and apply the content owner's policy." With the YouTube in Video Ads, organizations can market products, services, or other entertainment options.

Who Started It?

Chad Meredith Hurley, Jawed Karim, and Steve Chen are the cofounders of YouTube. Hurley and Chen wanted to "share some videos from a dinner party with a half-dozen friends in San Francisco. Sending the clips around by e-mail was a bust. The e-mails kept getting rejected because they were so big." The solution was YouTube. Google acquired YouTube in 2006.

Tool Scorecard for Chapter 27: Video

Instructions: Using the following five-point (0 to 4) scale, rate each tool in this chapter on the basis of how valuable it *might be* to the internal and external operations of your company. Make notes about which tools appeal to you the most.

> 4 = Extremely Valuable
>
> 3 = Very Valuable
>
> 2 = Somewhat Valuable
>
> 1 = Not Very Valuable
>
> 0 = No Value

Tool	Internal Value	External Value
Brightcove	4 3 2 1 0	4 3 2 1 0
Google Video	4 3 2 1 0	4 3 2 1 0
Hulu	4 3 2 1 0	4 3 2 1 0
Metacafe	4 3 2 1 0	4 3 2 1 0
Viddler	4 3 2 1 0	4 3 2 1 0
YouTube	4 3 2 1 0	4 3 2 1 0

CHAPTER 28

Microblogging

Microblogging is no more than text messaging on steroids. With the demise of Pownce, we're talking for the most part about Twitter for open text communication and Yammer for internal, or behind the firewall, communication. The reason for Twitter's success was best put by Samuel Clemens (Mark Twain), when he said in the late nineteenth century, "I apologize for the length of my correspondence. Given more time it would have been shorter."

We love the 140-character bite-sized messages because we can read and comprehend them in about five seconds. In that short amount of time we can fully understand what the author is trying to convey. With text messaging, you don't have the opportunity to drone on and on as we do in our e-mail correspondence. With Twitter, we read it, comprehend it, and move on.

This chapter provides you with a source of the different companies in the microblogging space. New ones are coming online and some old friends such as Pownce are going away. Let me know if there is a service you would like to be included in the next edition.

This chapter introduces you to three companies in this category:

- Plurk
- Twitter
- Twitxr

As you read each profile, keep in mind that its features and functions may or may not be right for your particular business. Use the Tool Scorecard at the end of the chapter to help you determine which of these tools qualify for further consideration when you begin creating your social media strategy in Part III of the book.

Plurk

Company Name:	Plurk
URL:	www.plurk.com
Location:	Mississauga, Ontario, Canada
Founded:	2008
Employees:	8
Revenue Model:	None; privately funded
Fees:	Free at this time
Tagline:	Your life, on the line

What Is It?

Plurk is a themed instant messaging service providing a medium to "showcase the events that make up your life, and follow the events of the people that matter to you in small messages or links which can be broadcast over the web through instant messaging, and text messaging on your mobile phone." Plurk combines instant messaging, texting, and blogging for communicating with friends, family, and coworkers.

How Can It Be Used?

Plurk is currently used for friend and family communications. Plurk could be an effective project collaboration tool or interoffice communication tool in a business environment, specifically if the organization is large or spread out across numerous locations. Plurk also has the potential for use as a word-of-mouth marketing tool. In an academic environment, it can be used as a collaboration tool for projects, for quick conversations between faculty and staff or students and professors, or for assignment clarification.

What Other Applications Does It Work With?

Images and video can be linked from YouTube, TinyPic, ImageShack, Flickr, or Photobucket, and Plurk provides a thumbnail reference in the time line entry for viewing within Plurk. Plurk has an embeddable widget to post on your web page or blog and is compatible with AOL Instant Messenger. Karma applications provide feedback for the most active Plurkers.

Who Uses It?

Plurk's primary user groups include family and friends, and it is used as an instant messaging and texting service, allowing them to stay in touch and share key moments of their lives. Although not heavily used in business, Plurk has the potential to be used for intracompany communication and collaboration, as well as a new type of market research tool. Plurk also has the potential to be used for viral (word-of-mouth) campaigns.

Should You Use It?

If you are looking for a way of communicating with friends, family, and coworkers, or journaling or chronicling your daily activities, Plurk would be an effective platform. Plurk is a newcomer in the social media marketplace but has grown rapidly in a very short time and holds significant potential for use as a social marketing tool, a means of collecting consumer feedback, or a communication platform in a variety of environments.

Who Started It?

"Plurk was envisioned as a communication medium meant to form a balance between blogs and social networks, and between e-mail messaging and instant messaging. After months of development, Plurk was launched in May 2008." Information on the founder of Plurk is presently unavailable to the public.

Twitter

Company Name:	Twitter
URL:	twitter.com
Location:	San Francisco, California
Founded:	2006
Employees:	25
Revenue Model:	None at this time
Fees:	Free at this time
Tagline:	What are you doing?

What Is It?

Twitter is a social medium specifically created to enhance communication. "Twitter is a service for friends, family and coworkers to communicate and stay connected." People can "share their current activity or state of mind with friends and strangers." Chris Winfield deems Twitter a "word of mouth engine" for small businesses to power better relationships. Users can receive updates through the Twitter web site, instant messaging, SMS, RSS, or e-mail, or through an application such as Twitterrific or Facebook.

How Can It Be Used?

Before its release to the public, Twitter was used as a research and development tool within Obvious, LLC. The majority of users just "tweet" updates about what they are doing to friends, family, and coworkers while many use Twitter for sharing business insights. Businesses have begun using Twitter as a free marketing research service and for feedback on products and services. Twitter has been in the news media over the last year due to its use as a "hyper-grapevine news resource," and has been credited with breaking news about significant current events and natural disasters.

What Other Applications Does It Work With?

Twitter works with authoring tools, such as Twhirl, in addition to numerous tools for mobile phones, and as browser extensions. Search engines such as TweetScan, FriendFeed, and Summize (which Twitter announced the purchase of on July 15, 2008) are other compatible applications, as are "Hashtags" trackers, such as Hashtags and Twemes, and Mashups, such as Twittervision.

Who Uses It?

Most everybody uses Twitter; from entrepreneurs, to Fortune 500 companies, from nonprofits to governmental agencies; most everyone who wants to stay in touch. The majority of users "tweet," as the company's slogan would imply "What are you doing now?" updates about their daily activities with friends, family, and coworkers.

Businesses have begun using Twitter as a free marketing research service and for feedback on products and services.

Businesses such as Cisco Systems, Whole Foods Market, Dell, Zappos .com, and Comcast use Twitter to provide updates to customers.

The Los Angeles Fire Department put the technology to use during the October 2007 California wildfires.

NASA used Twitter to break the news of discovery of what appeared to be water ice on Mars by the Phoenix Mars Lander. Other NASA projects, such as Space Shuttle missions and the International Space Station, also provide updates via Twitter.

Should You Use It?

If you are looking for an expedient method of communication for your organization, you should use this social medium. News organizations such as CNN and the BBC have "started using Twitter to disseminate breaking news or provide information feeds for sporting events." Twitter was used in the 2008 presidential campaigns of Barack Obama as a "publicity mechanism," and Ralph Nader "for real-time updates of their ballot access teams across the country." The Red Cross also uses Twitter "to exchange minute-to-minute" information about local disasters, including statistics and directions.

UC Berkeley graduate journalism student, James Buck, and his translator, Mohammed Maree, were arrested in Egypt while photographing a local antigovernment protest.

> On his way to the police station, Buck used his mobile phone to twitter the message "Arrested" to his 48 followers who contacted UC Berkeley, the U.S. Embassy and a number of press organizations on his behalf. While being detained, Buck was able to send updates about his condition to his followers. As a result of the message and the efforts of his Twitter friends, he was released the next day from the Mahalla jail after the college hired a lawyer for him.

Who Started It?

Twitter was initially used internally by Obvious, LLC as a research and development project. Its success led to the launch in 2006. Jack Dorsey is a cofounder and the CEO at Twitter. Evan Williams is a cofounder and chief product officer. Biz Stone is a cofounder and director of community.

Twitxr

Though this application has been categorized primarily as a photo sharing tool, it includes several features and functions of a microblogging tool. See the Twitxr profile and photo in Chapter 25 for a complete overview.

Tool Scorecard for Chapter 28: Microblogging

Instructions: Using the following five-point (0 to 4) scale, rate each tool in this chapter on the basis of how valuable it *might be* to the internal and external operations of your company. Make notes about which tools appeal to you the most.

4 = Extremely Valuable

3 = Very Valuable

2 = Somewhat Valuable

1 = Not Very Valuable

0 = No Value

Tool	Internal Value	External Value
Plurk	4 3 2 1 0	4 3 2 1 0
Twitter	4 3 2 1 0	4 3 2 1 0
Twitxr	4 3 2 1 0	4 3 2 1 0

CHAPTER 29

Livecasting

Livecasting isn't for everyone, but those who livecast are passionate about it. My friend Jody Gnant livecasted her life for nine full months, 24/7. Chris Pirello has been uStream'n his livecast of himself for years. Both have built a tremendous following and skyrocketed their music and careers.

Livecasting is broadcasting video live. It could be 24 hours a day or just for a simple one hour of television. Livecasting is the ultimate reality television and it's available for free to everyone. So if you've always dreamed of creating and starring in your own television show, the companies in this chapter will help you realize your dream.

This chapter highlights those companies that provide technology and services to assist you in your very own livecast:

- BlogTalkRadio
- Live 365
- Justin.tv
- SHOUTcast
- TalkShoe

As you read each profile, keep in mind that its features and functions may or may not be right for your particular business. Use the Tool Scorecard at the end of the chapter to help you determine which of these tools qualify for further consideration when you begin creating your social media strategy in Part III of the book.

BlogTalkRadio

Company Name:	BlogTalkRadio
URL:	www.blogtalkradio.com
Location:	New York, New York
Founded:	2006
Employees:	25
Revenue Model:	Advertising and a white-branded product
Fees:	Free to $99 per month for premium host packages
Tagline:	The best shows from around the Web on any subject

What Is It?

BlogTalkRadio (BTR) is a social network application that allows people to easily and quickly host their own online radio show. BTR provides robust production capabilities, such as allowing hosts to take live callers and play MP3s during a show. Listeners can subscribe to shows as shows are archived within 30 minutes or less and receive a unique RSS feed. BTR has thousands of active hosts as well as clients who use the platform in their own environments.

How Can It Be Used?

There are a variety of BTR clients. Educators use BTR to hold virtual classes and deliver their lectures or to conduct training among staff and faculty. Other clients include the U.S. Department of Defense, Sun Microsystems, *Golf* magazine, and the American Petroleum Institute, whose uses vary from entertainment to public service to education to sales to internal and external communications. The U.S. Department of Defense is using BTR to reach out to the American public in a way that was never before possible. The agency hosts live call-in shows on issues that affect average citizens and military personnel alike—such as homeland security, safety, health, and family. In this way, the public develops a greater understanding of the issues affecting our nation's military. Another example of BTR usage is host Marla "the FlyLady" Cilley. She brings her 500,000-plus Yahoo! member listening audience practical, solid advice for the many challenges they face while trying to organize their homes and lives. They interact with her one-on-one, giving her community the opportunity to take their journey one step further.

What Other Applications Does It Work With?

Many BlogTalkRadio hosts send a tweet (using Twitter) before the beginning of their shows to get people to call in or listen. The network is also incorporating short message service (SMS) tools into the platform. Distribution tools let hosts post a Flash Player featuring their last show in multiple social networking sites, such as Facebook, MySpace, Ning, and Typepad.

Who Uses It?

Most hosts create interactive live shows and take callers. Some shows are strictly for entertainment purposes, while others do it to demonstrate their knowledge or to generate sales leads. Organizations like Sun Microsystems, Golf.com, and the Department of Defense created interactive content through the network, engaging their customers and audiences in a unique way. Such conversations also improve search engine optimization for better Google rankings and create messaging that will exist online for years to come.

Should You Use It?

Yes. BTR serves a wide variety of needs for its hosts and users, but most of all it serves the most basic human need: freedom of speech. Unencumbered by government regulation of speech, users and listeners can communicate freely with one another. Whether for individual use, business, or education, any type of user can easily create and produce a program and reach a specific audience. With clients such as the U.S. Department of Defense, Fortune 100 companies, and educational clients, the spectrum of usage is limited only by the user's needs and imagination.

Who Started It?

Levy and Bob Charish founded BTR in August 2006. The original BTR concept was the dream and vision of Levy as he mourned his father's passing. Levy maintained a blog for his ill father so his family and friends could remain updated on his father's health—and later as a memorial to the elder Levy's life. However, Levy wanted more from his blog, and the seeds of live, interactive social broadcasting took root. Within months of its launch, BTR housed thousands of hosts and hundreds of thousands of listeners. Notable guests and hosts include Barack Obama, John McCain, Brad Pitt, Anjelica Huston, Oliver Stone, David Mamet, Salman Rushdie, Dennis Miller,

Margaret Cho, Yoko Ono, and Evander Holyfield, as well as owners of leading corporations and digital-media entities from around the world.

Live365

Company Name:	Live365 Inc.
URL:	www.live365.com
Location:	Foster City, California; Newport Beach, California
Founded:	1999
Employees:	39
Revenue Model:	Advertising, VIP subscriptions; range from $5.95 to 7.95 per month, and start-up fees
Tagline:	The world's largest Internet radio network

What Is It?

According to the "About Us" page on Live365's site, "The Company gives individuals and organizations a 'voice' to be able to reach a global audience, while offering radio listeners an unparalleled choice in music and other audio content. Through easy-to-use tools and services, anyone with a computer and an Internet connection can create his or her own Internet radio station. As a result, Live365 offers the most diverse array of high-quality radio available today, with thousands of stations spanning myriad genres and representing over 150 countries." In essence, you can be either a listener and listen to individual broadcasters, selecting your genre of choice, or you can be a broadcaster, transmitting material ranging from MP3 playlists to live talk radio format.

How Can It Be Used?

Live365's services have two audiences: the broadcaster and the listener. Listeners can listen with various media players, and broadcasters can broadcast by creating a "broadcaster" membership. Broadcaster packages vary in type, size, and price. At the most basic level, members can stream MP3 playlist files to listeners. Advanced broadcasters can install software and broadcast live using a computer, a stable bandwidth connection, a microphone, and a mixing board. Listeners listen on their computers or Internet browser–capable devices.

What Other Applications Does It Work With?

Live365 works with Mac, Linux, or Microsoft-based operating systems. To listen to Live365 on mobile devices, a user would use a Radio365 mobile player. Users can also use Winamp, Real Player, iTunes, and Windows Media Player to access Live365.

Who Uses It?

There are educational broadcasts such as "American University," a Japanese language-learning channel, transmissions of the entire air-to-ground communications of the Apollo 11 lunar landing, and "African United States Theory," to name a few educational topics. There are also business-related broadcasts such as "Smallbiz America Radio." The description provided states, "Listen to Interviews with BIG Thinkers in Small Business." Other examples of professionally oriented broadcasts include "Real Estate Nation" and "Trader's Nation."

Should You Use It?

In addition to the typically well-known music genre broadcasters that can be found on Live365, the talk radio genre allows for discussion of a wide variety of industries. No matter what the industry, there is likely to be an audience that would display interest in hearing the latest goings-on, technological advancements, business concepts, and economic influences. The mobility of Live365 means a listener can listen while working, traveling, or during leisure time and maintain a knowledge base with the selected station. Your business marketing can be enhanced by transmitting business meetings (live or on demand) or information about new products or technological breakthroughs, and customers can provide feedback, all through Live365.

Who Started It?

According to Wikipedia (but not otherwise confirmed), Nanocosm Inc. employee Andy Volk started up a hosted community radio project using SHOUTcast material. He shared the idea with Nanocosm CTO Peter Rothman. The two developed the concept of Live365. At the time, Nanocosm's start-up product was Nanohome, but once Live365 went live and exploded in growth, Live365 became the focus of Nanocosm. At launch, Live365 was free of charge and had a maximum listener cap of 365 as well as 365 MB of storage for music and audio per station. In 2001, Live365 began charging fees for broadcasting and for VIP subscription packages.

Justin.tv

Company Name:	Justin.tv
URL:	www.justin.tv
Location:	San Francisco, California
Founded:	2007
Employees:	27
Revenue Model:	Currently none; "building a 'transaction system,' which is a combination of pay-per-view, Craigslist, and eBay"
Fees:	Free; some services, however, may require a subscription fee
Tagline:	The place for live video

What Is It?

Justin.tv offers a platform to "enable viewers and broadcasters to interact and exchange ideas in real time through chat and live video." Initially, Justin.tv began as a single channel broadcasting the life events of one of its founders, Justin Kan, but is now a "network of thousands of diverse channels."

Justin.tv is still in stages of infancy, but is proposing future collaboration with media companies to "sell access to live sports like European soccer, Japanese baseball, or a closed-circuit music concert."

How Can It Be Used?

Justin.tv is currently used by private individuals looking to broadcast events occurring in their lives as they happen. The future potential exists, however, to implement media distribution of live events on a pay-per-view basis.

What Other Applications Does It Work With?

Justin.tv is compatible with Twitter, MySpace, personal web sites, and blogs by configuring the video to share with the site you wish to embed into. Justin.tv also has a free iPhone app.

Who Uses It?

Justin.tv is primarily used by individuals to chat with friends and share their life, musicians and DJs to broadcast music and chat with fans, artists to promote their work, and comedians and entertainers to host interactive talk shows. The potential exists for industry, education, government, and non-profit organizations to engage in live communication and collaboration. Justin.tv would be an effective tool for e-learning, as viewers can tune in to the presenter and interact in real time.

Should You Use It?

Justin.tv channels are open to the public and would not be an effective tool for broadcasting proprietary or confidential information. If your organization is looking for a way to demonstrate a product, however, increase awareness of a service, or conduct an interactive meeting, Justin.tv may be a possible solution. Should Justin.tv implement its transaction system, this application would be effective for revenue generation for media companies to sell access to live sports events that cannot be viewed from typical cable and satellite services.

Who Started It?

Justin.tv was founded by Justin Kan, "who decided it would be really cool if he could broadcast his entire life, 24/7, to the Internet." Justin "enlisted the help of his friends Michael [Seibel, chief executive officer and cofounder], Emmett [Shear, chief technology officer] and Kyle [Vogt, vice president, engineering], and raised a secd investment from Y Combinator."

SHOUTcast

Company Name:	Nullsoft
URL:	www.shoutcast.com
Location:	Dulles, Virginia
Founded:	1997
Revenue Model:	Advertising
Fees:	Free
Tagline:	Free Internet radio

What Is It?

SHOUTcast is a free online audio streaming system that works with Windows, Linux, and Macintosh computers. It permits users to broadcast their own audio from a personal computer to individuals online via the Internet or other IP-based networks. Broadcasters use SHOUTcast by either running their own server (with the SHOUTcast server application), or finding a third-party server provider who is willing to stream their audio broadcast. Once the server is set up, broadcasters can install the SHOUTcast radio plug-in to begin streaming their audio. Listeners can browse through the SHOUTcast broadcast directory and choose to listen to a stream through a compatible digital media player.

How Can It Be Used?

The most common use for SHOUTcast is to create and listen to online audio broadcasts. Audio streams can be broadcast for any particular theme. For example, broadcasts exist to play only certain genres of music, to play music from certain record companies, or to play songs from a given time period. A musician could use SHOUTcast to broadcast and promote music, a distribution company could use SHOUTcast to promote new albums coming out, or a traditional radio station could use it to reach listeners through the Internet. Another option is to use SHOUTcast to broadcast a private stream and allow only select users to listen to the audio. For example, a business could broadcast selected music to all its employees working within the business network.

What Other Applications Does It Work With?

SHOUTcast works with digital media players to broadcast and listen to the streaming audio feeds. SHOUTcast has recommended digital media players for listeners who want to access SHOUTcast feeds. Linux users should use XMMS, Windows users should use Winamp, and Macintosh users should use iTunes. For broadcasting purposes, the only promoted digital media application presently is Winamp, but alternative methods of broadcasting are available that are not officially supported.

Who Uses It?

SHOUTcast is used by a wide variety of broadcasters and listeners. Since stations exist for everything from polka to heavy metal, the listeners tuning into SHOUTcast audio feeds cover a very broad market spectrum. Proponents of record companies use SHOUTcast to broadcast their artists' music and to reach fans for promotional purposes. Radio stations that exist on traditional AM or FM channels also use SHOUTcast to extend their presence further on the Internet.

Should You Use It?

You should use SHOUTcast if you are interested in creating and broadcasting your own online audio stream, whether you are a radio network operator or a recreational broadcaster. SHOUTcast does have some advantages over traditional radio broadcasting, so it is an attractive option to many users. A radio broadcast conducted through SHOUTcast is notably less expensive than operating a radio network through more traditional means. A SHOUTcast network can also be assembled more quickly and easily than a traditional radio network, and with far less technical knowledge.

Who Started It?

Justin Frankel and Tom Pepper founded Nullsoft in 1997. Nullsoft, which also developed and acted as the driving force behind popular programs such as Gnutella and Winamp, designed SHOUTcast in 1999. On June 1, 1999, Nullsoft was sold to America Online, where it currently exists as a division of AOL Music.

TalkShoe

Company Name:	TalkShoe
URL:	www.talkshoe.com
Location:	Pittsburgh, Pennsylvania
Founded:	2005
Revenue Model:	Advertising
Tagline:	Your community is calling.

What Is It?

TalkShoe is an online social voice service provider. With TalkShoe, users can create live audio broadcasts, which other users can then join to either participate or to just listen. Live audio broadcasts, also called Community Calls, give individuals the opportunity to converse online in real time; and then, if desired, save these Community Calls for other people to listen to as podcasts or audio blogs. TalkShoe currently allows for 250 people to actively participate in a Community Call, with 1,000 users listening simultaneously. TalkShoe also has a mechanism that shares revenue with popular Community Call hosts.

How Can It Be Used?

TalkShoe can be used to accomplish any number of things. A business could use TalkShoe to market directly to an intended audience and gain valuable interactive feedback. A blogger could use TalkShoe to draw traffic to a web site or discuss the latest post. A health group could use TalkShoe to share information about a disease and act as a support group. An individual who hoped to gain a position as a radio talk show host could use TalkShoe to hone his skills to prove one's drawing power. Essentially, TalkShoe can be used in any instance in which someone wanted to communicate in real time with others online.

What Other Applications Does It Work With?

TalkShoe can be used with different applications to disseminate your podcasts to your audience. Among the applications that it works with are podcast directories (such as iTunes) and blogging applications (such as WordPress). TalkShoe also works with online voice programs such as Skype, so users can call into a live show through their computer as opposed to a regular telephone. TalkShoe also works with Facebook, Twitter, and Meebo.

Who Uses It?

TalkShoe is used by a wide variety of podcasters that host shows based on a multitude of topics. As a result, several different audiences listen to shows on TalkShoe. Some examples of the current shows running on TalkShoe are "Puppywishes," a show for expert dog training advice; "The New Wine Consumer: Wine Brands," a show that discusses everything from how to choose a wine to the historical factors of wine that influence the market today; and "The Unofficial Apple Weblog," a discussion of all things related to Apple Inc.

Should You Use It?

You should use TalkShoe if you are currently, or are looking to start, broadcasting audio in any form. Podcasters can schedule live shows and advertise the date, and then broadcast the show live while controlling the interaction of the participants. You should also use TalkShoe if you are interested in adding an audio aspect to your blog or personal web site. Once your show has been recorded on TalkShoe, it remains on the TalkShoe web site, and it can then be listed on a web site or podcast directory. Also, if you feel that you can create a popular TalkShoe podcast, the TalkShoe cash incentive program may be an appealing selling point.

Who Started It?

Dave Nelsen started TalkShoe in April 2005. Before creating TalkShoe, Nelsen had worked in telecommunications as an employee of both AT&T and FORE Systems. TalkShoe was kept intentionally low key up to, and during, its launch in June 2006. This was done with the intention of slowly scaling server operations with site traffic.

Tool Scorecard for Chapter 29: Livecast

Instructions: Using the following five-point (0 to 4) scale, rate each tool in this chapter on the basis of how valuable it *might be* to the internal and external operations of your company. Make notes about which tools appeal to you the most.

4 = Extremely Valuable
3 = Very Valuable
2 = Somewhat Valuable
1 = Not Very Valuable
0 = No Value

Tool	Internal Value	External Value
BlogTalkRadio	4 3 2 1 0	4 3 2 1 0
Live 365	4 3 2 1 0	4 3 2 1 0
Justin.tv	4 3 2 1 0	4 3 2 1 0
SHOUTcast	4 3 2 1 0	4 3 2 1 0
TalkShoe	4 3 2 1 0	4 3 2 1 0

CHAPTER 30

Virtual Worlds

When organizations such as the American Cancer Society, CNN, Dell, Disney, Harvard, IBM, MTV, Reuters, Starwood Hotels, Sun Microsystems, Toyota, and Wells Fargo are all participating in virtual worlds, there must be something to it.

The American Cancer Society has actually raised $650,000 in real dollar donations during their time there. IBM holds their monthly engineers' meetings at their headquarters in Second Life where engineers from all over the world, meet, talk, exchange ideas, and watch presentations.

I have some oceanfront land and a two-story Mediterranean mansion in Second Life where the first floor is a virtual store where you can purchase 3-D Internet adverting (paper models). My three developers meet me there from time to time to discuss projects and design ideas. They are in Ukraine and I have never personally met them other than our time in Second Life.

Upstairs in the amnion is the virtual office of *The Social Media Bible*. I use this space for commerce, meetings, presentations, or sometimes I just go there to hang out.

Stop by! Like nearly all social media, it's free! Come by and feel free to look around. Read the first few chapters of *The Social Media Bible*, watch the video of my interview with Second Life's CEO Mark Kingdon, take my sailboat for a spin, get a free cup of coffee, or just lie back on the beach and enjoy the waves and the sunset.

To help you get a better feel for how tools and applications in this category might be of value to your business, this chapter introduces you to four of the key players in this space:

- Active Worlds
- Kaneva
- Second Life

As you read each profile, keep in mind that its features and functions may or may not be right for your particular business. Use the Tool Scorecard at the end of the chapter to help you determine which of these tools qualify for further consideration when you begin creating your social media strategy in Part III of the book.

Active Worlds

Company Name:	Active Worlds Inc.
URL:	www.activeworlds.com
Location:	Las Vegas, Nevada
Founded:	1997
Revenue Model:	Advertising, premium subscriptions, servers
Fees:	$6.95 per month to become a citizen

What Is It?

Active Worlds is "a comprehensive platform for efficiently delivering real-time interactive 3-D content over the Web." Users create avatars that they use to explore worlds (some of which are created by other users) and engage in various activities such as online games, building their own houses and buildings (which can exist as a part of a town), and interacting with other user avatars. The program also has features that enhance the user's experience such as web browsing, voice chatting, and streaming media.

How Can It Be Used?

Active Worlds can be used in several different ways aside from the socialization and entertainment aspects. A business could create and maintain a functional world or environment in which current and potential customers can visit to receive technical support, interact with other customers, or learn about new products and services. An entrepreneur could even create a new online business specifically for Active Worlds by selling custom-made designs, textures, or objects to other Active Worlds users.

What Other Applications Does It Work With?

Active Worlds works with 3-D design programs to create the buildings, objects, and avatars that exist in the virtual environments, provided the programs can create within the supported formats. Active Worlds also provides a Software Developer Kit in both C/C++ and Visual Basic/COM versions, which allows users to create bots that can perform multiple automated functions.

Who Uses It?

Several different groups use Active Worlds to fit their own needs and intentions. Many of the users who use Active Worlds do so to interact with others and entertain themselves, but there is also a strong subset of users that treat Active Worlds as a functional networking tool. For example, educators often use Active Worlds as a virtual classroom or as a medium for students to collaborate in; there are pricing plans based on educators' needs. Businesses have also used Active Worlds for training employees and as an online meeting environment. There are even vendors who sell products, both virtual and material, in the online 3-D virtual mall.

Should You Use It?

You should use Active Worlds if you are interested in becoming a part of an active online community in a 3-D virtual environment. Active Worlds works well for educators and businesses by offering them the ability to collaborate online, demonstrate new products and services, and conduct lessons through the Internet; thus, you should use Active Worlds if you like the idea of owning a functional online world that you can moderate. You should also use Active Worlds if you have been looking for a way to reach a large, global audience for advertising, viral marketing, or e-commerce purposes.

Who Started It?

Richard Noll and J. P. McCormick founded Active Worlds. The company was initially created to design a 3-D web browser that combined the graphical elements of a virtual world with the functionality of a 2-D web browser. The company has undergone several layoffs, divisions, reformations, and acquisitions.

Kaneva

Company Name:	Kaneva Inc.
URL:	www.kaneva.com
Location:	Atlanta, Georgia
Founded:	2004
Revenue Model:	Microcommerce, premium subscriptions

What Is It?

The Virtual World of Kaneva is a 3-D environment that combines elements of web browsing, social networking, entertainment media, and massive multi-player online games into one online virtual world. Users create avatars that explore properties in the Kaneva world such as shopping malls, popular hangouts, or other users' apartments. While exploring the Kaneva world, users can meet new people, join communities, play games and puzzles, or just hang out with their friends. Users can also purchase items to decorate their apartment, modify their avatar's appearance, or give as gifts. Some of the features in Kaneva require Kaneva currency, which users must purchase.

How Can It Be Used?

Kaneva can be used as a socialization tool as well as a marketing vehicle. As a socialization tool, Kaneva offers several entertainment options, such as owning or visiting a dance club, watching videos at your virtual apartment with friends, or hosting your own social event. Anyone you meet in the Kaneva world who interests you can become your friend in Kaneva's own social network. If you are a photographer, musician, movie maker, or any form of artist, you can also use Kaneva as a marketing tool. Through Kaneva, your movies can be featured in virtual theaters, your photographs can be hung on walls or featured in showcases, or your music can be featured at parties.

What Other Applications Does It Work With?

Kaneva allows users to integrate YouTube with their virtual environment. For example, a user could watch videos from YouTube with friends on their apartment television, or play rock videos on a big-screen television inside their own nightclub. Kaneva also works with your web browser to fuse the Kaneva social network with the World of Kaneva. For example, clicking on a user's avatar in the Kaneva world can lead you directly to her Kaneva social profile on the Web.

Who Uses It?

Kaneva has over 1.3 million users and hosts over 22,000 communities, so it has a very large number of subscribers. Also, businesses use Kaneva to extend their online presence. Turner Broadcasting System currently has a contract with Kaneva to build virtual properties within the World of Kaneva. Users in Kaneva can visit the TBS headquarters, which offers televisions that play streaming videos of Turner content, posters advertising Turner products hanging on the walls, as well as an explorable version of the house from the popular television show *Family Guy*.

Should You Use It?

You should use Kaneva if you are interested in a 3-D virtual world that combines elements of social networking web sites (such as MySpace) with elements of virtual worlds (such as Second Life). You should also use Kaneva if you are interested in using a social application as a marketing tool. Every Kaneva community gets its own virtual hangout, as well as its own profile in the Kaneva social network; therefore, any business or individual that creates a community can interact directly with potential customers as well as garner publicity if the community hangout has drawing power.

Who Started It?

Christopher W. Klaus and Greg Frame founded Kaneva Inc. in 2004. Klaus is the founder and former chief technical officer of Internet Security Systems, while Frame is the founder and former chief technical officer of Indigo Olive Software Inc. The World of Kaneva was released in beta form in 2006.

Second Life

Company Name:	Linden Lab
URL:	secondlife.com
Location:	San Francisco, California
Founded:	1999
Revenue Model:	Microcommerce, premium subscriptions
Fees:	Free (basic membership) or $72 per year for increased technical support and a weekly stipend for an individual's avatar
Tagline:	Your World. Your Imagination.

What Is It?

Second Life is an online 3-D world that allows multiple users, called residents, to interact with one another as avatars in a virtual society. Residents can create their own buildings, own land, interact with other residents, and participate in individual and group-based activities. A large portion of the Second Life experience involves the economy, in which residents trade goods and services among one another in exchange for Linden dollars. Linden dollars, the currency of Second Life, can be converted through the Linden Currency Exchange for U.S. dollars.

How Can It Be Used?

Second Life can be used both recreationally and commercially. Residents who participate in Second Life for the recreational value can socialize, role-play, or engage in the various activities available. From the commercial perspective, Second Life is not only used by real-world business to extend their online presence, but it is also used by businesses that were initially created to operate within the Second Life universe. These businesses can use Second Life to reach their customer base through promotions and demonstrations or provide virtual services to residents.

What Other Applications Does It Work With?

Second Life works with SLurl.com, which is an external web site that allows residents to connect to locations inside Second Life, as well as locate other Second Life residents from outside the virtual world. Second Life also works with Vivox, a communications system, to provide voice chat and instant messaging capabilities between residents.

Who Uses It?

As of September 2008, Second Life had over 15 million accounts registered worldwide. In September 2008, Second Life also saw its largest concurrent user base online, with over 70,000 residents logged in to the world at the same time. Numerous businesses and organizations are using Second Life to their advantage, including 20th Century Fox, the American Cancer Society, Dell, Major League Baseball, Cisco, American Apparel, MTV, Toyota, the University of Southern California, and Harvard Law School.

Should You Use It?

You should use Second Life if you are interested in a 3-D virtual world that has a heavy emphasis on socialization and creating a virtual identity, with a well-established commercial presence. If you have a business or organization, Second Life offers the opportunity to establish publicity among its residents. For example, 20th Century Fox held an event for the premiere of the movie *X-Men: The Last Stand* in Second Life and the American Cancer Society held a Second Life version of its Relay for Life fund-raiser. If you are an entrepreneur, you could create an online business within Second Life that has the potential to generate a real income.

Who Started It?

Linden Lab launched Second Life on June 23, 2003. Linden Lab, founded by Philip Rosedale in 1999, was originally created to design hardware that could immerse computer users into a 3-D environment. That concept eventually evolved into the software application Linden World, which was later transformed into Second Life.

Tool Scorecard for Chapter 30: Virtual Worlds

Instructions: Using the following five-point (0 to 4) scale, rate each tool in this chapter on the basis of how valuable it *might be* to the internal and external operations of your company. Make notes about which tools appeal to you the most.

4 = Extremely Valuable
3 = Very Valuable
2 = Somewhat Valuable
1 = Not Very Valuable
0 = No Value

Tool	Internal Value	External Value
Active Worlds	4 3 2 1 0	4 3 2 1 0
Kaneva	4 3 2 1 0	4 3 2 1 0
Second Life	4 3 2 1 0	4 3 2 1 0

CHAPTER 31

Gaming

Online gaming might seem like an odd category for *The Social Media Bible,* but it isn't. Did you know that 17 million people are playing Halo3 or an additional 17 million are playing World of Warcraft? Any time you can measure a target audience in the millions, you need to be there.

Many Fortune 1000 companies have participated in gaming as a way to build brand recognition. Hewlett-Packard puts up billboards in auto racing games. An author friend of mine had a game developed for his web site for the release of his new book that cost only a couple of thousand dollars, but now has an 18 percent conversion rate on buying his book. And mobile phone game apps are one of the fastest-growing app categories for the smart phones.

Gaming isn't just about kids. The average age of the online gamer is 35 years old. The average gamer now spends eight hours per week online gaming and that number is increasing at more than 10 percent per year. Anytime you have millions of like-minded people in the same place sharing a similar experience, you as a company need to be there.

This chapter shows you three of the largest membership game site companies:

- Entropia Universe
- EverQuest
- World of Warcraft

As you read each profile, keep in mind that its features and functions may or may not be right for your particular business. Use the Tool Scorecard at the end of the chapter to help you determine which of these tools qualify for further consideration when you begin creating your social media strategy in Part III of the book.

Entropia Universe

Company Name:	MindArk
URL:	www.entropiauniverse.com
Location:	Gothenburg, Sweden
Founded:	2003
Revenue Model:	Microcommerce
Tagline:	The next generation of interactive entertainment is here.

What Is It?

Entropia Universe is an online virtual world that combines elements of massively multiplayer online role-playing games, first-person shooters, and economic practices. In the Entropia Universe, players assume the role of colonists who are exploring an untamed planet and must find resources, deal with wild animals, and trade with other colonists. Entropia Universe is a free game that functions off a micropayment system, wherein players convert real-world money to Entropia Universe currency for usage in the game.

How Can It Be Used?

Entropia Universe can be used in different ways by players and businesses. Many players choose to play the game for free, but many entrepreneurs invest money into Entropia dollars to try to turn a real-world profit. There have even been a few cases where large amounts of money—as much as $100,000—have been spent or earned by players. A business could also use Entropia Universe to market itself. For example, a business could buy a piece of virtual property and build something to attract users, such as a club or entertainment venue, and then advertise by networking with the players who come to visit.

What Other Applications Does It Work With?

Entropia Universe works with micropayment systems that enable the users to quickly convert real-world money to and from the Entropia Universe currency. There is also an ATM card that Entropia Universe participants can use to withdraw their Entropia Universe money as real-world money from certain ATM machines.

Who Uses It?

Entropia Universe is used by a large global audience. As of the fall of 2008, there were over 810,000 subscribed users from more than 200 countries around the world playing the game. Entrepreneurs, merchants, gamers, role-players, and more are all drawn to the virtual world created by Entropia Universe. A large segment of Chinese users are also participating in this online environment, with that user base expected to grow since Entropia Universe has been chosen by the Chinese government to create a cash-based virtual economy for the country.

Should You Use It?

You should use Entropia Universe if you are interested in a free online game that revolves around a massively multiplayer universe. Since Entropia Universe emphasizes the economy of the world, it draws a more varied player base than other massively multiplayer games. This position opens up a realm of possibilities for a business to network and market to users who are interested in both games and economies. From a business perspective, you should consider using Entropia Universe if you are looking to interact with, or broaden your understanding of, the Chinese market, as it will likely be branching out rapidly into the Entropia Universe.

Who Started It?

MindArk started Entropia Universe, which is a continuation of Project Entropia. Project Entropia was an undertaking initiated in 1995 by Jan Welter Timkrans along with some of his colleagues in Sweden. During the game's creation and testing in 2002, MindArk was raided by court officials as a result of a Microsoft claim that MindArk was using unlicensed software. By 2003, MindArk had launched its game commercially.

EverQuest

Company Name:	Sony Online Entertainment
URL:	www.everquest.com
Location:	San Diego, California
Founded:	1995
Revenue Model:	Subscription, merchandise, software sales, microcommerce

What Is It?

EverQuest is a 3-D massively multiplayer online role-playing game published by Sony Online Entertainment. In EverQuest, a user takes on the role of a character that exists in the EverQuest fantasy world, and then interacts with other users' characters, computer-controlled characters, and items. Users can trade, adventure, join groups of other users, socialize, or craft items in the EverQuest universe. The EverQuest franchise has had 16 expansions as well as a sequel released in 2004 and has received many gaming rewards since its initial release on March 16, 1999.

How Can It Be Used?

EverQuest can be used as a socialization and recreation tool, as well as an interactive story that the user engages in as an active participant. EverQuest can also be used as an effective viral marketing tool by advertising directly to potential customers while socializing with them. The game serves as an efficient vehicle for more conventional business marketing as well, as the now-defunct 2005 deal between Sony and Pizza Hut displayed. A user playing EverQuest 2 could type "/pizza" into a chat window and a web browser would launch, taking the user directly to the online ordering section of pizzahut.com. In EverQuest 2, Sony also implemented Station Exchange, which is an official auction system that allows users to transfer real money for virtual goods.

What Other Applications Does It Work With?

EverQuest works with web browsers by sending commands from the game that will result in the browser performing certain actions, such as in the pizza marketing deal with Pizza Hut. There are also numerous add-ons that are available for EverQuest, which modify the interface, game play, and visual appearance of the game. The EverQuest web site is compatible with Share-This, a widget for sharing web sites.

Who Uses It?

A global and varied audience of gamers uses EverQuest. Casual users play for the social and entertaining aspects of EverQuest, while some hardcore gamers play EverQuest often, and even use Station Exchange as a means of making money through the game's economy. The Pizza Hut deal, although now nonexistent, serves as evidence that businesses have, and may consider in the future, using EverQuest as a tool to increase business exposure.

Should You Use It?

You should use EverQuest if you would like to engage in a fantasy-themed massively multiplayer online role-playing game that has a large fan base and is well established. EverQuest may also interest you if you like the concept of a business relationship similar to the one between Sony and Pizza Hut. By participating in that deal, Sony showed that it was open to innovative ways in which games and businesses could collaborate.

Who Started It?

Brad McQuaid, Steve Clover, and Bill Trost are credited with the original design for EverQuest, with the original concept coming from John Smedley. Smedley was an executive at Sony Interactive Studios America in 1996 when development of EverQuest began. McQuaid and Clover were hired as programmers for the game, while Trost created the history, lore, and major characters. It was developed by Verant Interactive and 989 Studios, and then published by Sony Online Entertainment—all of which are, or were, divisions of Sony. EverQuest has survived various corporate restructurings of Sony since it was first conceptualized.

World of Warcraft

Company Name:	Blizzard Entertainment
URL:	www.worldofwarcraft.com
Location:	Irvine, California
Founded:	1991
Revenue Model:	Subscription, merchandise, software sales

What Is It?

World of Warcraft is a massively multiplayer online role-playing game that takes place in Blizzard Entertainment's evolving Warcraft universe. Players assume the role of a character belonging to one of the two available factions, and then explore the World of Warcraft while interacting with other users, computer-controlled characters, and various other items.

How Can It Be Used?

World of Warcraft, though primarily seen as a recreational activity, could be used as a tool for improving business. Consultants draw parallels between managing a World of Warcraft guild, which is an organization of players, and managing a company's networking, growth, and employees. Also, businesses have paired with Blizzard Entertainment to increase their own revenue through World of Warcraft's popularity. For example, DirectTV has offered a free 11-month subscription to World of Warcraft for any new customers who sign up for DirectTV services.

What Other Applications Does It Work With?

World of Warcraft is compatible with a multitude of third-party add-ons to enhance the social and game-playing experience of the players. These add-ons can modify many of the game's features, including the visual appearance, the interface, and the interaction between players. There are also add-ons that allow players to track the supply and demand of trade goods, which makes it easier for them to improve their status in the game's economy.

Who Uses It?

World of Warcraft is used by a massive number of subscribed players, with large segments of its player base in North America, Asia, and Europe. It is currently the world's largest massively multiplayer online role-playing game, with over 11.5 million monthly subscribers as of December 2008, while holding an estimated 62 percent of the massively multiplayer online role-playing game market as of April 2008. World of Warcraft also holds the Guinness World Record for the most popular game in its genre.

Should You Use It?

You should use World of Warcraft if you are interested in a massively multiplayer online role-playing game that takes place in the well-established Warcraft universe. You should also consider using World of Warcraft if you would like to interact directly with the players of the world's most populated massively multiplayer online game. World of Warcraft is also widely considered to be one of the friendliest games of its type for a casual user, so the market audience for the game covers a broader base than most other games in the same genre.

Who Started It?

World of Warcraft is a continuation of the Warcraft game series that Blizzard has been developing since 1994. World of Warcraft was announced in

September 2001, and underwent extensive testing and development prior to its first public release on November 23, 2004. Blizzard Entertainment was founded in 1991 as Silicon & Synapse by UCLA graduates Michael Morhaime, Allen Adham, and Frank Pearce. Since its founding, the company has undergone several name changes and acquisitions. It is currently known as Blizzard Entertainment and exists as a division of Activision Blizzard.

Tool Scorecard for Chapter 31: Gaming

Instructions: Using the following five-point (0 to 4) scale, rate each tool in this chapter on the basis of how valuable it *might be* to the internal and external operations of your company. Make notes about which tools appeal to you the most.

4 = Extremely Valuable

3 = Very Valuable

2 = Somewhat Valuable

1 = Not Very Valuable

0 = No Value

Tool	Internal Value	External Value
Entropia Universe	4 3 2 1 0	4 3 2 1 0
EverQuest	4 3 2 1 0	4 3 2 1 0
World of Warcraft	4 3 2 1 0	4 3 2 1 0

CHAPTER 32

Productivity Applications

The companies highlighted here offer the widest range of features of any category in *The Social Media Bible*. These are all part of the wide range of "productivity tools." These tools include event management, VOIP telecommunications, peer-to-peer downloads, alerts, word processing and spreadsheets in the cloud, and even online surveys.

These tools are especially worth exploring as they are readily available, highly feature rich, and free. As you read each profile, keep in mind that its features and functions may or may not be right for your particular business. Use the Tool Scorecard at the end of the chapter to help you determine which of these tools qualify for further consideration when you begin creating your social media strategy in Part III of the book.

Acteva

Company Name:	Acteva
URL:	www.acteva.com
Location:	San Francisco, California
Founded:	1998
Employees:	25
Revenue Model:	User fees
Fees:	Processing fees start at $1 and increase depending on plan
Tagline:	Marketplace for activities.

What Is It?

Acteva offers a secure online event management solution for corporations, associations, event planners, nonprofits, faith-based organizations, entertainment organizations, schools and universities, and other continuing education organizations. The service allows event organizers to focus on the event preparation rather than the administrative and attendance duties necessary for hosting the event, and offers a MultiVent option for organizations running numerous events. Acteva creates a secure page for the organization's event that processes the registration, payment processing, ticketing, and attendance verification, and provides response-reporting services that allow organizations to access data from one central location. Several different service plans are available, depending on the organization's needs.

How Can It Be Used?

Acteva provides a platform for organizations to organize, manage, and track an event. The event registration and management software can be customized based on the organization's needs and has been used for events such as conferences, conventions, meetings, symposia, workshops, webinars, classes, seminars, trade shows, user groups, trainings, festivals, fund-raisers, galas, concerts, tours, and reunions. The Acteva system enables organizers to create custom-tailored event registration pages that process the registration and payment, and then send an electronic confirmation to the registrant. The event management software facilitates the generation of attendee lists, meal preference lists, name tags, and badges; the ticketing option prints and mails tickets to the attendees.

What Other Applications Does It Work With?

Acteva is a self-contained application suite and was not designed to work specifically with other social media applications. It can be used in a complementary fashion, however, with a wide variety of other applications.

Who Uses It?

A variety of organizations, including corporations, associations, event planners, nonprofits, faith-based organizations, entertainment organizations, schools and universities, and other continuing education organizations use Acteva. Anyone needing event planning tools can use its services. Since its founding, more than 16,500 event organizers have relied on Acteva to help increase attendance, reduce administrative burdens, and provide an out-standing online experience for their attendees, participants, and customers.

Libby Craig of the Flute Bay Area stated, "Our guests registered with ease, and your reporting functions were a great help in our efforts to track activity and be certain special needs of registrants were met."

Marianne Leon of the NJ Green Building Council used Acteva and found that the "reporting features save a tremendous amount of time and I can make strategic decisions. I also target attendees with distinct offers to entice them to register."

Should You Use It?

If you are looking for a convenient package program to assist in event planning or do not have the time or personnel to handle the administrative functions of planning an event, Acteva could be a viable option.

Jennie Bolas of McKesson stated, "Acteva provides a professional registration solution that contributes to the success of our corporate events."

According to Darian Rodriguez Heyman (Craigslist Foundation), "There are so many different ways Acteva helps me accomplish my goals as an organizer. It's really made my job much easier. I have plenty of insight into who's coming to our boot camp, why they are coming, and what we can do to improve their satisfaction with the program."

Who Started It?

Pankaj Gupta is founder of zDegree, the parent organization of Acteva, and is cofounder, president, and CEO of Acteva. He worked for or founded numerous Silicon Valley technology companies prior to Acteva. Gupta holds degrees in electronic systems engineering and industrial systems engineering as well as a bachelor's degree in biological sciences.

AOL

Company Name:	AOL LLC
URL:	www.aol.com
Location:	New York, New York
Founded:	1983
Revenue Model:	Advertising, services
Fees:	Free and Premium

What Is It?

AOL is a company that serves two main functions: providing Internet services and providing online content. Both of these functions are derived from the company's older software application, America Online, which was at one time the most popular subscription dial-up Internet service in the world. America Online allowed users to access select areas of the Internet (users were eventually allowed to access the entirety of the Internet) and participate in the world's largest online community, complete with chat rooms, special interest groups, games, and a graphical user interface. These types of features later became key components of social networking.

How Can It Be Used?

The Internet service provider aspect of AOL manifests itself through services such as dial-up access to the Internet, AOL e-mail and chatting accounts, and security applications. There are also services available for users who have high-speed Internet access through a different provider. The content aspect of AOL can be accessed primarily through myAOL, which serves as a contact point for users to browse the Internet. The myAOL service offers several features, such as customizable content, RSS feeds, saved bookmarks, myAOL Favorites (a way to share your favorite web content with other users), and personalized content recommendations.

What Other Applications Does It Work With?

AOL works with Yahoo! and Gmail so users can check multiple e-mail accounts from the AOL homepage. AOL also works with Facebook, Twitter, and MySpace. The AOL Internet services do not rely on AOL Internet access, allowing users the ability to access AOL offerings through their chosen Internet access company.

Who Uses It?

AOL, when it was known as America Online, at one point had more than 30 million subscribers worldwide. This subscriber base has fallen considerably since 2001. AOL online content is accessed by a global audience, with large portions of the consumers coming from the United States, Germany, and the United Kingdom. Some of the partners that provide content for AOL include News Corporation, Sony, NBC Universal, and Warner Bros.

Should You Use It?

You should use AOL if you would like to consolidate and customize content from the Internet in one location through myAOL. You should also use AOL if you are interested in finding a variety of online content that includes offerings like news, horoscopes, entertainment, and job postings. AOL Internet services are useful as well if you are interested in different features such as Internet access, security software, technical support, video on demand, or insurance coverage.

Who Started It?

AOL first began as a company called Control Video Corporation in 1983, which was reorganized as Quantum Computer Services Inc., on May 24, 1985. The company focused on providing dedicated online services to Commodore computers. In 1988, Quantum created online services for Macintosh, and later IBM, computers. In 1991, Quantum became known as America Online Inc., AOL for DOS was launched, and Steve Case became the CEO of the company. Case decided the best direction for the company to take was to position AOL as the premier online service for those who were not particularly knowledgeable about computers. This strategy led to the company's biggest growth period. On January 11, 2001, America Online merged with Time Warner. It was spun off to be a completely independent company again on December 10, 2009.

BitTorrent

Company Name:	BitTorrent Inc.
URL:	www.bittorrent.com
Location:	San Francisco, California
Founded:	2004
Employees:	30
Revenue Model:	Advertising, paid downloads, and software
Fees:	Media downloads vary by content. Other services require contact with a BitTorrent representative.
Tagline:	Access the Internet's richest media.

What Is It?

BitTorrent is an avenue for high-quality media downloads over the Internet. The free BitTorrent software allows you to securely and quickly download TV shows, music, movies, and PC games on demand. Publishing your own films, music videos, and various media content is another service that BitTorrent offers to showcase your work on a global scale. Downloads from BitTorrent are compatible with select home entertainment devices for viewing TV shows.

How Can It Be Used?

BitTorrent is popular among movie studios, television networks, software developers, record labels, musicians, and others for distributing media for public download. It is a great way to develop your fan base, introduce a new product, and get the world familiar with your specialized offering. Many popular Hollywood studios are distributing content using BitTorrent to develop brand awareness online. Even radio programs are using BitTorrent to help dedicated listeners download podcasts of their programs. Using BitTorrent's DNA (Delivery Network Accelerator), companies can also take the pressure off of a company's server by using the service for downloads.

What Other Applications Does It Work With?

The BitTorrent store and software are compatible with any web browser. BitTorrent DNA is also compatible with any web browser, but carries the ability to apply its revolutionary protocol to your own personal web site. Content downloaded from BitTorrent is compatible with Windows Media Player and many other popular media storage programs.

Who Uses It?

Major motion picture studios, record labels, musicians, software developers, television networks, and others are releasing content for download on BitTorrent. NBC, MTV, FOX, Warner Bros., Comedy Central, and others have partnerships with BitTorrent for viewers to download programming. Small businesses that lack bandwidth on their web sites can use BitTorrent's DNA technology to unload stress on their server and relay downloads to other servers. BitTorrent currently has 160 million clients worldwide.

Should You Use It?

If digital distribution is a means of reaching your target audience, then BitTorrent is a service that would act in your favor. Whether you are launching a new product or trying to create hype for your new dramatic short film, BitTorrent provides effective online exposure. With today's impatient consumers demanding speedy turnaround, BitTorrent downloads are fast and efficient. BitTorrent's DNA technology can help a small business lacking bandwidth on its web site to improve the quality of downloads. Advertising on BitTorrent would reach a tech-savvy audience that depends highly on the Internet for common functionalities.

Who Started It?

Programmer Brahm Cohen developed the BitTorrent software in 2001. Using the popular peer-to-peer file-sharing protocol, Cohen and colleague Ashwin Navin began BitTorrent Inc., in 2004. The pair based the company on three levels of business: a web-based store with ad-based downloadable content, BitTorrent's DNA technology, and BitTorrent's Software Development Kit (SDK).

Eventful

Company Name:	Eventful
URL:	eventful.com
Location:	San Diego, California
Founded:	2004
Employees:	35
Revenue Model:	Series A & B venture capital funding, advertising
Fees:	Free
Tagline:	Life is short. . . . Make it eventful!

What Is It?

Eventful is a repository of events from all around the world. Whether concerts, art events, sporting events, or other entertainment venues, users can research or post them for other users to find. In addition to being an event-listing database, Eventful also allows users to post "demands" for venues, such as requesting a music performer to come to a certain location.

The specified performer can monitor the demand rate, and if the demand is high enough, plan a performance at that location.

How Can It Be Used?

Eventful is an Internet-based calendar database used by people around the world. Fifteen million people a week use Eventful to find out what is happening in their area. According to Eventful's "About" page, people use Eventful to import iTunes and Last.fm performer lists to keep track of local appearances; export events through feeds, calendar widgets, and more; keep track of favorite venues and performers; create customized e-mail event guides; add events to personal watch lists; and add and promote events for free.

What Other Applications Does It Work With?

Eventful works with a number of applications: iTunes (to include as an application for iPhone), Yahoo!, iGoogle, MySpace, Artist Data Systems, Clickable City, and Mapdango. All of these applications feature the ability to post calendar events with locations, and can be incorporated into Eventful.

Who Uses It?

Music performers, art show hosts, celebrities, stadiums, and marketing specialists can all use Eventful to broadcast awareness of their events or stir demand for future events. Eventful was even used in the 2008 political campaigns as candidates determined which location to target by monitoring user demand for candidate appearances.

Should You Use It?

Eventful seems to be gaining popularity for its global event tracking, and with the use of Eventful in political campaign strategy, it seems like a good idea. If political candidates can use it for assessing constituency demand, the same principle could be used in product-release events to build up interest in a new product. For example, what if Apple created the next-generation iPhone and used Eventful to hold some sort of locale contest to determine when and where a major release event would be held? Marketing strategies are endless, and obviously Eventful is useful for attracting local people as well as travelers to your major event.

Who Started It?

Brian Dear founded Eventful after experiencing routine frustration at finding out about events in San Diego after they occurred. In an interview on SoCaltech.com, Dear stated that he began researching Eventful as early as 2002. In its beta version, Eventful was known as EVDB, and in 2005 the name was changed to Eventful. Brian Dear started Eventful to facilitate sharing of event information on a global level. Prior to Eventful, Dear was the founding director of eBay Design Labs at eBay Inc. He also worked at Eazel, MP3.com, FlatWorks, RealNetworks, and Coconut Computing.

Google Alerts

Company Name:	Google Alerts (Google Inc.)
URL:	www.google.com/alerts
Location:	Mountain View, California
Founded:	2003
Employees:	20,000 (Google)
Revenue Model:	Advertising and premium subscriptions
Fees:	Free

What Is It?

Google Alerts allows you to create alerts against your Google searches and receive the results through RSS feeds or e-mails. You can determine how frequently you receive the alerts, and searches last for six months. You can renew the alerts or let them expire. Google Alerts are based on the six categories of Google information: news, Web, blogs, images, videos, and Google Groups. Users are allowed a maximum of a thousand different alerts.

How Can It Be Used?

Google Alerts can be used to track a number of items on the Internet. You can create queries to alert you when someone links to your web site, keep track of new web pages on a web site, track when your favorite blog posts new entries, receive alerts when someone quotes you or uses your name, or track news about a specific topic, product, or company. According to Blogstorm.com, you can even use Google Alerts to keep track of whether your web site has been hacked and had hidden links placed in the web page to elevate the ranking of a different web page, called a "black hat site."

What Other Applications Does It Work With?

Google Alerts works with Google Bots, but not with any other applications.

Who Uses It?

No specific demographic is attributed with using Google Alerts. Many people in business or engaged in research use it, whether to keep abreast of news on a topic of interest, or to track cross-links between web sites.

Should You Use It?

Google Alerts is a great tool for keeping up to date on new information, web updates, images, and other data that are available and constantly changing on the Internet. You just need a Google account, and you can establish up to a thousand alerts. It's a great tool for businesses, nonprofits, students, and private individuals who want to be updated.

Who Started It?

According to the Google Guide, in February 2003, Google engineer Naga Sridhar developed an application because he was tired of regularly visiting Google News to check for developments in the imminent U.S. war with Iraq. The application e-mailed him when a news story matched a specific query. Naga demonstrated his prototype to cofounder Sergey Brin, who set up a news alert for "Google." Naga continued his development of this application full-time with the encouragement of both Sergey and Marissa Mayer (Google's director of consumer products). Six months later, links to News Alerts were added to Google Labs' home page and to Google News. Google subsequently added Web Alerts to track changes to web pages. Eventually both News Alerts and Web Alerts were merged into a single service called Google Alerts.

Google Docs

Company Name:	Google Docs (Google Inc.)
URL:	docs.google.com
Location:	Mountain View, California
Founded:	2005
Employees:	20,000 (Google)
Fees:	Free
Tagline:	Create and share your work online.

What Is It?

Google Docs allows users to upload documents so that they are available on the Internet for use, collaboration, and travel. You can upload DOC, XLS, ODT, ODS, RTF, CSV, PPT, and other documents to a common place for keeping and accessing them. Google Docs also allows you to organize your data, control access, and work in real time, and instantly publish the document as a web page, to a blog, or within a specific group or company. Up to 10 people can edit a document at the same time, or 50 people for the same spreadsheet.

How Can It Be Used?

Google Docs has many collaborative and publishing options. With the variety of documents that can be used on Google Docs, collaboration is unlimited. Users can determine who has access to what document, and how it gets published. Google Docs can be used as a backup server as well as a central location point when employees travel. Another way Google Docs can be used is to create polls or surveys by creating a form, embedding the form into your web site or blog, and then collecting the data into a spreadsheet. Google Docs is limited in storage: word documents up to 500 kilobytes; up to 2 megabytes per embedded image; and spreadsheets up to 10,000 rows, 256 columns, or 40 sheets, whichever comes first.

What Other Applications Does It Work With?

Google Docs is viewable, but not editable, on mobile devices. Apple has created an interface for viewing Google Docs on the iPhone, and the Android but again, the data are not editable. However, the only other application that works with Google Docs is the Google Apps application geared for collaboration. Google Apps enables sharing of documents stored on Google Docs.

Who Uses It?

Google Docs offers a number of stories of how people use the application. Anecdotes range from the Red Sox fan who uses a spreadsheet to sell his season tickets for games he can't attend to author Ken Leebow who uses Google Docs to keep track of his book projects. There is a story of a Las Vegas drag strip operations coordinator who uses the Google Docs spreadsheet to keep track of employee time cards for payroll purposes. The uses are as endless as the office suite programs that people access on a daily basis on their PCs and Macs.

Should You Use It?

Google Docs is as useful as any other set of office suite programs. The difference is the location of the files and the ability to publish and share the documentation in real time in a number of ways and platforms. Google is a known name, which brings a sense of comfort and security to the user. The only downsides may be the amount of storage provided and the fact that other than embedding documents on web sites or blogs, there isn't a lot of third-party software compatibility.

Who Started It?

Google Docs originated from two separate products, Writely and Google Spreadsheets. Upstartle created Writely and launched the Web-based word processor in 2005. Writely's features included collaborative text editing and access controls. The graphical user interfaces were similar to those in Microsoft Word or OpenOffice. Writely maintained its own user system until its integration with Google Accounts on September 19, 2006.

Google Gmail

Company Name:	Gmail (Google Inc.)
URL:	gmail.com
Location:	Mountain View, California
Founded:	2004
Employees:	20,000 (Google)
Revenue Model:	Advertising, additional storage purchases, stock sales
Fees:	Free

What Is It?

Gmail, or Google Mail, is a free e-mail service that provides user accounts with 7 megabytes of storage for messages and attachments, helpful features like conversation threads and integrated chat sessions with AIM friends, and a search-oriented interface. Users can also integrate other e-mail accounts using Pop3 access and receive all their e-mail in one account. Gmail is available for use on any mobile device with Internet browser capability. Gmail offers features such as keyboard shortcuts, quick contacts, and specialized advertising focusing on the individual user and his interests.

How Can It Be Used?

Gmail can be used like any other e-mail application, but it does have some unique features. Google's search capability is integrated for easy searching of e-mails the same way you type in a keyword search in Google, only you select "Search Mail." The search query does not recognize symbols used in Boolean logic or other special characters. Gmail also allows users to receive e-mail from other accounts through Pop3 access. Gmail account holders have special features such as iMap, labels, and filters. Gmail also has chat sessions built right in to the e-mail interface that also allow users to chat with AIM friends as well as other Gmail contacts.

What Other Applications Does It Work With?

Gmail works with any mobile device with browser capability and AOL/AIM. Google has strict policies in place regarding no use of third-party software applications with Gmail. Some of the other Google tools enhance Gmail's capability, such as using Google Talk for leaving voicemail on Gmail, or using Picasa for image capability.

Who Uses It?

Gmail offers anecdotal reports of its usage. Much of it is personal, but highlights include a divorce lawyer who strictly enforces the use of Gmail accounts with his clients to prevent spouses from reading e-mails regarding legal strategy. Another story was from a pastor's wife who organizes activities and events at her husband's church. She must communicate with many people, and the ability to organize them easily into contact groups is a feature for her. Academic institutions such as Arizona State University use Gmail as their e-mail tool for these reasons.

Should You Use It?

Many e-mail applications are out there, and people use them for many of the same reasons: familiarity, ease of access, or features. Gmail incorporates several major needs into one package: e-mail, chat, and organization. The ability to have a number of tools combined into one package makes Gmail an attractive e-mail application. With the additional features of tools such as iMap, Mail Goggles (stop yourself from sending embarrassing e-mails late at night!), and labeling, Gmail gives other e-mail applications a serious run for the user's money.

Who Started It?

Paul Buchheit, founder of FriendFeed, was an early Google employee (the 23rd, to be exact) and is credited with the creation of Gmail. According to Buchheit's blog:

> I wrote the first version of Gmail in one day. It was not very impressive. All I did was stuff my own e-mail into the Google Groups (Usenet) indexing engine. I sent it out to a few people for feedback, and they said that it was somewhat useful, but it would be better if it searched over their e-mail instead of mine. That was version two. After I released that, people started wanting the ability to respond to e-mail as well. That was version three. That process went on for a couple of years inside of Google before we released to the world.

MSGTAG

Company Name:	Fisher Young Group
URL:	msgtag.com
Location:	Wellington, New Zealand
Founded:	2002
Revenue Model:	Premium service
Tagline:	Got the message?

What Is It?

MSGTAG is a desktop application that informs you whenever your e-mail messages are received and viewed by the recipients. The program works by adding a tag to your outgoing e-mail that tells the MSGTAG server details such as the date and time the e-mail was sent, the date and time the e-mail was opened, and the duration of time between the two. Three different versions of MSGTAG are currently available: MSGTAG Free, MSGTAG Plus, and MSGTAG Status 2. Each program ranges in cost (from free to around $60) and features (SMS notifications, compatibility, e-mail footers, and so forth).

How Can It Be Used?

MSGTAG can be used in time-sensitive instances—when it is vital to know who has received an e-mail and who hasn't—so alternative methods of communication may be pursued if necessary. MSGTAG can also be used to offer peace of mind to its users, who no longer have to wonder if e-mails have been received or read.

What Other Applications Does It Work With?

MSGTAG works with SMTP (Simple Mail Transfer Protocol) e-mail applications. Some examples of STMP e-mail applications are Microsoft Outlook, Microsoft Outlook Express, Eudora, Netscape Mail, and Pegasus Mail.

Who Uses It?

MSGTAG is used by anyone who is interested in knowing if and when her e-mails have been received. Businesses can use it to ensure their e-mails to clients are getting delivered, to figure out whether or not their employees have been too busy to respond to an e-mail, or to see if they just haven't received the message. Whether the e-mails are being sent among friends, family, or professional relations, users can use MSGTAG to determine if their e-mails are getting through.

Should You Use It?

You should use MSGTAG if you are ever in a position in which you need to know if your e-mails are being received and read. Since MSGTAG does not require you to change anything about the way you send your e-mail, it is an attractive option for those people who are not advanced computer users. With the availability of MSGTAG Free, you should also use MSGTAG if you need the basic functionality of the program without spending any money.

Who Started It?

According to Msgtag.com, "MSGTAG is a product of Fisher Young Group, a New Zealand company formed in 2002. The company contracted eCOSM, a Christchurch software development company, to create MSGTAG. eCOSM is the company that developed MailWasher Pro, the groundbreaking anti-spam application for Firetrust. With the debut of MSGTAG, Fisher Young Group is leading the way in the field of automatic e-mail read-receipt software."

ReadNotify

Company Name:	ReadNotify
URL:	www.readnotify.com
Location:	Sydney, Australia
Revenue Model:	Premium subscriptions
Tagline:	Track your e-mail.

What Is It?

According to readnotify.com, "ReadNotify is the most powerful and reliable e-mail tracking service that exists today. In short—ReadNotify tells you when e-mail you sent gets read/re-opened/forwarded and *so* much more." Though the features and tools of ReadNotify are complex, it is a relatively simple service to use. The service operates in one of two ways: through an Active-Tracker plug-in or by adding commands to the end of a recipient's e-mail address.

How Can It Be Used?

ReadNotify can be used to track several different details of e-mails so users know what is happening to their communication after it has been sent. Among the things ReadNotify can tell you are the date and time an e-mail was opened, the location of the recipient, the recipient's e-mail address, the length of time a recipient spent reading an e-mail, the number of times an e-mail has been opened, or if your e-mail was forwarded.

What Other Applications Does It Work With?

ReadNotify works with several different applications to notify you when your e-mails have been opened. These applications include ICQ, AOL Instant Messenger, IRC, Yahoo! Instant Messenger, and MSN Messenger. If used manually (without the ActiveTracker plug-in), ReadNotify is compatible with all e-mail programs and operating systems.

Who Uses It?

ReadNotify is used by anyone who wishes to track his e-mails' details. One large customer base is businesses, which take advantage of the different ReadNotify features. For example, if a user is sending confidential information to someone through e-mail, ReadNotify allows him to set up a "Self-Destructing" e-mail, which means the e-mail will destroy itself in a designated amount of time or if the recipient tries to copy, print, or forward it. This feature also allows for e-mails to be retracted before a recipient opens them.

Should You Use It?

You should use ReadNotify if you are in situations in which it would be beneficial to know detailed information about e-mails for any reason. Read-Notify is a great program to use when you need to track when e-mails were sent, when they were received, and whether the recipient has accepted a read guarantee. Also, with features such as court-admissible certification and notarization, you should use ReadNotify if you work in a highly sensitive field that often relies on e-mails.

Who Started It?

Christopher Drake founded ReadNotify in Sydney, Australia. The company originally operated from Drake's house. Readnotify.com was the recipient of the 2002 Yellow Pages Business Ideas Grant for the state of New South Wales. Drake is currently the company's chief technology officer.

SurveyMonkey

Company Name:	SurveyMonkey
URL:	www.surveymonkey.com
Location:	Portland, Oregon; Menlo Park, California
Founded:	1999
Revenue Model:	Service packages
Fees:	Basic: free; Monthly Pro: $19.95 per month and $0.05 for each overage; Annual Pro: $200 per year
Tagline:	Because knowledge is everything

What Is It?

SurveyMonkey offers users an effective tool for creating online surveys. Users are able to customize and design their surveys by choosing from numerous question options and are provided the option to "require answers to any question, control the flow with custom skip logic, and randomize answer choices to eliminate bias." SurveyMonkey offers creative control over the appearance of the surveys, allows users to upload logos for brand recognition, determine the collection method, send a survey invitation, track and manage results, and download summaries. SurveyMonkey has teamed up with Mail Chimp to provide a higher level of functionality to create e-mail campaigns, manage lists, and offer additional tracking and reporting tools.

How Can It Be Used?

With the pairing mentioned in the previous section, SurveyMonkey provides the tool to design, create, and implement a survey, and Mail Chimp is the application to control and manage its distribution. Users determine the type, length, design, and content of the survey through SurveyMonkey, create a link to the survey, and either post the link to a site or e-mail it to potential respondents. Mail Chimp allows users to build e-mail campaigns, manage e-mail lists, and track and create reports based on the campaign.

What Other Applications Does It Work With?

SurveyMonkey works with most Internet browsers, allows users to create links to their surveys from their web page, supports computer lab and kiosk setups, allows users to save their results in PDF formats, and exports surveys in numerous formats. Mail Chimp works with WordPress, TypePad, Open-Social, Joomla, Drupal, Foxy Cart, Zen Cart, blogs, and other applications by independent developers.

Who Uses It?

SurveyMonkey is widely used by businesses large and small, including many Fortune 500 companies. It is also used by students conducting surveys for courses or research projects, professional associations, non-profits, professional and personal services providers, recreation and enter-tainment groups, religious organizations, restaurants, retail outlets, and travel and tourism organizations. Mail Chimp can also be used by these organizations as a resource to deliver surveys to a targeted audience and glean insight into who reads, responds, or forwards the e-mails or news-letters. Using SurveyMonkey and Mail Chimp together provides an effective marketing tool.

Should You Use It?

If you or your organization are looking for a way to communicate with your audience and obtain feedback regarding products and services, expand and track marketing initiatives, and generate reports, these tools could provide an appropriate solution. Traditional advertising and marketing techniques reach just a limited target audience. Using Web-based marketing and surveys, organizations can reach and interact with a wider audience to target the customer's wants and needs.

Who Started It?

SurveyMonkey was developed in 1999 by Ryan Finley, a graduate student at University of Wisconsin in Madison, to "enable people of all experience levels to create their own surveys quickly and easily." Mail Chimp "started out as a web development company (The Rocket Science Group) back in April 2000." In recognizing an expanding need to resolve difficulties in sending HTML e-mail newsletters with limited options for the customer, Mail Chimp was developed.

TiddlyWiki

Company Name:	TiddlyWiki
URL:	tiddlywiki.org/wiki/Main_Page/and tiddlywiki.com
Location:	Menlo Park, California
Founded:	2006 (Now owned by the UnaMesa Association, a nonprofit)
Employees:	Not available
Revenue Model:	Corporate contributions, individual donations, grants
Fees:	Free
Tagline:	Send stuff to your friends.

What Is It?

According to the TiddlyWiki.org/wiki, the concept is "TiddlyWiki is a single-file, self-contained wiki for managing micro-content, written in JavaScript." It is also referred to as a nonlinear, reusable notebook. TiddlyWiki is intended to be a single file easily stored on your computer and thus easily stored and transferred through your USB flash drive or e-mail. TiddlyWiki is marketed as a simple, easy program that is usable on any operating system, and doesn't even require the Internet. It is a wiki, used like any other wiki for project collaboration or a personal notebook or journal.

How Can It Be Used?

UnaMesa describes TiddlyWiki use in the following wiki excerpt:

> TiddlyWiki itself is a unique piece of software that provides a complete, editable web document without the need for a network connection. This means that students can access educational materials "on the web" and record their own notes even if they do not have a live network connection, for example in unwired classrooms, at home, or remote villages. We have also demonstrated how to incorporate materials from several sites, such as Wikipedia, SocialText, and others, into a single file that can be easily shared, edited, and updated. This creates a much more dynamic learning experience and reduces most if not all technology barriers to sharing information.

What Other Applications Does It Work With?

TiddlyWiki works on any computer operating system. Additionally, Apple has included TiddlyWiki in the list of new apps available for the iPhone and iPod Touch. Generally the concept behind TiddlyWiki is that users can easily develop applications they need or want to work with their wiki. A Google search of associated applications shows users have done just that, as exhibited on the web site "Musings of Dawn." The owner of Musings of Dawn provides an editing application and a comment scripting application from another TiddlyWiki user.

Who Uses It?

TiddlyWiki in Action is a web site dedicated to showing how users use TiddlyWiki. One purpose is for presentation and pictures. User Dr. Robert Boss presents a study of eighteenth-century author Robert Fuller's work, "The Gospel Worthy of Great Acceptation," the focus of Boss's PhD thesis. Another example of a TiddlyWiki use is publication. User Lynsey Gedye published a book, *Japanese Haiku,* a compilation of ancient Japanese haiku poetry using TiddlyWiki.

Should You Use It?

Businesses can use TiddlyWiki for activities such as project management and collaboration, publication of user manuals and tutorials, discussion of products, and other topics of concern to company administration and consumers. Conversely, as part of UnaMesa's mission to provide free software tools for clinics, schools, and other community organizations, this tool fits in with the UnaMesa mission. Therefore, anyone who falls under one of those categories is philosophically the right entity to use TiddlyWiki.

Who Started It?

TiddlyWiki itself was created by Jeremy Ruston, who states on his LinkedIn bio, "I've spent my life inventing software products with great user experiences, and building the teams to develop them. Now I'm the creator of TiddlyWiki, a very popular open source personal organizer that's grown to be the platform for a whole new class of web applications. I lead the community around TiddlyWiki, and am dedicated to building a great product for users all over the world." He is the head of British company Open Source Innovation, a telecommunications company, and founder of Osmosoft, a consulting company. Jeremy provided TiddlyWiki to UnaMesa under a Berkeley Software Distribution open-source license, which makes it free software.

Yahoo!

Company Name:	Yahoo! Inc.
URL:	www.yahoo.com
Location:	Bangalore, India; Sunnyvale, California
Founded:	1994
Employees:	13,900
Revenue Model:	Advertising, subscriptions, and transactions
Fees:	Free (additional applications available by paid subscription)

What Is It?

Yahoo! is an Internet services company founded in 1994 by two Stanford PhD candidates, Jerry Yang and David Filo. Yahoo! offers "vertical search services such as Yahoo! Image, Yahoo! Local, Yahoo! News, and Yahoo!

Shopping Search . . . and communication services such as Yahoo! Mail and Yahoo! Messenger." Best known for its web portal, search engine, Yahoo! Directory, Yahoo! Mail, news, and social media web sites, Yahoo! is consistently expanding its range of services to meet the changing needs of the consumer.

How Can It Be Used?

Yahoo! provides free and paid services depending on the user's needs. Yahoo! can be used to search the Internet for a vast array of information and services, to purchase or sell items and services, to conduct research, to receive updates on financial services, to communicate with others, to play games or interact with others, to watch videos or listen to music, and to find and offer employment. Many other applications and services are developed and integrated into the Yahoo! family of services. A new service, Yahoo! Search BOSS, "allows developers to build search applications based on Yahoo!'s search technology." Currently in beta testing is Yahoo! Next, a forum community for user "feedback to assist in the development of these future Yahoo! Technologies."

What Other Applications Does It Work With?

Yahoo! works with most current Internet browsers and offers mobile service compatibility and a significant number of social media applications. With the implementation of Yahoo! Search BOSS, independent developers can create applications based on Yahoo!'s search technology, which further expands the possibility of compatibility with customized future applications.

Who Uses It?

Yahoo! is a free Internet services provider available to anyone with an Internet browser and Internet connection. The array of information available provides usability for a broad spectrum of users, and the ever-expanding list of services affords users flexibility on how it can be used.

Should You Use It?

Yahoo! offers myriad services to meet the needs of consumers. It is an effective tool to search for information, listen to music, find videos and other entertainment, communicate, and interact with others.

Who Started It?

Two Stanford engineering PhD candidates, David Filo and Jerry Yang, developed Yahoo! as a platform to track their personal interests on the Internet. The founders recognized the business potential of their web site as the popularity of the site spread. Yahoo! was incorporated in 1995 and continues to add features and services to meet its audience's expanding needs.

Zoho

Company Name:	AdventNet
URL:	www.zoho.com
Location:	Pleasanton, California
Founded:	1996
Employees:	1200
Revenue Model:	Subscription fees, program sale
Tagline:	Work. Online.

What Is It?

Zoho wants to be the IT department for businesses, providing a wide range of online applications needed for businesses and individuals. There are two categories of applications: the Productivity and Collaboration Application Suite and the Business Application Suite. Zoho is the only vendor that has this combination in the online application market, which not only makes Zoho unique but also defines the direction of the online business market when these two application suites come together. To date, Zoho has launched 22 different applications, and more are in the works. Zoho has received numerous awards, including a 2008 *PC World* 25 Most Innovative Products Award for Zoho Notebook and Best Enterprise Start-up at the 2007 Crunchies.

How Can It Be Used?

Zoho is used for creating and sharing content with other users. They use the Zoho tools for productivity and in some cases to run their business online. Zoho provides a number of applications that have similar purposes as Microsoft Word and other programs. A sample of the applications include a word processing application (Zoho Writer), a spreadsheet application (Zoho Sheet), a wiki (Zoho Wiki), and much more. These applications can be accessed from any computer, whether at home, at work, or during travel.

What Other Applications Does It Work With?

Zoho works with box.net and Entrepreneur Assist. Additionally, Zoho applications work with Microsoft applications, the iPhone, Jot, Twitter, and Facebook. Different Zoho applications may have specific interoperability with other applications—for example, Zoho Sheet works not only with MS Excel but also with box.net and Facebook. Zoho recently gave users the ability to log in with Google and Yahoo! accounts.

Who Uses It?

Zoho has five major categories of users: individuals, students, departments in larger organizations, larger organizations that are standardizing their applications, and government. Zoho is being recognized by users such as Pam Gaulin, a freelance writer, for the ease of uploading, sharing, and creating information in the Web 2.0 environment. Gaulin touts the use of Zoho Notebook over Google Notebook, applauding that Zoho Notebook allows for the incorporation of audio and video, whereas Google Notebook does not. One academic user is noted on the Zoho blog as using Zoho applications to post the results of a survey regarding online learning, as well as a presentation discussing appropriate computer usage at his college. Another academic user used Zoho Creator to conduct a survey and collect data on how library patrons selected books.

Should You Use It?

Company executives particularly recommend their Zoho line for educational institutions and students. If you are looking for an easier way to work and collaborate online, you should use this social medium. The ability to work on any computer from any location renders an environment of constant productivity. Zoho is compatible with so many applications and tools that the possibilities for usage are endless. For the individual user, there are no subscription fees; for the nonprofit/business/academic organization, there are fees depending on the applications being used and the number of employees. Fees range from $8 to $850 a month.

Who Started It?

During a 2007 interview about Indian start-ups, when asked about the trigger for creating Zoho, Raju Vegasna stated, "Around 2001 to 2003 after the telecom bubble burst, [AdventNet] had lots of engineering resources on hand. So we decided to enter different market segments. Online applications is one of them. We truly believed in online applications and Zoho was born from there."

Zoomerang

Company Name:	Zoomerang
URL:	www.zoomerang.com
Location:	San Francisco, California
Founded:	1999
Revenue Model:	Service packages

What Is It?

Zoomerang offers users an effective tool for creating an unlimited number of online surveys with up to 30 questions. Users are able to choose from more than 100 survey templates, and, depending on the tier, can send surveys to an unlimited number of respondents, and "download to Excel and create charts." The Pro and above tiers offer additional features such as the ability to customize the survey, images, logos, and links. They also provide "cross-tabulation, skip logic, filtering, report downloads, and customizable charts."

How Can It Be Used?

Zoomerang provides various tiered options to meet the needs of your organization, and has ready-made templates for customer satisfaction with products or services, the organization as a whole, technical support, and the buying experience or cancellation surveys. Zoomerang guides the user in determining the type of question to ask based upon the type of response you are looking for. With the reporting and analytics tools, Zoomerang offers the ability to measure your results accurately, determine trends, and develop future initiatives to build your business further.

What Other Applications Does It Work With?

Zoomerang works with Twitter and most Internet browsers, uses SMS messaging for mobile connectivity to provide instant feedback, or can be inserted into a blog.

Who Uses It?

Zoomerang is a popular survey tool now being used by businesses, educational institutions, and individuals worldwide. Richard Aaron, president of BizBash Media, stated, "By conducting Zoomerang surveys of our event's attendees, we better understand their needs, see how well we meet their expectations, and better tailor our future shows to meet their preferences."

Should You Use It?

Traditional advertising and marketing techniques only reach a limited target audience. Using Web-based marketing and surveys, organizations can reach and interact with a wider audience to target the customer's wants and needs. If you or your organization are looking for a way to communicate with your audience and obtain feedback regarding products and services, expand and track marketing initiatives, and generate reports, Zoomerang would be an effective tool.

Who Started It?

Zoomerang was started in 1999 by MarketTools, a technology and solutions provider offering online market research tools.

Tool Scorecard for Chapter 32: Productivity Applications

Instructions: Using the following five-point (0 to 4) scale, rate each tool in this chapter on the basis of how valuable it *might be* to the internal and external operations of your company. Make notes about which tools appeal to you the most.

> 4 = Extremely Valuable
> 3 = Very Valuable
> 2 = Somewhat Valuable

1 = Not Very Valuable
0 = No Value

Tool	Internal Value	External Value
Acteva	4 3 2 1 0	4 3 2 1 0
AOL	4 3 2 1 0	4 3 2 1 0
BitTorrent	4 3 2 1 0	4 3 2 1 0
Eventful	4 3 2 1 0	4 3 2 1 0
Google Alerts	4 3 2 1 0	4 3 2 1 0
Google Docs	4 3 2 1 0	4 3 2 1 0
Google Gmail	4 3 2 1 0	4 3 2 1 0
MSGTAG	4 3 2 1 0	4 3 2 1 0
ReadNotify	4 3 2 1 0	4 3 2 1 0
SurveyMonkey	4 3 2 1 0	4 3 2 1 0
TiddlyWiki	4 3 2 1 0	4 3 2 1 0
Yahoo!	4 3 2 1 0	4 3 2 1 0
Zoho	4 3 2 1 0	4 3 2 1 0
Zoomerang	4 3 2 1 0	4 3 2 1 0

CHAPTER 33

Aggregators

In this chapter, I highlight Aggregators, web sites that allow you to choose what type of content you want to see, where you want it to come from, present it to you all in an organized page, and do it automatically all of the time. Aggregators allow you to see all of the new blogs, web pages, news, audio, photos, and video updates all in one convenient web page location. This is like having an automated worldwide web clipping service and news agency at your fingertips. And, it's free. As you read each profile, keep in mind that its features and functions may or may not be right for your particular business. Use the Tool Scorecard at the end of the chapter to help you determine which of these tools qualify for further consideration when you begin creating your social media strategy in Part III of the book.

Digg

Company Name:	Digg
URL:	digg.com
Location:	San Francisco, California
Founded:	2004
Employees:	81
Revenue Model:	Series A & Series B funding, advertising
Fees:	Free
Tagline:	All news, videos, and images

What Is It?

Digg's purpose is for users to submit online sites and content they believe would be valuable to other Digg members. If enough Digg members vote on the submitted online site or content, the item is placed on the front page of Digg's web site for all viewers to read about. Those stories that don't do well get "buried," in Digg terminology. Not only does this approach encourage users to continuously provide content to Digg, it also ensures that they actively participate, assuming that maintaining a high status is important to the user. In this manner, the Internet audience drives the quality and type of information on the Web.

How Can It Be Used?

Individuals, groups, organizations, and businesses can use Digg to remain informed of web content of interest. Conversely, those users can submit links to web content. Digg says it best on its web site: "Because Digg is all about sharing and discovery, there's a conversation that happens around the content. We're here to promote that conversation and provide tools for our community to discuss the topics that they're passionate about. By looking at information through the lens of the collective community on Digg, you'll always find something interesting and unique. We're committed to giving every piece of content on the web an equal shot at being the next big thing to promote their specific interest."

What Other Applications Does It Work With?

Digg works well with a number of social media applications, including Facebook, Twitter, MySpace, Blogger, WordPress, and iGoogle. Digg also provides interesting capabilities such as Digg Spy, in which you can watch as stories are added to the queue and are read, dugged or buried, and reported. Digg offers one-click blogging with TypePad, Blogger, WordPress, Live Journal, or Movable Type.

Who Uses It?

Digg user profiles run the gamut, and included the 2008 presidential campaigns of Barack Obama and John McCain. Both camps used Digg to promote web content regarding their runs for the presidency. Digg isn't just for individual users. Companies use Digg as well. For example, you can find Digg profiles for Apple and Microsoft. There are specific categories of information, such as for technology and gaming, so users can click on the categories tab and catch up on the latest *diggs* for that particular category.

Should You Use It?

Digg can be a valuable tool for businesses that wish to either keep track of news regarding competitors or to make Digg readers aware of the latest news. It can, however, have some repercussions, as there is no editorial monitoring of Digg content. According to the web site "How Stuff Works," in 2006, four stories appeared on Digg stating that Google was buying Sun Microsystems. These stories resulted in pushing the value of Sun Microsystems stock to high levels. The stories were rated highly by Digg users, and once the realization was made that the stories were false, many wondered if the posters weren't somehow related to Sun Microsystems, trying to make more money off the stock.

Who Started It?

Kevin Rose founded Digg. Rose approached computer programmer Owen Byrne and paid him $10 an hour (for a grand total of $200) to develop Digg. Digg was fairly popular, but it wasn't until the news story of Paris Hilton's cell phone getting hacked broke on Digg that Rose realized just how big his idea was and how important his site would be to breaking news on the Internet. Kevin Rose is not only the entrepreneur and founder of Digg, he is also one of the founders behind the social media application Pownce and the Internet TV network Revision 3, as well as an investor in the online dating site iminlikewithyou .com. Among Digg's other principals are Owen Byrne, who has more than 20 years of experience in the IT industry and has spent the majority of those years as a freelancer. He was also a university professor for a short time. Jay Adelson, CEO, has experience in broadcasting and switched to the IT industry. He helped engineer Netcom (the first ISP in the United States) and Equinix.

FriendFeed

Company Name:	FriendFeed
URL:	friendfeed.com
Location:	Mountain View, California
Founded:	2007
Employees:	11
Revenue Model:	Currently venture capital backing. Facebook acquired the company in August 2009.
Fees:	Free

What Is It?

FriendFeed is a social aggregate (news feed) business in which people can keep track of the Internet contributions to applications such as Blogger, Twitter, LinkedIn, Flickr, and other social network services by peers, colleagues, friends, and family. It is being touted as a guide through the growing level of noise in Internet presence and use. Users create an account and provide the links or information for the social media networks to which they belong. The feeds from these accounts are aggregated onto a simple web page list. Users can subscribe to the FriendFeeds of other peers, business associates, colleagues, friends, and family.

How Can It Be Used?

Businesses can use FriendFeed to enable broadcasting of their news as well as monitoring developments of competitors. Interested members can subscribe to businesses that are FriendFeed members and keep up with blogs, Twitters, YouTube postings, and other social media applications that a business may use to relay company information. If an educational entity uses social media applications in the relaying of information, whether related to administrative, operational, or educational information, FriendFeed members with an interest in such information can subscribe and stay abreast of information feeds.

What Other Applications Does It Work With?

This is a relatively easy question to answer, since FriendFeed's purpose is to aggregate information from more than 40 social media web sites such as Flickr, Twitter, Facebook, Netvibes, and others. It would seem the simplest answer is "all of them." As a web site, if a device has Internet access, then, in essence, FriendFeed can be used with any of those devices.

Who Uses It?

Interestingly, bub.blicio.us, a web site that covers social media, has ranked in the top 30 users of FriendFeed. The list is based on Google ranking, and surprisingly consists of people whose career is the focus of social media, like Robert Scoble (a social media and technology blogger who has been pointed out as accounting for 20 percent of FriendFeed's usage), Muhammed Saleem (a social media consultant), and Brian Daniel Eisenberg (a social media and culture blogger). It would seem at the moment that those who are involved purely in the social media explosion are the biggest users. Again, time and more reliable research will determine the type of audience drawn to use FriendFeed.

Should You Use It?

According to the FriendFeed site, "FriendFeed enables you to keep up-to-date on the web pages, photos, videos and music that your friends and family are sharing. It offers a unique way to discover and discuss information among friends." The use of FriendFeed is widely debated on the Internet. Some users praise its simplistic approach; others declare it won't last very long. Given the relative newness of this business and its concept, it truly is a matter of time and its popularity with Internet users to determine just how valuable of a tool this application truly is.

Who Started It?

The executive (founding) team comprises former Google employees responsible for more than 25 Google products. Bret Taylor is not only a former Google employee, he is also an entrepreneur in residence at Benchmark Capital. He earned Google's highest award, the Founders' Award, for his contributions to Google. Jim Norris, like Bret Taylor, was also a former employee of Google and an entrepreneur in residence at Benchmark Capital. Norris worked on Google's core structure and Google Maps. Paul Buchheit is noted as the 23rd Google employee and is credited not only with the creation of Google Mail but also Google's slogan "Don't be evil." Sanjeev Singh, like his FriendFeed cofounders, contributed to Google's success working on Google Mail and the Google Search Appliance. Prior to working at Google, Singh worked at Third Voice and a government research lab.

Google Reader

Company Name:	Google Reader (Google Inc.)
URL:	www.google.com/reader
Location:	Mountain View, California
Founded:	2005
Employees:	20,000 (Google)
Revenue Model:	Advertising and sales of stock
Fees:	Free

What Is It?

Google Reader is another feature of Google Inc. It is a Web-based aggregator that provides you with the feeds of your favorite updated web sites so you don't have to spend time visiting all these sites. Google Reader is capable of reading RSS or Atom feeds both online and offline.

How Can It Be Used?

Google Reader has a number of features that make it a useful tool for reading the latest postings on your topic of interest, such as news on the top Silicon Valley companies. With the front-page configuration, you can see new items at a glance. You can import and export subscription lists as an OPML file. There are keyboard shortcuts for main functions. You have a choice between the list view or expanded view for item viewing, meaning you see either just the story title or a description of the story. As items are read they are automatically marked, just as in most e-mail software programs. Google Reader also gives you the ability to share your feeds with chat friends or a list of contacts. Finally, Google Reader searches in all feeds, across all updates from subscriptions.

What Other Applications Does It Work With?

Google Reader aggregates RSS and Atom Feeds. If someone posts a blog on a WordType site, Google Reader will pull that feed if you direct it to do so, but it isn't actually working with the WordType site; it's working with the feed. One cool little gadget that made the Internet buzz is that someone who helped develop Google Reader installed Konami code; users can type a certain sequence and a little ninja appears on the left side of the screen and watches you as you scroll through your feeds.

Who Uses It?

Not a lot of specific data are available on who uses Google Reader, but given the functionality, it is easy to see that just about anyone can find Google Reader useful. Most web sites use RSS or Atom feeds, and the relative audience would find Google Reader a useful application for keeping up with that site or related sites.

Should You Use It?

Yes. Many people like and prefer Google Reader to other feed aggregators. Mark Berthelemy, learning solutions architect for Capita Learning &

Development and director and lead consultant for Wyver Solutions Ltd., recommends Google Reader. On the web site for the Center for Learning and Performance Technologies, Berthelemy stated:

> Keeping up to date is a rapidly changing field, and knowing what the market is saying about learning, about technology, and about us is critical for success. An RSS reader allows me to do that without having to go to dozens of web sites to see if they've got anything new. Google Reader has been my reader of choice for a year now. I can use it from any Internet-connected browser. I can organize things just how I want. I can even share particular items, or whole groups of items, with other people in many different ways. I like the way it allows me to choose how I use it—its flexibility.

Who Started It?

At this time, the only available information on who created Google Reader is that it was allegedly developed by Matrix Systems and Technologies Inc.

iGoogle

Company Name:	iGoogle (Google Inc.)
URL:	www.google.com/ig
Location:	Mountain View, California
Founded:	2005
Employees:	20,000 (Google)
Revenue Model:	Advertising and sale of stock
Fees:	Free

What Is It?

Originally called the "Google Personalized Homepage," iGoogle is a feature of Google and is best described as a customizable AJAX-based start page. iGoogle's features include web feeds and Google Gadgets such as GoogleGram, Gas Buddy, and a YouTube Channel. You select the news, art, and gadgets you want to appear on your iGoogle start page, and when you open up iGoogle, those elements are updated and displayed, in essence creating a home page that provides you with the information and entertainment you desire. Last but not least, there is a Google Search query bar at the top so you can search the Internet for information.

How Can It Be Used?

The iGoogle aggregator is used to create a specialized home page by the user for the user. It acts as a news aggregate, and users can embed a number of gadgets in their iGoogle page to include themes for decorating the home page. Google also provides users with the ability to create their own gadgets without needing to know code. Users simply plug in the data feed and customize the appearance; the service does the rest. Users can also create their own themes and even submit their themes for the iGoogle theme gallery for other users to use. iGoogle is now available in 26 languages.

What Other Applications Does It Work With?

This is one Google feature that works with other applications because it allows and encourages users to create gadgets and applications to work with it. There are gadgets for users to access Digg, Facebook, MySpace, Hotmail, Pownce, Twitter, and Yahoo! Mail from the iGoogle page. Users can also use SlideShare to embed images into their iGoogle page. Hawidu is an application that enables users to create unique themes for their iGoogle page. The iGoogle feature is also usable with the Apple iPhone.

Who Uses It?

According to a May 2007 presentation on iGoogle by Marissa Mayer, vice president of search products and user experience, iGoogle has tens of millions of users. From that statement, you can conclude that just about anyone and everyone uses iGoogle to facilitate aggregating information to one easy page, whether to keep up on world events, financial news, business competitors, new technology, or research in academia.

Should You Use It?

There are other web sites with similar capabilities, such as Netvibes, Pageflakes, MyYahoo!, and Windows Live Personalized Experience. The determining factors for which application to use for aggregating information and multimedia services will be ease of use and implementation. iGoogle is immensely popular, and it provides an easy-to-use service for creating gadgets. These two factors alone make iGoogle an attractive tool for getting information in one place.

Who Started It?

Google's code name for the feature that came to be known as iGoogle was "Mockingbird." The concept was thought up in 2004 with the original name iGoogle as a result of Google's purchase of Kaltix, a company owned by Sep Kamvar. Kamvar's theories on personalized content search capabilities were the impetus behind iGoogle's creation.

MyYahoo!

Company Name:	MyYahoo! (Yahoo! Inc.)
URL:	my.yahoo.com
Location:	Sunnyvale, California
Founded:	1994
Employees:	10,000
Revenue Model:	Advertising, subscription, and transactions
Fees:	Free (additional applications available by paid subscription)

What Is It?

Yahoo! Inc. provides Internet services and is "known for its web portal, search engine, Yahoo! Directory, Yahoo! Mail, news, and social media web sites and services." Yahoo! implemented MyYahoo! to provide customers with the ability to create a customizable web page. MyYahoo! allows users to personalize their page with their favorite features, content feeds, and other information. Users can view information on one page, preview new items or feeds, search the Web, add and remove content, and modify layout.

How Can It Be Used?

MyYahoo! is an information hub where users can locate their favorite features, content feeds, and any other information added to the page. Users can designate the content they want displayed on MyYahoo! and determine the layout for navigational ease. This functionality allows the user to check the weather forecast; follow financial markets; see local, national, and international headlines; or subscribe to horoscopes, comic strips, quotes, or jokes of the day. Virtually any content the user desires can be added to MyYahoo!

What Other Applications Does It Work With?

The key benefit of using MyYahoo! lies in the extensive functionality with other applications which allows the user to add the content the user deems important. Some of the applications it works with are MyDrive, Evite, Flickr, PayPal, and Pingg invitations.

Who Uses It?

MyYahoo! can be used by anyone looking for a one-stop information center in which a quick glance at various feeds can tell you stock market quotes, weather forecasts, news and entertainment headlines, health risks and alerts, the latest movie schedules, and much more. The possibilities are only limited by the information the user wants displayed. The array of information available provides usability for a broad spectrum of users.

Should You Use It?

MyYahoo! is an effective tool if you are looking for a quick reference point to access myriad information based upon your personal needs. The primary benefit of MyYahoo! is the ability to customize the page, which allows you to change the page content as your needs change. Many people have specific information they search for each day. If you are looking for a way to effectively manage your time by consolidating each search onto one page, then MyYahoo! would be a valuable asset.

Who Started It?

Yahoo! was developed by two Stanford engineering PhD candidates, David Filo and Jerry Yang, as a platform to track their personal interests on the Internet. The two founders recognized the business potential of their web site as its popularity spread. Yahoo! was incorporated in 1995 and continues to add features and services like MyYahoo! to meet its audience's expanding needs.

Reddit

Company Name:	Reddit (owned by Condé Nast Publications)
URL:	www.reddit.com
Location:	San Francisco, California
Founded:	2005
Employees:	5
Revenue Model:	Advertising and merchandise
Tagline:	What's new online!

What Is It?

Reddit is a dynamic news web site that is socially driven by the community of users. Users post links on Reddit that lead to content found anywhere on the Internet. Once the link has been posted, the audience can determine how that particular link ranks against other links suggested by members of the community. Links are ordered according to how many positive or negative votes they have received. Discussions based on the linked subject matter also take place within the community in the form of comments attached to the links.

How Can It Be Used?

Reddit can be used as a vehicle for sharing and receiving information and as a social forum. Links are posted into categories, or "subreddits," such as economics, pictures, or technology. In this manner, users can browse specific media that interests them if desired, or browse all the links for a more general experience. A rather robust social system beyond comment discussions is a key component of Reddit. Some of the facets of this system include awards, private messaging, and befriending other members. By taking advantage of this social system, users can effectively network with others interested in the same subjects and even collectively vote on links. Additionally, a karma-based mechanism is used for members of Reddit, wherein users who consistently post popular links are rewarded with karma points.

What Other Applications Does It Work With?

Reddit works with several different web browsers to simplify the user's process of viewing and participating. A "Reddit Widget" can be incorporated into a web site's coding to display headlines from a user's preferred category. Another way Reddit works with web browsers is through "Reddit Bookmarklets." Reddit Bookmarklets are Java-based links that are added to your web browser like regular bookmarks, but these bookmarks perform actions such as submitting links to Reddit or taking you to a random Reddit link.

Who Uses It?

A number of different audiences use Reddit. Some members use it to discover new information on the Internet, whether for educational or recreational purposes. Some visitors use Reddit to comment on and analyze the links with the rest of the audience. Another user base of Reddit is web site owners looking to virally market their own web site to the vast community of Reddit users. Finally, some users choose to come to Reddit for the social aspect of the web site, such as sending and receiving private messages.

Should You Use It?

You should use Reddit if you are interested in being a part of a diverse community of users who all participate in the distribution of information. Reddit allows you to effectively look at intriguing content from all over the Internet by using this one tool, and then providing the capability to examine how fellow users view that content. You should also use Reddit if you have a need or desire to drive traffic toward a web site without paying for marketing or advertising fees. Reddit offers an interesting delivery of current news and entertaining links along a social backdrop.

Who Started It?

Two University of Virginia graduates, Steve Huffman and Alexis Ohanian, created Reddit in 2005. The initial funding for the company was provided by Y Combinator. In that same year, Christopher Slowe and Aaron Swartz joined the company. During October 2006, Condé Nast Publications, which also owns the publication *Wired*, acquired Reddit. The company name was suggested by Alexis Ohanian and is derived from the pronunciation of "read it."

Yelp

Company Name:	Yelp
URL:	www.yelp.com
Location:	San Francisco, California; New York, New York
Founded:	2004
Employees:	75
Revenue Model:	Some advertising; backed by venture capital financing
Fees:	Free
Tagline:	Real people. Real reviews.

What Is It?

Interested in the good (and bad) of a particular business or product? Someone has likely rated it on Yelp. Yelp's concept is to provide an online rating service for places to eat, shop, drink, and play. Members provide informed opinions of these places, and business owners can see what they need to improve upon to increase their customer satisfaction. With many categories of businesses and geographic locations, a site visitor can easily see what's hot and what's not in a specific locale. Yelp is not just limited to businesses in the service and entertainment industries; Yelp categories include businesses and organizations focused on day-to-day tasks and needs such as real estate, finance, and religion. Businesses can also use the reviews to see what their customer base says about them, good and bad, and use the reviews to market their business or improve it.

How Can It Be Used?

Members (consumers and businesses) create free membership accounts. Consumers provide reviews on businesses, and business owners create pages for their business to keep track of reviews. Businesses are listed by category and geographic location, so that users can search for a desired venue and see what rating the local populace gives that venue.

What Other Applications Does It Work With?

Yelp does not do a good job of broadcasting the applications it works with, but there is an ability to incorporate Yelp profiles and reviews with Facebook profiles. When a Yelp member posts a review, that review can show up automatically on the reviewer's Facebook profile. Users apparently use Flickr to post photos on Yelp, and Google Maps are used on profiles to identify locations of reviewed businesses. Yelp also has a mobile application so you can look up a needed service or business while on the go.

Who Uses It?

According to Yelp's web site, Yelp users are locals in the know about what's cool and who enjoy sharing the information, real people who have visited a place or used a service and want to share their opinions, visitors from other places or who have just moved to a particular city who want to quickly get an insider's local perspective, and anyone who wants current and reliable reviews in a specific location. In December 2009, Yelp had 26 million unique visitors.

Should You Use It?

If you are looking to attract a larger client base and are confident in your level of customer satisfaction, Yelp can be a huge asset in your online marketing tool bag. Yelp business owners are encouraged to use Yelp as a way of keeping track of what customers are saying, and establishing a more personal rapport with that customer base. There are some conflicting stories regarding Yelp and accusations of "paid reviews," as well as accusations of Yelp removing negative reviews, earning it the label of being a do-goody web site. Yelp does have review submission guidelines, and will remove reviews in circumstances such as when a review is from another business owner or a former employee, or reports secondhand experiences, personal attacks, employment issues at the business, irrelevant statement, or just a blank review with no text. There may have been some legitimate reviews deleted, resulting in the rancor about Yelp allowing only positive reviews. There have also been accusations in the San Francisco news media that Yelp asked restaurant owners for $150 presented as a sponsorship package "to guarantee a positive review to be posted first."

Who Started It?

In an interview conducted for the Web 2.0 Awards, CEO and cofounder Jerry Stoppelman stated, "A personal pain point came when I was looking for a doctor online and couldn't find any information other than the basics (name, phone, affiliations, et cetera). My cofounder Russ Simmons and I realized that word of mouth was the best way to find great local businesses, but we weren't sure how we'd bring that to the Web. We ended up building a web site about asking friends for recommendations and later realized some of our early users really just wanted a platform for sharing their favorite local businesses, which is what you see today." Stoppelman and chief technology officer and cofounder Russell Simmons are both former PayPal employees who met while part of PayPal cofounder Max Levchin's incubator during college internships at PayPal.

Tool Scorecard for Chapter 33: Aggregators

Instructions: Using the following five-point (0 to 4) scale, rate each tool in this chapter on the basis of how valuable it *might be* to the internal and external operations of your company. Make notes about which tools appeal to you the most.

4 = Extremely Valuable
3 = Very Valuable
2 = Somewhat Valuable
1 = Not Very Valuable
0 = No Value

Tool	Internal Value	External Value
Digg	4 3 2 1 0	4 3 2 1 0
FriendFeed	4 3 2 1 0	4 3 2 1 0
Google Reader	4 3 2 1 0	4 3 2 1 0
iGoogle	4 3 2 1 0	4 3 2 1 0
MyYahoo!	4 3 2 1 0	4 3 2 1 0
Reddit	4 3 2 1 0	4 3 2 1 0
Yelp	4 3 2 1 0	4 3 2 1 0

CHAPTER 34

RSS

RSS, or Really Simple Syndication, is the name of the technology and also the name of just one of the technology providers. An RSS feature on a blog or web site allows you to sign up and automatically get notified whenever there is an update to the site including a new blog or news. Rather than having to go from site to site every day checking to see if new content has been posted, RSS notifies you when it has. RSS automatically feeds you new content, from only the sites you want it from, and only when that content is new.

Try RSS by clicking the RSS button on your favorite blog site or try the Google landing page that aggregates RSS feeds from blogs, web pages, airlines, weather, or any changing information of interest to you. As you read each profile, keep in mind that its features and functions may or may not be right for your particular business. Use the Tool Scorecard at the end of the chapter to help you determine which of these tools qualify for further consideration when you begin creating your social media strategy in Part III of the book.

Atom

Company Name:	Atom
URL:	www.atomenabled.org

What Is It?

"Atom is an XML-based web content and metadata syndication format" developed to deliver dynamic content to a vast audience without the viewer having to visit each site individually. The user subscribes to a feed and receives consistently updated information. "Atom is designed to be a universal publishing standard for personal content and weblogs."

How Can It Be Used?

RSS/Atom feeds are used to provide subscribers with a dynamic stream of information that is supported in blogs, news publishers, government agencies, and personal and commercial web sites. Users create a channel for the content they wish to publish, and include "items for Web pages they want to promote." The "channel can be read by remote applications, and converted to headlines and links," which can be inserted into web pages or read in dedicated readers.

What Other Applications Does It Work With?

Atom works with other Atom-enabled software and services, and is compatible with dedicated readers and is World Wide Web Consortium (W3C) compliant. Personal aggregators were designed specifically to find, organize, and check for updates for the channels you subscribe to, enabling you to view them all, using the reader's interface.

Who Uses It?

"The U.S. Intelligence Community Metadata Working Group has issued a recommendation that the Intelligence Community, over time, move toward adoption of Atom Syndication Format as the Community's standard SML-based language for syndication feeds." Many private, professional, and commercial organizations use RSS/Atom feeds to notify their community of upcoming events, promotions, status, organizational changes, and much more. Atom claims it "is a simple way to read and write information on the web, allowing you to easily keep track of more sites in less time, and to seamlessly share your words and ideas by publishing to the web."

Should You Use It?

If you are looking for a way to track many sites or a simplified method to provide information to a large target audience, Atom may be an effective solution.

Who Started It?

"The Atom format was developed as an alternative to RSS." Sam Ruby is credited with spurring the movement toward a new syndication format to address the problems with RSS by creating a wiki as a platform for this discussion. In 2003, a project snapshot known as Atom 0.2 was released; discussion was later transferred to a different forum, resulting in the release of Atom Publishing Protocol as a proposed standard in 2007.

Google FeedBurner

Company Name:	Google FeedBurner (Google Inc.)
URL:	www.feedburner.com
Location:	Chicago, Illinois
Founded:	2004
Employees:	20,000 (Google)
Revenue Model:	Advertising and premium subscriptions
Fees:	Basic: free
Tagline:	Put your content in front of more eyeballs.

What Is It?

FeedBurner claims to be the leading provider of media distribution and audience engagement services for blogs and RSS feeds. FeedBurner helps Internet publishers (bloggers, podcasters, and commercial publishers) promote, deliver, and profit from their web content. They have unique tools like PingShot to make using RSS and Atom feeds easier. With the recent acquisition by Google, AdSense is now a part of their automatic feed, which enables you to generate revenue if your audience is large enough.

How Can It Be Used?

You use FeedBurner to notify your audience of new content on your blog, web site, or commercial publication. FeedBurner has 11 tools for publicity, optimization of subscriptions and e-mails, analysis and reporting, and revenue generation. There is the basic free account, or users can upgrade to a pro account, which charges by the number of feeds being managed.

What Other Applications Does It Work With?

FeedBurner works with Google applications, RSS feeds, Atom Feeds, iPhones and iPod Touch MP3 players, podcasts, videocasts, blog software, Newsgator, Netvibes, and Pageflakes.

Who Uses It?

A number of well-known companies use FeedBurner to push their new content to readers: Reuters, AOL, *Newsweek,* the *Wall Street Journal, USA Today,* and more. Entities that want to reach their audience immediately and easily use FeedBurner to push their new content.

Should You Use It?

For those who want to push their web site content but who may not necessarily be technologically savvy, FeedBurner takes the process of using RSS or Atom feeds and simplifies them for the average computer user. For just a few dollars a day, you can analyze your traffic and determine where your readers come from and what they view the most. With the acquisition by Google, you can now also earn revenue due to the automatic inclusion of Google AdSense: visitors to your site click on the ads, and you earn money for those outclicks. Another use for FeedBurner is by actually paying to advertise your business or service on FeedBurner. With over a million publishers, and too many subscribers to count, FeedBurner has a massive audience you can reach with your advertisements.

Who Started It?

Dick Costolo, Eric Lunt, Steve Olechowski, and Matt Shobe founded Feed-Burner. According to a March 2007 Startup Studio interview with Matt Shobe, the four cofounders met in 1993 on a project at Andersen Consulting. The four cofounders have started four companies together, including Feed-Burner. FeedBurner was derived from their second company, Spyonit, which was an early Internet service that notified Internet users of updates of many types of sites. FeedBurner took that aspect of Spyonit to the next level and made it easy to notify users of newly posted content through the use of feeds.

PingShot

Company Name:	PingShot (a feature of FeedBurner from Google Inc.)
URL:	www.feedburner.com
Location:	Chicago, Illinois
Founded:	2005
Employees:	20,000 (Google)
Revenue Model:	Advertising and premium subscriptions
Fees:	Basic: free
Tagline:	Trigger faster updates for subscribers.

What Is It?

FeedBurner claims to be the leading provider of media distribution and audience engagement services for blogs and RSS feeds. PingShot is a service of FeedBurner that quickly updates your feeds in the widest variety of places. The PingShot logarithm detects whether your feeds are a podcast or a nonpodcast and sends out the updates accordingly. As an example, if your feed is a podcast, PingShot notifies Odeo, but it won't notify Odeo if it is a nonpodcast feed. In general, feeds allow readers to subscribe to receive updated content for a web site. FeedBurner helps Internet publishers (bloggers, podcasters, and commercial publishers) promote, deliver, and profit from their web content.

How Can It Be Used?

PingShot is one of the more well-known FeedBurner tools. It updates your feeds as soon as you publish. Other similar services can take anywhere from 30 minutes to six hours to update the feeds, which means by that time your news is already old news. PingShot is also an open directory, so third-party members can use it once they register and provide their service method protocols. Publishers simply click the Publicize tab, and their update is sent out immediately.

What Other Applications Does It Work With?

By itself, PingShot does not work with other applications. It is a tool to send your feeds to feed services, which you select when you create your

FeedBurner account. FeedBurner works with Google applications, RSS feeds, Atom Feeds, iPhones and iPod Touch MP3 players, podcasts, videocasts, blog software, Newsgator, Netvibes, and Pageflakes.

Who Uses It?

There are no documented or advertised users of PingShot, but here are a number of well-known companies that use FeedBurner in general to push their new content to readers: Reuters, AOL, *Newsweek,* the *Wall Street Journal, USA Today,* and more. Entities that want to reach their audience immediately and easily use FeedBurner to push their new content.

Should You Use It?

As a matter of saving time, yes, PingShot (and hence FeedBurner) is a speedy tool for notifying subscribers of your new information. For those who want to push their web site content but may not necessarily be technologically savvy, FeedBurner takes the process of using RSS or Atom feeds and simplifies them for the average computer user.

Who Started It?

The founders of PingShot are the same guys who founded FeedBurner: Dick Costolo, Eric Lunt, Steve Olechowski, and Matt Shobe.

RSS 2.0

Company Name:	RSS 2.0 (Owned by Harvard Law School)
Founded:	1997

What Is It?

RSS is an acronym for Rich Site Summary; it is a format to deliver dynamic web content without the need to visit each site individually. The user subscribes to a feed and receives consistently updated information. RSS is supported in many blogs, and in the web sites of many news publishers, government agencies, individuals, and businesses. RSS 2.0 is the current specification, conforms to XML 1.0 specification, "as published on the World Wide Web Consortium (W3C) web site," and is backward compatible with the 0.91 version.

How Can It Be Used?

RSS feeds are used to provide subscribers with a dynamic stream of information. Users create a channel for the content they wish to publish, and include "items for Web pages they want to promote." The "channel can be read by remote applications, and converted to headlines and links," which can be inserted into web pages or read in dedicated readers. "It's also used for photo diaries, classified ad listings, recipes, reviews, and for tracking the status of software packages."

What Other Applications Does It Work With?

RSS 2.0 is compatible with dedicated readers, and is compatible with W3C-compliant web sites. Personal aggregators were designed specifically to find, organize, and check for updates for the channels you subscribe to, enabling you to view them all using the reader's interface.

Who Uses It?

RSS feeds are used by many media organizations and e-commerce as a way of delivering information. These feeds are similar in function to a news crawler in that they provide a consistent stream of information and are used in this capacity by news outlets. Many organizations provide RSS feeds to notify consumers of upcoming events, promotions, or organizational changes. The use of RSS feeds saves time for many organizations. The feed is updated and reaches everyone subscribed to that channel, which aids in reducing the amount of time previously spent sorting through the hierarchy of notification procedures.

Should You Use It?

If you are looking for a simplified method to provide information to a large target audience, RSS feeds may be an efficient solution.

Who Started It?

RSS was first invented by Netscape in 1997; UserLand Software took control of the specification, refined it, and released a newer version. The RSS 2.0 specification was donated to Harvard Law School by David Winer, and they are now responsible for future development.

Tool Scorecard for Chapter 34: RSS

Instructions: Using the following five-point (0 to 4) scale, rate each tool in this chapter on the basis of how valuable it *might be* to the internal and external operations of your company. Make notes about which tools appeal to you the most.

4 = Extremely Valuable

3 = Very Valuable

2 = Somewhat Valuable

1 = Not Very Valuable

0 = No Value

Tool	Internal Value	External Value
Atom	4 3 2 1 0	4 3 2 1 0
FeedBurner	4 3 2 1 0	4 3 2 1 0
PingShot	4 3 2 1 0	4 3 2 1 0
RSS 2.0	4 3 2 1 0	4 3 2 1 0

CHAPTER 35

Search

Internet search is one of the most important functions of the Internet. How else would you be able to find the one page you are looking for out of the one trillion Google-indexed web pages? SEO, or Search Engine Optimization, is as important as ever. And, as the number of web and blog pages grow, search will become even more integral to your Internet experience and to your customers and prospects.

If you want your customers and prospects to be able to find you and your company, you have to make it easy for them. SEO, tags, fresh content, external reputable links (Link Love), and keyword density, all add to your company's web and blog page's Google Juice. As you read each profile, keep in mind that its features and functions may or may not be right for your particular business. Use the Tool Scorecard at the end of the chapter to help you determine which of these tools qualify for further consideration when you begin creating your social media strategy in Part III of the book.

RAMP

Company Name:	RAMP
URL:	www.ramp.com
Location:	Cambridge, Massachusetts
Founded:	2006
Revenue Model:	Direct sales
Fees:	Third-party fees like Internet service

What Is It?

Previously known as Podzinger, then EveryZing, RAMP is considered a "media merchandising platform, which is actually a search publisher's solution that can make all audio and video content searchable, indexable by the major search engines through the text transcripts." RAMP provides "time-coded and full linkable transcripts, graphic indicators of key points in a video (which are also accentuated with a keyword search), and a video player with social bookmarking and sharing capabilities." RAMP focuses on multimedia search and publication of user-generated and client content.

How Can It Be Used?

RAMP uses speech text transcriptions in creating what it refers to as a "media merchandising platform." This technology enables users to search and index audio and video content through text transcripts. This further enhances the recall and optimization of your site, in addition to aiding with targeted advertising. RAMP uses its proprietary speech-to-text technology, which "automatically classifies spoken-word multimedia content into meaningful topics and keywords, which visually appear to the user as actual, clickable, and navigation-friendly text."

What Other Applications Does It Work With?

RAMP complements a wide variety of social media applications.

Who Uses It?

RAMP is used by companies large and small, including CNBC, P&G, Comcast, Fox News, and NBC Universe.

Should You Use It?

If you are looking for search engine optimization to enhance your online presence, RAMP may be the solution. RAMP enhances the recall and optimization of your site, in addition to aiding with targeted advertising, which presents better opportunities for consumers to find you.

Who Started It?

RAMP was developed by BBN Technologies and was "used for government purposes before becoming a commercial product." BBN (originally Bolt,

Beranek and Newman) is a high-tech company that provides research and development services and is known for the development of packet switching (including the ARPAnet and the Internet). In addition to its role as a defense contractor, BBN is also known for the 1978 acoustical analysis it conducted for the House Select Committee on the assassination of John F. Kennedy.

Google Search

Company Name:	Google Search
URL:	www.google.com
Location:	Mountain View, California
Founded:	1998
Employees:	20,000
Revenue Model:	Advertising via AdSense and AdWords
Fees:	Free

What Is It?

Google Search is Google's core product, so popular and embedded in our social culture that it has become a transitive verb in Merriam-Webster's dictionary. Features of Google Search are the Internet-crawling Googlebots and the PageRank algorithm, which is influenced by linking. Users type keywords in the home page search field and receive relevant results that can be further refined. There is also a more specific search capability for blogs, images, video, and news. Google Search can also be used to search your own computer files and e-mails through Google Desktop.

How Can It Be Used?

Google Search can be used from two perspectives: the user and the business or organization. From the user's perspective, Google Search allows a search of the Internet for information, images, news, videos, and more. Google Search provides definition links, optional search terms, and alternate terms in the event of a misspelling. Search syntax can be simple words filled in the search field on the home page or advanced search queries in which words or phrases can be specified or excluded, or Boolean logic can be used. From the business or organization perspective, paid advertisements and search engine optimization are considered key tools in Internet marketing. Google is now available in 114 natural languages and 5 artificial languages (for example, Klingon) for humor.

What Other Applications Does It Work With?

Google Search doesn't actually work with other applications. It works on computer and mobile devices that have Internet browser capability. Google Search is one of over 50 products in the Google Inc. inventory. From the Google Search page, users can go to the Google products page and select the desired Google application they wish to use. Google Search has a toolbar that you can permanently affix to your Internet browser page, making it easy to search, bookmark, and highlight your favorite pages.

Who Uses It?

Everyone who owns a computer has probably used Google Search at least once. Google is listed within the top 10 web sites on the Internet, and Google claims to be the number one search engine. In May 2008, Google had more than 130 million unique U.S. visitors to its web site. Having one's web site turn up on the first page of a search query is considered important in search engine optimization. Users are more likely to visit the web sites that appear on the first several pages of a query.

Should You Use It?

Google Search is a dependable search engine tool. In addition to finding links related to your search query, Google Search will display advertisements that relate to your search query and may provide additional information, which also means that as a business owner or an organization you can advertise and drive users to your web site. An additional way of sending users to your web site is through the use of associated metadata and keywords.

Who Started It?

According to Google's corporate page, Stanford graduate students Sergey Brin and Larry Page started the search company in a Stanford dorm room in 1996. Eventually Page and Brin moved the company to a Menlo Park garage, which the company quickly outgrew. The first investor was Sun Microsystems founder Andy Bechtolsheim, and other notable investors include Ron Conway, John Doerr, Mike Moritz, and Ram Shriram.

Ice Rocket

Company Name:	Ice Rocket
URL:	www.icerocket.com
Location:	Dallas, Texas
Founded:	2004
Employees:	Not available
Revenue Model:	None at this time
Fees:	Free

What Is It?

Ice Rocket is a dedicated Internet search engine that is extremely efficient in looking out for blogs. It functions like an invisible tracker that will keep a count of your blog visits and all other statistics pertaining to your blog. The company has mixed its own Web search technology with meta search features that can tap into rival search engines. Ice Rocket is a world leader in commercial search services on the Internet. It is a part of the latest generation of search engines, some of which hope to out-Google Google Search. Ice Rocket performs a number of search services.

How Can It Be Used?

Some interesting features of Ice Rocket are as follows:

- *Line Tracker:* This feature lets bloggers know the details of those who are establishing links to their posts.
- *Trend Tool:* This feature allows users to track the current word trends in a range of two to three months.
- *RS Builder:* This free service allows users to create RSS feeds for their sites. It provides a simple interface that allows users to add topics, links, and content. The feature is suitable for anyone who owns a web site that does not offer RSS.
- *Ice Spy:* This site allows users to view the topics that are being searched for by other bloggers.
- *Search Relay:* Here the user sends an e-mail with the search items to the specified e-mail ID, and Ice Rocket mails back the results. The same can also be done for news and pictures.

Ice Rocket performs several other interesting services like blog searches, phone images, multimedia searches, and so on.

What Other Applications Does It Work With?

Ice Rocket works along with Wise Nut, Twitter, MySpace, Rocket Mail, Yahoo!, and Teoma, as well as MSN, AltaVista, and AllTheWeb. As a result, all your searches in Ice Rocket are thoroughly indexed and answered. Ice Rocket has introduced an interesting feature that works well with your mobile phone, for the total benefit of the gadget-savvy.

Who Uses It?

Internet browsers and bloggers who are looking for specific videos and music for online downloading can make use of Ice Rocket. Web site owners who want to upgrade their sites by adding online videos to it would find this search engine as an inevitable tool of development. The search engine optimization strategy of Ice Rocket can be helpful in improving the quality of your web site by including relevant online videos in it, which in turn will increase the viewing of and subscription to your sites.

Should You Use It?

If you are an avid blogger or you own a web site and wish to include some online videos in it, then the search engine services of Ice Rocket may be useful for you. Ice Rocket has features like Blog Tracker, an invisible tracker that counts your blog visits and maintains other blog statistics. With the help of Ice Rocket, you can analyze and monitor all the visits to your blog in real time. Ice Rocket can save you valuable time as well as the trouble of tediously monitoring your blog visits.

Who Started It?

Ice Rocket was the brainchild of Blake Rhodes. Soon after its launch, Mark Cuban, who is an investor and owner of the Dallas Mavericks, signed an agreement with Rhodes and pooled in investments to the company. Cuban formerly founded broadcast.com and later sold it to Yahoo! for an estimated $6 billion.

MetaTube

Company:	MetaTube
URL:	metatube.net
Location:	La Jolla, California
Founded:	2006
Employees:	Not available
Revenue Model:	None
Fees:	Free
Tagline:	Browse 100 video sharing sites at once!

What Is It?

MetaTube is a simple yet effective method to browse 100 of the most popular video sharing sites around the world. When you want to view a particular video online, you would normally go to any one site like YouTube. If the video is not available, you would search other sites like Daily Motion, MySpace, AOL, and so on. The entire process of going into each site and entering your search query might be very cumbersome. This problem is solved in an easy manner with MetaTube, a search engine that simplifies the entire process and throws 100 search results all at once. This is a torrential multisearch engine that searches through its catalog of video sharing sites and gives you the results. The most important feature of this high-speed search engine is that it not only throws 100 search results but also allows you to see a list of the recent searches made by other users. This step makes it easy for the user to sift through the search results.

What Other Applications Does It Work With?

Normally MetaTube conducts its searches in YouTube, Google Video, AOL Uncut, Veoh, and others. Apart from these sites, MetaTube also searches lesser-known sites like iklipz, jublii, and Flixya.

Who Uses It?

MetaTube.net users come from all over the globe, including Saudi Arabia, Egypt, the United States, India, Syria, Sudan, Algeria, Germany, Libya, and Italy. By the end of 2008, the site had already performed over 12 million searches.

Should You Use It?

If you need an easier way to search hundreds of sites for online videos, then this high-speed video search engine could be your answer. It is the easiest way to browse 100 of the most popular video sharing sites. You can also add various videos to your web site and improve its viewership without having to open and close browser tabs or navigate tabs. With this online video search engine, you can make finding and viewing online videos an easy and trouble-free experience.

Who Started It?

The company maintains a low profile and information on MetaTube's founders is not readily available.

Redlasso

Company Name:	Redlasso
URL:	redlasso.com
Location:	King of Prussia, Pennsylvania
Founded:	2005
Revenue Model:	Advertising revenue share
Fees:	Free to users

What Is It?

Redlasso allows users to search television and radio broadcasts by searching for "relevant keywords, names or phrases," and capture clips to post on their blog or web site, or by sending links to friends. "Redlasso enables bloggers/multimedia content producers/creators/owners/consumers to monetize their content through a revenue share model." Redlasso touts its service as a "major plus for content owners who produce audio, video, streaming Internet programming or podcasts which they desire to publish internally, while maintaining content integrity."

How Can It Be Used?

Redlasso can be used to enhance a web site or blog by providing relevant audio or video clips to supplement text content. According to Redlasso's web site, "Users create their own community around the content which: improves the stickiness of the site, increases visits and page views (as well as time spent at the site), enhances advertising rates by driving more traffic, [and] creates additional advertising opportunities for revenue enhancement." The Internet community is consistently searching for the latest tidbit of information or sound bite to augment their argument or position; the tools provided by Redlasso make this possible.

What Other Applications Does It Work With?

Redlasso works with "virtually all media including broadcast television and terrestrial/satellite radio, streaming Internet programming and podcasts." It is compatible with most web sites and blogs, and currently "utilizes an embeddable Flash player."

Who Uses It?

In 2008, Redlasso was under a cease-and-desist order and therefore was only able to offer business-to-business products, including Radio2Web, TV2Web, and PR Clipping Service. Redlasso states, "We are actively pursuing licensing agreements with the publishers and will reopen the site to bloggers as we gain permission." Redlasso gained agreements with Fox and many others and has opened back up to bloggers.

Users of Redlasso reach a wider audience, provide accessible content, and generate revenue from existing content and enhanced advertising opportunities. Organizations use Redlasso as a means of redistribution of content to generate interest in particular subject matter or to further engage their audience.

Should You Use It?

With the technology offered by Redlasso, consumers don't have to wait very long for their favorite broadcasts to become available. Redlasso has almost real-time access to broadcasts to search for specific content, create clips to view, or post on any Internet site. If your organization is looking for a means to create interest in your site, expand the time spent at your site, and increase traffic and advertising opportunities, Redlasso may be a viable option.

Who Started It?

Redlasso was founded by Jim McCusker, chief technical officer; Kevin O'Kane, president; and Al McGowan, chief operating officer. The service was set up as a "defense against sites like YouTube.com" by partnering with content owners to monetize their clips.

Technorati

Company Name:	Technorati
URL:	technorati.com
Location:	San Francisco, California
Founded:	2002
Employees:	25
Fees:	Membership is free; some services have fees
Revenue Model:	*Time* magazine
Tagline:	Search the blogosphere.

What Is It?

Technorati is a powerful search engine with a special focus on blogs. Perhaps *Time* magazine said it best: "If Google is the Web's reference library, Technorati is becoming its coffee house." What sets Technorati apart is that it indexes the global online conversation, the blogosphere, by collecting, highlighting, and distributing online blog posts in real time. Since July 2008, it has indexed 112.8 million blog posts and more than 25 million pieces of tagged social media and also tracks the authority of blogs, an indicator of how many blogs are linked to a web site (the more, the better), as well as how much influence a blog has. Additionally, Technorati keeps the most current and comprehensive index of what is most popular in the blogosphere. It tracks top stories, news, photos, and videos across many venues that include, but are not limited to, entertainment, technology, lifestyles, sports, politics, and business.

How Can It Be Used?

Technorati is the ideal way to stay connected to the subjects and conversations that matter the most to your business. It's both a research tool and an application that enables you to develop a community around your content. Blogs offer a platform for publishing individual perspectives on a variety of subjects and Technorati helps you filter the blogosphere to find those blogs that correspond to your interests.

Besides a search function, Technorati has the following services:

- For bloggers and publishers: Technorati has a network designed to enable blog and social media publishers at every level to maximize online advertising revenues
- For advertisers: Technorati creates connections between influential bloggers and consumers through online conversation
- Self-service launch: A new function, in a limited beta version, that creates a self-service advertising network of blogs and social media sites

What Other Applications Does It Work With?

Technorati works with most browsers and mobile devices that can be connected to the Internet.

Who Uses It?

A typical blogger is educated, affluent, and a college graduate. Almost half have attended graduate school. More than 50 percent have a household income of more than $75,000. Individuals use blogging as a platform to express their ideas, concerns, and viewpoints. Professional and corporate bloggers provide insiders' perspectives on their organizations and platforms to interact with stockholders and consumers, or to follow trends in an industry. Politicians can communicate with the public, inform constituents about proposed legislation, and promote their individual platforms. Mothers can give tips on childrearing.

In addition to the bloggers creating content, users include the individuals who follow the blogs, who can be as passionate and influential about the subject matter as those who write the content. The number of those who participate in the blogosphere, whether by blogging, commenting, rating, sharing, or networking is staggering—about 75 percent of all Internet users (per global communications media agency Universal McCann).

Should You Use It?

Technorati recently sent a tweet, through Twitter, stating that 38 percent of the Fortune 500 companies are now blogging. Blogs have become full information and news outlets, with more than 90 percent of newspapers and media conglomerates now blogging. Blogs are being written by journalists, subject matter experts, advertisers, and entrepreneurs and are important connections between those writing content and those interested in that content. They provide ways for companies to engage their customers through collaboration, education, and entertainment. If you want to get connected to the content and the bloggers who influence your market space the most, Technorati is an essential tool to add to your social media toolbox.

Who Started It?

Dave Sifry, an Internet entrepreneur and thought leader in the areas of wireless technology, open-source software, and blogs, founded Technorati in 2002. He served as Technorati's CEO from 2002 to 2007 and presently serves as chairman of its board of directors.

Yahoo! Search

Company Name:	Yahoo! Search
URL:	search.yahoo.com
Location:	Sunnyvale, California
Founded:	1994
Employees:	10,000
Revenue Model:	Advertising, subscription, and transactions
Fees:	Free (additional applications available by paid subscription)

What Is It?

Yahoo! Search is a navigation tool to aid users in finding relevant sites and information based on the criteria entered in the search field. Users can narrow their search criteria to search images, video, local information, shopping, answers, audio, directory listings, jobs, news, the Web, or all of these. Yahoo! Search also provides advanced search options for users looking for very specific information, search preferences (saved settings), sponsor results (paid placement listings), shortcuts, and queries conducted by other Yahoo! users that are similar to your search criteria.

How Can It Be Used?

Yahoo! Search can be used to locate images, video, local information, shopping, answers, audio, directory listings, jobs, news, web sites, or all of these based upon the search criteria and user preferences. Yahoo! Search offers businesses paid placement results and listings that display when users enter specific search words relevant to your business's offerings. Sponsor Results provides enhanced placement on a pay-per-click basis, and Sponsor Listings is a "fee-based service that allows commercial web sites already listed in the Yahoo! Directory to receive enhanced placement in the commercial categories."

What Other Applications Does It Work With?

Yahoo! Search works with Internet Explorer, Mozilla, Firefox, Safari, Netscape, and various other applications based on specifications set forth in the Yahoo! Developer Network as well as with a variety of mobile applications.

Who Uses It?

Yahoo! Search is a free search engine available to anyone with an Internet browser and Internet connection. The array of information available provides usability for a broad spectrum of users.

Should You Use It?

If you are looking for information but don't necessarily know where to look, Yahoo! Search would be an effective tool to point you in the right direction and provide options you might not have considered. If you are looking for very specific information, Yahoo! Search can provide a vast number of possibilities to suit your needs and allow you to narrow the search parameters. The infinite number of available search results provides usability for almost every demographic.

Who Started It?

Two Stanford engineering PhD candidates, David Filo and Jerry Yang, developed Yahoo! as a platform to track their personal interests on the Internet. The two founders recognized the business potential of their web site as the popularity of the site spread. Yahoo! was incorporated in 1995 and continues to add features and services like Yahoo! Search to meet its audience's expanding needs.

Tool Scorecard for Chapter 35: Search

Instructions: Using the following five-point (0 to 4) scale, rate each tool in this chapter on the basis of how valuable it *might be* to the internal and external operations of your company. Make notes about which tools appeal to you the most.

4 = Extremely Valuable

3 = Very Valuable

2 = Somewhat Valuable

1 = Not Very Valuable

0 = No Value

Tool	Internal Value	External Value
EveryZing	4 3 2 1 0	4 3 2 1 0
Google Search	4 3 2 1 0	4 3 2 1 0
Ice Rocket	4 3 2 1 0	4 3 2 1 0
MetaTube	4 3 2 1 0	4 3 2 1 0
Redlasso	4 3 2 1 0	4 3 2 1 0
Yahoo! Search	4 3 2 1 0	4 3 2 1 0

CHAPTER 36

Mobile

Mobile marketing is the fastest-growing segment of technology-driven marketing. Kakul Srivastava, the general manager for Flickr, told me that there are three cell phones for every man, woman, and child on the planet. With that kind of technology penetration, you and your company need to be participating.

Mobile phones are less expensive than laptops, desktops, and broadband and are completely portable. Not many people in Third World countries can afford to have an Internet-connected PC, but they can all afford a mobile phone. It's through this technology that people from around the world are staying in touch with one another, accessing their e-mail, sending photos, audio, video, blogging, and surfing the Web.

People are using their iPhones, BlackBerrys, and Androids to download music, watch television shows, view movies, and connect with their friends. As a company that wants to connect with their customers and prospects, shouldn't you be participating in the most widely used technology on the planet? As you read each profile, keep in mind that its features and functions may or may not be right for your particular business. Use the Tool Scorecard at the end of the chapter to help you determine which of these tools qualify for further consideration when you begin creating your social media strategy in Part III of the book.

airG

Company Name:	airG
URL:	corp.airg.com
Location:	Vancouver, British Columbia, Canada
Founded:	2000
Employees:	150+

What Is It?

The airG service "is a global community service made available to end users through different mobile service providers." Customers of included service providers have access to an instant community network based on their interests and demographics.

How Can It Be Used?

"The mobile phone has proven to be a viable platform for bringing mobile users together in interactive communities, and with multiple access points including voice, video, SMS, MMS, WAP, Java, BREW and i-mode." The airG service can be used in an interactive community or as a GPS locator.

What Other Applications Does It Work With?

As a mobile networking device, airG offers a platform to interact with members of its community. It is interconnected to more than 100 million mobile operators and media companies.

Who Uses It?

Companies, including Sprint, Nextel, AT&T, Rogers, TELUS, Virgin Mobile, Orange, Boost Mobile, Vodafone, and MTV Asia, use airG.

Should You Use It?

If you are looking for a mobile social network, airG satisfies that need if you are covered under a compatible phone service provider.

Who Started It?

Technology entrepreneurs Frederick Ghahramani, Vincent Yen, and Bryce Pasechnik founded airG in 2000.

AOL Mobile

Company Name:	AOL LLC
URL:	mobile.aol.com
Location:	New York, New York
Founded:	1983
Revenue Model:	Advertising, subscriptions, services

What Is It?

AOL Mobile provides AOL products and services to users on portable devices. With AOL Mobile, users can access AOL content from categories like news, music, and sports. AOL Mobile also provides services like ringtones, AOL e-mail, and AOL Instant Messenger. The AOL Mobile site also gives information and reviews about different cell phones, cellular service providers, and cell phone accessories.

How Can It Be Used?

A user who wanted to find a restaurant in her area could use AOL City Guide to find the closest locations, browse reviews, and then call to make reservations. A businessperson who is out of town could use AOL Finance to access information about stocks or other companies. A user who wanted to see a movie could use AOL Moviefone to learn what movies are playing, read summaries of the plots, and find out what times the movies begin.

What Other Applications Does It Work With?

AOL Mobile compatible programs include MapQuest Mobile, City's Best, City Guide, and Moviefone. Also, through AOL Mobile you can access AOL Instant Messenger, AOL Mail, AOL Pictures, and a number of AOL Channels.

Who Uses It?

AOL is used by a wide variety of people to meet their various needs. Businesses can stay current with e-mails, find up-to-date financial information, and maintain an address book. Consumers can find new restaurants and clubs, read movie reviews, and get directions to a certain address.

Should You Use It?

You should use AOL Mobile if you are often away from your computer in situations in which you would benefit from being able to access AOL products and services. For example, if you need to always be available through e-mail, AOL Mobile allows you to receive and send e-mails through your portable device. According to AOL, AOL Mobile allows you to stay "entertained, informed and connected to your network of family and friends while on the move."

Who Started It?

AOL first began as a company called Control Video Corporation in 1983, which was reorganized as Quantum Computer Services Inc., on May 24, 1985. The company focused on providing dedicated online services to Commodore computers. In 1988, Quantum created online services for Macintosh and, later, IBM computers. In 1991, Quantum became known as America Online Inc., AOL for DOS was launched, and Steve Case became the CEO of the company. Case decided the best direction for the company was to position AOL as the premier online service for those who were not particularly knowledgeable about computers. This strategy led to the company's biggest growth period. On January 11, 2001, America Online merged with Time Warner. It was spun off to be a completely independent company again on December 10, 2009.

Brightkite

Company Name:	Brightkite (a division of No Sleep Media, LLC)
URL:	brightkite.com
Location:	Burlingame, California; Denver, Colorado; Helsinki, Finland
Founded:	2005
Employees:	5
Revenue Model:	Platform for third-party applications and presently evaluating location-based advertising
Fees:	For text messaging, service plan rates apply
Tagline:	No rest until the dream comes true.

What Is It?

Brightkite offers a location-based social networking medium that provides updates to friends on your location through a cell phone or Internet browser. Users can text message friends or create posts of text and images to create a virtual layer for that location. One of the advantages of location-based servicing is the similarity to a navigation device or GPS locator, so if users are in a crowded area, they can find who they are looking for through Brightkite.

How Can It Be Used?

Brightkite is currently a communication tool to update people within a social network on the user's location or as a navigational aid. By targeting bars, music venues, conferences, and symposiums, users can see who is there. Users can enter a business name into the search feature for possible locations in their proximity.

The potential for tracking previously uncharted locations and marking areas for research will expand as GPS capabilities expand, making it a useful tool for expeditions.

Brightkite is currently exploring selling real-world analytics to businesses for location-based targeted advertising and the potential for tracking consumer spending trends.

What Other Applications Does It Work With?

Socialthing! provides users with an all-in-one site to receive updates from those in your social network and recently integrated the Brightkite API (application programming interface). SPOT Satellite Personal Tracker is now supported by Brightkite and can "check you in anywhere on earth via satellite"; this is beneficial if you are out of range of Wi-Fi or cell signals. FriendFeed and Twitter also work well with Brightkite, and users can customize what is sent to Twitter.

Who Uses It?

Brightkite is currently used as a platform for people to update their social network with their location and can be used as a navigation tool. Brightkite is an effective tool for those who want to mark a specific location to return to later. Depending on the user's privacy settings, Brightkite allows users to send double-blind messages to other Brightkiters in their vicinity for networking purposes, which could be helpful if you are at a large conference or symposium and trying to locate people.

Should You Use It?

If you are looking for a method of communicating your location to a large number of people with minimal effort, Brightkite would be an effective tool. This application could be beneficial for corporations or news outlets as a means of checking in for employees who are often out of range of cellular or Wi-Fi services. In the future, however, this type of application could be essential for locating employees in remote locations. Some areas of academia, specifically field research or archaeological specialties, could benefit from the use of Brightkite as a means of updating locations and tracking previously uncharted locales, or simply as a method of verification of whereabouts.

Who Started It?

Brady Becker and Martin May are the founders of Brightkite. Brady Becker has a "passion for creating location-based services that challenge how we define and interact with [the] place-based community." Public information on Martin May is currently unavailable.

CallWave

Company Name:	CallWave
URL:	www.callwave.com
Location:	San Francisco, California
Founded:	1998
Employees:	~100
Tagline:	The new way to work together.

What Is It?

CallWave specializes in providing an integrated communication system that incorporates the most-used devices in the world today: the cell phone and the PC. The solutions offered enable the collaboration of Internet and phone from any device. The products are compatible with businesses of all sizes, and existing business enterprise tools can be merged to suit your needs and requirements.

In their own words, "Leveraging our wholly owned CLEC, Liberty Telecomm, and years of experience and innovation in making mobile phones and PCs communicate with each other, CallWave is in a unique position to provide a suite of secure, scalable, and cost-effective mobile communications tools."

CallWave is a publicly traded company with its headquarters in San Francisco, California, and has branch offices in Santa Barbara, California, and Sofia, Bulgaria.

How Can It Be Used?

CallWave has communication tools that can be used in conjunction with other applications for effective and efficient working. Some of CallWave's features and functionality include:

- Voicemail-to-Text application converts voice messages to text, enabling professionals to read their voice messages, send them by text or e-mail, and manage messages online.
- FUZE, which offers high-definition and synchronized video, audio conferencing, chat, and online media storage. Ideal for web collaboration and conferencing, FUZE can be hosted from any Internet-enabled device, allowing professionals to collaborate from anywhere and share documents and images in sync.
- The beta version of FUZE supports BlackBerry and Nokia devices and will soon support the iPhone and Windows Mobile–based phones.
- HD Audio Conferencing provides clear sound quality and conference plans to suit the needs of small to large businesses.
- Fax2E-mail allows professionals to send, receive, and save faxes to e-mail.
- Mobile IM securely extends IM to any smart phone and is compatible with all major IM Services: MSN, AIM, Jabber, Yahoo!, Google Talk, and ICQ.

What Other Applications Does It Work With?

IBM Lotus Sametime, Microsoft OCS, VoIP, Jabber, Google Talk, Yahoo!, AIM, MSN, and ICQ are social media applications that can be used by CallWave widgets and gadgets that come free with the service.

Who Uses It?

CallWave can be used by anyone. However, it is ideal for professionals on the move because it provides an ideal amalgamation of PC and mobile to conduct business effectively and efficiently from anywhere.

Should You Use It?

If you are on the move and multitasking, CallWave could be the solution for you.

Who Started It?

CallWave's chairman and cofounder, Peter V. Sperling, is also a founder and senior vice president of the Apollo Group Inc., the parent company of the University of Phoenix. Sperling is also the chairman and cofounder of Communication Services Inc., which serves the U.S. Coast Guard, FBI, and Department of Homeland Security, and the U.S. commercial wireless industry. Sperling is also the chairman of Ecliptic Enterprises, a provider of integrated space imaging and telemetry and payload deployment systems.

Jott

Company Name:	Jott Networks Inc.
URL:	jott.com
Location:	Seattle, Washington
Founded:	2006
Employees:	156,000 (Nuance)
Revenue Model:	Venture capital backing, but considering premium subscriptions and advertising
Fees:	Free and premium subscription plans
Tagline:	Get simple back.

What Is It?

Jott is a voice transcription service that allows a user to call 1-866-JOTT-123, provide the name of the person for whom they want a message transcribed (to include themselves), and Jott sends the message to that name. Whether responding to e-mails, establishing a calendar date, or reminding oneself of an idea or task, Jott provides the means to continue communication, collaboration, and creativity regardless of the time or the place. Jott even allows you to send messages to web services such as Twitter, for real-time communication to your web-oriented audience. In 2009, JOTT was acquired by Nuance.

How Can It Be Used?

Jott is geared toward those who need to multitask, whether because of hectic professional or personal lives or as a matter of safety by providing hands-free communication. Jott provides the ability to communicate without needing an Internet-enabled device, but with just a simple phone call. Lifehacker.com mentions other valuable uses of Jott, such as remotely shutting down Windows, controlling your Mac, or sending audio files to yourself, such as that fantastic composition you believe will fit in with your next ad campaign for your company.

What Other Applications Does It Work With?

Obviously, if you have a telephone or a cell phone, Jott works with your device, since the primary requirement to use Jott is the voice. Currently Jott has specialized services with BlackBerry, iPhone, and iGoogle. Jott in general works with web services such as Blogger, Zillow, Amazon, WordPress, and Twitter. The ability to post late-breaking news to your Internet-reading audience can prove valuable as a business tool. Conversely, the audience can also access your Jotts through Jott feeds (RSS feeds). Jott users simply dial 1-866-JOTT-123, say, "Jott Feeds," and then provide the name of the desired feed. Jott users can then listen to your latest Jott posting.

Who Uses It?

There are enough recommendations from individual users to support the apparent popularity explosion of Jott. It isn't just the individual user, though, who is finding Jott valuable. A number of Web-based companies are coming up with applications that play off of Jott's basic usage premise. One example is Tsheets.com. Tsheets is a time-tracking application that allows a Jott user to sign in and sign out. Users who telecommute or are on business travel would find such an application useful to help them keep track of time for time sheets and metrics.

Should You Use It?

Jott seems to be most useful for just about anyone who has a busy schedule or needs a technological tool to make notes and reminders. People are finding a number of reasons, professional and personal, to use Jott.

Who Started It?

John Pollard, one of the cofounders and CEO of Jott Networks Inc., has a solid foundation in the computer industry, with Microsoft, and subsequently Expedia, on his resume. Shreedhar Madhavapeddi, another cofounder and the vice president of products, also worked at Microsoft and was key in the development of MSN and Smartphone. Doug Aley, vice president of business development, most notably worked at Amazon in developing Unibox as well as becoming general manager of its third-party sellers' business. Dave Rich, vice president of business operations, has extensive experience in call center operations and voice recognition stemming from his work with companies such as American Airlines, SABRE, and Nuance. According to Jott's corporate overview: "Cofounders John Pollard and Shreedhar Madhavapeddi started Jott in response to a growing frustration: their lives were already full of technology, but they still felt they weren't staying on top of things. Jott was born from the promise of being able to help people remember anything."

Jumbuck

Company Name:	Jumbuck Entertainment Ltd.
URL:	jumbuck.com
Location:	Melbourne, Australia (headquarters); offices: Perth, London, Cologne, San Francisco, Rio de Janeiro
Founded:	2000
Employees:	72

What Is It?

Jumbuck Entertainment has the unique distinction of being a leading source of community messaging applications to worldwide wireless carriers. It sends out a wireless markup language (WML) page every year that crosses the 13 million mark each time. Jumbuck has branches in Perth, San Francisco, London, Cologne, and Rio de Janeiro, and its main headquarters are in Melbourne, Australia. Today, Jumbuck has effectively achieved a comprehensive distribution footprint wherein it has incorporated a network of more than 80 carriers internationally, including a community that easily exceeds 15 million users.

Jumbuck is a public company listed on the Australian Stock Exchange.

How Can It Be Used?

Jumbuck Entertainment Limited has put together a messaging and social networking service that enables mobile users to use services like chat rooms, blogging, dating applications, and other features using mobile phones. The company offers a variety of products that cater to different countries and various user requirements. For safety and proper use of its services, a moderation service is provided that ensures that all messages are reviewed and meet ethical boundaries as required by different communities in the world.

Some of its products are detailed here:

- *Power Chat* is an application that can be customized and allows users to interact the world over. Public and private rooms are available, and it supports multiple languages, including Italian, Spanish, German, English, Portuguese, and Polish.
- *Jumbuck Island* offers multiplayer chat applications in Java 3D. Play on a virtual island using your customized characters, use it separately, or integrate it with your Power Chat.
- *Jumbuck Blogs* is a blogging application in which users can text, comment, or insert images on their page.
- *Chat Del Mundo* is one of the largest mobile Hispanic communities in the world, where you can find members from the United States, Spain, and South America.
- *TXT chat* is a short message service (SMS) in which a single sent command enables the user to send messages and browse through chat rooms.
- *Chat do Mundo* is one of the major mobile Portuguese communities in the world. Members come from Portugal and Brazil where communication is by way of text, images, and video. Now available on TIM and Vivo in Brazil, and on Optimus, TMN, and Vodafone in Portugal, the Chat platform supports wireless application protocol (WAP), SMS, multimedia message service (MMS), and video.

What Other Applications Does It Work With?

Jumbuck takes you online and has integrated support with social media applications that meet technical connectivity requirements. For more information, it is important to check with the carrier or service provider you are subscribed to.

Who Uses It?

This is a user-friendly service for those who can put its various features to good use and help them increase their business, their friends list, or their social circle.

Should You Use It?

If you love to make friends, and you like staying connected and talking to people from all over the world, then this is a service to consider. There are a lot of features that can be used, and with a little bit of imagination, ingenuity, and smarts, you could use this medium to boost your business opportunities, too.

Who Started It?

Adrian Risch is the founder of Jumbuck. He was appointed CEO in July 2007. With his experience in web project management and applications development, and his exhaustive understanding of international markets in telecommunication and consumer consumption of mobile data services, he leads the company from the front. He is also a member of the corporate governance committee.

SMS.ac

Company Name:	SMS.ac Inc.
URL:	www.sms.ac.com
Location:	San Diego, California
Founded:	2001
Employees:	100 to 200
Fees:	Carrier charges may apply
Tagline:	Always connected.

What Is It?

SMS.ac is a mobile data and Internet communications company that offers a global system of Short Message Services (SMS) along with multimedia messaging services. It is considered to be one of the biggest mobile communities in the world today. Mobile and web distribution is provided to those who sell and buy digital content like music, videos, and other applications through the medium of SMS mobile billing. The web site has integrated social networking services like comments, photographs, music, and videos with its mobile billing technology.

How Can It Be Used?

SMS.ac is a medium through which text messages are sent to interact with other users. Once you are a registered SMS.ac user, you can use your account to send regular text messages, make your own greetings, and look for other profiles with similar interests as yours, which will help you increase your friends list. The methods for updating blogs; swapping photos, music, and videos; and many other features are updated and improved on a regular basis. All this is done using your cell phone. This service is free to join, and charges are levied depending on the country of residence and your service provider or carrier.

Besides the very obvious entertainment factor, this medium can be effectively used to spread messages of social awareness, alerts for imminent natural calamities, and so on. SMS.ac is a wireless e-mail provider, and as such it has tie-ins with many carriers or service providers worldwide. This network of carriers and technology combined can help avert many a disaster through timely news flashes.

There is a proposal for incorporating a tsunami warning system into this medium, the requirement for which followed in the wake of the disastrous tsunami that hit Indonesia, India, Thailand, and Sri Lanka in 2004. Those who do not have cell phones and are not registered users can benefit from news spreading by word of mouth.

What Other Applications Does It Work With?

Your cell phone can help you connect with other social media applications available on the Internet. The Wireless Application Protocol, or WAP, is a standard that makes available secure access to e-mail and web pages that are text based to handheld devices and mobile phones. From your WAP-enabled mobile phone, you can connect to the biggest mobile community in the world with SMS.ac.

Who Uses It?

Today SMS.ac has more than 50 million registered users in about 180 countries worldwide. It caters to varied tastes in music, videos, and other features. It also helps people stay connected in times of crisis. The network is spread out, and a new arrival in a city can easily make friends through this common medium.

Should You Use It?

If you are looking to make new business connections and stay in touch with coworkers, then this is an ideal platform for you. Apart from just messages, there is so much more you can do with this system. It would help you keep contacts for your business; you can download interesting videos and the latest music; and keep in touch with news and views from friends around the world. It can also keep you in the know with what's happening around the world, be it eventual natural disasters, aid required, and so on.

Who Started It?

Greg Wilfahrt is cofounder of SMS.ac, and he serves as executive vice president, office of the chairman. His portfolio involves corporate communications and public relations initiatives and development of a strategically sound road map for the company.

Greg took over this position after being vice president of public relations at MP3.com. He also had tenure with Ubrandit.com as vice president of communications.

Michael Pousti is CEO at SMS.ac. In 1993, Pousti cofounded College Club.com, where he was chairman. Pousti has also completed a stint as cofounder and CEO of Productivity Solutions Corporation. He saw the company from concept to subsequent acquisition by Unisys.

Tool Scorecard for Chapter 36: Mobile

Instructions: Using the following five-point (0 to 4) scale, rate each tool in this chapter on the basis of how valuable it *might* be to the internal and external operations of your company. Make notes about which tools appeal to you the most.

    4 = Extremely Valuable

    3 = Very Valuable

    2 = Somewhat Valuable

    1 = Not Very Valuable

    0 = No Value

Tool	Internal Value	External Value
AirG	4 3 2 1 0	4 3 2 1 0
AOL Mobile	4 3 2 1 0	4 3 2 1 0
Brightkite	4 3 2 1 0	4 3 2 1 0
CallWave	4 3 2 1 0	4 3 2 1 0
Jott	4 3 2 1 0	4 3 2 1 0
Jumbuck	4 3 2 1 0	4 3 2 1 0
SMS.ac	4 3 2 1 0	4 3 2 1 0

CHAPTER 37

Interpersonal

This is another category of seemingly unrelated technology. The common thread, however, is that they are all tools that allow you to connect and communicate with your customers and prospects. Some companies provide the means to host a meeting for your employees or perform a webbing for a thousand people. Some allow you to use the Internet like a free telephone service, while others allow you to convert your voice into text messages to be sent to your e-mail and other team members.

These tools are extremely feature rich, easy to use, and are mostly free. As you read each profile, keep in mind that its features and functions may or may not be right for your particular business. Use the Tool Scorecard at the end of the chapter to help you determine which of these tools qualify for further consideration when you begin creating your social media strategy in Part III of the book.

Acrobat Connect

Company Name:	Adobe Inc.
URL:	www.adobe.com
Location:	San Jose, California
Founded:	Adobe Systems 1982
Employees:	7,000
Revenue Model:	Software sales/upgrades
Fees:	Premium: $149 per year or Premium Plus: $390 per year

theSocialMediaBible.com

What Is It?

Acrobat Connect is the Adobe Systems Inc. solution for reaching a disseminated workforce or audience. Adobe markets Acrobat Connect as easy-to-use software that "can help break through technology barriers by letting virtually anyone participate in effective online communication and knowledge transfer." By providing web conferencing options such as screen sharing, whiteboard, chat video and audio, and options for archiving and editing recorded online meetings, Acrobat Connect reduces travel costs and increases productivity.

How Can It Be Used?

Acrobat Connect is used to communicate and collaborate through online conferencing features with the capability to screen share, to chat through audio and video, and to use a whiteboard to enhance understanding. This functionality allows users to conduct training or e-learning workshops, demonstrate a product or service, or host a meeting to review a variety of presentations.

For the individual, Acrobat Connect is a useful tool for sharing life events with extended family.

What Other Applications Does It Work With?

Any application that the host of the meeting has installed on his or her computer can be shared using Acrobat Connect. This capability is effective when conducting a sales demonstration so the participants in the online meeting can see the product or service firsthand, or for conducting a business meeting in which participants are spread across numerous locations so they can all view presentations.

Who Uses It?

Business and academic organizations use Acrobat Connect to enhance relations and improve productivity. According to Steve Bamberger, national training manager, eLearning, Toshiba America Business Solutions Inc., "Integrating Acrobat ConnectPro into our online training initiatives has been enormously instrumental in helping us enhance communications and grow business lines, and we've been able to extend this enrichment to other teams for use in product launches and customer meetings."

Should You Use It?

Acrobat Connect is an effective tool for communicating, demonstrating, presenting, or conducting meetings and conferences. If you are looking for a way to reach many people across a myriad of places, Acrobat Connect would be a viable option. As many businesses are recognizing the increased productivity and cost-effectiveness of telecommuting, Acrobat Connect would be a beneficial tool to keep the lines of communication open between on-site and remote employees, and to enhance training modules. In a sales environment, Acrobat ConnectPro offers a solution for presenting or demonstrating when it is difficult to reach multiple leads in one location.

Who Started It?

Adobe was founded in 1982 by John Warnock and Chuck Geschke on the principle of translating text and images from a computer screen to print. By introducing Adobe PostScript technology, they revolutionized desktop publishing; "a computer file could be printed exactly as it appeared on screen, with all formatting, graphics and fonts intact." After Adobe's acquisition of Macromedia, Macromedia Breeze became Acrobat Connect. Built upon Flash technology, Acrobat Connect is considered the next generation in the Adobe suite of products.

AOL Instant Messenger

Company Name:	AOL LLC
URL:	www.aim.com
Location:	New York, New York
Founded:	1983
Revenue Model:	Advertising, subscriptions, services

What Is It?

AOL Instant Messenger is a free online service that allows users to communicate with one or multiple users synchronously. There are versions for Linux, Macintosh, and Windows operating systems, and they are all able to communicate with one another. Users can add contacts to their AOL Instant Messenger Buddy List, which allows them to see when their contacts are online. Aside from synchronous text-based chatting, AOL Instant Messenger also offers features such as voice-based chat, video-based chat, alerts and reminders, file transfers, and text messaging.

How Can It Be Used?

AOL Instant Messenger can be used in any instance when people want or need to communicate over the Internet. People can use AOL Instant Messenger to maintain contact with friends and family that live far away, or businesses could use AOL Instant Messenger to communicate internally among employees or externally with customers. Also, with the ability to transfer files, it is a useful program for concurrent collaboration.

What Other Applications Does It Work With?

AOL Instant Messenger works with AOL Radio, AOL Explorer, iPad and Plaxo, mobile applications like the iPhone, Android, Windows Mobile, and BlackBerry. AOL Instant Messenger also allows third-party developers to create chat bots, custom clients, mashups, widgets, modules, and plug-ins. These applications do any number of things, such as allowing a user to post directly to a blog, allowing someone to track the cost of a meeting, or allowing a user to draw simultaneously with one of his buddies.

Who Uses It?

AOL Instant Messenger is used by a large and global online audience. It is estimated to have a large segment of the instant messaging market in North America. Businesses and private users both use AOL Instant Messenger to communicate and share media online.

Should You Use It?

You should use AOL Instant Messenger if you are interested in communicating with other users online, either professionally or recreationally. You should also use AOL Instant Messenger if you are interested in creating a third-party application that will serve a function through the chatting service. For example, a web developer could create an application that works as a part of an online marketing campaign to drive traffic to its web site.

Who Started It?

AOL first began as a company called Control Video Corporation in 1983, which was reorganized as Quantum Computer Services Inc. on May 24,

1985. The company focused on providing dedicated online services to Commodore computers. In 1988, Quantum created online services for Macintosh and, later, IBM computers. In 1991, Quantum became known as America Online Inc., AOL for DOS was launched, and Steve Case became the CEO of the company. Case decided the best direction for the company was to position AOL as the premier online service for those who were not particularly knowledgeable about computers. This strategy led to the company's biggest growth period. On January 11, 2001, America Online merged with Time Warner. It was spun off to be a completely independent company again on December 10, 2009.

GoToMeeting

Company Name:	Citrix Systems Inc.
URL:	www.gotomeeting.com
Location:	Fort Lauderdale, Florida
Founded:	1989
Revenue Model:	Subscriptions
Tagline:	Online meetings made easy.

What Is It?

GoToMeeting is an online meeting service that enables individuals, businesses, and organizations to collaborate and communicate through the Internet. Users pay a flat subscription fee, on a per-month or per-year basis, which allows them to conduct unlimited online meetings for the duration of their subscribed period. GoToMeeting also offers additional features such as VoIP (Voice over Internet Protocol), screen sharing, and meeting recording. Users on Windows and Macintosh operating systems can join a GoToMeeting session.

How Can It Be Used?

GoToMeeting can be used to promote collaboration and communication, demonstrate products or presentations, and share information. By using the audio and chatting components of GoToMeeting, employees of a business can communicate with one another while reducing travel expenses. With the screen-sharing feature of GoToMeeting, you can show a slideshow to multiple people or allow a group to edit a document together in real time. Since

GoToMeeting also allows guests to attend meetings for no additional charge beyond the subscription fee, you could invite a potential client to meet with you from anywhere in the world (with an Internet connection) to negotiate or view a product demonstration.

What Other Applications Does It Work With?

GoToMeeting can be integrated with several applications from which users can start an impromptu GoToMeeting session. These applications include IBM Lotus Notes, Microsoft Office, Microsoft Outlook, and some instant messaging applications. Recorded meetings can also be converted to the Windows Media format, enabling users to watch past meetings in Windows Media Player.

Who Uses It?

Several companies use GoToMeeting to manage and grow their business. GoToMeeting offers them the ability to save resources, communicate to a greater degree, and be more productive. Just a few of the companies that find GoToMeeting beneficial are Clarity, a company that provides Internet-based business solutions; e-Touch International, a company that designs automated hospitality technology; and xG Technology, a company that develops wireless communications technologies.

Should You Use It?

You should use GoToMeeting if you are interested in a collaboration tool with features like audio conferencing and screen sharing that allows you to meet with people online. Also, since GoToMeeting operates on a flat subscription rate, it is a good choice if you intend on meeting online numerous times within a given period. You should also use GoToMeeting if you need a method of sharing or discussing confidential information over the Internet, as GoToMeeting has several security implementations.

Who Started It?

GoToMeeting was developed in July 2004 by Citrix Online, a division of Citrix Systems Inc. GoToMy PC and GoToAssist, applications created to remotely access computers, were the basis for the technology that GoToMeeting utilizes. Version 4.5, the current release of GoToMeeting that was introduced in 2006, provides integration with Microsoft Office and support for Macintosh users to join meetings.

Apple iChat

Company Name:	Apple
URL:	www.apple.com/macosx/features/ichat.html
Location:	Cupertino, California
Founded:	2003
Employees:	75,000 (Apple)
Revenue Model:	Sales of hardware and software

What Is It?

Apple iChat is a video chat service offered with the purchase of Apple's Mac computer running the Leopard operating system. Apple publicizes, "iChat turns any video chat into an event." New features provide users with video backdrops, photo booth effects, comic book effects, and the ability to show photo slideshows, keynote presentations, and movies. Apple iChat also provides a screen-sharing feature that enables users to control a single desktop for collaboration, and automatically initiates an audio chat, eliminating the need for conference calling.

How Can It Be Used?

Apple iChat is primarily used to communicate with friends, family, and coworkers. Using the variety of special effects, and the ability to share photos and video, iChat provides a more comprehensive chatting tool. The built-in functionality of screen sharing, audio chat, and chat recording makes this an effective tool for business collaboration or educational presentations. The recording feature is beneficial for users working on a collaborative project or presentation in the event someone on the team is unavailable for the presentation.

What Other Applications Does It Work With?

iChat works with a number of other applications that allow users to share audio and video and do limited white-boarding. It is compatible with AOL

Instant Messenger, Google Talk, Facebook Chat, MSN Messenger, Yahoo! Messenger, and Quick Look, a file preview feature developed by Apple.

Who Uses It?

iChat is presently used by individuals, students, and businesses that use Macs. Users who have a .Mac account can use iChat instantly, and those who have an AOL or AIM screen name can also use iChat.

Should You Use It?

If you have a Mac and are looking for additional ways to communicate and collaborate, iChat is a viable option. The new features available with the photo and video sharing, and desktop sharing with audio chat, provide an all-in-one functionality that many businesses subscribe to using multiple vendors. Paid subscribers to Apple's .Mac service have encrypted communication support for more confidential or proprietary information.

Who Started It?

Apple Computer was founded by Steve Jobs and Steve Wozniak in 1976 in an effort to make "the easy and affordable personal computer become reality."

Jott

Company Name:	Jott Networks, Inc.
URL:	www.jott.com
Location:	Seattle, Washington
Founded:	2006
Employees:	150
Revenue Model:	Venture capital backing, but considering premium subscriptions and advertising
Fees:	Free
Tagline:	Get simple back.

What Is It?

Jott is a voice transcription service that allows a user to call 1-866-JOTT-123, provide the name of the person for whom they want a message transcribed (to include themselves), and Jott sends the message to that name. Whether responding to e-mails, establishing a calendar date, or reminding oneself of an idea or task, Jott provides the means to continue communication, collaboration, and creativity regardless of the time or the place. Jott even allows you to send messages to web services such as Twitter, for real-time communication to your web-oriented audience. In 2009, Jott was acquired by Nuance.

How Can It Be Used?

Jott is geared toward those who need to multitask, whether it's because of hectic professional or personal lives or as a matter of safety by providing hands-free communication. Jott provides the ability to communicate without needing the aid of an Internet-enabled device, with just a simple phone call. Lifehacker.com mentions other valuable uses of Jott, such as remotely shutting down Windows or controlling your Mac or sending audio files to yourself, such as that fantastic composition you believe will fit in with your next ad campaign for your company.

What Other Applications Does It Work With?

Obviously, if you have a telephone or a cell phone, Jott works with your device, since the primary requirement to use Jott is your voice. Jott currently has specialized services with BlackBerry, iPhone, and iGoogle. Jott in general works with web services such as Blogger, Zillow, Amazon, WordPress, and Twitter. The ability to post late-breaking news to your Internet-reading audience can prove valuable as a business tool. Conversely, the audience can also access your Jotts through Jott feeds (RSS feeds). Jott users simply dial 1-866-Jott-123, say, "Jott Feeds," and then provide the name of the desired feed. Jott users can then listen to your latest Jott posting.

Who Uses It?

There are enough recommendations from individual users to support the apparent popularity explosion of Jott. It isn't just the individual user who is finding Jott valuable, however. A number of web-based companies are coming up with applications that are based on Jott's basic usage premise. One example is Tsheets.com. Tsheets is a time-tracking application that allows a Jott user to sign in and sign out. Users who telecommute or are on business travel would find such an application useful to help them keep track of time for time sheets and metrics.

Should You Use It?

Jott seems to be most useful for just about anyone who has a busy schedule or needs a technological tool to make notes and reminders. People are finding a number of reasons to use Jott, both professional and personal. Scott Clark posted a suggestion to use Jott for keeping migraine diaries.

Who Started It?

John Pollard, one of the cofounders and CEO of Jott Networks, Inc., has a solid foundation in the computer industry with Microsoft, and subsequently Expedia, on his resume. Shreedhar Madhavapeddi, another cofounder and the vice president of products, also worked at Microsoft and was key in the development of MSN and Smartphone. Doug Aley, vice president of business development, most notably worked at Amazon in developing Unibox for Amazon as well as becoming general manager of its third-party sellers' business. Dave Rich, vice president of business operations, has extensive experience in call center operations and voice recognition stemming from his work with companies such as American Airlines, SABRE, and Nuance. According to Jott's Corporate Overview: "Cofounders John Pollard and Shreedhar Madhavapeddi started Jott in response to a growing frustration: their lives were already full of technology, but they still felt they weren't staying on top of things. Jott was born from the promise of being able to help people remember anything."

Meebo

Company Name:	Meebo
URL:	www.meebo.com
Location:	Mountain View, California
Founded:	2005
Employees:	52
Revenue Model:	Advertising
Fees:	Free
Tagline:	All your IM accounts in one place—chat, play games, and much more!

What Is It?

Meebo is the solution to a problem that many people encounter: too many Instant Message (IM) accounts (and the accompanying user IDs and passwords). Meebo allows IM users to consolidate their accounts and reduce the need to download different types of software that, while they enable communication with different online users, results in clogged computer processes and cluttered computer desktops. Meebo incorporates MSN Messenger, Yahoo!, AIM, Google, ICQ, and Jabber, and allows Meebo users to log in from any location (as opposed to being restricted to a particular PC where the user's IM software would be installed) and send IMs. Meebo can also be embedded anywhere online that an IM application can be embedded, such as in MySpace or blogs.

How Can It Be Used?

In today's world of networking for personal and professional needs, remembering and separating the various user IDs and passwords to each individual account can be difficult. Meebo allows you to have one central login and gives you the ability to log in from anywhere and IM someone at any time. Meebo also provides features such as Meebo rooms (chat rooms), Meebo Me (IMs on blogs and other web sites), Meebo Mobile for iPhones and iPod Touches, and Meebo extensions for Firefox users.

What Other Applications Does It Work With?

As mentioned in the previous paragraph, Meebo works not only with the major IM applications, but with iPhones and iPod Touches, Firefox, Facebook, and MySpace. According to an article on Reelseo.com, Meebo is a platform for multiuser and synchronous applications such as 3rd Sense, Absolutist, AddictingGames, BladeSix, Clearspring Technologies, Come2-Play, Feedhaus, Gamebrew, MeBeam, MediaGreenhouse, Mochi Media, Jiggmin, Kongregate, PlayFirst, Presidio Media, Pudding Media, TalkShoe, TokBox, Ustream.tv, uWink, wellgames, and ZeroCode.

Who Uses It?

Seth Steinberg, CEO and cofounder of Meebo, best points out the range of Meebo users in the following interview excerpt from Centernetworks .com:

Mostly people who are twenty-five years and younger. From there the demographic gets really wide. We have U.S. soldiers in Iraq and Meebo is the only way they can communicate live other than calling them. . . . Teachers are using Meebo on their class blogs to allow students and parents to communicate [with] them from the class blog. . . .

Thirty percent of people using Meebo are in America; the balance is abroad. Meebo is available in fifty-three languages and the way that came to be, our users really wanted Meebo in multiple languages, so we asked for help on our blog. So we threw up a wiki with the English strings and people came and helped translate the strings into fifty-three languages.

Every month, over a hundred million people utilize Meebo.

Should You Use It?

Meebo is a good tool for those who have multiple IM accounts. The ability to log in to a centralized IM location and use one user ID and password saves a lot of time, bandwidth, and frustration. IM'ing may not necessarily be perfect for everyone's business needs, but if it is, then Meebo can certainly save you time and give you mobility.

Who Started It?

Meebo originated from cofounder Sandy Jen's frustration at having 13 IM screen names and passwords to remember. Seth Sternberg, Sandy, and third cofounding partner, Elaine Wherry, played with Ajax IM as a way to solve the problem. The name Meebo was cooked up as the three sat in a California Pizza Kitchen restaurant trying to find a name that was memorable, easy to pronounce and spell, and of course was not already in use on the Internet.

Skype

Company Name:	Skype Limited
URL:	www.skype.com
Location:	Luxembourg, Belgium
Founded:	2003
Licensing Fees:	Licensing revenue, Skype credit, premium subscriptions

What Is It?

Skype is a piece of software that operates through VoIP to enable users to make, receive, and conduct phone calls over the Internet. If a user is calling another person who is also on Skype, the call is free. Calling someone who is not using Skype (for example, on a cell phone or landline) requires users to either become a Skype subscriber or use Skype Credits. Skype also offers a number of other features, including videoconferencing, call forwarding, and text messaging. Skype is the leading global communications company.

How Can It Be Used?

Skype can be used as a conventional telephone, but it is capable of doing much more. A business could set up an online number in a location within any of the supported countries (21 available currently), and anyone in that number's locale who calls the business pays the local rate, while the business can answer through Skype for free. Skype also allows for call forwarding, which allows users to redirect calls incoming to Skype to a cell phone or landline. This allows a user to only give out one number, their Skype number, and still receive phone calls even when she is not online.

What Other Applications Does It Work With?

Skype works with several mobile applications, so users can access Skype away from the computer. Any phone operating the Windows Mobile operating system can use Skype, and an official Symbian operating system version has been developed. There are also phones that are designed entirely for use with Skype, including Skype's own phone, known as the Skypephone.

Who Uses It?

Skype has a substantial, and still growing, user base. At the end of the first quarter in 2010 there were an estimated 560 million user accounts in existence around the world. Unfortunately, that number may include multiple accounts owned by the same user, but on September 17, 2008, Skype hit a peak with 13,230,315 concurrent users online at once. Skype is used by individuals who want to maintain contact with friends and family all around the world, as well as businesses that wish to communicate globally with employees or customers. Skype accounts for 8 percent of all international calls and at the end of the third quarter in 2009, Skype-to-Skype calls accounted for 27.7 billion minutes.

Should You Use It?

You should use Skype if you would like a VoIP-based program that is similar to conventional phone services, but also offers features beyond that of a conventional phone service. You should also use Skype if you would like to communicate with other Skype users around the world for free. Also, with the ability to register international numbers, Skype is great for those who need an international presence but are unable to establish themselves somewhere physically.

Who Started It?

Niklas Zennström, Janus Friis, and a group of software developers based in Tallinn, Estonia, started Skype. Zennström and Friis cofounded the file-sharing application KaZaA before founding Skype. Skype was acquired by eBay in September 2005 in a deal worth about $2.6 billion.

WebEx

Company Name:	WebEx Communications Inc.
URL:	www.webex.com
Location:	San Jose and Santa Clara, California
Founded:	1996
Employees:	2,189
Revenue Model:	User fees
Fees:	Fee schedule ranging from $49 per month
Tagline:	Vision: To use the Web to bring people together from around the world and work collectively on creative ideas and business.

What Is It?

WebEx is a Cisco company product that "creates on-demand software solutions for companies of all sizes." These applications include online meetings, web conferencing, and videoconferencing. The WebEx Application Suite is "designed for business processes such as sales, support, training and marketing processes."

How Can It Be Used?

WebEx advertising says "all you need to run effective online meetings is a browser and a phone," making their services available to virtually anyone. WebEx is used to conduct meetings, webinars, large-scale seminars, sales demonstrations, and training and support sessions. WebEx allows users to select the material they want to present or share so participants do not have access to someone's entire desktop or personal files, and permits changing the role of the participants at any time during the meeting. More advanced features include the ability to conduct polls and quizzes, videoconferences, and chat with participants.

What Other Applications Does It Work With?

WebEx is a versatile meeting application that uses the presenter's desktop and files, thus working with any applications on the presenter's system. According to the WebEx site, "With WebEx, users share presentations, applications, documents and desktops, with full-motion video and integrated audio, all in a rich multimedia environment."

Who Uses It?

WebEx provides on-demand collaboration, online meeting, web conferencing, and videoconferencing for financial services and high-tech industries; health care, pharmaceutical, communications, manufacturing, government, and educational organizations; and management consulting organizations. Organizations looking to improve productivity by reaching a wider audience through on-demand training and support or to conduct online sales presentations and demonstrations remotely use WebEx.

Should You Use It?

If your organization is looking for an application to conduct remote meetings or training sessions, WebEx can effectively meet those goals. WebEx provides a service that could increase productivity while reducing support costs through unattended and attended remote support sessions. One key benefit of using WebEx is the ability to share information without traveling, which increases productivity and time management, and reduces costs. WebEx web conferencing works across differing platforms, which allows users and presenters using different systems to collaborate effectively.

ZooLoo

Company Name:	Zog Media, Inc.
URL:	www.zooloo.com
Location:	Scottsdale, Arizona
Founded:	Zog Media, 2008
Employees:	30
Revenue Model:	Micropayments, creative services
Fees:	Free Trial; Monthly Packages from $1.99 to $9.99
Tagline:	Your Name, Your Domain, Your Life.

What Is It?

ZooLoo is the easiest and most innovative way for individuals and organizations alike to connect, promote, and share their interests and passions online. It allows the user to manage all of his social media outlets in one place, making it easy to share throughout the digital world. State-of-the-art Microblog technology allows users to post text, photos, videos, links, and more. The user has total control of the site from choosing a custom skin to a personal domain name. ZooLoo also offers a personal dashboard, bringing all one's online interests into one place.

How Can It Be Used?

The ultimate social media tool, ZooLoo connects the user with the digital world. The individual has a place of her own to connect, blog, and share with the rest of the world as well as having an organized web site to manage all of her social media accounts. An organization can use ZooLoo as a way to interact directly with its customers and target communities as well as allowing customizable ad space.

What Other Applications Does It Work With?

Compatible with Facebook, Twitter, MySpace, Twitter, and LinkedIn, Zoo-Loo combines all of these in an easy-to-use way in which the user is in total control. ZooLoo is also a part of the AddThis platform.

Who Uses It?

ZooLoo is for everyone.

Should I Use It?

You should use ZooLoo if you are interested in using a new social media technology platform that allows you total control. If you enjoy blogging and connecting with other people, then ZooLoo is for you. Whether you are a professional, student, or somewhere in between, ZooLoo is for you.

Who Started It?

Zog Media, Inc., was founded in 2008 by digital marketing leader Jeff Herzog with the goal of building technologies and services to help marketers use the power of digital marketing to make more valuable connections with their target audiences. Zog Media companies provide the technology, services, and design to help consumers find, engage, and interact with your brand.

Jeff, a visionary and entrepreneur, before beginning Zog Media, is recognized as the founder and CEO of iCrossing, which he began in 1998. In 10 years, Jeff took the company that he created from an inspired idea and turned it into one of the leading digital marketing companies in the world with annual revenues greater than $120 million.

Jeff also acquired five companies across North America and Europe, built a client roster of more than 40 Fortune 500 companies, created more than 600 jobs, and collaborated with investors, including Goldman Sachs, Oak Investment Partners, and RRE Ventures. Jeff has received several awards, including the New York Ten Awards and *B2B Magazine*'s "Who's Who" in Business. He was named to the Executive Council of New York's list of the "10 Most Prominent Innovators," and was a finalist for Ernst & Young's Entrepreneur of the Year.

Tool Scorecard for Chapter 37: Interpersonal

Instructions: Using the following five-point (0 to 4) scale, rate each tool in this chapter on the basis of how valuable it *might be* to the internal and external operations of your company. Make notes about which tools appeal to you the most.

4 = Extremely Valuable

3 = Very Valuable

2 = Somewhat Valuable

1 = Not Very Valuable

0 = No Value

Tool	Internal Value	External Value
Acrobat Connect	4 3 2 1 0	4 3 2 1 0
AOL Instant Messenger	4 3 2 1 0	4 3 2 1 0
GoToMeeting	4 3 2 1 0	4 3 2 1 0
Apple iChat	4 3 2 1 0	4 3 2 1 0
Meebo	4 3 2 1 0	4 3 2 1 0
Skype	4 3 2 1 0	4 3 2 1 0
WebEx	4 3 2 1 0	4 3 2 1 0

STRATEGY

The Five Steps to Social Media Success

Introduction

In *The Social Media Bible*, Second Edition, I want to take a completely different approach to the strategy of implementing your new social media marketing and communications plan from what was done in the first edition. Most everyone is now familiar with the Communication, Collaboration, Education, and Entertainment, Four Pillars of Social Media from the first edition and how to develop a SWOT analysis (Strengths, Weaknesses, Opportunities, and Threats) for one's company. You do need to go through that process. You need to do all of the exercises detailed in Part III—Strategy of the first edition. In this second edition, over the next five chapters, I am going to get more hands-on; show you more practical examples, and how to develop a step-by-step plan using the Five Steps to Social Media Success.

After consulting and speaking with many U.S. Fortune 1000 companies on down to the individual entrepreneur, and from governmental agencies to nonprofits, I am always asked the same thing: "Now that we have a Facebook page and sent out some tweets, where do we go from here? How do we integrate and implement a complete social media strategy into our existing marketing, sales, and communications strategy?"

Here are five easy steps (chapters) that explain how and why social media needs to be integrated into your marketing strategy.

Chapter 38—Analyze Your Existing Media

Chapter 39—The Social Media Trinity

Chapter 40—Integrate Strategies

Chapter 41—Identify Resources

Chapter 42—Implement and Measure

theSocialMediaBible.com

FIGURE P3.1

Fundamental Shift in Power

We are in the middle of a Fundamental Shift in Power that is taking place across the world in media and advertising that is having far-reaching effects in industries that used to dominate the businesses of marketing, public relations, advertising, media buying, television, radio, newspapers, magazines, billboards, and even the music and film industries. Newspapers are collapsing at an alarming rate, magazines are shutting down, radio stations are going syndicated to reduce costs and to amortize their ad revenues over a national area and no longer regional, and the music and movie industry is trying to cope with technologies such as iTunes, Netflix, and peer-to-peer distribution.

The Fundamental Shift in Power is shifting the power of the corporate messaging, the power of the news agencies, and the power of the ad agencies into the hands of the cyber-citizens like you and me. Our customers are now controlling our brands and our messages.

We are no longer in control of the media, the news, or the advertising, but our customers are. More and more and nearly exclusively, people are turning to peers for product and service recommendations. Facebook, with its 400 million members, are where most people now go to find out about how one automobile compares to another, or how good was that movie, or what is the latest news on, or what's the truth behind such and such.

CNN, Fox, ABC, the *Wall Street Journal*, and the *New York Times* are being replaced by the Internet, blogs, aggregators, Facebook conversations, and tweets. When the commercial jet landed in the Hudson River in New York in January 2009, it was a private individual who broke the news from the wing of the plane, with his cell phone and Twitter. When we watched the elections in the Mideast, it was Twitter again, coupled with a mobile phone. Unlike Desert Storm, when everyone, including the military, was watching Wolf Blitzer bringing us the play-by-play actions of the war on CNN, today it's we who are telling the story through our own technologies and social media.

TechNewsCrunch reported "More People Around the World Get Their News Online from Google News than from CNN." We are getting our news from social networks, Twitter reports, and blogs, while the social networks are getting their news from us!

A recent poll showed that:

37 percent of Americans regularly go online for their news.

27 percent picked up a newspaper on any given day.

39 percent turned to cable television.

Those who watched a nightly news bulletin on TV fell from 34 percent to 29 percent over the past four years.

There is a 30-second video from the Federal Trade Commission (FTC) that I use in my keynotes that really summarize this shift. While the video wasn't designed to address this shift, it certainly recognizes the implications. Here is a transcript of that video.

Mary Engle, Associate Director, Bureau of Consumer Protection, Federal Trade Commission (FTC)

Mary Engle, Associate Director Bureau of Consumer Protection

Mary Engle

There's been a lot in the news about the FTC Endorsement Guide, "What's the story?" Well, the FTC cares about protecting consumers. We know that nowadays when consumers want information about a product or service they are thinking of using, they often go online to see what other consumers have to say. Don't you want to know if the reason the consumer is giving a rave review is because they're being paid by the advertiser to say it or they're getting a steady stream of free products from that company? We just want to bring some transparency to the process, so that when there's a relationship between the advertiser and the reviewer, the reader knows about it.

"Transparency, Sincerity, and Authenticity," is what people are looking for in product recommendations and in advertising.

The primary cause for this shift is we are moving away from the age-old tradition of pontification and moving toward two-way communication. We are more interested in what a peer thinks about a particular product than what the company has to say about it. It's now peer perspective, not sponsor perspective.

For the first time in history, people are spending hundreds of dollars to buy and install technology that can remove or at least fast-forward through companies' commercials. In my presentations, nearly half of all attendees have purchased and installed a Tivo box so they can skip our messages. In many ways, we brought it on ourselves. For all of our lifetimes, we have been bombarded with commercials' hidden agendas and psychological hot buttons that make us react to the advertisers' commands. There're hidden messages and psychological hot buttons?

There better be! The average 30-second television commercial costs about $250,000 to produce; some more, some less. To play that commercial nationally just one time, prime time, costs about one and a quarter million dollars. So, if you were producing a commercial for your company and just spent one and a half million dollars, you had better get people to react, convert, and buy your products. Otherwise, you'd be out of a job and should be.

We, as consumers, are no longer falling for this. We have moved from being *con*sumers to *pro*sumers. We are professional consumers and don't want to be sold, tricked, or manipulated.

We now listen to commercial-free radio shows on our computers and mobile phones, watch live mobile phone TV, aggregate the news we want without advertising on our Google or Yahoo! home pages, watch live streaming video on uStream, and get our editorials from people we trust on blogs and Twitter.

The other reason for this Fundamental Shift in Power is because nearly all of the social media tools and implementation are free; no hard costs. And . . .

It's Word of Mouth at the Speed of Light . . .

CHAPTER 38

Analyze Your Existing Media

In this chapter we are going to get into the weeds with what you have been currently doing with your conventional marketing. As I refer to marketing, I am also referring to public relations, communications, sales, and marketing.

We are going to look at all of your efforts and determine return on investment (ROI), cost-of-customer-acquisition, and determine the overall effectiveness of how and how much you are spending on communicating your message to your customers and prospects.

When I speak about Entrepreneurship and always start with the business case, I say, "Plan your work and work your plan." Then I say, *"Yuck!"* The purpose of preparing a business plan isn't as much planning your work as much the value of a business plan lies in the process. When you get into the details necessary enough to produce a good business plan and understand the customer, the competition, the expenses, the SWOT (Strengths, Weaknesses, Opportunities, and Threats) to your business, then and only then do you understand your business well enough to start building it.

The same is true for this exercise. You need to go through the process described in this chapter so that you will understand how effective what you have been doing is, understand it enough to know how to integrate social media marketing into it, and finally understand it well enough to know what and how to measure it.

There will be a worksheet available to you in the Chapter 38—Analyze Your Existing Media Strategy section of the companion web site at www .theSocialMediaBible.com or just TSMB2.com.

Identifying Your Existing Media Mediums

To start off, you need to look at *all* of your existing conventional media mediums, whether it's print ads, newspapers, trade journals, trade shows, radio, TV, telemarketing, billboards, door hangers, direct mail, whatever. Lock yourself in your office, turn off the phone (and your cell phone), and start making a list.

Analyze Your Existing Media Strategy

Now that you have a complete list of your entire marketing media, let's take a look at what has been effective and what has not? I am sure you have some feelings about what has been effective, but we need something more tangible than that. Have you been accurately measuring your conventional media?

If not, don't feel bad; nearly no one does, or can, for that matter. In conventional marketing, we almost always use impressions. If you ask any newspaper how they measure the effectiveness of their medium and my advertising dollars, they tell you that for each ad placed, two and a half people per newspaper will view that ad. Do you actually believe that?

In my opinion, half of all printed newspapers go unread. And when read once, they either go into the landfill, the recycle bin, or at the bottom of a birdcage. I don't believe that two and a half people read each newspaper.

The same is true for magazine, radio, and television impressions. When was the last time you sat through and comprehended a television commercial or listened to a radio ad, or studied, let alone reacted, to a newspaper ad?

The next step is a valuable one and takes a little detective work. You will need to go to your accounting software or ask your accountant or accounting department for some numbers.

Expense/Conversion (ROI)

You need to get two numbers: the total amount your company spent last year on sales, marketing, and public relations (PR). Be sure to include all of the hidden costs beyond just what you paid for the media. Include all of the indirect costs such as payroll; add 32 percent for indirect costs associated with payroll such as taxes, sick days, vacation, and so on. Add in all of the travel costs for trade shows, visiting clients and prospects, and other sales and marketing-related activities. Add your lease and rent, telephone, automobile allowances, airfare, hotel, meals. . . . You're getting the picture. Another way of looking at it is to take your total expenses for last year and simply deduct the administrative (and manufacturing if applicable) costs and do not include any social media marketing in this number.

The next number you need is the total number of new customers you acquired last year. How many new customers did you gain for that year? Now, divide the new customers into the total expenses. Now, when you regain consciousness and look at that number, you will realize how incredibly expensive it was for you to acquire just one new customer. This is referred to as the cost-of-customer-acquisition. It is the best way to determine the effectiveness, or ROI (Return on Investment), of your conventional marketing. (Now clear, crumble up, or erase that number before anyone sees it!)

Who Is Doing It?

The next step is to take a serious look at how your marketing is doing, whether it's being executed in-house or out-of-house. If you're a small entrepreneurial company, you're probably doing it all. If you're a Fortune 1000 company, you probably use an outside agency. Take some time right now to seriously question the effectiveness of who's doing it. Is your time better spent on different activities, building your business, other marketing-related projects? Is the marketing and PR company the right choice? Have they done a really good job at a really good cost? Are there activities they are doing that should be brought in-house?

Analyze Your Many Demographics

In this next step, we need to look at *all* of your demographics. Oh, I know, you know your demographic. I am suggesting that you might not. First off, if you refer to it as your demograph*ic* and not in the plural, you don't know who your customers or prospects are. When utilizing social media marketing, one size doesn't fit all. You can try to make one size fit and your customers will look like they're wearing their parents' clothes.

Social media are most effective when you listen to the conversation and participate appropriately. The conversation you have at night with your kids is different from the conversation you had that day with coworkers. The conversation you have with your parents is different from the ones you have at church or hanging out with your friends. Social media conversations are the same.

Identify Your Demographic Groups

If you defined your demographic as male and female between the ages of 25 and 54 with a combined annual income of more than $50,000, that's a *huge* demographic and needs to be treated differently. What will motivate a

25-year-old is completely different from what motivates a 50-year-old. Men and women are different. You've heard of the whole Mars and Venus concept, and different income households buy differently.

They are different because they think differently. Their motivational psychological hot buttons are different and where they participate on the Internet and in which social networks they interact with are different.

There are also different ways that different people communicate. Which of your different demographic groups prefer audio? Which prefer text? Which are using text messaging and Twitter? Who hangs out on Facebook or MySpace? Who loves watching videos? Maybe some, maybe all, maybe different groups prefer different forms of communication, and maybe they overlap. Do they learn through text, audio, visual, or kinesthetic stimuli?

How Many Groups Are There and What Are They?

Take some time to calculate each group. I want you to understand them psychologically. What are they doing right now? What do they do after dinner and on weekends? Do they text? Do they watch video on the mobile phone, their computer, their laptops? Do they listen to podcasts at the gym? Do they even go to the gym?

Break them down into as many categories and subcategories as you can. You will see a pattern emerge. You will see several distinct groups appear. Now, you will better understand how to effectively reach each group with both conventional and social media marketing. Again, it's in the process.

You may discover that you have a category of customers that really do like to participate on Facebook or maybe MySpace. Some, if they're older, might still respond best to direct mail. Keep in mind that the fastest-growing single demographic population in social media is the 54-plus Baby Boomer age group. They also still have the greatest amount of disposable income. You may also have a very mobile 25-to-35 age group that does everything on their mobile phones.

By determining the ROI on each of your different demographic groups, you will suddenly see which form of communication is the most effective for each. When Bill Marriot, the second-generation head and CEO of the Marriott Hotel chain, was asked about why he loves to blog, he said, "I get to communicate directly with my customers. I find out what we are doing right so we can keep doing it, and what we are doing wrong so we can stop it." What terrific wisdom; listen to your customers, keep doing what's right, and stop doing what's wrong.

Determine what you are doing right and keep doing it. Find out what isn't paying off and stop it.

Who Are You?

The final step in this chapter is to closely analyze your communication strategy. Analyze each demographic group, and ask, "Who are you?" What persona are you or your company portraying? Answer the following questions for each demographic group:

- What is the description for the demographic group (for each)
- Who is your persona? (for each)
- What is your style? (for each)
- What is your message? (for each)
- What is your frequency? (for each)
- What is your call to action (conversion)? (for each)

Your persona is important. When you participate in an online conversation, who are you? Are you being Authentic, Transparent, and Sincere? You had better be or you will get flamed. You can still represent your company by being yourself. Someone would much prefer building a relationship with a person rather than a corporation. Most people would prefer buying something from a person and not a corporation.

You may have to change your style of communication with each demographic audience. I significantly change my use of "dude" according to who my audience is. I like using it and it's part of who I am, and I use it more or less freely, depending on my audience.

What has been your persona? If it's been all about features and benefits like we were taught in the 1970s, let it go. If it's been a corporate message, no one is listening, If it's been one of sell, sell, sell, you've been TiVo'd. It's about listening, participating, and being trusted; then they will buy.

Let's go to the next chapter, Step 2—The Social Media Trinity.

The ROI of Social Media

Exploding Book Sales through LinkedIn

Background

With my social media effort, I needed to attract interest in my book without being a pushy salesman, in a short amount of time with little or no expenses.

(continued)

(*continued*)

As a first-time author and unknown brand, the challenge was to gain attention and in the process generate interest in my book. Using LinkedIn to penetrate my market created no hard costs, only time.

Strategy

Sale without selling. Be visible, be controversial, be friendly, be open to get noticed. The target group was pretty wide, a book on creativity can reach across many niches and overall interests. The largest two target groups were business leaders and creative people. Being visible was achieved by answering questions on LinkedIn, posting questions that would draw combative or heated discussion postings by other posters. Being visible was also achieved by being friendly whenever I was able to help someone make a connection, by giving personal advice not posted to the public forums. Being visible was also achieved by being open with answers. The intuitive thinking would be to not give away the store when answering a question publicly but to give them just enough so readers would want to hire you, at which point you give a whole answer to the question. I found that the more advice I gave, the more I became visible and had an increase in connection requests.

Each tactic was taken without "selling" my book, but providing an opportunity for someone to discover my book when reading my posts.

Implementation

Online shops were set up on the publisher's site, my site, and major bookseller sites. I joined or created groups for members who might have an interest in my book.

Opportunity

To present me, the author, as legitimate, caring, and forthright; which makes post readers comfortable enough to relate that to how my book might be and is being worth buying.

Conclusion

Within two months, there was a 15,000 percent increase in hits to my web site, Amazon could not keep the book in stock and major booksellers like Borders and Barnes & Noble could not get the book reordered fast enough to keep up with demand. According to Alexa, my site is rated in the top 14 percent of all globally tracked web sites. By the end of the fourth month, my site had a Google ranking of four. There was a peripheral relation as well. One guest blog post I did for a site generated a 1,000 percent increase in traffic to their site.

Traffic generated: 40 percent of all traffic generated now is direct traffic, which means they go straight to my site because visitors either know the URL or have it bookmarked. Thirty percent of traffic is generated by referring sites, which means other sites are linking to mine from theirs. Thirty percent of traffic comes directly from Search Engine searches for things related to me or my book.

Gary Unger, Author
www.garyunger.com

Expert Insight

Chris Pirillo, geek and technology enthusiast, www.chris.pirillo.com

Chris Pirillo

. . . Every year something new pops up onto my radar; and a couple of years ago, it was the ability to livestream without really paying anything other than your ISP, so I thought, "Hey, why not!" . . .

. . . [Usually in the beginning of the interview, I'll just say, "Can you tell us a little bit about yourself" but I wanted the listeners to get a full appreciation of who Chris Pirillo is. So I threw out a few statistics: "You've recorded over a thousand videos in the past year, you cracked the Top One Hundred Most Subscribed throughout the whole of YouTube, your live stats are more impressive, with five million unique video viewers watching Chris do his thing in 2007 with a total of two-plus million live viewer hours with an average viewing of 25 minutes per visitor. This past August, your live video feeds recorded 279,000 viewer hours with over a million viewers; 827,000 unique viewers; 395 average viewers, and 707 hours of live broadcasting! In addition, in the first seven days of launching your Web community for geeks, you logged in 587,000 page views. I mean, this stuff is unbelievable and here's one that is just totally cool because it's so simplistic; you are the Number One hit on Google for the word "Chris." Now how cool is that?]

. . . Mostly that particular statistic will hold true for the duration of my life, I don't know. . . . There's only one place to head, and that's down, after you're [the] Number One "Chris" on Google; although I haven't had it happen yet. I'm praying that they never change their algorithms or another more important "Chris" potentially comes along and usurps my position. . . .

(continued)

(*continued*)

. . . I turned a personality disorder into a career, as I have been prone to say. There's really no one thing that I do. I'm an omni-geek, so some might call me; someone who has just always been attracted to technology, much like a bug may be attracted to a light hanging on the porch in the middle of summer.

Sometimes it works pretty well for me and other times not so much. Umm, but I'm a content publisher, I help other people publish content and now have gotten more and more into increasing and sharing my own video experiences when they're live or, of course, recorded on YouTube.

The direction that I have been going is just largely just being myself. I enjoy talking about technology during the sharing of information; and when that's directly with people like myself, or specifically in talking directly to companies either on a sponsorship level, or specifically, a consultancy. . . .

. . . When I started online, there really weren't a lot of pools to facilitate community building; it hadn't really grown. Today, those tools are plentiful. There are plenty of ways that you can build communities and draw people in to the things that you are interested in, and help build their interest and their experiences with you. The hope in community building is that you feel less and less alone in this world, and no matter your background and the chances of some other people sharing your similar interests, or similar enough, are pretty strong.

You know, the Internet is a big place and community ebbs and flows, but certainly the one thing that you're obviously going to have going for you is yourself. So as long as you are honest with yourself and with your friends and the people who are not yet your friends, the chances of you maintaining a level of integrity on an ongoing basis (no matter if the tools are not where you're at) are pretty strong.

It's all about being honest and direct and that really is. . . . It's not so much in the area of community building; it's just more in being (I guess) a good communicator in general. . . .

. . . Well, you can't talk about something if you don't know what you are talking about. . . . When people do that it's pretty obvious that they are just either a hired gun, hired talent, or shouldn't be doing the things that they are supposedly doing. . . .

. . . People come and opportunities come in a multitude of directions; and certainly I started cultivating a lot of it back in 1992, but unofficially (at least in the commercial path) in 1996. From that point forward, you know, it was kind of an uphill battle because I was left to my own devices. This was long before social networking was a word and we had other services like Facebook and MySpace and Twitter; and you name any one of those services that are really there to help give anybody a voice to share with the rest of the world. And, of course, that came not long after blogging.

I've surveyed the landscape of these services efficiently. There is always something new to look at. And so I look at all of these resources and being able to leverage my own knowledge and passions against these resources to reach the same people or potentially new people, is really kind of key to, I think, any success for community building.

It's not just being there, it's really getting what the tool is and where it fits, specifically in your modus operandi. I was doing all this stuff before I had started to work on a radio show as a host; and before I had done a stint at Tech TV. Some people believe that I got my start at Tech TV and they really don't know me at all [Laughter], if that's the case. And it usually is. They seem to believe that everything came because of Tech TV, but . . . Tech TV only happened because of everything that was done before that, including writing books, sending out newsletters, and doing community building a lot on my own. . . .

. . . I've been working with CNN.com, doing a live segment every week, and carte blanche in terms of the content part, but I'm looking to involve myself a little deeper with CNN.com as the tech expert. And that only came about because of everything else I am doing. So one thing builds on top of another, on top of another, on top of another. . . .

. . . If something couldn't be entertaining, why would anybody watch it? I mean that it should be informational and entertaining at the same time. I approached the classroom in much the same way when I was student teaching. I am a teacher by degree, but never actually became one in any kind of school.

Even if I've got my livestream going and nothing's going on and all that the people are doing is staring at the back of my head or listening to whatever I'm listening to, or whatever . . . then at least I've got a chat room that's integrated with the experience.

So even if I cannot be entertaining, well maybe I can be informative. . . .

. . . The airline safety instructions was the first video I uploaded to YouTube and it made it to the front page of YouTube. . . . It was three months into it, but it made it to the front page.

You know, I've been recording video since I could. I used to record videos, I'm pretty sure, on a Sony Mavica here and used a later series to actually record videos onto a floppy disc.

. . . And I was like, "Oh wow, I can record videos! This is so cool!" Of course, they were stamp-sized but they were still good. . . .

. . . Umm, you know, in respect, to livestreaming, I seldom move the camera. I usually play the Xbox 360. I just started to bring my laptop in there and then I switched the stream over to that. But usually I only keep one camera on, and I can leave the room at any time and not feel obligated to take the camera with me.

(continued)

(continued)

Umm, and because of that, I have set out that particular boundary. Some people violate that particular boundary, you know, whether they share personal information about myself that I would rather not have shared, like a phone number or what-have-you . . . anything like that, you know. But for the most part, I'm in control. My wife Ponzi can now watch . . . keep an eye on me throughout the day. Hey, you know, what wife would not want that? . . .

. . . It's all about sponsorship and those kinds of partnerships. And certainly other things come from it as well. Whether it's me, or Valunet . . . that's just the direction I've followed and that kind of stuff follows me.

Certainly sponsors have been extremely supportive in the things that I try to do and that's . . . not an uphill battle, necessarily, but since my model is usually a little different I have to, kind of, ride the cusp between what they're used to and what I think the next step is going to be. You know, it usually works out pretty well. . . .

. . . Usually I come up with a wacky idea that works and then find a way to underwrite it with the sponsor, and that's how it goes. I have never been asked to go out and speak on community building by any one of those companies. I would certainly welcome it, but I've never had the opportunity.

If it's kind of how my career path is going, and an opportunity will come up, and do I have the time and it's something that I'm interested in and will it be fun, . . . then I will give it a shot. . . .

. . . I love saving money and, more importantly, I love helping people save money, which I've done over and over and over and over again; and everybody loves to find a good coupon . . . and so now people will e-mail me and say, "Hey, I'm thinking about buying Product X. Do you have a coupon for it?" and I go find one. And then just sharing it with them, I share it with the rest of the world.

And so because of that, I'm able to close that loop between myself and the community and also create a value-add for everybody else. So, yeah, I like posting a lot of coupons on the blog. . . .

. . . Locker Gnome is what started it all on LockerGnome.com and that's still around. Now, well I guess, trying to build it into a blog network and a community and beyond. But unfortunately a lot of the platform choices out there are really limiting. I tried a lot, but unfortunately they're really, really expensive or really, really impossible to work with. So I try to find the "sweet spot" in the middle that I can give people a voice and give them a chance to get paid for what they know, like blogging. . . .

To listen to or read the entire Executive Conversation with Chris Pirillo, go to www .theSocialMediaBible.com

Conclusion

We discussed in this chapter the process of really analyzing your existing media, what you are currently doing to touch your customers, the definition and importance of ROI and the cost of customer acquisition. We also discussed your persona, how you communicate with your customers, the frequency, your message, and your call to action or conversation strategy.

Determining your ROI and cost of customer acquisition is more than an exercise. This process will be critical when you get to Step 4, Chapter 41, Identify Resources. The answers you get in this chapter will identify what you are currently doing that is effective and is returning a good ROI and what isn't. As Bill Marriott, the CEO of Marriott Hotels, says about his blog, "It will tell you what you are doing right so you can keep doing it and what you are doing wrong so you can stop."

Credits

The ROI of Social Media was provided by:

Gary Unger, author, www.garyunger.com

Expert Insight was provided by:

Chris Pirillo, geek and technology enthusiast, www.chris.pirillo.com

CHAPTER 39

The Social Media Trinity

We discuss in this chapter the importance of the Social Media Trinity: Blogging, Microblogging (Twitter), and Social Networks. Chapter 7—The Ubiquitous Blog, discusses blogs quite thoroughly, while Chapter 14—Thumbs Up for Microblogging discusses Twitter and other microblogs (mobile text message communication that is limited to 140 characters), and Chapter 2—Say Hello to Social Networking discusses social networks. Here, I want you to understand the importance of these three chapters and their associated technologies. If you understand the Social Media Trinity, you will have a good understanding of 90 percent of everything you need to be successful using social media in your marketing strategy.

At the risk of being redundant, I am going to list many of the particular features of each of these three technologies so you can go back and read or learn more. Let's start with blogs.

Trinity Number One—Blogs

As I discussed in Chapter 7, blogs are an integral component to social media marketing. Blogs help you and your company build a trusted following, allow you to brand yourself in a strong environment, get you and your brand in front of your audience automatically, and frequently, set you up as a perceived industry thought leader.

Get to know the five Ws of blogging: the Who, What, Where, When, Why, and How. The *Who* is two-fold: Who within your organization is the right person to blog on your company's behalf. Who likes to communicate through the use of text? Who would be willing to take the responsibility of blogging for your company? The second Who is who else is blogging about your industry out in the blogosphere?

The *What* is what are they blogging about? What should you blog about? What does your customer want to read? The *Where* is where will your blog reside? On another's web site, such as Blogger.com, or on your own URL with a blogging platform like WordPress. (Hint: The answer is on your server.)

The *When* is when are you going to blog? How often will you post new material? The *Why* is in Chapter 7 and this chapter; and the *How* is how will you find the time to do this? You'll learn more about this in Chapter 41— Identify Resources.

Understand the Terms

If you want to be successful at integrating blogging into your existing marketing strategy, you need to understand the jargon of the genre. Get familiar with terms such as: Posting, Publishing, RSS feeds (Chapter 18— RSS: Really Simple Syndication Made Simple), Tags, and so on. The more you become familiar with these terms, the better you'll understand how to take full advantage of all of the benefits of blogging.

Identify Your Tools

You will need to decide where your blog is going to reside. You can use other people's platforms to base your blog on because they're free, easy to use, but you don't get SEO (Search Engine Optimization) advantages. I discuss more about this further on. Choose an easy-to-use platform such as WordPress and have it installed on your root directory directly on your web site. WordPress is free. It's open source, so many developers are working on it from around the world, there are more widgets and plug-ins (which give it additional capabilities), and it takes about 15 minutes to download from WordPress .org, and ftp upload it to your web site. Whatever ISP or web hosting service you use, such as GoDaddy or BlueHost, they will do it for you while you are on their tech support phone line.

Identify Your Content

If you want to be successful at blogging, the first thing you must have is a strong What's in It For Me angle, or WIIFM, or you can add, IDKT (I Didn't Know That). You've heard me preaching about this throughout this bible. So now that we have established that, you need to consider how you will best convey those thoughts. Of course, there will be text, but also consider the photos you will use. What touches the psychological hot buttons of your reader? People love to look at photos, so give them some. Include one, two, or three photos in your blog, and if you have more photos that your readers can look at, give them a link. Put your photos up on a photo sharing site such as Flickr and share them with your blog readers.

Create and add links to podcasts and video. This adds interest and good content. Your readers would much prefer looking at you in a video explaining your thoughts than just reading them. Make it fun, interactive, and rich in content.

Identify Plug-Ins and Widgets

Take a look around at the plethora of plug-ins and widgets that can be added to your blog site to give it more capabilities. It really is amazing. If you can think of it, there probably is a plug-in or widget for it.

For my TheSocialMediaBible.com web site I wanted to add a countdown timer to when the book would be released. There was a plug-in for that. On my www.LonSafko.com web site, I wanted to add an unlimited number of my personal quotes, which would rotate randomly. I found a plug-in for that. A WordPress blogging platform is in many ways much more versatile and component rich than a standard HTML web site, and it's easy, and it's free.

SEO Advantages

By running your blog directly off your own web site (in your root directory), you can take advantage of a great deal of SEO perks. The two I like the best are Google Juice and Link Love.

Google Juice is a fun term that means the number of links to web (or blog) pages that Google has indexed in its search engine that refers to you, your company, and your web site. In the world of SEO, there are an estimated 140 different tests that each search engine performs on every web page to determine where in the rankings that web site or web page should reside. Each test is weighted and some math is applied and your web page gets a ranking from one to nine. Google Juice, or the number of links to your web pages along with the page rank, will push you higher on the SERP, or Search Engine Reply Pages.

By creating a lot of blogs, you are creating a lot of different web pages for the search engines to find and to index. Also, blog pages get a significantly higher priority than does a standard HTML web page. Here's the reason.

The only purpose for a search engine is to return the most relevant results for your query. The better the results, the happier you will be using that search engine. The Google indexing algorithm is the best in the industry. It's what gave them the advantage over Yahoo! even though Yahoo! has a few years' head start in the search engine business.

So, when you ask Google (or any search engine) for the most relevant pages to your query, should it return blog pages, which by definition are new, timely, and fresh, or web pages that probably haven't been updated in two years? It's the blog pages.

When I was first doing the research for the blog chapter back in 2007, I wrote a blog about when Subway sued Quiznos for defamation of sandwich. See my blogs for the story. I wanted to see how Google indexed my blog page. With a strong background in SEO, I knew that a standard web page could take as much as 12 to 14 days for Google to find and index my new page.

Thirty minutes later, Google sent me a Google alert that my blog page had been indexed. Thirty minutes instead of 12 to 14 days! I then wanted to see how well it was indexed. I chose not to use my name in the search query. I am the only Lon Safko there is and already have about 158,000 references to me personally on Google. I went to Google and entered the terms *Subway, Quiznos,* and *social media.* I wanted to see if those terms would deliver good results.

The term *Quiznos* had about 585,000 SERPs, while *Subway* had 33,700,000 (mostly because of the underground rail system), and *social media* had about 185,000,000, none of which should have taken you to my page. In December 2007, I ranked first place, second place, and fourth place on the Google search results. And the last time I checked, in March of 2010, I still held first, second, and fourth position for the terms.

As a result of this occurrence back in 2007, I formatted my web site hard drive (completely erased), all 102 pages, and recreated my entire web site using only the WordPress blogging platform. Now, any time I create a new blog, a new page, or just update a page, I get priority search engine rankings.

I don't recommend that you erase your entire corporate web site, but I do strongly recommend that you add a WordPress blog for the same results.

RSS and Readers

There are a lot of other technical reasons for creating and maintaining a blog. Having your blog pages automatically delivered to your customers and prospects every time you create a new blog is priceless. By providing an RSS button so your followers can click and have your updates delivered to their reader or an e-mail notification be sent within seconds of your new blog post is unbelievable.

Interconnection

And with many of the new tools such as ZooLoo, Google Buzz, and others, you can directly interconnect your blogs with your Facebook, e-mail, Twitter, and social bookmarking sites.

Blogging Conclusion

Determine your strategy, your conversion, your persona, develop a strategy for your content, frequency, and type of interaction. Make your blog posts full of hyperlinks to interactive rich media, with photos, audio, and video, and interconnect with all of your other community social networking sites.

Trinity Number Two—Microblogging (Twitter)

Everyone is talking about Twitter. Ashton Kutcher is challenging Larry King, Ashton and Ellen DeGeneres have more followers than the combined populations of Ireland, Norway, and Panama, and Oprah has more than 1,000,000 followers. This is all reason enough to take Twitter's capabilities seriously.

If you don't fully understand microblogging (Twitter), and have begun using it, now is a good time to go back and read Chapter 14—Thumbs Up for Microblogging. As with the previous Trinity category, you need to get into the five Ws: Who, What, Where, When, Why, and How, again.

The *Who* is who in your organization will be tweeting and managing your Twitter account. Microblogging also has a second who and that is, who is out there in your industry who is tweeting? Identify some of the thought leaders in your industry and follow them. See what they have to say. Look at the number of followers they have. Look at how many people are following them. Look at the frequency and the content of their tweets. Are they providing their customers with a good WIIFM or IDKT?

The *What* is, what are those leaders tweeting about. What do your customers want in their tweets. The *Where?* The Where is any place you can tweet: the office, the coffee shop, the airport, at home, but *not* while driving. . . .

The *When* is as often as you have good content. If you are going to use Twitter for business, please don't tell me your plane is late, or you're having bacon with your eggs, or the sunset is pretty. I will un-follow you as fast as my thumbs can move. On my personal account, that's okay. On my business account, not so much.

The *Why* is because I want you to amass as many customers and prospects as Ashton and Ellen. The *How* is right here.

Coming to Terms

You need to understand the basic vocabulary of microbloging: Following, Followers, Tweets, ReTweets, Direct, Hash Tags, and so on. Hash Tags are particularly useful, so be sure to understand them.

You will also need to identify the right tools. Twitter is the most popular microblogging platform, while there are others, such as Yammer, which can be used behind your firewall for internal use only; Tumblr, which combines microblogging, blogging, aggregation, and social network integration, and Twitpic, which lets you upload a photo and post the shortened URL for that photo you tweet.

Manage the Tweets

Part of the responsibility of participating on Twitter is its management. Once you begin to play, it's good to stay in the game. You need to do some cyber surveillance. This sounds all CIA-ish, but just means monitoring what's being said about you and participating in that conversation. People *are* talking about you, it's not the schizophrenia talking. People are having conversations about you, your company, and your brand.

There are quite a few really good tools out there to manage the tweets. Applications such as Tweetdeck and Seesmic Desktop are great. You can download them for free and they all work on Windows, Mac, and Linux operating systems. Either of these apps will let you see all of the tweets from every one of your followers, see all of your direct messages, allow you to send messages, and provide a great search capability much like Google Alerts, in which you can set up search terms such as your name, your company name, product names and so forth. Then, anytime, anywhere in the world, someone tweets about you, you get a copy of the message at the same time the recipient does.

There are other helpful tools such as URL shorteners such as Bit.ly and Tr.im. these allow you to put in a large URL and it assigns a small, usually 4 character URL to paste into your tweet so as not to hog up your 140 characters with one URL.

Determine Your Strategy

As has been stated before, you need to determine your strategy. Are you going to use Twitter to sell, educate, add value for your followers, create personal interaction to build trust, or the always-present brand awareness? The answer is "all of the above" and more.

As with all communications with your customers, you have to provide that strong WIIFM content and be the cognoscenti of your frequency. As long as the content is good, the frequency on Twitter is better high, unlike e-mail, in which if the frequency is too high, people will unsubscribe. This is because it's only 140 characters, about 5 seconds to comprehend, which is a small investment of time.

Here's another friendly reminder: Do not sell on Twitter. Don't spam Twitter. Build trust, let your customer get to know you, stay in front of them, and when they are ready to buy, they will.

Trinity Number Three—Social Networks

The third and last part of the Trinity of Social Media is Social Networks. Now is a good time to reread Chapter 2—Say Hello to Social Networking.

Once again, it is in your best interest to understand the five Ws—Who, What, Where, When, Why, How. The *Who* is you, or someone who can manage the social network site. That person needs to stay active, participate, kick out advertisers and spammers, post new content, and have a social presence.

The *What* is your content. You are building a friendly web site that uses you as the representative of your company. Understand what persona you are going to use. It should be much different from the persona you use when you are interfacing with college classmates, or the teen you dated in high school.

The *When* is now. The earlier you get a presence and a following the better. The *Why* is because any time you have a "watering hole" (a marketing term for a place that like-minded customers and prospects gather), with 425,000,000 members, you need to be there. You need to be available to participate in that conversation. If Facebook were a country, it would be the second-largest country in the world, exceeding the 309,409,364 total population of the United States. For the *How*, reread Chapter 2 and read on.

What Are the Terms

Again, with each of the three technologies described in this chapter, you will need to understand the vocabulary. You need to understand what a profile, group, fan page, in-mail, questions, and so forth are. That's your homework assignment.

Identify the Tools (Sites)

You really need to have a profile on most every social network site you've ever heard of. Why not? It's free and if you don't sign up for your account, someone will eventually take your name, either because it's theirs also, or on purpose to sell back to you later when you realize the importance of it. It's easy to do. Use Open Social and with one click, your new profile is completely filled in using the information from an existing social networking site.

Facebook—Fastest-growing U.S. network, with more than 425 million members

LinkedIn—Professional network

MySpace—Becoming more of an entertainment network

Ning—Usually themed within a niche or interest

Plaxo—Large alternate to Facebook

Others—Which are the right ones for your demographic? If you've heard of it, go sign up.

Determining the Strategy

As with the other categories, you will need to develop your strategy for interaction. Play with each network to help you understand the culture of that network and how the members interact. Each network is different, with a different basic purpose: Facebook to interact on a personal basis; LinkedIn to provide an online individual directory; MySpace, music and entertainment; Ning, to create your own vertical niche social networking site. Then refer to all of the strategy advice from this section; determine the frequency of participation, listen before you speak, provide strong content, and never sell.

The ROI of Social Media

Adobe Asks Students, "Is it Real or Fake?"

Background

College students are a vital audience for the long-term success of Adobe. These are the future creative professionals who will buy Adobe products like Photoshop and Illustrator. It's essential that they be exposed to them when they are young, so they will want to use them when they enter the workforce. They also happen to be incredibly skeptical of marketing. Adobe engaged Traction to break through to this challenging target.

Strategy

Create relevant value. Clever advertising wasn't enough for Adobe to successfully reach this challenging audience. They had to provide relevant value—relevant to the audience, relevant to the brand, and relevant to the medium through which our message would be delivered. The Millennial audience was the first to grow up with technology as a ubiquitous part of their lives. They were not afraid of it and we had to respect them. The brand's flagship product was Photoshop—a tool that gives users powerful capabilities to manipulate photos. The medium was Facebook, where our audience was spending an average of 22 minutes a day at the time. It was an entertaining diversion for our target and the value we would provide would be an entertaining diversion as well.

Implementation

Seizing upon the cultural insight that Photoshop was famous for faking photos (think Sarah Palin in a bikini holding an assault rifle), Traction created a Facebook game called "Real or Fake?" that challenged users to guess if a series of images were real or fake? If the answer was "fake," a tab popped up that provoked users to "See how we did it" and showed them a brief tutorial of how to use Adobe products to create the effect in the image.

Opportunity

The opportunity was threefold. One was to provide a simple, yet compelling brand experience that would re-engage audiences again and again. The second was to educate while we entertain— the potential to make players feel like experts and thus have a greater emotional investment with the brand. Finally, there was the opportunity to drive sales. Adobe had terrific student-only pricing offers for this audience designed to make their products affordable to future customers. By engaging audiences again and again, we were able to expose them to offers again and again.

Results

Adobe "Real or Fake?" garnered results on all three opportunities. First, 40 percent of people who played the game returned to the site to play again. Twenty-one percent of game plays resulted in players experiencing a tutorial and another 6 percent clicked to check out the offer.

Adam Kleinberg
CEO, tractionco.com

Expert Insight

Michael Naef, CEO and cofounder, Doodle, www.doodle.ch/main.html

Michael Naef

Doodle takes the pain out of scheduling. It helps people find a common date and time for their next conference call, project meeting, business lunch, family reunion, barbeque—any group event. It focuses on delivering a very simple and usable service, which is free to end users. . . .

The service was conceived and implemented in 2003 and the idea for it was born from my personal need. I wanted to schedule dinner with some friends. The process of finding the right time was very inefficient, involved a great number of e-mails. So I concluded that there has to be an easier, more efficient way, and implemented Doodle. The service attracted a large and growing user base quickly. In 2006, I decided to professionalize the service, so Paul Sevinç and I decided to found the company that still runs Doodle. . . .

We launched the service in Switzerland, but our biggest growth is outside Switzerland. Doodle is used in many countries worldwide and is translated into 30 languages. What's interesting is that almost all of these translations are the work of volunteers from these various countries. . . .

Translations are important to our users. We provide a very simple service, and one could think that it's okay to have it in English only, but it's important to have it in the local language of the people who are using it. Our target audience is not only the Internet professional, but everyday people who might not be familiar with an English application. . . .

Localization is very important and I think that as a Switzerland-based company we are in a perfect position for that, considering that Switzerland is a country with four official languages. We are quite used to providing just about everything in several languages. . . .

People are using Doodle for all kinds of use cases, both for business and private events like family reunions, ski weekends (in Switzerland, obviously), et cetera. Our users appreciate Doodle's simplicity, high usability, and low entry barrier. They don't have to download anything or even register for the service. These factors have contributed to our high number of users; we're currently reaching way more than five million each month. . . .

The typical use case is that the event organizer visits our site and creates a poll of sorts, which offers a number of dates to choose from. Then the organizer receives a unique web link provided by Doodle, which he or she can send to the event participants. The participants use that link, then, to access the poll and indicate their availability. The organizer uses the same link to monitor the poll's progress and determine the best option at the end. That's it, in a nutshell. This explains that Doodle is a scheduling service . . . not a calendar. It connects with calendars, however, providing the missing link between people who use electronic calendars, paper-based, or none at all. . . . Many of our more experienced users connect Doodle with their calendars to help them schedule even more efficiently. They can set up and participate in polls in the context of their calendar information, and they can book tentative and final appointments directly to their calendar. . . .

Because Doodle itself is not a calendar, we are not competing with companies like Google or Microsoft or Notes and their respective calendars. We help them coordinate the process of finding the dates and time. . . .

We have loads of user success stories and some of them are listed as testimonials on our web site. I just had a call from one user who said that, "My work is driven by conference calls, and it is a pain to arrange an appropriate time among several parties. We have ended this heartache and trouble with this brilliant polling system." This is the type of feedback that we get. There are also people telling us that they're using Doodle to schedule a meeting with people at seven different hospitals where they need a hundred percent attendance, and they're very happy with our service because it allows them to schedule a meeting and coordinate and accommodate the time usually within minutes. . . .

We offer. . . . time zone support, which is easily activated when creating a new scheduling poll. If activated, Doodle will display the times in the time zones of each participant so they get their time correct automatically. . . .

We also offer users some social media tools. Doodle integrates with all major calendars like Microsoft Outlook, Google Calendar, Lotus Notes, iCal. Integrating Doodle with your calendar will make your scheduling experience even more efficient and seamless. It will help you determine your available times easily, book your appointments automatically, and help you prevent double bookings. We also offer integrations into a number of social networks and portal sites like Facebook, Xing, and iGoogle. And we provide a number of APIs to help developers implement their own extensions or integrations. . . .

So how do we monetize all this? We currently have three revenue streams: One is based on advertising and monetizes the free service. The other two are based on paid services. One is called *Branded Doodle;* it allows an enterprise or other forms of organizations to run their own Doodle, hosted on our servers, with their branding, additional features, and security options. The other one is called *Premium Doodle* and offers a similar feature set to private individuals. Both paid services are subscription-based. . . .

To listen to our interview or read the entire Executive Conversation with Michael Naef, go to www.theSocialMediaBible.com.

Conclusion

We discussed in this chapter the importance of the Social Media Trinity. If you know these three categories, you know enough to really make an impact for you and your company's marketing and brand recognition. These three categories are the most effective way to build a following and build trust. I may require a little homework, but the juice will be worth the squeeze.

Credits

The ROI of Social Media was provided by:

Adam Kleinberg, CEO, tractionco.com

Expert Insight was provided by:

Michael Naef, CEO and cofounder, Doodle, www.doodle.ch/main.html

CHAPTER 40

Integrate Strategies

Integrate Your Existing Strategy into the Trinity

The third step in your Five Steps to Social Media Success is Integration. This is when you take all of what you learned from Step 1, Analyze Your Existing Media, filter out what is ineffective with a low ROI, what you learned in Step 2, the Social Media Trinity, and combine the two into one integrated cohesive marketing strategy. Remember, social media isn't a stand-alone set of tools that must be dealt with as a separate strategy. It has to be integrated.

I am often asked when consulting with Fortune 1000 companies, "Does my company need to do social media marketing?" or "How much should my company spend on social media marketing?" I say, remove the term *social media* and ask those questions again: "Does my company need to do marketing?" or "How much should my company spend on marketing?" When put that way, it sounds silly. Just like in the previous chapter, you will now need to develop an integrated strategy that includes your existing conventional marketing and the new digital tools.

Selecting the Best of Both

When you develop your integrated marketing strategy, you will need to identify the best media for each demographic. Sometimes it will be conventional marketing tools such as selling RVs to the retired; direct mail might still be the best way to reach your targeted demographic. Sometimes it might be a combination such as selling RVs to the retired. The fastest-growing demographic is the 54-plus-year-old. Or sometimes it might be just social media such as selling RVs to the retired, as Facebook's fastest-growing and most active population is the 54-plus-year-old.

Remember that when you craft your message, it will be different for each medium you use. The copy in a newspaper article will be significantly different from a tweet or what you post in a blog. They're different audiences even if they are the same people. When we're hanging out drinking a beer, I would expect your language to be different from when you come over for Thanksgiving with the family. Remember your audience, the platform (be it conventional or social media), the culture, and the rules within that environment.

Develop Clear Individual Goals (Conversions)

When you craft your message it has to have a clear call to action: clear goals, or conversions. The whole reason you are participating in that conversion is to build trust to sell. Be sure each message meets a predetermined definition for conversion. Here are some examples:

- Increase revenue through e-commerce
- Collect user-generated content
- Increase web traffic
- Product or service awareness
- Loyalty and peer support
- Collaboration
- Innovation (ideas)
- Promote events
- Sale or closeout
- Reduce tech support
- Increase e-mail subscriptions
- Drive telephone sales
- Build brand awareness

Develop one call to action (conversion) per message, especially when using e-mail. More than one call to action per message will confuse and weaken your conversion.

Quality Content, Not Quality Production

As I mentioned in the earlier chapter, you, me, and your customers have become pro-sumers, professional consumers. We know that if a company spends a quarter-million dollars to produce a television commercial, there has to be a hidden agenda, some psychological hot buttons being pushed to get us to do something, which is convert. As a result we subconsciously tune out polished expensive advertisement productions. We, the people, want content, not polished agendas.

Our messages still need to be professional-looking without typos, but the overall quality can and should be lower. Even a hi-def video uploaded to YouTube (regular account), looks pretty bad once YouTube uploads and degrades it for distribution. We are accustomed to it. A blog should be 400 words without typos, and an image or two, with a few hyperlinks. Most videos on YouTube are shot with inexpensive video cameras and flip phones. That's what we want. The days of the glossy one-sheet and B-roll are over. Embrace it.

Integrate Existing Conventional and New Digital

I have been talking so far about integrating the two technologies: conventional media and social media into different demographic groups. Now I need you to take it one step further by integrating each of them into each other.

Here are some examples:

- Place all of your major social network links on your stationery, your sales literature, and your business cards. Use the little chicklets (small avatar-type icons that represent those companies).

- Put your Twitter account on your business card. If you want people to follow you, you have to tell them how. A few years ago, if you wanted people to call you, you made it easy for them. Do the same thing with social media.

- Create a social media interactive e-mail signature. Put all of your social media addresses in your e-mail signature. Or, if you think that looks too cluttered, put all of them in your Google profile and put the link to your Google profile in your e-mail signature. I am surprised (shocked) at how many people still don't use an e-mail signature, let alone include their social addresses. Are you trying to keep them a secret?

- This is one where I get everybody, is your web address on your return mailing label? Why not? The post office doesn't care. They ignore it. Do name, street, city, state, zip, and URL. Put your web address everywhere.

- Is your Twitter web address in all of your print advertising?

- Is your blog address on your brochure and business cards? You do want people to read them and follow you, right?

- Do you tell your customers your web address in company voicemail? They are on hold, they have one hand free, tell them to use it to go to your web site while they are waiting.
- Is your URL and Twitter account watermarked on your videos? Do you mention them in your podcasts?
- Do you mention your blog address in your podcasts and videos? Is it in your e-mails?
- Do you print your web address on your brochures and in your direct mail pieces with a "Visit Us at . . ." or "Follow us on @YourName"?
- Is your blog address with a hyperlink in every one of your e-mails?
- Do you mention your Twitter address in your blogs in which you microblog tweets with the address to your social networks that display your web address, where they can download your product PDF that contains your telephone number, from which they can call you to find out your address? I think you're getting the picture.

Is all of this making you think a little differently?

The ROI of Social Media

Hotels Use Twitter to Increase Revenue, Customer Service

Background

Provenance Hotel Group owns and operates five boutique hotels in Portland, Seattle/Tacoma, and Nashville. Because of the economic conditions in late 2008, the hotel was looking for additional sources of revenue and traffic. Social media was the quick answer, as it was a hot new buzz/trend that didn't carry huge startup costs. The barrier to entry was minimal because there were few hotels doing anything noteworthy or extraordinary, so there was an opportunity to jump on Twitter and create a name for Provenance and its hotels, Hotel Lucia (Portland), Hotel de Luxe (Portland), Hotel Max (Seattle), Hotel Murano (Tacoma), and Hotel Preston (Nashville).

Strategy

Anvil was to create Twitter accounts and provide Twitter training to the key contacts at each hotel so they understood what it was, how to use it, and why we were using it. Once they understood the potential, each contact began creating tweets based on events, deals, packages, free giveaways, random thoughts, and so forth for their respective hotels. We quickly noticed two big opportunities. The first was folks looking for hotel recommendations. These folks were immediately tweeted back, offering a special Twitter rate to stay at a Provenance hotel in that area. This started a conversation and established credibility for the hotels. The second opportunity was more of a customer service/concierge role in which guests were asking questions about the hotel, restaurants, dog parks, and so on. Anvil worked directly with the hotels to provide answers to these people as well. Many times it helped solidify a booking, or made the difference between a great stay and an okay stay. Customer service will always win over guests.

Implementation

Anvil worked with a design company to create unique Twitter accounts for each hotel, as well as include social media icons on each hotel's web site to increase visibility. Anvil then worked with each hotel to create a process for Twitter, which included an editorial calendar and a process for reviewing tweets.

http://twitter.com/hotel_deluxe

http://twitter.com/hotel_lucia

http://twitter.com/hotel_max

http://twitter.com/hotel_murano

http://twitter.com/hotel_preston

Opportunity

The opportunity was to drive increased revenue through a special Twitter follower rate, increase the credibility of the hotel among the social media community by building trust, and providing top-notch customer service.

Conclusion

Since the Twitter strategy has been rolled out, Anvil and Provenance have seen huge success, coming in many different forms. Each hotel is consistently booking rooms through Twitter (and a special 15 percent Twitter rate code) on a monthly basis, as well as building credibility for working so hard to engage and communicate with the Twitter community. Provenance has been recognized for its efforts, with Provenance getting mentioned in a CBS News Travel article (and CBS *Early Show* video). Additionally, Provenance has received mentions on industry-relevant blogs like Hotel Interactive (specifically for their Facebook campaigns) and Hotel Marketing Strategies due to activity on Twitter (Anvil helps cross-promote blog posts and Facebook through Twitter).

(continued)

(*continued*)

John McPhee
Web site URLs:
www.hoteldeluxeportland.com
www.hotellucia.com
www.hotelmaxseattle.com
www.hotelmuranotacoma.com
www.hotelpreston.com

Expert Insight

Bill Jula, CEO and founder, Fast Pitch!, www.fastpitchnetworking.com

Bill Jula

. . . I graduated from the University of Florida in the mid-1990s, and went on to get a master's degree at the University of Kentucky. I then took a job in Major League Baseball with the Tampa Bay Devil Rays for a season, doing some sales and marketing.

Then I really got into the world of technology. I met up with a couple of colleagues of mine from the University of Florida, moving down here to where we're located right now with Fast Pitch! here in Sarasota, Florida, just south of Tampa. We're doing some very high-end Web development kind of stuff for ERP systems such as SAP, PeopleSoft, and different systems like that. And that's what really got me involved in technology, truly understanding it, and, more importantly, with my background being more of the marketing side of things, how to market a company that's involved in the Internet age.

From there, I worked in a couple of different capacities with a couple of different companies, eventually breaking off and starting to do my own thing with Fast Pitch! It initially started out in 2003 as a networking event company where we did what we called at the time "Speed Networking" events. It's like a "Speed Dating" concept, but for business people. To my knowledge, we were the only company in the world where we actually had these events going in about 20 different states at any one time. I had different people contracted out around the country hosting these events on a regular basis. It was my technology background and my marketing background, but the experience of dealing with literally thousands of business professionals around the country, that led to the creation of what Fast Pitch! is now, which is an online business network for professionals. And a lot of that experience that we had, one-on-one, with a lot of the people that we connected with in all these different states and cities has lead to the creation of a tool set and the feature set that we developed that's unlike any other network on the market right now. . . .

. . . First of all, we're obviously excited about some of the accolades we've been getting over these past few months. We're about to celebrate our four-year anniversary from our official launch, which was in July of 2006. Despite being the second-largest online business network in the U.S. and one of the top five in the world, we've kind of flown under the radar a little bit, which has actually been fine for now and just recently, as you've said, MSNBC and some other big networks have picked up on us, and so we're excited about that.

Let me tell you a little bit about what makes our network and why people are becoming so excited about it. Part of the reason we built our network is this. We were looking two to three years ago at the landscape and some of the dinosaurs in social networking are sites like MySpace and Facebook. Obviously, those are very socially oriented.

And then in the business world on the other end of the spectrum we have the networks that have been around the longest, like LinkedIn, which is very career-oriented. It allows you to really promote yourself in terms of your resume and your work experience and those kinds of things.

And so we took a look at the landscape and we said, "Okay, there's a lot going on in the social world; that's tough to compete in. There's a lot going on in the resume/career world with LinkedIn and Monster.com and those kinds of sites. But there really was nothing filling the void left for business professionals who actually are involved in a company who are given the task of either marketing or doing sales or promoting from a PR standpoint."

So we looked at it from the standpoint of a typical small business owner. What kind of tools would they need in an online network and what can we build? And going back to those experiences of having done a lot of events and the feedback we'd received, we came up with a couple of different tool sets within our system that really are designed to help people promote their business.

The experience when you come into Fast Pitch! is really driven by your company. It's not as much about you and your career path, although you can promote that within our network. The basis is for everything you do is your "pitch" and that's why the name is Fast Pitch! It's a really concentrated way to promote your company; what makes it great, what makes it different, the types of companies you are also trying to connect to, and providing a number of different ways for you to promote yourself within that network. . . .

. . . It's more or less your elevator pitch put front and center of the experience. And then around that there are a lot of opportunities for you to add a personal side to it. And that's where your personal networking comes in;

(continued)

(*continued*)

being able to link to other people that went to your colleges, or maybe people that are involved in other networks you're a part of, like Chambers of Commerce, and leads groups you can leverage. And all of those things are within our network, as well. The idea for us is to become a one-stop shop for all of these things. You can come here and you can look for career opportunities as well. But while you're there and you're already working a job, there's opportunity to really push your business. And that's what most people are there to do. Our goal is to make our community very, very active and very, very valuable to everybody, to the point where they're actively logging in on a daily basis and leveraging our system.

We don't necessarily want to become one of these monster networks that have 20, 50 million users because we don't really want to have 10 million profiles that aren't necessarily being used or are inactive. There's not much value in that, in our opinion. . . .

. . . So what we're looking for is the opportunity to build a very vibrant network. . . .

. . . When we think about networking here at Fast Pitch!, we try to impress on people to really make a calculated decision about who you're going to connect to and be a little bit smarter about it from that standpoint. Now you're obviously going to get those people that are kind of taking a blanket approach or shotgun approach where they connect to everybody and anybody. You know, who's to say whether which is right or wrong. For some people, that may work well for. So we're not going to inhibit that, by any means, but all the messaging on our site is really geared toward telling people to make this a valuable experience, connect with people you know, look for real opportunities here, not just opportunities to spam people for whatever reason.

The idea is to really create value. One of the unique things that we do is actually force our members to become active on the system. Periodically, we'll send out alert messages to members that we see haven't logged in in quite sometime. Perhaps their e-mail is getting bounced back. They might not have made any connections, or their profile is not even close to being complete. We'll send a message periodically over the course of a month or two, reminding them to do these things. And quite honestly, at some point, if we're getting no response back from those people we will actually purge the profile from the system. It won't get purged completely, the person can ultimately come back in, log in, and do all these things, but in terms of the experiences for the people that are actively using our site, that person won't show up.

That will make the person who's really using the site have an experience that is much more fruitful because they won't be wasting their time trying to connect to somebody that's obviously not engaged. . . .

. . . Everybody's time is valuable these days. The last thing you want to do is log in to a system and spend an hour connecting to 10 or 20 people and only have two or three reply, and to have part of the reason why they're not replying be that they're not even really there. That's why we're not in that market at all. We're not trying to play that game. We're not an advertising-based company; we're not dependent on advertising revenues by any means. So we have the luxury of not having to worry about click-throughs and impressions and all these different things. We're approaching it from a subscription-end. . . .

. . . There's definitely etiquette to it. And we're very conscious of it. Any time somebody on our network sends us an e-mail to report somebody doing something inappropriate, we'll keep a close eye on it. I think there have been maybe only a handful of times we've actually had to kick somebody off of the network. So I think it all starts with your initial approach as a company. And a lot of the messaging and things that you're conveying, from the top down, to impress on all of the members that, "Hey, this is the attitude we're taking here on this network; and if you are looking to just spam people and take these shotgun approaches, there may be other networks that give you a better opportunity to do that."

. . . The way we present Fast Pitch! to people is to think about it in terms of two major things: One, obviously, networking. That's a huge component to it. The first thing you are going to want to do is to go to our profile, put your pitch on there, and put together a good message. So then when you are communicating with people and making that first impression you have a nice picture up there. You've got a fully completed profile that really tells a nice story.

That's your first step to networking. Two, the second, and in my opinion, the more important aspect to social networks like Fast Pitch!, is the marketing side of things. And that's where a lot of people actually do not pick up on when they join a social network. It's the power of marketing within the network. And let me give you an example. On Fast Pitch!, a lot of the features we've created allow you to add a lot of content above and beyond just your initial pitch about your business. We've got an entire press distribution system within our network, which helps our members receive immediate syndication to Google News, which ultimately improves their organic search rankings as a company. We've also got a blog syndication feature you can import all your blogs from your blog to your profile and out to our blog site, which gets picked up on a feed.

We've got a whole event-distribution section where you can promote events and highlight events you may be attending to help market those. There's a classified section and there's the opportunity to post video and podcasts and really make your profile interactive. There's also the opportunity to attend what we call "virtual" trade shows. That's a really popular section of our site where a lot of our members will go to a certain page at a certain point in the day and have

(*continued*)

(*continued*)

one-on-one communication with other members, via live chat or two-way streaming video. And that's something that no other network has rolled out.

It's all about networking, but more importantly, it's about marketing. The more content that you can add to your profile, the more colorful it becomes and the more opportunity there is when people are searching Fast Pitch! for certain types of people and certain types of industries for your content to get served up in those results. So somebody makes a search for a financial planner in Phoenix, Arizona, and ultimately comes across your press release that you posted, which is tied to your profile, which is tied to your web site, which, hopefully drives some business in your direction.

Not only by posting content in our network are you putting a footprint on our network, but you are also building your footprint outside of Fast Pitch!, which is probably even more important. There's opportunity now as search engines like Google pick up your press release or pick up the keyword in an event announcement. So now people outside of Fast Pitch! are coming across your profile or your press release and then taking that cycle into seeing your profile, learning about you, learning about where you went to college, learning about your company, and hopefully contacting you. . . .

To listen to or read the entire Executive Conversation with Bill Jula, go to www .theSocialMediaBible.com.

Conclusion

We are now three for five. By now you should have a good strategy or at least a good idea about how to develop one. Look at your existing media, determine what's working and keep doing that. Figure out what's not and stop doing that. Take the time to understand the three most important tools in social media: The Trinity—blogging, microblogging, and social networks. Take the time to really identify all of your demographic groups. Integrate your conventional marketing into social media marketing. And develop a strategy for each using the most appropriate tools for each group. If you do this, you will win.

Now that you see the amount of work ahead of you, how are you going to get it all done? Where will you find the resources? Read the next chapter to find out.

Credits

The ROI of Social Media was provided by:

John McPhee, www.hoteldeluxeportland.com

Expert Insight was provided by:

Bill Jula, CEO and founder of Fast Pitch!, www.fastpitchnetworking.com

CHAPTER 41

Identify Resources

The three previous steps (chapters) are mostly your responsibility to implement. Now that you have a comprehensive integrated marketing strategy developed, you have to figure out who is going to be responsible for implementing and maintaining all of these new tools and efforts. I'll bet right now it seems like it would take a team of people to execute your plan. Don't worry; here's how we'll get it done.

The last couple of years were tough ones for businesses around the world. The economy affected all businesses from the Fortune 500 down to the one-person sole proprietor. It had the same effect on nonprofits and governmental entities as well. Marketing budgets and personnel were cut, fewer people had to do more work, and now in the middle of all this, we have a whole new way to market using social media.

This is actually good news. While all marketing takes human resources to implement and social media is no different, social media is free and doesn't require huge media buys, creative, and production. Here's some of your resources right here.

Going through the process in the first step showed you what marketing efforts were effective and what weren't. Now is the time to make a list of all of the efforts you are going to put on hold in place of using social media. Grab your yellow pad or erasable whiteboard and start making a list.

List all of your previous activities that didn't return the return on investment (ROI) you had hoped for. List print advertising, your direct mail, your trade show sponsorship. Next to each category, list the number of hours it took for each activity and subactivity associated with that effort. Now make three columns: one for hours; one for the cost of those hours, which will include the base hour wage plus 32 percent for indirects; and in the third column list the hard costs.

Right away, you can see extra hours or money to purchase outside assistance or to bring someone in, and more money from the hard costs that can be added in. This can become substantial even if you are a one-person team or had a relatively meager budget to begin with.

In my companies, I pretty much do it all with the exception of hiring outside help on a project-by-project basis. What I found was that there were many marketing activities I simply don't do anymore. When I did my analysis, I realized I would never have to do a direct mail campaign again. This pleased me. They're expensive, time consuming, and the national average conversion is one-half of 1 percent. That's 0.005 percent conversion. This freed up a chunk of time and a chunk of money that I can now spend on other social media–related activities.

I also found that print ads weren't generating the type of ROI I expected, so I am much more cautious where, when, and how much I advertise. And finally, trade shows and conferences were another place I cut budgets without any noticeable reduction in sales from those activities.

Once you see the inordinate ROI of using social media in your marketing strategy, you are going to want more resources than just the ones you saved. That leads us to upper management. I do realize that you may be one of the more than 21 million entrepreneurial companies in the United States and there may be more outside the country, in which case upper management just might mean your spouse.

Management Buy-In

One of the more frustrating conversations I have been having with Fortune 1000 companies across the United States is that while the folks in marketing, PR, and communications get it—they understand the ROI of using social media in their marketing strategy—the corner office folks don't get it, which is unfortunate. For the most part, the "C Suite": CEO, CFO, COO, CIO, and so on, are over 50, and we didn't grow up with this technology. It was handed to us after college. We've had more than three decades of success without using the newfangled social media.

I joke in my keynotes that when my granddaughter was a baby, I gave her a rattle: one of my old cell phones. She was figuratively weaned on technology. It comes easier to the Generation Xs, Ys, and Millenials. For those of us over 50, not so much, but hey, I'm over 50 and I wrote the book on it, so get over yourself and get into this century.

The hard facts are that you need upper management's buy-in for you to secure human and financial resources. Now that you have your plan, go to work on them. Here are a few tips to help win them over.

Give them a copy of this book. I know it sounds self-serving (which it is), but it's effective. Just buy another copy and leave it on their chair when they are out of the office. Put a yellow sticky on this chapter so they can read the Over-50 Speech I just gave you. Also, they will thumb through the book and not be embarrassed by asking for answers to all of the questions they didn't already know the answers to and felt that they should have known.

Next, give them some ROI case studies. There are 27 of them in this book. Nothing pleases the C Suite more than success stories. They feel it limits their liability for trying someone new and untested.

Next is third-party credibility. For some reason, even though you've been telling them about social media for some time now, they will believe it more if it comes from an outside source. Again, a consultant's recommendations sound better than an internal recommendation. So hire me to come and say what you've been saying all along (too self-serving?). Then hire someone, but be really careful. If anyone calls himself a social media expert, ask him to leave your building. I take here more than 700 pages to explain social media. If I wasn't forced to understand all of the many facets of this technology well enough to write the book on it, I would never have become an expert.

If you want my 10-Question Social Media Expert Test, go to www .theSocialMediaBible.com (www.TSMB2.com) and download your free copy. If your expert can correctly answer 7 out of the 10 questions, she might know something about social media, but that won't mean she's an expert or a guru.

Reputation Management

Another reason to engage in social media is that you have responsibility for reputation management. As I stated earlier, people are talking about you, your company, your products, and your brand. You need to be aware of those conversations and you need to engage in them. You need to encourage good behavior (press) and you have responsibility to defuse negative press.

If someone writes something good about your product or service in his blog, don't you want to know that? Don't you need to know that? Don't you want to encourage that? Drive customers and prospects to that unsolicited rave review?

If someone says something negative, don't you want to know that, too, and feel a responsibility to engage with that person? Unlike conventional media (press), it's okay to engage. It's preferred. Many times the author of the negative press is only looking for engagement, but your customer doesn't know that.

Rule Number One: Always take the high road. Never condescend, get snarky, use inappropriate language, or belittle the author. Everyone has a right to one's own opinion, even if it's an idiotic one.

Engage with "I understand your point of view, however, . . . " and state your case. If you do it correctly, the reader will side with you and discredit the author. Set the book aside for a moment, think about this, and let it permeate your thoughts. This is a completely different wisdom from what we've used in the past. It works.

The same is true for Twitter. Retweet good tweets; disarm bad ones. Use this opportunity to drive customers away from having this conversation on Twitter, where you are limited to 140 characters, and drive them instead to your blog or your Facebook Fan Page. The same is true if the confrontation erupted in a social network. One more note: Never, ever, delete a bad comment on your blog. If it used inappropriate language, though, delete it. If it hurts your feelings, don't. Post it and address it.

Successful Campaigns

The next effective solution to upper management buy-in is success. For example, run a Twitter campaign to build your e-mail list or create a giveaway on your Fan Page. Closely monitor and measure (next chapter) your before-and-after result. Set a benchmark, implement measurement tools, run a small campaign, measure the results, create a small white paper, and slip it on to the CEO's desk along with your request a new hire or budget increase.

This test campaign along with most of your social media strategy implementation can be executed with you and some existing staff or just you. It's about managing your time and reappropriating resources to activities with a greater ROI. The great feature about social media is there are no hard costs and it delivers an inordinate ROI. Upper management loves this kind of talk.

Identify Resources

If you weren't previously convinced about the effectiveness of social media before running one or two simple test cases, you will be. You will want to begin testing different tools in different ways and eventually you will need or want help.

In-House

Existing Staff

Even if you are just a one-person show, there might be others within your organization who would love to help. Is there someone passionate about your company who likes to write? Invite her to write your blog. For someone else who is a social butterfly and loves his own Facebook page, have him manage your Facebook page. If there is another who likes to tweet, then you've got yourself your new Twitter rep.

In most cases, they will require only a little guidance to get them started. Have your blogger write a blog (only 400 words or so), look it over for grammar, punctuation, legal perspective, intellectual property issues, and if it's on corporate message. Remember that if you are a publicly traded company, there are a lot of SEC rules about what you can and cannot say in your communications. Guide them without a heavy hand, as they are volunteers, and let them go. It should require much less effort to manage than to do it all yourself.

Outside Staff

If there just isn't anyone you can recruit, then look for help outside that you can bring inside. There are interns, college students, temps, craigslist, eLance, and so on.

I know that managing interns is like herding cats, but once you get them pointed in the right direction with proper training, they're pretty good, and in most cases, they're free. College students are awesome and inexpensive. The best way I have found to identify the brightest and best is to call the dean of communications or marketing at your local university. Ask the dean to recommend their best student. They know who's best and will get kudos for getting them employment.

When I was building my computer company in 1986, I did just this and the student I hired eventually graduated, worked full time for me, became my vice president of engineering, and worked with me for more than 10 years.

Craigslist and eLance are two other places to find great inexpensive help. I found one person on eLance who did 24 hours of interviews for the Expert Insights for this book entirely through eLance. She was half the cost of even getting translations done in India, and English is, of course, like a native language to her.

Warning: I mentioned Generation X, Y, and Millenials earlier. Just because they understand the technology doesn't mean they understand marketing, communications, sales, and public relations. They may have a

Facebook page and use text messaging, but don't assume they understand how to communicate on a corporate level. Guide them or provide them with the content and let them execute.

Changing the Mind-set Challenge

Overall, we have to realize there is a different mind-set when using social media. Not all uses are intuitive, especially when we've had two or three decades of doing things differently and having success without the new ways. Some techniques are the same and some are different. The key to your success is knowing the difference.

Out-House

Marketing and Public Relations Firms

I get teased about using this descriptor. I have worked with a lot of outside agencies in my career. Some were good, but most knew about as much as I did and often less. Please be wary of service agencies and marketing and public relations firms selling social media services. Most companies know less than you do by now (unless they also read this book).

I can't tell you how many times I have been asked to present and talk about social media with some of the world's largest firms only to find out that they know less than average and have been selling social media services to their clients for several years now. Have them take the earlier-mentioned test as well. Make up a list of questions you have.

Consultants

The same goes for consultants. Within the past two years, almost everyone is now calling herself a social media expert or guru. She's not. If you are going to hire a consultant, please interview her extensively. Quiz her on specific IDKT (I Didn't Know That) moments you had when reading this book. If she can't answer most of your questions, invite her to leave and you should try again with someone else.

Warning: Out-House firms don't want you doing your own marketing, social media or otherwise. If you do it yourself, they get no billable hours. They will often obfuscate the execution and insist you leave it to the experts. You are the expert here. No one knows your company, your product, and your services the way you do.

The ROI of Social Media

Exclusive Blogger Event Results in Widespread Social Media Buzz

Background

Moving away from the big box, sterile office supplies world, OfficeMax is targeting women with stylish, affordable private brand lines that encourage creativity, productivity, and efficiency. To support its new positioning, Office-Max and nationally renowned organizational expert, Peter Walsh, partnered to boost organization and innovation in the workplace with the launch of a new product line—[IN]PLACE SYSTEM by Peter Walsh.

Strategy

To introduce Walsh's line and bring his workspace organization expertise to life, OfficeMax and Peter Walsh selected to host a sneak preview web event with influential women's interest bloggers. OfficeMax chose to inform and educate women's interest bloggers about office organization and give them special access to celebrated organization expert Peter Walsh. Taking place at the start of spring, OfficeMax also leveraged the timeliness of the announcement during spring when organization and spring cleaning are common interest areas to engage its social media audience and offer them useful tools and advice.

Implementation

To generate anticipation and excitement leading up to the product launch, OfficeMax selected 250 influential women's interest bloggers to participate in a sneak preview of Peter Walsh's new product line and attend a live event titled "Work Life Organized Blogcast." The bloggers were selected for their readership and focus including parenting, professional women and moms, organization, and product reviews. One week before the blogcast, the women's interest bloggers received product samples of [IN]PLACE SYSTEM by Peter Walsh, product brochures, and an introduction letter.

On April 2, 2009, Peter Walsh and OfficeMax's VP of marketing and advertising, Julie Krueger, met the women's interest bloggers online for a 40-minute blogcast live from a Los Angeles studio. During the blogcast, Peter and Julie shared organization tips and strategies for addressing clutter, answered live blogger questions and demonstrated Peter's new organizational system in relation to common workspace organization challenges. To facilitate real-time conversation, a TweetChat room was arranged using the hashtag, #OfficeMax, where hundreds of bloggers discussed workspace organization and the new product line on Twitter.

(continued)

(*continued*)

Following the blogcast, the bloggers received Peter Walsh's "Work Life Organized" tip sheet, product images, and links to the recorded blogcast and [In]Place System microsite.

Opportunity

To offer bloggers high quality content they can leverage for their blogs in combination with the introduction of a new workspace organization product line.

Conclusion

OfficeMax's "Work Life Organized Blogcast" with Peter Walsh attracted over 200 live participants, including some of the highest-ranking women's interest bloggers in social media. The web event resulted in more than 125 favorable blog posts about office organization and [IN]PLACE SYSTEM by Peter Walsh with a total of 2.75 million audience impressions. Furthermore, its hashtag, #OfficeMax, became the Number 2 trending topic on Twitter and secured over 1,000 tweets with a total of 2.3 million impressions. The social media coverage eventually led to traditional media coverage from 15 news outlets with a total of 2.1 million audience impressions. In sum, the web event contributed to a successful product launch at OfficeMax with widespread social media and traditional media coverage focused on the product line and its many uses for home and business office organization.

OfficeMax PR team, OfficeMax.com

Expert Insight

Gary Vaynerchuk, Wine Library director of operations and host and founder of Wine Library TV, www.WineLibrary.com.

Gary Vaynerchuk

In October 2007, I decided to start videoblogging under my name—GaryVaynerchuk.com—to kind of talk about the business behind *Wine Library TV* and just business in general—something I'm obviously very passionate about as well. I wanted a platform for that; and so that's been quite successful for me and has led to a lot of speaking engagements, consulting, and opportunities on that level.

So being very entrepreneurial, that's been fun; being artistic with the wine stuff, that's been fun. So I've been, kind of, scratching multiple itches. . . . I come from the lemonade-stand world, and the baseball-card world, and the snow-shoveling world . . . so I've been very, kind of, entrepreneurial my whole life. What's great about social media and where the world's at now is [that] you have the ability to build much bigger brands much quicker and at much lower price points; and that's a very big change in the way business is done in America.

The gatekeepers are [slightly] out of control . . . have *lost* control, actually. No more editor/producer telling you what you can or cannot be, or deciding whether you can speak to the American people or the people of the world, actually. We now have tools that allow us to communicate our message, whatever that may be, with zero cost; just the time and effort we put into the community. That is the fundamental shift of what we're living through right now. . . .

And commitment to our community. I think that's really . . . that's the real equalizer to money for somebody small, like myself, compared to the *Wine Spectator,* or a comedian compared to a top-notch comedian who's on Comedy Central. Whoever leverages their community and whoever builds a community better is in a position to win, whatever that may be. And so time, once again, continues to become important; time has become more valuable than ever, and I've already cited that people who care and give back are going to win. And I think that's a very powerful message, a very good message, and a very big opportunity for a lot of people. . . .

I think it's one step at a time. I think a lot of people ask me, "What was the tipping point: When you got on Conan, or you were on Leno, or *Nightline,* or in the *Wall Street Journal?*" And I think when you don't focus on tipping points and just focus on pumping out good content—and you focus on hustling every day and answering your e-mail and caring about your community, putting out good content . . . I think you start realizing that you don't need a tipping point and that that's not really what fundamentally separates a victory from a loss. I think that for me it was just pumping out good shows every day and becoming part of the community; leaving comments and blogs and answering my e-mail and creating accounts in things like Facebook and Twitter; you know, just working it. And I think that that is the way to success; it's always been. And the only difference is that now your fans and consumers and the people who care about you have the ability to build you quicker and easier and better because they have tools. Word of mouth has changed; not the way you build a brand. . . . Yeah, I mean, I think the message is the whole game. I think the less polished it is sometimes, the better. I think that the lighting or the mike or the camera you use is so irrelevant and just such a stumbling block by many producers. Many people who want to get into the game spend so much time on trying to figure that part out and that part has no value . . . none! I really think zero. Some of them, you know I mean . . . it's got to be watchable, you've got to be able to hear it, but outside of that, that's the threshold. . . . I think authenticity of the message is what really attaches people to the product, to

(continued)

(*continued*)

the service, to the individual. And I think it's quality of message, not quality of the way we consume it, or the video or the sound. So I think it's very obvious what works.

You know, people like tradition, and commercials didn't need to get into million-dollar budgets; they just did because they had the money and people weren't making smart decisions, really! I really believe that. So I think that, you know, you've got to really take a step back and understand what people react to; and people react to things that are authentic, real, transparent, and deliver. And listen . . . some people really love watching something in HD; I get that! But I don't think that's going to be the differentiator from victory or defeat. I really don't! . . .

Building community is about giving a crap! That's where I separated myself from everybody else, or whoever else. . . . I mean, those other people do a great job, but to me it's about really caring about your user base: listening to them, making them involved, letting them participate, caring about their thoughts, letting them have their say in molding the direction of what you do. And so to me, it's just about caring. It's about taking the extra effort to read your e-mails, to respond to them, to meet them in person, to send them little gifts. To just care. I mean, it's a very simple process. It's just one that's costly of time and money and that's something people aren't willing to invest.

To listen to or read the entire Executive Conversation with Gary Vaynerchuk, go to www.theSocialMediaBible.com.

Conclusion

The reality is, if you want to incorporate social media into your marketing, sales, public relations, and communications plan, you can. The resources are there. You may have to be a little creative in where you find them. You may also have to educate upper management to the effectiveness of the combination of conventional and social media marketing. You may have to reprioritize your activities and you may have to look at marketing a little differently. When you do finally implement your Phase One strategy and realize the ROI and effectiveness of adding social media, you will be hooked like I am.

Let's go to the final step and talk about implementation and measurement.

Credits

The ROI of Social Media was provided by:

The OfficeMax PR team, OfficeMax.com

Expert Insight was provided by:

Gary Vaynerchuk, Wine Library director of operations and host and founder of Wine Library TV, www.WineLibrary.com

CHAPTER 42

Implement and Measurement

Implementing Your Strategy, Metrics, and Analytics

Dr. W. Edwards Deming has been incorrectly credited with saying *"You Can't Manage What You Don't Measure."* No truer words were never spoken. If you want to measure your return on investment (ROI) and determine your conversion rate, you do need to have measurement tools in place.

I wrote earlier that nearly every newspaper claims that every printed copy of their newspaper is read by two and a half people. Not likely. That's been the problem with measuring conventional marketing. If we learned anything from the late-1990s–to–early-2000s dot-bomb era is that impressions may add to additional brand recognition, but had little measurable value beyond that.

Measuring ROI, or responses using conventional marketing, has always been difficult. We used multiple post office boxes to track ads, we've used coupon and discount codes, and we've used different telephone numbers. At one time, Hewlett-Packard maintained more than 4,000 different telephone numbers just to track the responsiveness to all of their different advertising. The problem has been that there wasn't a way to run the responses through an automatic counter until the advent of the Internet.

Because the Internet is managed by computer systems and networks, everything that passes through the system can be measured. Over the past 10 years, we even used the Internet and unique landing pages to measure unmeasurable conventional responses. Today, there is a myriad of tools, mostly free, that can help us measure and manage all of our marketing efforts.

theSocialMediaBible.com

Determine Your Measurement Tools

There are a ton of different tools for every category of social media distribution and communications channels. Unfortunately, there just isn't enough space to go through all of them with their features and benefits in this book. You will have to accept their research as a homework assignment. I will discuss some of the more popular and feature-rich tools and their advantages, but do your homework. I will be calling you shortly to grade you.

Web, Blog Page, and Tweet Measurement—Check the Pages

The easiest and freest way to monitor every web page and every blog page in the world is through Google Analytics. If you aren't using Google Analytics, you need to. Go to Google and google Google Analytics. You need to have a Gmail e-mail account, and you should have one anyway; it's free.

Once you have access to all things Google, select Google Analytics and set some up. You create a new Google search term by typing "whatever you want Google to notify you about." I have Google notify me of every occurrence of "Lon Safko," "*Social Media Bible,*" my other companies and products, my partners' names, and more.

This way, any time there is the use of that exact text on any web page, any blog page, anywhere in the world, I get a notice with a clickable link that allows me to view that page. Think about that for a minute. Any time anyone mentions me anywhere in the world, I get a notice and a link within 30 minutes of it happening.

Being the first to know about my mention gives me the opportunity to maintain my reputation as I discussed earlier. I am often the first to comment on the blog either thanking the author for the good mention or offering my point of view.

Listen for the Tweets

While this takes care of nearly all of cyberspace, there still is the SMS text messages, or tweets. What if you could monitor every tweet sent from anyone on Earth who mentions you, your company, your products, or services and actually get the exact tweet at the same time the recipients get it? You can with Seismic Desktop or TweetDeck.

Both of these products are free, easy to set up, amazingly powerful for managing your brand, and even have mobile versions so you can manage your brand from your mobile phone. You set up searches the same way you set up searches in Google, using text within quotes.

You can also read all of the tweets from the people you are following, read all of the tweets and replies you send out, and all of your direct messages without having to log on to Twitter. Every minute or so, the screen refreshes and there is all of your company's Twitter activities right there on one screen, and it runs in the background.

A quick way to check every tweet worldwide is Search.Twitter.com. Here's an example of a quick search for "Social Media Bible":

marconabu: Espero q n la office el boss entienda q si me llevo el social media bible pa la choza es porq quiero q me pasen al dpto de redes sociales!!

about 5 hours ago from TweetDeck · Reply · View Tweet

marconabu: yo sé q hoy s jueves pero cómo yo nunca sigo las reglas! mi #librorecomendado de la semana será Social Media Bible!!

about 5 hours ago from TweetDeck · Reply · View Tweet

njhogan: @Sarah_Tweeds I was unaware social media was in the bible!:P

about 6 hours ago from web · Reply · View Tweet · Show Conversation

lilymafiette: Nerd-out bedtime reading with The Social Media Bible. This book is my new religion. @nguyener0127 Thought you'd appreciate this!:)

about 15 hours ago from HootSuite · Reply · View Tweet

If you don't read or speak Spanish, I will let you look up the first two in iGoogle Translator.

More Sophisticated Surveillance

If you want more sophisticated analysis, you can opt for a pay service such as Radian6, which with one piece of software, will do all of the Google analytics, all of your Twitter tweets, all of your Facebook and other social network comments and wall writings, and . . . look for trends, both negative and positive, for your keywords and notify you of any negative trend or discussion taking place about your company or brand. This service does have a price tag associated with it, but it's well worth the price.

If you are using video sharing as part of your strategy, which I highly recommend, and are posting videos on YouTube, wouldn't it be great if you could see how many times the video was downloaded and viewed? What if you could know the number of views per day your video received, where those viewers are in the world, how popular your video is compared to other videos in a given period of time, popularity by country, by U.S. state, track the life cycle of videos, including how long it takes for a video to become popular, and what happens to video views as popularity peaks, and a lot more metrics? You can, for free; it's called "YouTube Insight."

Video Sharing

If you post your videos to more than one video sharing site (and you should), there's TubeMogul, which allows you to view statistics from all of your video sharing web sites.

Traffic Analytics

If you really want to monitor your web traffic (and you do), then Google Analytics and Alexa are the tools you need to become familiar with.

Google automatically generates an analytics code that can be placed in any HTML web site or blog site, and the amount of data that is now available to you, in real time, in incredible detail, is amazing. Try it and see for yourself. Honestly, it's worth the effort.

Alexa is known for its data collection and reporting on browsing behavior. Alexa uses toolbars on Firefox and Internet Explorer that collects the data and reports back the web pages' popularity as measured against all of the web pages in the world with similar keywords and other metrics, including page views, bounce rates, and time-on-site.

External Reputable Links

As External Reputable Links are one of the most important and heavily weighted criteria search engines used, it might be good to know how many external links there are coming in to your web site. Interested? Then just go to Google and type in "links:www.YourDomain.com," and there they are! Here is every web site that has ever linked to yours.

You may want to go back to Google and type in "site:www.yourdomain .com." This tells you every page that Google has indexed for your entire web or blog site. This way, if you have an imported page or pages, you want to be sure they are getting indexed.

Cyber Surveillance

All of these tools are used for reputation management and what I call Cyber Surveillance. Tools that allow you to monitor your brand. There are many other tools, including Spyfu.com for PPC (Pay-Per-Click) monitoring, a general Google Search, Google Universal Search, Google Blog Search, Google Social Search, Forum Search, and even Flickr and YouTube Search.

Know Your Competition

Here's something that most people don't think of: you can use all of the preceding tools to monitor and surveil your competition. Yes, monitor everything they are doing in cyberspace. By using the same tools, you can know every minute of every day what social media tools they are using, where they are engaging with their customers (Facebook, blogs, Twitter), where they are advertising, read their blogs, their tweets, and follow them in the Google shopping search.

Analyze Each Marketing Channel

Once you have set up all of your tools with the appropriate keywords, be sure that you do this for each campaign and not just overall. This way you can monitor specific keywords and the ROI for each campaign and for each activity. Your ROI will be different; some good, and some not so good. As in the previous chapter, either change the way you are performing the activities with the lowest ROI or just stop them altogether. This will allow you to relocate resources to the activities with the best ROI.

Once you have them working for you, lather, rinse, and repeat. Keep perfecting what's working. Also remember that even the activities with a lower ROI are generating a great deal of brand awareness and recognition. It's also building a good reputation and trust in those areas.

Note: I would love to know which genius wrote those three amazing words: *luther, rinse, repeat*, which doubled his client's shampoo sales from just this marketing message. If anyone can tell me who was responsible, I will give any free product that person wants from my www.PaperModelsInc .com store.

Managing Your Expectations

Manage your expectations and the expectations of upper management. While social media is an amazing set of technologies, they still take time. Trust isn't something you can buy or trick someone into giving you. It's earned. Total success will not be measured overnight. Like all marketing, social media marketing is a long-term strategy that needs to be coupled with your conventional long-term marketing strategy. Social media is inordinately effective and in most cases nearly free. Keep at it and it will pay off.

Putting the Pedal to the Metal!

Keep your enthusiasm. Don't give up. Stay current on the technology by setting some time aside each week and looking around on the Web. Read some of *Tech News World*'s articles. Renay San Miguel writes some great stories on all of the cutting edge technologies. Look at SocialMediaOptimized .com, TheSocialMediaBible.com, and my ExtremeDigitalMarketing.com for how-to videos on everything I discussed here in this book.

The most important element of a Five-Step Social Media Success Plan is Commitment!!!

The ROI of Social Media

Increasing Attendance and Revenue to Peabody Rooftop Parties

Background

We needed to increase our attendance and revenue for a series of 16 hotel rooftop parties lasting from April to July 2009. We also wanted to target a younger demographic. Social media was a cost-effective way to promote all the parties in a short amount of time. Because our target audience had begun to adopt the technology, social media provided an efficient channel for us to tap the market.

Strategy

Visibility on the social networks of our target audience was our main focus. We created episodic content to gradually grow our audience week by week. Our two platforms were Facebook and Twitter. Facebook served as more of a weekly publication of invitations, party information, photos, and video. Twitter served as a real-time broadcast of updates, links, and stories our rooftop audience would find valuable. We created the hashtag #pbodyroof for all rooftop-related content.

Implementation

We created a Facebook group, The Peabody Memphis Events and Rooftop Parties. The landing page featured this year's prices and music lineup. We ran a two-week Facebook advertisement in April 2009 about the group. Clicking on the ad brought the viewer to our group. We created 16 rooftop party events and sent invitations to each party on a weekly basis. During the parties, we took photos and recorded video. Photos were posted the next day to the group. We tagged all of our friends, radio station hosts, DJs, and bands and encouraged [that] they tag their friends and share content with their fans and listeners. A rooftop recap video was posted each month that highlighted the month's music lineup.

On Twitter, all of our posts included the hash tag #pbodyroof. We posted party updates, including last-minute band additions and weather updates. We answered questions from our followers about the parties. We also posted twitpics of the parties in real time.

Opportunity

The opportunity was to establish the Peabody Rooftop Parties as the premier social event in Memphis throughout spring and summer. It also built credibility with our online audience because of our engagement on Facebook and Twitter. The Peabody Memphis also earned credibility in the industry as an effective social media marketer, being featured in trade magazines such as Hotels Magazine and Hospitality Technology

Conclusion

We increased our attendance in 2009 by 113 percent from 2008. Beverage revenues also increased 83 percent from 2008 to 2009. Before Twitter, 700 people would be considered a huge turnout for a rooftop party. Today, the average number is a thousand to twelve hundred, with upward of seventeen hundred in attendance. Our group page grew from eight hundred members in April to more than twenty-two hundred members by the end of July. The rooftop parties were featured in local blogs as being a successful turnaround from the previous year. Local bloggers and community influencers also praised the Peabody for listening to the community putting on the acts people wanted to see.

You can currently find the Peabody Memphis on the web at:

peabodymemphis.com

facebook.com/peabodyducks

twitter.com/peabodymemphis

The Facebook group is "The Peabody Memphis Events and Rooftop Parties."

Jonathan Lyons, marketing and PR coordinator, The Peabody Memphis

Expert Insight

Rishi Chandra, product manager, Google Enterprise, www.google.com/apps/intl/en/business/index.html

Rishi Chandra

The Google Apps is a set of business applications, which are hosted on the Internet, or . . . on Cloud. The idea is—if you have heard of some of Google's more famous consumer products like Gmail, Google Calendar, and Google Talk—[that] we actually take those consumer technologies, package, and bundle them in a way that enterprises and businesses can actually use.

So, for example, instead of having a Gmail.com e-mail address where you use the Gmail product, you can use your own company's e-mail address, and access the power of your company's e-mail infrastructure. . . .

So, as I said, there are two core components to Google Apps. There is a messaging component, which includes Gmail, Calendar, and Contacts. And on the collaboration side—the other element of Apps—includes Google Sites, Google Docs, and a new product we have just recently launched, called Google Video for Business . . . the difficult thing is that we launched [it] only two to three weeks ago [September 2008]; and [again], we are really excited about taking this idea of Google's Consumer Technologies—in this case, YouTube—and being able to apply [them] to a business setting. So being able to allow companies to upload their own video content and within their company—just as you see YouTube do in the consumer world for them. . . .

We have done a couple of things that . . . work in a business environment. . . . Businesses love the fact that we have very easy-to-use and powerful tools [that] can be hosted on the Web. They get all the benefits of Google hosting it for you. You do not have to worry about it; [and since] it works in a browser, you do not have to install or maintain any type of hardware or software. At the same time, businesses have a higher level of expectation around certain features than [consumers do]. You need to have more control, more security, and more functionality targeted for specific business-use cases. And that's actually what we have done with the video product, for example. We actually have it at higher resolution; it's more secure because you can actually share it with a set of people; and only a small set of people so that they will be the only ones to have access to that information. And we have administrative controls in there, so that your administrator can administer the product just as you could with any other product. . . .

That is really one of the key benefits of Cloud computing . . . this idea that you have a single place for your information—in this case, it is on the

Internet—[that] most people can access from [wherever they are in the world]; whatever company they are a part of, or whatever device they are accessing it from, whether it be a mobile device or a computer or a laptop. . . .

That is one of the great benefits: anyone can access [the information] at any point in time. The other benefit—as you [pointed out]—is this idea of collaborating with multiple people in different places. You know, the biggest challenge we heard from both businesses and consumers is this idea of collaboration through e-mail is a pretty broken process. . . . So, for example, if four or five people wanted to work on a document today, most people actually just e-mail that out to five different people; each of them downloads an individual copy of that document, work off their own copy, and send it back. Now [the original] person has to recompile those different changes; and if multiple people are working off of it with different revisions, you can see yourself getting into a pretty easy nightmare, pretty quickly . . . and so, . . . we are thinking of a new way for people to interact with each other and actually share information and collaborate on information.

That is really one of the key benefits of Cloud computing. . . . And what that product does is actually a wiki. A wiki is [a document or web page] that anyone can edit a piece of . . . and you can easily create multiple pieces of data in one single place. So, for example, if I have a Project Team, I can embed a Google Calendar in that Google Site; I can embed a document associated with that Project Team; I can associate videos with that Project Team. You can bring together all of these different types of rich, social information into one single place and have people collaborate on it in a very easy way. . . .

It is a monumental change with how people interact with web pages today. [When] most people hear the word *web page,* they get really intimidated. It certainly makes them think of things like HTML and how complicated those are. Google Sites wants to make it as easy to edit a web page as it is to use *edit* in a document. Anyone who has permission to that site can go do it, and it is as straightforward as editing a document. You can edit text, you can pull different pieces of information in very quickly and easily, and with one button you can publish it to the set of people you want to share that information with. That's the real philosophy behind Google Sites. . . .

It is a great product, because it brings together a lot of different places that use information; and really highlights to business users in particular. There are certain technologies that they are just not used to using, but it really does enable much richer collaboration. Video is a great example of this. You will find in the consumer world [that] video is actually very pervasive. Lots of people interact with video content all the time, but somehow it never made the transition to the business world. And we believe that there are a couple of reasons for that. . . . One is that it is just not simple and easy to do so. . . .

(continued)

(continued)

That is where Google can really change the game there with our simple user interfaces, which are incredibly powerful, to enable much richer collaboration. But at the same time it is incredibly expensive for most business to do something like that, because video is a very intensive application and most companies do not have the time, the bandwidth, or even the costs to actually make it work for them. And that is really where Google Apps can change the game. We can bring these really great, compelling, new social technologies into the enterprise and do so in a way that is very cost-effective for most businesses. . . .

It is pretty amazing actually, when you think of what's happened in the consumer world, where storage has become much and much less of an issue for most users. In the business world, it actually still is a really big problem. One of the greatest examples and what really highlights that is, if you go to Gmail.com, for free you can sign up for a 7-gigabyte e-mail storage on your inbox . . . and most companies today still only give 500 megabytes to their users; even though they pay lots and lots of money to actually make the technology work for their employees. Somehow, we have gone completely backward. . . . And that is why Google technology can really change the game here. With the premier edition of Google Apps, we give our users 25 gigabytes of e-mail storage—which is just monumental compared to what most businesses already give their users. So we can really change the game by giving more storage at a better price and giving more tools that actually incorporate these new social technologies in an easy way for the end user.

To listen to or read the entire Executive Conversation with Rishi Chandra, go to www .theSocialMediaBible.com.

Conclusion

Developing an integrated conventional and social media strategy isn't difficult. It will take a little time to go through the steps. The toughest part is changing the way you think about marketing and finding the time and support to implement your effort.

You still have to focus on the message. That is the reason you are communicating. Never sell or you will get flamed. Remember, it's like walking into a networking event; there are a room full of small groups between three and five people all talking, all holding the tiny wines. If you walk up, push in and start telling everybody that you sell . . . and the next time someone needs a . . . and that you are the person to call, you will get slapped in the lips. That is inappropriate behavior. You know that.

The same goes for online. Listen first, and when it's appropriate to add something to the conversation, slide it in. After that, you are part of that group and will be treated as such.

Listen, Participate, Trust. Authentic, Sincere, Transparent. Rinse, Lather, Repeat.

That's all there is to it!

Credits

The ROI of Social Media was provided by:

Jonathan Lyons, marketing and PR coordinator, The Peabody Memphis

Expert Insight was provided by:

Rishi Chandra, product manager, Google Enterprise, www.google.com/apps/intl/en/business/index.html

Krista Canfield
PR Manager for LinkedIn

Before working for LinkedIn, Krista Canfield was a senior account executive for the Horn Group, and has a background in journalism as a news reporter. She has extensive experience in media relations and all PR account activities including analyst relations, press releases, and competitive and company news tracking. In the public relations capacity, she has worked with many software companies, securing some of them feature stories with *USA Today*.

Marc Canter
CEO of Broadband Mechanics

By his own words, "a toolsmith by trade," Marc Canter has been creating digital software and tools for 25 years. A founder of Macromedia, he has been watching the blogging world and social media evolve over the past two decades.

Vint Cerf
One of the Fathers of the Internet and Futurist

Vint Cerf was at Stanford in 1973 when Bob Kahn came to him and asked for help in hooking different nets together. Together they created the basic design of what would become the Internet. He is amazed at how quickly the public has absorbed the different ways of interacting on the Web and that the original consumers of information are now producing information, hence social media.

Rishi Chandra
Product Manager for Google Enterprises

A Stanford MBA, Rishi Chandra has been with Google for two years, working exclusively on Google Applications, the newest being Google Sites, a suite of products continuously updated by Google that resides on the Internet, not the desktop, and consists of everything from word processing and spreadsheets, to presentations and e-mail.

Scott Clough
Avid Online Gamer

Scott Clough started gaming as a teenager in the 1980s with "Dungeons and Dragons." He gravitated to role-playing games on the computer such as "Zork," then to the online "D&D," among others. In 1997, with much time on his hands, he went to "Ultima Online," and then to "EverQuest," which he feels made the role-playing game genre successful with its amazing graphics and realistic world. Now prudent with his game time, he tries to make sure gaming doesn't dominate his life, but he is always looking for new entertainment. He has an understanding of the user's side of gaming and why businesses should watch the $1 billion-plus, multimillion-player industry.

Angela Courtin
Senior Vice President, Marketing Entertainment and Content for MySpace

A veteran of MTV where she was vice president of integrated marketing, Angela Courtin was also vice president of Rock the Vote, where she partnered with MTV's Choose or Lose campaign and corporate America to get young people across the country to get out and vote. Her work in politics spans the Human Rights Campaign to the Democratic National Committee. At MySpace, she is responsible for leading the marketing, branding, promotions, events, content, and entertainment teams with the objective of increased growth, public awareness, and driving revenue through marketing programs.

Neal Creighton
Cofounder and Chief Executive Officer of RatePoint

Neal has more than a decade of experience in information security, identity verification, and Internet business markets. Formerly, as cofounder, president, and CEO of GeoTrust, Neal was responsible for providing the leadership, strategic direction and management for the company. Neal led the efforts to raise $24 million in venture financing and sold GeoTrust to VeriSign (NASDAQ: VRSN) for $125 million in September 2006.

Neal also led the spin-off of ChosenSecurity from GeoTrust as part of the VeriSign merger agreement. In 2010, ChosenSecurity was acquired by the PGP Corporation and Neal is currently serving as a member of PGP's Technical Advisory Board. Neal considers his most meaningful professional experience graduating from U.S. Army Ranger School in 1990. Neal received his BS from the United States Military Academy at West Point, and holds an MBA and Juris Doctor from Northwestern University.

Jody Gnant
Livecaster, Community Marketing, and Musician

Jody Gnant is a Phoenix-based singer and songwriter who grew up with the Internet. She gained notice by broadcasting her life, a livecast 24 hours a day, for nine months. She also participated in Kyle MacDonald's historic venture, *One Red Paper Clip*, the journey of turning a paper clip into a house through cyber-trading. She uses the Internet to be independent—she sings, writes songs, and puts them out for people to listen to.

Jack Herrick
Founder of WikiHow

Jack Herrick founded WikiHow with the intent of building the "world's largest, highest quality how-to manual." Expanding the definition of how-to manuals, it deals with subjects as diverse as car repairs and relationships, with content submitted and maintained by readers.

Gretchen Howard
Director, Online Sales and Operations for Google AdWords

Gretchen Howard has held this position for almost three years and previously worked in financial services and as a consultant. She explains how Google AdWords works, and how to set up an account and start a campaign with little or no effort and a limited budget.

Stephanie Ichinose
Director of Communications for Yelp

Stephanie Ichinose managed a public relations team for Yahoo! for years before becoming director of communications at Yelp. Yelp is an Internet tool that accesses and creates local reviews rating restaurants, auto mechanics, dentists, or any company by building a community of individuals who communicate by digital word of mouth.

Bill Jula
Founder and CEO of Fast Pitch!

After earning a master's degree, Bill Jula entered the workplace, working in marketing and business development, and found himself learning how to market in the Internet Age. He started his current company, Fast Pitch! in 2003, based on the ideas that the most powerful ways to grow a business and a brand are through word of mouth and building a strong referral network, and that there should be places on the Internet for businesses to interact.

Mark Kingdon
CEO of Linden Labs of Second Life

Mark Kingdon joined Linden Labs in 2008 as CEO and creator of Second Life Virtual Environment, an online program used by individuals for socializing and companies for meetings, educating their customers, and even prototyping products. Mark served as CEO of Organic Inc., a digital communications agency; Idealab, providing strategic guidance and operational support to emerging companies and was a partner with the consulting division of PricewaterhouseCoopers, LLP. He holds an MBA from the Wharton School of Business and a BA in economics from UCLA.

Alan Levy
CEO of BlogTalkRadio

Alan Levy created the concept for BlogTalkRadio as a means for friends and family to be updated on his father's health that would become a memorial upon his father's passing. BlogTalkRadio is now the leading social radio network, enabling millions of bloggers to interact with an audience in a live, real-time manner.

Tony Mamone
Founder and CEO of *Zimbio*

An engineer by training, Tony Mamone gravitated toward business and used his interest and passion for Internet content to create Findarticles.com. A few years later, after selling that site, he caught the entrepreneurial bug again and created Zimbio.com, an online magazine with more than 13 million unique visitors a month that caters to style, entertainment, current events, and sports. While similar in content to other magazines on the market, like *Elle, Vogue, Newsweek,* and so on, *Zimbio* is fundamentally different in that its members and readers are creating much of the magazine's content.

Dharmesh Mehta
Director of Product Management for Windows Live Instant Messenger

Dharmesh Mehta is the director for Windows Live Messenger at Microsoft in Redmond, WA, and lives in the greater Seattle area. Dharmesh is a graduate of the Harvard Business School and the Massachusetts Institute of Technology specializing in strategic analysis, project management, team management, growth analysis, financial modeling, and analytical reasoning.

Matt Mullenweg
Cofounder of WordPress, President of Automattic

Matt Mullenweg created WordPress, in part, to give people a better means of personal expression through blogging. Matt's company has helped democratize publishing blogs, making them more accessible to writers and others who can now share interests on a global scale. WordPress also enables individuals and companies an unparalleled ability to listen to their community. Current WordPress users include Ford Motor Co., the CIA, FBI, Homeland Security, the *New York Times*, Fox News, and CNN.

Michael Naef
Founder and CEO of Doodle.com

Michael Naef holds an MS in computer science from the Swiss Federal Institute of Technology, Zurich, and is the inventor of Doodle as well as its original developer. Incorporated in 2008, Doodle is located in Zurich, Switzerland, and runs the online scheduling service doodle.com.

Chris Pirillo
Geek and Technology Enthusiast

Chris Pirillo has recorded more than 1,000 videos in the past year, made the Top 100 Most Subscribed on YouTube and has the distinction of being the number one hit on Google for the word *Chris*. He has been participating in Internet conversations since 1992, is a monthly columnist for *CPU Magazine*, has authored books on business and personal technology, and produces weekly video segments for CNN.com.

John Pollard
Founder and CEO of Jott

John Pollard holds an MBA from the University of Michigan and has been in the technology industry for 20 years, including Microsoft, where he was involved in Sidewalk, Office, and Expedia, which he took internationally. While he considers working on the projects at Microsoft some of the highlights of his life, he decided to become an entrepreneur, leaving Microsoft in 2006 to create Jott. Jott is the culmination of things he's seen in his long career—something with global impact that worked on mobile devices like cell phones, was simple, and that people found very valuable.

Patrizio Spagnoletto
Senior Director of Marketing, Yahoo! Search Marketing

A Yahoo! employee for almost eight years, Patrizio Spagnoletto's current role is managing the marketing team for the Search Marketing product, the sponsored links that appear on Yahoo! His team is instrumental in making sure customers get a good return on their investment through education, communication, and product innovation.

Biz Stone
Cofounder of Twitter

Biz Stone has published two books about social media. Besides Twitter, he helped create Xanga, Odeo, and Obvious. He also worked for Google on the blogger team. He describes Twitter as a short messaging service that communicates everything from "What are you doing?" to immediate disaster reports.

George Strompolos
Content Partnerships Manager for YouTube

George Strompolos reaches out to content creators and helps them engage on YouTube, distribute their content, and connect with audiences globally.

Linh Tang
Author of *Launching Your Yahoo! Business* and *Succeeding at Your Yahoo! Business*, and entrepreneur

Linh Tang is the author of two e-commerce books on how to use Yahoo! Stores to build and market an online business. He is also the coowner and founder of vCentives, an online resource to help online retailers acquire new customers with no risk and zero acquisition costs. An award-winning Web designer, he has been designing web sites since 1995 and developing Yahoo! Stores since 2000.

Evo Terra
Coauthor of *Podcasting For Dummies*

Considered an "old man" in podcasting, Evo Terra started podcasting in October of 2004 and had the 40th podcast on the planet. Coming in on the ground floor, as it were, he collaborated with Tee Morris to write *Podcasting For Dummies*, now in its second edition.

Gary Vaynerchuk
Wine Library Director of Operations, and Host and Founder of Wine Library TV

Starting out literally with just a liquor store, Gary Vaynerchuk has built a successful online retail store into a $50 million enterprise as well as Wine Library TV.com, with 600 episodes and an audience of more than 80,000 viewers per show, and his own blog, through which he shares his experiences behind the scenes.

Peter Booth Wiley
Chairman of the board of John Wiley & Sons, Inc.

Peter Booth Wiley is the sixth generation of Wileys involved in the publishing business, in a company that was founded when Thomas Jefferson was president. Chairman since 2002, he has 25 years of his own experience in the publishing world and as an author and journalist, and understands the historical evolution of social media. At the same time, his sons are actively working in social media, ensuring their future involvement in the Wiley legacy.

theSocialMediaBible.com